History of Portsmouth, Virginia

by
Mildred Holladay
&
Dean Burgess

The Portsmouth History Commission
in commemoration of the 400th anniversary of
the landing of the first colony at Jamestown
Portsmouth, VA 2007

© Dean Burgess
for the Portsmouth Historical Commission
Red Lion Square Stutios
P. O. Box 126
Portsmouth, VA 23705-0126
redlion3@juno.com
www.deanburgess.com

ISBN 978-0-9792491-0-5

Forward

The History Commission of the City of Portsmouth, as part of the Jamestown 2007 Community Program, is proud to present *A History of Portsmouth, Virginia* by Mildred Holladay and Dean Burgess as one of the city's "legacy projects."

Portsmouth's tomorrows are found in the footsteps of the richest traditions of America, from the earliest days of Colonial Virginia through participation in every one of America's wars, the victories of equality, dignity and diversity. As guardian of the collective heritage of many people, we have become one. The Portsmouth family preserves the proudest traditions of the past as the compass for our future, drawing the grace of our spirit into the nobility of what we have become."

The Historical Commission of the City of Portsmouth

Table Of Contents

Introduction	VII
Chapter 1: In the Beginning	1
Chapter 2: The Founder	7
Chapter 3: The Town Begins	17
Chapter 4: A Royal Capital	25
Chapter 5: The Revolution: Collier's Raid	39
Chapter 6: The Revolution: General Leslie's Occupation	49
Chapter 7: The Revolution: Benedict Arnold's Occupation	53
Chapter 8: The Revolution: Cornwallis' Occupation	57
Chapter 9: Portsmouth's Revolutionary War Veterans	61
Chapter 10: The Ferry and the Tunnels	85
Chapter 11: "The War of '12" - Craney Island	97
Chapter 12: Portsmouth Veterans of the War of 1812	107
Chapter 13: The Great Fire of 1821 - Fire & Police	117
Chapter 14: Lafayette's Visit	129
Chapter 15: Sail, Steam and Stage Make the Town	135
Chapter 16: "Where Rail Meets Sail"	139
Chapter 17: Yellow Fever	151
Chapter 18: Returning To the Growing Town	163
Chapter 19: Ante-Bellum Days, Nat Turner, The Mexican War and John Brown	169
Chapter 20: Secession	175
Chapter 21: Capture of the Naval Shipyard - "The Pawnee War"	179
Chapter 22: The City Prepares for the Storm	183
Chapter 23: The CSS "Virginia"	187
Chapter 24: The Union Occupation and "The Beast"	199
Chapter 25: Portsmouth's Civil War Veterans	211
Chapter 26: The Spanish American War	217
Chapter 27: The Navy Yard	223
Chapter 28: The Naval Hospital	257
Chapter 29: The Coast Guard Base	279
Chapter 30: A City of Neighborhoods	285
Chapter 31: How We Lived	303
Chapter 32: Etiquette Lessons From the Past	315

Chapter 33: Some Early African American History
 and the Institution of Slavery 323
Chapter 34: Walking the Streets of the Olde Towne 349
Chapter 35: Amusements 377
Chapter 36: Getting Educated 399
Chapter 37: The Town's Business Begins 415
Chapter 38: More Businesses, Cemeteries and the Courts 437
Chapter 39: Taverns and Hotels : 455
Chapter 40: Getting Religion 469
Chapter 41: A List of Mayors, Managers and First Citizens 513

INTRODUCTION

Miss Mildred M. Holladay's delightful *History of Portsmouth* has been virtually inaccessible for seventy five years, existing only in yellowed, crumbling newsprint, or blurry typescript with a separate index which I first commissioned to be handmade by volunteers in the library local history room of the public library in the 1970s.

Miss Holladay is less a historian than a journalist. She is the first in a line of journalists which includes that wonderful old *Virginian Pilot* gossip and historian George Tucker. Many of his columns have been anthologized into his books about South Hampton Roads, known to those who really love the place as simply "Tidewater," and are well worth searching out; Margaret Windley who put out her own Portsmouth newspaper, *The Portsmouth Times* and Alan Flanders who has puttered about Portsmouth's past for many years publishing a column in *Currents*, the Portsmouth supplement to the *Viginian Pilot*, which I occasionally quote here.

But the ultimate Portsmouth journalist in Miss Holladay's line is that irreplaceable and irrepressible Portsmouth cheerleader and gadfly, Ida Kay Jordan, who has devoted her life to delighting the citizens, harassing the politicians and describing in her long-running column in *Currents* this special place. I hope that some time in the future someone, perhaps Ida Kay herself, will compile her columns into an anthology, as the old *Portsmouth Star* did for Miss Holladay. It would be as useful, as entertaining, and as enlightening about the period after Miss Holladay's *History*.

Portsmouth's story is not trivial, for it is the site of the world's largest and the nation's oldest naval shipyard, the largest U. S. naval hospital on the Atlantic Coast and the oldest in the nation; it is headquarters for the Coast Guard and its predecessors and the city has been a prize in every war fought on American soil and a supplier of men and ships to every one of our foreign wars. Portsmouth history is really America's history. For a short time it was Virginia's third largest city with a population of 114,775 citizens. More to the point, however, it is a quirky, funny, lovable place, full of outrageous characters, heroes and villains, and one of the nation's largest assemblages of surviving historic houses. In the Olde Towne you can actually walk through excellent examples of every period of American architecture from Colonial times to the present in three-quarters of an hour. The whole of Olde Towne was added to the *National Register of Historic Districts* in 1969 and is so indicated by a marker beside the Hill House. This registration resulted from an architectural survey in 1963 by architect John Paul Hanbury which was followed by the adoption of architectural guidelines for the district in 1967.

Portsmouth has been blessed with people who loved it so much they felt compelled to record its past, among them John Clloyd Emmerson who compiled the valuable gleanings from old newspapers called "the Emmerson files," often cited in this work and "Some Fugitive Items . . . " both surviving only in typescript. He published three volumes on the coming of the steamship to the Chesapeake Bay as well. The elder Marshall Butt collected every document he could find about Portsmouth, and published the basic history of the city called *Portsmouth Under Four Flags* and other more specialized histories of its first settlers, place names and physicians. William H. Stewart documented all of Norfolk County's history, Portsmouth being its county seat, in his book *A History of Norfolk County* carefully republished by General Hank Morris in the 1990s. John Porter also recorded the town's Civil War history in a volume now long out of print. To this list I must add several citizens who compiled and published from the vast accumulation of pictures of this most photogenic, and most photographed historic old port, among them Bob Wentz, Alf Mapp, Casandra Newby-Alexander, Mae Breckenridge-Haywood and Robert Albertson. Part of this photograph collection is available on the INTERNET through the Library of Virginia. The library also has the collected papers of Mrs. Bertha Edwards (unpublished) on African American history, the *Portsmouth Star* on microfilm; the clipping morgue of the Portsmouth section of the *Virginian Pilot* and its picture file, also stored in the library history room. They have been invaluable sources for my part of this work. I will often refer to *Portsmouth and Norfolk County Documents* a multi-volume collection of copies of letters, legal papers, memorabilia and narratives which this author started collecting in the library forty-five years ago, a work that is still in progress.

I have taken advantage of the encyclopedic memory of Barnabas (Billy) Baker, a past mayor of the city and its *real* historian, although he refuses to collect his vast store of facts on paper: Mrs. Alice Haynes, who succeeded Marshall Butt as Director of the Portsmouth Naval Shipyard Museum with its small research library and was president and a driving force in the Portsmouth Historical Association; my successor, Susan H. Burton and finally the current keepers of the Portsmouth Public Library local history collection, which I believe is among the most comprehensive of such collections in the Commonwealth, Edith Carmichael and Ed Rakowski. Some of my other sources and reviewers also need mention: J. Brewer Moore, past City Planner; William A. Brown III, past Assistant Director of Libraries; Ned McCabe who inspired me to put down what I knew in print after hearing my regular presentation on the city's history for the Vann Lefcoe Workshop; Gabrielle Maupin Bielenstein and Fleet Murdaugh Carney Morgan. I must also give credit to my wife, Marguerite Barco Burgess, for her tireless editorial work.

My purpose is to make Miss Holladay accessible again, identifying the places she describes, correcting what more recent research has revealed to be wrong, bowdlerizing Miss Holladay's unfortunate references to race, and adding some of my own insights into what later became of the places and people she describes.

The reader may be concerned about the owners of this intellectual property. Foreman's and Emmerson's works were written so long ago they are now in the public domain.

As compiler of most of the primary source collections in the library I give myself permission to use them. Miss Holladay wrote for the newspaper, making her part "work for hire" belonging to the old *Portsmouth Star*, now departed, with any claim to copyright. The *Star* added its name to the old *Norfolk Ledger Star*, now also defunct. I checked with the *Virginian Pilot* as to whether it claimed any rights to Miss Holladay's work. Marian Anderfuren, Director of News Operations, *The Virginian-Pilot* replied: "We hold no copyright on the material referenced below (i. e. *History of Portsmouth* by Miss Mildred M. Holladay). I think this response clears the way for your publication." Based on that, I believe Miss Holladay's work to be in the public domain as well. I claim copyright only to my comments and additions.

    The *Portsmouth Star* added a forward, which I have not included, by her neighbor and friend the editor Norman Hamilton, who later went on to represent the area in Congress. In this he tells us she was born and brought up in the town. Miss Holladay lived on Dinwiddie Street just south of its intersection with London, on the west side of the street. The house still stands. She was a school teacher in the time when teachers were not allowed to marry. Her cousin, Gabrielle Maupin Bielenstein, remembered her as a "charming and individualistic lady who was planning to vote for the first time when women's suffrage passed, but died before she could fulfill that dream.". Barbara Grace, who was one of her students, remembered that Miss Holladay had studied abroad at Oxford University she thought. Her use of British sources, not now available in Portsmouth, suggests this may be true. Mrs. Grace said Miss Holladay always came to class in a black crape dress lightly dusted with chalk. Her students loved her. Another student, the local historian Barnabus Baker, said she asked him to go to her house and give a note to her maid instructing her to give him an old flintlock pistol so she could show it to the class. Baker peeked in the note and found that along with the pistol she wanted her false teeth which she had forgotten to put in that morning.

    I hope my copious notes will fill out the stories told by our primary narrator. You can tell what is hers and what is mine because my notes are in italics, when they are inserted, and her text is in normal type. Otherwise, my only changes to Miss Holladay's work are corrections to regulate her eccentric use of punctuation.

Dean Burgess, 2007

ELIZABETH RIVER (CRAWFORD BAY)

ORANGE ROW		MARSH ROW	
NORTH STREET			
BOSTON	CHATHAM	CORNWALL	GREENWICH
GLASGOW STREET			
ASHBURN	BOUSH	SUSSEX	WESTMINSTER
LONDON STREET			
CARLISLE	MIFFLIN	BON	CAMBRIDGE
QUEEN STREET			
ARLINGTON	WASHINGTON	DEVONSHIRE	OXFORD
HIGH STREET			
	MONTGOMERY	CHESHIRE	DINWIDDIE
KING STREET			
PRESTON	PROCTOR	HERTFORD	PRINCESS
COUNTY STREET			
BURLINGTON	CLERKSON	LEICHESTER	COUNTY
CRAB STREET (now COLUMBIA)			
GRANBY	HAMPSHIRE	DOVER	VIRGINIA
SOUTH STREET			
HOLBORN	DARBY	SOHO	SALISBURY
BART STREET			

EFFINGHAM STREET

GREEN STREET

WASHINGTON STREET

This map shows the names of the squares.

ELIZABETH RIVER (CRAWFORD BAY)

HAMPTON ROW		ELIZABETH ROW		
NORTH	STREET			
HAMPTON	ELIZABETH	NORFOLK		NORFOLK
GLASGOW	STREET			
BARCELEY	GLASGOW	RED LION		ROW
LONDON	STREET			
QUEEN	HANOVER	LONDON		
QUEEN	STREET			
PRISON	COURTHOUSE	GOLDEN		WATER
HIGH	STREET			
CHURCH	MARKET	BLOOMSBERY		
KING	STREET			
KING	ST. JAMES	EDINBURG		ROW
COUNTY	STREET			
PORTSMOUTH	BRISTOL	CAVENDISH		
CRAB	STREET			
LINCOLN'S INN	MIDDLE	CRAB		
SOUTH	STREET			
ESSEX	FERRY	BUCKINGHAM		
BART STREET				

DINWIDDIE ST. | COURT STREET | MIDDLE STREET | CRAWFORD ST.

Chapter 1: In the Beginning

Miss Mildred Holladay starts her narrative of Portsmouth history with the speculation that the Norse had a settlement on the south end of the Chesapeake Bay, and that this may have been on the site of Portsmouth. It was a common claim by Atlantic Coast cities in her time, including Newport, RI, but excavations of a Norse settlement at L'Anse au Meadow in the 1960s by Helge Ingstad places the Norse settlements in maritime Canada. Farley Mowat in his book <u>Farfarers</u> has added to that evidence the sites of Norse longhouses, beacons and possible walrus fat-rendering sites on Baffin Island, Labrador and Newfoundland. He also identifies the Vikings' primary goal as walrus ivory rather than settlement or exploration. That would preclude any motive for sailing down to the Elizabeth River.

To Miss Holladay's credit, however, she presents her theory only as a speculation and reviews work by the Norwegian historian M. Meljde in an article about Lief Ericson and G. H. Gathorne-Hardy in his book <u>The Norse Discoveries In America</u> as evidence supporting her claim.

One source attributes the discovery of the Elizabeth River, on which the town stands, to Sir Ralph Lane in 1586. He was an officer on the ship <u>Tiger</u> commanded by Sir Richard Grenville and was made "Governor of Virginia" while at the Roanoke Island Colony. His murder of the Native American chief Wingina may have doomed the colony. He did send out expeditions to map the Virginia Coast and his "Discourse On the First Colony" was included in Richard Hakluyt's <u>Principle Navigations</u> in 1592. He jettisoned his original records, unfortunately, to lighten the load on his hasty return to Plymouth, England, and so we will really never know exactly what area he mapped.

The Elizabeth River, however, was named for Elizabeth Stuart, the daughter of James I, called the "Winter Queen of

1

Bohemia" for her short reign there after marrying the Elector (a state historical marker on Crawford Parkway tells this story). It was, of course, Charles who gave Virginia its nickname, calling it "My old dominion."

Surprisingly, Miss Holladay does not present the evidence for Native American settlement at what would become the site of Portsmouth. Marshall Butt, in his 1960s history of Portsmouth, <u>Portsmouth Under Four Flags</u>, tells us Captain John Smith, while reconnoitering the new Jamestown Colony in September 1608, mentions a village where the city now stands. Smith says the village is deserted, located on the southern bank of the Southern Branch of the Elizabeth River - Portsmouth. Smith tells us he crossed the Hampton Roads with twelve men in a small boat and, "Sayled six or seven myles" up the river and saw "garden plots." He also says the shore was, "overgrown with the greatest pyne and firre trees we ever saw in the country.".

Based on a map in <u>The Indian Tribes of North America</u> by John R. Swanton [Pub Washington : U.S.G.P.O., 1952] this settlement would be in the nation of the Chesapeake tribe. Just before the arrival of the colonists at Jamestown the Powhatan Confederation (formed around 1500) made war on the Chesapeakes, decimating them. That could explain why John Smith saw a deserted Indian village in 1608 where Portsmouth now stands.

The Elizabeth River location described by Smith in his journal in 1608 may be confirmed by the excavation made in the year 2000 when the commander's quarters was moved to allow for the expansion of the Portsmouth Naval Hospital (now Naval Medical Center Portsmouth). As I will note later, archaeologists were hired by the federal government to survey that part of Hospital Point which juts into the Elizabeth River in what is now Portsmouth and they discovered artifacts from an Indian settlement there.

Miss Holladay will tell us that Indians still lived in the city within the memory of her sources and were a common sight on its streets up to the 20th century. It is probable, however, that the Indians to whom she refers were from the Nansemond tribe which centered on what was called Nansemond County and is now the city of Suffolk, but also held land within what is now Portsmouth city limits based on the map mentioned above and Miss Holladay's contemporary accounts.

One last connection with the establishment of the first English colony in America at Jamestown took place in 1956 when the Curtis-Dunn Marine Shipyard in Portsmouth built the first full-scale reproductions of the three little ships which brought the settlers: The <u>Susan Constant</u>, the <u>Godspeed</u>, and the <u>Discovery</u>.

Miss Holladay continues, History shows no more favors to Portsmouth for many years and then legend tells us that it was on the site of our city that the first shipload of slaves landed in 1619. We have found no record of this; but the tradition has been handed down and persists. It is said that the Jamestown planters came to this point and purchased them.

Out in the harbor between what is now Norfolk and Portsmouth, there was a battle fought in 1667 between Dutch men-of-war and a fleet of English merchant ships, and the Dutch ships were driven away. Perhaps these ships carried some slaves and have been confused with the Dutch ship *said to have* brought them to Virginia in 1619.

The first slave ship did come to the Jamestown settlement in 1619, but there is no evidence that it stopped at Portsmouth, which would have been recently chartered plantation land at the time, and an unlikely site for this dubious honor.

Shipbuilding projects on the site of what would become Portsmouth start very early. The shipbuilder John Wood recognized the possibilities of this river front when he applied for a land grant here for that very purpose on July 12 1620. He is mentioned on the state historical marker on Crawford Parkway. He said of the location: "thereon is timber fitting for his turne and water sufficient to launch such ships as shall be there built."

Norfolk County, of which Portsmouth would become the county seat was established May 15 1637.

Portsmouth as a town dates back to 1752: but her history really commences with Bacon's Rebellion In 1676, when Capt. William Carver the owner of the plantation on which the city was built (it was granted to him *September 15 1664 - actual this is his second patent, his first was on June 15 1659*), followed the Rebels and gave his life in the cause of liberty. Since a part of Bacon's plan was to kill Indians, "liberty" may be an exaggeration. A state historical marker in the median at the foot of High Street gives the date the land was first patented to Captain William Carver in 1659.

The records of Norfolk County show that Carver was a man of weight in the community. In addition to serving as justice, Burgess and high-sheriff for that county, he held the position of Purveyor for the southern and eastern sections of the Elizabeth River.

In his early deeds he is styled "mariner"; but in later ones he calls himself "merchant", thus conveying land at Church Point (*Scott's Creek*) to his "well-beloved cozens, Edward Davis and Rachel, his wife". In 1666 he appears as "merchant".

Carver married twice; but of his two wives history tells us nothing beyond their names. The first wife was called Elizabeth and her successor Rose. Richard Carver, his son, owned the tract of land now known as Lambert's Point (*now a part of the City of Norfolk*).

Though we know little about the private life of this doughty old captain, we are not without some record of his official career. As justice he was active and alert and while on the bench he in person presented Jone Jenkins as being too familiar with evil spirits and using witchcraft. When the Quakers were tried, he was one of the justices who sentenced them.

One of the local Quakers owned the plantation which is now City Park in Portsmouth. These Quakers would become strong opponents of slavery and among the papers of old Norfolk County, of which Portsmouth was the County seat, preserved at the Chesapeake Clerk's Office, are their declarations issued when they freed their slaves, saying that they do it because of their conviction that it is morally wrong for one man to hold another in servitude. Some Quaker narratives also relate how they would visit their neighbors in an attempt to convince them to release their slaves. I suspect that this activity did not make them popular among the large landowners of Virginia.

As elsewhere in the Colonies citizens of Norfolk County were required to attend the state church - the Church of England - and dissenters were not tolerated. A painting survives of vestrymen dunking a Baptist in the Nansemond River in what is now Suffolk. Methodism, however, was tolerated as a "prayer meeting" of the Church of England.

In the Reverend Mr. John Henry Wingfield's plan of the colonial church in Portsmouth there are pews designated for African Americans - presumably both free and slave.

Our next account of Carver is very painful one: telling us that in 1672, while attending a dinner party, he turned suddenly upon Thomas Gilbert, who was seated next to him and stabbed him to death. The trial shows that Carver was perfectly unconscious of his crime, as he was "laboring under a mental aberration" at the time that the murder was committed.

The most important episode in Carver's checkered life can best be told by one of his associates, Edward Good, secretary to Nathaniel Bacon (*of Bacon's Rebellion*). Good tells us that he had been busy with Bacon nearly all night helping him fill in the blank commissions that the Governor had finally been induced to give him. Bacon had scarcely left him, says Good, "when in came Captain Carver who told me he had been to wait upon the General for a commission, saying that he had decided to risk his old bones against the Indian rogues. The next news that I heard after going home, was that the General had marched against the Indians with a thousand men. Then came the Governor's call to the militia of Middlesex and Gloucester to suppress Bacon. When Bacon had burned Jamestown he pressed the best boat on the James River into his service. and placed his lieutenant-general on board with Captain Carver, formerly in charge of a merchant vessel, to curb the small ships sent out by the Governor."

At this point we must leave Good's narrative for a while and follow an account that gives us more details of the work planned for Carver. The ship referred to by Good was a large one that belonged to Capt. Larramore. It was then armed with a number of cannon and manned by two hundred men. Bacon gave secret orders to Carver, but being a little uncertain of his lieutenant, Bland, failed to inform him of his designs. Carver he said he could trust entirely. They were to go to Accomac, *on the Eastern Shore of Virginia*, for the purpose of capturing *Royal Governor* Berkeley, who was to be seized and carried to England as a prisoner, to be tried before the King for the treatment of his subjects in Virginia. After peace was declared between Berkeley and Bacon, Good tells us that the former sent for Carver, "who would not agree to go to Berkeley until his written pledge had been given him. This done Carver went to the Governor, who feasted and petted him offering large promises if he would quit Bacon and serve with him. Carver told him if he had served the devil he would be true to him; but he thought he would go home and live quietly."

From the source before quoted, we learn that while Berkeley and Carver were together that Berkeley had a secret message from Larramore, telling him that he would seize his *(Carver's)* ship if he would send him men and seamen. The Governor was delighted with this news, and complied at once with the request. While doing this, however, he had to stretch out the interview with Carver who, when finally dismissed, started out to join his ship. He was amazed to find it under attack by the enemy and decided to run away. "He changed his mind" says Good. "and went tamely on board."At all events, he was savage enough when he reached Bland, whom he cursed and raved at as a traitor who had ruined the cause. The vessel was recovered by Larramore, and Bland and Carver both put in irons and three days later hanged.

Marshall Butt, Sr., compiled a list of all of the landowners who owned property in Norfolk County in the seventeenth century, It is in a card catalog at the library.

Chapter 2: The Founder

Carver's property was forfeited and the Portsmouth tract was re-granted to Col. William Crawford In 1715 *(in another source this is listed as 1711, as we will see later. On the city website it appears as 1716, but I believe 1711 is the correct date. The original spelling of the name, Craford, will also be addressed later).* It is probable that the Crawford family took up the land soon after the forfeiture, the legal title not being established until later.

Roughly speaking the bounds of this patent were Crab Creek *on the south*, a small stream that once separated Portsmouth and New Town, *now Port Center, but originally called Gosport Village. It was to become the site of the Gosport Yard, later the Norfolk Naval Shipyard. The creek sometimes reasserts itself at high water between the Downtown Tunnel and the WAVY-TV station and is facetiously called "Lake WAVY". There was a ferry across this navigable waterway until the latter part of the 1790s, when it was replaced with a bridge. On Marshall Butt's list of the names of the blocks in the town you will find one called "Ferry Square," which was the point of departure from Portsmouth to Gosport Village. Another block on its banks is called Crab Square for the creek it bounded. Continuing the bounds of Craford's land we find* Paradise Creek, also on the south, and Church Creek *now Scott's Creek. It may have been called Church Creek because the land adjacent to it, now the neighborhood called Port Norfolk, was the glebe for Portsmouth Parish, now Trinity Church* on the west. The northern boundary was the land of Joshua Curle, now included in the Naval Hospital property and also a small body of water called Island Creek. This creek is now being reclaimed and filled in by the Government and the owners of the land known as Craford Place. *This landfill now marks the southern boundary of the Naval hospital grounds. Craford Place is now a street in the Swimming Point neighborhood of Portsmouth.*

In the documents signed by the Colonel in <u>Portsmouth and Norfolk County Documents</u> *it appears he never signed himself "Crawford," but always Crafford, or more often Craford. He appears as Crawford only in public documents. A clerk obviously read the double "f" as a "w" making it into a more common English name. His name is correctly spelled on the statue of him placed in front of Towne Bank on the northwestern corner of Crawford and High streets, erected in 2006, facing the location of his old plantation house. A Crafford family, who spell their name occasionally Craford, was prominent in Kent in the years before the colonization of Virginia, which may be one in the same with Norfolk County's Crafords. That this family with this spelling was elsewhere in Virginia is demonstrated by the Crafford House built in 1749 at Mulberry Point in Newport News now a part of Fort Eustis. Col. William Craford's grandfather, a major Norfolk County land owner, also spelled his name Craford - we know this is the town founder's grandfather as he mentions his grandson and granddaughter Abigail (later Abigail Conner) in his will.*

Returning to the bounding of the Craford property Miss Holladay says: in old times, this creek (*Island Creek*) ran well into *what is now the* Park View *neighborhood*. It took its name from an island at its juncture with the Elizabeth River. This island was gradually submerged but could be seen plainly into recent times (*the 1930s*). The eastern boundary, of course, was the *Southern Branch of the Elizabeth* River.

It is strange that so little is known of the man who founded our town, and to whom she owes some of her greatest privileges. One tradition tells us that Colonel Crawford was born in Portsmouth, England, and named his town for his native city. *The great shipyard there is also called Gosport and its main street runs from the Gosport shipyard to its naval hospital as Effingham Street does in Portsmouth, Virginia.* Another legend says he was born in Hull, England, and laid out the town after that city. *The "English Basement" houses so characteristic of Portsmouth's Olde Towne today are said to resemble houses of the same style surviving in Hull. Only two of the streets in the town are named for British cities: London (an obvious choice) and Glasgow (which has caused some to speculate a Scottish connection).*

We do not know when he was born; but it is more than likely that Norfolk County was his birthplace, since his grandparents, and perhaps his parents *George Craford and Abigail Mason Craford*, lived there. The will Of William Crawford, Gent., *Col. William Craford's grandfather*, is on record at the Clerk's Office in Portsmouth, dated 1699. *These records were moved to the municipal complex at Great Bridge in Chesapeake, VA, by Clerk of Courts for Norfolk County, Charles Cross, but most of them are available on microfilm, or in copies at the Portsmouth Public Library.* Though slightly mutilated its contents are plainly set forth. He left no children, his heirs being his grandson, William, and his granddaughter, Abigail Crawford *(later Conner)*, "both minors". *They were orphans. The grandfather, presumed to be the immigrant, was a large land owner - whose holdings included property in Norfolk County, Princess Anne County, now Virginia Beach, and even well into North Carolina as far as the Pasquotank River.* There is one English city mentioned in this will - Plymouth. It requests that his man servant be sent back there as it is his home. Mr. Craford also appointed a Plymouth man as his attorney in England. *Based on the fact that both William and Abigail were minors at the time of their grandfather's will it is reasonable to say the Colonel's birth was no later than 1680.* Colonel Craford's father was Robert Craford, but of his mother there is no mention *(as you can see from the previous Miss Holladay has the father's name wrong and his mothers name is now known - see the <u>Dictionary of Virginia Biography</u> now in draft and my notes above).* His sister Abigail married a gentleman named Keader Connor, from an old Norfolk County family, and lived in Portsmouth. Colonel Crawford himself never married. His will dated 1761, is on record at the Clerk's office *and the Portsmouth library.* The bulk of his property was bequeathed to his sister, Mrs. Conner. A portion of his estate was left to the children of Mary Veale, "deceased," but not as a whole - that is, each child was called by name and had a separate legacy. *Mary Veale is referred to as his "housekeeper." In the complete list of the earliest purchases compiled by the elder Marshall Butt many of the lots were sold by the Veales. Craford also left some land to his plantation overseer David Dale who will be mentioned later.*

We know that in 1710 Col. Craford was caring for his paternal grandmother in her second widowhood. In 1711 he patented 173 acres in Nansemond County, now the city of Suffolk and on 31 October 1716 he patented 1,129 acres in Norfolk County across from the town of Norfolk. This latter would, of course, become the town of Portsmouth.

Craford was a partner in the construction of a mill in Norfolk County and a wharf, presumably at Portsmouth. He appears in at least one deed of sale for an enslaved woman, but it is not know if he was a large slaveholder. Col. Crawford was on the bench of Norfolk County for years, *and was appointed by the Royal Governor as Sheriff of Norfolk County on 4 May 1725. He was a Colonel of the Militia by 1742 and County Lieutenant, that is commander of the Militia, in 1748.*

He served in the House of Burgesses a number of terms. *He was first elected to the House in 1712 representing Norfolk County and served with only one short break for thirty years. He sat three times on the Committee of Claims (1723, 1744 and 1746) and twice on the committee that drafted a reply to governor's messages. His last service was to manage for the House £600 for the support of British soldiers blown into Virginia while sailing to Cape Breton.*

That he was a man of broad vision and great ability, there can be no doubt. It was to his liberality and wide outlook that we owe the ferries (*in fact, the ferry service substantially pre-dates Colonel Craford; when it was closed in the 1950s it was the longest continuously operated ferry service in the nation, but he did continue it and it would become the property of Norfolk County*), the County Court and many of our other assets.

A very intelligent and gifted lady of a past generation, Miss Louisa Emmerson, has done more than anyone else to interest us in the founder of our city. She has preserved for us a picture of the times of Col. Crawford in Portsmouth, as it was represented to her by the older people of her own day. *Her full account survives in the Emmerson file at the Portsmouth library.*

She remembered the Crawford homestead and tells us that, "it stood at the southeastern corner of High and Crawford streets *on Bloomsbery Square*; a comfortable brick dwelling built in the colonial style. *The Dale-Reed house on Swimming Point Walk was the home of Craford's overseer David Dale. It is the only manor house surviving in the two cities from the eighteenth century.* One local historian believes it is older than the 1735 date attributed to it and that it was once Craford's home. It is said to have been built with brick imported from England. It certainly illustrates what Craford's home in town probably looked like. There are descendants of David Dale still living in Portsmouth today.

High Street was then the private plantation road leading to the County Road *(the King's highway)* about three hundred feet to the east, and directly in front of the house was the Elizabeth River with its healthy breezes and pleasant odors. *The house lot ran 113 feet south from High Street on Crawford.* When the condominiums now there were under construction in 1987 Alan Flanders excavated bottles, plates, pipe stems, a baby's shoe and a part of a brick wall, but then City Manager George Hanbury refused to halt construction saying there were no artifacts of interest there. To return to Crawford's residence, the pleasure grounds are said to have been well shaded; and certainly he did not have to go far for his shade trees; and it is said of the variety that he planted, the oak, sycamore and beech *which* long survived him. New settlers, as these died out, planted the streets of our town with Lombardy poplars, Pride of China, elm, and paper mulberries. *The Pride of China and mulberries survive in the Olde Towne now as persistent weed trees.* The northern border of the plantation was planted with swamp laurel, jessamine, fringe tree, myrtle and woodbine; forming a screen beautiful to view and conducive to health, *by* warding off malaria. *It was believed when Miss Emmerson was writing that malaria was caused by "miasmas," or unhealthy breezes from swamps like the Dismal Swamp, just south of the city.*

"Here too were the sportsman's pets, partridges, robins and wild ducks; here too singing birds built their nests, and martins and hummingbirds. On the plantation grew crops of Indian corn and tobacco beside all the succulent vegetables of the day, ready for the master's table."

Our chronicler gives us, too, a graphic account of Col. Crawford's pleasures, reminding us "that in colonial days as planters were separated from one another by watercourses, the sailboat and bateau were their only conveyance, and that when Mr. Crawford went to Jamestown, Hampton or Smithfield he would be conveyed in one of these boats. *The explanation for the earlier development of large cities in the Northern Colonies, but not around the Chesapeake Bay is a consequence of each large landowner having his own wharf from which he sent his goods directly to England and from which he would receive imported manufactured good directly to the same wharf, without transshipment. It was said the nearest town to the Chesapeake planters was London. In Portsmouth's case this is bourne out by a bill of lading signed by Craford for the direct export of his tobacco crop* .

When Mr. Crawford and his friends from the adjacent waters of the Nansemond and the Lower James and branches of the Elizabeth proposed a fishing trip, we are told that Craney Island, *now a part of Portsmouth,* was their rendezvous. The little fleet made a gay appearance rowed by black oarsmen with flags flying. When the fatigue of drawing in the lines and hauling in seines was over, the slaves were called and matters were turned over to them. Now the gentlemen, having nothing else to do, talked politics, told jokes and discussed the absorbing news of the day - the Spanish War, France and Sir Robert Walpole. In the beautiful autumn with which this land is blest, Mr. Crawford and his friends would hunt through the extensive range offered for the purpose in the land bordering on the Dismal Swamp. Suffolk was the meeting place and there would gather hunters from Southhampton *County* and Surry to try their luck with those of the water sections. When the field sports were over, then would follow dinner; sitting late into the night these mighty hunters would doubtless discuss the neglected duties of the

County Court *and* suggest improvements for the roads. Many plans no doubt, were brought out for increasing the wealth of the county. Indian problems were debated with solutions offered by all. Surry friends would tell the latest news from England, which had reached them by the way of Williamsburg."

When his duties were over, and his pleasures had been laid aside we can picture this fine old gentleman sitting on his porch gazing across his well-cropped lawn at the river, dreaming dreams and seeing visions of its usefulness. His liberal mind doubtless planned the city which should arise from his fruitful acres, and in the distant future rank with the great ports of the New World. Turning his eye to the west he saw a more convenient spot for the County Court House than the one at Washington Point - *now the Berkley section of Norfolk city. The new courthouse he built stood on Courthouse Square where the Ocean House, later called the Hotel Monroe would be built in the 1850s after the courts were moved to the new 1846 Courthouse location on Prison Square, across Court Street. This would be followed on Courthouse Square by the Famous Department Store owned by Bernard and Zelma Rivin, after the hotel burned down, and in the late 1990s by the Tidewater Community College Visual Arts Center);* already he had given a landing placc on his farm for the ferry to Norfolk (*on Ferry Point, now called North Harbor, or Portside after a public amusement center under a tent, much loved by Portsmouthians, which stood there until it was blown down by a storm in the 1990s).* The dream must come true; and to make it a reality, Col. Crawford gave up some of his fairest land for this purpose. We can picture him as he goes about his little town, encouraging the struggling shipbuilders and merchants who had flocked to the, newly-fledged city, attracted by the cheapness of the lots and the abundance of the work to be found there. *Another account says the first settlers were mainly Scottish merchants from Norfolk, as Andrew Sprowle was, attracted by the cleanliness of the place compared to our sister across the river.* Crawford lived to see the town outgrow the bounds that he had given it; and arrangements were being made to add more lots at the time of his death in 1762. *A full list of all of the original purchasers was compiled by Marshall Butt and is in the library collection.*

Be it said to Portsmouth's everlasting shame, that she has done nothing to honor the name of her founder *apart from naming two streets after him. Since Miss Holladay this has been remedied by a state marker in the median of High Street east of Crawford Street indicating the location of his town house at the southeast corner of Crawford Street and High Street and, of course, the statue of him across the street.* His grave has been trampled out of existence and his burial place forgotten. It is possible that he was laid to rest in Trinity churchyard. *Although a monument there names him as a member of the first vestry, no grave stone was listed among those copied from the first Vestry Minute Book by this writer and the elder Marshall Butt.* It is more likely that he was buried in a private cemetery on his own plantation, according to the custom of the day. Some years ago when the workmen were digging a foundation for the annex to the Merchants and Farmers Bank, they disinterred some human bones, among them three skulls. *Miss Holladay does not mean the site of Towne Bank (previously Merchants and Farmers) on the northwest corner of Crawford and High streets, directly across the intersection from the site of his town house, but the bank's earlier location on the south side of High Street between Crawford and Middle streets.* It was suggested at the time that this spot was once the Crawford burying-ground. It was certainly a part of his garden. *The Towne Bank location is where his statue, dedicated in 2006, now surveys the town he created.*

  The act creating the town says: "Be it enacted by the Lieutenant Governor, Council and Burgesses of this present General Assembly, and it is hereby enacted, by the authority of the same, That the said piece, or parcel of land be, and is hereby constituted, appointed, erected and established, a town, in the manner it is already laid out, by said William Crawford, in lots and streets, to be called by, and retain the name of Portsmouth, and that the freeholders of said town, shall forever hereafter, enjoy the same rights and privileges which the freeholders of any other town, erected by an act of Assembly, in this colony, have and enjoy." The act was signed by Royal Governor Robert Dinwiddie, for whom a street in the town is named. Another street in the town was named for then Governor General, Francis Howard, Baron Howard of Effingham.

The town of Portsmouth became the county seat of Norfolk County on January 20 1801.

Chapter 3: The Town Begins

The town of Portsmouth entered upon its municipal existence on February 27 1752. The Act of Incorporation says. "It has been represented to the General Assembly that William Crawford, of the County of Norfolk, Gentleman, hath lately laid out a parcel of land on the south side of the Elizabeth River, opposite to the town of Norfolk, into one hundred and twenty-two lots, commodious streets, places, courthouse, market and landing, for a town by the name of Portsmouth, and made sale of the said lots to divers persons who are desirous to settle and build thereon, and also that the said town lies very convenient for trade and navigation; be it enacted that said piece or parcel of land be hereby constituted, appointed, erected and established as a town to be called by the name of Portsmouth."

This act forbade the construction of any wooden chimneys within the town limits *as a fire precaution, no doubt*; and furthermore granted it all the same privileges accorded to other towns in the state.

Portsmouth was surveyed and laid off by Gershom Nimmo of Norfolk, and the original plan is still in existence; and can be seen at the office of the Clerk of the Court of Hustings. *There are copies in the Portsmouth Public Library and the Portsmouth Naval Shipyard Museum. It was laid out like an English county town with broad streets alternating with narrow ones in a grid pattern..*

The eastern boundary of the town was, of course, the Elizabeth River, which also marked its northern limit. The north side of South Street and Crab Creek bounded it on the south, while what is now the eastern side of Dinwiddie Street was the western border. Crawford Street, at first called Main, was the last street on that side of the town, Water Street being added later,.the lots on the eastern side extend*ed* to the water. Next to it and running parallel to it was Middle Street so called from its position Court Street being the only one west of it. North Street was originally called Ferry Street, the Norfolk ferry then running from the end of it, where the Seaboard warehouses now stand. *The Seaboard Warehouses stood where the Holiday Inn, its parking ramp, Harbor Tower and the Visitor's Center now stand, on North Landing, near where the ferry still runs. This whole area was, at one time, called Ferry Point. These wharves were removed in the 1950s, but once characterized the waterfront, as illustrated in postcards, photographs and engravings from this time. One long time resident remembered chasing rats in the decaying wharves. There is a plan now to remove the Holiday Inn and replace it with condominiums.* Columbia Street was called Crabbe until about thirty years ago *(1905)*, when its name was changed at the request of the property owners on it; the African Americans living in the lower part of it had brought the name into such disrepute, *they argued.* It was originally "Crab," so called from the creek of that name which flowed through a part of it, cutting off Crawford and Middle Streets and running far up into *Norfolk County, now Chesapeake.* At this time there was only one sufficient land above high water mark to make one large lot at the southeastern intersection of South and Court streets. What is now the rest of the block was then under water at high tide. The lot was called Widow's Point, probably from its first purchaser, Mary Avery, widow, as she is styled in the deed for it. Mrs. Avery was the ancestress of many families in town and two of her sons fought in the Revolution.

Portsmouth was laid off in squares, each of them bearing a good old English name, Buckingham, Golden, Red Lyon, etc. *Portsmouth is one of the few American cities in the nation to retain the original names of its blocks. Some businesses have taken their square names in the past - Prison Square Antiques, the Oxford Square Restaurant, the Bristol Square Office Complex, and the Cheshire Grill. Ida Kay Jordan has suggested that markers be placed in the pavement of these squares to identify their original names.* The squares bounded on one side by the river were called rows, and took their names from the square next to them. The lot frontage on the streets running east and west was 360 feet while on those extending north and south the frontage was only 226 feet.

Only four lots were allowed to a square and tradition says that the narrow streets, such as Glasgow, King and Bart were meant for alleyways or back entrances. *Another explanation for this layout of alternating wide and narrow streets is that the elegant houses stood on the broad streets and the homes of the artisans and lesser lights on the narrow streets; and indeed the houses on the wide streets are large and the ones surviving on the narrow streets are modest.*

Though each owner had plenty of lot the houses were all on the corners directly on the street line. Behind them was the kitchen, vegetable garden and space for drying clothes. The remainder of the lot was generally a flower garden; but the whole lot was fenced in the English fashion with a fence too high to show it off. The larger houses in the town had English basements, that is a story with its floor right on the street level and built of brick; the rest of the house being wood. Quite a number of these houses remain, but the basement story has in most instances been changed into stores marring their quaint air. *This was true in Miss Holladay's time. All have been restored now to private homes and the businesses, often little groceries, removed. Some were lowered when the English basement style became unpopular. To do this massive dollies were placed in their basements and the "basement" removed by lowering.*

Moreau de St. Mery, an exiled French gentleman and refugee from the Island of San Domingo, in the 1700s tells us: "The roads leading to Portsmouth are mere tracks, large enough for wagons, occasionally bridged across ditches, streams, or mud holes, by small tree trunks placed close together. . . One meets coaches, wagons and carts on these roads, the carts sometimes drawn by yoked oxen; and occasionally one passes a horse with a husband in the saddle and his wife riding behind, which indicates that the horses are stronger than they seem." This small pillow mounted behind the saddle is called a pillion. He goes on to tell us, "I will close my account of Norfolk, Portsmouth and Gosport by remarking that the women in these places, as elsewhere in Virginia, have the sweetest of voices; and this charm, perhaps *one of the greatest the fair sex can possess, is so pronounced that the English language, far from sweet, becomes something quite different on their seductive lips."*

In 1763 the town was extended, incorporating certain lands devised to Thomas Veale by Col. Crawford. This addition included the west side of Dinwiddie Street, Washington from Bart to North, *and* a part of Green Street; and South Street was extended across the new streets. Bart Street, too, was added at this time. The new squares were also given names *which they retain to this day.*

This same year (1763), by act of the Assembly, the town was empowered to appoint nine trustees. Those selected were Andrew Sprowle, Thomas Veale, Charles Stewart, Humphrey Roberts, David Purcell, Francis Miller, James Rae and Amos Etheridge. The first official act of the new body was the laying off of the lots in the newly annexed territory.

Meanwhile Andrew Sprowle, one of the richest merchants in Virginia, had purchased land across Crab Creek from Thomas Bustin and there started the village of Gosport, establishing a marine yard (present navy yard), and many other industries in his little settlement. *Sprowle selected the location because it was protected water with a sandbank at the correct angle for careening ships. This process which predates dry docks is illustrated in* <u>*Images of America, Portmouth , VA*</u> *from contemporary drawings. To careen a ship you would run it out above a sandbar, wait for the tide to leave it high and dry, and then pull the ship over on its side with a team of oxen and clean and repair that side of the ship. When the tide came in again you would turn the ship and at the next low tide repeat the process on the other side. This was the only place on this part of the Atlantic Coast where a protected sandbank of this sort was available to deep water. Long after this practice was replaced by dry docks this sandbank still appeared on nautical charts of the Elizabeth River as "Cox's Island," for which the annual Cock Island sailing regatta and race is now named, although locals will tell you it came from houses of prostitution surviving near there until the twentieth century.* He also built a fine residence for himself just behind his marine yard *which he named Soul's Point.*

Portsmouth was not very old herself when her first suburb came into existence. *Gosport Village was annexed to Portsmouth in 1784.* So useful did Mr. Sprowle's shipyard prove that soon the British government kept it busy and found it necessary to place a navy agent there. Mr. Sprowle filled this office until the outbreak of the Revolution.

We get a glimpse of Mr. Sprowle's little village in the days before the Revolutionary War had spoilt it, from a French traveler who visited this country in 1764. *Moreau de St. Mary's diary is dated in Portsmouth records as 1794, but that date cannot be correct because he describes meeting Andrew Sprowle, who would have been long dead, Gosport as a separate village, which it would not have been at the later date, and refers to "the King".* This confusion which places the Frenchman's visit at least thirty years after it took place probably rises from the publication date of his diary, not when it was written. The diary of this gentleman has recently come to light in the archives of Paris. The writer's name is not given and the manuscript is incomplete. While its author is entirely unknown, *or was at Miss Holladay's time,* it is believed that he was what might be called a secret agent sent out by the French Government to get information about the Colonies. The traveler came to Norfolk and stayed there, a few days; but upon visiting Portsmouth he liked the smaller town so much better that he immediately engaged lodgings at Roberts' Ordinary, taking up his quarters there on April 17, 1764, and dining at 6 o'clock. "Portsmouth," he tells us, "has the advantage of Norfolk, having deeper water on its side. Ships of any size can come to their wharves, of which there are several very convenient.—This harbour is safe for ships of any burthen. It is the only part of Virginia where they build anything of ships. They have all the conveniences possible for that purpose. There is a fine ropery here; and there are plenty of masts of all proportions to be had, and great quantities are shipped to all parts, especially to Havana, where they have a contract for that article.—I look upon this place as one of the properest on the continent for a King's port. As to the harbour, none can be better, and the country is well stocked with timber; they make their own cordage; have plenty of iron and all kinds of naval stores. The drinking water at Norfolk is bad, but very good in Portsmouth. Both places are chiefly inhabited by the Scotch, all Presbyterians; and though the most bigoted set of people in the world, have no house of worship of their own. There is a church in both places of the English Establishment *This would be Trinity Church, then Portsmouth Parish, completed in 1762 and Old St. Paul's in Norfolk.*—Dined today with Andrew Sprowle, Esq. the 'headman' of Portsmouth, He lives in a pleasant place separated from the town by a creek. His house goes by the name of Gasporte *(Gosport takes its name, as mentioned earlier, from the great shipyard at Portsmouth, England)*, and he has a very fine wharf before his door where the King's ships generally heave down. This merchant is a gentleman of great reputation." Our traveler goes on to describe the launching of a ship at Western Branch; and there he met with an accident, his horse having run away. He treated his cuts and bruises very lightly. Dr. Purcell cured them by frequent bleedings. The ferry at that time, he tells us, used three boats, and covered a distance of three quarters of a mile.

Gosport was partially burned in 1776. Sprowle's house was set on fire by an infuriated mob in retaliation for Dunmore's bombardment of Portsmouth. *The details of Dunmore and Sprowle in the first year of the American Revolution will be covered in a later chapter.*

Mr. Sprowle being one of the Governor's intimate friends, they had left Portsmouth together. Sprowle's property was forfeited and in 1784 the General Assembly of Virginia appointed three commissioners to sell these lands.

Gosport was to be laid out in conformity with the town of Portsmouth, as far as possible, the lots corresponding in size. Before the year was out the lots from 1 to 212 were sold with the exception of those reserved for the navy yard—from 19 to 56. Many of the purchasers of these lots did not live in this vicinity, and deeds were recorded in various clerks' offices. Bonds were given with payments at the end of the year. Many of them did not comply with their contracts; and the land purchased by them was sold again with the remainder of the public lands in 1795. This sale was made by lottery, bringing the sum of four hundred and ninety dollars. This amount was applied immediately to the building of a road to Deep Creek, and a causeway between Portsmouth and Gosport *at Court Street*.

This bridge had draws near each end, for Crab Creek at that time was a busy thoroughfare. It was an outlet for the farms in the nearby section and ran far into the west; and schooners and sloops plied its waters, carrying necessaries to the farms and bringing from them the crops and timber.

Portsmouth, too, was growing rapidly, and as time went on the residents of the town felt the need of a street nearer the water. The river front on the east was lined with shipyards, sail lofts and machine shops. A street was opened up by those who owned lots on the east side of Crawford Street; but the right of way was subject to the will of the property owners, who could close it whenever they chose to do so.

In 1791 an appeal was made to the General Assembly for right to lay off a water street in the town. The petition was granted, and the property owners were authorized to lay off the street. This act forbade injury to private property if the owners objected. Naturally, with such a proviso, the street was not legally laid off at this time. Forty years later there was another appeal made to the General Assembly, with better results. The Act this time authorized the Town Trustees to lay off a street forty feet wide; beginning 216 feet from Crawford Street, and running from one end of the town to the other. Should any property owner be unwilling to cede the required land, twelve impartial freeholders were to be selected and empowered to condemn the land needed. Many of the Water Street lots were sold off in 1839.

From the time that Gosport was rebuilt, the east side of First Street was lined with docks and warehouses used for the East India trade. These wharves were owned chiefly by the Dickson family *(Buried in Trinity Churchyard, see <u>Surviving Graves In Trinity Churchyard, Portsmouth</u> by Dean Burgess for further details on their extensive land holdings and business.)*, the Young family *(also buried in Trinity churchyard)* and Coxe family *(for whom Cox's Island in the Elizabeth River was probably named)*. These with several other families had handsome brick residences on First Street; Captain James Young's house is the only one left now *(torn down in the 1930s and now a part of the Port Center industrial park)*, the others having been razed to make room for business. The Young house has an interesting history. It is now *(1935)* called the Neville house, having been occupied by that family for two generations. It was the birthplace of General Wendell Neville, the hero of Chateau-Thierry *in World War I*, who also won laurels in the Spanish-American War. General Neville's father fought in the Confederate service in the War Between the States; the builder of the house was James Young, a captain in the Revolutionary army. This house stood on part of the land now used by the Government as a buoy yard *which was, until the construction of the nTelos Pavilion on this site. This buoy yard was landmark of the Coast Guard presence on the Portsmouth river front of which we will hear more in the chapter on that service.*

The Dickson home was razed many years ago. One of these brothers died under very sad circumstances. He had married a young Scotch lady, whom he had met on one of his voyages. She was always so much troubled whenever he started out to sea that he finally yielded to her wishes to settle down to land duties. He was pledged to one more voyage, but it was to be the last one. This was so, but not in the sense in which he had intended it to be. The ship was lost at sea, and he was drowned.

The Coxe home stood on the western side of First Street and was torn down in 1928. Capt. Coxe's story *will be* told elsewhere in this book.

At this point Miss Holladay continues to identify houses and businesses, but I will take her work out of order and continue the history of the town. The social history of the town; the houses, surviving and lost; the businesses and particularly the unusually handsome and historic collection of churches will be deferred to later chapters.

Portsmouth played its part in the French and Indian War as the point of debarkation in 1755 for British troops on their way to join General Edward Braddock's ill-fated campaign in Pennsylvania.

A scale model of the town as it looked before the American Revolution is on display in the Naval Shipyard Museum.

CHAPTER 4: A ROYAL CAPITAL

Portsmouth having been a garrison town since colonial days has had wide scope for service in time of war, and has done a noble part in the wars both of her country and state. At the outbreak of the Revolution there was in the town a large Tory element, and her first service at this time was of a dubious nature, becoming the seat of the royal governor in 1775. In May of that year the ship *Roebuck* of his majesty's navy entered the harbor and quietly proceeded up the river to Sprowle's shipyard *now the Norfolk Naval Shipyard in Portsmouth, then called Gosport Shipyard*. Repairs were not the object of her visit; more important matters had brought her here. *John Murray, Earl of* Dunmore, *Vicount Fincastle, Barron of Blair, of Moulin and Tillymount, better known as simply Lord Dunmore,* the governor, was on board. He had become convinced that the ships around Yorktown were not a safe place for him *and* had decided to take up his quarters in Portsmouth with his friend, Mr. Sprowle. Dunmore brought with him many stragglers, among them a number of runaway slaves.

 Gardner W. Allen in his <u>Naval History of the American Revolution</u> quotes the following description of Dunmore's fleet from various sources: "Governor Dunmore of Virginia employed a considerable fleet in Chesapeake Bay, which in July comprised more than forty vessels. Whatever British men-of-war happened to be stationed in the bay, and there were generally a few at least, were attached to this fleet. A family of Tories, John Goodrich and several sons (from Portsmouth), also cruised about the bay in Dunmore's service (elsewhere in American accounts called "pirates"). The chief function of the (Virginia) state cruisers was to check the ravages of these vessels along the shores of the bays and rivers. Several of their prizes were recaptured by the navies of Virginia, Maryland, and North Carolina, and other captures, some of them important, were occasionally made ." From another source we have a clearer idea of the forces the Royal Governor had with him. Virginia Militia General Charles Lee says, that Dunmore's force was lying between Tucker's Mill, now the location of the Portsmouth Naval Hospital on Hospital Point, and Gosport, the shipyard, in a line running between the inlets at more than six hundred. Portsmouth, as we have seen elsewhere, was cut up by many little waterways and really stood on several points of land. Forty of Dunmore's troops were marines from Liverpool, the sort of professionals you would expect to have on hand to defend a governor's home; several hundred were untrained loyalists. When Dunmore first settled at Sprowle's home, Soul's Point, he took one of his ships up the Elizabeth River to Kemp's Landing, the primary town in Princess Anne County, now the city of Virginia Beach, and "raised the King's banner:" the traditional symbol to call up troops when a revolution was in progress against the rightful authority of the King. The organization raised by the Loyalists there was to be called the Princess Anne Rangers (a name also used in the Civil War for a Confederate unit). Miss Holladay calls them "Queen's Own," and I think she is right, as the "On Line Institute for Advanced Loyalist Studies" identifies them by that name as one of two Loyalist companies at the Battle of Great Bridge, the other being the Ethiopian Brigade.

    The following is from a biography of the founder of the Queen's Own, "Jacob Ellegood was a native of Virginia. He owned a plantation called Rose Hall on the Lyn Haven River in Princess Anne County, and another plantation called Chapel Hill. At the start of the American Revolution he actively supported Governor Lord Dunmore, and in November 1775 six hundred militia men accompanied him to serve in support of the Governor. Lord Dumnore proposed that Jacob Ellegood raise and command a corps of Loyalists for the defense of Norfolk (and the Governor's headquarters in Portsmouth), and issued a commission for him to form the Queen's Own Loyal Virginia Regiment. The officers and men of this regiment were later incorporated into the Queen's Rangers in the Canadian Army. Ellegood commanded this regiment at the Battle of the

Great Bridge where the British were defeated, and later while escorting women and children to the Eastern Shore of Virginia he was captured."

Dunmore, after leaving Princess Anne County, went to Norfolk where he was met by the mayor and two hundred citizens (most of the population) who all swore allegiance to the King. The rest of his small army was to be made up of the Ethiopian Brigade. Dunmore, desperate for troops, had issued an emancipation proclamation at Portsmouth promising freedom to any African slave who ran away from his master and joined the British Army (this Emancipation Proclamation survives). Later in this book I will list some of those slaves who came from Portsmouth. At this point there were at least three hundred African Americans in the Ethiopian Brigade, all uniformed with sashes across their chests emblazoned with the word "liberty". He also had his ships lying in the river with their sailors available if needed.

The Virginians were horrified at Dunmore's freeing slaves and Richard Henry Lee wrote: "Lord Dunmore's unparalleled conduct in Virginia has, a few Scotch excepted (by which he probably means the Scottish merchants at Portsmouth and Norfolk), united every Man in that Colony. If [the British] Administration had searched thro the world for a person the best fetted to ruin their cause, and procure union and success for these Colonies, they could not have found a more complete Agent than Lord Dunmore. The last Post produces a proclamation fro Ld. Dunmore declaring Liberty to the Slaves and proclaiming the Law martial to be the only law in that Colony. And all this he says is done 'in virtue of the power and authority to me given by his Majesty.' Is it possible that his Majesty could authorize him thus to remedy evils which his Lordship himself had created? It is impossible that vice can so triumph over virtue, as that the slaves of Tyranny should succeed against the brave and generous Assertors of Liberty and the just rights of humanity."

Emboldened by the forces he had raised, Dunmore decided to retake Norfolk County and sent the Queen's Own and the Ethiopian Brigade to Great Bridge. We will get to the details of the battle, and its hero, William "Billie" Flora, who was a free black from Portsmouth, later.

For five or six months *Lord Governor Dunmore* remained at Mr. Sprowle's house, while his followers were barracked in the warehouses of his friend. *Tradition says Andrew Sprowle's wife, Catherine, found Dunmore's Liverpool marines boorish, and didn't hide the fact from the Governor, and that was why Dunmore treated her so badly later. Miss Holladay will presently tell us about this in more detail.*

Andrew Sprowle had started the little town known as Gosport about 20 years before and there established his marine yard, which was soon taken over by the British government for the repair of ships. Sprowle was appointed navy agent and placed in command of it. This yard stood on the site of what is called the old part of the present U. S. Navy yard (the Norfolk Naval Shipyard in Portsmouth).

Here Dunmore, it is said, found many recruits among the Scotch clerks employed in the busy town. He now formed two regiments from his followers, the "Queen's Own" and the "Ethiopian," the latter of course composed of the fugitive slaves. John Hunter, a lad of sixteen, Mr. Sprowle's stepson, was lieutenant in the Queen's Own. This regiment was later merged into the Queen's Rangers.

There is now in Richmond, in the archives room in the State Library *(now the Library of Virginia)*, the petition of Mrs. Catherine Douglas, formerly Mrs. Andrew Sprowle, dated 1784. If we may take the word of this lady, "Lord Dunmore was a most unwelcome guest, living riotously upon his friend." Mrs. Sprowle was called "a very untrustworthy and dangerous woman" by the Patriots.

Tradition tells us nothing about the private life of the Governor while in Portsmouth, where he was doubtless well received owing to the strong Tory feeling existing in the town. There remains in Portsmouth what may be a relic of his sojourn here. Years ago a package of old books was purchased by a gentleman of the town. Among them was one with Lord Dunmore's name on the flyleaf.

In December 1775, soon after Dunmore rejoined his fleet, Mr. Sprowle having incurred the enmity of the town, with his family sought refuge with him. They were most courteously treated and assigned quarters on the <u>Roebuck</u>, in command of Captain Hammond. When Dunmore bombarded the towns of Norfolk and Portsmouth on January 1, 1776, the Patriots of Portsmouth were so enraged that they burned down Sprowle's house, seized his marine yard, took possession of his plantation, Soul's Point, and declared all his other property forfeited. We learn from the aforesaid petition that Mr. Sprowle was very old at this time, and was so overcome by grief that he died of a broken heart, on shipboard in May 1776. *Sprowle was on the list of the first trustees of the town of Portsmouth when it was formed, no wonder he was heartbroken as his fellow citizens drove him out of his town and took his property.*

This is the first mention of Portsmouth being bombarded. Later we will find out this consisted mainly of the shelling of Hospital Point. The damage to Portsmouth town itself was actually done by General Charles Lee and the Virginia Militia, as detailed in Lee's court martial in Williamsburg before the Committee of Safety. It was after Miss Holladay's time that documentation was found to prove that Dunmore's damage to Norfolk in this bombardment was minor and that the majority of the damage in Norfolk was done by the Virginia Militia under Colonels Woodford and Howe and their "red shirts" shouting "Keep up the jig!" on orders from Governor Thomas Jefferson. Jefferson, furious at the Norfolk citizens' support for Dunmore, said in a letter to John Page (Oct. 1775), "Delende est Norfolk!" (Norfolk must be destroyed) quoting Cicero on the destruction of Carthage by the Romans. From this point on Portsmouth was the only town left of any size in South Hampton Roads.

Dunmore eventually left the Elizabeth River for Gwynn's Island (sometimes called Governors Island) off Mathews County in the Chesapeake Bay and consequently out of our story.

Soon after the death of her husband Mrs. Sprowle was granted permission to visit her son, the young lieutenant, who was in the patriot jail in Halifax, North Carolina. His Majesty's ship *Otter* was put at her disposal for the trip. Her passport was refused by the Patriots at Williamsburg, on the plea that she was a most dangerous character.

That she and Dunmore fell out is quite certain; for he treated the widow of his old friend not only with indifference but with positive harshness. Her name, which had been placed on the Virginia pension list, was scratched off by him with no apparent reason. He gave her no assistance in getting to England. Had it not have been for Capt. Hammond of the ship which was for some months the home of the Sprowles, she would *indeed* have been in sore straits. He procured her a passage to Glasgow, where to use her own words she was, "thrown on the world in a helpless condition with seven children to care for." Romance followed hardship in the case of Catherine Sprowle. She met young Francis Douglas *who was* a kinsman she tells us of the Duke of Queensbury, who "took pity" on her and gallantly married her. She urges in her petition that she and her husband and her son John Hunter may be allowed to take up their residence in Virginia, as well as come into possession of the property of the late Andrew Sprowle. Mrs. Douglas in this document makes no allusion to the seven helpless children and we are at a loss to know what became of them. The Sprowles appear no more in the history of Portsmouth; but Mr. Sprowle's shipyard which had been taken over by Great Britain just before the outbreak of the war, with a view to equipping it and making it a great navy yard, has played a considerably part in the development of the town, as the United States Navy Yard.

At this time Portsmouth was in great danger of being wiped out by fire, as can be seen by a letter of Gen. Charles Lee to Edmond Pendleton. In 1776 General Lee had been sent to Portsmouth to crush dissatisfaction there. He certainly created much amusement there by his long green trousers called "sherry-valies" and his litter of dogs. *An amusing painting of the general so dressed and lead by his dogs survives.*

His letter to Edmond Pendleton, dated at Portsmouth, May 4, 1776, plainly shows the state of mind prevailing in that town. He says, "found the inhabitants of Portsmouth had universally taken the oath to Lord Dunmore; and as the town was, I believe justly, reputed the great channel through which his Lordship received the most exact and minute intelligence of all our actions and designs, I thought it incumbent on me and agreeable to the spirit of your instructions to remove the people without exception, for even the women and children had learned the art and practiced with address the Office of Spies. Considerable quantity of valuables *were* found in the houses of Messrs. Jameson, Sprowle and Goodrich, such as molasses, salt and other things wanted by the public. *You will remember the Goodrich clan was with Dunmore's fleet from the start and were later called pirates.*

"As the town of Portsmouth will afford so convenient a shelter and quarters for the Enemy, on supposition that they make this part of the world their object, it would (strictly speaking) be just and political to destroy it totally—but I thought it a matter of too serious concern for me to execute without the Injunction or sanction of the Committee - the houses indeed of some of the most notorious Traitors I ventured to demolish with a view of intimidating the neighborhood from trifling any longer, or flying in the face of your ordinances. Sprowle, Jamison, Goodrich and Shedden's houses have on this principle been demolished."

Charles Lee was a rival to Washington for the job of commander of the Continental Army, but his actions at Portsmouth, taking the wives and children of Tories to Suffolk in chains and holding some Tories while he burned their houses, scotched that plan. The Virginia Committee of Safety was not happy with his actions in Portsmouth. When Lee arrived in Portsmouth he calculated that half of Dunmore's small army was dead of the fever, or had deserted, making his work easy. Some escaped from Dunmore's fleet, swimming to the mainland, and some locals took pleasure playing pranks on those who remained. Norfolk historian George Tucker tells of Hummingbird Jasper who got his name by convincing some British officers in one of Dunmore's ships that he would give them some rare Virginia hummingbirds. He took them out to the fleet in a box, telling the officers they must not open the box until he was gone as the hummingbirds so loved him they would follow him back to Portsmouth. When the officers opened their prize they found an angry hive of bees.

Another Tory of note among the inhabitants of Portsmouth was Humphrey Roberts, a merchant of some means..

At one time he fled to the Eastern Shore, where he did all that he could for his cause. There are letters extant warning the people of Portsmouth of his activities. Whether Roberts changed his side or kept away from the town until after the bitter feelings due to the war had subsided, we do not know, but he lived in Portsmouth for many years much respected, and died there. His tombstone is in Trinity Churchyard, near the Court Street wall, where he was buried with other members of his family. *In my survey of the churchyard I did not find his grave, but that of his wife Ann is there. At that time I found he was also one of the first Trustees of the town when it was formed, along with Andrew Sprowle, and he lived on the Court Street side of Middlesex Square. Miss Holladay earlier mentioned that the Frenchman so often quoted stayed at Roberts Ordinary.*

Perhaps none of the Portsmouth Tories was as energetic in stirring up strife and making trouble for the Patriots as the Rev. John Agnew. Now his name is not even remembered in the town and the only association connected with him is the name which clings to a certain corner, the Tory Parson's Corner, where his house stood at the southwest angle of Crawford and Glasgow Streets. *This reference by Miss Holladay has caused some Portsmouth historians headaches, as there is no question Agnew lived on the corner of North and Crawford, now the site of the Patriot Inn, and not where Miss Holladay places him. In the Colonial deeds (Book 26 page 5) it clearly says lot 4 at the intersection of Crawford (then Main Street) and Ferry Street (now North Street) was sold by Col. Crafford to Francis Miller, 16 July 1752 and that he transferred it to John Agnew by a deed of lease "for a dwelling house and a garden." An old map titled "Map of Portsmouth in 1780" also shows the property on the corner of North and Crawford with the note that it is owned by Agnew and was burned in the "1700s." Agnew did not own land on, or near Glasgow Street. I think legend placed it there in Miss Holladay's time because the lot was vacant. It is still vacant, being the long front yard of the Irish Row house, about which more later. Agnew's house was burned, as General Charles Lee tells us, and another house was built in 1784 on its foundations at North and Crawford Streets. That house, built by Thoroughgood*

Keeling, is now the Patriot Inn bed and breakfast, owned by Ron and Verle Weiss, who have a copy of the original papers, naming the builder. In the basement you can see a rough-hewn beam which appear to be charred. As Miss Holladay will tell us, this was the place where returning Tories camped out in hopes of regaining their land before they were driven away. It is possible heirs of Agnew were among them and that that is why they chose "the foot of North Street" for their gathering place - another Tory home burned by Lee was across North Street. This house *(Miss Holladay is again talking about Rev. Agnew's)* was burned by the Patriot troops in 1776 and the lot has been vacant ever since except for a brick kitchen *(by which I think she means the Irish Row house, which is certainly not a kitchen)*, now the home of an African American. Parson Agnew had been forced to leave Nansemond County, where he had been rector for twenty years, having charge of the Chuckatuck and the present Glebe Churches. He became very active in the Tory Cause, much to the annoyance of his parishioners, who noticed that he was visiting the women of his flock most assiduously, urging them to attend the services on the approaching Whit Sunday.

The congregation was fully prepared for some demonstration from their rector in behalf of the Royalist cause; and the church was crowded when Sunday arrived. In fact several hundred people had gathered outside.

We are told that the services started, and when the prayer for the King was read, no one was in the least disturbed; but when he read his text, "Render unto Caesar the things that are Caesar's," the congregation was on the elect *(alert)*.

He commenced to inveigh against the crime of disloyalty to the government. Immediately one of the magistrates left his pew, walked to the pulpit steps and ordered the preacher to leave the chancel.

"I am about my Master's business." was the reply.

"Which one," said the Magistrate: your Master in Heaven, or your master over the seas? Leave this church at once."

Agnew thereupon declared that he would never breed riot in his master's house, left the pulpit and passed down the aisle, through the crowd at the doorway, where they parted to make way for him. He never again entered the church which he had served for so many years. It is probable that Parson Agnew read at this service Lord Dunmore's Proclamation. This document was found among his papers and across it was written "Complied with."

This was probably the cause of the inquiry concerning his behavior for we find in the old vestry book of St. John's Chuckatuck, that Col. Anthony Holladay, Maj. Thomas Godwin and Mr. John Gregory were appointed to investigate it. We know also from the fragment of a record found at Williamsburg, that Agnew was sentenced by the court of commissioners of Nansemond and made appeal; beyond this record the fragment tells nothing.

History records that he came to Portsmouth and mention is made of his efforts in the cause so dear to his heart, in contemporary letters. The Parson remained in Portsmouth until his son's regiment was quartered there in 1779; he then became chaplain of the Queen's Rangers, that being the regiment in which his son, Stair Agnew, was a lieutenant; for this staunch old Tory was willing to do more than talk for the cause. In 1780 both father and son were in the town again with their regiment. Toward the close of the war they were captured by the French and taken to France; but the vessel on which they sailed was wrecked in a fearful storm and the Agnews given up for lost. But after twenty four hour's exposure to the sea they were rescued.

Upon regaining their liberty they settled near Frederickton in New Brunswick: *a separate colony in these years before the unification of Canada.* where Captain Stair Agnew served in the Assembly for nearly thirty years. The gallant old Parson died there in 1812, at the age of eighty-five.

In addition to the Tory sympathizers who stirred up strife in the town there was another element who were a great menace to the Patriot cause. This element consisted of a number of merchants who were first on one side and then on the other, lending their ships and aid to the side which paid most for their services. *On their hats men would wear a rosette of ribbons indicating their loyalties. One story says that the men of Portsmouth kept both a Tory and a Patriot badge handy and would change them based on who held the town. These were mainly Scotsmen.* Their livelihood depended on trade. Their loyalties often went to those who would buy their goods. Some of these finally went over to the Tories, while others made a better bargain with the Patriots, and Portsmouth took her stand strongly on the side of the Americans.

All who could bear arms rallied to the colors. Sprowle's Marine Yard had been seized by the Patriots, and was a hive of workmen, ships building, and stores loaded and unloaded, for this yard was the supply base in the region of the Chesapeake *and on to the Northern Colonies* for the Continental Army. Fort Nelson, which had been finished and manned, protected the town and outlying section. *This fort stood on what was then called Mosquito Point and now is called Hospital Point. There is a historical marker on the Naval Hospital grounds. We will hear more about it in the chapter on the hospital*

Dunmore, as we have said, bombarded Portsmouth and Norfolk in 1776. He damaged the former to the extent of ten or twelve thousand dollars and burned about eighty houses in Norfolk, but in that town much property was destroyed by the Continental troops. Many of the houses which they occupied as barracks were injured by them. *As mentioned earlier, in the twentieth century, but after Miss Holladay's time, the records of the burning of Norfolk were found among the state papers and the number of building destroyed by Dunmore was actually 19 businesses and 32 houses. The Virginia Militia burned 863 buildings, destroying the city.* In 1833 the State of Virginia paid to the owners of the destroyed and injured property, or their heirs, the amount asked by them for damages. From the state papers relating to this settlement we get a list of those whose homes were burned or injured.

Among the houses destroyed *in Portsmouth* were those of Robert Sheddon, John Goodrich, John Goodrich, Jr., Alexander Love, John Agnew, Duncan McNiell, John Morris, Isaac Luke, Samuel Veale, Amos Etheredge, and Andrew Sprowle. The town market house, too, fell a prey to the flames. *Robert Sheddon was a "merchant of Norfolk County."* He *lived on Lot 9 on the northeast corner of Crawford and High, where a bank now stands. The lot originally belonged to James Marsden, who, when he went bankrupt in 1767 conveyed the land to Shedden. This was probably his place of business, as he also purchased from David Dale, Craford's overseer, in 1769, the lot on the northwest corner of North and Crawford, where the Grice-Neely House now stands. Dale had built a brick house on it, right across the street from the Rev. Mr. John Agnew's home. The next in the list is probably the same John Goodrich who, with his son, added his ships to Dunmores, continued to raid American ships in the Chesapeake after Dunmore went to Gwynn's Island and was called a pirate in the <u>American History of the Naval Engagements in the Revolution</u>. Duncan McNiell lived on the southwest corner of Crawford and Queen Streets on London Square. Isaac Luke and his wife Rachel are buried in Trinity Churchyard, by the High Street gate. He is the one who allowed the Methodist preacher to preach from his front porch on Court Street and is credited by Margaret Windley in her history of Monumental Methodist Church as being the founder of the Methodist church here. He had more than one house. His descendants in their account of him in the library collection say the house from which Methodism was preached survived the Revolution and we will hear about it in the chapter on "Getting Religion." Amos Etheridge was one of the first nine Trustees of the town when it was formed and Hannah Etheridge, the wife of Powers Etheridge, who I believe to be his daughter-in-law, is buried in Trinity Churchyard near the wall of the Commodore Theater. Her grave tells us she was born in Ireland and died here in 1798. Samuel Veale was one of the heirs to Col. Craford, among the first Trustees of the town and listed on the large Celtic cross in Trinity Churchyard as among the first Vestry of the church; he owned two lots on the northeast corner of North and Middle Streets running to where the Glencoe Bed and Breakfast, currently owned by Anne McGlynn now stands.*

Thomas Veale had a house demolished by cannon, it being used as a target for trying them out. His windmill was also destroyed. *You will remember that after Col. Craford's death many of the unsold lots in Portsmouth went, by way of his housekeeper, to the Veale family. The windmill is probably the windmill which gave its name to Windmill Creek which ran from Washington Street via Dinwiddie Street to Crawford Bay. The creek reappears whenever there is a hurricane, or a strong northeaster.*

Those whose homes were used as barracks and claimed damages were John Brannon, Thomas Toomer, Humphrey Roberts, Samuel Sandfoot, Walter Gwynne, Henry Culpeper, William Roberts, Michael Fredly, Francis Hatton, Richard Tishman, Samuel Veale, John Lello, George Lesley, Sophia Hancock, Elizabeth Hall, Jane Butler and Patience Nicholson.

The sites of many of these houses have been located, and we know in some instances the history of their owners. John Brannon lived at the northeast corner of North and Court Streets, where Judge Bain resides in the 1930s, *currently owned by Amy Manning and believed to be the location of General Cornwallis' headquarters. He owned two lots on Elizabeth Row facing North Street between Middle and Court streets. His deed mentions an "alley" as part of its boundary which is probably what used to be called Hunters Lane and is now returned to its original name: Gaskin's Lane.* He proved a good patriot, fighting at Great Bridge, at Cowpens and in other battles. His granddaughter, Mrs. Wm. M. Peters, inherited a part of this lot and in turn gave it to her two daughters, Mrs. Legh R. Watts and Mrs. E. M. Watts. *Thomas Toomer's home, built in 1775 survives on the west side of Court Street. It has a long porch across the front. Humphrey Roberts, called a merchant, is mentioned elsewhere by Miss Holladay. He had at least three lots and maybe more: on the southeast corner of Middle and High Street, between North and Glasgow on the west side of Middle, on the southwest corner of Crawford and High and on the east side of Crawford at the foot of County which may have been a shipyard, or the ordinary which bore his name. Samuel Sanfoot is surely related to William Sanfoot who was a "bricker and bricklayer" living in a brick house on the northeast corner of Court and Glasgow, now a parking lot. Henry Culpepper lived on the northwest corner of Middle and Glasgow where the handsome carpenter-Gothic Gill House now stands. He was a "shipwright" and also had a lot on*

Westminster Square just outside the town proper. Michael Fredly, spelled Freedly in the deed book, was a butcher who lived on the Dinwiddie Street side of Back Creek Square. The Hatton family, as we will see later, owned the plantation called Alabama where Park View now stands. John Lello's wife, Susan Lello, is buried in Trinity Churchyard. John was the town cordwayner, the man who made elegant lady's shoes from Cordoba leather, and they lived on the corner of Middle and County Streets on St. James Square in 1770. This is the house which was damaged. Buried in Trinity Churchyard, Jane Butler bought her lot from Thomas Veale in her own right on the Dinwiddie Street side of Oxford Square between Court and Queen in 1772. She was 70 years old at her death.

Richard Lishman owned the lot on Middle Street, now occupied by the Rudwall and Monterey Apartment houses and the private residence number 200 *torn down when Olde Towne was renovated in the 1960s.* Lishman was killed in the Revolution but his ghost up to recent years still haunted that square of Middle Street. He was seen and heard by people walking up the block as soon as daylight faded. *He is, however, not one of the ghosts visited on the annual Olde Towne Ghost Walk which has been held the Friday before Halloween every year since 1980.* His daughter, Mrs. Forsythe, built the house torn down after a hundred years of service, to make room for the Rudwall Apartment. George Lesley lived on High Street where the County Clerk's Office now stands - *now the gift shop for the 1846 Courthouse.* Patience Nicholson was probably the mother of that great Patriot and useful citizen, whose story is told on another page.

The town was now occupied by the 4th Virginia Regiment and Fort Nelson constructed on Hospital Point to protect the entrance to the Elizabeth River.

CHAPTER 5 - THE REVOLUTION: COLLIER'S RAID

When war was declared the men of Portsmouth joined the Patriots and took up arms, all who could do so. The little town which had developed so rapidly now felt the pinch of war. Luxuries could not be had at any price. Tea *and* coffee were cheerfully given up with other things; but the question of clothing was a serious one. Cloth could not be obtained; women turned to the spinning wheel with avidity and every one was glad to wear the homespun garments. Life went on peacefully; the people had grown used to privation, and danger had not assailed them since the cannon of Dunmore had been silenced. All through the spring of 1779, the good house mothers of Portsmouth set their homes in order, worked in their gardens and plied their shuttles, unaware that a great British Fleet was bearing down on their homes. There was neither telegraph nor wireless to tell them that Hampton had already been fired on. Quietly, as usual the townspeople went to their beds on the night of the eighth of May, ready to resume their labors on the morrow. Down at Fort Nelson, garrisoned by a mere handful of soldiers, all were equally undisturbed, with "no visions of tomorrow's strife."

So while the good people slept *on May 11 1779*, that gray array of British ships passed almost into the harbor. The enemy did no sleeping, (of that we may be sure). They were on the alert and with the first streak of dawn, Sir George Collier, the commodore of the fleet, left his flagship and boarded his barge guarded by armed schooners and started down the river to reconnoiter the fort and get information as to the enemy's strength. As he approached her shores the town was still asleep. Two loafers lounging on the waterfront, however, were not averse to giving the Commodore all the information that he desired. They told him that the fort was held by a handful of men, the troops having been ordered from this post to points where they were more urgently needed. Collier was also informed that the inhabitants of the town were unaware of the approach of the fleet. He hastened back to the mouth of the harbor where the ships had anchored, to confer with Gen. Mathew. They agreed between them that it would be best to attack the fort immediately and simultaneously from land and sea.

We know the makeup of the fleet from an account in A Naval History of the American Revolution by Gardner W. Allen. Admiral Gambier sailed for England April 5, and the day before his departure, Collier "received a commission as Commodore and Commander-in-Chief of the King's fleet in America." Of the condition of this fleet he complained, saying that "the weak enfeebled state of the ships, both in point of numbers and of most painful sensations. I ardently wish to prove myself deserving of the great trust I am honoured with, by the most spirited exertions." These exertions were first directed towards Virginia, "the province which of all others gives sinews to the rebellion from its extensive traffick. (Stopford-Sackville MSS., 125, 126 (Collier to Germain.) The British fleet, which sailed May 5 from New York for Chesapeake Bay under Collier's command, consisted of the sixty-four gun ship Raisonable, the Rainbow of forty-four guns, "the Otter (which we saw earlier in Dunmore's fleet), Diligent and Haerlem, sloops, and Cornwallis galley, together with several private ships of war and twenty-two transports having on board" about two thousand troops under General Mathew. The Diligent must have been captured before the squadron arrived in Chesapeake Bay. "At sunrise" on the 10th, says Collier, we saw some rebel ships and vessels in Hampton Road with their sails loose, who, as soon as the tide admitted of it, got under weigh and ran up the Elizabeth and James Rivers; our fleet also weighed and the Raisonable anchored shortly after in Hampton Road, her great draught of water not admitting of her going further with conveniency. I immediately shifted my broad pendant to the Rainbow and proceeded with the fleet up the Elizabeth River, till a contrary wind and the ebb tide obliged us to anchor. The next morning being calm prevented the ships from moving with the flood, on *account of the narrowness and intricacy of the channel." The troops advanced, nearly to Portsmouth, supported by a galley and two gunboats; and a breeze springing up, the ships soon followed. The American fort on the river (Fort Nelson) was evacuated. Much property was destroyed and many vessels were seized by the British, others being saved from the same fate by destruction at the hands of the Americans. The <u>Otter</u> and a number of other small vessels were sent up the Chesapeake. "The movements of this little squadron were so judicious that the enemy were much harassed and distressed; they destroyed many vessels and captured others." (Almon, viii, 290, 291, 293)*

Meanwhile the awakened town had heard of its danger, and in it all was tumult and confusion. Frightened women and children running hither and thither, many of them seeking safety in the Dismal Swamp. At Fort Nelson the soldiers were ordered to fire upon the enemy, but to evacuate upon their near approach, as it was impossible to hold out against them. They were to leave the fort and march to Washington Point (Berkley) and with a view to fooling the enemy and thus gaining a little time; the flag was to be left flying on the staff.

The day was very calm and the transports could not move, and though they were nearly five miles from the fort, General Mathew undertook to bring the soldiers in detachments in flat boats. Another difficulty arose, the flagship, the *Raisonable*, was considered too large to enter the inner harbor. Sir George Collier promptly hauled up his broad pennant on the <u>Rainbow</u> and transferred his quarters to her.

Commodore and General took up their positions on the barge, which was escorted by the *Cornwallis* Galley and a number of gunboats. Scarcely had they gone two miles when a strong breeze prevailed and the transports followed quickly.

An eyewitness has described the journey of the fleet to our very doors. "It was," he says, "the most beautiful scene, making the finest regatta in the world. Signals were occasionally given from the Admirals' barge, to advance or halt, by small red or blue flag: had there been a necessity for retreating a white one would have been used. When the leading boat was within less than a musket shot of the intended place for landing, a signal to halt was made; the galley and gunboats then advanced, and kept up a warm cannonade toward the shore for several minutes, which the Rebels returned from the fort but most of their shot fell short.

The gunboats ceasing firing and the troops were landed on a spot called the Glebe, *now the neighborhood of Port Norfolk in Portsmouth,* about two miles from the fort."

Into our harbor came the great procession, with swelling sail and flying flags—The *Rainbow, Otter,* the *Diligent* and other men-of-war, followed by numerous gunboats and galleys, protecting some twenty-eight transports bearing two thousand troops, divided into four regiments, or more—the Forty-second, Prince Charles own Hessians, the Guards and Volunteers of Ireland. From Maj. Gen. Mathew's letter to Sir Henry Clinton, dated Portsmouth, VA., May 16, 1779, we get some other details of the landing of the soldiers at the Glebe. He says "About three in the evening we landed at Glebe on the western shore of the Elizabeth River, just out of cannon shot of the fort. As the troops landed, the column moved to invest the fort." *This would have been across West Parkview, a plantation owned by the Matthews family and Parkview, a plantation owned by the Hatton family and called Alabama. In the history of the 42nd Royal Highlanders it specifically mentions this engagement, but they are not mentioned by Miss Holladay.* "The enemy perceiving that their retreat would be cut off evacuated before we could reach the southern branch of the river. Having taken possession of the fort and placed guards in the town, I encamped in two lines, right to the fort and left to the south branch. On the 11th the flank companies of the guards took a strong position ten miles in front of the right wing. The Volunteers of Ireland took one equally strong *position* seven miles in front of the left wing. The center of the line was covered by an impenetrable swamp. The Volunteers of Ireland have done some slight skirmishing in which they have suffered little."

Collier's letter of the same date and heading adds a few particulars to the story of the capture of Portsmouth by the British. He says, "The enemy fired some heavy shots at the galley, which were rendered harmless by the distance. He urges that the British hold Portsmouth saying, "Permit me as a sea-officer, to observe, that this port of Portsmouth is an exceeding safe and secure asylum for ships against an enemy, and not to be forced even by great superiority. The marine yard is large and extremely convenient, having a considerable stock of seasoned timber, besides great quantities of other stores.

"From these considerations joined to many others, I am firmly of opinion that it is a measure most essentially necessary for his Majesty's service, that this port should remain in our hands, since it appears of more real consequence and advantage than any other that the Crown possesses in America; for by securing this, the whole trade of the Chesapeake is at an end, and consequently the sinews of rebellion destroyed."

To return to the capture of Fort Nelson—the British found there what is said by military authorities to have been an unprecedented state of affairs. When Gen. Mathew's men entered the fort and gained the ramparts, they found it commanded by a British officer, who at that moment was engaged in hauling down the stars and stripes. This officer proved to be Lieut. Dickey, who until its evacuation an hour or so earlier, had been a prisoner there. Commodore Barron, for some years a resident of Portsmouth and a boy at the time of the Revolution, has preserved for us the story of this gallant lieutenant, who he says commanded the British schooner *Fortunatus;* and in her fight with our armed schooner *Liberty*, off Hampton Roads, fought with the odds greatly against him until all but one or two of his crew had been killed. He was much admired for his gallantry. When he was sent to Portsmouth to be imprisoned in the fort, he was paroled with almost unlimited liberty; and was a welcome guest at the homes of the best citizens of the town. The Lieutenant was fond of walking and took a daily constitutional in the country back of the fort. Returning from his walk on this historic ninth of May, he found Major Matthews and his men about to leave. He waited quietly until the last soldier had disappeared and then returned to the deserted stronghold and assumed command, where he had hitherto been a prisoner.

To say that Commodore Barron, who tells this part of the story, was a "boy" is a slight exaggeration, as he served on *his father's ships in the Revolution. His father was an important member of the Virginia Navy. A dispatch of June 20, 1776, says "Captain James Barron of the Virginia Navy took the <u>Oxford</u>, one of the fleet of Scotch transports bound to Boston, and brought her into Jamestown (Am. Arch., IV, iv). The younger Barron's interesting story will be told subsequently.*

It is certain that Portsmouth fared well at the hands of Commodore Sir George Collier and it has been suggested that this leniency was due to the intercession of Lieut. Dickey, who was mindful of the courteous treatment that he had received from the people of Portsmouth. This may be true, but there can be no doubt as to Collier being a generous foe. He had given strict orders to prevent all acts of cruelty, the burning of houses or the molestation of innocent people.

Some wanton acts were committed; but they were due to stragglers who had joined his army. Sir George's generosity was shown on several occasions. Some of these followers had set fire to a house in the neighborhood of Cheriton; and in reply to the complaints of the people of that vicinity, he sent them a shipload of salt, a commodity that they needed sorely at that time. So favorable an impression did he make upon the people there that they immediately sent him a present of some freshly killed lambs, a great treat as fresh meat could scarcely be procured.

Collier refused to serve it on his own table; but sent it instead to the sick soldiers.

When orders came to evacuate the town we can understand that Collier was much distressed, since we have quoted his letter in which he refers to the importance of holding Portsmouth.

Preparations were at once made for the departure; and there was much to be done. The most difficult job was that of destroying the fort, which they declared to be of amazing strength toward the river. The parapet was fourteen feet high and fifteen thick, surrounded by strong timbers dovetailed, the middle part filled with dirt and hard-rammed. A great number of heavy cannon were taken in the fort, with a large amount of ammunition and provisions. There were forty-two embrasures; and the fort resisted all efforts at destruction. Every attempt of troop and battery failed to demolish it;: fire was resorted to as a last hope and its ruin was successfully accomplished.

At the navy yard, which was the largest in the country, similar measures were taken. Before evacuating the Patriots had displayed a fine ship of twenty guns, ready for launching: and left on the stocks another of thirty-six guns, as well as several smaller ones and some brigs and sloops. They had also set fire to two French merchantmen, one loaded with bale goods and the other carrying a thousand hogsheads of tobacco. The British were amazed at the immense supply of naval and other stores in the yard, besides ships loaded with mahogany and other woods.

The following is the accounting made by the British of what they found ready for shipment to the Continental Army: at Fort Nelson, 285 cannon, 1.472 shot, 51 barrels of powder, at Suffolk a powder magazine, naval stores and 3,000 barrels of pork; at the Gosport yard 25 vessels, including three frigates, 28 cannon, 400 firelocks, 263 bayonets, 10 barrels of powder, 193 hogs heads of tobacco, 43 barrels of rum, 117 barrels of pork, 113 barrels of flour and naval stores and at Kemp's Landing 7 ships, 8 cannon and 200 barrels of pine tar.

The arsenal was well stocked and the warehouses filled with tobacco and other commodities. Much of this the enemy could not remove, so the yard like the fort was set on fire; and in addition to the aforesaid stores, five thousands loads of fine oak knees for shipbuilding, as well as an infinite number of masts and like material went up in flames. It was said by an eye witness that the conflagration made a magnificent sight, probably unsurpassed in this way by anything of the kind until that historic night in April, 1861, when this yard was again set on fire, by the enemy.

Many of our ships and privateers had taken refuge in the Southern Branch; but the British suspecting this sent Capt. Creyke on the *Otter* to bottle them up. This he succeeded in doing; and when the British left Portsmouth on May 24, for New York they carried with them seventeen of our ships. The entire number of ships taken, burnt and destroyed while the British fleet was in the river was "one hundred and thirty-seven sail of vessels."

The worst had happened, so the sorely tried people of the town felt, and with thankful hearts they saw the enemy embark. On this occasion they did not take ship at the Glebe, but left right from Fort Nelson, now the Naval Hospital Point. The hospital ship carrying some few men wounded in the skirmishes in and about Portsmouth, sailed first, followed by the artillery, cavalry baggage; next came Prince Charles' Own, the Hessians, the Volunteers of Ireland and the Guards.

Collier describes his departure in this way: (Collier to Clinton, May 16, and to Stephens, May 17, 1779): "The fort was raz'd, the season'd timber for ship building burnt, the buildings and storehouses of the finest yard on this continent underwent the same fate; the sufferings of individuals I endeavoured to prevent all in my power and in general happily succeeded, and by it I hope have procured many friends to the royal cause." (Stopford-Sackville MSS., 129.) Collier wished to remain longer and to keep possession of this valuable naval station, but General Mathew insisted that their orders required their return to New York. The two large men-of-war and the transports thereupon sailed out of the bay, leaving the others to continue their depredations. A hundred and thirty American vessels were destroyed or taken as well as amount of property on shore (Almon, viii, 289-295; Penn. Gazette, June 9, 1779; Town's Detail of Particular Services in America, 76-87.) Richard Henry Lee, writing June 26 to William Whipple of the Marine Committee, says of the operations of these smaller vessels, left in the bay: "They have already burnt several private houses and one public warehouse with between 2 & 300 hhds of Tobo. and carried off much plunder & many negroes. Soon as they see the Militia gathering they embark and go to another unguarded place. They have 6 Vessels: <u>Otter</u>, 16, <u>Harlem</u>, 12 Guns, King's Vessels; <u>Dunmore</u>, 16, Schooner <u>Hammond</u>, 14, <u>Lord North</u>, 12 Guns, & <u>Fin Castle</u>, 2 three pounders. The 4 last are [Goodrich's] Pirates." You will remember the Goodrich family whose home at Portsmouth was burned after Dunmore's defeat. "They say the orders are to burn and destroy all before them; an Eastern Man whom they had captured . . . escaped from them when they were burning the Warehouse and gave us the above account of their force, which is confirmed by others. They land between 60 & 70 men when they mean to do mischief." (Penn. Mag. Hist. and Biogr., January, 1899.) Lee requests the Marine Committee to send two frigates into the bay, a force sufficient, he says, to destroy the enemy's fleet. The Marine Committee had already issued orders for the purpose. As early as the previous November and again in January they had expressed a desire to capture or destroy "the infamous Goodrich," and June 25, Captain Nicholson of the <u>Deane</u> was "directed to proceed in company with the Frigate <u>Boston</u> from the Capes of Delaware into Chesapeake Bay and on your arrival there, at Hampton or any Other way, endeavour to Obtain the best intelligence if any of the enemies Ships of war or Privateers are in the Bay, and if you find there are any of such force as you are able to encounter, you are to proceed up and attack them . . . taking or destroying as many of the said Vessels as may be in your power." (Mar. Com. Letter Book, 223.) The <u>Confederacy</u> was ordered up to Chester to prepare for other service, but on July 2 was directed to cruise ten days longer with the <u>Deane</u> and <u>Boston</u>. Accounts of this service in Chesapeake Bay are lacking, but that it was performed may be inferred from Lee's letter of August 8 to Whipple, saying: "We are much obliged to the Marine Committee for their attention. I see the frigates have taken and sent in two prizes, vessels of war." (Penn. Mag. Hist. and Biogr., January, 1899; Mar. Com. Letter Book, 187, 193 (to Navy Board, Boston, November 16, 1778, January 9, 1779), 223, 224, 225 (to Nicholson and to Harding, June 25, July 2, 1779); Penn. Gazette, August 4, 1779.) Upon the return to New York, May 29, of the British fleet from Chesapeake Bay, says Collier, "I found Sir Henry Clinton on the point of setting off on an expedition up the North River and I immediately determin'd on assisting in it, carrying with me the <u>Raisonable</u>, <u>Camilla</u>, <u>Vulture</u> and three row galleys and two gunboats with the transports and troops." This excursion up the Hudson resulted in the capture of Stony Point and other successes, which induced Collier to observe: "I hope I may now say with some confidence that rebellion is thrown on its back and that this campaign will be the last of this unnatural civil war." (Stopford-Sackville MSS., 129 (Collier to Germain, June

15, 1779) . *Lord Germain was roughly the English equipotent to our Secretary of War and we will hear from him again about Portsmouth. Collier's Raid, as it is called, is commemorated by a state historical marker on Crawford Parkway by the river.*

CHAPTER 6 - THE REVOLUTION: GENERAL LESLIE'S OCCUPATION

After the departure of the British from Portsmouth no time was lost in rebuilding the marine yard and soon ships were ready for launching. The town resumed its former life, but the people were in constant dread of another invasion. Their fears were realized in October of the next year (1780) when another great fleet of sixty sail sweep into the harbor. Gen. Lesley, who commanded the troops, at first divided them between Portsmouth, Hampton and the shore side of Princess Anne *County, now Virginia Beach. Norfolk needed no troops as it was a smoldering ruin.* His orders were soon changed and the entire force of three thousand men were concentrated in Portsmouth. They immediately commenced to re-fortify the town.

Previously it had been the plan of General Sir Henry Clinton, the overall commander of British forces in America, to sandwich between his garrison in New York, and British Canada what was thought to be the most dangerous part of the rebellion in New England and let the Southern theater go its own way. But in this year that strategy changed. General Cornwallis thought he could easily secure the South for the British, believing that there was a great reservoir of Loyalists there. This ambitious plan was started by the taking of Charleston, South Carolina. It was Cornwallis' plan to move his army up from Charleston through the Carolinas to Virginia, thereby securing all of the South, except Georgia, for the Crown. The Georgia Navy had been virtually destroyed at the same time Collier had come into Portsmouth and so it was eliminated as a threat. Leslie's retaking of Portsmouth was a part of that larger plan.

On 7 October 1780 Major General Alexander Leslie departed New York City with a half dozen ships, including the transports Diligence *and* Peggy *and troops from The King's*

American Regiment (3 companies serving under Fanning), a company from the Provincial Light Infantry (commanded by John Watson of the Guards), the Hessian Regiment Von Bose, chasseurs from New York and, if what we were told earlier about Stair Agnew is correct, some part of the Queen's Own Regiment, the whole force numbering about 2,200 men at arms. Their destination was Portsmouth where they arrived 21 October 1780. They went on to take Hampton two days later, but, as Miss Holladay has told us later consolidated their force at Portsmouth.

Lesley's men had not been here long when there was a ripple of excitement among them. Just outside of the town a spy had been caught by some of the Patriots. The man was apprehended on his way to *South* Carolina and when told that he would have to be searched, he made no objection to the proposition. He carelessly drew from his pocket what appeared to be a quid of tobacco and put it in his mouth. His chew was interrupted by the order of his captors, who demanded the quid of tobacco. This dainty bit proved to be a letter from Gen. Lesley to Lord Cornwallis, telling him of his establishment at Portsmouth, where he was forming a post. The latter was written on silk paper; rolled up in a gold beater's skin, nicely tied at each end, making it not much larger than a goose quill.

The original plan was first to divert American forces from Cornwallis in the Carolinas and second to be ready for Cornwallis to come up from Charleston through the Carolinas where he would join forces with Leslie. Cornwallis, however, hearing of the defeat of Ferguson at King's Mountain retreated to Charleston. He did not know that the American general, Nathaniel Greene, in North Carolina had refused to enter Virginia, leaving the state practically undefended. Leslie began to fortify Portsmouth, expecting to stay here. It is probably around this time that Johann Conrad Doehla wrote his journal from Portsmouth describing Trinity Church as "a poor meeting house," the church celebrant was a British chaplain, William Andrews, its regular priest, John Braidfoot, having fled and joined the Virginia Militia as a chaplain for Washington. Doehla also tells us the Germans were much amused by seeing hay growing in the trees (Spanish Moss) and that the young ladies of Portsmouth were much taken with the handsome blond Hessians.

Cornwallis did not meet Lesley here; but whether the intercepted letter had anything to do with the failure of their plans we do not know. At all events Lesley was much disappointed at his failure to do so; and left Portsmouth suddenly on November the fifteenth, embarking on the same ships that brought the troops, the *Romulus*, commanded by Admiral Rodney, the *Blonde*, the *Delight*, and a twenty-ton ship and some galleys under command of Commodore Grayton. *They were on their way to reinforce Cornwallis at Charleston. A substantial number of Virginia irregulars had been assembled to retake Portsmouth, but they disassembled when the British threat appeared to have passed. It took Leslie more than a month to reach Charleston. The winter of 1779-80 was one of the most severe in history with ice floes in the Chesapeake.*

When the refugees entered the town they found much unfinished work which the British had made no effort to destroy. They had also left great numbers of slaves, who had gone over to the enemy; but had to remain in Portsmouth for lack of ship room.

The homes of the people had not fared so well this time. Their owners were mightily grieved over their well polished floors. From them the rough cuts and drawings made by the soldiers swords could never be effaced by any amount of dry-rubbing. Some of the old houses torn down in comparatively recent years showed these marks. No skill could repair the portraits wantonly used as targets, in many instances.

This is probably true, but contradicts Thomas Jefferson's letter praising General Leslie for his chivalrous behavior at Portsmouth. There is no marker to commemorate Leslie's visit.

The town had been saved and as far as we have ascertained, no houses were burned or destroyed: the inhabitants settled down with the hope of a quiet Christmas, for none expected a merry one. Their hopes were barely realized, for at that very time the British were planning another attempt on Portsmouth.

CHAPTER 7 - THE REVOLUTION: BENEDICT ARNOLD'S OCCUPATION

Early in January *(on the second) another* fleet of twenty ships came into the river and the troops invested the town under command of Benedict Arnold, who took up his quarters in a house on the northwest corner of Dinwiddie and London streets. *I am sorry to say Miss Holladay is wrong again about a location. Arnold's headquarters was on the northwest corner of Middle and High Streets. The original tax-dodger style house in which he presided is pictured in Lossing's* Field Book of the Revolution, *published in 1859 in the library. The original house no longer exists. Currently the coffee shop called the Daily Grind has taken its place in a Federal Period house on that corner. For many years it was marked by a sign identifying it as the site of Arnold's headquarters, but the sign was removed when the house changed hands and has never been replaced. On the other hand, Arnold may have had several buildings. The one I mention may have been his headquarters and the one Miss Holladay mentions his residence, or the headquarters could be the tax-dodger across High Street in a photo of this intersection from the 1870s.*

While in Portsmouth Arnold acquired a slave named James Armistead, or he was somehow insinuated into Arnold's service. We will hear much more about him when he continues in Cornwallis' service after Arnold departs the town.

Arnold, who had been appointed by Sir Henry Clinton, entered the Capes on 30 December 1780. Clinton did not trust him, reasonably, since he had just turned his American General's coat in for a British Major General's. Clinton also thought him rash, because of an ingenious proposal he had made to capture George Washington, which the British thought would be bad form. Clinton sent two majors to restrain him from rash action, but it didn't work. In stead of landing at Portsmouth as earlier

British commanders had done he first went up the James River with a force of sixteen hundred men and twenty ships. He was joined by his then commanding officer Major General William Phillips with two-thousand men. There was no Virginia Army to face them, some being in North Carolina and some with Washington in New England. Hood fired on Arnold's fleet from some earthworks along the river, but to no effect. Arnold landed his force on the wharf at Westover Plantation, destroyed the Westham Foundry which produced cannon for the Continental Army, a mile downstream from the Huguenot Bridge and took Richmond on 5 January 1781. He destroyed the military stores, except for a few the Patriots slipped across the river, and the public buildings in the new capital. The militia finally blocked him from taking Petersburg and he retreated to Portsmouth, the town Clinton had told him to take in the first place.

As soon as he got to Portsmouth he began building strong fortifications. These have been mapped by William A. Brown III from contemporary records. A brick wall started about where the Holiday Inn now stands and ran along the old coastline of Crawford Bay to Washington Street where it turned south to the shipyard. Two state historical marker describe the defenses Arnold left behind in Portsmouth in this way: "A brick windmill near here was close to the southern limit of the line of the British redoubts erected in March 1781by order of Brigadier General Benedict Arnold who, under Major William Phillips, commanded British troops occupying Portsmouth. The line of fortifications extended in an arc along Washington Street from the northern waterfront to Gosport Creek and defended Portsmouth from American attack from the west." During the restoration of a brick English basement style house, identified later in this work as the Hartt House, on the west side of Court Street, where Arnold's defenses crossed the street, a British cannonball was found and another was found under Trinity Church. The windmill is probably the one which gave its name to Windmill Creek which once ran where Dinwiddie Street is now situated. There was a parade ground and powder magazine where the entrance to the Downtown Tunnel is now and Arnold reinforced the walls of Fort Nelson with granite. After this fort was dismantled the granite was used to rebuild the north wall of Trinity Church and when the bronze plaque to the American patriot Rev. Mr. John Braidfoot was put in place the screws on the left caused the workman to burn up his drill bit, because he hit that granite (Arnold's last revenge).

Jefferson's militia was formed under Generals Steuben, Nelson, Weedon and Muhlenberg with the intention of driving the British out of the Commonwealth. Washington hatched a plan to capture Arnold. He requested Rochambeau to send the French fleet then commanded by D'Estouches, and a land force to the Chesapeake. He also asked Lafayette to attack Portsmouth by land with a force of 1,200 infantry, preventing Arnold from escaping. The French admiralty, however, only sent a small force under De Tilley. They destroyed ten small vessels and captured the capital ship <u>Romulus</u> at the entrance to LynnHaven Bay and then went back to Newport, Rhode Island. Washington tried again with Rochambeau, who agreed to send another French fleet to capture Arnold. this effort was prevented by British Admiral Arbuthnot who met the French fleet at the mouth of the Chesapeake. The two fleets drew up in battle order, eight on a side, but after a few shots the French withdrew and Lafayette, without naval support, also withdrew, leaving Arnold strongly fortified at Portsmouth. Arnold and Phillips took all the James River land as far as City Point with a force of only twenty-five hundred troops.

It is evident that Arnold made some attempt to enjoy social pleasures and at least one invitation issued by him while in this town, is extant; dated "Portsmouth, VA., February 22, 1781: *Another, in the form of a copy, is in the library collection. The original was found behind a drawer in a chest purchased at a Virginia Beach auction in the 1960s. The new owner brought it to the library to look up the value of the signature and allowed the library to copy it.*

"Brigadier General Arnold presents his compliments to Col. Edward Moseley, Sr., requests the pleasure of his and Mrs. Moseley's company to dinner and pass the evening on Wednesday next."

We do not know whether or not the invitation was accepted, but it is certain that nothing but a sense of duty could have induced any Patriot to break bread with the traitor. Arnold was superseded in his command at Portsmouth by General Phillips. *This is not exactly the case. Sir Henry Clinton sent Phillips to Virginia as commander of all forces in the Commonwealth. There is no evidence he ever stayed in Portsmouth, but went to Petersburg. Phillips died of an illness in Petersburg, leaving Benedict Arnold as the commander of all British forces in the Commonwealth, to the apparent embarrassment of the British high command.*

Meanwhile the British ships at Portsmouth had been warned by Admiral Arbuthnot, from Newport that a French fleet was approaching them. Knowing that the enemy's fleet was much larger than their own, they could only find safety by withdrawing their ships so far up the river that the enemy could not follow, owing to the great size of their ships; and there they bottled up all the summer of 1781.

This contradicts the account from a history of the Revolution in Virginia I quoted previously. I think that version is more likely to be the case than Miss Holladay's account, but I really don't know since she does not cite a source. Miss Holladay says nothing about Arnold's departure from Portsmouth. He left the town to be with his wife Peggy, who was having their second child in New York. Peggy is often cast as one of the villains of the Benedict Arnold piece as she came from a Tory family in Philadelphia and is credited with wooing Benedict to the dark side. If so Arnold got the last word. When he died in London he requested that Peggy bury him in his American general's uniform.

CHAPTER 8 - THE REVOLUTION: CORNWALLIS' OCCUPATION

Lord Cornwallis was then in command of Portsmouth, though it was much against his judgment that he remained here, saying plainly that he thought it a bad place from which to make an attack, telling his superior officer, Sir Henry Clinton, that Portsmouth could not be made strong without an army to defend it; that it could give no position to ships of the line; and was above all not healthy. *This confirms, in a way, the popular story in Portsmouth that Cornwallis left the town for Yorktown because he didn't like the mosquitoes. His headquarters, as mentioned earlier, was on the northeast corner of Court and North streets.*

Now we must explain what Cornwallis was doing in Portsmouth. He started his Virginia campaign in May 1781. With his own troops, Leslie's reinforcements and the army under General Phillips at Petersburg (Phillips would die soon) the British had a force of 7,724 men. The only effective force to face them was Lafayette with 1,200 Continentals, 2,000 Virginia Militia and 50 dragoons. Lafayette said, "Were I to fight a battle, I would be cut to pieces, the Militia dispersed and the army lost. Were I to decline fighting, the country would think itself given up. I am therefore determined to skirmish, but not to engage too far, and particularly to take care against their immense and excellent body of horse, whom the Militia fear as they would so many wild beasts . . . Were I anywhere equal to the enemy, I should be extremely happy in my present command, but I am not strong enough even to get beaten." Faced with this situation Cornwallis split off General Leslie with the seventeenth regiment and two battalions of Anspach to secure Portsmouth as Cornwallis' headquarters in Virginia. This brought more Germans to our town. Cornwallis then turned to take Richmond. Clinton had advised caution, as the disposition of the French fleet was not known. Tarlton, with his usual dash, went on to take the new capital of Virginia at Charlottesville and Cornwallis made a try at Fredricksburg, but seeing that Lafayette now had reinforcements from Pennsylvania with him, he felt he was too far from his base at Portsmouth and withdrew to Richmond and then on to his base on the Elizabeth River, pulling Tarlton back as well. A descendant of Tarlton sold American regimental banners he had captured in America at auction in 2006.

While lying south of Richmond in June, Von Steuben joined Lafayette bringing the armies to virtual parity. The small force of Colonel William Campbell, the hero of the Battle of King's Mountain, also joined Lafayette and that allowed the Americans to go on the offensive, engaging our old friend Stair Agnew's Queen's Rangers, now under General Simcoe (for whom the first British capital of Lower Canada would be named). The British withdrew. On June 22 Cornwallis reached Williamsburg where he found a message from Clinton telling him to send some troops to Clinton's support in New York City and take a defensive position with the rest at Portsmouth. He did that, as we have seen, reluctantly, leaving Tarlton to skirmish and harass the Americans. The campaign had been a failure. Cornwallis now held only the south side of the Hampton Roads and the town of Portsmouth. Norfolk, of course, was still totally in ruins.

It was from Portsmouth that Cornwallis went to Yorktown in order to meet the Patriot army. *A state historical marker on Crawford Parkway marks the point from which his troops debarked.*

There were spies in Portsmouth again this summer, among them Lord Cornwallis' faithful servant, who was, for a certain sum of money, keeping the Governor of Virginia well informed as to his lordship's movements. This honest valet could glean no information from his master's papers as he kept too tight a hand upon them. He reported that certain officers had left the town, but Col. Simcoe and Gen. Tarleton remained in Portsmouth. As to the ships only nine of them remained in the harbor. The big fifty-gun ship, two thirty-six gun frigates, as well as eighteen sloops loaded with horses had gone to Hampton Roads. All were preparing to leave. His lordship's servant was evidently truthful on this occasion, and Portsmouth was evacuated by Lord Cornwallis in 1781.

The spy Miss Holladay is referring to is the slave we first saw in Benedict Arnold's service: James Armistead. There is some disagreement about his service. What is known is that he was born in New Kent County in 1748, the slave of William Armistead who offered his services to Lafayette. Lafayette saw how intelligent he was and recruited him as a spy. One source tells us he was in Arnold's headquarters at Portsmouth and then transferred to Cornwallis, also in Portsmouth, after Arnold departed. Cornwallis also saw his usefulness as a spy and sent him to spy on Lafayette, which allowed this patriot to pass back and forth between the lines carrying intelligence to Lafayette and hoodwinking Cornwallis. Another source says that Armistead was recruited by Cornwallis in Yorktown, but that is obviously wrong, as by that time anything he discovered would have been of no use to either side. This version states that all he passed to Cornwallis was an exaggerated count of the Patriot strength. This seems unlikely; passing back and forth between the lines during a battle would be impossible and Cornwallis could already see that he was outnumbered. No spy was needed to tell him that. I am sure Miss Holladay's description of the facts when he was with Cornwallis, where, and what he passed on to Lafayette, is the correct version, assuming this Lafayette could have contacted the Compte de Grasse as to the disposition of the British fleet and Washington as to where and when Cornwallis would move. After the war Armistead was returned to his master. On his visit to Virginia Lafayette embraced Aristead and publicly told his story. Armistead then added Lafayette to his name.

This old spy won his freedom in an unusual way. On 4 July 1787, James Armistead Lafayette, using a letter from Lafayette issued in 1784 about his service, petitioned the Virginia House of Delegates to grant him freedom. After the war he is known to have himself owned slaves. A portrait of him survives in the Valentine Museum in Richmond and can be seen on the INTERNET. He died 9 August 1830.

We Americans have no good word to say for Cornwallis, remembering his ungenerous behavior at Yorktown, in the sword episode *(where he at first refused to relinquish the weapon to Washington: the traditional mark of defeat)*. We do not remember that he bitterly opposed the strenuous methods applied by his government to the Colonies, and that he openly voted against those measures, in opposition to his party. He had won a high place among British leaders before the American campaign, and after his great defeat received no word of criticism from his government; but was loaded with honors, first made governor-general of India, and then invested with the Garter.

In 2006 a cannon was put on display in the Portsmouth Naval Shipyard Museum discovered during the construction of the condominium complex called Admirals Landing. The British cannon had been spiked to keep it from being used by the Patriots. It is believed by the museum to have been left by Cornwallis' troops.

Chapter 9 - Portsmouth's Revolutionary War Veterans

The patriot priest John Braidfoot returned to Portsmouth and the bell in the tower of Trinity Church was cracked ringing the victory at Yorktown.

All through the Revolution, as we have said, Portsmouth was in a perilous state. Invasions by land and water from the legal sources of war were frequent and she was also beset by attacks from privateers.

Just on the edge of the town was the Patriot camp, known as Camp Carson, which occupied part of what is now comprised within the two squares on Washington Street, between High and County, *Cheshire and Hertford Squares*. Some of the older people of the town remember when some of the barrack foundations could be traced. Affidavits of old soldiers once encamped there keep its memory alive. John Bradshaw, in his application for a pension, tells us that he marched to Camp Carson at Portsmouth in January, 1781, and spent the winter there, taking part in an engagement there in sight of the town. Another veteran, William Sharpe under Capt. Kinkead, makes a similar affidavit. Both of these men left Portsmouth in April, 1781.

From the records of Norfolk County we get an interesting glimpse of the burning of a French vessel in front of the Marine Yard in 1779. The owners of the ship later made claim for damages. This protest was made by Pierre Raphael Chariot, commander of the ship *Le Soucy* of Bordeaux, who declared that his ship was at anchor in the harbor when the English Fleet was sighted on the ninth of May, 1779. He carried a cargo of hogs and tobacco, and fearing that his vessel would be plundered he went up the "Southern River" *meaning the Southern Branch of the Elizabeth River,* where he went aground in front of the shipyard, having no pilot. Capt. Charlot tells us something of conditions not only in the town but bears out the testimony concerning the handful of men at Fort Nelson, where he says there were so few soldiers there that it was impossible to make any defense. The town he says was in wild confusion; everyone scuffling for himself. When he saw the strength of the British forces he called his lieutenant in consultation. It was decided between them that with only seven guns on their vessel resistance was out of the question. If it was captured it could easily be converted into a frigate of war, and thus be an aid to the British. They agreed to burn her; and prepared to do so. Everything was made ready and the long boat filled with provisions, then he and the crew took to the woods, leaving the boatswain to set fire to the ship. He did so successfully and joined the crew and officers in the woods. The first lieutenant was Pierre Vollet; Louis Vignier and Arnie Bougeous were second lieutenants.

Though it did not take place near Portsmouth, one of the most daring exploits of the Revolution was accomplished largely by a Portsmouth man, Capt. John Coxe of Gosport, who early in the war received his commission in the Navy of Virginia. He was sent by the Governor Patrick Henry on a special mission to the French West Indies, to establish an entrepot for arms and ammunition. This undertaking he accomplished in a most able manner. He then fitted out the schooner *Sally Norton* and with her was sent to perform some duty at St. Croix. There he was captured by a British ship, but not without a gallant struggle, and imprisoned on the Island of Tortola where he underwent severe hardship for about a month and then escaped, and fell in with the American brig *Renown*. He reached home early in 1781 and was sent to the Eastern Shore *of Virginia* to impress ships for another expedition. This exploit proved to be the celebrated affair at Bermuda, when Judge Tucker assisted by Capt. Coxe landed on the island, captured all the powder and brought it to Williamsburg. This gallant officer lived to be eight-five years old; spending the remainder of his life in Portsmouth, carrying on a large shipping business. He died at his home on First Street Gosport in 1837. Capt. Coxe had but one child, a daughter, who was remembered by the older generations of the town as Mrs. Swift. Her descendants moved away from Portsmouth many years ago.

Capt. Coxe's neighbor, Capt. James Young, who at the outbreak of the war was a lad, but nevertheless entered the service and did good work in the army. Capt. Young's father was a Scotch lawyer who came to Portsmouth and became King's counsel for the county. Capt. Young's home, a handsome brick house on First Street, has recently been pulled down to make room for activities connected with the United States *Coast Guard* Buoy Yard. *It was located where the nTelos pavilion now stands.* It was for many years the home of the Neville family, the birthplace of Gen. Wendell Neville, the hero of Chateau-Thierry *in World War One.* One of Captain Young's daughter, *Ann Ballard Maupin, buried in Trinity Churchyard,* was the first wife of Dr. George W. Maupin *of whom much more later,* and the other married Dr. Leigh of Norfolk *who is also buried at Trinity and of whom we will hear more when we identify his house on the northwest corner of Middle and North streets.*

The daring exploit of the armed ship *Marquis de la Fayette* in the interest of the colonies, has been preserved for us by one who took part in the venture, John Cowper, Esq., for many years editor of the old *Public Ledger.* Mr. Cowper was born near Suffolk but his father moved to Portsmouth just at the outbreak of the Revolution. The firm of Willis Cowper and Brothers had large shipping interest in Portsmouth and Suffolk at this time. The Cowpers lived in Norfolk after the war and built the house now occupied by the Virginia Club. This house is the last one on the south side of Bute Street, and was for forty years or more the home of the Cooke family, now torn down.

The ship *La Fayette*, Mr. Cowper tells us, was frigate-built and a fast sailor. She was built near Suffolk and was ready for launching, which was to have been done the next day, when news came that the British had reached Portsmouth and were about to march to Suffolk. Plans were changed and the *La Fayette* was launched at once to keep her from being burned on the stocks.

She was scuttled and sunk in eighteen feet of water but the sinking was imperfectly done, so the British raised her and sent her to Portsmouth for repairs. Fortunately her sails and rigging had been hidden in one of the warehouses below Suffolk and *were* not found by the enemy.

At Portsmouth she was fitting out for New York when the British evacuated. She was sunk again and this time raised by her owners. When ready for her hazardous enterprise, Capt. Meredith took charge of her and with great difficulty manned her, and she lay in the Nansemond *River* ready for her journey, waiting for a dark night. *Benedict* Arnold's arrival in Portsmouth made it imperative to leave at once, though the moon was shining brightly.

"Upon reconnoitering," says Mr. Cowper, "we found the enemy's ships distributed nearly as follows: One ship of the line, a frigate and a sloop of war lay under Newports Noose *(Miss Holladay's spelling, not mine, or perhaps the spelling of the man who set the type, or the way Mr. Cowper said it.)*; two frigates and two sloops lay off Hampton bar, about a half a mile from each other, three vessels of war at the entrance to the Elizabeth River, and several vessels of war, of what description, or number I do not now remember were near Old Point Comfort. The transports and merchant ships, some eighty or a hundred in number, lay in different parts of the Roads; but we apprehended nothing from them, unless those higher up should give warning of our approach. Captain Meredith had ordered that no spirits should be used on board that day. After entering the Roads the duty of the ship was to be carried on in so low a tone as not to be heard outside of the ship; the guns were to be loaded, but not to be fired even if fired on, Capt. Meredith explaining to his officers that by not returning fire of the enemy we might pass for one of their own ships, and it might cease; but if we fired our character could not be mistaken.

He tells us that Capt. Meredith planned to get among the transports and keep one or more of them between him and the ships of war. The river was cleared and all went well until just after the pilot had returned, then a dead calm prevailed. "It was," said Cowper, "an awful moment—to return was impossible on account of the tide. Nothing could be done but anchor and that must be done at once. Orders were given to let anchor go, when Capt. Meredith called out, 'Stop,' I was near to him and heard him exclaim, 'I see a cloud from whence we shall have wind.' This was true and all at once the sails swelled, for a northeast wind had come up with the usual effects. The first ships we passed were those at Newport News, but they gave us no signal, probably not seeing us." He tells how they passed the frigates and got among the transports, so near them that they could sometimes hear conversations on board them. They were not afraid of the transport, knowing that they were much too fast for them; the danger was from the ships ahead. Passing the vessels at Old Point, things were looking brighter, when a large frigate appeared off Willoughby Point. She hailed the *La Fayette* but had no answer; and it was never known what she was. Cape Henry was passed and then *they found* safety on the open sea. Mr. Cowper had volunteered on this ship; his father at the time was imprisoned in Portsmouth and told him that the British were not on the lookout for the ship that night, never dreaming that they would come out on a moonlight night.

The ship made many more thrilling voyages and was finally lost, but not while the gallant Meredith was her captain.

The Cowper Brothers carried on an extensive business after the Revolution was over. They owned the wharf property on the waterfront of Water Street from Queen halfway to London Street.

Another Portsmouth youth who entered the Revolutionary Army was Spivey Wyatt. He too, was noted for his intrepid conduct on the field of battle, distinguishing himself on several occasions. Wyatt never lost his interest in military affairs and at the time of his death was a major in a regiment of militia. He lived at the northeast corner of Queen and Dinwiddie streets, in an old-fashioned house torn down in recent years. He has many descendants in Portsmouth, among them the Williams and Foreman families.

Speaking of Captain Jesse Nicholson, a veteran of the War of 1812, who knew him well says that he came originally from the up country and that he was a faithful soldier and a devoted friend to the "Great American Cause." He was a rifleman during the Revolution; and although a very strict Methodist preacher, he was very fond of talking of the Revolution. I used to love to hear him fight his battles o'er again. The old Gentleman always kept his rifle in order. He was appointed Postmaster of the town of Portsmouth under Jefferson, and died in Portsmouth while holding that office. "The Volunteer companies did him all honor," says the narrator and he was buried with every mark of respect in the Methodist Churchyard, and his funeral was attended by throngs from both cities. Another chronicler tells us something of the gallant old soul. In appearance, "he was a very handsome old gentleman, dressed always in the old English style, velvet coat, knee breeches and silk stockings and silver buckled shoes, hair in queue tied with a ribbon." He was ordained a minister in the Methodist Church in 1789 by Bishop Francis Asbury, who had himself been for a time pastor of this church in Portsmouth. He became pastor of the Portsmouth church in 1790.

Jesse Nicholson was a very busy man, but found time to teach school and some of Portsmouth's most prominent citizens of a bygone day were his pupils. They always reverenced his memory.

His tombstone has been removed to the yard of Monumental Methodist Church. It bears this inscription: "Sacred to the Memory of/ Jesse Nicholson/ A patriot of the American Revolution/ A most exemplary Christian." *The stone is now in Cedar Grove Cemetery at the western end of North Street.*

Mr. George Myers was another of the Portsmouth lads that joined the army and did good service. Mr. Myers died at his home on the southeast corner of South and Court Street in his ninety first year. He has a number of descendants in Portsmouth.

At the Battle of Great Bridge *(the first battle of the Revolution in the South and described earlier, as it involved Dunmore's troops)* there was a generous proportion of Portsmouth men to the fore, said one of their comrades—"Wilkinses, Branons, Herberts, Nashes, Porters, Wattses. Brookses, Formans, Etheredges, Hodgeses, Moores, Culpepers and Wilsons. It was in this battle that Gen. *William* Woolford had his horse shot under him; and his friend Col. John Wilson called his young son and made him dismount and give his horse to Woolford. Young Wilson was then *hoist* on *the* mount with his father. Col. Wilson's four sons were all in the army.

Captain Nash, one of the heroes of this battle, was captured by the British with some of his comrades and with them imprisoned in the "Sugar House" *in Portsmouth* which in those days was the Provost prison. Later he was transferred to the *Cornwallis* prison ship at Yorktown and thrown in the hold. Capt. Nash used to tell harrowing tales of his life there, made more horrible by the filth and vermin to which the prisoners were subjected.

The old Provost Prison recalls the story of the wonderful escape of Capt. Cunningham, who was imprisoned there during the Revolution. Commodore James Barron has preserved this story for us and tells us that, "When Virginia was invaded Capt. Cunningham of the Navy took up his landtracks and joined the army on the southern side of the James River. He was not much at home on land as he was on sea, and was captured while on a foraging expedition. He had been recently married and his wife lived with her family on the borders of Gosport. He said to his uncle, Commodore Barron, "I will see my wife tonight or perish in the attempt." The prison which was situated on the corner of Crawford and County Streets *(later the site of the Armory, now a bank buildings - before the war some of these lots belonged to Andrew Sprowle)*, and strongly enclosed by a stockade fence, the principal gate opening on the southwest. At sunset every evening the guard composed of forty or fifty men was relieved by fresh troops; on their arrival the guards with their officers paraded in front of the prison on both sides of the pathway leading to the gate. At this hour on this occasion the ceremony was in progress; the relieved guards had stacked their arms and were looking up to their baggage; the fresh guards were relieving the sentinels, and in a degree at their ease. As the sentinel turned and moved toward the gate Capt. Cunningham darted from the house and overtook him before he turned, knocked him down at his full length by a butt of the head, for which he was famous. It was dark, and confusion reigned, shots were fired, some of them whistling over Cunningham's head; but he kept right on, and just before he reached the Navy Yard he plunged overboard; swimming for a half mile until he reached his wife's home. He found the house deserted as the family were hiding from the enemy. He found there, however, two faithful servants who helped him equip an old horse, and started him out to find the family which had hidden in the woods nearby.

    Capt. Cunningham's joy must have been much clouded by the sad fate of his friend, Lieut. Church, who had served under him and was devoted to him. When Church realized what Cunningham was about, he too attempted to escape, thinking that he might serve his friend. He left the prison without interference in the scuffle that followed Cunningham's flight, but he disappeared and was never heard of again. It is probable that he jumped overboard to escape capture and was drowned.

    The most famous of all Portsmouth's fighters was Richard Dale. He was born at Dale's Point *(in the Waterview neighborhood)* the home of his grandfather, a plantation, which had been in the family for some generations since 1756. He was the son of Winfield and Ann Dale and as Miss Seawell says, "the future commodore had not much opportunity for an education, as at twelve years of age he determined to go in to the sea service *and* took up that work at once. Though in after years he made up for his lack of schooling, he could never learn to spell; and it has been said of him that his daring and recklessness in spelling was only surpassed by his boldness in the fray." It has been said that Dale had no great intellect, but in addition to his good sense and the constancy of his nature, he was gentle, courageous and just. His great probity won him the esteem of all. Cooper called him, "a truth-loving, truth-telling officer." "He was," said one of his biographers, "well up in all the little courtesies of life; his manners polished and his person handsome."

    His first voyage was made in a merchantman, of which his uncle was captain. Here his career of hard knocks began; and his biographers tell us that few men had more of them. He began by falling down the hold of his ship, breaking practically all the bones in his body except those in his neck and back. Then followed the experience of being knocked overboard and battling in the sea an hour before being picked up. Scarcely was he over this when he was struck by lightning, remaining unconscious for hours. From the time he joined the navy of the Colonies, he was never in action without being wounded or captured, and sometimes both. Three times was he badly wounded, and captured five times: yet he managed to be in active service during the greater part of the war; and died at last peacefully in his bed, at a good old age."

When war was declared Dale enlisted at once, and was immediately captured by the British, placed on the prison ship at his home, Portsmouth, where he met an old schoolfellow, who persuaded him that he was serving the wrong cause and succeeded in making him enlist on the opposite side. His first fight in the British Navy was against American pilot boats and with his usual luck he was captured and badly wounded. He was again brought to Portsmouth and during his long convalescence he saw his mistake and bitterly regretted it. One of the finest things about Dale was that he never attempted to disguise or belittle his early lapse. He was always expressing the deepest sorrow for it saying, "I knew no better at the time. *Adding: "Never again to put himself in the way of the bullets of his own countrymen."* Upon his recovery his one desire was to join the Continental Navy. He managed to get on a merchant ship with this in view.

The ship that hid him was the *Lexington* and he lost no time in enlisting on her as a midshipman. This ship in her scuffle with the British ship *Pearl* was captured and Dale was again a prisoner. Owing to the heavy seas the captain of the *Pearl* only transferred a few of the *Lexington's* men to his own ship, but placed the vessel under a prize crew, giving orders to follow the *Pearl*. As night came on the gale increased greatly and the waves were so boisterous that the captain of the *Pearl* felt no anxiety about his prize, and became less vigilant than he should have been. Later In the night in company with the officer of the deck, he went below to have a toddy. Scarcely had the officers disappeared when the Americans knocked the British sailor from the tiller and also the guards from the deck. The next step was the securing of the companion way against the exit of the officers. The Americans now had everything their own way *and* sailed immediately to Baltimore. Richard Dale was the leading spirit in this adventure. The next year 1777, the *Lexington* with other small vessels was sent to British waters to harass trade. There can be no doubt that the English commerce got a bad jolt; but the *Lexington* was caught off Plymouth and her crew imprisoned there in the Mill Prison, for high treason. Another account says its captor was the English ship <u>Allert</u> off the coast of France in 1777. They were cruelly treated, and deliberately starved. Appeal was made to the British Government, but without avail. Private subscriptions, however ameliorated their condition to some extent.

Dale's adventurous spirit soon found a way of escape, and he with other shipmates tunneled their way to the outside. When they reached London they were caught by the press gang and imprisoned again. When Dale had been in prison about a year he procured a British *(naval officer's)* uniform, donned it and boldly walked out of jail. Where he got the uniform has remained a mystery, which he refused to solve: refusing to tell even after the war had long been over. It was supposed by some that it was gotten for him by a woman.

Another source says at this point he went to France where he met John Paul Jones and joined his crew.

The most glorious achievement of our hero was accomplished as John Paul Jones' lieutenant on the *Bonhomme-Richard*. The details of this fight are too well known to need repetition here. At the critical moment when the ship was sinking and confusion reigned below, Jones sent his lieutenant to take charge; the resourceful Dale was ready for the emergency, though the prisoners had been turned loose, enemies and all. Everyone was clamoring for surrender. Above the confusion they heard Dale's call and listened. He told them that the *Serapis*, for it was in charge of the captured ship that Dale had been put in command, was sinking rapidly and the only hope of being saved was to stand by the ship, every man to his post. Order was restored and the day won. Dale had been wounded in the fight but did not know it until he had retired after the battle to rest.

On the chance there are those among us who do not know the story , the full account of the battle was told by Dale himself, and here it is: "On the 23d of September, 1779, being below, was roused by an unusual noise upon deck. This induced me to go upon deck when I found the men were swaying up the royal yards, preparatory to making sail for a large fleet under our lee. I asked the coasting pilot what fleet it was? He answered, "The Baltic fleet under convoy of the Serapis of 44 guns and the Countess of Scarborough of 20 guns." A general chase then commenced of the Bon Homme Richard, the Vengeance, the Pallas and the Alliance, the latter ship being then in sight after a separation from the squadron of nearly three weeks, but which ship, as usual, disregarded the private signals of the Commodore. At this time our fleet headed to the northward with a light breeze, Flamborough Head being about two leagues distant. At 7 P.M. it was evident the Baltic fleet perceived we were in chace from the signal of the Serapis to the merchantmen to stand in shore. At the same time the Serapis and Countess of Scarborough tacked ship and stood off shore, with the intention of drawing off our attention from the convoy. When these ships had separated from the convoy about two miles, they again tacked and stood in shore after the merchantmen. At about eight, being within hail, the Serapis demanded, 'What ship is that?' He was answered, 'I can't hear what you say.' Immediately after, the Serapis hailed again, 'What ship is that? Answer immediately, or I shall be under the necessity of firing into you.' At this moment I received orders from Commodore Jones to commence the action with a broadside, which indeed appeared to be simultaneous on board both ships. Our position being to windward of the Serapis we passed ahead of her, and the Serapis coming up on our larboard quarter, the action commenced abreast of each other. The Serapis soon passed ahead of the Bon Homme Richard, and when he thought he had gained a distance sufficient to go down athwart the fore foot to rake us, found he had not enough distance, and that the Bon Homme Richard would be aboard him, put his helm a-lee, which brought the two ships on a line, and the Bon Homme Richard, having head way, ran her bows into the stern of the Serapis. We had remained in this situation but a few minutes when we were again hailed by the Serapis, 'Has your ship struck?' To which Captain Jones answered, 'I have not yet begun to fight!' As we were unable to bring a single gun to bear upon the Serapis our topsails were backed, while those of the Serapis being filled, the ships separated. The Serapis bore short round upon her heel, and her jibboom ran into the mizen rigging of the

<u>Bon Homme Richard</u> *In this situation the ships were made fast together with a hawser, the bowsprit of the <u>Serapis</u> to the mizenmast of the <u>Bon Homme Richard</u>, and the action recommenced from the starboard sides of the two ships. With a view of separating the ships, the <u>Serapis</u> let go her anchor, which manoeuver brought her head and the stern of the <u>Bon Homme Richard</u> to the wind, while the ships lay closely pressed against each other. A novelty in naval combats was now presented to many witnesses, but to few admirers. The rammers were run into the respective ships to enable the men to load after the lower ports of the <u>Serapis</u> had been blown away, to make room for running out their guns, and in this situation the ships remained until between 10 and 11 o'clock P.M., when the engagement terminated by the surrender of the <u>Serapis</u>. From the commencement to the termination of the action there was not a man on board the <u>Bon Homme Richard</u> ignorant of the superiority of the <u>Serapis,</u> both in weight of metal and in the qualities of the crews. The crew of that ship was picked seamen, and the ship itself had been only a few months off the stocks, whereas the crew of the <u>Bon Homme Richard</u> consisted of part Americans, English and French, and a part of Maltese, Portuguese and Malays, these latter contributing by their want of naval skill and knowledge of the English language to depress rather than to elevate a just hope of success in a combat under such circumstances. Neither the consideration of the relative force of the ships, the fact of the blowing up of the gundeck above them by the bursting of two of the 18-pounders, nor the alarm that the ship was sinking, could depress the ardor or change the determination of the brave Captain Jones, his officers and men. Neither the repeated broadsides of the <u>Alliance</u>, given with the view of sinking or disabling the <u>Bon Homme Richard</u>, the frequent necessity of suspending the combat to extinguish the flames, which several times were within a few inches of the magazine, nor the liberation by the master-at-arms of nearly 500 prisoners, could charge or weaken the purpose of the American commander. At the moment of the liberation of the prisoners, one of them, a commander of a ?-gun ship taken a few days before, passed through the ports on board the <u>Serapis</u> and*

informed Captain Pearson that if he would hold out only a little while longer, the ship alongside would either strike or sink, and that all the prisoners had been released to save their lives. The combat was accordingly continued with renewed ardor by the Serapis. The fire from the tops of the Bon Homme Richard was conducted with so much skill and effect as to destroy ultimately every man who appeared upon the quarter deck of the Serapis, and induced her commander to order the survivors to go below. Nor even under the shelter of the decks were they more secure. The powder-monkies of the Serapis, finding no officer to receive the 18-pound cartridges brought from the magazines, threw them on the main deck and went for more. These cartridges being scattered along the deck and numbers of them broken, it so happened that some of the hand-grenades thrown from the main-yard of the Bon Homme Richard, which was directly over the main-hatch of the Serapis, fell upon this powder and produced a most awful explosion. The effect was tremendous; more than twenty of the enemy were blown to pieces, and many stood with only the collars of their shirts upon their bodies. In less than an hour afterward, the flag of England, which had been nailed to the mast of the Serapis, was struck by Captain Pearson's own hand, as none of his people would venture aloft on this duty; and this too when more than 1500 persons were witnessing the conflict, and the humiliating termination of it, from Scarborough and Flamborough Head. Upon finding that the flag of the Serapis had been struck, I went to Captain Jones and asked whether I might board the Serapis, to which he consented, and jumping upon the gunwale, seized the main-brace pennant and swung myself upon her quarterdeck. Midshipman Mayrant followed with a party of men and was immediately run through the thigh with a boarding pike by some of the enemy stationed in the waist, who were not informed of the surrender of their ship. I found Captain Pearson standing on the leeward side of the quarterdeck and, addressing myself to him, said, 'Sir, I have orders to send you on board the ship alongside.' The first lieutenant of the Serapis coming up at this moment inquired of Captain Pearson whether the ship alongside had struck to him, To which I replied, 'No, Sir, the contrary.' The lieutenant renewed his inquiry, 'Have *you struck, Sir?' 'Yes, I have.' The lieutenant replied, 'I have nothing more to say,' and was about to return below when I informed him he must accompany Captain Pearson on board the ship alongside. He said, 'If you will permit me to go below, I will silence the firing of the lower-deck guns.' This request was refused, and with Captain Pearson, he was passed over to the deck of the <u>Bon Homme Richard</u>. Orders being sent below to cease firing, the engagement terminated, after a most obstinate contest of three hours and a half. Upon receiving Captain Pearson on board the <u>Bon Homme Richard</u>, Captain Jones gave orders to cut loose the lashings, and directed me to follow him with the <u>Serapis</u>. Perceiving the <u>Bon Homme Richard</u> leaving the <u>Serapis</u>, I sent one of the quartermasters to ascertain this, and asked the helm whether the wheel-ropes were cut away, supposing something extraordinary must be the matter, as the ship would not pay off, although the head sails were aback, and no after sail; the quartermaster, returning, reported that the wheel was hard a port. Excited by this extraordinary circumstance, I jumped off the binnacle, where I had been sitting, and halling upon the deck, found to my astonishment I had the use of only one of my legs. A splinter of one of the guns had struck and badly wounded my leg without my perceiving the injury until this moment. I was replaced upon the binnacle, when the sailing-master of the <u>Serapis</u> coming up to me observed that from my orders he judged I must be ignorant of the ship being at anchor. Noticing the second lieutenant of the <u>Bon Homme Richard</u>, I directed him to go below and cut away the cable, and follow the <u>Bon Homme Richard</u> with the <u>Serapis</u>. I was then carried on board the <u>Bon Homme Richard</u> to have my wound dressed.*

When honors were showered upon Jones and his officers, Dale modestly kept in the background; but he was appreciated in spite of his modesty. Jones and Dale were devoted friends and Jones wished to keep his lieutenant with him, but Dale was anxious for sea service. This he got, nor did he escape his usual wound and capture. He soon exchanged, however, and by that time the war was over.

Dale, who had been first lieutenant on the <u>Bonhomme Richard</u> until it was sunk, continued to serve with Jones on *the Alliance and the Ariel.* "He returned to Philadelphia on 28 February 1781, and was placed on the list of lieutenants in the Continental Navy, and joined the Trumbull, which was captured in August of that year by the [HMS] Iris and the [HMS] Monk. Dale received his third wound in the engagement. Dale was exchanged in November, obtained a leave of absence, and served on letters of marque (this was a private ship authorized by its government in a "letter of marque" to act as a privateer and attack and capture enemy ships - this was often done by a government to augment its navy) and in the merchant service until the end of the war. He was appointed captain in 1794 on a short cruise in the Ganges.

Admiral Lord Horatio Nelson said, observing Dale's seamanship, "There is in the handling of those trans-Atlantic ships a nucleus of trouble for the Navy of Great Britain." This would prove true in the War of 1812. In 1796 the Pasha of Tripoli demanded the tribute paid by the United States (then $56,000) be increased if we did not want our shipping in the Mediterranean harassed. Jefferson did not approve of this tribute and pointed out it would be cheaper to build a navy. He sent an expeditionary force with four ships under Dale. When they arrived Dale was told at Gibralter that Tripoli had declared war on the United States. He had no orders to fight a war and so he took his little fleet to blockade Tripoli and escort American shipping near it, but the captain of the Enterprise took on the Barbary Pirate ship Tripoli and handily defeated it. Although Dale leaves this story in April 1802, I will continue to tell it, as two men who will take a place in Portsmouth history now come on stage. Dale's successor, Morris, continued Dale's passive policy and was recalled for it by Jefferson and drummed out of the Navy. The new commander, Edward Preble, gave his captains, among them Stephen Decatur, a free hand. Decatur's heroics gained him a commission at age twenty-five, making him the youngest captain in the navy and a national celebrity. This hotdogging lost several ships and did not win the war. James Barron then pulled up with reinforcements and, as he outranked Preble took over as commander. Barron stopped the grandstanding and won the war by convincing the British in Egypt to help overthrow the Pasha.*

Dale wished to spend the rest of his life in the Navy, but resigned owing to an affront put upon him as head of the Navy, by the Government. *(This may have been criticism for not having been more aggressive in the War With the Barbary Pirates, after the swashbuckling of Stephen Decatur).*

He spent his remaining years at his home in Philadelphia; dying there in 1826. He had two sons: his namesake who was killed in the War of '12 and another who lived in Philadelphia, where he has descendants now. Dale had a large family of sisters and brothers who lived in Portsmouth, and left descendants, among them the Luke and Colter families. The old Dale home in which the Commodore was born has long since been destroyed, but the house in which he spent his childhood is still to be seen on Swimming Point, and is now the residence of J. Davis Reed, Esq. *and later by Robert and Shippie Reed.* This house was built for Dale's father by Col. Crawford and devised to him in his will.

Dale was a deeply religious man and had the spiritual welfare of his men constantly on his mind. He organized a mariner's church in Philadelphia, making every effort to get sailors to attend. For thirty years he faithfully went to this little chapel every Sunday evening.

Bishop Meade tell us this story in <u>Old Churches and Families of Virginia</u>: *"The magnificent gold-hilted sword presented by Louis XVI has an added interest to us. When John Paul Jones was on his deathbed he requested Governor Morris, then American Minister to France to present it to, "Good old Dickie," as he affectionately called Richard Dale) who did more than any other to help me win it. This sword is now in the Pennsylvania Historical Museum."*

Dale was buried in Christ Church yard near his old friend Benjamin Franklin in Philadelphia, with the following inscription "In memory of Commodore Richard Dale, born November 6 1756, died February 24 1838. An honest man, an incorruptible patriot. In all his dealings a Christian without guile. He departed this life in the triumphant hope, well founded, and of the blessedness which all who like him died in the Lord." His body was moved in Victorian times to Laurel Hill Cemetery in Philadelphia; where there is another marker to him.

A simple but beautiful monument was erected in Portsmouth in memory of Dale, and unveiled with great ceremony on the ninth of May 1917. The stone work of the monument was done by Archibald Ogg *(from a stone cutting family still in business in Portsmouth)*; the bronze tablet is considered a very fine piece of work, designed by the well known artists Coupes. It was made especially for Col. Wm. Lamb of Norfolk, but proved not available for his purpose. It was sold to the monument committee by his heirs. The heads of the rivets that hold the small tablet to the stone were buttons from the uniform of Capt. Kenneth McAlpine, U. S. A., a distinguished officer, who rendered valiant service as Chief of the Engineers on the *Texas* in the Spanish-American War.

The United States Government named the fine ship of war, *Dale* in his honor, and like the Commodore she saw much hard service. *This monument stands on the median in the middle of Washington Street at its intersection with North. One of the two local Daughters of the American Revolution chapters is named for Richard Dale, the others for Fort Nelson and Great Bridge. I can find nothing about the artist Coupes.*

By the twenty-first century five ships have been named for Dale: the USS <u>Dale</u> (1840-1921); the destroyer #4 USS <u>Dale</u> (1902-1920); destroyer #290 and later DD-290 USS <u>Dale</u> (1920-1931); DD353 USS <u>Dale</u> (1935-1946) and DLG19 later CG19 USS <u>Dale</u> (1963-2000).

Dale's final military service station did find its way into the Marine Corps. song - "From the Halls of Montezuma (the Mexican War) to the shores of Tripoli (The War With the Barbary Pirates)."

A report discovered in the files of the Fort Nelson Chapter of the Daughters of the American Revolution adds some names to Miss Holladay's list of Revolutionary War veterans. It includes references, which I have omitted here, but it can be found in <u>Portsmouth and Norfolk County Documents</u>. The DAR thinks it was put together by Dorothy Monroe. There is a longer list in Stewart's <u>History of Norfolk County</u> page 52.

* *Rev. Thomas Armistead: 15 Sept. 1777 enlisted as 1st Lieut. in the 1st VA Regiment, 8 April 1779 became Captain and mustered* *out in 1780. He is credited with starting the first Baptist Church in Portsmouth in 1789.*

* *William Halley Avery: 1st Lieut. 6th VA 1 March 1776, Capt. 4 Jan. 1777 and resigned 28 June 1778. He and James are the sons of Mary Avery mentioned earlier in reference to her property at Court and South streets.*

* *James Barron will appear later in this narrative. He was very young at this time, but the DAR papers say, "toward the end of it (the Revolution) was initiated by his father into the service of the state and continued in it until the small remnant of Virginia's little navy was disbanded in 1788."*

* *Antonio Sylvestre Bilisoly was born in Ajaccio, Corsica, in 1758, the son of Charles and Olivia Bilisoly, and died in Portsmouth in 1845. He is buried under the Roman Catholic Church, but his marble slab is in Cedar Grove Cemetery. He joined the navy of French Admiral Compt de Grasse in the West Indies. He was sailing master on the French ship <u>Carvette Pucelle</u> in the Battle of the Capes which prevented the resupply and reinforcement of Cornwallis at Yorktown.*

* *Brannon has already been mentioned. He served at the Battle of Great Bridge.*

* *Thomas Bowers Dickenson, who appeared elsewhere in Miss Holladay's narrative as Thomas Bowers (her error), buried in Trinity Churchyard.*

* *Captain John Cox (or Coxe) story has already ben told by Miss Holladay. Record of his funeral was in the First Vestry Book of Trinity Church (now lost). He left a daughter, Mrs. Swift.*

* *Davis Day is listed among those held prisoner at Antigua taken to New York 15 September 1780, "on giving and signing their parole of honor to surrender to the governor, or commandant of New York on their arrival."*

* *Thomas Edwards, also a prisoner at Antigua.*

* *Captain Robert Elliott's story is told in an affidavit by Captain William Moffat before Samuel Watts, Justice of the Peace of Norfolk County 20 July 1834: Captain Moffat was the mate of the brig <u>Neptune</u>. "He saw the ship <u>Renown</u> which was built at the State Navy Yard at Gosport by Stoddard, the master ship builder, and commanded by Captain Robert Elliott, drop down*

from the Navy Yard, and when she passed the wharf where the Neptune lay, Captain Elliott enquired when the Neptune would be ready for sea and expressed a wish that she would get ready and proceed to sea under convoy of his ship. The Neptune followed the Renown and when they reached Hampton Roads they found 16 or 17 sail of other vessels waiting the departure of the Renown, and wishing protection under her, Captain Moffat further made oath that in May of the year 1779, a sloop of war was burnt at the Gosport Navy Yard by the enemy, and that the ship Renown was built on the same stocks and was pierced to carry 20 odd guns, but at the time of her first sailing in April 1780, in consequence of the great deficience of arms at the time, she had only eight or ten guns, that the Renown went into the port of Eustalea and there fitted with her full compliment of guns and returned to the colonies. He further made oath that Captain Elliott went to sea a second time in the Renown and was chased into St. Martin. The Renown was captured and Captain Elliott taken prisoner. This deponent did not return to Portsmouth until after the peace, being more than three years from the time of Captain Elliott's first cruise in the Renown. This affiant does not know at what time Capt. Robert Elliott entered the service, but he supposed the sloop-of-war that had been built in 1778, and was burnt in May 1779 was designed for his command, as he commanded the sloop built in place of that sloop-of-war. On the return of this affiant, it was then peace and Captain Elliott was at home. He does not know how long Captain Elliott was in prison." We, however, know he is listed as a 2nt Lieut. 20 March 1779 and that he served as a Captain in the VA Militia (probably mistaken for the Navy) and died 4 June 1838.

* Amos Etheridge was among the first trustees of the town. Miss Holladay lists an Etheridge as at Great Bridge. It could also be his son: Powers Etheridge.

* I have outlined the life of William "Billie" Flora and his exploits earlier.

* James Gaskins was Portsmouth's first silversmith, a Revolutionary War veteran, for whom Gaskins' Lane, off North Street between Court and Middle is named. Some of his silver survives.

* Levin Gayle: his obituary in the Portsmouth newspaper *Palladium* in June 1827 says: "Col. Levin Gayle, formerly of Mathews County, . . . was actively employed as a soldier during the Revolutionary War, particularly so at the siege of Yorktown, and was present at the surrender of Cornwallis. In the last struggle with England, he commanded a force of Virginia troops in and about the County of Mathews. Col. Gayle died in Portsmouth.

* Laban Goffigan served in the Virginia State Navy. He is mentioned in the Naval Board Letter as being on the *Scorpion* 18 Jan. 1777 with the following orders: "If the river should be frozen in such a way as to prevent your going on with your vessel, you must apply to Mr. Hunter to procure wagons for the purpose of conveying your goods down there to your vessel." In these days the weather was colder than it is now, the river three times froze over and, as Miss Holladay told us earlier, tropical plants which now grow well here did not survive the colder weather then. His wife is buried at Trinity Churchyard.

* Lieut. William Ham, Sr., served in the Virginia State Navy, commanding the schooner *Nicholson* on the James River during the siege of Yorktown and was at Portsmouth; although he was born and died in Elizabeth City County.

* Joseph Hay was among those taken as prisoners to Antigua (see David Day above).

* William Hunter was paymaster of the 1st Virginia Regiment for 1777-78.

* John Kay, is mentioned as an ensign in the Virginia 12th Infantry with a marker in Trinity Churchyard and at Cedar Grove Cemetery.

* William Kirby was born and died in York County and may be in this list because descendants live in Portsmouth.

* Lieut. Thomas Mathews is buried at Wallaceton "on the banks of the Dismal Swamp Canal."

* Capt. James Murdaugh is on this list because so many of his descendants were so prominent in Portsmouth's history, settling here right after the war. He, however, was born and died in Nansemond County. He was captain of a company of minute men appointed by the House of Burgesses under the local Committee of Safety in 1773.

* Jesse Nicholson's service is outline by Miss Holladay earlier, but this list says that her informant is mistaken in saying that he came from the "up country," and that he was born in Portsmouth in 1759, that he was seventeen when he enlisted and served with Washington throughout the war and was ordained a Methodist minister in 1789.
* We have already covered the distinguished career of Major General Josiah Parker, but this source adds that his country home was Macelesfield (?) in Isle of Wight County, and under Lafayette he was commander of forces in Norfolk County, Princess Anne, Nansemond, Southampton, Isle of Wight and Surry. His winter home was on the northwest corner of Glasgow and Crawford Streets, as mentioned earlier. He spent the last years of his life in Portsmouth, where he had been our first member of Congress and first Postmaster. His grave was found in 2005 at his summer home in Isle of Wight.
* Thomas Pollard has also been mentioned earlier. He was a first lieutenant in the Navy and then commander of an artillery company at Yorktown.
* Captain John Porter was mentioned at the Battle of Great Bridge. One of his descendants would build the C. S. S. *Virginia* and the family would be influential in the founding of Monumental Methodist Church.
* William Porter, although a Portsmouth man, is buried at Old Saint Paul's Church in Norfolk.
* Charles Stewart was a lieutenant in the 15th Virginia Regiment.
* John Thompson is covered in greater detail elsewhere in this work.
* Jacob Valentine is one of those taken prisoner at Antigua (see David Day above).
* Richard White who was born in England served aboard the provisions ship *Betsy Loyd* out of Portsmouth.
* James Williams is mentioned as a captain and then a brigade major.
* John Wilson we heard of earlier in Miss Holladay's narrative when he had his youngest son give his horse to Colonel Woodford at the Battle of Great Bridge. These papers add that he was in

command of the Norfolk County Militia during Patrick Henry's administration. His estate was at North Landing in Norfolk County, and after his death his wife put in a claim for the warehouse there which had been burned during the war.

* Willis Wilson's epitaph at Trinity Churchyard is worth looking up in <u>Surviving Gravestones at Trinity Church, Portsmouth, VA.</u>

* Spivey Wyatt kept his interest in the military and at his death was a major in the militia. His father and mother were John and Sarah. He was born February 24 1760 and lived on the southeast corner of Queen and Dinwiddie streets.

* Captain James Young mentioned elsewhere in this book.

Several others appear on this list, but will be covered when we begin to describe their homes in the Olde Towne.

In a letter from the Rev. Mr. Charles H. Holmead, Rector of Trinity Church, dated July 17, 1941 is in the DAR file - he lists the Revolutionary War veterans buried in Trinity Churchyard known to him at that time (all of them can be found by using <u>Surviving Gravestones At Trinity Church, Portsmouth, Virginia</u>): "Col. Bernard Magnion (spelling error - Magnien), near the Court Street gate to the left of the entrance; Lt. Edward Ouley (spelling error, it is Onley, his grave says he was killed in a duel in 1806 at age 38) of the British Navy, near the King Street wall; Capt. Thomas Bowers (this stone is now lost, the Vestry Book calls him Thomas Bowers Dickenson who died in 1785 at age 36), front of the Parish House (this is the old Parish House, replaced in the 1950s); Col. Willis Wilson, front of the Parish House; 1812; Com. James Barron, opposite High St. side of the Parish House, also Revolution; Capt. Jacob Stobo, rear of Com. Barron (by which he means toward the Commodore Theater, which had not been built at this time, the stone is missing and may be buried under the turf), it says he is "late of Philadelphia" which is confirmed by a relative, H. Frederick Fishel Jr. of Wildwood, MO, who came searching for him in 2003. He died Jan. 30, 1794, age 34; Ens. John Kay (spelling error - Key) - south side of the church (there is a marker for him in Cedar Grove as well, but this marker at Trinity, placed later, marks his burial); Rev. Chaplain John Braidfoot - south side of *the Parish House near the High St. gate. He was the 2nd Rector of the Parish" and his body was moved to its present location from the glebe.*

Chapter 10 : The Ferry and the Tunnels

It could be argued that the ferry to Norfolk made the town. Portsmouth is essentially a peninsula and a dead end at the Elizabeth River; and Norfolk, to which the ferry connects, is essentially an island. Miss Holladay says - It is to the generosity of Colonel Crawford that we owe our share in the ferries, for when the farmers of this section petitioned the General Assembly for a ferry in 1705, it was agreed upon by those interested in the plan that a point on the Crawford plantation would be the most suitable spot on this side of the river. This public-spirited gentleman gave them the land required for the purpose. *The ferry itself, however, existed long before this time having been started in 1636 by Adam Thoroughgood.*

The place given was at the extreme eastern point of what is now North Street, where the Seaboard warehouses stand today. *The warehouses are now gone, replaced by Harbor Tower. When ferry service was resumed in the 1970s, at the urging of then City Manager George Hanbury, the North Harbor was reopened to the river and a ferry landing again stands near the place where it did in Colonial times. City Manager Hanbury grew up in Berkley, now a part of Norfolk, but then an independent town served by the ferry, and remembered one night missing the last ferry from Portsmouth and swimming across the Elizabeth River to get home.*

When the committee *in 1705* undertook to raise the money to put the ferry into operation Norfolk refused to subscribe her quota, saying that the ferry gave her no advantages. This lack of foresight that city has regretted more than once, since she has never in any way been able to reap the profits arising from this venture.

Of course the ferry antedated our town by many years, but when Portsmouth was laid off as a town the ferry was within its limits.

On this side of the river the landing place has been changed several times, first in 1834, when it was moved to the foot of High Street for the convenience of the newly established railroad. Then it was changed to a point on Water Street just north of High, but in later years it has taken over its High Street wharf again. *The Portsmouth Naval Shipyard Museum, now a part of the Portsmouth Museums, is a fragment of the old ferry building complex. This is the location where it is most remembered by old citizens and seen in many postcards of the early twentieth century. Alice Haynes, curator of the Portsmouth Shipyard Museum and President of the Historical Association, said, as a teenager, she would go across on the ferry with her friends to a Chinese restaurant in Commercial Place in Norfolk where they could get lunch for a quarter. The lunch was large enough for three of them to share. In the closing days of the twentieth century the High Street Landing was excavated and the ferry slip situated there again. During the excavation for the new High Street Landing, which opened July 18 1997, the well-preserved remains of a wooden ship from the end of the 18th, or early days of the 19th century was discovered. The front section was removed and, since Governor Wilder had just done away with Virginia's Department of Archaeology, sent to North Carolina. Its whereabouts are now unknown. The rest of this ship was left in place for later excavation. Its sides were held together with pegs and made of local wood, but thicker than most hulls of the time suggesting that it was a ship of war. Also in the muck at the foot of High Street the workers found an automobile with two dead Navy men in it. Apparently they had run off the end of High Street into the excavation at night. This ferry was, when it was discontinued, the oldest continuously operated ferry in the nation. It was discontinued when the Downtown Tunnel took its place. Hereby hangs a tale: Vernon Asbury Brooks, Portsmouth's councilman from 1920 to 1934 and mayor from 1926 to 1930 proposed building a tunnel from Portsmouth to Norfolk under the Elizabeth River. His political opposition obstructed the plan for decades. They were mainly stockholders in the ferry, among them the editor of the <u>Portsmouth Star</u> Norman Hamilton (which may explain why Miss Holladay demurred on this debate) and* who was then our Representative in Congress. The State finally set up a commission and appointed Brooks to it. The Downtown Tunnel was opened 23 May 1952 and the last ferry left Portsmouth August 25, 1955. The tunnel connected Portsmouth with Berkeley. The Berkeley Bridge already existed, connecting Berkeley to Norfolk. It was an iron span across which the trolleys ran. The trolley from Berkeley would stop before crossing the bridge and the conductor would collect two cents from each passenger to cover the cost of the toll.

Brooks also was the first to suggest the dredging of Scotts Creek in 1921, but that good idea still languishes on a shelf at City Hall.

George Hanbury, when he was City Manager, arranged to replace the small Admiral's gig in use as a temporary pedestrian ferry with the handsome ships now plying this old path across the Southern Branch of the Elizabeth River. The man contracted to provide a very elegant product was never able to deliver, to the great embarrassment of the city administration, but soon a more workable product was found; and now several boats, belonging to Tidewater Rapid Transit (later Hampton Roads Transit Authority) and managed by the Jordan brothers leave from the Norfolk side on the quarter and three quarter hour and from the Portsmouth side on the hour and half hour. For details of the long ownership controversy about the ferries see <u>Portsmouth and Norfolk County Documents</u> in the library.

The Norfolk dock has never been changed, though by purchase more land has been added to it. *Of course, this is no longer true. The remnants of Commercial Place where the ferry docked on the Norfolk side are now inland around the Confederate Monument. The new dock was finished as a part of the shopping complex and marina on the Norfolk waterfront called Waterside. A history of the earliest ferries is outlined on a historical marker at Waterside.*

In early days the ferry was operated by Col. Craford on this side and he received for his trouble six thousand pounds of tobacco. In 1753, the year after the town was incorporated, the ferry was leased to Mr. Alexander Bruce and Mr. Francis Miller for about the same amount.

The first glimpse that we get of the ferry fleet is from the diary of a Frenchman who visited Portsmouth in 1764, and tells us that there were three boats plying between the two towns. *This French traveler we have heard so much about, Moreau de St. Mery, tells us that the boats were rowed by two slaves. The rule was that as soon as a passenger presented himself they were to row him, or her, across. To avoid this requirement the slaves would hide in the reeds until they thought they had enough passengers to be worth their efforts. He also tells us the fare was equivalent to two French pennies.*

In 1784 George Dyson was ferry keeper. The fleet had grown a bit since the days of our French traveler. The rowboats had increased to five in number and there were two barges and a horse boat. We know nothing about the management of the ferry in those early days. There were doubtless complaints but they have long since been forgotten. Neither do we know the cost of a trip across the water until 1792; in fact we do not know the cost of a single trip *at this time*, but find that the use of the ferry could be had for a year by the payment of six dollars.

In 1813 the lease of the ferries brought $4,900, while in 1831 they were leased for $3,000. The money arising from this source was used in lowering the county levy. The late Thomas Rowland, Esq., of Norfolk, who lived to be over ninety, has given us a description of the old team boats which were introduced by Mr. W. H. Wilson in 1820 while he was lessee of the ferries. These were the first boats which could carry vehicles. The stables for the ferry horses stood where the Macon House *Hotel,* or rather the apartments into which it was converted, stand *on the south side of North Street between Middle and Court Streets.*

"After some ten years of use on the ferry these old blind horses were turned over to the mud machine," Mr. Rowland says," I have an indistinct recollection of the old team ferry boats which were used between Norfolk and Portsmouth. My aunt, Mrs. Selina Dickson lived on First Street, Gosport, on the corner opposite the present officers' quarters, and the building is still standing. *Now long gone.* The family would go over to spend the day with her. The so-called boats were lighters with square ends. There was a circular pit on the deck; horses were used to operate the wheels, which were three or four feet in diameter, for propelling power. I cannot remember that there was any shelter for passengers. The boats left the ferry dock on this side, *Norfolk,* and landed at the foot of North Street *in Portsmouth.* The voyage was full of vicissitudes.

The steam-propelled ferry boats that followed the horse boats were of small dimensions, but amply filled the demand for all purposes of the time. Accommodations for the traveler were scant, and boxlike rooms about six feet by twelve furnished shelter from the weather. If they had outside windows to draw the complaint of leakage, I do not remember. The engine was on deck fully exposed, and the engineer backed or went forward as he saw fit, without any orders, for there was no lookout forward; and the steering was done with a long wagon pole tiller, which, when unshipped, was laid upon the deck in a way for everyone to stumble over.

The hours were from sunup to sundown. When the dinner hour arrived Engineer Childs went home and the schedule took a vacation until he returned.

The Junior Military Company was once invited to some jollification at Deep Creek, and chartered one of the steam ferry boats piloted by Captain Cornick, who issued orders to Engineer Bayea, to 'back her and go ahead one turn!' 'Half a turn sideways, Mr. Bayea,' said some wag. The whole crew consisted of fireman, deck hand and engineer.

What night service was required was done by Captain Jarvis' small boats. His oarsmen were two African American men, each with a wooden leg. It is said that a man once applied to him for a place on the boats. He replied, "Yes, I will take you. Come, Bill, bring the bucksaw and saw this fellow's leg off." It is needless to say that the applicant did not accept the job. It was not until April, 1898 that the ferry boats ran all night. This change was made when Gill & Thomas leased the ferries.

In 1839, Norfolk established a ferry on her own account, but it did not succeed; in fact was never really operated. Their appeal to the Legislature was not granted, and at the end of a year the company found that they would have to sell out. There was one loyal soul at least in the borough, who made appeal after appeal to the newspapers, urging them to find some way to save the ferry "Anything rather than let the Norfolk County Ferry have the equipment at cost." That seemed to be the burden of his song, or what was worse, "probably below cost."

The newspaper offering no suggestion—the gentlemen offers one to the paper: "Let our ferry run for one year, and for this term pass all passengers and freight of all kinds free." This he felt sure would build up a clientele. He acknowledged that it would prove a costly venture but that the citizens of Norfolk should be public-spirited enough to subscribe the requisite amount.

We do not know what became of the "equipment." It would be interesting to know whether the county ferry got it at a bargain or not. We do know, however, that Norfolk made no more attempts to run a rival ferry.

On April 2 1839 the ferry slip was moved from its old location of Ferry Point at the end of North Street to the foot of High Street.

In the early *eighteen* fifties there was a perfect howl set up about the ferries. It was claimed that they kept to no schedule, ran only as long after dark as the superintendent pleased, took their own time in crossing, and moreover had not enough room on the boats for the crowds that they had to handle. To add to the inconvenience of the people of Norfolk and Portsmouth, an order had been given by the superintendent of the ferry, requiring all boats to stop at Washington Point (Berkley) for passengers and freight. After a mighty protest from the Portsmouth people, this order was withdrawn. As far as we have been able to find out, this was the beginning of the ferry boats making the Berkley run *mentioned earlier. There is a photograph in the library of a ferry with a sign showing it was dedicated to the Berkley run.*

We learn that this storm of criticism was not without its effect, and that in the course of the year conditions were much improved. The steering gear on the boats had been removed to the upper deck, thus giving passengers more room below, but the boats were not nearly large enough. A two-cent fare was demanded, and the five cent fare reduced to that amount. This arrangement was declared by all to be most satisfactory. At this period the ferry was yielding an income of about twenty thousands a year. The superintendent's troubles were by no means over yet. He was soon involved in a spicy newspaper controversy. A gentleman who was shocked by the obscure (obscene) writings and drawings that he had observed on the walls of the ferry waiting room, wrote a long and indignant article on the subject and sent it to the paper. After some sharp letters on both sides, the superintendent closes the matter with a letter saying that his duties do not allow him to spend his time in the waiting room, watching the walls. In order, he tells us, to get rid of this nuisance, the walls would have to be freshly painted every week. "In future," he says to this correspondent, "go into the waiting room, and sit quietly down, not wasting your time reading the scribbling on the wall." *Graffiti is not a new problem.*

Twice in their history the Norfolk County and Portsmouth Ferries—for that *was* the official name—have been taken over by the Federal Government, once as an enemy, when Portsmouth fell into the hands of the Federals, and again when in the *First* World War she took them over as a war measure.

The Federals enlarged facilities. In 1862 going to Norfolk or coming to Portsmouth was no easy job. A passport had to be issued at the Provost Marshal's office, which of course made delay, and was often a very disagreeable necessity. *This office was on the first floor of the Pass House on the northwest corner of London and Crawford Street. The house is still there and the current owner has marked the room with a sign saying "Provost General's office." This was the same place you would go to get a pass through the Union lines to visit the Confederate Army lying in Suffolk, or to swear an Oath of Allegiance.* As a rule permission was readily granted, but when a rude or ungentlemanly officer was on duty, a person demanding a permit was sometimes subjected to insults. People were often asked all kinds of questions and occasionally searched before the permit was made out. Some vary amusing stories are told by those who frequented the Provost's office. It is said that the Federal officers of the better type hated this duty, as many of the applicants made things as difficult as possible for those in charge.

After the Civil War the City of Portsmouth and the County of Norfolk made a claim against the Government of the United States for $100,000 in payment for the use of the ferry, through their counsel, James G. Holladay, Esq. Many years later the claim was paid, but the amount reduced to one-half the sum asked for.

From this time the ferries have gone on quietly serving the public, with little of interest to note. There have been few accidents and the few that have occurred have not been of a serious nature. One of the boats sank, in the *eighteen* fifties in fifteen minutes. Nothing worse was recorded than a fainting fit of one of the fair sex aboard. In the *eighteen* eighties there was an accident of a more serious nature, which resulted in one or two deaths. In the early days of the Civil War when there was uncertainty as to who would hold the Navy Yard; the ferry boats were mounted with cannon, but there is no record that they were ever fired.

In the old days being on the water was thought to be an excellent thing for sick babies, and the ferry boats were very convenient for this purpose. The decks were often crowded with the nurses and their charges. In 1873 an order was issued by the ferry committee forbidding nurses in future to blockade the outside decks of the ferry steamers with baby carriages for several trips at a time. If the nurses were to ride back and forth they were told to leave the carriages in the ferry house, where they would be cared for. So popular were these excursions for sick babies that at a later period there was a latticed enclosure built on the roof of the ferry steamer *Manhasset*, where the nurses and babies could be more comfortable, and quieter.

About twenty-five years ago, *(1910)* the ferry schedule was changed from twenty to ten-minute-trips. This was accomplished by running two boats. The law required the schedule to be kept and the lessees forfeited a certain sum if they did not keep up to the requirements. At this time the ferries were leased for about one hundred thousand dollars a year. Perhaps the hardest times the ferry ever had were when we entered the *First* World War, everything then being inadequate for the immense amount of traffic due to the importance of this port for war needs.

As a result, the Government took over the ferries on terms most detrimental to their owners, running them as they chose. The old waiting-rooms were torn down and new ones, inconvenient in construction and cheap in type, replaced them. The fare for passengers and vehicles was doubled without gain either of comfort or time. The repairs cost an enormous amount and the owners had to pay for them. It was thought by many of our citizens that the ferries would be retained by the federal authorities, but this proved a groundless fear and the county and city *were soon* in possession of them *again,* and also possessed of a heavy debt due for the aforesaid improvements made by the Government for its own use.

The last lease before the *First World War* was for one hundred and fifty thousand dollars a year. Since that war they have been run on a little different basis. It is said that on some days during the tourist season that cars from every State in the Union cross the ferry. *Until the ferries were discontinued when the downtown tunnel was opened on May 23 1952 the ferries carried automobiles. Photographs in the library show lines of automobiles waiting for the ferry, stretching all the way up High Street to Washington Street. On August 31 1955 the last Elizabeth River ferry ran from Portsmouth to Norfolk. When reinstated in the 1960s the ferries became pedestrian only, as they are today.* At present *(1935)* there is great talk of tubes being built between the two cities and doubtless this will be done in the course of time.

Norfolk has several times tried to claim *the dock on her side* as her own property. It was part of the original fifty acres bought of Nicholas Wise in 1683, as the site for a future city. It was set aside for a public dock, and used by the county in undisputed possession until 1811, when Norfolk refused to allow the ferry committee to repair it.

On May 11, 1811, the County Court had appointed commissioners to see to the repairing of the county wharf. The gentlemen appointed were all residents of Portsmouth—Tapley Webb, Jordan Marchant, Holt Wilson, Mordecai Cooke and William Pritchard. They were authorized to contract for the best material and to have all repairs made that seemed suitable to them.

The commissioners having done their part, work on the dock was started on August 12, and progressed for two days. Then appeared the town sergeant of Norfolk on the scene, commanding all repairs to stop by order of the Borough Court. That body, it seems, had empowered the sergeant to pull down anything erected on the wharf. The sergeant urged the superintendent of work not to proceed with the repairs, as it would be his duty at night to pull down all that was done in the day. When the superintendent reported this threat to the commissioners they told him to continue his work until stopped by force. These gentlemen then went to Norfolk to watch for results. In due time the sergeant appeared with an armed bodyguard, bearing a new order. The guard consisted of Norfolk citizens, Samuel Moseley, Joel Hodges, Nathaniel Burgess *an original purchaser in Portsmouth who apparently departed to Norfolk during the Revoluiton)*, Godfrey Coxe, James Gleason, Henry Guy and George Evans. The matter was carried to the County Court, which summoned the sergeant and his escort to appear before it to show why they interfered with a court order to repair the County Dock. Meanwhile the Borough Court filed an injunction which was never executed, Norfolk having backed out of the scrape.

The work went on without further molestation and was finished in due season. The whole matter of ownership was then looked into, to save further trouble.

A prominent lawyer, Mr. Swepson Whitehead of Portsmouth took the case in hand; commencing with the deed of Nicholas Wise, the original owner of the land, and laid the evidence before two of the best-known lawyers of the state. John Wickham and Daniel Call. These gentlemen were from Richmond, and they decided in favor of *(Norfolk)* County, *Portsmouth benefiting, because it was the county seat..*

It may be interesting here to know what this suit cost; and to satisfy our curiosity there is on record at the Clerk's Office an itemized account of it. Mr. Whitehead's fee was seventy-five dollars. The last two charges are listed as "for advice." The expense of the two gentlemen, which included fare back and forth from Richmond was nineteen dollars. That, too, is itemized. It cost them by stage coach from Richmond to Petersburg two dollars; from that town to Sleepy Hole *in Norfolk County* another six dollars. The last lap of the road cost only one dollar and fifty cents. Breakfast and dinner for both at the Eagle Tavern in Portsmouth cost four dollars, the whole cost of the suit being one hundred and seventy-five dollars and ninety cents.

For forty years Norfolk made no more claims to the ferry dock; but in 1850 she demanded that Norfolk be paid fifty cents for every load of wood landed on the wharf. The county again had recourse to the law and was again victorious. In the *eighteen* seventies Norfolk made another grab at the ferry dock, ordering that a certain part of it be set aside for the city fish market. This time *Norfolk* appealed to the Legislature in order to get her way, but was unsuccessful.

In 1764 it was decided that the ferries were not obliged to carry passengers across the river earlier than sunrise or later than nine in the evening.

It was decided in 1796 that the lessees of the ferry should turn over one-third of the amount they paid for the ferry to the parishes of Portsmouth, Elizabeth River and St. Brides, for the poor of those parishes. The first horse boat, which was the immediate successor of the rowboats and lighters, was built at William Dyson's shipyard in Portsmouth in 1821. We do not know that it had a name. At all events, we have no record of one. Ten years later steamboats were introduced while William Wilson was lessee. The first one was called *Gosport*, and was followed by the *Portsmouth*, *Union* and *Norfolk*.

Acts of 1857-9 incorporating the City of Portsmouth gave her a half interest in the ferries. One-third of the profits from the ferries was to go to the schools of the city and the county, and the rest divided between the two communities.

About this time, or perhaps a little later, the ferries were managed on a different basis, run by the owners, who appointed a superintendent to take care of them. In the course of the years there were many of these officers to be named; but the service rendered by Capt. William H. Murdaugh, who was superintendent several times, and the Porters, and Capt. George Chambers are still gratefully remembered. In more modern times the ferries became still more efficient under the management of Franklin Gill and his partner, Cornelius Thomas, who leased them, the former method of control having gone into effect again.

The Elizabeth River froze over in 1815 and again in 1836, but the "Great Freeze" was in 1857. The rivers froze all the way to the Hampton Roads. Passengers for Portsmouth were unloaded at Craney Island and carried to the city by sled. The snow was so deep cows could walk across their fences on the snow. An effort was made to cut a path through the ice for the ferry, but it failed. The temperature reached nine bellow zero. This was Portsmouth's participation in the "Little Ice Age." Now the parts of Portsmouth nearest the water are in gardening zone eight, the same zone as coastal South Carolina, and inland areas are only just in zone seven - one snow a year is normal and accumulation is unusual. The river now never freezes.

In the 1930s there was one oil-burner in *the* fleet, and it was built in Portsmouth.

The second crossing of the Elizabeth River, the Midtown Tunnel, was opened on September 6 1962. In the 1990s a second tube was added to the Downtown Tunnel and in 2005 the entrance to the Midtown Tunnel was rebuilt to accommodate the Pinners Point Connector described later in this book. A badly needed second tube for this tunnel is in the state's highway budget.

As mentioned elsewhere the ferries are now run by the Hampton Roads Transit Authority, and managed by the two Jordan brothers who have been with the system since it was re-opened

Now there are several ferries with decorative paddle wheels on the back and one which is diesel powered. As well as the regular half-hourly runs from each city there is a special ferry to carry Portsmouth people to the baseball park.

Chapter 11 - "The War of '12"
- Craney Island

In 1813 Portsmouth again heard the call to war; and nothing daunted, she accepted the challenge *to* do gallant work in the defense of the two cities.

Early in January it was known here that a British Squadron with a large number of troops had landed at Bermuda, well supplied with bombs, Congreve rockets and ammunition of other sorts. It was thought that preparations were being made to attack some of our most exposed southern cities. By the fourth of February alarm spread here, for this squadron under Admiral Sir John Borlase Warren took possession of Hampton Roads; and it was plain that the attack was to start on the Virginia cities. *The little community of Seatack in Virginia Beach was the place where the first British troops landed and it may have been named for this "sea attack" by the British there, but there is another possibility - it may have gotten that name because it was at the point of the last tack a sailing ship would make before exiting the Chesapeake Bay.*

This *British* fleet consisted of two ships of the line, four frigates and several smaller vessels of war. Before the attack was made Warren sailed for Bermuda again and returned early in June with considerable reinforcements. With him was the One Hundred and Second regiment of infantry, the Royal Marine Brigade, two companies of Canadian Chasseurs and about eight hundred foreign renegades and prisoners, called Chasseurs Britannique, under the command of Sir Sidney Beckwith and Lieut.-Col. *Charles* Napier. The whole force amounted to five thousand men, commanded by Admiral Warren and Rear Admiral *Sir George* Cockburn. Hampton Roads had been in a state of blockade since the first part of February.

Meanwhile the Americans had bestirred themselves and, though our forces in this neighborhood consisted largely of militia, they accomplished wonderful results. Added to these companies, which had been gathered from all parts of the state, were some regulars and the officers and crew of the *Constellation* and the gun boats. *Your compiler had an ancestor, Abednmego Kiser, from Russell County in the mountains of Southwest Virginia who served in this campaign and died in Norfolk of the fever before the battle started. From his wife's pension application we know the Virginia mountaineers called the War of 1812 the "Norfolk War."*

The Constellation was the fastest ship in the U.S. Navy at the time (pictured on a postage stamp in 2004). It was the secret weapon of the new nation in the Quasi War With France. It had been sailing down the Chesapeake Bay on its way to sea when it spotted the British fleet entering the bay. It, however, had not been seen by the British. It made a run for the Elizabeth River where it was kedged up the river to the shipyard. The British were furious when they realized what a prize they had lost. They first tried to follow up the river, but a chain which ran across the river from Fort Nelson to Fort Norfolk was raised and some floating gun platforms (what Miss Holladay calls gun boats) moved into place, refusing them access. That is why the British decided to seize Craney Island so they could take the town, with its shipyard and the Constellation, overland from the rear as Collier had done in 1779.

The following is Miss Holladay's account of the battle using the information she had at the time. There is an eyewitness account in the library collection called "the Jarvis Papers." After the battle, the only victory for the Americans on land in the War of 1812, there was a hot controversy as to whether the Navy or the Army should get credit for this victory. To get a full picture of the battle, the controversy and its resolution, you should read John M. Hallahan's The Battle of Craney Island: a Matter of Credit.

The *American* regulars and militia were stationed in the immediate vicinity of Norfolk and Portsmouth, mainly at Fort Nelson, *Fort* Norfolk *(which still stands)* and *Fort* Barbour. The *Constellation* rode at anchor between the two cities. The gunboats were moored east of Craney Island, in crescent form, extending from Lamberts Point *in Norfolk* across the channel.

Craney Island, where the battle was fought, lies just north of Portsmouth, near the mouth of the Elizabeth River, commanding the approach from Hampton Roads to that city. This island is very small; at that time about nine hundred yards long and in width about two hundred and thirty-three yards. There was no house on it and but one tree, a lone cedar. It was separated from the mainland by a narrow inlet, which could be forded at low tide, or even half tide. *The island is now much larger as it has been used for dumping spoil dredged from Hampton Roads and its waterways, making it ideal for seabird watching. It is also now the home for the ships of the Fifth Coast Guard District, with its offices in the Federal Building on Crawford Street in Portsmouth. Eventually the Federal Government is supposed to close the landfill there and the island revert to one of the local cities. In the 1960s Hampton tried to claim ownership of the island, but research in the Portsmouth library copy of* Hennings Documents, *a collection of Colonial court cases, convinced the legislature that the island rightfully belonged to Portsmouth, should the Federal Government ever let it go. In 2006 efforts began to have the federal government turn it over to the Ports of Hampton Roads which would deny Portsmouth the island again, giving it to the state of Virginia.*

"This," *Craney Island,* said one who described the battle, "was the most exposed of our military line, the nearest in contact with the enemy—a position of great importance as a key to the harbor, and it was indispensable that the enemy should possess it before they could reach the ultimate object of attack—the cities of Portsmouth and Norfolk. A small breastwork had beer thrown in on the east end of the island, but it had not been finished. There were mounted three cannon, two twenty-four pounders and one eighteen-pounder.

On the twenty-first of June, the whole force on the island consisted of two companies of artillery, Captain *Arthur* Emmerson's and Captain *William Harvie* Richardson's, under command of Major *James* Faulkner of the State Artillery, Captain *Burrell* Roberts' company of riflemen, and four hundred and sixteen infantry commanded by Lieut. Col. *Henry* Beatty and Major *Andrew* Waggoner.

It was remarked upon at the time, that though the force on the island was so small and so exposed to the assault of superior numbers and with scarcely any means of retreat, every one was calm and collected, wishing the attack rather than fearing it.

On this same day the twenty-first of June, it was learned that the enemy had anchored their ships east of the mouth of the Nansemond River, about five miles from Craney Island. Immediate steps were taken to reinforce the troops on the island with such forces as could be spared, for judging by the enemy's movements the attack was imminent.

Gen. *Robert Barraud* Taylor came in great speed to Fort Norfolk and ordered Capt. Pollard of the United States Army, who was stationed there, to send thirty men of his company and that he would add thirty men and two officers. This detachment with Lieut. Johnson of Culpeper and Ensign Archibald Atkinson of Isle of Wight were promptly at Fort Norfolk, and embarked in boats wildly cheered by the garrison, for Craney Island, where they arrived about twilight on the twenty first of June. In the meantime General Taylor had applied to Captain *Joseph* Tarbell of *Constellation*, urging that he add such forces to those on the island as he could spare from the frigate - officers sailors and marines. As a result of this request Captain Tarbell despatched first Lieut. Neale with one hundred officers, midshipmen and sailors, and Lieut. Brackinridge with fifty marines. This contingent arrived at night. The whole force on the island on that eventful day numbered fifty riflemen, four hundred and sixteen militia infantry of the line, thirty regulars of the United States Army, ninety-one State artillery, one hundred sailors and fifty marines.

About twelve o'clock that night a *shot* from one of the sentinels who had made a mistake, thinking that he saw a boat pass between the island and the mainland, gave the alarm. The troops were called to arms and remained so until dawn of the twenty-second, when they were dismissed.

Scarcely had they been disbanded when a horseman dashed across the inlet; *he* reported that the enemy were landing in great numbers near Maj. Hoffler's, about two miles west of the island. *This is now the beautiful wildlife refuge called Hoffler's*

Creek. Quickly every man reached his post; and as it became lighter the enemy's boats could plainly be seen passing from the ships to the shore, landing great numbers of troops.

The three heavy cannons, which had been placed in the unfinished fort on the east end of the island were promptly brought to the west by order of Maj. Faulkner, where the four six-pounders had already been installed. At this time there had been a low breastwork temporarily erected and the cannon were posted immediately in the rear of it.

These seven pieces were all that composed the battery. The infantry and riflemen with Captain Richardson's company of light artillery, with their right resting north, behind the low breastwork were arranged, the six four pounders to the north; next to them the eighteen pounder, and on the left of the battery were placed the two twenty-four pounders.

Every arrangement was made for our defense and all felt that we could put up a pretty fair fight; our troops were full of ardor and we were in fact eager for the fray. There was one thing, however, that we had overlooked; there was no flag staff. A long pole was soon gotten and the colors nailed to it. It was planted in the breastworks and soon the Stars and Stripes floated in the breeze. Maj. Faulkner then assigned the guns, one twenty-four pounder to Capt. Arthur Emmerson and the other to Lieut. Thomas Godwin, assisted by Corp. Rourke of the ship *Manhattan*. The four six pounders were in charge of Lieut. Howie. Corporal *William* Moffat and Sergeants *Samuel* Livingstone and *William P.* Young. The whole battery being thus arranged was under the orders and direction of Major Faulkner of the State Artillery.

In the interim the British had landed about twenty-five hundred infantry and marines. They could be distinctly seen marching and countermarching on the beach, the weather being very calm and clear, and the sunshine directly upon them. After forming a column they took up the line of march; but owing to the dense underbrush near the beach they were soon lost to view. Two hours later they emerged from the woods and appeared on the point of land made by the junction of Wise's Creek with a narrow inlet which separates Craney Island from the shore. From this point a detachment of British were sent to cross Wise's Creek with a view of reaching the island on the south; and the enemy to divert the attention of our forces from that movement, commenced the action by a rapid discharge of Congreve rockets upon the island. *These rockets were a regular part of warfare at the time, but in retrospect they were ineffective, except to intimidate the foe. They are the "rockets' red glare" referred to in the "Star Spangled Banner" by Frances Scott Key, at a later battle in this war. W. A. Brown thinks the cannon set muzzle down in the pavement on the northwest corner of High and Court Streets may be an American piece from 1812. Three cannon from 1795-6 can be seen in front of the Naval Shipyard Museum at High Street dock, and one made in Spain from 1801, plus various naval ordinance on the Elizabeth River side of the Admirals Landing condominium complex.*

Our battery was promptly directed at the column in sight, keeping up, for some time, a galling and destructive fire of canister and grape shot. The enemy soon sought protection behind some woods and a house belonging to Capt. George Wise; but the shot directed at the house through the trees, soon tore off the roof and threw down the chimney. It was soon perceived that these shelters provided no safe retreat against the accuracy and precision of our fire, *the men* fell back in dismay, having many killed and wounded, two officers among them. They then went beyond the range of the guns, awaiting the result of the movement of their barges to the south of the island; the attack now being made from the water. By this time two of our guns had become disabled. Scarcely had the enemy been driven, by our well directed fire, from their assailing position on the land when fifty of their largest barges, filled with men from their ships, supposed to contain about fifteen hundred sailors and marines, began to approach within the range of our artillery. They were advancing toward the island in column order, in two distinct divisions, one following the channel, between the mainland, led on by the Admiral's barge the *Centipede*, a boat upwards of fifty feet long, rowing twenty four oars. *This elegant boat was painted bright green.* There was a brass three-pounder in the bow under command of Capt. *John* Hanchett, of His Majesty's ship *Diadem*. The other division directed its course to some point on the north of the island.

While they were approaching Capt. Emmerson observed to Maj. Faulkner, "Are they near enough for our fire?" "No Sir," replied the Commandant, "let them approach a little nearer." The time had come and the gallant Emmerson called, "Now boys are you ready?"; most of them were boys. The answer came "Ready." The next word was "Fire," that thick and galling was the fire that they turned and beat a hasty retreat.

The barges however, continued to advance in the face of this destructive fire until they could no longer maintain themselves under it, when the *Centipede* and the boats immediately following her were observed to change their direction towards the division of barges aiming at the north end of the island, at which moment the *Centipede* was sunk by a shot from one of the guns, passing through the boat and wounding several, and among them Captain Hanchett, the commanding officer of the division, severely in the thigh.

At this time so quick and galling was our fire that the enemy were thrown into the greatest confusion and the order was soon given for a hasty retreat to the ships. Five of their boats were sunk. One of them, as before remarked, the Admiral's barge, and many others were so shattered that it was with difficulty that they were kept afloat. The firing was kept up with round shot until they got beyond the reach of our guns. No sooner had the enemy made good their retreat in their barges when orders were given to Lieut. Neale to send a detachment of his *in*trepid sailors, to haul up the boats which had sunk and to secure the British sailors and marines who were making for safety to the shore. That duty was promptly and gallantly performed by a detachment of sailors under the command of Midshipman Bladen Dulany, and acting Master George F. de la Roche. The prisoners secured and the *Centipede* drawn up. To Acting Master de la Roche, after she was subsequently made tight, was assigned the honor of taking to the navy yard at Gosport that beautiful specimen of naval architecture: *the Centipede* . In her was found the small brass three-pounder, before mentioned, a number of small arms and a quantity of pistols and cutlasses, placed there for use if the enemy had succeeded in getting a landing. Twenty-four of her men were brought to the island with her and surrendered themselves as prisoners of war.

Among them a Frenchman, with both legs shot off, was brought in a hammock. He died in a few hours.

After the battle about thirty deserters came to the island. In this warm and spirited engagement British soldiers, sailors and marines, led on by brave and inexperienced officers, were opposed to 544 Virginia militia and volunteers, 30 soldiers of the regular army, and 150 sailors and marines; but in active participation, less than two hundred of our troops were engaged *and* the loss on the side of the invaders in killed and wounded and drowned was upwards of 200, exclusive of 30 prisoners and 40 deserters. Indeed if we may credit the statement of Capt. *William* Travis, the commander of the revenue cutter *Surveyor*, who prior to that time had been taken prisoner by the British, *and* conversed freely with the British officers after the action, and who arrived in Norfolk on his parole on the 6th of August 1813, *learned that* the fire from the battery at Craney Island was far more destructive than we had any idea of. A single shot, as he learned from them, cut off the legs and feet of nearly a whole boat's crew. Another shot struck among a crowd of soldiers and killed seven. Nothing, he added, could exceed the confidence of the enemy in taking Norfolk on the 22nd of June except his astonishment and mortification at being beaten: *Norfolk Herald* August 10, 1813.

Admiral Warren in his official report of the repulse of Craney Island, dated on board the ship *San Domingo*, the 24th of June, 1813, sets forth the necessity of his obtaining that island, to enable the light ships and vessels to proceed up the narrow channel towards Norfolk; *and he* acknowledges the failure of the attempt and his repulse by the militia of the state and the seamen assisting them; *he* compliments his men and officers for their bravery, and expresses his regret that Captain Hanchett, who had volunteered with so much bravery and led the foremost division of boats, was so severely wounded. This Captain Hanchett, says Chas J. Ingersoll in his history of the war, was a natural son of King George III, born sometime after his marriage to the Queen.

Some of the prisoners and deserters were sent on to the penitentiary at Richmond until arrangements were made to send them to Annapolis; they gave the following information—That the British were so confident of victory that they brought their dogs and shaving material and extra clothing. The French prisoners stated that Cockburn assured them that they would have no difficulty in getting the island, and when that was won they could march right to Norfolk and have three days pillage and a reward of 25 pounds sterling if they exerted themselves. He also told them of the beauty of the women and promised to place them at their disposal. This could scarcely be credited but for the subsequent events at Hampton. "By sunset of the evening of that memorable day, all the forces under Sir Sidney Beckwith returned discomfited to their shipping. All the British officers, of whose opinions we have heard since the action, have expressed their unqualified astonishment at the precision and accuracy of our guns."

This same British force went on to burn the city of Hampton and then went up the Chesapeake to the District of Columbia. President Madison fled the town and the British took Washington, burning the Capitol Building with the loss of the first Library of Congress, then housed in the Capitol, and the White House, Dolley Madison having saved what she could, including a portrait of George Washington. The Americans also lost the Battle of Lundy's Lane near Niagara Falls, Canada, when they tried to cross the river and take Lower Canada. The only victories for the Americans were naval ones on the Great Lakes and the stand-off immortalized by Francis Scott Key. It is surprising that the treaty which finally ended the war, however, was favorable to the United States.

"It may be said with great propriety, that every officer and soldier on the island upon that occasion is entitled to some credit and some share of the glory which was added to the national arms. Each must be content with the share which fortune allots to him. In this engagement that distinction belongs to the Artillery. The enemy was at no time able to approach within the range of the rifles or musketry. The repulse, both by land and by water, was effected by the guns of the battery. Upon this point there is no contrariety of statement to be found anywhere. The officers of the navy who came upon the island to aid and assist in the defense, took their position as volunteer artillerists, subject to the lineal rank then in command. The constituted no separate corps, but were throughout the whole action as completely under the direction and command of Maj. Faulkner, as the officers of the Portsmouth Artillery were. *There was* some dispute as to who fired the gun which sunk the *Centipede*. But to whichsoever gun it may be awarded, it can detract nothing from the efficiency of the others. All concede that Lieut. Neale fired his gun with extraordinary skill and gallantry, and with most effective execution; the same may with equal justice be said of Emmerson, Godwin, Howie, Young and Moffatt.

The muster roll of the Portsmouth Artillery on the morning of the Attack of Craney Island: Arthur Emmerson, Captain; Parke G. Howie, First Lieutenant; Thomas Godwin, 2nd Lieutenant, Nansemond; Wm. P. Young, 1st Sergeant; William Drury, 2nd Sergeant; James B. Butt, 3rd Sergeant; Samuel Livingston, 4th Sergeant; William Moffat, 1st Corporal; Daniel Cameron, 2nd Corporal; John M. Kidd, 3rd Corporal: Privates—Richard Atkinson, Will Kelly, John Lawton, Aaron McAdow, Abner Nash, Lame Owens. George Pell. John Pully, John Roper, Francis Lousedo, J. H. Simmonds, Nicholas Scott, George Sweeny, Nathaniel Walker, John Newell and Joseph Whiterock. *Add to this list Dr. George Washington Maupin, a medical officer originally from Williamsburg, who took part in the Craney Island battle. He remained in Portsmouth after the war. His first wife died in childbirth and is mentioned elsewhere in this book, his second was a grand-daughter of William Craford's overseer, David Dale. Many of these soldiers and sailors are buried in Cedar Grove Cemetery and Arthur Emmerson is commemorated in a window at Trinity Church.*

At the time of the Civil War the name of this company was changed to Grimes Battery. It is still in existence, commanded by Captain Arthur Emmerson, the great grandson of the Hero of Craney Island. *There is a book about this company and its history in the library collection and there was once a monument to it at the corner of Washington and South streets, but it is now gone.* It has the honor of being the second oldest artillery company in the United States, the "Ancient and Honorable Artillery Company of Boston" being a little older.

Chapter 12 - Portsmouth Veterans of the War of 1812

One of the most important services of this defense, *in 1813*, was assigned to one of our Portsmouth citizens, Captain William Tee. When the attack on Virginia and the South became imminent, Capt. Tee was employed by the Government and made sailing master in the Navy and made chief-pilot of the Fleet, which consisted of the Frigate *Constellation*, some gunboats and smaller vessels and barges. It was said of him, "During the whole of the war he most faithfully and successfully discharged his duty, serving in every important occasion undertaken with martial intention, whether in the pool, *presumably Hampton Roads,* or at sea in the expansive Chesapeake, the James, Potomac and York, or in all the waters of the Virginia Capes." He superintended the blockading of the harbor, sinking the wrecks in the channel to prevent the approach of the enemy's vessels. When the war was over Capt. Tee was again employed by the Government to lift the wreckage and clear the channel for navigation.

When the first light-boat was placed at Craney Island Capt. Tee was put in charge of it, and held the position for over thirty years. He had many thrilling stories to tell of his life there. *Now these are called lightships, and it is the placing of this one at Craney Island, one of the first lightships in the nation, that convinced the Coast Guard to offer the lightship which is now a museum of that service, called the Lightship Portsmouth, at the eastern foot of London Street, although that ship is actually from the early years of the twentieth and not the early nineteenth century. It was added to the official list of National Historical Landmarks in 1989.* Mr. Tee's home in Portsmouth stood on the northwest corner of Washington and London Streets, on the site now occupied by St. John's Church. He died in 1849 in his ninety-first year and is buried here in Cedar Grove Cemetery.

Among his descendants here are children of the late John C. Tee; the Stevens and Gibbs families and Miss Annie Veale, and her sisters.

One of the queer incidents told after the actual fighting on the island was over, was the finding of a leg with the silk stocking still on it. It was not for many years that the mystery of the leg was cleared up.

De la Roche, whom we have mentioned several times in this narrative, met on the Baltimore boat one evening a British officer, Col. Lester, who had served as a subaltern in the One Hundred and Second regiment at Craney Island. Col. Lester told him the story of the "leg." He went on to say that a British officer, keen to see what was going on among the enemy, took his spyglass and climbed a pine tree. As the column passed him, an officer observed to him that he had better look out, for those "Yankees" would knock him down. He answered, "Oh, I'm too high for them." Just at that moment a ball struck the tree, breaking it down. In the fall his leg was so badly injured that it had to be amputated on the spot.

Almost at the same time, said Col. Lester, he was shot and another ball struck four men and killed two of them. By this time the captain called to his men, "Push on! Push on! This is only a random shot." At this an old sergeant remarked, "If this is only random, what will the point blank shot be." Lester added that all were astonished at the wonderful precision of the firing. He acknowledged that they had lost in the battle many more officers and men than were reported; but even then refused to give any definite number.

Jarvis, in his account of the battle, tells us the only American casualty was a Quaker who refused to participate in the battle. He was set to protect the ammunition dump on the island. He decided to smoke his pipe and a spark from it blew him and much of the ammunition away. Fortunately the British had withdrawn by this time.

One of the sad events of this period was the assassination of Lieut. Ball of Winchester, adjutant of the Fourth Virginia Regiment. He was stationed with his company at Fort Nelson, *on Hospital Point in Portsmouth,* in 1813; and in May of that year he started from the fort to carry orders to Norfolk, and was accosted by a sentinel. He answered but the sentinel apparently was not satisfied, called again and started toward him, fired at Ball and wounded him fatally. It proved to be an intentional murder and was done in broad daylight. We learn from one who knew Ball well and was barracked in a neighboring camp that the excitement here exceeded any that he had ever witnessed, that the entire state was wrought up. Ball was a great favorite with all. He was a man of unusual ability and an artist in etching and line engraving, in fact almost a genius along those lines. He was buried in Portsmouth in the burying ground of the Methodist Church on Glasgow Street, and in addition to the men of the many companies encamped in the vicinity who were ordered out, there was an immense gathering of civilians. *The site is now a vest-pocket park on the south side of Glasgow Street between Court and Dinwiddie, in the middle of the block. For a time it was a playground for a private school mistress who lived across the street, then for many years there was a quonset hut on this site used by the Boy Scouts for meetings, but now the lot has a marker identifying it as the site of Glasgow Street Methodist which would become Monumental Methodist Church. This lot was also the first separate home of Emanuel AME before they built on North Street. Ball's stone and two others were returned to the lot in 2006.*

The murderer, who was a soldier in the United States Army, was tried and given eighteen years in the penitentiary. A marble slab was placed over *Ball's* remains by his fellow soldiers, bearing the following inscription: "In memory of William Ball, Jr., of the Winchester Rifle Company, (late adjutant in the 4th Regt. Va. Mil., in the service of the United States) who was inhumanly shot by a sentinel at Fort Nelson, on the 24th day of May, 1813. He was born in Winchester, Frederick County, the fourteenth day of October, 1792. As a son dutiful and affectionate, as a friend faithful and sincere, as a man scrupulously honorable. He was endowed with talents of a superior order, in an evil hour cut off in the morning of a military career. His companions in arms of the 4th Regt. as a lasting testimony of their high respect for his virtues have erected this monument."

In 1815 the papers of the day report the death of Capt. William Miller of Gosport, in Halifax, Nova Scotia. Capt. Miller had been captured by the British and remained in Halifax as a prisoner-of-war.

In 1854 the friends and admirers of Capt. Edward Carter met at his home just outside of Portsmouth, situated on a beautiful stretch of land just opposite Fort Norfolk and bordering on the river. The object of the meeting was the presentation of a cane to Capt. Carter in appreciation of his gallant services at the Battle of Craney Island. The cane was made from a piece of the old frigate *Constellation*. Beautifully carved around the sides was the inscription, "Young America to one of its old defenders." It was capped with a handsome gold top. Capt. Jarvis, *who was the author of the papers mentioned earlier giving an eyewitness account of the battle,* a veteran of Craney Island himself, was chairman of the presentation committee. The address was made by Mr. Claudius Murdaugh, a prominent young lawyer of Portsmouth, and told in eloquent terms of Capt. Carter's gallant services at Craney Island. After the presentation formalities were over a handsome collation was served to the guests.

In 1853 there is a report in the daily paper of a meeting of the veterans of the "War of '12." A list of veterans present will be of interest inasmuch as it gives the names of many who fought for us at that time. Those from Portsmouth were: Chichester Walker, *born in 1795, served in the 6th Regiment*; John N. Ashton, Sr., died at Portsmouth in the yellow fever epidemic of 1855; Ben'j Spratley, *among the first to solicit funds to create a Fire Department in Portsmouth. on Feb. 16, 1830*; Michael King, Merritt Parsons, William R. Guy, John H. Pollard, Thomas Johnson, Sr.; Richard Baugh, Jas. A. Williams, Charles Cassell, James Bowers, James Atkinson; William Masling, William Wood, John Borum, *of the family who's 1860 house survives on Middle Street,* M. S. Moore, John Maclin, Sam'l Lewis, Benj. Deans, William Whidbee, John Watts, Thomas Wrenn, Alexander Cunningham, Lewis Jones, Amos Edwards, Elias Bullock, John Luke and Charles Grice who built the fine old residence on the southwest corner of Court and London Streets and was the father of the late Mr. Charles Grice and the late Mr.

Alexander P. Grice. *For many years this Grice house mentioned by Miss Holladay was Mechanic's Union. The core of the old house was built about this time. It had a new front put on in the 1860s then another added about the time of the First World War. As a result it does not look as old as it is unless you go a few steps down London Street and notice the Federal Period granite lentils and the Flemish bond brickwork. As handmade brick was porous it was laid in double thickness with stringers set crossways to hold the two together. The 1860s brickwork, also visible, was intended to be painted to seal it and remnants of the paint can still be seen on it. The current facade is made of modern machine-made and sealed brick. It is now a private residence again. While the Mechanics Union hall, the basement was a meeting place with a long bar. The mens' room off this barroom had three unusual plumbing fixtures. Being set in concrete they could not be removed, making it the only house in the Olde Towne with three urinals.*

Those present from Norfolk County were, George W. Parker, John Wilkins, J. C. Hyslop, George McClenny, Maurice Tabb, Robert Carson, Sam'l Carney *of one of the most prominent families in what would become the Churchland neighborhood.* Of course there are many other names that could be added to the list of veterans. The names above refer only to those who were present at a particular meeting.

The soldiers encamped at Craney Island were like all others soldiers and many stories are told of their pranks and fun.

There was one neighbor, from whose land extended the bridge from Craney Island; it was through his farm the Island was reached by land. One of the old soldiers has told us how they plagued its owner who was in constant complaint about the soldiers' shortcomings, and, said the old soldier, we did not fail to annoy him all that we could, but perhaps we would not have been so inconsiderate had he not always been so rude to us. On one occasion he found one of our youngsters doing nothing worse, probably, than stealing a peach from his orchard. The youth was captured and taken prisoner. When convenient Mr. S—— brought the captive to camp; but just as he reached the island the soldier escaped him; rushed to a tent and changed his clothes and mingled with the other soldiers. When the officer asked Mr. S—— to point out the offender, he was at a loss to do so. When the angry gentleman started home and passed over the bridge which was thronged with soldiers fishing, a young man very much like the offender stepped behind him and pushed him overboard, and with the help of a brother soldier nearly drowned him.

When Mr. S—— appealed to the commanding officer for redress it was promised him. Every soldier in camp was called, even the fatigue squad. They formed in lines and the injured gentleman looked them carefully over and finally picked out the culprit. He was mistaken. It was one of the fatigue squad who proved that he had not been at camp that day.

The soldiers always called this "S———'s Inspection" and laughed over it for years.

Miss Holladay discretely omits the end of this farmer's name, but it may well be Andrew Stewart whose slave, Jane Bush, was transported to Nova Scotia from "Crane Island near Norfolk" in 1783 with others freed by Governor Dunmore, to fulfil the Governor's promise to resettle black recruits.

When the British finally cleared out from these shores they had a chorus that they were fond of singing, which went this way: "Ross, Cockburn, Beckwith, Warren/ With twenty thousand men,/ Came sailing into the Chesapeake/ And just one half went back again."

England certainly sent some of her most noted officers to command her troops in Virginia. Admiral Borlase Warren stood high among the British and afterwards was invested with the "Garter," an honor only given for rare service. Cockburn, who was at the Battle of Craney Island, was also a noted officer, and the one selected in 1821 to carry the Emperor Napoleon to his cruel exile at St. Helena.

There was another call in the summer of 1814 when the British got to Washington. "I was fortunate enough to get with my own company from Portsmouth, with Colonel Sharpe, and Major Dempsey Watts, afterwards Colonel Watts of the Seventh Regiment; Major Foreman, afterwards General Foreman."

"Colonel Magnien was with his regiment at Fort Nelson; he received general orders, having the whole history of the transactions at Hampton. Whilst the regiment was on parade Colonel Magnien caused the two wings of it to be wheeled in, forming three parts of a hollow square. The colonel called on his clerk to read the general orders. Mr. Beavan, who was the clerk, read them and as soon as he had finished Colonel Magnien addressed the troops. He said, "Sojers you her dat. You see dem dam Anglois, dey bin Hampton, dey steal, dey rob, and de dam rascals dey mudder and ravish you fader, your mudder and your sister, we will have satisfy for dis—outrage. What say you my mans. Mr. Beavan read that general order one more time."

Col Magnien was a Frenchman and as a Grenadier of the French Army was at the Siege of York*town* and in many of the skirmishes and battles in which the French troops engaged. He was a citizen of Portsmouth, and a good one, from the end of the Revolution to the end of his life. *He died at age 65 in 1819 and is buried in Trinity Churchyard with his wife, whom he met here. She is identified as Margaret from Port le None, Ireland, and died at 70 in 1817. I can find no listing for a Port le None in Ireland, or anywhere else. He is said to have been an aide-de-camp to General Lafayette in the Revolution. His obituary in the Emmerson Papers says he "owned several houses in Portsmouth and Gosport and 60 acres around his mansion house and another 100 acres within a mile of Portsmouth (remember at this time Portsmouth ended at Washington Street) and another 50 acres a mile and a half from the town on the 'Old Western Branch Road,' probably High Street. John Foreman says he died without heirs.*

When on parade, if he discovered any of the troops he was familiar with in private life, carrying their musket awkwardly or not keeping step, he would sing out, thus, "You, Mr. William M— just dou hold up your gun. Left foot stand fast; right foot no move, march." He would frequently make his pronunciation of the English language as far out as he could for the purpose of causing merriment. He once told the regiment that when "two guns were fired by der self and one gun together dat was de relarm."

His last parade was in Portsmouth. When the Seventh Regiment had formed for inspection, (some years after peace was proclaimed betwixt Great Britain and the U. S.) the adjutant, in reporting the regiment *was* ready and in saluting the Colonel, with a "present" with the sword. "The brightness of the sword or the plume in the adjutant's cap frightened the colonel's horse. Colonel Magnien was thrown and very much injured. He lived to get partly over the fall, but he resigned, and in a year or less died.".

Colonel Magnien was born in Lunevulle *(Lunville)* France, and came to America with LaFayette. He was a mere youth when he settled in Portsmouth, where he became a prominent citizen. He was one of the founders of the Masonic Lodge here in the latter part of the Eighteenth Century. *The French Masonic Lodge he founded was on the Middle Street side of Bloomsbury Square.*

As has been said, General Robert B. Taylor, of Norfolk was in command of the forces assembled for the defense of the two cities. He must have had a hard billet, judging from the reminiscences of some of those who served under him.

"It was under Gen. Taylor," said one of his old men, "that the organization" was adopted. This had to be done because there was too much intimacy between the officers and the privates of the militia companies. It is a fact that most of members of these companies were blood relations. In most of them the captain would have at least three brothers, one or two uncles and perhaps ten or twelve cousins; then in consequence of intermarriages the balance of the company were half-brother, etc. Here was a pretty mess for discipline. It was not unusual for a private to call out to his captain, "Nat, what in the devil do you keep us marching all day for?" The captain being the brother would pass over such as this without notice. Gen. Taylor soon found out that this sort of soldiering would not do, and determined upon the celebrated "Organization." He saw that for the time, "Auld acquaintance (must) be forgot"; the troops were "fellows and brothers," too nearly allied ever to become disciplined troops.

They were too congenial. "The Organization" he tells us took place on Briggs Point, (end of Holt Street, Norfolk).

The privates of these nearly related companies were divided up among some twenty other companies, and men from these companies swapped for them. Swapping of the officers was not so drastic; but there was a shake-up there, too. All the companies were then counted as new companies further organized into battalions and then consolidated in a regiment.

Also in the letter from the Rev. Mr. Charles H. Holmead, Rector of Trinity Church dated July 17, 1941 to the DAR he lists the following veterans of the War of 1812 buried in Trinity Churchyard known to him at that time (all but one of them can be found by using Surviving Gravestones At Trinity Church, Portsmouth, Virginia*): "Com. James Barron, opposite High St. side of the Parish House, (two of his grandchildren, who died in infancy, are buried in the same iron fenced enclosure); Capt. James Fowler (actually Capt. Samuel Fowler, 'of Salisbury, Massachusetts) who died in 1814. He lived near the Naval Shipyard in Gosport. Near the rear of the chancel (now in the part of the churchyard south of the Court Street gate); Capt. John Paulsin, (I can find no record of this stone, and it is not listed in* Surviving Gravestones, *but during the Union occupation of the town many stones were destroyed by the troops and he may have been using the old Vestry Books); Lt. James R. Mason (his stone says that he comes from Loudoun County, VA, and died 28 Oct. 1814, aged 27 years) on the Court St. side (the stone is now just outside the All Saints Chapel's east wall, toward Court Street); Capt. John W. McRae (this stone is missing in the church records, but may be the badly damaged stone by the path south of the church which says "McR . . . his soul . . ."; several of his family are buried in the churchyard. He lived in the house on the north side of London Street nearest Crawford Street, currently owned by Denton and Michelle Weiss. He owned a small shipyard on the Elizabeth River in the trade described by John Foreman - these small yards built ships which the captains sailed to the Carribean and sold for rum, which they then imported to the U. S. for sale; legend says he died at sea, but his obituary in the Emmerson Papers says he was buried from his home on London Street)- rear of chancel (his wife and children are buried just outside the west wall of the church); Capt. Samuel Trevett (identified* *on the stone, which is excellently preserved New England slate, as Capt. Samuel Russell Trevett, M. D., "late surgeon in the U. S. Navy, born in Marblehead, Mass., Aug. 20, 1783, died Nov. 14, 1822, on this island, soon after his arrival from a cruise in the West Indies") - front of the Barron tombstone (by which he means east of Com. Barron stone, hard against the colonnade).*

Chapter 13: The Great Fire of 1821 - Fire & Police

Like almost all of the small towns Portsmouth was without any means of fighting fires; and it was not until there had been many severe ones, that any effort was made to get a fire engine. *The first volunteer fire companies were first formed by veterans of the War of 1812*

What is known as the "Great Fire" occurred in March 1821. It was of incendiary origin, starting in a vacant house (118, *by the old numbering system*) on the corner of High and Crawford streets. The fire spread with great rapidity, burning every house from High almost to Glasgow Street on Crawford. Then it swept the corresponding blocks on Water Street; burning every house on London, Queen and High streets, east of Crawford. At the foot of High Street the town market house fell a prey to the flames. This was a brick building with an upper story of timber *which resembled the Red Lion Tavern now standing on London between Middle and Crawford.* Six large warehouses on the water front as well as three ships at their wharves were burned beyond repair. The handsome brick residences of Dr. George Maupin and Col. Richard Blow were destroyed on Crawford and a fine house, the home of Capt. Joseph Seward on Water Street. *This would be George Washington Maupin who is buried in Trinity Churchyard just to the east of his first wife's grave, Ann Ballard Maupin. It was the custom to be buried with your first wife. He had children with his second wife, later buried in Cedar Grove Cemetery, but because of this custom he was not buried with her. Apparently the second wife did not like this arrangement as his grave at Trinity is not marked..* Wild confusion reigned in the neighborhood of the fire and the furniture and other articles that were carried to safe distances from the burning area were injured by thieves and looted. Desks were broken open and robbed. The

Norfolk fire company came to our assistance and the officers and men from the Navy Yard rendered heroic service, aiding Capt. Jarvis and his Portsmouth Rifles.

When the alarm sounded every man took his bucket and formed two lines to the water *in the Elizabeth River*. One line passed the empty buckets and the other the full ones. Large supplies of these regulation leather fire buckets were kept at the Navy Yard gate in case of emergency.

An account of another fire has been handed down to us from an old resident, a child at the time of the fire. She says, "Ten years had passed since the fire of '21, when one day great excitement prevailed in the town. The courthouse bell rang violently, followed by the cry of fire. There was consternation when it was learned that the Sugar House was burning. The alarm spread from South Street to North Street; and black and white went to the fire. A bucket brigade was quickly formed; and old men and young boys worked hard to save the building, but it was doomed. Being very combustible, it soon burned to the ground. This fire inspired our citizens to work for a fire engine, which they did with great unanimity and success. *A history of the Portsmouth Fire Department written in 1915, called The Fireman's Red Book survives in the library local history room.*

After this fire the town was divided into fire districts and nothing but brick or stone buildings could be erected east of Middle Street or north of the Creek. *That would include Norfolk and Water Rows running along the bank of the Elizabeth River, from where the Holiday Inn now stands to the entrance to the Downtown Tunnel. This rule was violated by the Seaboard Airline Railroad which built wooden warehouses on its piers, now the site of the Holiday Inn. It would also explain why Benthall-Brook Row, built in 1841, is brick, but not why the house on the north end of the row, which is said to have been the home of the town baker in the 1840s (a stone for rolling out bread was found in the house in use as a hearth stone during renovation) is built in wood. An insurance map of the county and city survives from 1915 showing which parts of the area were covered by fire companies. Even as late as that time most of Norfolk County was served only by volunteer companies.*

Another fire of incendiary origin which made a great impression was started with a view to freeing some prisoners from the jail. *This then stood on the southeast corner of Washington and High Streets where the Professional Building now stands. The Roman Catholic Church was directly across High Street. This was the second Catholic church on this site, the first one also being destroyed by fire. From this we can tell Miss Holladay is talking about a fire in 1897 which she will describe more fully in a few pages.* The firemen, we are told, did wonderful work and succeeded in saving the jail; but in spite of their heroic endeavors, they were unable to save the Catholic Church, which had caught from the sparks from the jail.

The exceedingly fine record of her fire companies has been one of Portsmouth's proudest boasts, and the history of the origin of some of these companies will be of interest.

On the sixteenth of February, 1830, a meeting of the citizens of the town was held at Runald's Tavern, with a view of organizing a fire company and of raising sufficient money to purchase a fire engine. Capt. Arthur Emmerson was appointed chairman of the meeting and Mr. Wm. P. Young, secretary; Col. Mordecai Cooke and Messrs. Benj. Spratley, Charles Grice, and Geo. Reed formed a committee to solicit funds. Capt. Emmerson was appointed treasurer of the organization, while Capt. Samuel Watts, Messrs. Henry Singleton and Charles Grice were to select and buy the engine. Capt. Watts, Messrs. Grice, Spratley, Edward Williams and John Collins were the committee for soliciting membership. These committees were to meet every week to report progress.

In February 1830, there appeared an editorial in *The American Beacon*, a paper whose subtitle was *Norfolk and Portsmouth Advertiser*, published in Norfolk, urging the people of that city to give largely to the fund for the Portsmouth fire engine. It also stated that books had been opened for contributions on both sides of the river and that Portsmouth had already subscribed $800. *In these days of private volunteer companies you would mark your house with a symbol of the company and if your house had the correct marker the fire would be fought - you had paid your fire insurance to that company. Reproductions of some of these old fire company markers can still be seen on several of the Olde Towne houses today.*

The early records of the fire department are scanty; but occasionally we get a glimpse of their work and management from scattered sources.

Up to 1854 the fire companies were independent and voluntary in service; but at this time some change in their management was introduced. At a meeting of the town council a letter from Mr. George Chambers was read in which he declined the office of chief engineer of the fire department. Mr. Chambers stated that he had been with the company for about twenty-five years and in charge of it for fourteen of them. He felt unable to accept the office under the conditions. Just what the conditions alluded to we have not ascertained. The office had no salary attached.

The company referred to was the Resolute Fire Company and for years did marvels in fire fighting.

It had just finished its new building on Court Street. In its lower story was housed the engines and other fire fighting apparatus. Above it were the mayor's office and station house. This building was torn down in 1880's to make room for the present city hall. The stables for the engine horses were in the rear of the building. The fire department still uses the lower floor of the city hall for its equipment. *Of course that is not true today. The building Miss Holladay is describing as the "present city hall" is the Bangle law building, the one with the clock tower, across from Trinity Church. When it was built there was some debate as to who would keep the clock in working order. Finally it was decided that the town jeweler, C. S. Sherwood, would keep it telling the correct time for $25 a year. Now, unfortunately, it has stopped and is correct only twice a day, Mr. Sherwood being long gone. Even in Miss Holladay's time many of the functions of City Hall were carried out in the Courthouse Annex, added in the teens of the twentieth century. That building is also gone; although pictures of it survive. It stood where the parking lot of the 1846 Courthouse Gallery is today.*

When the Seaboard Airline gave up its passenger station south of High Street Landing in the 1950s, that became city

History of Portsmouth, Virginia

hall, called the Municipal Building. The Mayor at the time was Barnabas "Billy" Baker and the City Manager Aubrey Johnson. A plaque on the south side of the building commemorates this event.

The current city hall was built in 1981 and given a new more modern and elegant exterior in the 1990s. It was originally built on speculation along with the adjoining office tower by a private developer and rented to the city. This obviated the need for raising money through a bond to pay for the new construction. In May 2007 a two-million two-hundred thousand dollar decorative traffic circle is to be added in front of it.

Upon Mr. Chambers' retirement *from the Fire Department* he was presented with a silver trumpet, and at this time or a little later the company changed its name to that of Chambers. Mr. Chambers had not only been a loyal member of this company, but a valued citizen of the town, giving his life in its service, staying in Portsmouth during the yellow fever epidemic in 1855, though he had no tie to bind him here but a setup of duty.

Later Mr. George O'Neill Palmer gave an engine to the town. There was great rivalry between these engines and the youngsters used to have heated discussions as to their relative merits.

There is a singular coincidence in the death of Mr. Chambers from yellow fever. His wife died here of a sporadic case of the same disease in 1845. Their only son died of yellow fever in New Orleans a few years later.

The old Chambers engine did much good work both for Portsmouth and Norfolk. Mr. Thomas Rowland, a very competent volunteer fireman himself, tells us that when Vauxhall Gardens *in Norfolk* burned in the fifties that, "Capt. George Chambers came over from Portsmouth with his Resolute Fire Company, and took water from the river at Union Street." This was a wonderful feat in fire fighting with hand engines, so that many can scarcely credit it in this day.

It is a great pity that we have no personal recollections of this famous old company, as it merits a more complete history than we have been able to give. *An article in The Portsm9uth Star in its issue of August 21, 1902 does tell us the name of their* fire engine - it is described as *"a steamer, the Vigilant, run by a hand engine of colored men."* In 1853 this company became the Independent Fire Company with 35 men and lasted through the yellow fever epidemic and the Civil War. Miss Holladay was apparently not aware that this old company had evolved into the Independent.

Of the Independent Company we can speak a little more at length, through the printed recollections of its former chief, Capt. Knott. an intrepid leader. *Its nickel-plated hose cart was said to be one of the best in the Commonwealth.*

Another of the old companies was the Phoenix, and between these companies there was a great deal of good-natured rivalry and badinage. We are told by an old citizen that the Independents had a song with the following refrain:

> "Resolute in the mud,
> Phoenix in the mire
> Looking at the Independent
> Putting out the fire."

These companies were like gentlemen's clubs. One had a master-at-arms who responsibilities included ejecting drunks from their premises. In the rule book of the Chambers Company the driver's duties included feeding and grooming the horses.

Odel Benton who, when he retired as Fire Chief in the 1980s, was the city official with the longest service - having started with the department as a teenager, was famous for his irascible pride in the department. When "Fireman's Bride" was played as he and his wife arrived at a department heads party he turned on his heel and left. Once he came into a City Manager's meeting cursing. The Portsmouth department had been called to aid Chesapeake in putting out a brush fire on the city line. Their firemen had arrived out of uniform he said - without their shirts.

The Independent Fire Company was established in 1853, with thirty-six men under Francis Jordan, who is said to have been a born fireman, absolutely fearless and brave. The company fought thrilling fire battles and have many testimonials to show for their efforts.

In 1873 they fought nobly to subdue the great fire in Norfolk which raged for two days. In appreciation of this work the city presented the company with a handsome silver water set, consisting of a large waiter *(tray)*, pitcher and goblets, on them inscribed, "Presented to the Independent Steam Fire Company, No. 1, of Portsmouth, VA., by the Council of the City of Norfolk, VA., in grateful remembrance of service in subduing the disastrous fires which occurred in Norfolk. 25, 26 of July, 1873."

A suspicious fire broke out October 7, 1869 damaging the old Masonic lodge and Odd Fellows Lodge on Court Street. A gas lamp exploded, but the members swore the lights had not been used for days. The building was insured for $5,000 by Richmond Mutual. This lodge building still survives. The best known Masonic Lodge, however, is the "Scottish Rite" on Cedar Lane in Churchland.

Other highlights in this experience were the incendiary fire of March 29, 1897, and the fire that destroyed the Glasgow Street Pier of the Seaboard Railway about a quarter century ago, *(1905)* along with Peters and Reed's stave wharf to the south of it, clearing the waterfront from North to London streets.

The blaze, which started in Whitehurst's Hall *in* 1897, on Glasgow Street, with a northwest wind blowing, caused one of the most dangerous and erratic fires that Portsmouth has ever seen. In a few minutes sparks had ignited houses on the north side of London Street. The houses on the south side of London, between Green and Washington, were next to go; and sparks drifting against the high slate roof of St. Paul's Catholic Church, at High and Washington streets, found a crevice and set the church ablaze. The church and adjoining dwellings on that side of the street were destroyed and all the dwellings on the opposite side followed in the wake of destruction.

The fire then skipped nearly three blocks and ignited a house on Dinwiddie near South Street. Thence it leaped nearly half a mile, setting fire to a house on Third Street near the Navy Yard. This dwelling was destroyed and marked the farthest progress of the blaze. The streets were full of household belongings; the military companies were called out to prevent looting. Some forty houses, as well as several public buildings, among them the Catholic Church, were burned to the ground. For weeks the citizens of the town divided themselves into groups and patrolled the town at night, for the protection of the people, as it was feared that other fires would follow. No one felt safe until the incendiaries were caught. *Miss Holladay told us earlier that these arsonists were trying to divert attention from a jail break at the city lockup on the southeast corner of Washington and High Streets where the Professional Building now stands.*

The recent fires in Norfolk which the Independents have been called upon to aid were the Atlantic Hotel fire, the St. Vincent Hospital, and in January 1918 the great Monticello *Hotel* fire, when excitement ran high, as the fire was thought at first to have been the work of German spies. Both towns were placed under martial law until investigations could be made as to the origin of the blaze. *Picture postcards survive of this conflagration, showing the fire equipment encased in solid ice.*

Soon after its organization the Independents purchased out of their own funds, for five hundred and seventy five dollars, a small double-cylinder, hand-worked, man-drawn engine with side and gallery streams and jumper, with two hundred and fifty feet of hose. After a while this old engine was made over at the Gosport Iron Works and did 'yeoman's' service for a long time. It was then turned over to fire company in the county. The new engine purchased in Philadelphia was called John Agnew. She was re-christened Franklin; the old name perhaps had very unpleasant associations for Portsmouth. *This is a reference to the Tory Priest, John Agnew, described in the first chapter on the American Revolution.*

The Company has had its vicissitudes, sometimes dwindling to almost nothing in ranks; and at other times needing longer ropes to accommodate its members in parade. *To the present time the fire companies exhibit their equipment in parades, such as the Memorial Day parade, the oldest continuously operated parade of its kind in the nation, started in 1918. Miss Holladay surely attended it often. Among the marshals of the parade in 2004 was Senator John Kerry, during his unsuccessful Presidential campaign along with Portsmouth's own Delegate and Senator Johnny Joannaou. Portsmouth remains one of the few bastions of the Democratic Party in Virginia.*

On one occasion the company sacrificed its own engine house to save the surrounding property.

The company was for a long time a purely independent volunteer body of men, amenable to its own officers only; and as Capt. Knott avers, "We were as lively a set of boys as ever pulled a rope."

Amazing stories are told of the town's four volunteer companies, which were only exceeded by the rivalries between the fire organizations of the two cities. The companies were eternally ready for fight, frolic, or serious work. When in times of fire stress either city called on the other for assistance; then the visiting companies made a supreme effort to throw more water than the home companies.

The Independents were motorized a few years ago *(1920s)*. They own the thousand-pound bell for alarms, hanging in their engine house on South Street *now just a memory* ; and their parade carriage, surmounted by the great nickel fox has won numerous prizes in parades. *A picture of the parade rig for the Chambers Company can be seen in <u>Images of America: Portsmouth, Virginia</u>, by Robert Brooke Albertson. The Chambers Company was badly depleted during the Union occupation in the Civil War and the city began to consolidate the small volunteer companies into what would become the Portsmouth Fire Department. Firemen were occasionally paid and in 1885 the Virginia Fireman's Association was formed in Portsmouth.*

In the early years of the twentieth century Rescue Fire Company #1 was formed. It was the first all black volunteer company. The Portsmouth Fire Department didn't add African Americans to its ranks until 1965.

In 1920 a Portsmouth man, Jordan W. Grant, designed a new form of nozzle for fire hoses. The Grant Multiversal nozzle saw duty around the world during World War II during bombing raids. Alan Flanders says this nozzle: "fixed to fire trucks was able to harness the power of four hoses and could be set at a target without constant manning by a fireman." It is memorialized in a monument which once stood on Effingham Street across from the main fire station, but was moved in the 1990s to the new headquarters building. This monument is pictured in Alf Mapp's *Picture History of Portsmouth*.

Another Portsmouth innovation was a two tank air-supply which could be rotated without a break in air. Previously single tanks were used and when the air in that tank ran out the fireman would have to break off the fight to resupply the tank.

Motorized fire-trucks were added in 1917 and in 1924 the Portsmouth Fire Department began regularly paying its firemen.

The officers of the company in 1923 were Chas. R. Lively, foreman, G. M. Corprew, first asst. foreman, W. L. Bennett, second asst. foreman, Dr. F. S. Hope surgeon, Geo. Peed rec. sec., M. T. Cain treasurer and F. K. Holborn, financial secretary.

In 1906 the Seaboard Building at the foot of High Street had a fire which destroyed its upper floor. At that time it was a three story building. When rebuilt two stories were added.

In February 1958 a massive fire destroyed the Seaboard Airline Railroad wharves on the Elizabeth River effectively clearing the city's river front for development.

One of the most spectacular fires on High Street took place after an explosion in March 1965, when the Merchants and Farmers Bank and M. M. Crockin Furniture store were destroyed and the Leggett's Department Store damaged by smoke and water. Bank records were spread out across the street. A suppliment to the old *Fireman's Red book* is long overdue.

The early history of the police department is told in *The Policeman's Blue Book* in the library and so I will just add some highlights here.

Portsmouth for the first hundred years of its existence did without regular police, the town sergeant and the magistrates looking to order by day, with the volunteer soldier companies keeping guard at night. In that very progressive age in the history of our town, the *eighteen* fifties, the soldiers tired of the watchman role and refused to serve longer as guards. The Council forthwith divided the town into two districts, appointing two policemen for night duty. When necessary they could be called on to serve in the daytime.

The first Town Constable was I. Driver in 1845. Three years later the responsibility for collecting taxes was added to the job. All the watchmen carried a copy of the ordinance authorizing their service to show to anyone who might question their authority.

By the yellow fever epidemic there were two policemen and eight watchmen. Watchmen came on duty a half-hour after sunset and patrolled until sunrise. The watch also lit the gas lamps. None of these officers carried weapons; in stead they had a sort of rattle they would twirl over their heads with a tongue which would click on the teeth of a ratchet-wheel to alert the citizens that something was afoot. In June 1858 they were given pistols.

In 1859 Southall Cummings was the first to be elected permanent police watchman.

The jail was in the 1846 Courthouse. This was replaced by a stand-alone facility on the corner of Water and County streets in 1926. It was said to be one of the best in the state with not just cells, but a courtroom and offices for the Police Court, the Civil Court and the Circuit. Even this elegant location, quite near the present jail and courts, became outdated and in 1951 the department and jail was moved to the northeast corner of North and Green street where the Comfort Inn now stands across from the main fire station. After a spate of escapes from this jail it became apparent it was not secure and the jail and police station was again move to its present location in the Civic Center on July 8 1970.

During Reconstruction after the Civil War there were African Americans on the police force, but on November 11 1871 one of these officers, John Wilson, was standing guard at the corner of Middle and High street while a political speech was being delivered by Judge Watts from the balcony of the Ocean House. Suddenly a shot rang out and Wilson fell mortally wounded with a shot to his forehead. Several prominent citizens were suspects in this case. To avoid a repeat of this African Americans were forbidden to serve as policemen. This continued until 1952 when Willie Cooper joined the force. The first African American to make sartgent was Charles Neal in 1966.

The actual date of the founding of the Portsmouth Police Department in July 7 1873 when C. W. Hill, the judge of the Court of Hustings, appointed a board of Commissioners to create and oversee a force. The members were John Nash, John S. Thomas, William G. Maupin, James E. Stokes and the Mayor James S. Watts. They authorized uniforms for the new department.

In 1903 there was an effort to rid the town of public gambling. They would raid the places where "craps" and "skin" were being played - particularly at the corners of Green and Queen streets and at the corner of Clifford and Chestnut streets. This met with only moderate success.

In 1914 the first auto patrols were added with Gamewell Police Telegraph, a sort of steel call box with a wheel and sometimes a red light originally invented in 1888. In this same year the first motorcycle officer, Johnny Dowson, began his rounds.

In 1923 a darkroom for police photography was added and in 1926 stop lights were placed at some street intersections in the city. Radios were placed in the police cars in 1939 and added to the motorcycles in 1942.

There is a history of the Portsmouth Police, and some crimes they solved, published in 1915, called _The Police Blue Book_ in the library and a history of the force drawn from Council minute-books by Suan H. Baker (now Susan H Burton) the current Director of Libraries. Most of what I have to say about the police comes from these sources.

Although the Regional Jail is in Portsmouth, managed by retired city finance officer Roy Cherry, the city still maintains a lock up run by the sheriff.

Chapter 14 - Lafayette's Visit

This account of LaFayette's visit to Portsmouth was written by miss Louisa Emmerson. A much more detailed account of his visits to this city, and also Norfolk, Yorktown, Hampton and Richmond exist in the Emmerson file.

"In 1824 when it was announced that LaFayette was coming to Norfolk and Portsmouth for a visit, there was a great stir among the military companies of the two towns and it was not long before they received orders for drilling and practice parades, preparatory to going to Yorktown to celebrate the arrival of LaFayette there.

When the Yorktown honors are over the people of Portsmouth must make their own preparations for entertaining their gallant guest. This they did with zeal and success. In both towns cannons were placed at intervals along the line of waterfront; at the intersection of High and Crawford streets a fine triumphal arch was built; forty or more bonfires were ready on the waterfront to blaze up when darkness came. Meanwhile flags and evergreen decorated the town. Several companies of soldiers from the two cities were stationed on the wharf in Norfolk to await the Marquis' arrival. Those from Portsmouth were the Rifles under Capt. Young and the Grays under Capt. Langhorne. When the *Pocahontas (Petersburg)* appeared in sight the cannon along the river shore saluted the Nation's Guest and notified the people of his approach. LaFayette was escorted to his quarters in Norfolk and all night the bonfires blazed along the water and the two towns were brilliantly illuminated.

In the morning *of October 25 1824* LaFayette was escorted to Portsmouth and received by the trustees of the town. Captain Emmerson made the address of welcome and he *(LaFayette)* was then conducted to the arch. LaFayette remarked to his escort that he well remembered a former visit to

Portsmouth, when he tried to capture Arnold, who was quartered here, but the traitor escaped him. The General went on to speak of the changes in the town since that time and remarked, "How different everything is."

We have an account of the arch from one who saw it as a little child. 'The arch through which our General passed was not only decorated with flowers, evergreens and flags, but some of the schoolchildren were placed about it like statuettes. The most beautiful of the girls who figured on this occasion was Nancy Collins, *later Mrs. John Nash.* She was chosen to recite some verses of welcome to the "Nation's Guest." *She said, "General, your love of liberty, your disinterested labor for the independence of these United States, endears you to our fathers and mothers, whose recapitulation of your valor and your friendship for our beloved Washington have awakened in our young hearts feelings of gratitude which we cannot express. Be so kind, sir, as to receive from our hands this wreath . . ." Mr. James Murdaugh, thinking the ordeal might be too much for the young lady, procured a glass of water from the office of Dr. Butt, but her nerves were steadied by a kiss from the gallant Marquis."* Winchester Watts recited some verses of welcome from the boys *now forgotten*. The procession left the arch passed through some of our principal streets and crossed "Lafayette Bridge' on its way to the Navy Yard.

The arch covered the whole intersection of Crawford and High streets, and was large enough so that the children actually stood up in the arch itself. A letter published in the <u>Portsmouth Star</u> *in 1880 adds: "The landing was made at the old ferry, foot of North Street; and entering carriages, the Marquis and attendants were driven slowly along Crawford Street, ladies occupying the sidewalk to the right and gentlemen to the left hand side, as they proceeded toward the Navy Yard. On Crawford Street, between what is now Baine's Bank and the American House an arch had been erected, tastefully decorated with fruit and flowers, many made in wax; and here were thirteen young misses to represent the original states, also the pupils of the Lancaster School of Portsmouth. The Marquis alighted and the following verses were recited in full chorus:*

It is a maxim of our school,
And certainly a golden rule,
That nothing is without grace
If only in its proper place.
And where is ours on this free day,
When all come out in fair array
To welcome one? Where should we be
Out here to show ourselves to thee,
The nation's guest, the nation's joy,
And dear to every girl and boy,
Whose name we never shall forget
The great and gentle LaFayette?"

On the return to Portsmouth, LaFayette and his party went to Webb's hotel and were entertained at a banquet. At night there was a great ball given for him in Norfolk. The writer has one of the invitations to this ball, and as far as she can learn it is the only one in existence. *The letter writer mentioned earlier had a kid glove with a portrait of LaFayette with the inscription "Welcome LaFayette," which were given out to the young ladies designated to greet him.*

Webb's Hotel is still standing but in the last few months it has been greatly changed, the lower front having been removed and store fronts substituted. It stands on the southwest corner of Court and South streets. *This old hotel is now long gone, but a house in which the General was entertained on this visit survives on Middle Street between London and Glasgow. It is marked with a state historical marker. At the time of LaFayette's visit it was on Crawford Street, but moved later to Middle.*

In 1976 the little park between Crawford and Water Street near the Renaissance Hotel was laid out and the brick arch there dedicated by Pierre Schimitz, the then French Consul to the Hampton Roads cities, to commemorate the general's participation in the American Revolution. The stone lions set into the arch were carved by an itinerant artist in the 1920s and originally decorated the American National Bank building on the northeast corner of Middle and High streets.

Some of the bricks in the paving have dates on them and profiles of George Washington. Alf Mapp was chair of the committee which oversaw the placement of this memorial to the distress of Portsmouth Redevelopment and Housing which had other more commercial plans for that piece of land. On the Water Street side of this little park is a memorial to those men from Portsmouth who were honored with the Congressional Medal of Honor and another commemorating Portsmouth sailors lost in the first and second World Wars. A more complete listing can be found on the plaque at the High Street Landing flagpole. At various times in the year the Grand Union Flag is flown to commemorate Portsmouth's service in the American Revolution and at others the fifteen star flag is flown to commemorate Portsmouth's part in the War of 1812.

The Portsmouth servicemen cited for winning the Congressional Medal of Honor are Lt. Richard T. Shea, Jr, for his service in the Korean War, killed in action; Charles Veal, a sargent (actually corporal) in the 4th U.S. Colored troops in the Civil War; Major Raymond H. Wilkins of the 5th Army Air Force in World War II, killed in action; Seaman David D. Barrow of the U.S.S. Nashville in the Spanish American War off Cienfuegos, Cuba; William M. Carr of the U.S.S. Richmond in the Civil War; Jesse W. Covington of the U.S.S. Stewart in World War I; Quartermaster Thomas H. Jordan of the U.S.S. Galena in the Battle of Mobile Bay in the Civil War; Joseph Mitchell of the U.S.S. Newark in the Boxer Rebellion; General Wendell C. Neville, of whom we will hear much later in this book; Landsman James F. O'Conner of the U.S.S. Jean Sands for jumping overboard near the Navy Yard to save a young girl from drowning in 1880; Master-At-Arms August Ohmsen of the U.S.S. Tallapoosa for bravery during the sinking of the ship and Samuel Woods of the U.S.S. Mount Washington in the Civil War. On the Navy memorial to sailors lost in the two World Wars, placed by the Seaboard Airline Railroad are: in World War I W. O. StClair, C. Jackson, M. Oliver, G. H. Langton and in World War II J. P. Gray, A. E. Lassiter, J. S. Whitehurst, Jr, J. Burch and M. Power of the "Colored" troops.

Two other Portsmouth sailors are particularly worth

mention. Rear Admiral Edward C. Allen, Jr., served on the _Alexander Hamilton_ when it was sunk by a u-boat off the coast of Iceland in World War II, he then served on the _Leonard Wood_ in the invasion of North Africa, Sicily and nine of the Japanese held islands. He then commanded three ships for the Coast Guard and left the service with the bronze star, nine battle stars and the Navy Citation. Rear Admiral Herman Joseph Kossler was commanding officer on the submarine _Cavilla_ in World War II and then was commandant of the South Carolina Naval District where, after retirement he became director of the Naval and Maritime Museum at Patriot Point.

For many years a marker on the northwestern corner of Crawford and High streets marked the spot where the wooden arch described earlier stood. During the reconstruction of the bank in 2004 that commemorative marker was moved to the second garden planting west from the Crawford Street intersection on the High Street front of Towne Bank.

Another marker commemoration LaFayette's visit is attached to a rough stone in City Park which is illustrated in Alf and Ramona Mapp's _Picture History of Portsmouth_.

Chapter 15 : Sail, Steam and Stage Make the Town

Before the days of railroads the good people of Portsmouth had not grown dull-witted by staying at home. At the end of the eighteenth century there were regular lines of sailing ships for passengers from this port to New York and Philadelphia, as well as to Charleston and other Southern cities. These ships had regular days for sailing and advertised to carry the mails. Indeed the *nineteenth* century had not gone much beyond its first decade when a steamboat line was established here.

One July day in 1815, great excitement prevailed in the town. War in Europe was forgotten; the fate of Napoleon was no longer of any moment. A topic of greater interest occupied the thoughts of the people, who had thronged the shores to watch for the arrival of the steamboat. Eagerly their eyes scanned the harbor for the wondrous sight, for few if any on the crowded waterfront had ever seen a steamer. On this third of July the first steamboat of any kind to enter this port reached here, having started from Richmond the day before. Amid the roaring of cannon and the blowing of whistles the *Eagle* glided gracefully to her wharf, with flags flying, *and* made her landing cheered by the admiring multitude. She deserved their appreciation, having covered the distance in nineteen hours. *For a full account of this business check out John Clloyd Emmerson's three volume* <u>The Steamboat Comes To the Chesapeake</u>, *in the library collection. Miss Holladay gives us a date in July for the first steamboat landing, but another source sets the date as May 24 1815.*

The *Eagle* had been purchased by a company composed of Norfolk and Portsmouth men, in New York. She was commanded by Capt. Rodgers, but did not stay long on this run, being taken over by a company from Alexandria to ply between that city and some nearby point. In fact the *Eagle* had but a short span of years and met with the fate of most of her kind—her boiler burst. In the newspapers of that day the bursting boiler was as commonly reported as are the airship accidents now. *Miss Holladay was writing just after the crash of the Zeplin Hindenburg.*

In 1816 the *Powhatan* came to serve on the Richmond route. Her trial trip was made, and the proprietors announced that they could with some degree of certainty tell the periods of her arrivals and departures from the places en-route. She left this port on Mondays and Wednesdays at 3 p. m., and it took her about twenty-two hours to make the trip. The fare between the two points was $10, which included everything but liquor, that very necessary commodity being extra.

We find that the *Powhatan*, like all the Richmond boats that followed in her wake, paid no respect to her schedule; and her tardiness caused much anxiety in the community. The managers of the line were so often appealed to by those grown weary of waiting for her arrival that they issued a statement in the newspapers, stating that the late hour at which the *Powhatan* arrived so frequently was not due to any mismanagement, and there was no occasion for fear. Her slowness was entirely due to the difficulty of procuring fuel. The wood was bought by contract and was often of so poor a quality that the requisite amount of heat could not be maintained.

We find no complaints from these travelers of early days. Perhaps they were not recorded,
or probably they did not expect all the luxuries of a palatial home on the high seas.

On March 18, 1817, when the *Powhatan* was within eight miles of Richmond, the engineer had to leave her and go ashore in search of fuel. During his absence there was no one on board capable of managing the machinery; her steam was greatly increased and the boiler burst. In addition to the loss of the vessel, a number of people were killed. The successor to the *Powhatan* was built in Norfolk at the shipyard of Wm. F. Hunter, at the foot of Newcastle Street. This boat was christened *Richmond*, and we are told that she served the line for a number of years.

Before the opening of the nineteenth century, there were several stage lines from Portsmouth to various points. The route to Petersburg then followed the present new or short way, branching off from the Suffolk Road at Drivers, past Bing on to Sleepy Hole, where it made a stop, and then crossing a bridge, or perhaps ferrying, to Holladay's Point. *When the park called Sleepy Hole was laid out in the 1960s by the Portsmouth City Planner, J. Brewer Moore, he gave it that name. It is interesting to see there was a place by that name in Norfolk County as early as the 18th century. It was not where the Sleepy Hole Golf Course is now, however, because the Old Suffolk Road through Driver would not have gone along what is now route 17, but by way of what is now route 264. The Sleepy Hole Mr. Moore gave the name to was the plantation of Amadeo Obici, an Italian, and a benefactor of the hospital in Suffolk that bears his wife's name. His elegant home is preserved in the park around the golf course and is used for a golf shop, wedding parties and workshops. Mr. Obici was a very short man and the stair railings in the house are unusually low as a result. Although situated in Suffolk, the whole complex was owned by Portsmouth until fairly recently when it was traded back to Suffolk for other considerations.*

There was another *stagecoach* line that went to Suffolk, and at a little later date one to Elizabeth City. The coaching office was at the old Bell Tavern (Mansion House) *on Market Square on the southeastern corner of High and Court Streets.* Here arrangements for the trips were made and from this point the stagecoaches left.

Would that we had had a Dickens in the community so that these trips might have been chronicled for the pleasure of future generations.

Chapter 16: "Where Rail Meets Sail"

The title of this chapter is the city's official motto to this day.

Railroads had scarcely proven successful when Portsmouth was on the alert to build one. It was not long before a number of citizens banded together for that purpose, subscribing what seemed a sufficient sum of money to carry it through; and thus Portsmouth was the pioneer in this section in railroad building. On March 8 1832 the Portsmouth and Roanoke Railroad Company was incorporated by act of the General Assembly. The contracts were given out and building operations commenced at once. The newspapers carried an advertisement for two hundred laborers for work on the road. It was plainly stated that the wages would be ten dollars a month; and moreover, they must have a spade, or be responsible for the one lent them by the company.

Work continued but the undertaking soon proved difficult for the capitalists of so small a town; and consequently the Company appealed to the Legislature for financial aid from the State. There was a stormy time ahead for the incorporators, as the bill met with violent opposition in the Assembly. The wrangling in that body continued until the end of the year when things took a brighter turn for the *rail*road.

On the nineteenth of January the Portsmouth and Roanoke Railroad Bill passed the Senate. The good news reached Portsmouth on Sunday, by special messenger; but that made no difference in the rejoicing. Cannons had been placed at intervals along the road to Suffolk so that the news might reach there quickly. Rockets were shot across the river and for two hours pandemonium reigned in the land.

Financial troubles were not the only ones encountered in this great venture. The engineers found, when their work was finally accomplished, that it was considered quite a feat in engineering. Moreover all the rails had to be made in Great Britain.

In spite of trials and disappointments, the track had reached Suffolk by July 1834; and on the twenty-ninth of that month the train was to make its first trip from Portsmouth to Suffolk. Schedules had been duly advertised. There were to be two trips a day to each place, at a cost of $1.50 for the round trip.

The depot, or passenger station, was at that time at the junction of High and Chestnut Streets, placed there, so the "old inhabitants" used to say, because in that remote spot horses would not be frightened by the locomotive, and children would not be in danger. The Chestnut Street station was known as the "upper depot" when the tracks were afterwards extended to the ferry at the foot of High Street.

It is easy to turn our thoughts back a hundred years and imagine the interested community awaiting the great day. Few, if any, of the people had ever seen a locomotive for as we have said Portsmouth was a pioneer in this section. How eagerly everyone was to see the great iron monster that was to perform such miracles. Each day the question was asked, "Has the engine come?" Every day the answer brought disappointment to the interested throng.

There were scoffers, too, who put no faith in the newfangled things, and timid souls who would never risk their lives on a train. Horses could carry them fast enough and were far safer. Many, however, had the money for the fare ready, eager to be among the first to experience the thrill of being carried by the iron horse. All, however, were sorely disappointed as July drew rapidly to its end and no engine came. Like the rails, *the engins* were made in England and there had been some delay about their delivery. The looked-for twenty-ninth arrived and still the locomotive had not come. The Railroad Company was on its mettle; proving itself equal to the emergency, and *it* sent out the train to Suffolk, drawn by horses in lieu of the engine. And thus the trip was made twice a day from each town according to schedule, until the eleventh of October when the engines arrived.

One of these locomotives was a Watt engine named "John Barnett"; of the other, we have no record of its name or maker.

There is a picture of this locomotive in Miss Holladay's original. At that time, and in fact for many years, engines bore names just as the vessels do now. We call to mind the old "Joe Sam," named for one of the most popular men ever in Portsmouth, an official of the road, and the mighty "Ajax" as they puffed up and down London Street, into the *eighteen* eighties.

On October the eleventh, 1834, the train made its first trip to Suffolk in due form, drawn by its mighty engine, and filled with invited guests. It left town, with flags flying and the Grays band dispensing joyful music. *The Portsmouth Grays was one of the local militia companies.*

Early in 1835 the tracks had been extended to the foot of High Street, where it adjoined the ferry landing, which had been changed from North Street. *The ferry dock from Colonial times to this time had been at North Harbor, the second stop in Portsmouth for the current ferry. That point of land, where the Harbor Tower now stands, was called "Ferry Point." On the Norfolk side ferries landed at what was then called Commercial Place, approximately where the Confederate Monument stands on Main Street in Norfolk.* These changes had been made for the convenience of Norfolk, that city having invested a sum of money in the road on that condition.

Norfolk was not satisfied, however, to stick to her bargain *and began* trying to force the company to make its terminus there. In 1835 she petitioned the Legislature to this effect. There was a stiff fight put up in the Assembly over this measure. The representatives in both houses were Portsmouth men, Col. James Langhorne and Capt. Samuel Watts. Both gentlemen made eloquent speeches against the bill, and Col. Langhorne, it is said, caused much mirth in the Senate by his witty account of the squabbles between Norfolk and Portsmouth. The claim that the company had promised to make Norfolk its terminus proved groundless, the records showing that it had agreed to bring the tracks to the foot of High Street and to move the ferry to the same location. The measure was defeated.

The charter of the road made Portsmouth its terminus, and that instrument could not be changed without the consent of every incorporator.

Our Sister City, having failed in her attempts to make trouble at this end of the line, immediately turned to the other end, causing some disturbance at Margaretsville, which had recently been reached by the backs of the road *that is its far western end). Margaretville is no longer on the Virginia map.*

In 1836 the railroad again had trouble; but this time it was not of Norfolk's making. On the eleventh of August its first accident occurred. Upon the return of an excursion train to Suffolk there was a collision with a heavily loaded freight train from McClenny's Station. The excursion train carried about two hundred passengers. Forty of them were injured and four killed. The dead were all women, Misses McClenny, Roberts and Eley of Suffolk and a maid. The accident occurred just outside of Suffolk; and physicians from both towns hastened to the place, and Dr. Williamson, in command of the Naval Hospital *in Portsmouth* sent a relief squad to their aid. Mr. Richard Godwin, who owned a large house near the scene of the accident, turned it over to the doctors for a temporary hospital.

The accidents were not over, even for the day; the engine that carried up the relief squad, returned that night in a blinding storm, and two men walking on the track, unaware of its approach, were run over and killed.

This terrible accident made a stir in the community. The Town Council of Portsmouth *which was still a town, not a city,* ordered an investigation, appointing Samuel Watts, Richard Blow and Robert Taylor a committee of inquiry. Their report exonerated the conductor of the excursion train, placing the entire blame on the freight conductor, who left town before the investigation.

The next interesting event in the history of the road proved to be a very trying one. The Petersburg and Weldon *Rail*road, with which it had some conflicting interest at Weldon, made several attempts to put *the Portsmouth and Roanoke* out of commission. By devious methods it succeeded in beguiling the owner of certain lands in Southampton County, through which the Portsmouth road had right of way, to allow a squad of laborers to wreck the tracks on his land. The matter was taken to court and the Petersburg road ordered to relay the tracks without delay. The officials of the road were severely reprimanded, and came near going to the penitentiary.

Except for financial difficulties from time to time the road continued its services without anything *unfortunate* occurring, but in the early *eighteen* fifties the stockholders were in need of greater capital to extend and improve the road.

Dr. William Collins of Portsmouth was then its president. At this time it was taken over by Philadelphia capitalists. The road was then almost entirely rebuilt *and* new tracks laid; and these rails, too, were made in Newport, England. Two new engines were bought, the "Romulus" and the "Remus." Mr. Tee tells us that the boys of the town were divided in opinion as to their merits. Some bet strongly on the Remus, while others were champions of the Romulus. It is said that these old locomotives can still be seen at the Seaboard shops. *Not only can these locomotive not be seen any more, but neither can the Seaboard shops that held them. There is, however, a display of antique railroad cars on the old Seaboard line near the nTelos pavilion that locals one day hope will be the seed of a railroad museum in Portsmouth. If you follow that line a little further toward Effingham Street you can see a beautiful little example of a brick railway station, long closed. This might be a good home for the museum. Since Portsmouth was the first city along this part of the coast to get a railroad it would seem a reasonable project. The model railway collection in the Children's Museum of Virginia on Middle Street is one of the best in the country.*

There is extant a printed schedule of the Seaboard and Roanoke Railroad, made out by the late O. D. Ball in 1859. The following regulation concerning the speed of the trains is found as a note to the timetable. The speed of trains shall in no way exceed the following rates: of the Express twenty five miles an hour; accommodation and freight twelve miles an hour; in passing over bridges, over trestles and through towns six miles an hour."

It was in the *eighteen* fifties that a spark from the engine set fire to the house of Mr. Schultz on Crawford Street, and stirred up trouble. It was declared dangerous to property to have the engine come into the town and the road was ordered to switch off the passenger coaches and bring them down town by horsepower.

After its reorganization in the *eighteen* fifties the road forged ahead rapidly. Warehouses were built along the waterfront on Water Street, which had been gradually acquired, and an outlet was needed from the upper depot to the new wharves reaching from London to Glasgow streets. Right of way was granted and a track was laid on London Street as far as Middle *which* there branched diagonally through the block to Crawford Street and the river. In order to reach the waterfront the historic old house, now number 213 Middle Street *(by the old numbering system)* had to be moved from its site on Crawford. *O. D. Ball, mentioned earlier, was the owner of the house now called the Nivison-Ball house. To get it out of the way of the railroad he moved it from Crawford Street to its present location on the east side of Middle Street between London and Glasgow Streets.*

There is a house on London Street just beyond Middle that still bears record of the changes made to accommodate the road. About 1870 a room in this house abutted on the line of the road. The room was cut also diagonally across and keeps its half-square shape today. *This house no longer exists, but the angle of the track can be seen in a fence line on the west side of Crawford Street between London and Glasgow.* The Crawford Street tracks, *which ran right down the middle of the street,* were not laid until 1890, nor were they laid without violent protests on the part of many of the property-owners on that street. Threats were made and excitement ran high in the town. A temporary injunction was issued by the court, which expired on a certain Friday night; and a permanent one was to be asked for when court convened on the next Monday. Now was the Road's chance—if a train could use the track, it was said that it would be too late to get the injunction. Saturday morning by daylight Crawford Street was alive with workmen, who busily plied spade and pickax. Work progressed rapidly and at two o'clock Sunday morning the track had been laid from one end of Crawford Street to the other, and the train filled with a noisy and jubilant throng passed over it.

The matter was not, however, satisfactorily adjusted for some months. The property owners who had protested against the tracks were brought to terms, and received damages. There were two of the landowners, and the two who had protested most violently, who were not entitled to damages, because the road made a curve near their property just a few feet beyond the legal limit.

The new tracks did away with the need of those on London Street. This proved an opportune thing for the Portsmouth Street Railway, who purchased them for the new road they were building to Port Norfolk. *The line in Port Norfolk was called the Port Norfolk Electric Railway Company.* One railway train a day passed over these tracks in order that the railroad could keep her right of way. *When Middle Street between Queen and London had its paving ground off after 2004 to make way for new paving in front of the Virginia Sports Hall of Fame parking ramp, the old trolley lines could be clearly seen in the brick, making a curve off Middle onto London that almost cut the southwest corner. The joke about the new pavement running from London to High Streets on Middle is that it appears to be brick, but isn't. A machine was brought in to make striations in the pavement to look like bricks and then one morning, to the amusement of the neighbors, a crew of men went out with push brooms and painted it brick color. One wag said it reminded him of the gardeners in <u>Alice In Wonderland</u> repainting the colors of the roses to satisfy the Red Queen. The street now has imitation brick laid over real brick.*

At first the Portsmouth Street Railway operated horse drawn streetcars, but in 1901 the lines were electrified.

The Portsmouth and *Roanoke* Railroad of 1832 was one of the oldest in the South, and in the course of time has developed into the great system known as the Seaboard Air Line serving a large area in the southern and eastern section of our Country. *The offices for this line were originally in the round-fronted building at High Street Ferry Landing, but on August 22 1958 they were moved to Richmond.*

The road at first was entirely a Portsmouth venture and it is natural that it should have availed itself of Portsmouth talent in selecting its officers. Its first president was Capt. Arthur Emmerson, who with his Artillery had defended us at Craney Island. Capt. Emmerson was the son of the Rev. Arthur Emmerson, the third rector of Trinity Church. Captain Emmerson himself was a warden in this church for many years; he inherited the house built by his father on High Street opposite the courthouse in 1784. *Three generations of Emmersons appear on a dedicatory window in Trinity Church. The old Emmerson house stood where the Commodore Theater now stands.*

While on the subject of railroads, it may be interesting to note that the first American to run a locomotive was a Portsmouth man, Edward E. G. Young, who made the trip between Frenchtown and Newcastle, Delaware, on November 26, 1832. *There are several claims to this honor, but Miss Holladay is correct that this was among the earliest.* The company which employed Mr. Young presented him with a handsome gold watch and chain as a testimonial of their appreciation of his skill in handling the engine.

In the early years of the twentieth century Pollard's <u>Sketchbook of Portsmouth</u> *tells us Portsmouth was the largest port for the export of cotton on the Atlantic Coast. This may be true because the city was the terminus of three rail lines. The Seaboard, which ran down the coast all the way to Atlanta and west to Roanoke carried 175,000 bales in an off-year. The Atlantic and Danville ran 281 miles inland to Danville and cotton was its most important freight. The Norfolk and Carolina, which came into Pinners Point from Rocky Mount, North Carolina, where it had a connection to Florida with another line, carried an additional 107,000 bales in that same poor growing year. Both the A&D and the Seaboard had wharves dedicated to cotton in the city. A private cotton warehouse, Heath and Smith, stood at the corner of Water and London streets, but the cotton exchange itself was in Norfolk. Cotton was also spun here at the Tidewater Knitting Mills and the Parker Hosiery Company. Not only cotton was important, but the oil made from its seed was a major industry. The Portsmouth Cotton Oil Refinery Corporation was one of the city's major industries in 1915. Portsmouth was certainly an important adjunct to King Cotton the industry that remade the ruined South after the Civil War.*

An insight into the cotton trade is provided by an October 1880 account of a ship fire at the wharfs. The ship was called the <u>Isaac Bell</u> of the Old Dominion Steamship Company. It was loading 750 bales of cotton destined for New York City. The steam fire engine <u>Virginia</u> of the Independent Fire Company was called, but it could not control the blaze. To protect thousands of bales of cotton on the wharf the ship was towed out into the river by four tugs. It blazed, an observer said, "with the brilliance of a lightwood knot . . . The whole vessel was wrapped in flames, and the scene though terrible was sublime."

The Seaboard brought its passengers directly into the city with a terminus at the foot of High Street where they could take the ferry to Norfolk. The Norfolk and Carolina dropped its passengers at Pinners Point near Port Norfolk with its hotel and resort and offered ferry service on to Norfolk from there as part of the fare. The Atlantic and Danville went into West Nrofolk, now a part of Portsmouth.

Two of these three major rail lines which entered Portsmouth by the end of the nineteenth century created two of her neighborhoods, West Norfolk and Port Norfolk, but we will deal with that later. In the twenty-first century, rail declined; all passenger service was suspended and only one railroad remains carrying products to and from the International Terminal. The old rail lines have now been replaced by three interstate highways: I-264, built in the 1950s to carry traffic from the south to the Downtown Tunnel bisecting the city, I-164, built in the 1980s and expanded by the Pinners Point connector in 2005 to carry traffic from the west to the Midtown Tunnel and I-664 completed in the 1990s to carry traffic from the north via the Monitor Merrimac Bridge Tunnel to 264 and into the city. These three interstate highways again place the city at the nexus of Hampton Roads traffic. She will always be at the area's geographic center.

It was not only rail and highways carrying goods to terminals which fed Portsmouth, but also canals.

In 1762 George Washington surveyed the Great Dismal Swamp, which extends into what was Norfolk County, crosses the state line in North Carolina and is only a few miles south of the City of Portsmouth. He thought the swamp would make good *farm land and in 1764 organized the Adventurers for Draining the Great Dismal Swamp. He planned to do this through the Washington Ditch, which still exists, but the drainage plan failed.*

In 1793 The Dismal Swamp Canal Company was formed to connect the Elizabeth River with the Albermarle Sound in North Carolina. This would be a particular benefit to Portsmouth because in those days it would connect with the deep water on the Portsmouth side of the Elizabeth River. It took slaves with picks and shovels fifteen years to complete the canal, which was 22 miles long, 15 feet wide and only 18 inches deep.

Miss Holladay says: The Dismal Swamp Canal was opened for business in 1828, after forty years spent in its construction. Apart from its commercial value to the community it is interesting as the work of George Washington, who planned and superintended its building, his work often bringing him to Portsmouth. There is an ancient and spreading oak tree on the canal bank called "Washington's Oak;" for under its boughs he often rested. When the road to Elizabeth City was built recently this tree was in the way. It was agreed that the oak must be saved, so the road curved in order to spare it. Washington had a personal interest in this section, owning a vast tract of swamp between Portsmouth and Driver. *This village is now a part of Suffolk. The drive by the canal became one of the most dangerous roads in the area, and in 2006 a new road was built parallel to it and the old road made over into a hiking and bicycling path.*

The canal passed through a densely-wooded section; and ships heavily laden with lumber regularly plied its waters. Its trade was practically ruined when the Government took over the Albermarle Canal, and made it a freeway. Within the last five years this canal too *(the Dismal Swamp Canal)*, has become a freeway *(i. e. 1930). In fact what doomed the old canal was competition from the railroads and not its takeover by the federal government which began in the 1850s. Its shallowness also made it impractical for steamers. The Dismal Swamp Canal is now used only by pleasure boats.*

In 1859 the Albermarle and Chesapeake Canal was dug parallel to the old Dismal Swamp Canal and it was 40 feet wide and five feet deep. It is still in use for heavy shipping.

Miss Holladay's lament at the canal being taken over by the federal government was premature, however. In 1908 Teddy Roosevelt awakened interest in an inland waterway linking New England and Florida and the government bought the old canals, widened them, deepened them and put them under the control of the Corps of Engineers. Then in the mid-1930s the Atlantic Intercoastal Waterway was completed from Boston to Key West. Portsmouth stands at the zero mile marker on this 2000 mile waterway where shipping is safe from the "graveyard of the Atlantic," running from Cape Charles through Cape Lookout to Cape Fear. The zero-mile marker is near Crawford Bay where Tidewater Yacht Marina has been since 1961. The new yacht marina at the south end of the seawall on the Elizabeth River is another example of the value of this waterway to Portsmouth, as is the Ocean Marine Yacht Center with yacht repair facility where the old banana pier used to be, behind the nTelos Pavilion. It has a massive syncrolift, an 80 ton marine travelift and indoor facilities where the shafts and propellers of the largest pleasure crafts in the nation can be repaired. It has indoor storage for up to 320 boats.

If Scott's Creek were ever dredged, as Mayor Brooks suggested in 1923, that waterway could be the best mooring in Hampton Roads and one of the best on the waterway.

The seawall which now stretches the length of the Elizabeth River frontage of the downtown replaced the remnants of decaying docks and mud-banks in 1969.

CHAPTER 17 : YELLOW FEVER

Perhaps the greatest setback that Portsmouth ever had was the yellow fever epidemic of 1855. There had been one or two mild epidemics in the two towns many years before this one *and an epidemic of cholera in 1832,* but they did not reach alarming proportions.

I will not expand on Miss Holladay's account, except to locate places and identify people because several excellent accounts of the fever here and in Norfolk survive: two contemporary publications, many letters, a modern account called "The Fever" by Lon Wagner, published in the Virginian Pilot and issued in monograph, and an excellent website by Donna Bluemink who is constantly expanding the site to cover all of South Hampton Roads history.

The official chronicler of this dread time tells us that "on the 8th of July, 1855, a perfect tremor of fear swept over the town; when it was learned that a young workman had died of yellow fever in Gosport. It was Sunday, but the Town Council met in extraordinary session, to hear the reports of the various physicians who had attended the man; Carter, for such was the victim's name, had been working on the *Ben Franklin*, a vessel which had recently come to Page and Allen's shipyard for repairs The *Franklin* had been in tropical seas and upon reaching here had discharged her bilge water. Evidence convinced the Council that the ship was the source of infection; and orders *were* issued to the Town Sergeant to have the vessel removed to quarantine. The captain, after much controversy and not until he had taken legal advice, moved her out of the harbor.

Meanwhile new cases were developing in Irish Row, just opposite the shipyard, on First Street. *This is Not to be confused with the Irish Row in Olde Towne, of which only one house remains, on the southwest corner of Glasgow and Crawford*

Streets. These "rows" were settled by Irish immigrants in the second decade of the 19th century. Some of the permission papers to immigrate survive in <u>Portsmouth and Norfolk County Documents</u>, *in which these Irish men and women disavow their allegiance, slight as it must have been, to the English Crown. The remaining house in Olde Towne has a walk-in fireplace and a 24-inch stairway leading to its loft, in the style of cottages in Ireland. The ones by the shipyard are now gone, but must have looked like the one on Crawford Street.* By July 27 the fever was rapidly spreading in Gosport. This suburb was found to be in a filthy and crowded condition; and the newly organized sanitary committee decided that the patients must leave it for healthier quarters. They determined to build a hospital at once in the town proper, where no case had yet appeared. Procuring the site for one proved a difficult proposition. At last one was found near Portlock's *(Oak Grove)* Cemetery.

By this time so great was the need for the hospital that not only the carpenters, but the other citizens of the Town, went to work with hammers and nails, completing *the hospital* building in two days.

On the last day of July it was opened to receive patients, with Dr. George W. O. Maupin and Dr. John Trugien in charge, both gentlemen serving without charge. Unlooked-for difficulties arose when the attempt was made to transfer the patients to the hospital. The Rev. James Chisholm, Rector of St. John's Church was present at this time. *Chisholm was acknowledged as one of the great heroes of the epidemic in Portsmouth, being one of the few clergymen to remain in the city throughout the fever and one of its final victims. He gives the* following appalling picture of it, quoted front his diary. "The wretched and squalid patients in Irish Row positively refused to leave their pestilential abodes. These *were* in number between two and three hundred, reeking in nameless abomination of filth and stench, and exhibiting in their conduct to one another a hard heartedness of which we would not have dared believe human nature capable of under such circumstances; reveling, fighting and quarreling amongst the dying and over the dead, they refused to stir." Mr. Chisholm goes on to say that Father Devlin, the Priest *at St. Paul's Roman*

Catholic Church had to be sent for to use his official authority. In fairness it should be said that the Irish had learned their mistrust of authority in a bitter school in their own occupied country.

"When he had gained their consent by mingled ecclesiastical threats and promises, a new difficulty arose. Wagons in which to move the poor creatures, nor hands to lift them, could not be obtained for any consideration. As the day wore on I have never seen a more disheartened set of men in my life than our physicians!"

The next morning, a few wagons having been procured, the doctors themselves with the aid of Mr. Chisholm and Father Devlin, lifted the patients into them. Nine wagons were filled with them. "Some" said Mr. Chisholm, "lying prostrate," others in a sitting posture, all with agonized faces and uttering fearful groans.

"By noon every bed in the hospital was filled and new cases *were* developing hourly. So far no cases had occurred in Portsmouth proper except one or two that could be traced to people who worked in Gosport." *The shipyard was, at this point, still a part of Norfolk County and not yet within the Portsmouth town limits.*

Dr. Schoolfield, the chronicler before alluded to, says in his *History of the Epidemic*, "That in the history of Portsmouth the blackest day the sun ever shone on was the first of August, 1855. The day was hot and sultry and the streets were alive with people. A single object enlisted their attention—a wagon covered with white, having a mattress on the floor, attracted the gaze of the terrified inhabitants. Nothing was thought of but the impending calamity, as the vehicle freighted with its fevered occupants passed slowly through the city on its way to the hospital. What had been feared and hoped against had become a reality. The sanitary committee had given publicity to the fact that yellow fever was epidemic in Portsmouth."

A delegation had been sent to Washington to petition the secretary of navy to turn over temporarily the Naval Hospital to the town for the use of the fever patients. The committee returned with good news. The building was placed at the disposal of the sanitary committee and the surgeon and his staff were to remain in charge of it. *After the epidemic five doctors at the Naval Hospital were struck gold medals for their diligence and bravery. One of those medals was recently on view at an antique store on High Street. Miss Holladay will give their names in a moment.*

Hundreds of the inhabitants were now leaving by every train and boat; and by the middle of August all who could go from the pest-ridden community were hurrying to do so. It was rapidly becoming impossible to find a place of refuge. Suffolk and Smithfield had quarantined against both Norfolk and Portsmouth. The stagecoach to Elizabeth City had been turned back when within ten miles of the town, and only the mail bags sent on. *Remember that, at this time, no one knew how the yellow fever was spread. It would be a half a century before the true vector, mosquitoes, would be identified by Walter Reed in Cuba.*

Every available building in the countryside was used by the distracted refugees; barns, churches and schoolhouses were alike pressed into service, while the poor creatures who could find no other shelter built huts along the Suffolk Road.

The boats to Old Point *Comfort* were the only means of delivery; and it was not long before rumor announced that they would no longer touch at Norfolk and Portsmouth. Frantic throngs crowded the wharf before each trip fearing lest it should be the last. There is a letter in the possession of the writer, from one of the citizens who stood nobly by his native town in this dark hour, describing the scenes which took place on the wharf. "I never witnessed such a panic as 1 encountered this morning. Nearly an hour before the boat started, the whole space was covered by trunks, carpet bags and boxes; thronged by an immense mass of human beings, of all ages and conditions, *there was* such a number that it was feared that the boat could not take all on board. When she made fast there was not only pushing and shoving, but actual fighting occurred."

It proved a fruitless trip to many who did embark for upon the arrival at Old Point *Comfort* the refugees met a detachment of soldiers from the United States Army who ordered them back to the boat at the point of the bayonet. Some of the passengers were fortunate enough to get on the Bay Line steamer leaving

Old Point *Comfort* for Baltimore. Upon their arrival in that city they received a hearty welcome.

The African Americans in both towns were thoroughly demoralized, though they seemed to be practically immune from the fever. No amount of money, no appeal of any kind could induce them to nurse the sick, or indeed render assistance of any kind to the sick or the dead. *Recently a medical reason African Americans would experience milder cases of the yellow fever has been suggested in <u>Guns, Germs and Steel</u> by Jared M. Diamond. It is the theory of partial genetic immunity. The disease originated in Africa where the natives had existed along side it for millennia. Over time a partial immunity had to evolve, or the population would by wiped out.*

An analogous case involved the European invaders and the Native American population of the new world. The Spanish in the south and the French, Dutch and English in the north brought with them smallpox. Although some Europeans die from this disease most survive. There are accounts, however, of conquistadors entering Mexican villages and finding the entire population dead from smallpox. Another example is the swine flu, to which Europeans had a resistance, but Native Americans, never having domesticated peccaries, had no natural protection.

By Miss Holladay's own account, African Americans were no different from the general population which also fled in panic. That this contention of Miss Holladay is not universally true is also illustrated by the fact one of the heros of the plague, who is mentioned by her in the next paragraph, was African American.

The doctors had usually to carry the sick to the hospital, and often found it necessary to shroud the dead. This duty however, consisted in wrapping them in winding sheets, there being no time for more formal shrouds. Only one undertaker remained in the town, and he could not supply the demand for coffins. Again the Government came to our aid; the workmen in the Navy Yard were ordered to make them. *There were sail makers and carpenters in the yard with the required skills.* The coffins were called for before the patient died in many instances.

The town grave-digger old Bob Butt was as faithful to his duties as any gentleman in Portsmouth. He did not spare himself, for when the epidemic was at its worst he spent the night as well as the day in the cemetery, snatching a nap there as he had opportunity. An amusing story is told in connection with one of Bob's naps. He had just prepared a grave and while waiting for the corpse to arrive, he fell into a doze by the grave side. Presently the hearse rattled up and two young men, who were at the beck and call of the community, lifted out the body. As they did so, there was a muffled sound from the grave and from it slowly arose a figure. The young men said that they thought the dead were beginning to return; but they recognized the old grave-digger just in time to keep from dropping the corpse. *Bob Butt, then a slave, is always acknowledged as one of the heros of this terrible time.* When the epidemic was over and the situation in the town had become normal, the citizens started a movement for raising a sufficient sum of money to purchase Bob Butt from his master, Mr. Britton, in order to give him freedom. This was successfully accomplished and this faithful man spent the rest of his life in Portsmouth, much respected as sexton of Trinity Church.

As the epidemic progressed, graves could not be opened fast enough so it became necessary to dig trenches in which eight bodies could be buried at one time. A portion of Portlock's *(Oak Grove)* Cemetery was purchased, then consecrated and set aside for those who died in the Catholic faith.

By the tenth of August famine stared the town in the face and her entire doom seemed certain. Relief, however, was at hand. The cities of Baltimore and Philadelphia came to our aid, not only supplying food and medicine, but also sent us doctors and nurses when the call to them came. To these cities Norfolk and Portsmouth owe a debt of gratitude which they can scarcely repay.

At this period we get another picture of the pest-ridden city from Mr. Chisholm's diary. He says, "The situation is awful beyond conception. The eye must see; the ear must hear; fancy cannot furnish the deep dark shadows of the picture, On Sunday thirty-two deaths, on Monday twenty-two, and today by eleven o'clock seventeen more have died. The only stores open on High Street are dispensaries, whose doors are beset by an anxious throng. There are no sounds of mirth or business in our main avenue, no groups of grave men on our pavements, no bands of frolicsome children in the highways and byways, no social gatherings, no hearty salutations and accostings when men meet, for everyone seems dubious about approaching his neighbor, no bridals, no baptisms, not even dirges due in sad array at the constantly recurring funerals. The sick wagon with its tall canopy dashes up and down the street and the black hearse bearing its coffined burdens, for there is usually more than one carried out at the time, rattling with an indecent and revolting haste, not one emblem of sorrow relieving its sinister aspect" Again some time later he says, "at this moment an astonishing spectacle is presented to our gaze. A schooner under full sail is entering our harbor, probably bringing ice; for the supply in both cities has given out. *This was necessary to preserve the newly dead, as refrigeration had not yet been introduced.* There has been nothing seen like this for the last six weeks. Sept. 4— Today the Baltimore boat came into port, among other things to land a load of coffins; and so great was the need for them that there was actually quarreling and fighting over them. In the wake of pestilence follows famine; its pinching horrors are already felt by a large part of our population, though the genial atmosphere of summer lingers with us and autumn is pouring her abundant stores around, there is not one grocery open in the place. A depository of provisions, sent us by the noble cities of Baltimore and Philadelphia, has been opened, and from this source the stricken and needy sufferers are supplied."

At this juncture, an offer made by the city of Baltimore suggests some idea of the conditions existing in the two towns. This generous city offered to convey "the whole population that has remained in Norfolk and Portsmouth to any salubrious point that could be obtained, guaranteeing them all clothing, bedding and provisions," in fact *to* care for them entirely just as long as it should be necessary. This proposition could not be accepted for many reasons. In the first place every well person was needed to help care for the sick.

Every church in the city closed its doors but St. John's. It's rector Mr. Chisholm did not succumb to the fever until the epidemic was well over. In this church he held services for all denominations but as can be imagined the congregations were not large. The Catholic Church too, was open until near the end, when its priest fell a victim to the fever. *There is a monument on High Street by St. Paul's Church honoring this brave man.* Mr. Chisholm in a letter of this period says, "Mr. Eskridge, *of Monumental Methodist Church,* and myself are the only resident ministers who can go about and visit the sick, the dying and the bereaved. Devlin, Handy, *of Emanuel A. M. E.* and *Thomas* Hume *of Court Street Baptist* are now convalescent of the fever; the others are away. The few men who remain on their feet to constitute the administrative council of this town are at their wits' end. Noble men, their number is sadly decimated.

Several of the best have fallen; but God still mercifully preserves some. They are men who merit more than the hero's amaranth. First and foremost among them, from the twentieth of July onward, has been and is your friend Gustavus Holladay. You would scarcely credit what this more than hero has suffered, has endured, has done, has sacrificed."

The members of the relief committee referred to by Mr. Chisholm were Winchester Watts, James Gustavus Holladay, Holt Wilson, Samuel Hartt, George Chambers, D. D. Fiske, and Joseph Schoolfield *who published an account of the disaster.* There were ten physicians who remained in Portsmouth during the epidemic. Five of them died of the fever; Trugien, Parker, Nicholson, Collins and Lovitt. Maupin, Bilisoly, Hatton, Cocke and Schoolfield were stricken with fever but recovered.

When the cry went forth for doctors, twenty-eight responded and came to Portsmouth. Eight of these died of the fever. It is not known just how many nurses came to our aid, but of the number nine fell victims to the plague.

So entirely was the town cut off from the outside world that those who recovered from the fever and needed purer air for recuperation, had to ride for some distance on the Suffolk Road, and at some points on the Nansemond River take a rowboat to meet the little steamer that plied between Suffolk and Newport News, at which port the Bay Line steamer landed.

Perhaps no buildings in Portsmouth was more useful during this scourge than the old "Academy." *This brick building, which was later Portsmouth's first high school stood on Glasgow Street between Middle and Crawford where there is now an off-street parking lot. Miss Holliday will describe it further in another chapter. It is pictured in the report of the Relief Association.*

At first many of the terrified inhabitants of Gosport wandered to the Academy seeking a sleeping place in the healthier part of town. They threw themselves down on the steps and porches of the building for the night. For a number of them it proved their last resting place above ground, the disease having already attacked them before they sought refuge there. As time went on it became necessary to take over the Academy for an orphan asylum. The number of homeless children had become a grave problem. At first they had been cared for at the Naval Hospital; but every particle of space there was needed for the ever increasing number of patients seeking admittance. The Academy was officially taken as an orphan asylum. Col. Winchester Watts, who had taken upon himself the care of the orphans, secured the services of a faithful and devoted Sister of Charity, Sister Isadore, who took charge of the institution. We learn from a letter written by Mr. Watts at this period of the difficulty he had in moving the orphans from the Naval Hospital to their new home. It proved impossible to get slaves to drive wagons or in any way help. He had to take *them* with Sister Isadore's aid, the young children in his own carriage, making trip after trip. He then forced his coachman to drive the older ones to the Academy.

When the epidemic was over the official list showed that nearly four hundred children had been cared for as orphans, though in some instances only one parent had died. Many of these children were taken by relatives afterwards; and a large number of them were taken over by the City of Richmond and placed in the orphanage there. The present orphans' home in Portsmouth was endowed with the funds left over from the Howard Association money, subscribed for the fever sufferers. *This report survives in the library.*

In the census report for 1850, Portsmouth is credited with 8,000 inhabitants; but it is estimated that the number of people had reached ten thousand at least by 1855.

About four thousand people remained in the town during the epidemic, the population evenly divided between white and black, thus making two thousand white *citizens* here. Of this number one thousand and eighty are known to have died of the fever.

The report of the Treasurer of the Howard Association shows that this organization paid for the burial of seven hundred and fifty persons, at the cost of $10,314.95. The earlier victims of the disease were buried by their families before the organization took charge of affairs. Bob Butt, the gravedigger, kept an account of the graves which he dug.

Irish or Leigh's Row, where the fever first broke out and which remain*ed* the center of the stage *was* still standing on First Street *in Miss Holliday's time* . It is but little changed, the basements having been turned into stores. It consisted of eight tenements with two stories and basements, two rooms on each floor. At the time of the fever every room was said to have been the home of a large family; pigs and calves in some instances lived in the basement rooms with the families. Filth abounded throughout the row, even in the grog shops *(bars)* which were kept in some of the basement rooms. The families occupying the Row had not long been over from Ireland and were desperately poor. The development of the Navy Yard had brought an influx of people to the town and housing conditions were acute. *("Pulled down lately," has been added parenthetically at this point in my copy of Miss Holladay)*

It would be impossible to give here a sketch of the many noble men who helped the town in her hour of need; but some memorial of those who gave their lives in her service can be found in *The Portsmouth Relief Association*, the official history of the yellow fever written by Dr. Schoolfield. *The Life of Rev. James Chisholm* by Conrad, which includes parts of his diary and a number of letters written in Portsmouth during the fever epidemic, furnishes an interesting though appalling picture of the plague.

During that awful summer of 1855, Mr. Chisholm labored night and day among people of every denomination. He was, however, spared to comfort the pest-ridden sufferings until the disease had abated; then his frail body, worn out by privation and toil, succumbed to the fever. He was stricken with the premonitary chill at the grave-side of a victim; the victim was buried, and as soon as the rites were over he asked to be taken to the Naval Hospital, and from there he passed to the reward of a martyr on the 15 of September 1855. He was buried in the family lot of his friend Mr. John Hatton, in Cedar Grove Cemetery, and a monument was later erected over his grave by the citizens of the town.

Portsmouth did not forget the services of the naval surgeons who rendered such devoted assistance during the epidemic. In 1856 the Council of the town appropriated a sum with which to purchase medals for these surgeons.

These medals were made of gold and were nearly three inches in diameter, costing two hundred dollars each. The gentlemen to whom they were presented were Doctors Lewis Minor, Randolph Harrison, James F. Harrison, Frank Anthony Walke, Thomas H. Steele and John C. Coleman. Dr. James Harrison and Dr. Minor had both been presented with medals by the French Government In 1854, in appreciation of their care of the yellow fever patients on the French man-of-war *Chimere*, which was anchored in this harbor at the time. On Jan. 12, Captain Thompson of Philadelphia arrived here to act as escort to the bodies of the doctors and nurses of that city who lost their lives in the fever. All the shops closed that day and the bells tolled as the remains of the heroic dead passed through the city, escorted by the military, the Masonic Fraternities and the Howard Association. The Philadelphians who died in Portsmouth were Doctors Cortlandt Cole and Edwin Parrett: the nurses and druggists were R. W. Graham, Henry Spriggman. Singleton Mercer, E. Perry Miller, Fred Mushfeldt, Charles Shrieve, William Husen, Mrs. Clive Whittier, and Miss Lucy Johnson.

Among other physicians who died here of yellow fever were Dr. J Clarkson Smith of Columbia, PA., Dr. Thos. P. Howie, of Richmond, and Dr. Marshall of Baltimore.

So quietly did the Sisters of Charity perform their ministrations in the ward at the Naval Hospital set aside for women and children, that they are in danger of being overlooked in distributing the meed of praise. These three Sisters, Isabella, Urbana and Bruno volunteered their services and were willing to help in any way. It was said of them by one who worked with them that they were ministering angels.

With the cool weather of October the fever disappeared, and by the middle of the month the inhabitants returned to the deserted town.

To the Physicians of Portsmouth it was clear that the yellow fever had been spread in this community by the *Ben Franklin*. That her discharged bilge water carried the germ, or rather infection as they called it in those days, so they thought. Another thing had been noted during the epidemic of 1855 as well as in the other epidemics of yellow fever in this section—a fly, they said, of rather unusual kind, seemed very plentiful. They were called "yellow fever flies," and it was not uncommon in the warm weather to hear the older people say of some fly—"that looks like a yellow fever fly."

Though science had not advanced to any great extent in those days in medicine, yet doubtless deep down in the minds of these Portsmouth physicians there were groping in the right direction. They would have rejoiced greatly in the work done by that noble son of Virginia, Dr. Walter Reed.

There were several clues to the correct cause of the disease in Portsmouth: that the infection spread from the Navy Yard across the town in the direction of the prevalent winds (bearing the mosquitos); that the infection ended with the cool weather (killing that particular variety of tropical mosquito); that some insect infestation unfamiliar to its citizens seemed to be observed and that African Americans seemed to experience milder cases. All were reported at the time, but correct inferences not drawn.

Chapter 18: Returning To The Growing Town

About 1841 First Street lost its prestige, and rapidly declined. Since that time it has been given over to sailors, or to those having dealings with them. Prohibition has pretty well wiped out the street, many of the houses being vacant and many more torn down because they were in a ruinous state.

This street in Southside, or old Gosport Village, led to one of the main gates to the Norfolk Naval Shipyard. It never fully recovered after Prohibition and is, of course, now long gone as a residential street. One English basement house survived the federal redevelopment project of the 1960s and a search of the pictures in the Portsmouth Public Library collection reveals it as Miss Holladay knew it.

Crawford Street had long been the favorite residential section of Portsmouth proper; but the lower part of it was soon given over to shops; and after the great fire of 1821, which destroyed several blocks of houses, many of them the handsomest in town, its popularity declined. Many of the homes were rebuilt after the fire, but in a much cheaper way, we are told.

Miss Holladay refers to the section south of High Street which now has bank buildings on its west - one designed by John Paul Hanbury in 1973, between King and County streets, with its mirror glass, is a fine example of mid-twentieth century modernism. On the east of Crawford street south of High is a complex of shops, condominiums and city offices built in the 1990s and the massive civic center with its two courthouses, underground parking, jail, police station and City Hall designed by the architect Glen Yates in the 1960s. The city hall, with a new facade added in the 21st century, was originally built on speculation, but at the behest of the city, by a private contractor, and rented to the city. This section was the anchor of an ambitious *plan to rebuild the waterfront developed in the early 1960s, and still in progress in the 2000s. The use of the land for a civic complex has become controversial and considered by some as a waste of excellent waterfront property. A plan to relocate these city building and redevelop this whole area was presented in 2005.*

Among the shops Miss Holladay would have known here would have been Robertson's Hardware opened on the corner of Crawford and County streets in 1903 by W. F. Robertson. It was later called Robbie's Home Center when it moved to High Street. It was a Portsmouth landmark until it closed in 2004 after one hundred years of service. The then proprietor Saunders Early, remembered the old Crawford Street store where clients gathered around a potbellied stove to haggle about the price of horse collars, and nails were sold by the handful out of kegs. Portsmouth Hardware, across from Maryview Hospital on High Street, also went out of business in the early years of the twenty-first century, but Dail's Hardware on Portsmouth Boulevard has held on since 1956.

In the Public Library, there is a bound volume of an ancient paper published in Portsmouth in 1827 called "*The Palladium.* Who its editor was or how long it furnished the town with news, we do not know. We find in it a poetical description of the town, written by one who calls himself a "Countryman."

> "First Water Street at water's edge
> Receives the passing stranger,
> Where blacksmiths wield the heavy sledge,
> 'Mid fire and smoke and danger
> Here vessels too, are built in style
> To suit the wealthy buyer,
> Team, row, or other boats meanwhile
> That move by steam or fire.
> Next into High Street quickly go,
> A street for business made, Sir,
> Where everything is sold so low
> You'd be compelled to trade, Sir.
> And here's the market house so neat,

With fruits so seasonable
And Old Virginia's greens and meat,
At prices reasonable.
Strawberries, peas and cherries sweet
All kinds of vegetation
You'd surely be compelled to eat
So great is the temptation.
On right, on left the houses fine
Look spacious neat and airy.
There you'll see a grocer's sign
And here an apothecary,
A tinker here, a goldsmith there,
Each at his trade so nimble,
A merchant with his goods so fair
A tailor with his thimble.
In Crawford Street there's various things
To please the eye or passion,
And here the barber shaves and brings
His patients into fashion."

    Mr. John Foreman, who was born in Portsmouth in 1811, wrote some recollections of the town, in the early nineties *(1890s)*. In them he tells us that in his boyhood Newtown (South Portsmouth, *old Gosport Village*) was the hunting ground of the boys, overgrown with chinquapin bushes and trees. *Your compiler has added later on some of Mr. Foreman's recollections from a copy in <u>Portsmouth and Norfolk County Documents</u>. In these he describes every building and street in the town with information about who lived and worked in each in the 1820s and 30s.*

    There was a house on Wythe (number 315), in his day the property of Mr. Robert Jones. There was but one other house over there. It was on a street leading west from the Navy Yard and was owned by Mr. Wakefield. This house has not been identified.

    At this period two bridges besides the Gosport causeway spanned Crab Creek: La Fayette Bridge, which extended from a point on South Street to Third *and* Union Bridge *which* started at the foot of Court and joined it to Fourth Street. Both bridges had draws. La Fayette Bridge was not used within the memory of any now living; but Union Bridge remained until the part of the creek that it crossed was filled in to make a roadway for the streetcars.

In 1811 the limits of the town were extended again to the west and included the eastern side of Chestnut Street. This remained the boundary line until 1899. The children living on the east side, of course, attended the city schools, while those on the other side had to go to school in the county.

The newspapers of 1825 make frequent allusions to the rapid growth of Portsmouth; and from this time on until the awful setback of 1856 *(the Yellow Fever)* she developed along all lines.

Sometime in 1857, Mr. Fiske, the editor of the *Portsmouth Transcript*, gave us in that paper the benefit of a walk that he took around the city. So much had it grown, and so fast was it growing, that he prophesied the need of omnibuses *(of course, horse-drawn)* in the near future for the convenience of those who lived in the suburbs. When Mr. Fiske took that walk some seventy years ago *(1850s)*, North Street stopped at Court, starting again at Washington to end in the marsh at Green. On the south side of North Street, there were several Dutch-roofed houses set far back into the square. *This style is now called "tax dodger" because it involved a false roof, not a mansard, hung on the front of the house to make it look like a one-story house when it was actually two full stories - the story goes that the King taxed houses by the number of floors and this architectural style was intended to avoid that tax; two houses in this style survive in the Olde Towne and several more which no longer survive can be seen in the library's photograph collection.* A bridge ran to *these houses on North Street* diagonally from Court Street, in order to give their occupants an exit at high tide. To get to Ben Lomond, *(Hampton Place)* the home of Capt. Samuel Watts it was necessary to go by way of Glasgow Street, and over a bridge that extended on it from Dinwiddie almost to Washington Street. The creek ran through nearly to Queen Street; London from Dinwiddie to Washington was all creek except the trestle for the Seaboard Railroad. There was a narrow walkway there on each side of the track. Continuing the journey to Ben Lomond, it was necessary to walk down Washington Street to North, where it ended. Stretching from what is now Mrs. Woodley's corner to Mr. Barlow's was a high fence, with a gateway for carriages, which was kept carefully closed. Pedestrians had to use the stile at Mrs. Woodley's corner. The enclosure was a beautiful spot, with its green lawn shaded by two rows of immense sycamore trees, sloping to the water. On one side of this lawn was the home of Mr. George M. Bain which was remodeled from one of the oldest houses in town, once owned by Mr. Joseph Pritchett. *This large yellow house beside the park in the 500 block of North Street between Dinwiddie and Washington streets was built in 1775.* On the other side and covering what is now Hampton Place was Ben Lomond. This house was built in 1799. *It remains in its new location and is called "The Watts House." It has a historical marker.*

The houses on the north end of Dinwiddie begin appearing in the City Directory in 1904. C. T. Phillips who was Clerk of the Court of Hustings is not at his Dinwiddie Street address in 1886, but is there in 1892, suggesting that the creek was filled in and development of that end of Dinwiddie took place in the 1890s. W. H. Baker, who lived at 534 Hampton Place is listed as the Secretary/Treasurer of the Dinwiddie Realty Corporation, which is probably the entity created to sell lots when the creek was filled in. Hampton Place first appeared in the City Directory with seven houses in 1911 (but not in 1910). By 1917 it was fully built up. The Maupin house on Court Street was built in 1895 on a lot which had been unsuitable because of the dampness rising there from the creek which at that point affected land almost to Court Street.

Chapter 19 - Ante-Bellum Days, Nat Turner, The Mexican War and John Brown

In 1831 the Portsmouth soldiers again were called to arms; but this time it was not war but massacre that made it necessary. The Nat Turner's Insurrection had sent a thrill of horror through the State. Seventy-five people in Southampton County had been murdered by *Turner* and his followers; those who were left in the neighborhood fear*ed* another massacre and appealed to the Governor for troops. This request was granted, the Governor selecting for this duty the Light Infantry Grays of Portsmouth, commanded by Captain Samuel Watts, and the Junior Volunteers of Norfolk under Captain George Newton. These companies were only on duty a few days; things having quieted down in Southampton *County* with the capture of those who had instigated the plot and their subsequent punishment.

Nat Turner was a slave, born October 2, 1800 in Southampton County, just south and west of Portsmouth. he was considered a profit, because as a child he seemed to remember things which happened before he was born. As an adult he avoided contact with others; fasting and praying. In 1821 he ran away from his master, but returned after a vision which told him he should return to his "earthly master" Samuel Turner. The next year, after the death of his master, he was sold to Thomas Moore. The next year he had a vision of lights in the sky and droplets of blood on the corn he was cutting. In the woods he found "hieroglyphics" depicting people he had seen in his visions. On May 12, 1828, he had another vision which he described in this way: "I heard a loud noise in the heavens, and the Spirit instantly appeared to me and said the Serpent was loosened, and Christ had laid down the yoke he had borne for the sins of men, and that I should take it on and fight against the

Serpent, for the time was fast approaching when the first should be last and the last should be first... And by signs in the heavens that it would make known to me when I should commence the great work, and until the first sign appeared I should conceal it from the knowledge of men; and on the appearance of the sign... I should arise and prepare myself and slay my enemies with their own weapons."

In 1831 he was transferred to the home of his master's new wife, Joseph Travis, there was an eclipse of the moon and an atmospheric anomaly which caused the sun to show blue-green. He took this as a sign and planned an insurrection. He and his companions killed the Travis family in their sleep and went on to kill every white person they encountered. At its zenith he had as many as forty followers, mostly on horseback. When captured he was taken to prison (the key to his cell survives in the Courtland Library) and ultimately hung on Hanging Tree Road in Courtland.

Many years after this occurrence one of our citizens, Mr. Henry V. Niemeyer, married Miss Mattie Vaughan of Southampton county, who had been the only member of the family to survive the massacre. The father, mother and five children were murdered. Mrs. Niemeyer at that time was about three years old and her nurse, who was much attached to her, was aware of the plot and dared not disclose it to the family; determined to save the child's life, *she* did so by hiding her until everything was over.

The Mexican War was unpopular in the North philosophically on the ground it was invasion of a foreign country and practically because any land acquired would go to the slave states, but it was popular in the South. Men who would become the leaders in the Civil War made their reputations in the Mexican War. Alf Mapp tells us a contingent of Portsmouth men joined the cause, marching out from High Street in the year the 1846 Courthouse was completed. They made up Washington Company F, First Regiment, Virginia Foot, called Portsmouth's Own.

Portsmouth companies were again called to suppress massacre, when John Brown made his raid. In fact the military companies of the town offered their services to the governor, who sent the "*Portsmouth Light Infantry* Grays to Charlestown, *now in West Virginia* on November 6, 1859.

John Brown, a radical abolitionist planned originally to set up a base in the Blue Ridge Mountains from which to help runaway slaves and attack slave holders through guerilla warfare, but his decision to take arms by force from the federal armory at Harper's Ferry, Virginia, and hold citizens as hostages made him a federal criminal.

Mr. Hanrahan, the father of Mr. Frank Hanrahan, formerly city manager of Portsmouth, who went to Charlestown with his company has written a very interesting account of his experiences there *(now lost)*, for his granddaughter, Miss Lucille Hanrahan, from which we quote: "I was at that time a member of the Portsmouth National Grays, a part of the Third Virginia Regiment. . . When the news came to our captain that we had been ordered to go to Harper's Ferry it was morning and we could hardly wait until evening, when the Bay Line boat left. We had to take the train in Baltimore, over the Baltimore and Ohio Railroad to Harper's Ferry. Our company was selected on account of its being the best drilled, and because we could muster more men than any other company in the Third Regiment.

"We were accompanied by the Woodis Rifles,- a company from Norfolk. When we arrived in Baltimore the next evening it was hardly light. I shall never forget how the ladies waved to us as we marched through the streets to get to the train and I shall never forget how we suffered with cold during the three weeks we were gone; but it seemed to me that when we came back to Portsmouth that every one was as glad to see us as if we had been gone three years. We did look like veterans with our long winter coats on, that the state had furnished.... It is a matter of history that John Brown and his men were soon captured, and that they all had a trial and John Brown was condemned to be hung. He was hung in a field not far from Charleston, Virginia *(before the days of West Virginia)*, about fifteen miles from Harper's Ferry.

"At the time of Brown's hanging I was among the members of the Grays left in charge of a battery of artillery at the courthouse at Charleston, and did not go with the troops, but

I saw Brown as he was taken out of jail just across the street and I was standing at one of the guns when the procession passed on its way to the gallows."

This interesting letter was signed "J, W. Hanrahan," and written when Mr. Hanrahan had passed his eightieth birthday.

The Portsmouth Rifle Company was commissioned on October 29, 1801. This company was organized by Captain Jesse Nicholson, who was its first captain. He was followed in turn by Francis Benson, Richard Kelsick, John Kay, James Jarvis, Wm. D. Young, John P. Young, Nat Gayle, and Wm. P. Sanger, and again in 1846 by John P. Young.

Their motto was, "Don't tread on me," placed on *a flag with* a rattlesnake twined around a tree. Also on its banner was a female figure, holding a staff with a liberty cap on it.

This company was called out twice in the service of the United States during the War of '12; and were in a fray on the Bay Shore when attacked by the guns from a British ship. Those of the company present at this time (1846 *which suggests the Mexican War, not Harper's Ferry, which was later*) were: Capt. Richard Kelsick, Lieut. John Kay, Ensign Edward Dunn, 1st Sgt. Geo. Leslie, 2nd Sgt. John Wyatt, 3rd Sgt. James Eccles, 4th Sgt. Lewis Granberry, 1st Corp, Jesse Kay, 2nd Corp. James Bain, 3rd Corp. Allen Copeland, 4th Corp. Amos Edwards, privates Alexander Etherage, Francis Armistead, John Hokwood, Dempsey Cherry, Christopher Hodges, John Pell, John McGun, John Watts, James A. Williams, John Harper, George Dyson, James Bingham, Edward Boutwell, John Jarvis, Nelson Miller, George Collins, John Shepherd, Moses Etherage, James Waughop, Nathaniel Whitehurst, John Kelsick, Tenant Scott, Basset McCoy, Wm. Broughton, Thomas Wotten, Joel Mathews, Wm. Owens, David Odean, William Luke, Joseph Wagner, Richard P. Owens, Edward Denby, Charles Holland. George Scott, John Luke, Wm. Barnard, Richard Jenkins, James Wilkins, Richard Ballance, James Wood, George Grant, Benjamin Deans, Peter Deal, Samuel Smith, Jesse Howell, William Hodges.

Portsmouth was just beginning to rally from the ravages of the yellow fever epidemic which had swept the town in 1855, when "war clouds rolling down" blackened the horizon. The

Portsmouth newspapers, of 1859 and 1860, sounded a note of warning. In editorials, letters and articles they expressed indignation at the interference of certain sections of the North with what might be termed our domestic affairs; and *they* bitterly resented the insults heaped upon the South by many Northern editors whose articles at first were injudicious, but later became malignant *in Miss Holladay's view*. Non-intercourse, direct transportation from Europe, establishment of factories in the South - in fact every remedy was suggested before secession was considered.

CHAPTER 20 - SECESSION

Portsmouth remained loyal to the Union until the bitter end; and elected by a large majority, the Union candidate, James G. Holladay as her representative at the convention called to consider seceding. The county *(Norfolk County of which Portsmouth had been the county seat until recently designated a city)* equally strong for the Union, also chose a nominee of that ticket, Dr. William H. White, of Deep Creek. *Much of Portsmouth's trade was with the North and it was dependent on federal facilities like the Ship Yard.* Both of these gentlemen voted against a secession until Lincoln called for troops. *The President's call would, of course, have included Virginia.* Then on April 18, 1861 Virginia seceded by the unanimous vote of those assembled in convention, this body agreeing however, that their decision should not be made public at once.

On Saturday morning, April 20, Mr. Holladay returned to Portsmouth bringing the news of "Secession." The town was thrown into a furore at once, and rioting barely averted. Many of our best citizens as well as many of our skilled mechanics were from the North.

Exulting cheers mingled with groans of anguish; life-long friends became enemies, and in some instances brother opposed brother. As soon as the news of "Secession" spread abroad an immense throng of people gathered at the vacant lot now covered by the Bank of Tidewater and part of the Old Kirn Building, *on the south side of High Streets between Middle and Court.* The bank was where the New Kirn Building now stands. This lot was rallying place for political speeches and open-air demonstrations of the municipality. In the center of this space was the city flagstaff, from which "Old Glory" then waved. Riot was again threatened when the order came to tear her down. *An engraving of this event appeared in <u>Harper's Weekly</u>.* The noise of shouting was dulled by the voice of weeping; for many who saw that old banner furled had enshrined it in their hearts; they had fought under it at Mexico and defended it at Craney Island, when the foes were at their very gates. Men stood there who had helped our Country grow and served her as good patriots; to them it was as the bitterness of death to fight against the country that they had loved so well. *That there were those who went North at this time is illustrated by the two Congressional Medal of Honor winners from Portsmouth who served in the U. S. Navy was noted in chapter fourteen.*

The flag was torn down hastily; but there was a pause—what flag was to replace that hallowed emblem? Not the Palmette flag of the Confederacy—South Carolina's contribution—no, not the most ardent Secessionist wanted that—Only one flag could replace it—that of Virginia and so old "Sic Semper Tyrannis" was hoisted amid chastened cheers.

Excitement grew more intense in the town with every hour. With the news of Secession had come Governor Letcher's call for volunteers; and by two o'clock on that historic Saturday, six Portsmouth companies had assembled at the parade ground, where High and Court Streets intersect.

We are told by Mr. John W. H. Porter, in his invaluable history written for the Stonewall Camp C. V., that these companies slept on their arms that night; some at barracks at the courthouse and the rest of them in the city hall *A few steps down Court street from the intersection with High, now the Bangle law office..*

Porter's excellent history of Portsmouth in the Civil War survives in the library local history room, as well as the minute books of the Stonewall Jackson Chapter of the Confederate Veterans: the local chapter. When the bank building on the corner of High and Middle Streets where the Virginia Sports Hall of Fame now stands was being torn down a woman who worked for the bank came into the library and said she had seen a filing cabinet she thought held papers of some historical value in the exposed basement. When salvaged this turned out to contain the original applications for membership in the Portsmouth camp, written in the various hands of the veterans and telling their experiences fighting for the Confederacy. These are now bound up in two large volumes in the library history room. Since most of the people Miss Holladay tells us about during this conflict have told their stories there in their own words, I will not add much in the way of detail about them and their service, other than that provided by Miss Holladay. The deaths of many can be found in the minute books of the chapter as well. Many are buried in Cedar Grove Cemetery, as all public burials were stopped at Trinity when the new public burial place was opened in 1832.

As you walk through that old walled cemetery at North and Effingham streets , added to the National Register of Historic Places in 1992, you will see the stones marked "CSA" for Confederate States Army and "CSN" for Confederate States Navy. Among the Navy men are James Cook of the CSS Albermarle, William Henry Murdaugh of the CSS schooner Manassas and CSS Beaufort, John L Murdaugh of the CSS Nansemond and Hampton and Eugene Alexander Jack of the CSS Virginia.

Meanwhile a plan had been formulated for blocking the harbor, and six young men had been detailed for this duty. They were Henry C. Hudgins and Joe Sam Browne of the old Dominion Guards; John C. Tee, Veale, Nicholson, William Hanrahan and Henry Allen.

The work was to be done by two vessels, which were to be towed down to Sewall's Point by the tug *Jane Smith*. One boat was quickly put in position; but the other one proved harder to manage, and while working on her the *Pawnee* appeared at dawn and gave chase. Mr. Tee says the *Pawnee* pursued them quite a distance before they escaped. The youths engaged in this perilous undertaking were all from Portsmouth and lived to do gallant service on the field of battle.

Chapter 21 - Capture of the Naval Shipyard - "The *Pawnee* War"

While the town was marshaling its forces, consternation reigned at the Navy Yard. When the workmen left it at 12 o'clock for their dinner hour, the gates were closed to the public. The commandant Commodore *Charles S.* MacCauley was probably too old and nervous to cope with the situation. He has been severely criticized by some for giving up the yard without a struggle, but his hasty action in leaving the yard which he could so easily have held was doubtless owing to a ruse of the president of the A. and M and C. *rail*road (now Norfolk and Western), William Mahone, afterwards so celebrated as a Confederate general and whose fame is forever linked with that of the Crater *at the Battle of Petersburg*. A sentinel in the crow's nest of the *Cumberland* saw trainload after trainload of Confederate soldiers brought to the outskirts of Portsmouth. Thousands of them had disembarked, so the watch reported. The sentinel in his lofty perch did not see the soldiers carried away from here, just a little bit farther up the road. That was beyond his ken. Mahone had really succeeded in filing one train of cars with soldiers and drew it down from Petersburg. When it reached the neighborhood of Portsmouth the men disembarked; fell into ranks and apparently marched to camp, but in reality *re*joined the train, which was waiting for them at some distance *back* up the road. This was repeated throughout the day, coming from Petersburg with band playing and colors flying, they returned with heads below windows, and silence prevailed.

Meanwhile frantic rumors had spread in the town; Norfolk and Portsmouth were to be bombarded and the populace was at its wit's end. A number of citizens banded together and attempted to block the harbor; but it proved a failure. This was the crowning blow to Commodore MacCauley, who after some correspondence with *U. S.* General Taliaferro, who was in command of the two cities, agreed that there should be no bombardment, provided the harbor was not blocked. This agreement was strictly kept.

A mass meeting of citizens had been held, and Capt. Samuel Watts, James Murdaugh and Wm. H. Peters, Esqs., were appointed a committee to confer with the commander of the yard. As they approached the gate they met a number of officers who had just resigned and left their ships. They told the committee that MacCauley would not see them, and this proved to be the case. Morning wore to evening—to an evening never forgotten by the people then in Portsmouth. At dusk the *Pawnee* of hated memory sailed into port her band playing the national anthem, and with colors flying, with loaded cannons pointed menacingly from her ports. The "*Pawnee* War" commenced, for thus many of the old people of the town designated that awful night of the twentieth of April, 1861. For many months afterwards the people here lived in dread of the *Pawnee's* return.

It was the *Pawnee's* commanding officer, Capt. Paulding, who gave the order to burn the yard and its contents; and his crew left the ships and joined the wrecking force in the yard. Many gallant vessels were berthed there at this time — some of them of glorious memory, like the *United States*, who under Decatur, had captured the *Macedonia* in one of the most thrilling exploits of our Navy *in the War With the Barbary Pirates*. The *Cumberland* was towed down into the harbor and like the *United States* escaped the fire. The *Dolphin, Plymouth, Raritan, Germantown, Merrimac* and *Pennsylvania* were burned to the water's edge. Why they did not set fire to the *United States* was never known.

Hundreds of oxen and horses were burned alive, and what could not be burned was destroyed in some other way; stores were thrown overboard, and heavy cannon spiked. When the liquor supplies were poured out so many of the sailors and workmen became drunk that they were unable to do their work properly, and some of the big guns were not well spiked. In consequence of this the Confederates repaired them and made good use of them. Just before dawn the Navy Yard was a seething mass of flames, and from the water great pyramids of fire ascended heavenward as ship after ship fell a prey to the flames. *This conflagration is also graphically illustrated in Harper's Weekly.*

The terrified inhabitants of the town were roused from their slumbers by the crackling of the fire, and the noise of a maddened populace. Adding to the horror was the booming of the *Pennsylvania's* guns which had been left loaded and fired as they became heated. Fortunately they did no harm, only one of the shots reaching the shore; and that one struck the Eagle House on First Street, and injured the doorway.

Lincoln Street was soon ablaze and but for the shifting of the wind to the south the city would have been wiped off the face of the earth in a few hours. *Lincoln Street was then in Gosport and is now in the industrial park called Port Center.* Many of the men were at camp; the terrified women and children thronged the street in desperation. Some of them had gathered together their most cherished possession, seeking a way to safety but unable to find it. When the sun rose on that April morning the Navy Yard was a mass of blackened ruins. From those ruins however, the Confederates were to accomplish miraculous feats—and with hope only exceeded by courage they prepared to rebuild the yard. The *"Sic Semper Tyrannis" blue flag of Virginia was first raised over the yard, as it had been in 1775, but soon replaced by the* Confederate flag on the yard staff, and Capt. French Forrest was placed in command of the yard, with Capt. Sidney Smith Lee, a brother of Gen. Robert E. Lee, as executive officer.

To the surprise of some of the Portsmouth soldiers who walked down to the stone dry dock, *Dry Dock Number One, the oldest in the nation and added to the <u>National Register of Historic Places</u> in 1970,* the morning after the fire, they found it uninjured. These two privates Mr. David A. Williams and Mr. Joseph Weaver examined it very carefully and found a train of powder laid, leading to a culvert at the northwest corner. Mr Weaver ran down to the dock and broke connection by kicking away several places. They then hunted for the fuse or slow match; but it could not be found. Later when water was turned into the dock some thirty barrels of powder floated out of the culvert. Mr Weaver and Mr. Williams concluded that the order to destroy the dock had been countermanded, or that there had been some hitch in the arrangements.

The mystery was solved the next spring by a singular coincidence. Mr. Weaver had been commissioned a carpenter in the Confederate Navy, and had been captured by the Federals and placed *as* a prisoner on one of their gunboats. The prisoner became very intimate with a master's mate who ate at the same mess with him. When the Mate heard that Mr. Weaver was from Portsmouth, he questioned him about the dry dock at the yard and then told him why it was not destroyed. The mate himself had been in command of the squad of sailors detailed to destroy it. When everything was in readiness for the match the sailors were ordered back to their quarters. As soon as they left the mate lighted the fuse. He did this in order to be able to report that he had done so. Instead, however, of applying it to the powder train he threw it overboard: feeling sure that his omission would never be found out as nobody was likely to return to see if he had obeyed the order. The mate's reason for not destroying the dock was a humane one. He went on to say that had it blown some of the great stones would have been thrown beyond the walls of the yard, injuring many homes and probably killing a number of people. Near the yard lived many families who had been kind to him; and he did not wish to hurt them, nor in fact, any women and children. The mate's description of the powder train tallied exactly with what Mr. Weaver had seen with his own eyes, and he believed the mate's story to be absolutely true. Both Mr. Weaver and Mr. Williams were living in Portsmouth when Mr. Porter published his book; and they vouched for the facts in the case.

Chapter 22 - The City Prepares for the Storm

Meanwhile the city was making every preparation for defense. The ferry boats had been armed with cannon belonging to Grimes' Battery. Cannon had been placed at intervals along the entire water front, from the Navy Yard to the hospital, at a distance of a hundred feet apart. Camps surrounded the town, placed a half a mile from each other. Breastworks were thrown up near the Navy Yard at Third Street and later the wall was lowered in places to afford a lookout.

All day Sunday troops poured into Portsmouth; and the first outside company to reach the city was the Columbus Life Guards of Georgia, under Col. *Alfred* Colquitt. They encamped at the Naval Hospital, where bales of cotton had been hastily piled to form temporary breastworks. The commandant of the hospital had not resigned; but he was waited upon by a committee, who were authorized to find out where he stood. *Samuel* Barrington when called upon to declare himself, resigned. The Confederate Government immediately appointed Dr. *George* Blacknall as Commandant of the Hospital.

On the afternoon of Sunday, April 21, the Rev. Mr. Peterson of the Methodist Church held a service on the steps of the hospital building. With him was an improvised choir, gathered from some of Portsmouth's best singers. Its leader was Capt. James Brown; T. Phillis Weed of the Rifles and Moses Young of the Grays sang tenor, while George Porter took the basso parts. It was said that they sang as they had never sang before, and that the entire audience was completely thrilled. When the religious services were over the crowd adjourned to the spot designated for the batteries. Here men and women and children took spades in hand and commenced to throw up earth for the batteries; Mr. Peterson himself having thrown up the first shovels full. With such vim was the work done that the earthworks were soon ready for the guns which were being salvaged from the wrecks at the navy yard. By the end of the week twelve of these cannons were in place, and the Hospital Point ready for attack. *Rev. P. A. Peterson served only one year in Portsmouth, leaving when the Union occupied the town to become a chaplain in the Confederate Army.*

The old frigate *United States,* which had not been burned when the Federals set fire to the yard, was re-christened *Confederate States* and placed at the mouth of the harbor to guard it. What eventually became of this frigate we have not ascertained. *The United States was the first frigate build for the U. S. Navy in 1797, designed by Joshua Humphreys, and William Doughty, and built at the Philadelphia Shipyard. It had been named by George Washington. Other sources say the Confederates kept its old name simply adding CSS, which may explain why Miss Holladay could not discover its fate. It was broken up in 1865, at the close of the war, but as a part of the display of the Monitor at the Mariner's Museum opened in 2007 in Newport News parts of this old ship have been reconstructed. Visitors can walk through this reconstruction.*

Pinners Point and Pig Point had been fortified and garrisoned, and it was at the latter place that our soldiers had their first engagement. *The Confederate fortifications at Pig Point still survive.* This was a skirmish with the *Harriet Lane.* Capt. Pegram in his official report of the battle said that the Confederates had no casualties; he praised the soldiers, giving especial credit to the Portsmouth companies. The *"Lane"* was put out of commission and found it necessary to go to Washington for repairs. About the same time the Georgia troops had some brush with the enemy off Sewalls Point and it was noticed that they had no Confederate flag, and used their own state flag. The ladies of Portsmouth at once set to work to make them one. When it was finished it was presented to the Columbus Life Guards with great ceremony, Miss Belle Bilisoly, one of the beauties of the town, making the presentation. Miss Bilisoly was afterwards the wife of Mr. Griffin F. Edwards, a prominent lawyer of Portsmouth. Mrs. Edwards is still in Portsmouth, universally loved and admired. Some of her war recollections are given on another page of this book.

In spite of the regiments and forts protecting the town the enemy were getting information of value, but the spies could not be found. It was learned, however, that like the Pied Piper their work was done at the river's brink. Men disguised as fishermen gathered all the information that they could get, then wrote it on scraps of paper, which they enclosed in bottles and attached to them a small flag or signal of some kind, setting them adrift at the proper tide. Thereupon a harbor police force was organized under Capt. John Young of Norfolk, which soon put a stop to this game.

In June, 1861, when the Confederate States laws went into effect here, John K. Cooke, Esq., a veteran of the Mexican War, was made postmaster at Portsmouth and the first Confederate stamps were sold here. Mr. Cooke's son, Giles Buckner Cooke, who after the war became a clergyman, was a member of General Lee's staff. *Confederate currency issued at Portsmouth still survives and copies appear in* <u>Portsmouth and Norfolk County Documents</u>.

The Confederates lost no time in repairing the Navy Yard and from the chaos there wrought what were almost miracles. The *Plymouth, Dolphin, Germantown* and *Merrimac* were raised by the Baker Salvage Company, under the Confederate authorities. Work on the first three was commenced at once, but the *Merrimac* was rejected as worthless. Many guns had been repaired and shipped to other parts of the Confederacy. One of the skilled workmen at the Yard, Mr. Thomas Carr, of Portsmouth, after seeing the Perrott guns used by the Georgia troops stationed at the Third Street Battery, had an inspiration. He decided that he could rifle the six-inch Dahlgren guns which had been left at the Yard half spiked, just as the Perrotts were. To do this it was first necessary to make a machine, which he promptly did. Then he talked the matter over with Capt. Fairfax, in command of the ordnance department. His plans were approved by this officer. Work was commenced at once. When the Dahgrens had been rifled, Capt. Fairfax took the tug *Harmony*, owned by Capt. James Brown and used to carry freight between the two cities, mounted one of the guns on board and went down the river to Hampton Roads to meet the Federal fleet anchored there. He first attacked the frigate *Savannah* lying at the mouth of the James River. The rifled gun did its work nobly, throwing the shot well into the frigate, while the return shot fell far short of the little craft. Capt. Fairfax continued, to shoot until his ammunition was exhausted, and then returned quietly to Portsmouth, well satisfied with the experiment. Under him was a Portsmouth mechanic, Mr. George Maxwell, who manipulated the gun. Mr. Carr himself never received the credit due him for his skill and ingenuity. Mr. Carr spent his life in Portsmouth, dying here much respected.

Another Portsmouth inventor of this period was Thomas W. Cofer who invented a 36 caliber percussion revolver here in 1862 for use by the Confederate Navy. One of these rare side arms sold recently at auction for more than $86,000. An example survives in the collection of Lee Hall.

On July 12, 1861, work on the old frigate *Merrimac* was commenced; she was to be converted into an ironclad ship, a unique experiment. She progressed very slowly, owing to the difficulty in getting the iron necessary to cover her. The iron plates with which she was covered were rolled from the rails of the *rail*road *and fabricated at the Tredigar iron works in Richmond and shipped to Portsmouth. A piece of the iron cladding can be seen on display at the Portsmouth Naval Shipyard Museum.* At the same time the *Richmond*, another ironclad vessel was building at the Yard as well as the gunboats *Hampton*, *Nansemond*, *Escambia* and *Elizabeth*. Many of the Dahlgren and other guns were rifled, only to fall into the hands of the enemy a few months later.

Chapter 23 - The CSS "Virginia"

Early in March, 1862, the *Merrimac*, then called the *Virginia*, was nearing completion. Built at Portsmouth by a Portsmouth man, John L. Porter, a constructor in the Confederate States Navy; this remarkable craft on the 8th of March sailed quietly down by the shore of the town and not far from it fought the battle that revolutionized naval warfare.

Porter designed the ship. The Secretary of the Confederate Navy, Stephen Russel Mallory, attempted, after the war, to take credit for its design, but, since he had no shipbuilding experience, was in Richmond at the time, and had never designed a ship in his life, his claim seems unlikely. He authorized John Porter's work and considered that more important than it was. Many of John Porter's descendants still live in the city. A committee was formed in the 1990s to mark his home, but never completed their work. There were two sets of plans for the CSS Virginia*. One, signed by Porter, remained in the Porter family until the end of the twentieth century when it was sold; the story of the other is very interesting. A black woman working at the Shipyard named Mary Louveste, stole that set of plans from John Porter's desk, put it under her dress and left the Yard. She went through the Union lines to Washington. The rest of the story is told in a letter from Secretary of War, Gideon Wells, written in his own hand from his home in Massachusetts 17 August 1872 in an effort to get her a pension for her service (the letter was purchased from his estate and is now in the Portsmouth Public Library). Wells says in the letter: "It was whilst we were in this state of anxiety (they were trying to decide if they could get to Portsmouth in time to destroy the ironclad in the dry dock before she sailed), with but vague and indefinite information, that this colored woman, Mary Louveste, came to the Navy Department, and requested to see me alone. Not a word would she communicate in the presence of* *anyone, but when we were alone she informed me she was from Norfolk, told me the condition of the vessel, and took from her clothing a paper written by a mechanic who was working on the 'Merrimac' describing the character of the work, its progress and probab completion."* Alan Flanders said in the <u>Virginian Pilot</u> at the time of the purchase that the Union did not need the plans, because they had been published in an article in a British journal and in the <u>Scientific American</u>. Indeed, reporters had seen the ironclad and there was a news note in the <u>Scientific American</u>, but its coverage was too general to be of any use, although it did have a rough sketch of the ship. Without airmail the British journal would have had to cross to America by steamship and not have arrived in Washington before the battle was fought. There can be little doubt the Secretary is telling the truth in his letter and Mary Louveste's spying was central to the Union's knowing the details of the <u>Virginia's</u> design and launch date before it met the <u>Monitor</u> in the world's first battle of ironclads.

The wonderful story of the *Virginia* has perhaps never been more faithfully or vividly told than by her chief engineer, Capt. Henry Ashton Ramsay from whose article published in *Harper's Weekly*, years ago, we quote freely.

There are a number of first-hand accounts from both sides in the battle preserved in the library collection. This one omits the fact that the officers came to Trinity Church before departure, where they were blessed by the Rev. Dr. John Henry D. Wingfield, His description of the blessing of the officers and later the ship survives in a letter he wrote June 8, 1895, after becoming the first Bishop of California. The following is from that letter quoted by Bishop C. Claude Vaché in his history of the church: "Yes!—I have not forgotten the fight in the Hampton Roads. Didn't I go by special invitation to hold a special service of Holy Communion in Trinity Church, Portsmouth, Va., for the Officers before going into the Battle, and didn't I accept a call to offer prayers and thanksgiving for the Victory on board the gallant ship <u>Virginia</u> March 10th, 1862? Can I forget that solemn, most impressive and affecting scene as those valiant men of war fell to the deck upon their knees, bowing their heads in reverence and godly fear? The weather-beaten faces of many of the brave seamen were observed to be bathed in tears, and trembling with emotions under the influence of that memorable occasion."

Now returning to Captain Ramsey's account: "The Merrimac was built in 1856 as a full-rigged frigate," says Mr. Ramsay, "of thirty-one tons burden, with auxiliary steam power to be used in case of head winds. She was a hybrid from her birth, marking the transition from sail to steam, as well as from wooden ships to ironclads. I became her second assistant engineer in 1859, cruising around the Horn and back to Norfolk. Her chief engineer was Allan Stimers. Little did we dream that he was to be the right hand man of Ericsson in the construction of the Monitor, while I was to hold a similar post in the conversion of our own ship into an ironclad, or that in less than a year we would be seeking to destroy each other, he as the chief engineer of the Monitor and I in the corresponding position on the Merrimac."

The designer of the Union ironclad Monitor was John Ericsson of Sweden. It was built at Green Point, Long Island for the specific purpose of meeting the Virginia in battle. It was initially called "Ericsson's Folly," and selected from several plans presented to the U. S. Naval board hurriedly assembled to mount a response to the Merrimac (now officially called the CSS Virginia, - I will, however, call it by its popular name as we continue the story, in part because Miss Holladay and Captain Ramsey use that name). It was completed January 30, 1862 at a cost of $275,000 to $280,000. It lay almost flush to the waterline with a turret holding an unrifled Dahlgren gun, but it was unusually seaworthy and strong in its construction. A letter from Gideon Wells as to how she should be manned survives which illustrates he was directly involved with her preparation and planning. As Captain Ramsay tells us, construction started on the Merrimac on July 12, 1861, and was delayed for a year while the iron plates were made. Clearly the Monitor was built as a reaction to news of the Merrimac. The official launch date for the Merrimac, as opposed to the one reported here, was February 17, 1862, a month after the Monitor, but, where the Merrimac took more *than a year to complete, the <u>Monitor</u> was rushed into service in only 100 days.*

Capt. Ramsay goes on to tell how the *Merrimac*, after being set on fire when the Federals evacuated the yard, the workmen scuttled her, thus putting out the flames. When raised by the Confederates she was only a blackened and burned hulk. "Naval officers were skeptical as to results. The plates were rolled at the Tredegar Mills, Richmond, and arrived so slowly that we were nearly a year finishing her. We could have rolled them at the yard here and built four *Merrimacs* in that time had the South understood the importance of a navy at the outbreak of the war.

"Rifled guns were just coming into use, and Lieutenant *John Mercer* Brooke, who designed the *Merrimac*, considered the question of having some of her guns rifled. *Francis Booke and John Porter were both contracted to work on the plan for the CSS <u>Virginia</u>. They were at each others' throats from the start and both took credit for her construction. It is thought that the final product was a compromise between the ideas of the two men, however, based on what is said here it seems more likely to this author that John L. Porter designed the ironclad itself (his name is on the surviving copy of the plan and that detailed drawing was passed down in his family) and Brooke designed the ordinance, not the ship itself.* How to procure such cannon, was not easily discovered, as we had no foundries in the South. There were many cast-iron cannon that had fallen into our hands at Norfolk; and he conceived the idea of turning some of this ordnance into rifles. In order to enable them to stand the additional bursting strain we forged wrought iron bands and shrank them over the chambers, and we devised a special tool for rifling the bore of the guns." *The <u>Merrimac</u> was 280 feet long with ten guns. She would face wooden warships with a total of seventy guns and defeat them.* "Many details remained uncompleted when we were floated out of the dry dock, but there was great pressure for us to make some demonstration that might serve to check *Union General* McClellan in his advance up the peninsula."

"The ship was full of workmen hurrying her to completion, when Commodore Franklin Buchanan arrived from

Richmond one March morning and ordered everything out of the ship except her crew of three hundred and fifty men, who had been hastily drilled on shore in the management of guns, and directed Executive Officer Jones to prepare to sail at once." After some discussion of details with his commander, Mr. Ramsay decided that a trial trip would be necessary, as they would have to go several miles down the river, and everything could be carefully watched at that time.

"Across the river at Newport News gleamed the batteries and white tents of the Federal camps and vessels of the fleet blockading the mouth of the James, chief among them the *Congress* and the *Cumberland*, tall and stately, with every line and spar clearly defined against the blue March sky, their decks and ports bristling with guns, while the rigging of the *Cumberland* was gay with the red, white and blue of the sailors' garments hung out to dry.

"The ship had been sighted from Old Point and help was sent to the Federal vessels," Mr. Ramsey goes on to say that "the *Congress* shook out her topsails and the clothesline on the *Cumberland* was hauled down.

"Our crew was summoned to the gun deck, and Buchannan addressed us, 'Sailors in a few minutes you will have the long-looked-for opportunity of showing your devotion to our cause. Remember that you are about to strike for your country and your homes. The Confederacy expected every man to do his duty. Beat it to quarters.'

"As we approached the Federal ships we were met by a veritable storm of shells that must have sunk any ship afloat except the *Merrimac*. They struck our sloping aides, were deflected upward to burst harmlessly in the air, or rolled down and fell hissing into the water, dashing the spray up into our very ports. As we drew nearer the *Cumberland*, above the roar of the battle, rang the voice of Buchannan: 'Do you surrender?' 'Never,' retorted the gallant Morris.

"The crux of what followed was down in the engine room. Two gongs the signal to stop, were quickly followed by three, and the signal to reverse. There was an ominous pause, then a crash, shaking us all off our feet. The engine labored. The vessel was shaken in every fibre. Our bow was visibly depressed. We seemed to be bearing down with a weight on our prow—We had rushed on the doomed ship, relentless as fate, crashing through her heavy barricade of spars and torpedo fenders, striking her below her starboard forechains and crushing into her. For a moment the whole weight of her hung on our prow, threatening to carry us down with her, the return wave of the collision curling up our port bow. The *Cumberland* began to sink slowly, bow first and continued to fight desperately for the forty minutes that elapsed after her doom was sealed. We had left our east iron beak in the side of the *Cumberland*." *Illustrations of this ramming device survive. In ancient times rams were used on galleys but at this time it seemed a new innovation. The Confederate submarine* <u>Hunley</u>, *recently raised from Charleston, SC, harbor, also did its damage with a similar ram.* "Like the wasp we could sting but once, leaving the sting in the wound."

"Our smokestack was riddled and our flag shot down several times, and was finally secured to a rent in the stack." *A photograph survives of the stack, after she was scuttled, full of holes.* "On the gun deck our men were fighting like demons. They gave no thought to the wounded and dying as they tugged away at their guns, training and sighting their pieces, while the orders rang out, 'Sponge, load, fire.' 'The muzzle of my gun has been blown away,' cried one of the gunmen. 'No matter keep on loading and firing, do the best you can with her', said Lieut. Jones. All were in high courage and worked with a will; they were so begrimed', with powder that they looked like negroes. Human hearts were beating and bleeding there, human lives were being sacrificed. Pain, death, wounds, glory—that was the sum of it. On the doomed ship *Cumberland* the battle raged with equal fury. The sanded deck was red and slippery with blood. Delirium seized the crew, who cheered and fought as their ship sunk under their feet. The ship listed; a pivot gun broke loose, leaving a mass of mangled flesh in its wake.

"The *Congress* was then attacked. She tried to escape but went aground and after desperate fighting the orders came, 'Cease firing.' The *Congress* had surrendered; the white flag had gone up. Orders were given and each man was ready for what might come after the lull.

"The whole scene was changed; a pall of black hung about the ships and obscured the clean outline of the three frigates, *St. Lawrence*, *Roanoke* and *Minnesota*, also enveloped in the clouds of battle that now and then reflected the crimson lightnings of the god of war. The masts of the *Cumberland* were protruding above the water. The *Congress* presented a terrible scene of carnage. The gunboats *Beaufort* and *Raleigh* were summoned to take off the wounded and to fire the ship. They were driven away by sharpshooters on shore, who suddenly turned their fire on us, notwithstanding the white flag of the *Congress*. Buchanan fell severely wounded in the groin."

"While being carried bellow Buchanan said to Jones, 'Plug hot shots into her and don't leave her until she is on fire. They must look after their own wounded since they won't let us.' Buchanan's brother was pay master on the *Congress*."

After the burning of the *Congress* the *Merrimac* next attempted to attack all three frigates at once; but they made off with the exception of the *Minnesota*, who could not be reached by the *Merrimac* sufficiently to do her serious damage. The ironclad then pulled up to Sewall's Point for the night, planning to make short work of the *Minnesota* in the morning. What happened in the morning can best be told in the exact words of Mr. Ramsay, who says, "We left our anchorage shortly before eight o'clock in the morning, and steamed across and upstream toward the *Minnesota*, thinking to make short work of her.— We approached slowly, feeling our way along the edge of the channel, when suddenly a black object that looked like the historic description, 'a barrel head with a cheese box on it' moved slowly out from under the *Minnesota* and boldly confronted us. It must be acknowledged that both ships were queer-looking craft, as grotesque to the eyes of the men of '62 as they would appear to the present generation." *The wreck of the Monitor, which was lost in the same year while being towed around the Outer Banks of North Carolina to participate in another battle, was discovered in 1973 turret down in the sand. This turret of the Monitor was raised in 2002 from its wreck. The turret was "excavated" by* *archaeologists at the Mariners Museum in Newport News and was put on display with a full-size reconstruction of the ship made at the Norfolk Navy Yard in Portsmouth, ironically. With a $30,000,000 display this reconstruction and the real turret with its artifacts was opened in March 2007.*

"And now the great fight was on, a fight, the like of which the world had never seen before. With the battle of yesterday old methods had passed away, and with them the experience of a thousand years of 'battle and of breeze' was brought to nought. The books of all navies were burned with the *Congress*, by a conflagration as ruthless as the torch of Omar. A new leaf had been turned, a virgin page on which to transcribe and record the art of naval warfare.

"We hovered about each other in spirals, gradually contracting the circuits until we were in point-blank range, but our shells glanced from the *Monitors'* turret, just as hers did from our sloping sides. *This battle is a popular subject of paintings, the most recent being by Bob Holland in 2006 and the careful reconstruction of the battle, down to the angle of the sun, done by the Mariner's Museum for its exhibit space. Even a series of post cards illustrating each of its key events was issued.* "For two hours the cannonade continued without perceptible damage to either combatant.—Then an accident occurred"—The *Merrimac* was aground."

The use of coal for two days had made the ship much lighter, thus exposing the part of the vessel which was not covered with iron. She was hurried out of the drydock before the plates of metal could be put much below the water line. Had the *Monitor* known this, she could have put the *Merrimac* out of commission without any trouble. Mr. Ramsay says, "Fearing that she might discover our vulnerable 'heel of Achilles' while she had us 'in chancery,' we had to take all our chances. We lashed down the safety valves, heaped quick-burning combustibles into the already raging fires and brought down the boilers to a pressure that would have been unsafe in ordinary circumstances. The propeller churned the mud and water furiously, but the ship did not stir. We piled on oil cotton waste, splints of wood, anything that would burn faster than coal. It seemed impossible that the boilers could long stand the pressure that was crowding upon them. Just as we were beginning to despair, there was a perceptible movement and the *Merrimac* slowly dragged herself off the shoal by main strength. We were saved."

"The enemy had not noticed the trouble of our ship, and it made a sudden dash for her; but decided not to risk the collision just then; gliding by the *Monitor* unscathed we fired upon the *Minnesota*. The *Monitor* gallantly came to her rescue, and we fired at her. The shot carried away her steering gear, injured the conning tower, and blinded Captain *John* Warden. The *Minnesota* was about to give up ship, but at this juncture she saw the *Merrimac* turn toward Norfolk. It was decided at a consultation of the officers on board that the *Merrimac* would not attack the *Monitor* until the needed plates could be put on; at that time she was *no longer* an iron clad.

"As the *Merrimac* passed up the river trailing the ensign of the *Congress*, under the stars and bars, *(The "stars and bars" is usually the term for the national flag of the Confederacy: a blue jack with seven white stars arranged on it in a circle and three vertical stripes, from the top red, white and red, but the Naval ensign was the familiar battle flag with a St. Andrews cross filled with stars against a red background, but rather than being square, drawn out into a rectangle. In most of the illustrations it is the national flag pictured on the <u>Merrimac</u> as Ramsay says it should be)*, she received a tremendous ovation from the crowd that lined the shores, while hundreds of small boats, gay with flags and bunting converted our course into a triumphal procession. In about three weeks the ironclad was ready to renew battle, but the *Monitor*, though reinforced by two other ironclads, the *Galena* and the *Naugatuck*, and every available vessel of the United States Navy, was under orders from Washington to refuse our challenge and bottle us up in the *Hampton* Roads. This strategy filled us with rage, but it proved very effective.

The new commandant, Josiah Tatnall was growing impatient to distinguish himself, and almost disobeyed orders on one occasion. After discussing affairs with President *Jefferson* Davis, the ship was ordered out one night, and she slipped by Old

Point and was making for the *Chesapeake* Bay, *with access to the open sea*, when signals recalled her. It was deemed inexpedient for the *Merrimac* to risk capture lest *General* Huger's army at Norfolk and Portsmouth should be left unprotected." *Major General Benjamin Huger, CSA, of Charleston, SC, who later distinguished himself at Roanoke Island, Seven Pines, White Oak Swamp and Malvern Hill was at this time commander of all Confederate troops in this area.* "We were to receive a signal when Huger evacuated, but this we never got. Learning that part of the waters that we had to cross in following Huger up the James River drew only fourteen feet of water, and when we prepared to risk this, the wind changed and blew the water off the bar. It was decided to abandon the vessel and set her on fire. We took the *Merrimac* to the bight of Craney Island, and about midnight the work of disembarking the crew began." *This contradicts another account which says she was blown up in Scotts Creek. Based on the fact the troops could easily join Huger I think Ramsay's account is the correct one.* "We had but two boats and it was sunrise before our three hundred and fifty were ashore. Cotton waste and trains of powder were strewn about the deck, and Executive Officer Jones, who was the last to leave the ship, applied the slow match. Still unconquered we hauled down our drooping colors, their laurels all fresh and green, *and* with mingled pride and grief, gave her over to the flames, and set the lambent fires roaring about our shotted guns. Then we marched silently through the woods to join Huger, who was on his way to Suffolk. The slow match reached the magazine, and that last low deep mournful boom told our people, now far on the march, that their gallant ship was no more." Among the officers and crew of the *Merrimac* there were a number of Portsmouth men.

Some years after the "Surrender" parts of the *Merrimac* were recovered and many trophies were made of her timbers and steel. Crosses made of the liveoak beams tipped with gold are possessed by many of the people of Portsmouth. One of her bells, in pretty good shape, was brought up in dredging some years ago, and is now in Norfolk. *Two bells claiming to be from her appeared, one the one Miss Holladay refers to, but the only one authenticated was apparently taken as a souvenir by a Union soldier and put on display in 2007 at the U. S. Naval Museum. In 1970 a plaque was commissioned showing the ship in metal on a wooden base with a small fragment of the iron-cladding set in it.*

The Confederate Navy was formed at the Shipyard after it was taken by the South. That is why the Confederate Monument in the middle of Court Street at High is one of the few such monuments to honor that small force. The figures are done from life, representing the four services, Infantry, Cavalry, Artillery and the Navy - the Navy is on the east side of the monument facing the Tidewater Community College Visual Arts Center. The monument was designed and built by Charles E. Cassell in 1876. A photograph of its dedication has recently been given to the library.

It was the custom for the United Daughters of the Confederacy to decorate this monument on Confederate Memorial Day. The memorial day for the Confederate dead was set on a different day, as the victors bitterly opposed Confederate dead being remembered on the national day of remembrance. In the 1960s the City Council thought it not politically correct to have Confederate flags on display in the city center and sent workmen in to remove them. Mrs. Marian Rawls, then the president of the local chapter of the United Daughters of the Confederacy, stood in the iron gate to the little compound and would not let the city workmen pass. The City Manager then asked me to research the monument to be sure it was city property. I found it was not. The monument had been built by the Stonewall Camp of Confederate Veterans and given to the local chapter of the UDC. The city had deeded the land on which the monument stands to the UDC as well. As a result, neither the monument, nor the land on which it stands belongs to the city. The City Manager decided to just ignore the problem. There was, at one time, a suggestion the monument should be moved to facilitate traffic flow, but this also ended with the realization this was not city property and would have to be condemned if it was to be taken, a process which might not be smart politically, and might not be decided in the city's favor if it were opposed and went to court. In 2006 vandals painted parts of the monument. Aware of its historic importance, the city quickly repaired the damage.

It could be said that the loss of the shipyard at Portsmouth would doom the Confederate Navy. It was certainly the finest shipyard available to the Confederacy and Hampton Roads the best harbor.

Chapter 24 - The Union Occupation and "The Beast"

The story of the *Merrimac*, or *Virginia*, has led us away from the almost superhuman efforts that our city was making for the cause of the Confederacy.

From the very first the women of Portsmouth gave themselves heart and soul to this cause. They were as earnest as our men, but their first weapon was the needle, which they used with invincible industry; sewing night and day, they made the uniforms for the soldiers in the newly-formed companies in Portsmouth. These gallant men not only went to war in homemade uniforms, but could at first find no better arms than the old-fashioned pikes.

The pinch of war was soon felt in the town. Commodities jumped to unheard-of prices in 1861, when leather for boots could not be purchased at any price, and shoes of the commonest kinds could not be had for less than $10. Women's shoes of the same type cost $6.50 a pair. Flour rose rapidly and was considered enormously high at $8.50 a barrel, while a few weeks later it was double that amount. The cheapest sugar was 15 cents a pound; butter 65 cents and lard 35 cents a pound. Trousers of the most inferior quality cost anywhere from $12.50 to $18 a pair. To us who are accustomed to habitually inflated prices, these prices do not seem remarkable; but compared with the normal cost of things in the *eighteen* sixties they were amazingly high.

Sewing societies were organized throughout the town, and garments were made for the needy, specially for those of the soldiers' families. Moreover, these devoted women took it upon themselves to provide the Portsmouth soldiers with blankets and shoes.

In July, 1861, there was so much poverty in the town that the Council came to the aid of the women and appropriated

$1,000 for the poor of the city. In August of the same year this body appointed a committee composed of David Griffith, Arthur Emmerson and John S. Stubbs, Esqs. to enquire into the needs of the soldiers' families. These gentlemen reported four hundred needy ones; and recommended that $5 a month be paid to each family. The Council acting on the advice of its committee immediately set aside $10,000 for this purpose.

As soon as war had left its red marks, the women volunteered to nurse the wounded. The Naval Hospital like the Navy Yard had been taken over by the Confederates. Dr. Blacknall, who had been in command of this hospital before, had now joined the Confederate Navy, and was placed in charge of the Hospital. Dr. Blacknall had married a Portsmouth lady, Miss Blow and had many ties with the city. In the Hospital cemetery today the Confederate dead sleep, row after row, close to their brothers in Blue; and their graves receive the same tender care. *Unfortunately federal government security after 2001 has stopped access to this interesting cemetery, of which we will hear more later.*

There was nothing that these women did not undertake; no risk was too great. Fearlessly they ran the blockade, and when a spy was wanted they did not falter; more than one was ready for the dangerous work. One of the noted spies of the Confederacy was a Portsmouth woman, formerly Miss Mittie Williamson, a daughter of Dr. Thomas Williamson, so many times surgeon in charge of the Naval Hospital. Dr. Williamson's home was on London Street. Miss Williamson married Dr. Wysham of Maryland.

Another daring Portsmouth woman was Miss Louisa Riddick, who helped the cause wonderfully; giving her time to running the blockade. Many were the interesting stories she told and many hair-breadth escapes fell to her lot; but danger did not daunt her.

At the outbreak of the War and for years before it the white petticoat, now but a memory, was an indispensable garment. Its popularity was only exceeded by its width, which was at least four yards. Embroidery or flounces on undergarments of this kind were considered a little risque in the *eighteen* sixties, and fortunately for the soldiers a deep hem was the correct finish for the underskirt. On the inside of these hems letters were written in lead pencil to those beyond the lines; money was stitched into them and other articles that no guard thought of. It is said that when the hems were ripped out by those to whom the garments were sent, that these petticoats proved veritable newspapers. *Medicine, in very short supply in the Confederacy, was stolen by these women from the Federal hospital in the Macon House Hotel on North Street, hidden under the stone threshold of a door on Washington Street next to St. John's Church and then carried in the hems of petticoats through the Union lines.*

    Miss Riddick would at intervals collect the petticoats and articles she expected to carry to the soldiers and others in the Confederate lines, and then start out on her journey. She was joyously received in Portsmouth when she returned with news from the refugees and soldiers. Sometimes Miss Riddick would say, "That hem is too deep; the guard will suspect. He knows how scarce cotton is," Grudgingly the garment was re-stitched.

    Mr. Hamilton, an old citizen of Portsmouth, tells of another blockade runner among the Portsmouth women, Mrs. Cox. On one occasion this brave woman was put to it to get a letter through and was resourceful enough to bake it in a loaf of bread. *The bread was.* remodeled, *even though* its curtailment meant that some loved one would be deprived of something that would give him pleasure or comfort.

    We must not forget the faithful services of a slave belonging to Mr. Logan Hurst. This African American carried letters back and forth from Portsmouth and the Confederacy by "underground railroad," and never betrayed the trust.

    Late in April, 1861, it was rumored that Portsmouth *troops* must be evacuated. With the cry of the Federals, "On to Richmond," came the necessity for the fifteen thousand soldiers that guarded the two cities to join Johnson's army; so Huger and his division had orders to march.

    Mr. William H. Peters who had been commissioned paymaster in the Confederate Navy *and* had charge of all the stores at the yard, received orders to move them to Charlotte, N.

C.. Mr. Peters was quietly going on with the work of removal and had nearly finished it, when it was learned that we had harbored a traitor. On the tenth of May, Capt. Byers with his tug, *J. B. White,* deserted and joined the Federals at Old Point, giving them information as to what was transpiring in Portsmouth and Norfolk.

As soon as his defection was known orders were given for immediate *military* evacuation of the city. The remaining stores at the Navy Yard were destroyed, as well as the ordnance; and for the third time in her history the torch was applied to the Navy Yard. The *Escambia,* the *Elizabeth* and the *Yadkin* were still on the stocks, and they too fell a pray to the flames. The historic stone dry dock was slightly injured. Meanwhile Huger had ordered all barrooms closed and liquor destroyed. Col. Stewart has described its destruction, much of it in front of the courthouse, where the gutters he said, literally ran brandy. Much liquor has been destroyed in the gutters of Portsmouth since that historic day; but it was destroyed in a much less worthy cause. *This would be the 1846 Courthouse on Prison Square, now the 1846 Courthouse Gallery. Miss Holladay is obviously not a wearer of the white ribbon: the symbol of those favoring prohibition.*

As soon as the Confederate flag was hauled down at Sewell's Point, 6,000 Federal troops advanced from Willoughby Spit to Norfolk and entrenched in camps. At 4 o'clock that afternoon the Mayor of the city met them and formally surrendered *in front of the old Courthouse, now the MacArthur Memorial. A man in my wife's family from Princess Ann County said it was the most impressive military display he had ever seen, and he was a Southern sympathizer.* The next morning a force of Federals crossed the river and took possession of Portsmouth.

As can be understood, the orders for *military* evacuation struck terror to the hearts of the Portsmouth soldiers. To leave their town, abandon it to the enemy with all they held dearest left to the mercy of the foe, leaving them until war was over; for well the soldier knew that the city would never be regained.

It was with despairing hearts if not with lagging steps, that they pressed on to Suffolk to join their division. On May

10 the last Confederate soldier left the town: the old "Rifles" bringing up the rear. *The local unit called "the Portsmouth Rifles," of which more later.*

More than two thousand Portsmouth and *Norfolk* county men marched away that day; and says Mr. Porter, "fully one fourth of this number died on the field of battle or of disease contracted in the service." Many of them followed the army to Richmond, to work in the foundries and workshops there; and the town was without men practically. A few gentlemen had been appointed by *Confederate* Governor *John* Letcher *of Virginia* to remain in the city, to aid the people left there, in the hands of the foe.

Nor did the hand of the enemy fall lightly on our city. Martial law in all its rigor prevailed. Our churches were seized. Trinity, *later in the occupation,* for an African American (military) hospital, and St. John's for something more offensive. From its pulpit the missionaries of the Northern Methodists proclaimed their obnoxious doctrines - *presumably abolition*. The Methodist church too was seized; but was accidentally destroyed by fire before it was used by them. *See Margaret Windley's* Brief History of Monumental Methodist Church *on the INTERNET. It was thought that the Union occupation had deliberately destroyed the church.*

The Macon House *Hotel on the south side of North Street between Middle and Court* and the Ocean House *where the Tidewater Community College Visual Arts Center now stands* were used as hospitals. Families were ordered out of their comfortable homes and crowded into houses occupied by several other families. Soldiers were quartered on unwilling hostesses.

Homes were plundered frequently and subject to search at any hour of the day or night. It was always a Confederate soldier that they looked for, supposed to be hiding. They did their work thoroughly as a rule, not forgetting to look into bureau drawers and bandboxes. The searchers took whatever they found of value, in lieu of the Confederate soldier they did not find. Silver and portraits seemed irresistible to the searchers. Mr. Hamilton, whom we have quoted before. says that it had been bruited abroad that they had a Confederate flag from the

Merrimac in their home, and reports to that effect led to frequent raids on their premises. The flag was never found, as Mrs. Hamilton had carefully sewed it up in a bed comfort.

Sometimes the searchers met with a just reward, and many funny stories are told of the punishments meted out to them by the defenseless women whom they annoyed. In justice to some of those who were sent on the house-searching expeditions, they hated the work and never failed to do it in a way becoming to a gentleman.

In the basement of the Murdaugh residence on the northwest corner of Crawford and London Streets, *now called the Pass House,* the provost marshal established his headquarters; the house having been vacated by the family who had gone into the Confederacy. This office was the scene of many unpleasant as well as amusing episodes.

In order to cross the ferry it was necessary to go to this office and get a permit to do so. This required red tape which meant delay. To go out of the city limits required the same trouble; and moreover the provost martial claimed the right to search the persons of those who came for permits. This right was sometimes used, but not often. Occasionally when a blackguard was on duty things were made very annoying for those who came for passports.

Gen. *Egbert L.* Viele was for some time in charge of this district and was very unpopular. *He lived in Norfolk in the year of Lee's surrender.* Mrs. Viele used to ride *around Portsmouth* in a very handsome equipage gorgeously decorated with red, white and blue. On one occasion as she drove through the town a very ordinary woman made some offensive remarks about her in a voice loud enough to reach her. Mrs. Viele had the woman arrested. The next day she was summoned before Viele, accused of insulting his wife. All that the prisoner could be induced to say in her own defense was that "A woman could not insult a lady, and a lady would not insult a woman." The culprit was returned to the jail, where she stayed for some time.

General Viele's tyranny was forgotten when the "Hero of Five Forks and Ten Thousand Spoons," Ben Butler, reigned in his stead, and ruled as only a man of his caliber could.

General Benjamin Franklin Butler was widely called "Beast" Butler in Portsmouth (of which more later), and sometimes "Spoons" Butler, because of his fondness for other people's silverware. The quote from Miss Holladay refers to a banner put across a Portsmouth street when he ran for president on the Greenback ticket - it read "Vote for the Hero of Five Forks," a battle in which he served, to which a local wag added "and God knows how many spoons." In Rev. Wingfield letter, quoted earlier, he is simply called "The Beast."

Butler was born on November 5, 1818, in Deerfield, New Hampshire. He became a criminal lawyer, and an important state legislator in Massachusetts. In 1860, he was a delegate to the Democratic Convention in Charleston, South Carolina. Believing that only a moderate Southerner could hold the Union together, he voted fifty-seven times to nominate Jefferson Davis for the Presidency. For the same reason, he supported John C. Breckinridge at the Democratic rump convention in Baltimore. When the Civil War began, however, Butler did not hesitate to enlist in the Union armed forces. A week after the attack on Fort Sumter, Butler facilitated the secure and free movement of Union troops to and from Washington by calming the Baltimore Riots.

He was appointed major general of volunteers from May 16, 1861. Although he was the first major general of volunteers appointed by President Lincoln, Butler became one of Lincoln's worst "political" generals. While in command of Fort Monroe on the Virginia peninsula, he led his troops to humiliation in a struggle at Big Bethel. Newspapers reported displays of ineptitude among the Union troops, including leaving behind valuable equipment while retreating. Butler barely maintained his commission after that incident.

Later, when Southern slaves fled to the North through Butler's Fort Monroe he freed them and the fort was called "The Freedom Fort." Many of these slaves were recruited into the Union Army - for a record of the service of these troops see William Paquette's list in the Portsmouth library developed as a part of the project called "Lower Tidewater In Black and White." It also lists where these soldiers mustered out. There is a monument to the African Americans who fell in the Civil

War in Lincoln Memorial Cemetery on Deep Creek Boulevard in Portsmouth. Butler declared these freed slaves as "contraband of war." He made the declaration because the government had not provided any guidance on how to deal with the problem. Southern slave owners were angered, because they regarded Butler's action as a confiscation of their property.

The president of the Portsmouth bank, George Washington Virginius Maupin, who had ten children, refused to tell Butler who had money deposited in the bank and admitted he had been carrying out charities for the relief of Confederate soldiers families. He was taken prisoner to Fortress Monroe. He kept a pencil list of civilians held there, the only such list to survive, a copy of this list is in <u>Portsmouth and Norfolk County Documents</u>. Of his ten children, two, Dawson and Alliene, lived unmarried at their home on Court Street until they were both almost 100. They recounted their memories of visiting their father in prison to their twin Maupin nieces.

Another Portsmouth family had their valuable piano confiscated by Butler. They were told it was lost. A relative, visiting Fortress Monroe after the war, looked into a window and saw the piano. The family petitioned President Johnson for its return. Johnson instructed Butler to give the piano back. Butler did dispatch it to the dockside in Norfolk, but, since he did not tell the family it was there, it was ruined by the weather. When the family retrieved what remained of it they made it into a coffee table.

Hoping to improve his military reputation, Butler tightened up his ranks, and scored a victory at Hatteras Inlet. After this he returned to Massachusetts to recruit new troops in the New England area. In 1862, he went to New Orleans when the city surrendered to the Union fleet, and was appointed military governor of the state. Although his political allies considered him a competent administrator, Confederate President Jefferson Davis called him an outlaw.

Butler was also known as "Beast" Butler in New Orleans, although the name originated in Portsmouth, and became the center of national controversy when he issued his "woman's order." Many women of New Orleans had been *insulting and verbally abusing Union soldiers. One woman even emptied a chamber pot on a Union captain. The Union officers, however, restrained themselves from reacting. In exasperation, Butler issued the "woman's order" (General Orders No. 28), which stated that: "when any female shall, by word, gesture, or movement, insult or show contempt for any officer or soldier of the United States, she shall be regarded and held liable to be treated as a woman of the town plying her avocation." Although Butler's "woman's order" was effective, it lowered Butler even further in the estimation of the community. There were chamber pots in Portsmouth with butlers face painted inside.*

 He was removed from the military governorship in December of 1862. In 1863, he was placed in command of the Department of Virginia and North Carolina, but later reduced in rank. He was transferred briefly to New York to deal with election riots there. Gen. Grant sent Butler home to wait for further orders. When Butler found out that Grant intended to mount a campaign against Fort Fisher, North Carolina, the last Confederate port open on the east coast, he demanded that Grant give him command. Because of seniority, Butler received the command, but seriously mismanaged it. It was the last assignment he was given, and he retired his commission in November of 1865.

 After the war, Butler became a Republican congressman, and played a significant role in Andrew Johnson's impeachment. In 1878, he was elected to the House of Representatives, this time as a Greenbacker. He ran for governor in Massachusetts several times, until he was finally elected in 1882. Two years later, he ran for President as a Greenbacker, but lost the election. Butler died on January 11, 1893, in Washington, D.C.. (All but the local history details in the above biography come from "History Central.")

 While in Portsmouth Butler lived in the handsome Peter's house, confiscated by him. That house still sands and is the home of Thomas McDowell Williams and his wife Sally Macon Porter Williams: a descendant of the designer of the CSS <u>Virginia</u>.

 Miss Holladay continues: Butler was hated by all classes in both cities - *Norfolk and Portsmouth.*

Some years after the close of the war, he came to Norfolk to attend to some business affairs. Signaling a hack, he was about to step into it, when the hackman thrust him aside and closed the carriage door in his face. He had recognized Butler, who as may be imagined, was greatly astonished at such treatment and asked for an explanation. The hackman's reply was, "No Sir, Gen. Butler doesn't ride in my hack."

So exactly did the hackman voice the feelings of the times that the people of Norfolk and Portsmouth took up a collection and bought a new hack for him, with the proceeds.

Perhaps one of the funniest occurrences that ever took place in the Provost's office was an oath of allegiance taken by a very ignorant old woman from the country. When told that she must take an oath she partly refused to do so. To the poor old soul an oath had but one meaning, and from her youth up she had been taught to abhor cursing. She begged to be released from the necessity, but the officer failed to understand her point of view and thought she was unwilling to obey those in authority. He did finally make her understand that she must take the oath or go to jail. The threat was sufficient—to go to jail would be a disgrace not to be borne. Immediately she announced her readiness to take the oath, and without delay exclaimed, "God damn every Yankee soldier to hell." Then with an earnest prayer asked forgiveness from heaven, saying. "While I was taking an oath I thought I might as well make it strong." Whether the oath was satisfactory or not, no other one was required and the old woman went back home in peace.

One of the punishments inflicted by the conquerors was stoning the houses of those who failed to obey orders or offended them in any way. Mrs. Belle Edwards, formerly Miss Belle Bilisoly, tells of her home being thus treated on several occasions. She lived on High Street and in those days the Seaboard train ran down the middle of that street. Her family was sewing on black jackets at the time it passed on one occasion. The train was filled with Federal soldiers who waved at the young girls sewing. The girls thoughtlessly waved back at them with the black garments upon which they were working. That night the house was roughly stoned. It was afterwards explained by the soldiers that it was done in revenge. They thought that the black jackets were waved in insult to them. On another occasion quite a general stone bombardment occurred because the townspeople refused to illuminate and decorate their houses for some Federal victory.

Once, Mrs. Edwards tells us that upon looking out of her window she saw a cart go by. In it was a Federal soldier, seated on a coffin. This man it seems was a deserter, on his way to the gallows, and the coffin was to be used for him when the hanging was over.

We learn from another source that this man was a Southern spy named Barnett. He posed as a Northerner and boarded with Mrs. _____ *(this blank is Miss Holladays, not mine)*, in the house on the southeast corner of Court and South streets, where many of the Federal workmen and soldiers boarded. It seems that he played his part badly—overdoing it. He was so ardent a "Yankee" that he was suspected and watched. He was soon captured, with the result that was related above.

There was great excitement among the people when the African American regiment passed through the town, but fortunately no tragedy occurred. *Their service in many battles, but particularly in the battles in the North Carolina sounds and their service in the Indian Wars, illustrates the resolve of these troops. As mentioned earlier, a list of local black troops who enlisted at Fort Monroe, many of whom mustered out in the Southwest as "Buffalo Soldiers", is in the library collection.*

Among the many hard things that the women had to bear was the lack of information concerning those in the line of duty. One of the youngsters, afterwards a prominent citizen, Mr. Wm. S. Langhorne, was on the *Stormy Petrel*, a vessel in the signal service, when it was wrecked. There was no way of letting his mother know that he had been rescued, and the suspense was weighing heavily upon her. After a while a friend in government service in Richmond, who knew officially of his safety, devised a scheme to let his mother know the facts. He put a "personal" in the *New York Herald*, knowing that this paper was much read in Portsmouth. *One Langhorn family lived in the second house south of the intersection of Glasgow and Middle on Red Lion*

Square on the east side of Middle Street after the Civil War. The house was removed when Olde Towne was laid out in the 1960s.

In spite of all the trials and hardships to which they were subjected, the Portsmouth women never lost their indomitable spirit. They were never conquered. A very kindly-disposed guard quartered at Mrs. Mercereau's, the fashionable milliner of the town, expressed great admiration for these women. He said, "I have not yet been called to the front, and do not know the Southern men; but if their spirit matches that of the Southern women, I hope to God I never may." "Yes," said Mrs. Mercereau, "When the Southern men are all killed the women will continue the fight if it is with nothing better than broomsticks."

While the women of Portsmouth were bearing the burden and heat of the day at home, the Portsmouth men were reaping laurels on the field of battle; but, alas, those laurels were too often stained with blood.

Chapter 25 - Portsmouth's Civil War Veterans

In 1861 Portsmouth had a little less than six thousand white inhabitants. She sent to the Confederate Army more men than those enrolled as voters. One thousand, two hundred and forty-two men answered the call to arms. Of this number one hundred and ninety nine died in battle or of disease contracted in the service.

It is a well-established fact that in every battle worthy of the name, fought east of the Mississippi River, there was at least one Portsmouth man in the ranks.

With the news of Crampton Gap came also the story of how our men had been officially complimented. At Malvern Hill Grimes Battery had won glory and its commander the gallant Grimes had been cited for bravery. Again at Sharpsburg, fresh laurels were added to its list of honors; but they were overshadowed by sorrow for the loss of their intrepid leader. This Battery, the second oldest in the United States, fought wherever the fight was thickest until the end; and then returned to Portsmouth with its ranks greatly thinned: twenty-six of its hundred men were numbered with the dead.

The Dismal Swamp Rangers, under Capt. Thomas Hodges, too were ever in the forefront of the battle, they made a gallant charge at Cemetery Hill at Gettysburg with Pickett's Brigade. This company lost twenty of its men; though new to military life, and largely made up of skilled mechanics, this company fought with the best. Their ranks were at first depleted by men being called to work in their own line; and afterwards by exposure to fearful weather. When the order to advance to Gettysburg was given only six men remained in the company, Capt. W. H. Lumber, Lieut. Gleason, Serg. R. A. Hutchins; privates Wm. Moran, Wm. Fiske and Wm. Herbert. All of them but Fiske were captured. This company (B) was next to the colors and when the standard-bearer fell mortally wounded, Hutchins seized the colors and rushed with them to the stonewall behind which the enemy were driven.

The National Grays had begun their work in the skirmish at Harper's Ferry when John Brown was captured *as we have seen earlie*. They fought gloriously at the second battle of Manassas and Jon Yost, their color bearer, was the first man to reach the Federal battery, which it was charging. Yost fought gallantly until 1865, when he died at Dinwiddie Courthouse from wounds. At Five Forks the color-bearer of this company was M. D. Monserrate, who refused to give up the colors though wounded in both arms. Fifteen of the Grays gave up their lives for "the Cause."

The Virginia Artillery was a new company, who gladly donned the uniforms made by the loving hands of Portsmouth women and took the old pikes found in the ruins of the Navy Yard in lieu of guns, changing them later for flint lock muskets. This company was know as Richardson's "Wild Cats," owing to their agility in climbing over the barriers placed to keep then in camp. It is unnecessary to say that it was young ladies that made them so eager to break bounds and it was the young ladies who gave them the nickname. They proved to be as skillful fighters as climbers. They opened the battle of Mechanicsville on June 26 by shelling a long range piece of woods in which the enemy were lodged and from which they were driven. At Malvern Hill they made their last fight as a separate company, so reduced were their ranks by death and disease that the remaining men were transferred to another regiment. Sixteen of their men were dead when the troop came back to Portsmouth in '65.

The Portsmouth Rifles, like Grimes Battery, had in its sixty-nine years of existence passed through two wars and received its baptism of fire at the heroic defense of Craney Island. They mustered in with the old types of rifles and bayonets. The Council, however, appropriated a sum of money to fit the guns with saber bayonets and these weapons were made in Portsmouth at the Union Car Works.

This company won its first laurels at Pig Point *(where the TCC campus now stands in Suffolk)* in the skirmish with the *Harriet Lane*. Its captain; John C. Owins, made a glorious record as a fighting man and became colonel of the regiment, where he won more honors. Col. Owins' grandson, John C. Owins, of Portsmouth, still has in his possession the tattered and stained banner of the Rifles.

At Gettysburg this gallant band did heroic work. Its color-bearer, Sergt. Grimes, carried the flag to within twenty yards of the stone wall, where he was shot. As he fell, Corp. Lemuel Williams seized the colors and took them to the farthest point then reached by the division. In the act of planting the colors on the stone wall, he, too, received his death wound. In this charge at Gettysburg this company had forty-eight men in the thickest of the fight. The morning after the battle only seven answered roll call, the others being either wounded. or dead. *This is the group of Portsmouth men led by General Armistead, who appears in the "Confederate Window" at Trinity Church, and for whom there is a monument on the Gettysburg battlefield.*

In the Craney Island Artillery were some of Portsmouth's bravest men, among them John Vermillion and John Christian Niemeyer. Vermillion was captured at Gettysburg and remained a prisoner until after the war closed. Niemeyer was killed in the same battle.

The Old Dominion Guards had only been organized a few years at the outbreak of the war, and when the call to arms came about one half of the company were under twenty-one years of age. These soldiers were full of life and spirit and very fond of society. They were barracked at Pinners Point, and their superior officers always said that this company was a handful to manage. It was impossible to keep these youths from "going to town." Much guard duty fell to their share in consequence of disobedience. When the fighting time came, none surpassed them in bravery.

While stationed at Pinners Point the ladies of Portsmouth presented the Old Dominion Guards with a banner. The presentation was made by Miss Handy, and Captain Kearns received it in behalf of the company. He attempted to make a speech of acceptance, but forgot it. After several times repeating, "If I falter," finally added, "may Christ kill me," *and* retired. The banner was left in Petersburg during the war for safekeeping, but disappeared.

This company fought in a long array of battles, winning glory everywhere. Of the nineteen men who went in the fight at Gettysburg, eighteen of them were killed, captured or wounded.

When the Ninth Regiment was fighting Sheridan at Dinwiddie Courthouse, it was marched to the left when the fight was at the hottest and thrown in the reverse in order to check the flood. Thus they bore the brunt of the charge, standing their ground until overwhelmed, as the enemy came faster than they could load and fire. Almost all of them fell, or were wounded.

When this regiment was taken from the center of the brigade it passed the Fifty-sixth North Carolina, in command of a Portsmouth man, Col. G. G. Luke. George H. Barnes of the Old Dominion Guards was color bearer for the Ninth, and when he recognized Luke, gave him a cheer which the Portsmouth companies in the regiment took up, though every one of them knew that they were a sacrifice in order to give the other regiments time to escape. They took up the cry, "Here goes old Portsmouth, Col., good bye."

This regiment not only fought at Seven Pines, Malvern Hill, Warrenton Springs, Second Manasses, Harper's Ferry, Sharpsburg, Fredericksburg, Suffolk, Gettysburg, Newberne, Drury's Bluff, Chester Station, Dinwiddie Courthouse, Five Forks, Saylor's Creek, but at as many other battles.

The Bilisoly Blues became Company 1 of the Sixth Regiment and its first captain, Charles McAlpine was promoted to a colonelcy. John Hobday succeeded him as captain; and it was due to him that the Confederates won at Wilcox's Farm. With a small command of 21 men, he passed down the enemy's line a distance of two hundred yards, and demanded their surrender. Another member of this company, Charles W. Collins, performed a gallant feat at the Battle of Shady Grove, May 8, 1864, and was reported for special mention for distinguished gallantry. Young Collins who was only fifteen when he enlisted, passed unscathed through twenty three battles, always in the midst of danger, and fell at the Battle of Davis Farm in 1864.

To this regiment was also attached the Jackson Light Infantry and the Virginia Rangers. Fifty-nine men left Portsmouth with the infantry. Sixteen of their number died on the battlefield or from wounds received there. The Rangers like the other Portsmouth men were in the thick of the fight. They fought in Mahone's Brigade and many laid down their lives at the Crater. Ten of their number were killed.

The Virginia Defenders fought in many battles and won fame at Crampton Gap. Nearly the whole regiment was captured and only four of the Defenders escaped, but they saved Harper's Ferry. The Secretary of War pronounced the defense of Cramptons' Gap to be one of the most gallant performances of the war; and "certainly it was a glorious exploit for eight hundred men to hold at bay twenty thousand for three hours."

After the Battle of Sharpsburg, "rations became scarce and the men were given ten ears of corn for a day's feed. One day one of the men in the Virginia Defenders was seen coming from the direction of Gen. Mahone's headquarters, with his ten ears of corn upon his arm, and upon being questioned said he had been to the General to complain of the shortness of his rations. He said that Gen. Mahone told him it was the best that he could do, that he had nothing else for himself, and he had informed the General that he did not object to ten ears of corn, that was all right as far as it went, but that five bundles of fodder should accompany it as a "feed." He did not repeat Gen. Mahone's reply. *The corn would be the appetizer and the fodder the meal.*

The druggist Joseph E. Weaver who lived at 517 South Street was a carpenter on the confederate ship Sea Bird, *the flagship of Commodore Lynch. This ship was lost in the North Carolina sounds and Weaver taken prisoner.*

As I have told you at another place in this narrative, I will not try to outline the military careers of all the soldiers Miss Holladay lists, or leaves out, because they have left better personal accounts of their service in their applications for the Stonewall Camp of the Confederate Veterans on file in the library collection. Some Portsmouth Civil War buff should compile their stories, perhaps using Miss Holladay as a guide, adding the accounts in Stewart and Porter, and issue a book about the service of individual Portsmouth men in the Confederate Army. These accounts are worth the effort. I remember reading one where a soldier remembers pulling his wounded officer to safety and then another by the officer telling the same story from his point of view. Transcribed and edited they would make a good first-hand account of Portsmouth men in the war. There are some other primary source materials in the library which could round that narrative out - I particularly remember some letters we were allowed to copy from a war widow trying to locate her husband after the war. She discovers that his slave, whom he took with him as a body servant, killed him.

Alf Mapp tells us that: "On April 30 1870, less than three months after the end of Military rule in Virginia, General Robert E. Lee visited the city on a tour of the South. The white haired general stepped off the Seaboard and Roanoke Railroad train and . . . walked with his escort toward the ferry wharf (near the present day High Street Landing). A large number of men and women cheered him and the thunder of artillery sent echoes bouncing off nearby walls. A small brass cannon was fired in salute from a group of young men . . . As Lee stepped aboard the ferry rockets and Roman candles were fired by Portsmouth citizens." Mapp continues, "Less than six months later Lee would be dead."

Chapter 26: The Spanish American War

In April, 1898, the United States, though not formally declaring war against Spain, admitted that she was in a state of warfare with that country and sent a fleet to Cuba and land forces as well. Portsmouth, as usual, took an active part in the war preparations. The navy yard was in a hum and the militia companies of the town preparing to go to war.

The Old Dominion under Capt. George Brooks, and the Portsmouth Rifles were called into the service of the Government. Two of the ships that were built at this navy yard formed a part of the fleet sent and became famous. The *Texas* was commanded by Capt. John Philip, and her chief engineer was a Portsmouth man, Captain Kenneth McAlpine. The *Texas* was known as the backbone of Admiral Schley's "Flying Squadron," doing good work at Guantanamo, and taking part in the destruction of Cevera's great fleet at Santiago *de Cuba. There is to this day an American base at Guantanamo.*

In the thick of the fight, when the *Maria Theresa* was going under, her decks covered with flames, the *Texas* crossed her bow and as was natural the sailors began to cheer. "Don't cheer," said Philip, "the poor devils are dying."

Again Capt. Philip gave utterance to an unforgettable speech from the decks of the *Texas*: when the Spanish fleet was ruined and the battle over, Captain Philip called his men to the quarterdeck, and, with bare head, said, "I want to make public acknowledgment here that I believe in God the Father. I want you all to lift your hats and from your hearts offer silent thanks to the Almighty."

Capt. McAlpine's duties were arduous on the *Texas* and much depended on his management of the engines. His work was highly praised by the Government. The *Portsmouth built*

Texas practically put the *Reina Mercedes* out of use. When the war was over, this vessel, the *Reina Mercedes*, was taken over by the Government and added to our naval forces.

The *Mercedes* was brought to the Portsmouth navy yard to be refitted and repaired and Portsmouth was ready to receive her. A bulletin announced that she would arrive at the yard promptly at one o'clock. She came in on time, and from a contemporary account we learn that "She hove around the Hospital light*house* and slowly made her way up the river to the navy yard. amid the applause of the people, the waving of handkerchiefs and umbrellas; the roaring of the cannon of Grimes Battery.

Such a sight has never been witnessed in this city, and the steamboats of every description, dressed as they were in gay bunting, with their whistles sounding a welcome to the new American cruiser, followed in procession. A feeling of pride rose in the bosom of every person who saw the pageant and the true spirit of patriotism prevailed. Upon the arrival of the cruiser at the yard the band played the *Star Spangled Banner* and the procession broke line, the boats scattering in many directions to make way for the tug *Merritt* to bring the prize ship to 'a comfortable position alongside the North pier.' This was successfully done in the presence of thousands of people, many of them wearing the uniforms of American soldiers or sailors, and who cheered lustily as the boat landed."

The *Riena Mercedes* served the United States Navy for many years in active duty; and has now won a well earned rest as receiving ship at Annapolis.

Captain McAlpin served with distinction through another war, World War *(I)*, and died at his home in Portsmouth.

The *Raleigh*, the other ship built at the yard, went to Asiatic waters as part of Admiral Dewey's fleet and participated in all the movements about the Philippine Islands, in the Battle of Manila Bay, in the capture of the Corregidor forts, the bombardment and capture of the SuBig Bay and the capture of the gun boat *Callao*, and in the bombardment of the Malata Fort, forcing the surrender of Manila.

The *Raleigh* was the first of Dewey's fleet to return home, and her journey was almost a triumphal procession. Her officers and men were feted and decorated at all of the British stations along the way. At Singapore there was an unusual occurrence. Though the *Raleigh* was flying a warship's pennant when she met a Spanish transport having on board troops and sailors from Manila, the transport lowered her colors and permission was given to the Spaniards to visit the *Raleigh*, where they fraternized with the American sailors who supplied them with much needed clothing and money.

Our soldiers, too, won laurels in Cuba. The Old Dominion Guards, a company which had won glory in the Civil War, was commanded as we have said by Capt. George Brooks. The Rifles were commanded by Capt. Edwin W. Owens, who was the son of Capt. John Owens, who, as a captain in the Civil War, made a heroic record and gave his life. When the time arrived for the return of the Old Dominion Guards, a thrill of interest pervaded the town and every one was alert to do them honor upon their arrival.

At eight o'clock in the morning of the day set for their return the people thronged the streets; the Naval Post Band was out in full array followed by Grimes' Battery The newspaper offices were besieged by those whose patience was ebbing, asking when the soldiers would arrive. Finally the Seaboard Air Line *Railroad* announced that it was thought they would reach Portsmouth about a quarter to ten o'clock. Later news said that the train would certainly be in at two thirty and as that hour approached the train came, heralded by the martial music of the Post Band, and salutes fired by the cannon of Grimes Battery and the Portsmouth Rifles. Bunting waved from the buildings and enthusiastic cheers rent the air as the first section of the train rolled in.

"But lo" said one who was at the station, "a great disappointment was in store for thousands of people who thronged streets; for the Old Dominion Guard were not on the train. There were a few Portsmouth soldiers however to appreciate the welcome, for Lieutenants Epps and Hutchins, Quartermaster Sgt. Bennett, Sgt. Williams and privates Majette,

Lynn and Brown and Dr. George Peed, assistant surgeon of the Fourth Virginia Regiment, stepped off the train.

There was some feeling of anger among the crowd at their disappointment; and inquiries went forth as to the cause of the non-arrival. There had been a slight accident which had caused a delay; but the second section of train was to bring the Old Dominion Guards and that was due at six o'clock. Six o'clock came and the train did not arrive. At seven there was the sound of a locomotive whistle and enthusiasm was rampant again. Grimes Battery fired another salute and cheers rent the air. Disappointment again—the Guards were not on this train; but the Norfolk soldiers were and they received a hearty welcome from the disappointed crowd.

At eight-thirty o'clock the Old Dominion Guards arrived and when the cheers and excitement had subsided to some extent the companies formed into a parade and started on the line of march, stopping in front of the home of the mayor, the late J. Thompson Baird, who made a stirring address of welcome, in which he said that the keys of the city had been lost and the city was theirs for the night.

When the march was over the companies and many invited guests adjourned to the armory *at the corener of Crawford and County streets* where a sumptuous banquet was served. Capt. Richard Marshall and Claude Markham made addresses of welcome, followed by numerous toasts. Some of our Portsmouth men have done great service and braved many dangers at the seat of war.

The death of Mr. Evan Hunley, custodian of Woodrow Wilson High School for many years, recalls one of the most gallant exploits of the Spanish American War. It was said of him that he had served in his early days in the United States Navy and was with Dewey at the battle of Manila Bay and enjoyed a heroic record. On one occasion, to save what might have been a disaster to his ship, he crawled through a hot boiler and accomplished that which none thought could be accomplished under the circumstances presented. The act was a trying one. It turned the then young Hunley's hair gray but he never spoke of it unless others spoke first.

It was to Portsmouth that some of the captured Spanish sailors and soldiers were brought for treatment at the Naval Hospital, where Admiral Cevera visited them twice. *A photograph of the Spanish Admiral taken during this visit survives in the library's collection.* Among the Spanish officers treated at the hospital was Cap*tain Victor M.* Concas, who had been in command of the *Infanta Maria Teresa* and chief of staff of the Spanish Squadron. The other officers were Lieutenants Ardurius, Nobal, an Fajardo and Dr. Gomez. Three the Spanish enlisted men died at the hospital, one from disease, the other two from wounds.

As will be mentioned in the chapter on the hospital, some were buried in the Hospital cemetery.

The story of the visit of President Theodore Roosevelt to honor those killed in this "bully little war," and the two monuments in Portsmouth to the war will all be covered in the chapter on the Naval Hospital. The war had established the American Navy as second only to the British on the high seas.

A framed copy of the roster of one of the Portsmouth companies that served in this war is on display in the library local history room.

Grimes Battery would be called to serve in 1916 with General John L. Pershing in his expedition against Pancho Villa in Mexico. That company would then serve with him again as part of the 29th Division in Europe in the First World War.

Chapter 27 - The Navy Yard

The navy yard here was usually known as the Gosport Yard until the Civil War: Afterwards it was called the Norfolk Navy Yard; and the mail sent there went through the postoffice at Norfolk. About twenty-five or thirty years ago *(1890-1900)* there was a change made in its designation. It is now officially named "The Norfolk Navy Yard at Portsmouth, Va.;" and the mail passes through the postoffice in this city. *It could not be called the Portsmouth Navy Yard as one by that name existed in New England.*

Its location and strategic points have made it the most important one on the Atlantic Coast. Commodore Sir George Collier as far back as 1779 told of its advantages in a letter, *quoted in part in Miss Holladay's description of Collier's Raid in her earlier section on the American Revolution.*

The site of the yard was used by the ships of his "Britannic Majesty" as a careening ground, long before our town was in existence. *I described how a ship is careened earlier and it is illustrated in <u>Images of America: Portsmouth, VA.</u> by Robert Albertson.* It is certain that Portsmouth had scarcely been established, when Andrew Sprowle, a Scotch merchant, who had made his home in the new town, purchased a tract of land across Crab Creek, from Thomas Bustin, and built thereon not only a handsome residence for himself *called Soul's Point*, but warehouses and tenements as well, thus giving Portsmouth her first suburb, which he named Gosport. *The shipyard itself dates to November 1 1767.*

Crab Creek, as mentioned earlier, was a navigable river crossed by a ferry until it was bridged in 1789. The grave of Rees Bartle in Trinity Churchyard, who died in 1822 at age 21 is that of the man who was engineer on "a replacement for the drawbridge over the Eastern Branch of the Elizabeth River to replace one blown down by a 'memorable gale'" He probably died building that bridge. It led to the shipyard from the Berkley side.

But the most important work that Sprowle established in his little town was the marine yard which he built and equipped on the site of what is now known as the oldest part of the navy yard. Gosport was soon a flourishing village and the Marine Yard was so much in favor with the British ships that the government in a sense took it over and appointed Mr. Sprowle as Navy Agent here about 1754, an office which he held to the outbreak of the Revolution. *This being the earlier than the traditional date attributed to the construction of the yard suggests the yard may be older than currently thought.*

At this time Great Britain was preparing to enlarge and equip the yard; and it appeared for a time that she could hold the port, which was in the beginning of the war a hotbed of Tories. It became the last seat of the Royal Government in Virginia in May, 1775, when Lord Dunmore came quietly up the river on the *Roebuck* and moored at Mr. Sprowle's wharf. The great warehouses were filled with his soldiers who used them as barracks. Mr. Sprowle was one of Dunmore's most intimate friends and doubtless gave him a hearty welcome. His Lordship and his followers remained at the yard for six months.

Dunmore in 1775, the first of January, *departed.*

The Colony of Virginia immediately took possession of all the Sprowle property *in 1775* and confiscated it. They developed the Marine Yard and stocked it with things necessary for warfare.

The Colony of Virginia in June 1776 declared herself an independent state and in the October following the Virginia convention directed the Commissioners of the Virginia Colonial Navy to provide materials for building two thirty-gun frigates and four galleys; and authorized the enlistment of crews for these ships to serve three years from March 1, 1777. The Commissioners of the Navy at this time were Messrs. Paul Loyall and David Stoddard. It was estimated that it would require two hundred oak and one hundred and fifty pine trees to build these two ships. The contract for furnishing this timber was awarded to

Thomas Talbott and the price was three thousand, three hundred, thirty three dollars and thirty three cents.

Over this yard five different flags have been unfurled; first as we have seen *was* the standard of Great Britain—lowered to make room for the flag of the Colony of Virginia; which after the Revolution was replaced by the flag of the State. After 1800 the banner of the United States waved over the yard in undisputed sway for sixty one years. On April 20, 1861 the stars and stripes gave way to the flag of the Confederacy. For one short year this flag floated from the yard staff and since that time the emblem of our country has waved there in unchallenged supremacy.

Three times has this yard been burned in warfare, first by the British under Commodore Sir George Collier, when he evacuated Portsmouth in May 1779. Collier, as stated elsewhere in this volume, considered this port a very important one, and the marine yard most convenient and well-equipped. On *April 20* 1861 the torch was again applied to the yard, this time by the retreating Federals. Scarcely a building was left standing; and as the work had to be done hurriedly the oxen, for hundreds of them were used there, were burned alive. A year later *on May 10 1862* the Confederates before evacuating set fire to the yard, but this work had been so thoroughly done before it fell into their hands that the conflagration did not amount to much.

The stone dry dock, the oldest in the navy yard, and the oldest dry dock in the country was practically uninjured.

So few records of the Virginia Navy are forthcoming that we know little or nothing about the ships built at this yard during this period. *We know that Samuel Barron was made Commander-In-Chief of all vessels in Virginia and* we know that the *Sally Norton* was fitted out there for one of the most daring exploits of the Revolution; and under Capt. John Coxe, a Portsmouth man, she went to Bermuda as St. George Tucker's aid in capturing the powder from that Island and bringing it to Williamsburg. At this yard, too, was the celebrated *Marquis de Lafayette,* repaired after being burned at Suffolk. From this port she went on another hazardous undertaking for the Patriot Cause; passing out of the harbor on a moonlight night, making her way through the British Fleet which had blockaded it, as told earlier.

When the war ended in 1781 Virginia reorganized her navy, putting Commodore James Barron in charge of it. *This is the elder, the father of our Commodore James Barron, whose story will be told in a moment.* Under him were his two sons, Samuel and James Barron, both to be commodores later, and Richard Dale, a native of Portsmouth, who had won fame as John Paul Jones' lieutenant on the *Bohomme Richard*, having himself taken a prominent part in the fight with the *Serapis*, as told at length earlier.

In 1794 when the Algerian pirates menaced the commerce of the world, the United States was in sore need of ships and men. Virginia came to her aid and turned over to her temporarily the Navy Yard. Richard Dale was placed in charge of the construction department; and William Pennock was made Navy Agent. Pennock by virtue of his office became custodian and administrator of the entire yard. This method of managing the yard was in vogue until about 1810.

As soon as the Federal Government took over this yard a forty-four gun frigate was commenced; but the declaration of peace between the United States and Algiers made work at the yard unnecessary and there was a halt called. Another impetus was given by war with France. *The war with Algeria was called The War With the Barbary Pirates, of which more later, and the war with France called the Quasi War With France.*

Although he was not a Portsmouth man by birth, Alan Flanders tell us that one of the heroes of that war does have a place, or his name does, in Portsmouth history. The Portsmouth neighborhood built by the federal government for African American shipyard workers in the first World War is named for Thomas Truxton. Truxton was one of our nation's first six Navy captains. He was born on Long Island and distinguished himself in the American Revolution. George Washington said that his service was worth that of a regiment, and he has had four U. S. Navy ships named for him. He went to sea in the British merchant marine at age 12 and by the outbreak of the Revolution was captain of the <u>Andrew Caldwell</u>, famous for bringing gunpowder to the Patriots in Philadelphia. After capture and release he was lieutenant on the <u>Congress</u> which captured English ships off

Havana. Then as captain of the <u>Independence</u> he took British ships off the Azores and then the British ship <u>Mars</u> in the English Channel. He continued this daring-do on two other ships until the end of the war. He was the first commander of the <u>Constellation</u>, which has sailed through these pages earlier. On 9 Feb. 1799 off Hen Island he took the much stronger French frigate <u>L'Insurgente</u> in the Quasi War With France, establishing the reputation of the <u>Constellation</u> mentioned earlier. For taking the <u>L'Vengeance</u> he won the Congressional gold medal. He returned to Portsmouth in 1802 to take command of the <u>Chesapeake</u>, about which we will hear from Miss Holladay in a moment. He wrote a letter concerning the chain of command which Alan Flanders tells us was misinterpreted as a resignation and left the service and Portsmouth, but his grandson, William Talbot, was commander of the shipyard in the 1880s.

The Quasi War With France started when the alliance formed during the American Revolution collapsed during the French Revolution. It did not end until 1803 when Napoleon sold the Louisiana Territory to America in Thomas Jefferson's administration. A final Portsmouth remnant of this conflict was the privateer (essentially a pirate working for the French during wartime) <u>Revanche de Ceri</u> under Captain John Jaques which had been taken by Commodore Rogers and held off Hospital Point. In 1811 it was blown up in the harbor.

A *Federal* Navy Department was created which ordered the purchase of some vessels and the construction of others. Richard Dale was put in command of one of them, the *Ganges*, the first of our vessels to get to sea. It was from this yard that she sailed in 1798.

To return to the forty-four gun frigate mentioned before, it is interesting to know that it was afterwards the celebrated *Chesapeake, although reduced to 38 guns during construction*, the first ship of the United States Navy to be built at this yard. She was launched here in 1799 and was called an unlucky ship from the start and so the end proved.

Though she went down in defeat she was not captured without a gallant fight. As this ship was a product of this yard her history has unusual interest for us and it has been briefly told in some reminiscences from which the following account is taken.

In 1794, in order to protect our commerce from Algerian pirates, Congress authorized the purchasing or building of six forty-four-gun frigates. The yard here was selected to build one of them *to be a sister ship to the <u>Constitution</u> and one of the first six ships built for the new nation.* At this time Dale was made superintendent of the yard and Josiah Fox, naval constructor or master-builder. An agent was at once dispatched to Georgia for the best pine; and by December, 1795, two thirds of the oak frames for the *Chesapeake* and most of her material were in store. The keel had been laid *on December 10 1798* and most of the frames bolted together when peace was declared with Algiers. Then came the war with France and work on the frigate was renewed; but she was cut down to thirty-six guns. It is not known why she was thus reduced; perhaps in order to build her in a shorter time. She was launched in 1799 at a cost of $220,678.80. Her first cruise was under Commodore Samuel Barron, *Commodore James Barron's brother*, to the West Indies in 1800, where she captured the *Young Creole*, and remained off Bermuda until recalled in 1801 (as we have seen, her second commander was Thomas Truxton).

In June 1807 *the Chesapeake* came to Portsmouth to be fitted out and while there a stroke of bad luck happened. Seven men declaring under oath that they were American citizens were taken on as part of her crew. When she sailed out of the Capes the British ship *Leopard* was seen hovering near. Hailing the *Chesapeake* she asked for a messenger to carry letters. The letter demanded the return of four of the sailors, recently enlisted, as British subjects.

This was a great surprise to the captain, who was James Barron, the brother of her first commandant. He refused to deliver the men. The *Leopard* then made fight, firing a shot across the bow of the *Chesapeake*. Being wholly unprepared for action the *Chesapeake* could make no reply, and remained helpless while the *Leopard* shot masts and rigging to pieces, wounded eighteen of her men and killed three more. Seeing that his men were being killed uselessly Barron hauled down his flag. She fired one shot as a matter of honor, delivered the four supposed deserters to the *Leopard* and sailed away, *but the impressing of sailors on American ships became one of the causes cited later for the War of 1812, possibly caused in part by this incident.*

A court-martial followed and *Commodore Stephen* Decatur was given command of the *Chesapeake*. The sequel to the story was of course the celebrated duel between Decatur and Barron.

The court-marshal found that Barron was not a coward and had acted in a prudent manner, but as a consequence of losing his ship at sea Barron lost the right to command at sea again, which is still the rule in the Navy. He was angry about that, blaming Steven Decatur for the order. There was already bad blood between the two men. Decatur had been one of the young captains showing off his heroism when Barron came to command the fleet in the War With the Barbary Pirates. When Barron arrived in the theater of war in North Africa he outranking the commanding officer of the fleet at that time who had promoted that behavior. Barron took command and, without a battle, managed to end the war through diplomacy. In the duel Barron shot Decatur dead. Dueling was perfectly legal at that time, but Decatur had come home from the War With the Barbary Pirates a hero, and Barron's killing him did not make him a popular figure nationally. The duel did not, however, impede his Naval career. He became the most noteworthy of the commanders of the Shipyard and at his death the ranking officer in the U. S. Navy. He is buried in Trinity Churchyard. The Commodore Theater on High Street is named for him. His home, at the north end of Middle Street, is now gone.

The *Chesapeake* had already won her name as an unlucky ship and it was difficult to find a crew for her. Officers, too, were prejudiced against her. The gallant *Captain James* Lawrence himself was much opposed to commanding her in 1812, and it was with the greatest difficulty that he manned her. The crew that he gathered together was a motley one and soon mutinied. When she met the *Shannon* off Boston *(another source says off Nova Scotia)* she had no chance of winning. She was captured after a hard fight and carried into Halifax.

The *Chesapeake* had not yet reached the worst of her humiliation; her end was ignoble. She was sold to a miller of Wickham, in Hampshire, England, who used her timbers to build his flour mill. They could be seen with the battle scars on them and probably still remain. *Alan Flanders, in another article in the <u>Currents</u> brings this story up to date telling us that this building does still exist today, but is now a pub.*

The Government now realized that the Navy Yard was indispensable so they decided to purchase it from Virginia. In January, 1800, the Legislature of Virginia passed an act authorizing the governor to convey it to the United States. Mr. *William* Pennock was to represent the Government and Mr. Newton the State in fixing a fair price for the property.

In 1801, James Monroe, as governor of Virginia, conveyed the sixteen acres of land then occupied by the navy yard to *U. S. President* John Adams and his successors in office, for the sum of $12,000, an amount considerably larger than the Secretary of the Navy had named as the price he was willing to pay. In 1827, we are told in a recent article by Lieutenant Carey, the navy yard included all the ground south of Lincoln Street and all east of Third Street to a creek (which means some point half a block from Jefferson Street) and small parcels of the creek - *perhaps Paradise Creek, may be meant*. When the Government acquired possession of such parts of Nelson, Jefferson, Fayette and Second Streets as are included in its plant, it did so without legal right, and it was not until 1833 that this land was conveyed to the Federal Government by the trustees of Portsmouth. The sum paid for it was $4,779.

During the administration of the first President George Bush the government went through a round of base closings, and the Norfolk Naval Shipyard at Portsmouth was on the list to be considered for closing. The then member of Congress from the Fourth District, Norman Sisisky, made the compelling argument that its proximity to the concentration of Naval forces at the Navy Base in Norfolk and Oceana and to the Naval aircraft at Langley and its central position on the Atlantic Coast made Portsmouth a location of more strategic value than Charleston, S. C.. This argument prevailed and the base remained, the base at Charleston being closed. It could be said that this was a bad bargain for the City of Portsmouth, if a good one for the region and the state. Along with St. Julians Creek and the state port facilities, federal and state-owned land now take almost a third of the land here off the local tax rolls, with only minimal state and no federal contribution, denying the city the use of some of its best industrial land on deep water. The counter-argument has always been the employment the shipyard provides, which was true through much of the twentieth century, but now most employees of the Yard live outside Portsmouth city limits. The influx of shipyard workers also had an adverse impact on the quality of housing in the city as we will soon hear. The Shipyard also contributed to making the Southern Branch one of the most polluted rivers in America at one time.

The Elizabeth River Project, however, formed in the 1990s with offices in Admiral's Landing at High Street in Portsmouth, has mitigated that last problem in part by removing old shipwrecks and rotting hulks, renewing the river's wetlands, demanding reduced runoff from the cities and the shipyard, with noteworthy results. When a person fell into the river, before, they would have been taken to the hospital for observation, but now people are again fishing in the river and wildlife, including porpoise, have returned to Crawford Bay.

A creosote plant south of the Shipyard has been closed; and the Project is now preparing to use a private grant to remove a pool of this noxious pollutant from the river bed.

St. Helena was purchased in 1846, for ordnance purposes, at a very reasonable price. This was due to the cleverness and foresight of Commodore Jesse Wilkerson, who foresaw the need of this tract. Commodore Wilkinson was from this section, having been born in Nansemond County and was familiar with the land and people about here. He quietly purchased this tract and held it until the government wanted it. He sold it to the government for $2,403.50. This was the same *price* that he paid for it plus the interest to date. Cedar Grove which is included in the present St. Helena, was purchased in 1900 for $135,000. Other tracts have been added to the Yard until it includes about three hundred and sixty acres on this side of the river.

The federal government, after having purchased the yard in 1801, immediately built a few warehouses and shops. In 1804 Mr. *William* Pennock, the Navy Yard agent, built a house for the commandant, *now Quarters A,* and erected the wall on the north and west sides of the yard. *Quarters A, B and C were added to the* National Register of Historic Places *in 1974. A part of this old wall, originally pierced with openings for guns but now bricked up, can be seen behind the officers' club.* The wall was finished under Commodore Stringham in 1805, thus enclosing the entire plant with the exception of the east side which was bounded by the river. From an old inhabitant of the town, Mr. Richard Hamilton, we quote the following interesting account of the patches on the yard wall in various places: "The patches on the Navy Yard wall on Lincoln and Third Streets are due to the filling in of openings in the wall—loopholes that were made during the Civil War for defensive purposes to shoot, had there been an approaching enemy. There was also a large battery on Third Street, at the corner of Lincoln, also built for war purposes, and at each end of the battery the Navy Yard wall was built up higher than the rest of the wall for protection from view, I suppose in event of the enemy capturing the battery just outside of the wall."

The first commandant to occupy the house built by order of Mr. Pennock was Samuel Barron. The present house for the commandant on Lincoln Street was built in 1824, and two others on the same street were added two or three years later. Few of the buildings now standing antedate the burning of the yard in 1861.

Some of what Miss Holladay has told us here is contradicted by the state historical marker by Quarters A and the marker in the park across from it. That says that on a map of the yard from 1827 the spot on Lincoln Street where Quarters A now stands was labeled "proposed commandant's house" (these records indicate that Captain Lewis Warrington was the first to occupy the house and it has been the home of every commandant since that time), Quarters B labeled "proposed master commandant's house," and Quarters C labeled "proposed surgeon's house."

Long before the Naval Hospital was established here there was a hospital in the yard. It was a wooden building standing at the foot of the southern drawbridge, so we learn from an advertisement in a newspaper of 1830 wherein this hospital building is offered for sale. The southern drawbridge ran from some point in the bounds of the present yard to the Berkley side. *This drawbridge was mentioned earlier.* The first commandant of the Naval Hospital as we will hear in the next chapter was Dr. Thomas Williamson, who had been surgeon in charge of the hospital at the Navy Yard on 1827.

We get a glimpse of the yard from a traveler, who tells us that four hundred men were working there, building the *Delaware* and the *New York*. Among the ships there for repair or for other purposes were the frigate *Guerriere* the sloop of war *Natches* and the *Alert*, a British vessel captured in the "War of 12" by Commodore Porter.

The *New York* for some reason was never finished and was still on the stocks in 1861. She was burned when the Yard was set on fire in April of that year. The *Alert* was captured by Porter after a fight lasting only about eight minutes.

Commodore David Porter of Boston was a midshipman on the Constellation in the Quasi War With France, taken prisoner in the War With the Barbary Pirates, but it was his capture of the Alert that made his reputation. He then went around Cape Horn on the ship Essex to the Pacific where he attacked British shipping, but was forced to surrender when faced by the Phoebe and the Cherub off Valparaiso. A man who died in Portsmouth and is buried in Trinity Churchyard, Edward Linscott, was with Porter on this expedition. His obituary says, "In action Mr. Linscott was distinguished, and at its close most grievously wounded by an explosion of cartridges . . . . he was some time after the war transported to the Gosport Navy Yard. He left a widow and three infant daughters" in Portsmouth. Porter went on to fight pirates in the Carribean, was commander-in-chief in the Mexican Navy, and died while serving as ambassador to Turkey.

One of the lieutenants who took an active part in the capture *of the Alert* was *David* Farragut, afterwards a well known admiral.

Admiral David Farragut entered service as a teenager in the War of 1812. He served in the War With the Barbary Pirates and then chased pirates in the Carribean. He was married at Trinity Church, Portsmouth, but settled in Norfolk. He transferred to New York when the Civil War broke out; he was 60 years old but continued to serve. It was in the Battle of Mobile Bay where he made his famous quote, "Damn the torpedoes! Full speed ahead!"

Later in this year—1827 in November orders were issued by the Navy Department to commence work on the stone dry dock - *dry dock number one*. The actual work began on the first day of January 1828. *The official Navy term for the dry dock is a "graving dock:" an old term for cleaning the bottom of a ship. John Quincy Adams and Congress authorized two such dry docks; one to be built in Boston and one in Gosport. Work on the Boston dock started first, but due to delays there the dock at Portsmouth was the first to be completed. They were designed by civil engineer Col. Loammi Baldwin at a cost of $974,365 each.*

This season was long remembered in Portsmouth for the mildness of the weather. Flowers and shrubs were blooming freely and the markets offered home-grown asparagus and other vegetables.

The dry dock was formally opened on Bunker Hill Day *June 17* 1833, to receive the line of battleship *Delaware*, the first of such ships to be built at this yard and the first ship ever to be docked in a government *dry*-dock; for this is the oldest dock in the country in a navy yard. *The <u>Deleware</u> was thus the first ship to be dry-docked in the Western Hemisphere.*

The *Delaware* was built here and her figurehead, which represented, Tecumseh, an Indian Chief of the Delaware Tribe, was carved by a Portsmouth carver, Mr. William Luke, who did much carving for the navy. *His house was torn down in the 1960s, but stood on the southeast corner of Court and London streets. His figurehead* was considered a masterpiece of its kind. This old figurehead has been preserved and can be seen in the grounds at the United States Naval Academy at Annapolis. *Undergraduates touch it for good luck when grades are issued.*

The Delaware, which was launched on October 20 1820, was the first 74 gun man-of-war to be built at the shipyard and the largest warship in the world at that time.

The opening of the dock was a great event in Portsmouth. Andrew Jackson who was president at the time, came with his cabinet for the ceremonies. *In fact, he visited the town twice in this period.* An interesting story is told in connection with his visit to the yard, in another part of this book.

The *North Carolina* was the next ship to use this dock. The voyage was delayed *as we will hear later* for three months, until a stock of hardtack could be provided, the first one having been lost with the bakery when it burned. The *North Carolina* was the first seventy-gun ship to repair at this yard.

In 1830 the John Adams was launched and in 1839 the sloop Yorktown.

In 1837, we again get the benefit of a visit to the yard. We are told that it at that period employed 1,200 men, all as busy as possible. At the various docks were an array of fine ships fitting out for an exploring expedition. Among them were the *Delaware, Relief, Consort, Pioneer*, and the schooner *Pilot*. The visitor's attention was particularly called to the *Macedonia*, which he described as a beautiful ship and noted that her cannon bore the insignia of George III, which made them very interesting, as they were the guns taken from the British ship *Macedonia*, captured by Decatur; the ship itself having been named in honor of that victory, was given the guns. The receiving ship at this time was the *Java*. She, too, was named for a captured British ship, in a fight of glorious memory. The *Java* was no longer seaworthy. "Her last sea fight was fought; her work of victory done." *The battle between the HMS Java and the Constitution (Old Ironsides) in December 1812 is immortalized in Master and Commander by the British Author Patrick O'Brien, and in the film based on the events surrounding it.*

In the dry dock was the *Columbian* and nearby were the frigates *Brandywine, Potomac* and *Guerriere*.

In 1847 the sloops Laurence and Perry were finished.

It was from this yard that Perry went out on the *Susquehanna* in 1851 to join his fleet for the opening up of Japan.

Japan had been closed to trade with any country other than the Netherlands until Matthew Calbraith Perry, eager to open her ports for the resupply of American whaling ships, sailed in: "On July 8 1853 four black ships, led by USS <u>Powhatan</u> (built at Portsmouth and described by Miss Holladay in a moment) and commanded by Commodore Matthew Perry, anchored at Edo (Tokyo) Bay. Never before had the Japanese seen ships steaming with smoke. They thought the ships were 'giant dragons puffing smoke.' They did not know that steamboats existed and were shocked by the number and size of the guns on board the ships." The treaty opening her ports was signed 31 March 1854.

In 1804 Capt. Stephen Decatur was sent to this yard to superintend the building of four gunboats. He was again stationed here in 1812 when his fleet was fitting out to enforce the "Embargo". In fact, so often was he quartered at this yard that this port must have been a second home to him. He was much interested in this harbor and wrote a long article about it which was published in the *American Beacon*, a newspaper whose subtitle was *Norfolk and Portsmouth Advertiser*. Though Decatur did not die in Portsmouth, he met his death at the hands of a man who had spent his boyhood in and around Portsmouth, as well as many of his later years. *We told the story of the duel with Commodore Barron earlier.*

Commodore Barron's second wife was a Portsmouth girl, Miss Mary Ann Wilson, who is remembered by many of the older people of the town. Commodore Barron's grandson, James Barron Hope, for many years editor of the *Norfolk Landmark* and a distinguished poet, was born in Portsmouth. Barron, with several members of his family, are buried in Trinity Churchyard.

In 1821, when Commodore *Lewis* Warrington was in command of this yard for the first time, he established a school for midshipmen, on the Frigate *Guerriere*, under the instruction of Chaplain Adams. Warrington was stationed here frequently and made Portsmouth his home. He built a fine brick house on First Street near the old timber dock. It was occupied by his descendants for many years. He was a member of St. John's Church and when it was building he presented it with a font, the pedestal made from one of the live oak stanchions of the old *Constitution*. The bowl, too, was of live oak. When old St. John's was torn down this font came into the possession of Dr. Gray Holladay, of this city. *It has now ben restored to St. John's Church.*

In 1850 the <u>Powhatan</u>, *which would become Perry's flagship when he entered Ido harbor,* was launched from this yard. The town made a gala day of the occasion, it being a very proud day for her. This great ship was a Portsmouth product from stem to stern. She was built by Constructor Samuel Hartt, who had made Portsmouth his home port and married a Portsmouth lady, Miss Celestia Pendleton. The *Powhatan* was designed by Mr. Francis Grice,, another constructor, who had adopted Portsmouth and was one of her prominent citizens, a founder of the Presbyterian Church here: *First Presbyterian on the northeast corner of King and Court Streets on Market Square.* He built and lived in the large brick house, 202 North Street, for many years the home of the Neely's: *the Grice-Neely House which survives on the northwest corner of North and Crawford streets, now the home of David Dixon; it has a memorial plaque.* Hartt ranked with the ablest men in the navy in his line and was one of our best citizens. He lived in an old fashioned brick house on Court, which is still occupied by his descendants: *the Hartt house, a handsome brick English basement house survives on west side of Court Street between North and Waverly Place.* He *(Samuel Hartt)* stood by his adopted city nobly when she was ravaged by pestilence in 1855. He was a member of the "Relief Committee" and rendered invaluable aid to the community.

Mr. Hartt's grandsons, William and Beverley Hartt, of Portsmouth, are at present officers in the United States Navy. *One would go on to become a much-loved Admiral and a parishioner at Trinity Church.*

The *Powhatan's* great engines were built at Mahaffy's Iron Works on First Street. *Another source, however, attributes their construction to the Gosport Iron Works, which at the time employed between three and four hundred workers. Of course, this may be another name for Mahaffy's as that foundry was in Gosport.* She was launched here in 1850; and was one of the most brilliant events that ever took place in the town. Capt. Farragut's and Lieut. Gleason's *homes* were thrown open to the public, and elegant collations were served at each house. The town was decorated and thronged with visitors. Farragut perhaps had a peculiar interest in Portsmouth; his first wife was born here in 1805, and he was married to her here by Rev. Mr. *John Henry* Wingfield of Trinity Church. Mrs. Farragut's family the Merchants went to Norfolk soon after the marriage. Farragut was stationed at this yard several times. His second wife, too, was from this vicinity, Miss Loyal of Norfolk.

Under Commodore *Silas H.* Stringham, who succeeded Commodore *John D.* Stoat, there were many improvements at the yard. This gentleman had the same views about liquor that Josephus Daniels held when he was Secretary of the Navy, and absolutely refused to serve it at his table, but he was too good an American to attempt to force his opinions on others. His dinners were lavish, the table it is said groaned under the weight of the choice viands served thereon; but many were the jokes and gibes at his expense. Like all heroes he had his need of praise, in spite of the unkind criticisms. One of the Portsmouth papers took up the cudgels in his defense and praised him nobly.

Commodore Silas Stringham, commander of the Atlantic blockade squadron for the Union Navy, conducted the first amphibious assault the Navy had attempted since the Mexican War when he landed troops under Benjamin Franklin (Beast) Butler on Hatteras Island, 27 August 1861. It was the largest Union naval operation up to that time in the war and the little Confederate fleet of surf boats, called the Mosquito Fleet, had no chance against it. Stringham's object was to capture the two forts guarding Hatteras Inlet. After a short skirmish the Confederate commander, Samuel Barron, was forced to surrender the island.

The Yard practically closed down as far as work was concerned in the summer of 1855, when the two cities were ravaged by the yellow fever. The number of men working there had been reduced from fourteen hundred to four hundred. By order of the Government the yard turned out coffins for the plague-stricken victims. So sorely were the coffins needed that when a batch of them were finished, relatives of the dead often fought for them.

The Yard soon recovered from this setback and the frigates *Roanoke* and *Colorado* were launched there. The *Dakota* was soon afterwards built, followed by the *Richmond* in 1860. The *Richmond* lived to win fame. It was this ship that led the blockading fleet up the delta of the Mississippi River in 1863. It had the distinction of serving through three wars—The Civil War first and then as receiving ship in the Spanish American War and as quarters for the Commandant of the Naval Training Station at St. Helena during the *First* World War. It was at one time Admiral Farragut's flag ship and the vessel selected to take Gen. Grant on his tour around the world.

This gallant ship returned to Portsmouth to spend her last days, first taking the place of the *Franklin* as receiving ship and later as we have said serving the Training Station. At this time she had much more the appearance of the typical Noah's Ark than of the battleship, so carefully was she housed over to make life more comfortable for the commandant's family. In 1900 the *Richmond* was towed away to the junk pile and scrapped. Like so many of her gallant predecessors. The *Richmond* is but a memory. *A photograph of her, however, survives in the library's collection.*

Speaking of receiving ships recalls memories of the *Pennsylvania*, perhaps the most noted of those who filled their posts at this port. *Her final commander in her post at Portsmouth was Hugh Nelson Page who was the last officer surviving from the Battle of Lake Erie.*

Anchored for more than twelve years off the Hospital Point, the *Pennsylvania* became part and parcel of the life of Portsmouth, taking an active part in the social life of the town. It was the *Pennsylvania's* band that was at the beck and call of all who wanted to dance—twice a week it gave a concert at the parade ground *(the junction of High and Court Streets)* and in many other ways served the people. Our mothers never forgot the balls on the *Pennsylvania* and talked of them as long as they lived. One of the young lieutenants serving on this ship fell overboard and was drowned. This was a personal grief to the community with whom he was popular. His ship mates erected a monument to his memory in Cedar Grove Cemetery, where he is buried—a pedestal with a broken column.

The *Pennsylvania* was built in Philadelphia; she was considered a fine ship and elaborately fitted out, but she had little scope for fame or adventure since she never made but one voyage—the trip from Philadelphia to Portsmouth in 1848. Why she remained so long in one port we have not been able to ascertain. Her colossal figurehead was considered a masterpiece of carving, the work of a Philadelphia artist, Mr. John Rush. It represented Hercules with his lion skin and club. The *Pennsylvania* met a tragic end, having been towed to the Navy Yard and burned with many other gallant ships on that historic night in 1861. Nor did she go to her fate without something to mark here going. Her guns, which had not been unloaded, exploded from time to time as the flames reached them, adding a horrible din to that already existing in the distracted town. Fortunately for the city but one shot did harm and that one struck the Eagle House in Gosport, causing some minor injury.

There are several pictures of the harbor in existence showing the *Pennsylvania* anchored off the Hospital Point.

In 1861 the threatening war clouds had caused much speeding up of work at the yard and by the first of April there were many ships at the wharves and in the docks; the *United States, Raritan, Plymouth, Dolphin, Cumberland, Merrimack. Columbia,. Delaware* and the *Pennsylvania* which had been recently towed there. The *New York* was also there, where she had been for half a century on the stocks.

At this point Miss Holladay repeats, in abbreviated form, her account of the capture of the shipyard by the Confederates, the building of the CSS Virginia and the subsequent loss of the shipyard again to the Union. Rather than read it again, you can turn back to the chapter on the fall of the Navy Yard. As Miss Holladay's part of this work was compiled from a series of newspaper columns, you may have noticed Miss Holladay sometimes skims over the same material again in almost the same words, and presents the material out of chronological order.

In January and February 1877 Grand Dukes Alexis and Constantine Romanov, heirs to the Russian throne, and Prince Oblinski visited Hampton Roads and on January 13 visited the Shipyard. They landed on the frigate <u>Svetlana</u> commanded by Admiral Bontakoff and on February 8th they were entertained at a grand ball.

Dry dock number two was built of wood in 1887; it would not be converted to concrete until 1933.

After the Civil War the yard gradually developed. About 1889 a new era of prosperity set in, and about this period the *Texas,* and *Raleigh* were built here and the *Amphitrite* finished. The *Texas,* launched here June 28 1892, was the first battleship in the U. S. Navy. Both the *Texas* and the *Raleigh* won fame in the Spanish American War, the former at Santiago, where with the help of the *Massachusetts,* she sank the *Reina Mercedes.* The *Raleigh* brought home laurels from the thickest of the fight at Manila Bay. The captured Spanish ship *Reina Mercedes* was brought to this Navy Yard where she was received with much pomp and clamor.

The first American submarine built for the U.S. Navy was the U.S.S. <u>Holland</u>. The second and third were the U.S.S. <u>Moccasin</u> and <u>Adder</u> launched here in 1903. A photograph survives in the library collection of Victorian ladies visiting these little submarines at the yard. Dry dock three was added in November of 1903.

On the 16th of December 1907 the Great White Fleet sailed out of The Norfolk Naval Shipyard in Portsmouth on a sixteen month world tour. It was the first circumnavigation of the globe by a fleet of warships. Teddy Roosevelt planned this as a demonstration of American Naval power. It consisted of 16 battleships all painted white, except for elaborate gilding. The first division was commanded by Rear Admiral Robley D. Evans and the second by Rear Admiral William H. Emory, the third by Rear Admiral Charles M. Thomas and the fourth by Rear Admiral Charles S. Sperry. Photographs survive in the library of various of the ships in the fleet moored at the Shipyard. Teddy Roosevelt welcomed them home at the shipyard on February 22, 1909.

The first flight deck was fitted to the U.S.S. Birmingham at the yard and Eugene B. Ely took off from it on November 14 1910 intending to land back in the Marine parade ground at the shipyard, but he finally brought his little plane down on the beach at Willoughby Spit in Norfolk.

The Yard was rapidly developing at the outbreak of the *First* World War, and as the war clouds gathered, work was speeded up.

The converted cruisers, *Crown Prince Wilhelm* and *Prince Eitel Frederick* were interned here, and the German sailor became a familiar sight on our streets. *The United States was, at this time, technically neutral and so they were not actually prisoners of war, or the ships prizes of war.*

Perhaps the most interesting thing at the Navy Yard at this time was the German Village, complete in every detail, a veritable bit of Germany amid forge and foundry. There were streets and avenues carefully laid off and named, cottages by the scores, covering a large area, each surrounded by a garden with an attractive fence. In some of the gardens flowers bloomed, while in others vegetables were raised. Almost every house had its pet; there were dovecotes, chicken coops and rabbit hutches. Everything was gaily painted and a homelike atmosphere prevailed. There was a chapel, a station house, a windmill and all the appurtenances of a real village. This remarkable little town was built practically without cost. The German sailors did the work, using scrap and salvaged material. A pass was necessary, not only to enter the yard at this period, but a special one was required to see the village. Hundreds of people visited it every day and people came from all parts of the country to see it. In front of the village the German sailors had their drilling ground and occasionally they could be seen practicing the goose-step. When work on the new dry dock commenced the interned ships were sent to the Yard at Philadelphia. The village was carefully torn down and packed, to be rebuilt in the new quarters. *A postcard of this village survives in the collection of Arthur Lerman.*

A man who worked at the Shipyard at this time put another spin on this apparently idyllic scene. Guards had noticed the Germans with wheelbarrows lingering about dry dock number one, but had thought nothing of it. After they had been transferred to internment at the Philadelphia Yard, where they built another German village, it was found they had been pouring sand around the dry dock gates in an effort to sabotage it.

By February the second the gates of the Yard which had been closed to the public for some time were put under a double guard. A number of the ships taken from Germany after the United States entered the war were sent to this Yard to be converted. Among them the *Bulgaria,* the *Neckar* and the *Rheine,* The first was re-christened *Nansemend*; the second became the *Antigone* and the *Rheine* was known as the *Susquehanna.* These ships were added to the transport fleet.

All during the period of World War *One* an immense amount of work was going on at the Yard. Forces were busy day and night; *three new* drydocks were built, *a shipbuilding way, twenty-four major ships completed* and activities of all kinds were carried on. *Dry dock number four was completed on April 1 1919, dry dock five was never built (although the number was reserved) and dry docks six and seven were opened on October 31 1919. They were engineered by the Fleet Emergency Corps, then part of the U. S. Shipping Board chartered by Woodrow Wilson.* In December 1917 there were nearly eight thousand men employed there, with a yearly payroll of eight millions of dollars. *Miss Holladay does not tell us, or may not have known, that women were employed for the first time at the shipyard in this effort. A photograph survives of some of them. By* January, 1919, there were a little over eleven thousand men *and women* employed with a payroll of about fifteen millions. *Employment went up from 2,718 in 1914 to a top employment of 11,234 in 1919.*

Of course, the city housing could not handle such crowds of workers and so in 1919 the United States Housing Corporation, created in Woodrow Wilson's term as President, built two communities; both were put on the Register of Virginia Landmarks in 1966 and placed on the Virginia Landmark Commission's <u>Registry of Historic Places</u> in 1974. Then part of Norfolk County, but now part of Portsmouth, built to *accommodate the influx of workers, they were the first planned military housing communities in the nation.*

The planned community built for whites was Cradock, named for the British admiral, Sir Christopher Cradock, who was commander of the combined allied fleet in the Atlantic in World War I. A painting of him hangs in the Cradock Branch Library and a relative visited on the city's 250th birthday celebration in 2002. Laid out on land belonging to the Barclay family the new town was designed by George Post and Sons of New York City, aided by the engineering firm of Hill and Ferguson and by A. L. Sheeler, who settled in the new village. A photo of its construction is also in the library. Cradock was laid out in the form of an anchor, its entrance (the shaft of the anchor) being Afton Parkway, the axis Prospect Parkway and the crossbar at its top being George Washington Highway, with Cradock High School (now a higher education center) across from the community. The curve of the anchor surrounded the central square with its bandstand, restored in 1999; there was a post office, now closed, fire hall, shops and movie theater called the Afton, opened in September 1937. Its grocery was Chapman's and it even had its own bar: the Academy. It was a self-sufficient little community with all the amenities of a small town. After school in the 1940s the students would stop at Red's Drug Store on Afton Square. Spaces were left for churches of every denomination, and elementary and middle schools. Among the churches built were the Episcopal church, Emanuel, which is still a mission. The Roman Catholic Church of the Holy Angels (said to have been named for its nearness to Paradise Creek) was started as a modest mission of St. Paul's Catholic in Portsmouth in 1919 at Gillis and Phelps roads. It became an independent parish and was expanded in 1933 on land acquired at the corner of Afton Parkway and Prospect Parkway, when it became independent, and took its current form in 1950 and was again expanded in 1987. The Presbyterian church and the Methodist church also rose from modest beginnings to become the handsome buildings you can see today off Afton Parkway.

A streetcar line ran down Afton Parkway to the shipyard. A bridge to the shipyard was planned, but never completed. Many of the street names memorialize naval heroes: Burtis, Cushing, Decator, Erickson and Farragut Streets: Gillis, Harris, roads: and Irving, Jenner Places. On its south is Paradise Creek.

The area was innovative for the time in the location of its electrical lines away from the street fronts, electric street lights and water and sewage lines.

Some of its notable citizens have been Tommy Newsome, long-time bandleader on the Johnny Carson Show on late night television; John Casteen, President of the University of Virgina; Harvey Bryant, City Attorney for Virginia Beach and Randi Strutton who spearheaded the creation of the Hoffler Creek Wildlife Preserve mentioned earlier.

Cradock has inspired great loyalty and is the site of frequent "Come Home To Cradock" celebrations. A renovation project was initiated there by the city in 2005. It has an annual flag-raising on July 4th and a popular "starving artists" show.

The Yard also hired African Americans, which resulted in a great migration from rural North Carolina of immigrants hoping to replace stoop labor or tenant farming with something more rewarding; but this was still a time of segregation. Although blacks and whites had lived next to each other in the city of Portsmouth (Mayor Holley grew up in Olde Towne), the government built a separate village for the black shipyard workers called Truxton, named for Admiral Truxtion, whom we met earlier in this book. Promotion was still limited for blacks in the Yard, but that would soon change, and Truxton would be the home for what would become Portsmouth's strong black middle class. Such later leaders of the community as Horace Savage, educator and manager of the Vann Lefcoe management workshop, would be born there. Mr. Savage's father worked 44 years for the shipyard and was one of the first purchasers when the property was given up by the government; and his grandfather, Thomas Tucker, was the Truxton Town Council President. This would spawn the other predominantly black middle and upper class section of the city: Cavalier Manor, the first of the nation's wealthy black suburbs.

Truxton was located on what was then called Key Road, now Portsmouth Boulevard. It was made up of 250 five-room homes on an 87 acre site and was to have had a business district like Cradock, but that was never completed. Part of the land it was built on was owned by J. A. Codd, a farmer and butcher. The Codd home, built in 1880, is still standing at 3325 Deep Creek Boulevard.

The head of the U. S. Housing Corporation, L. K. Sherman, called it an experiment to be watched. It was designed by the Norfolk architectural firm of Rosell Edward Mitchell with the assistance of the then City Planner, H. P. Kelsey. Many of the homes here were duplexes of as little at 800 square feet, with three rooms downstairs and two bedrooms and a bath above. The houses rented for $17.50 a month. When the war ended the whole was sold to two African American businessmen.

Among its early inhabitants were a teacher Edna Falls Atkins whose grandson and granddaughter became noted physicians; Delores Overton who was long-time Registrar for the city, and George Moody who was football coach for Norcum High School, Virginia State University and Elizabeth City State University and who is still active in city development projects, as we will see much later.

Truxton soon had its own church. In 1921 Portsmouth ministers realized they needed more room to accommodate the influx of shipyard workers. A Baptist congregation of 25 began worshiping in Truxton School, and by 1925 started building a small church, known as "the little white church on the hill," but officially called First Baptist Church. In 1938 it changed its name to Mount Carmel Baptist. Its new building was completed at 3310 Deep Creek Boulevard in 1945.

The really unique thing about the houses in both Truxton and Cradock was the fact that they did not look prefabricated. There were a number of component pieces which could be fitted together in 50 different ways so that they appeared to have different designs. Each was built on a 50-foot-square lot. The original report of the Housing Corporation, with plans and elevations, survives in the library collection. Cradock was added to the _National Register of Historic Places_ in 1974 and Truxton in 1982

After World War I ended the government withdrew support and the houses were opened for private purchase. There was a failed effort to incorporate the village as a separate town in Norfolk County, but it opened a school covering the first through the eleventh grade in 1920 with 16 teachers and 546 students. It willingly annexed itself to Norfolk County in 1922 and in 1960 it was annexed by Portsmouth.

In the 1920s the Navy Yard built six battleships: *Texas, Nevada, New York, Arizona, Mississippi,* and the *Idaho,* but its most famous ship of this period was the *Langley* built in 1919. It was the nations first aircraft carrier

In December, 1920, the number of employees had dropped to seven thousand, while the payroll was over twelve and a half millions. When the King and Queen of Belgium visited the United States in 1919, the *George Washington*, the Presidential ship which had been put at their service, was docked at the Yard while they traveled through the country. On the 31st of October, 1919, the King and Queen came to Portsmouth and were present at the flooding of dry docks 6 and 7.

"Today," *(1935)* says Lieutenant Carey, "this yard stands in equipment, facilities and accessibility unsurpassed by any other establishment in this country as a naval repair plant. Approached by Hampton Roads, with a channel forty feet deep, and a width at minimum of four hundred and fifty feet, ending at the south of the yard in a turning basin, large enough to accommodate the largest ships afloat, this yard is equipped to build, dock and repair such vessels as the *Majestic* and the *Leviathan* on down to the lesser tonnage of liners.

"The yard also manufactures turbine blades, paint, buoys, gas engines, metal furniture, gas for industrial purposes, coal and oil burning ranges and small boats."

Lieutenant Ashbrook has recently discovered that the nine o'clock gun was first instituted by Rear Admiral Stephen Rowan in 1866. He has been unable to find anything before that date concerning this all-important feature of the yard. However, there are old citizens of the town today who are prepared to say that it sounded their bed hour some seventy years ago or more *(1860).* Lieutenant Ashbrook probably meant that the gun ceremony was restored in 1866. In 1909 or thereabout, Admiral Taussig stirred up a hornets' nest when he issued an order abolishing the nine o'clock gun. "The entire population of both cities rose in an uproar. The affairs of the community could not be regulated without the cannon's roar at nine o'clock. Delegations were sent to the Navy Department to protest, but Admiral Taussig would not come to terms. He could not be made to understand that, as one paper said, "From a time to which the memory of the oldest inhabitant did not reach, the nine o'clock gun had been a sacred rite. It had been a thing to set watches by, and to those who had no watches an admonition to get to bed. Shirt-sleeved men immersed in the fury and heat of the game would lay down a queen full to see if their time was right; and young lovers in shady places were warned to break away. The whole town adjusted itself to the nine o'clock gun."

In March, 1910, Admiral Marshall won the affection of the entire community by restoring the nine o'clock gun. Great was the rejoicing when its warning boomed again. It is thought in the two cities that it will take a very bold and daring admiral ever to issue another order to silence that beloved gun.

Research since Miss Holladay's time places the start of the cannon in 1847. It was only silenced for a few months, after Miss Holladay's time, when a rear-admiral said it disturbed a child. It fell silent again when the Marines, who had protected the base since the formation of the Marine Corps., and fired the gun, were replaced by paid guards, but public complaint brought it back again. After the terrorist attack on the Twin Towers in New York City the Navy used that catastrophe as another excuse to silence the 44 mm gun for "security reasons." Since then it was used only to signal the completions of major projects. The Navy did, however, agree to resume firing the gun in 2004, but has apparently again reneged on that promise. It is a shame that the tragic loss of life in the Twin Towers has been misused so often to justify unconnected decisions. There remains a tug-of-war between the Navy and the community which loves the nine o'clock gun and considers it an important part of the town's patriotic legacy.

In 1933 the National Industrial Recovery Act, giving work to the unemployed, commissioned the Yard to build nine destroyers: <u>Tucker, Downes, Bagley, Blue, Helm, Rowan, Stack,</u>

Morris and the _Wainwright_. On October 16 of the same year Admiral Richard E. Byrd departed from Portsmouth for his famous Antarctic expedition.

On November 25 1941, before America entered the war, a British aircraft carrier damaged by German dive-bombers off Malta entered the Shipyard for repairs. Her commanding officer was Lord Louis Mountbatten, the great-grandson of Queen Victoria. He would later become Supreme Allied Commander in Southeast Asia, and after the war Viceroy at the time India and Pakistan were granted independence and a close confidant of his nephew, Charles Windsor, Prince of Wales. He would eventually be killed when his yacht was blown up by the Irish Republican Army in the Irish Sea. While Mountbatten's ship was at the shipyard it was visited by the Duke of Kent: the King's brother.

Admiral Simons built the Yard up until in 1944 it reached a peak employment of 42,893.

The twenty-story-tall hammerhead crane which is the most visible mark of the Yard - it can see and be seen from almost 15 miles - was started in December 1939 and completed in June 1940 in preparation for the U. S. to enter the Second World War. It is designed to lift 350 tons and has been used to lift sixteen-gun turrets onto battleships, the entire superstructure of a Liberty ship and tugboats. The apparently small crane on top of it can actually lift 25 tons and is used to repair the larger crane. The Hammerhead crane is the largest in the world.

In July 1942 dry dock number eight was completed to accommodate the massive keel of the battleship _Kentucky_. That ship, however, was never completed. To get an idea of the size of the modern dry docks at the yard one has held fourteen ships in it simultaneously: ten submarines and four target ships housed in dry dock four in October 1920.

During World War II the shipyard built 101 major ships including the aircraft carriers _Tarawa_ , _Shangi-La_ and _Lake Champlain_; battleships _Alabama_, _Kentucky_; the escort immortalized in song _Reuben James_, sunk October 31, 1941 by a German U-boat (before Pearl Harbor). The old song goes: "Tell me their names/Wont you tell me their names/ Did you have a *friend on the good Ruben James." A postage stamp was issued commemorating the loss after the war. The <u>Shangri-La</u> got its name from the Japanese reaction to James H. Doolittle's raid on Tokyo. The Japanese could not imagine where the airplanes had come from and Roosevelt said they came from the mythical Himalayan valley of Shangri-la from the novel <u>Lost Horizons</u> by the British author James Hilton. The carrier was christened at the shipyard by Doolittle's wife with 100,000 in attendance and and listened to by millions on the radio. President Franklin D. Roosevelt himself visited the shipyard during the war.*

During the war, apart from its major ships the shipyard repaired, or built 6,850 other U. S. and allied vessels including 20 tank landing ships and 50 medium landing ships for the invasions in Nromandy and on the Japanese held islands in the Pacific. the shipyard now encompassed 747 acres with ten miles of shoreline. Employment at the shipyard in 1940 reached 43,000 - larger than the population of the city when the war broke out.

The impact of World War Two Naval construction on the city was mixed. The housing built for workers was very cheaply constructed and not sufficient to accommodate all the workers. This purpose-built housing was privately built by Frederick Beasley, not intended for long-term use, and quickly deteriorated to substandard; but it was not replaced until sixty years later when the last remnant of what had been called Academy Park, and later was called Fairwood Homes, was torn down to make room for better housing, an office park and the proposed site of the Tidewater Community College campus, to be moved there from Suffolk. The private, segregated, golf course, Bide-a-Wee, was also purchased by the city and upgraded to municipal golf links.

In 1938, to address the need for worker housing Portsmouth built the first public housing projects in Virginia: Dale Homes and Swanson Homes.

The overflowing number of Shipyard workers were on their own to find places to live. The citizens of old Gosport, now Southside, began to rent out parts of their homes, in patriotic zeal at first and then for profit, to the workers; even back porches were rented. The crowding soon caused the owners of what had been handsome homes to move to better parts of the city and become absentee landlords in their old neighborhood. When the war was over they did not want to return to their now-ruined old dwelling. They rented them out to the poor until the area became one of the most notorious slums in Hampton Roads.

The Rev. Mr. C. Charles Vaché, rector of Trinity Church, finally shamed these owners by reading their names at a Rotary Club meeting, where some were in attendance. Little objection was then made to the city accepting a Federal Government grant to clear cut that whole part of the city, good and bad, and make the vacant land into the industrial park now called Port Center. Much of Portsmouth's history fell under that wrecking ball and it was several decades before the area again generated any tax revenue.

In the Korean War the employment at the Shipyard rose from 9,000 to 16,100; two ships, the Bold and Bulwark, (wooden-hulled non-magnetic mine sweepers) were completed and 1,275 ships were repaired.

In 1956 the yard's largest dry dock, number 8, was expanded to accommodate the largest warships in the world at the time.

The shipyard was certified to repair nuclear submarines in 1962 and the nuclear submarine Skate was overhauled at the Yard in 1965. The Skate was the first to transit the Atlantic completely submerged and the first to surface at the North Pole. In 1968 the nuclear submarine Scorpion received the least costly and fastest overhaul in the history of the Navy, but was lost at sea later in that year.

The U. S. Congress decided ship building would be moved to commercial yards, like the Newport News Shipbuilding & Drydock Co., now Northrup-Grumand, and the Naval shipyards would be used only for repair. Portsmouth did benefit somewhat from this decision, however, in that it still has some private shipbuilding at what was the old Moon Engineering at the foot of Harper Street on Scotts Creek, since 2004 a part of Earl Industries and National Ship Repair and Construction Corp. opened in the city in 2000.

The most memorable event in the Vietnam War was the fire on the aircraft carrier Forrestal off Viet Nam on 23 July 1967 with the loss of 134 lives. Portsmouth citizens gathered at the High Street waterfront to watch her pass on her way to the shipyard. The damage was obvious, but the crew in their summer whites stood in a proud line on the margins of her decks as she limped into the Yard.

A detailed history of the Yard in the first half of the twentieth century can be found in a clipping file assembled by wives of officers in the yard, now in the public library.

The center of the Yard has always been the parade ground for the public called Trophy Park, near the old Marine barracks. This barrack was the second oldest Marine barracks in the nation, the oldest being the one in Washington, D. C..

Trophy Park now houses relics of all America's wars at sea including: Perrott rifles from the Civil War used on the Kearsarge, the sidewheeler Florida, the Franklin in the 1870s, some cannon recovered from the wreck of the Sumter and the training ship Wyoming,; Dahlgren guns and shells from the Trenton, Wyoming, Chimo/Piscataqua, Tennessee, Enterprise in the 1880s, William G. Anderson, Mahopac,, the Pennsylvania about which Miss Holladay told us earlier, the iron gunboat Richmond of which we heard earlier, the Sabine from the 1870s, and the Constellation of which we also heard in the section on the War of 1812; among other ordinance is a 32 pounder from the Congress, lost in its battle with the CSS Virginia (Merrimac), the Huron lost off Nags Head, and many others from more recent wars.

In the past the park with its handsome bandstand was open to invited guests for summer concerts on its broad lawn, and events; the officers' club was used for wedding receptions and meetings by the townspeople and the historic trolley tour regularly visited its collection. Security concerns since the attack on the Twin Towers on September 11, 2001, however, has closed the Yard to most civilians.

In 1987 The commander of the Shipyard revealed a plan for cooperation between the town and the Shipyard. He proposed a garbage-fueled power plant built by the Navy which would resolve the city's waste disposal problem and create needed power for the Shipyard. This arrangement worked well until Congress ordered military bases to divest themselves of any in-house power generation. The facility was turned over to the regional waste authority SPSA in 1999.

A love-hate relationship with the city has existed at various times in the Yard's history. Distancing the shipyard again from the community which has faithfully hosted it since before America was a nation by silencing the nine-o'clock gun and restricting access to Trophy Park seems a sad and perhaps unnecessary outcome of the tragedy of September 11, 2001.

The Portsmouth Naval Shipyard Museum, founded in the shipyard in 1949, was moved to one of the old ferry buildings at the foot of High Street in 1963 with its longtime director Marshal Butt senior, the historian of the town. His successor is Alice Haynes and the museum is now a part of the Portsmouth Museums department.

A small park was opened in 2006 across from Quarters A between Lincoln and WAVY streets just outside Shipyard gate three. It was created as part of the "Path of History" in commemoration of the first landing of English settlers in Jamestown in 1607. It contains two massive <u>Cimarron</u> class oiler propellers cast in 1981. These 28 foot wide 75,000 ton screws enabled the ships to make 20 knots. This class of oilers serviced the fleet's aircraft carriers until the class was upgraded in 1987 from five-thousand to seven-thousand five hundred gallon capacity. It also has large naval guns taken from scrapped ships, including a gun from the German battleship <u>Ostfriesland</u> which was given to the United States after the First World War as a part of war reparations, used as a bombing target, and finally sunk off the Virginia coast July 20-21 1921. The most impressive exhibit is the superstructure of a submarine. The park has illustrated markers outlining the history of the Shipyard. Unfortunately this excellent historical park is remote from tourists on foot, parking at the entrance is limited by Lincoln Street being a no parking zone and the nearby parking lot is restricted to workers at the yacht repair facility. The yacht repair yard, visible from the park, is interesting in its own right. Quarters A and the Hammerhead crane can be clearly seen from the park. Should the historic trolley tours be reinstated it would certainly be a popular stop: particularly if other exhibits were moved there from Trophy Park.

COMMANDERS OF THE SHIPYARD

Captain Richard Dale 1794 to July 1794
William Pennock July 1794 to 30 April 1798
Captain Thomas Williams 30 April 1798 to 16 July 1799
Captain Samuel Barron 16 July 1799 to August 1799
William Pennock August 1799 to 26 April 1802
Daniel Bedinger 26 April 1802 to 10 February 1808
Theodorick Armistead 10 February 1808 to 7 July 1810
Captain Samuel Barron 7 July 1810 to 10 November 1810
Lieutenant Robert Henley 10 November 1810 to 1 May 1811
Captain Samuel Evans 1 May 1811 to 10 August 1812
Captain John Cassin 10 August 1812 to 1 June 1821
Captain Lewis Warrington 1 June 1821 to1 December 1824
Captain James Renshaw 1 December 1824 to 25 May 1825
Captain James Barron 25 May 1825 to 26 May 1831
Captain Lewis Warrington 26 May 1831 to 7 October 1840
Captain William B Shubrick 7 October 1840 to 1 October 1843
Captain Jesse Wilkinson 1 October 1843 to 1 October 1846
Captain Charles W. Skinner 1 October 1846 to 1 June 1847
Captain Lawrence Kearney 1 June 1847 to 19 January 1848
Captain John D. Sloat 19 January 1848 to 17 February 1851
Captain Silas H. Stringham 17 February 1851 to 1 April 1852
Captain Samuel L. Breese 1 April 1852 to 10 May 1855
Captain lssac McKeever 10 May 1855 to 6 May 1856
Captain Thomas A. Dornin 6 May 1856 to 30 April 1859
Captain Charles H. Bell 30 April 1859 to 1 August 1860
Captain Charles S. McCauley 1 August 1860 to 20 April 1861
Captain Robert B. Pegram 21 April 1861 22 April 1861 (Virginia State Navy)
Captain French Forrest 22 April 1861 to 1 July 1861 (Virginia State Navy)
Captain French Forrest 1 July 1861 to 15 May 1862 (Confederate States Navy)
Captain Sidney S. Lee 15 May 1862 to 20 May 1862 (Confederate States Navy)

Commodore John W. Livingston 20 May 1862 to 16 November 1864
Captain John M. Berrien 16 November1864 to 31 October 1865
Commodore Robert B. Hitchcock 31 October 1865 to 7 August 1866
Rear Admiral Stephen C. Rowan 7 August 1866 to 15 August 1867
Commodore Augustus H. Kilty 15 August 1867 to 1 October 1870
Rear Admiral Charles H. Davis 1 October 1870 to 1 July 1873
Commodore Thomas H. Stevens 1 July 1873 to 1 July 1876
Commodore J. Blakeley Creighton 1 July 1876 to 1 July 1879
Commodore Aaron K. Hughes 1 July 1879 to 3 July 1882
Commodore William K. Mayo 3 July 1882 to10 April 1885
Commodore William T. Truxton 10 April 1885 11 March 1886
Commodore George Brown 11 March 1886 to 14 January 1890
Commodore Aaron W. Weaver 14 January 1890 to 16 January 1893
Captain Edward E. Potter 16 January 1893 to 29 July 1893
Rear Admiral George Brown 29 July 1893 to 1 June 1897
Rear Admiral Norman H. Farquhar 1 June 1897 to 5 October 1899
Rear Admiral Albert S. Barker 5 October 1899 to 16 July 1900
Rear Admiral Charles S. Cotton 16 July 1900 to 1 April 1903
Rear Admiral Purnell F. Harrington 1 April 1903 to 7 July 1906
Rear Admiral Robert H. Berry 7 July 1906 to 26 December 1907
Rear Admiral Edward D. Taussig 26 December 1907 to 20 November 1909
Rear Admiral William A. Marshall 20 November 1909 to 1 November 1911
Rear Admiral Robert M. Doyle 1 November 1911 to 1 December 1913
Rear Admiral Nathaniel R. Usher 1 December 1913 to 25 Sept 1914
Commodore Louis R. deSteiguer 25 Sept 1914 to 4 January 1915
Rear Admiral Frank E. Beatty 4 January 1915 to 25 November 1915
Rear Admiral Walter McLean 25 November to 4 February 1918
Rear Admiral Augustus F. Fechteler 5 February 1918 to 10 April 1919
Captain Benjamin F. Hutchison 10 April 1919 to 15 November 1919
Rear Admiral Guy H. Burrage 15 November 1917 to 1 July 1921
Rear Admiral Philip Andrews 1 July 1921 to 6 June 1923
Rear Admiral Henry J. Ziegemeier 6 June 1923 to 10 January 1925
Captain Clarence S. Kempff 10 January 1925 to18 May 1925
Captain William T. Tarrant 18 May 1925 to 16 November 1925
Rear Admiral William C. Cole 18 May 1925 to 2 July 1928
Rear Admiral Wat T. Cluverius 2 July 1928 to 31 May 1930
Rear Admiral Frank H. Brumby 31 May 1930 to 28 Sept 1932
Captain William N. Jeffers 28 Sept 1932 to 14 February 1933

Rear Admiral A. St. Clair Smith 14 February 1933 to 23 July 1935
Rear Admiral Charles S. Freeman 23 July 1935 to 15 October 1937
Captain Lawrence P. Treadwell 15 October 1937 to 22 November 1937
Rear Admiral Manley H. Simons 22 November 1937 to 17 June 1941
Captain Lawrence P. Treadwell 17 June 1941 to 1 August 1941
Rear Admiral Felix X. Gygax 1 August 1941 to 19 October 1944
Rear Admiral Carl H. Jones 19 October 1944 to 1 December 1945
Commodore Lisle F. Small 1 December 1945 to 1 November 1946
Captain Noah W. Gokey 1 November 1946 to 19 March 1947
Rear Admiral Homer N. Wallin 18 February 1949 to 15 February 1951
Rear Admiral David H. Clark 15 February 1951 30 June 1953
Captain William H. Leahy 30 June 1953 to 11 August 1953
Rear Admiral Logan McKee 11 August 1953 to 13 September 1956
Rear Admiral George A. Holderness, Jr. 13 Sept 1956 to 30 June 1958
Rear Admiral William H. Leahy 30 June 1958 to 29 June 1960
Rear Admiral William E. Howard, Jr. 29 June 1960 to 28 June 1963
Rear Admiral James M. Farrin 28 June 1963 to 30 June 1965
Rear Admiral James A. Brown 30 June 1965 to 27 June 1970
Rear Admiral Jamie Adair 27 June 1970 to 24 June 1972 who settled in Olde Towne and became a central figure in many of the city's charities.
Rear Admiral Randolph W. King 24 June 1972 to 22 June 1973
Rear Admiral Joe Williams, Jr. 22 June 1973 to 31 August 1974
Rear Admiral Elmer T. Westfall 31 August 1974 to 25 June 1977
Captain Alfred Kurzenhauser 25 June 1977 to 26 July 1980
Commodore David P. Donohue 26 July 1980 to 29 April 1983
Captain Michael R. Gluse 29 April 1983 to 12 June 1987
Captain Edward S. McGinley 12 June 1987 to 11 May 1990
Rear Admiral James L. Taylor 11 May 1990 to 12 August 1994
Captain Willam R. Klemm 12 August 1994 to 8 August 1997
Captain Timothy E. Scheib 8 August 1997 to 18 August 2000
Captain Mark A. Hugel 18 August 2000 to 7 November 2003
Captain Joseph Campbell 2003 - 2005
Captain Richard D. Berkey 2005 -

Chapter 28 - The Naval Hospital

When Quarters C was relocated in the hospital expansion in 2000, Native American artifacts were found. This may mark the site of the abandoned Indian village described by Captain John Smith on the southern bank of the Elizabeth River in his survey in 1608.

The point was originally a part of the 1636 plantation of William Willoughby granted him by King Charles I.

At the outbreak of the Revolution the Patriots built a fort near Portsmouth for the protection of the harbor *as we have seen in the chapter on the American Revolution.* The point selected for its erection was known as Windmill Point *(or Tucker's Mill Point)* and was then the property of William Tucker Esq., of Norfolk; and was a part of the patent of Joshua Curle, from whom Tucker purchased it. When the purchase was made this tract was known as Mosquito Point; but the Tucker family, who owned it for three generations, built windmills on it and it thus acquired its new name.

The third Robert Tucker, by will, desired that this land be sold to pay a gambling debt which he had incurred while visiting in Williamsburg. He tells us he had perhaps taken more wine than he should, and had fallen into the hands of sharpers who had soon done for him.

It seems that his wishes were not carried out as far as selling Mosquito Point to pay the debt *was* concerned; this land was not sold until 1749 or thereabouts.

The land occupied by Fort Nelson was a part of the estate of Robert Tucker, and later of his son-in-law, Thomas Newton, until 1799, when it was sold to the United States government. We learn that at the time that *Royal Governor* Lord Dunmore bombarded the towns of Norfolk and Portsmouth that there were two large bake-houses and several windmills on the point and all of them were injured by Dunmore's cannon. These bake-houses were a good investment in the old days for in them was baked the hard bread or hardtacks which supplied the ships of the day with bread *that was slow to spoil* for their long voyages.

When Fort Nelson was completed the point was renamed Fort Point, or sometimes Musket Point. For a history of the fort in its earlier days we are indebted to Sir George Collier, whose capture of it in conjunction with General Matthew took place in 1779. *This is covered in more depth in an earlier chapter "The Revolution - Collier's Raid."*

He declared it to be of amazing strength: the parapet fourteen feet high and fifteen feet thick. It was surrounded by strong timbers dovetailed—the middle part being filled with earth hard rammed. There were forty-two embrasures in the fort; and there were a great number of heavy cannon and an immense amount of ammunition; as well as large stores of food to be found on hand.

Admiral Collier goes on to say that when the order came to evacuate Portsmouth in May 1779 that all attempts of troops and battery failed to demolish the fort, and fire had to be resorted to before its destruction could be accomplished.

Here we have the first recorded quarrel between Norfolk and Portsmouth. Just what the point at issue was we do not know; but we are told that it delayed the work for some time. We get another glimpse of Fort Nelson in 1809, when we learn from Simmons' *Directory of Norfolk* that Fort Nelson on the Portsmouth side of the river was a star fort, occupying about six acres of ground and holding a commanding position. At this time, it was undergoing extensive repairs; it had a bomb-proof magazine and they were now mounting forty-two pieces of ordnance.

Several places on the point have been designated as the site of this old fort, but a survey made by the old Revolutionary soldier Jesse Nicholson has recently been brought to light, and gives us the position of the fortification. It stood on the point but farther down than the present hospital building. At this time a small creek separated the land on which the Medical Director's house and the officers' houses stand from the point on which the hospital is situated. *During the building of the new addition to the hospital in 2000 the commandant's house was moved from its location by the beach adjacent to the point onto the southern side of the point itself and the other quarters were removed. It was said at this time that the quarters had been returned, by chance near to the place where the original quarters had stood. I am not sure, however, where they stood in Miss Holladay's time but her text suggests it was in the same spot it was before the 2000 renovation: on an extension of Swimming Point Walk just north of the current bridge.* There is a drain now that shows where the water *from the old creek* once ran.

The land on which these quarters stand was not then the property of Fort Nelson or of the Government but was owned by Richard Nestor, whose claim to it is obscure. He had purchased land from Thomas Edwards across Island Creek on Swimming Point in 1787 but Island Creek separated the two tracts. The land when first purchased by the Government was used for a powder magazine.

When the British left and the Americans returned to Portsmouth the fort was hurriedly rebuilt, but we find no further details concerning it until 1794 when the Government of the United States sent an engineer, J. Ulrich-Ricardi to lay off plans for the fortification of this harbor and Congress appropriated three thousand dollars to build Fort Nelson and Fort Norfolk. *Only Fort Norfolk survives in the twenty-first century.*

Island Creek was named for an island of small size which stretched out east of the Hospital bridge and for a smaller one in the middle of the creek which then reached almost to the land now occupied by the King's Daughters' Hospital. *Much has changed here since Miss Holladay's time, but the bridge remains. It was once used by the citizens of Portsmouth to picnic on the hospital grounds and swim off its beaches. It has, however, been closed for fifty years. There are photographs of Victorian ladies and gentlemen swimming on the beach at the other end of the bridge on Hospital property in the library collection. The remains of the filled-in creek still can be seen in the back yards of people in the houses on the southern border of the hospital property and it makes building on that land impracticable.*

The King's Daughters' Hospital Miss Holladay refers to was built with private money raised by the women of Trinity Church. It later became the not-for-profit Portsmouth General Hospital which had its entrance at the east end of Leckie Street between that street and Parkview on land now occupied by a very large apartment complex, built there in 2005. The creek must have run through this land just outside the Naval Hospital's main gate. The hospital was bought in the 1990s by Bon Secours hospital group, which had just acquired Maryview Hospital. It was purchased with the intention of demolishing the older hospital to eliminate competition. This closing and demolition was a matter of bitter controversy, as many doctors and citizens felt it gave better service than Maryview and that the city needed more than one hospital. Among its most active opponents was Dr. Emil Sayegh. Since it was not-for-profit its assets did not revert to any existing organization and they are administered by a Foundation (the Portsmouth General Hospital Foundation) whose first director is Alan Gollihue, its income to be used for projects promoting the health and well-being of the city.

There was no connection between Fort Nelson and Portsmouth *in the early years*. No bridges had been built and to reach it from the town it was necessary to go by way of Fort Lane, and when the Government took over the site for the Naval Hospital, Fort Lane was claimed as private property and the United States had to buy the lane.

In 1811 there were five hundred men barracked at Fort Nelson.

No vestiges of the old fort remain on the Hospital grounds, but physical Fort Nelson, if we may term it, still lives in our town: nearly six hundred thousand bricks from the fort were used in building the *King's Daughters'* hospital and much of the stone *was used to repair* the *north* wall of Trinity Church which was rebuilt in 1829. *An additional mass of brick from the old fort was used in the foundation of the Naval Hospital.*

The site of the fort has been marked by a monument placed there by the Daughters of the American Revolution *and one of its chapters in Portsmouth is named for the old fort.*

It is not the brick and stone of Fort Nelson that we love,

but the historic memories that cling to it which appeal to us. We go back to those May days in 1779 when Admiral Sir George Collier and Gen. Matthew sailed into our harbor. Again in the War of 1812 when the British attacked Craney Island there was a skirmish at the fort but they were soon driven off.

The glory of Fort Nelson waned, the building of Fortress Monroe had made her useless, and she was given over to decay and actually offered for sale.

After considerable looking around for a site for the hospital which was to be built for the convenience of the men and officers of the United States Navy, the government decided to buy Fort Nelson and steps for its purchase were commenced in January 1827. Soon after this decision the old fort was demolished and the construction of the hospital commenced. Its cornerstone is dated April 2, 1827.

It may be interesting to know just where the funds for the erection of naval hospitals come from and how they are supported. The Naval Hospital fund, says Captain Richmond Holcomb in his interesting history, *A Century With the Norfolk Naval Hospital*, grew out of a tax imposed upon the pay of officers, seamen and marines of the United States Navy. *This tax was suggested by a similar tax in the British Navy which supported the construction of the naval hospital at Portsmouth, England.*

For many terms the matter of raising money for hospital purposes was discussed in Congress and the various bills met with more or less opposition. An act for this purpose was finally passed by Congress in 1798. This act, however, only applied to seamen on merchant vessels and twenty cents a month was deducted from their pay for this tax.

In March 1799 the act of the previous year was made to embrace the governmental and the naval service as well. The same amount of money, twenty cents, was deducted from the pay of every seaman, officer and marine. The fund accumulated for years before any steps were taken to build the hospitals. The first of them erected was the Naval Hospital at Portsmouth, which, as we have said, was commenced in 1827. This predates the Naval Medical Service. At this time doctors worked for the military served as private surgeons under contract to the government

In March of that year, the Hon. Samuel Southard, Secretary of the Navy, with Commodores Bainbridge, Warrington and Morris, with other naval officials and the Hon. James Barbour, Secretary of War, arrived here on the 18th of March and selected the actual site for the building. *The park encompasses 112 acres.* In December 1826 John Haviland, a well-known architect of *the firm of Wood, Don and Deming in* Philadelphia, had drawn the plans for the hospital. He came to Portsmouth to take charge of operations. He received the munificent sum of two thousand dollars a year salary and was allowed forty dollars a month for a clerk.

Haviland's job was an arduous one, but he stuck to it and in the course of some years the hospital was ready for service, and in 1830 *it* received its first patients.

The building was in the form of a hollow square, the front of it extending one hundred and seventy-two feet. Its most remarkable feature was the magnificent Doric portico, with its ten columns. Leading up to this porch were twenty steps running the whole ninety feet of its length. This portico remains today as it stood originally. The hospital was constructed of freestone and granite and was fireproof. The roof was covered with Welsh slate. As the construction of the hospital advanced, it was necessary to appoint a surgeon to work with the architect, and Dr. Williamson, then on duty at the hospital in the Navy Yard, was appointed to act as adviser. *The resulting building is thought to be the finest Federal Period building in the South. Its most innovative detail is the use of what appear to be Greek Revival triglyphs, but are actually windows illuminating the operating room.*

Several ghost stories center on this building. There is an area under the entrance called the "dungeons" from which strange sounds are heard. The two new hospitals have also gathered ghost stories. The Hospital's first war casualties came from the Mexican War in 1847.

The old building was added to the <u>National Register of Historic Places</u> in 1972 and rededicated October 11, 2002

as administrative space and renamed Naval Medical Center, Portsmouth.

In 1830 Dr. Williamson was appointed as surgeon in charge and ordered to get the hospital in readiness for patients. Dr. Williamson's term of office was short; in less than a month, he received orders to sail on the *Brandywine*.

Dr. Williamson again held command of the hospital in 1831. Indeed, he served many terms there and eventually made Portsmouth his home. He married Miss Caroline Doulton of Portsmouth and lived on London Street in an old-fashioned Dutch-roofed house *(a tax-dodger style house which no longer stands)*. They had a large family and some of their sons became prominent men. Dr. Williamson had a large private practice here and was much beloved and respected in the town.

In 1830, when Dr. W. C. P. Barton succeeded Dr. Williamson, there were many changes made in the management of the hospital. Dr. Barton evidently had a leaning towards economy; and it is interesting to know that he succeeded in feeding the patients and servants in the hospital at the rate of 12 ½ cents a day each. So pleased was he with the result of his calculation that he cut the rations of officers and men as well.

There were the pleasantest of relations always between the hospital and Portsmouth. In 1835, when the Seaboard *Railroad*, or, as it was then, the Portsmouth and Weldon Railroad, had its first accident the hospital sent a relief squad up the road to help the doctors attend the wounded; and twenty year later, in 1855, when the yellow fever raged in the town, the Naval Hospital opened its doors to the orphaned children of its victims. The little temporary hospital which had been built in the town was soon filled to overflowing and the citizens of Portsmouth sent a delegation to Washington to ask that the *Naval* hospital be turned over to the city. The request was granted and in addition to the use of the building the surgeons on duty there were to remain and help care for the fever patients.

The orphans were removed and the sick brought in. There were about two hundred patients there throughout the period of the epidemic.

The commanding officer at this time was Dr. Lewis Minor, and under him were the following surgeons, Randolph Harrison, James F. Harrison, Frank Anthony Walke, John C. Coleman, and Thomas B Steele.

The Common Council of the Town of Portsmouth in February 1856, directed that gold medals with suitable devices and inscriptions should be presented to the Surgeon of the Hospital and his assistants. At the next meeting of the Council fifteen hundred dollars was appropriated for this purpose, and the medals were made. On one side was a relief of the old Hospital; on the other was the inscription "Presented by the Council of the Town of Portsmouth, Virginia." One of the metal patterns or models for the medals is in possession of the writer's family; but only one of the medals is known to be in existence today. One of them we learned was pawned by its owner, then a Confederate soldier, while on duty in Petersburg, who was anxious to get a sufficient sum of money to pay his way home while on furlough. It was never redeemed. *A second medal came into the possession of one of the antique stores on High Street in 2004. A photograph of the medal is on display in the Path of History park by the hospital gate.*

Dr. Minor was much beloved in Portsmouth and interested in all that concerned the town. His last years were spent in Norfolk and at his own request he was buried in the Hospital cemetery.

One other Commandant of the Hospital was buried there, Dr. James F. Harrison, who after the Civil War was for many years Professor of Surgery at the University of Virginia.

In 1861 the Surgeon in charge was Dr. Samuel Barrington, who caused some embarrassment by his attitude at the outbreak of the War. He was a Northern man and it was hardly possible that he was going to throw in his lot with the South, and yet he made no effort to declare his status. The story goes that a committee was appointed to wait on him and ask his intentions. The result of this step was the resignation of Dr. Barrington.

On the 20th of April, 1861, the Dismal Swamp Rangers, Marion Rifles, Grimes Battery and National Grays, *three days after secession* the Third Virginia Regiment marched to the hospital Point and took possession. Two days later they compelled Barrington to resign and Dr. Blacknall who had commanded the Hospital from 1839 to 1842 was again made surgeon in chief. He died while on duty in 1862. Dr. Blacknall who was a North Carolinian by birth had married Miss Blow, a Portsmouth lady.

The Hospital Point as we have said was fortified and again called Fort Nelson, and so listed in official reports; for one brief year the Confederates held the Hospital and were then forced to evacuate and the Stars and Stripes once more floated over the reservation.

In 1865 thirteen hundred patient were being treated at the hospital.

Miss Holladay skips on to the Spanish American War, but the history of the hospital on its official website adds some details. By 1877 the number of patients fell to an all-time low and the Navy was unwilling to pay for officers ashore and afloat, almost closing the facility, but by 1883 the number of patient had risen to 26, among them a four-year-old boy, Malcolm MacArthur, whose younger brother, Douglas, would become commander of American forces in the Pacific in World War II. Unfortunately, Malcolm did not survive.

Scott's Creek began to see more traffic, the north side as a precursor to the Portsmouth Marine Terminal, and the south side whose piers led directly to the hospital grounds. By 1889 city water was available across Gashouse Creek, where Fort Nelson Park now stands, and the marsh and so the hospital no longer needed to rely on its cisterns. In 1890 the "Russian Grippe" filled the hospital. Two years later electricity came to the hospital, replacing the gaslight.

To the staff were added six volunteer women nurses, maintained by the Daughters of the American Revolution and five Sisters of Charity from St. Vincent's Hospital, Norfolk. A number of local surgeons offered their services without pay and one of them was selected for this duty, Dr. Gray G. Holladay, who served at the hospital during the term of the *Spanish American War*.

A number of Spanish prisoners in need of treatment were brought to this Hospital *(55 sick and 48 wounded)*, among them Captain *Victor M.* Concas, who had been in command of the *Infanta Maria Teresa*, the chief of staff of the Spanish squadron *as mentioned in the chapter on the Spanish American War*. Admiral *Pasqual* Cevera twice visited the Hospital during this period. He was at the time himself a prisoner at Annapolis and applied for leave to visit his men. Several of the Spaniards died and were buried in the old cemetery.

While the Spanish prisoners were at the Hospital a detachment of marines were encamped upon the Hospital reservation to guard them, and many restrictions placed upon the freedom of the grounds; they were open to the public to a very limited degree.

The first hospital ship, the <u>Solace</u> was launched at Newport News and sailed out from Portsmouth's Naval hospital to Cuba during the Spanish American War.

The X-ray was invented in 1895 and the hospital had one the next year - it was operated by wet-cell batteries.

Many years ago the medical director of the day placed a fence across the bridge which connected the Naval Hospital with Swimming Point *Walk*, now Crawford *(since change to Craford)* Place. In the fence was a small gate which he ordered locked at a very early hour against all civilians.

The director remained obdurate when asked to remove the fence and refused to change his original order. Then one of the citizens living on Swimming Point immediately extended his fence across the walkway leading to the bridge, thus causing much inconvenience to all those connected with the Hospital staff. At this time the entrance at Fort Lane and the bridge alluded to were the only ways of reaching the hospital.

Some years later the hospital grounds were closed again to the public, and so great was the indignation in the town that Congressman *Horace* Maynard *of Tennessee who son was a Naval hero of the Spanish American War* reported matters to the authorities, and by order of the Navy Department the grounds were reopened.

Access through this bridge was again closed in the 1950s and after the Twin Towers disaster in 2001 access to the hospital grounds by civilians has been severely restricted. This put an end to the 1970s bicycle route designed there and elsewhere in the city by City Planner J. Brewer Moore.

The next event of interest in connection with the hospital was the project to widen the river at the Point. This was accomplished by removing about four hundred feet at the Point. The old lighthouse which stood there had been blown down in the "August storm" in 1879.

The new bridge was built about this time. The land has been much extended by filling in and the little islands that gave the name to the creek were submerged in the process of filling in.

The Army and Navy Union *(the Veterans of the Spanish American War)* had erected a shaft in memory of deceased comrades in the cemetery and in May 1906 the monument was unveiled by President *Theodore* Roosevelt. *Theodore Roosevelt's visit to Portsmouth appears in a photograph in the library collection. It is hard to make him out without magnification. He is in an open Victoria carriage in a parade on what appears to be Court Street at its intersection with Bart.*

Another monument to the Spanish American War veterans stands in the median at the intersection of North and Crawford streets and a roster of some of the Portsmouth men who served in that war is framed in the library local history room. At the end of the inscription on the back of the Crawford Street monument is a reference to the "relief of Peking," modern day Bejing. The Portsmouth Shipyard, as mentioned earlier, was home to the second oldest Marine barracks in the nation, after the one in Washington, D. C.. Marines from that barracks participated in the relief of the embassies there in the Boxer Rebellion and a Portsmouth man, Wendell Cushing Neville of the Fourth Marine Regimen, was awarded a Marine medal for his service in this campaign and another Portsmouth man, Joseph Mitchell, the congressional Medal of Honor. While in China Neville served in the battle at Tientsin. After the rebellion was suppressed he served as military governor of Basilan in the Philippines. He won the Congressional Medal of Honor for his service in Nicaragua and at Vera Cruz. Returning to China he commanded the combined forces in Peking in 1915. He was appointed Commandant of the Marine Corps on March 13 1929.

The Boxers wanted to drive all Westerners out of China, and surrounded the British, French, German, Russian, Japanese and American embassies in Bejing. The dowager Empress Tsu Si, probably agreeing with their motives, refused to intervene and so America sent a detachment of Marines to save the ambassadors. This substantially increased the stature of the United States in the eyes of the world powers and may have been a factor in Teddy Roosevelt being selected to mediate the treaty ending the Russo-Japanese War.

This day, *the visit of Teddy Roosevelt,* was a gala one in Portsmouth. A general holiday was declared; there was a grand parade in which the President rode. He made a speech from the portico of the hospital and the grounds were thronged with those who wished to do him honor.

At this time the two residences for junior officers were erected near the house of the medical director. Since then a number of houses have been built to accommodate others connected with the staff. *All of these were removed in the construction of the new three-hundred-million-dollar hospital addition in 2000.*

In 1898 President William McKinley authorized the creation of the Hospital Corps. The first corps School to train corpsmen in nursing and healthcare was opened at the hospital on January 17, 1898. This corps would turn out to be one of the most decorated in the military service.

In 1899 aspirin was prescribed for the first time here and the roads on the grounds were "reshelled," that is new oyster shells were laid on them. It was said they showed "most beautifully" on a moonlit night. Of course, these roads are now paved. Some of the roads in the town were also paved with oyster shell.

In 1902 the school of instruction was formed. Quarters B and C were built in 1909.

One of the landmarks of the hospital grounds was the "Pest House", an old wooden building west of the main building, near the beach. This barn-like structure was used, of course, for isolating smallpox patients or those with other contagious diseases. *It was called "Cubicle Two" by the Navy. Typhoid fever was treated here as well.* When exposed to *smallpox* in the wards, half the staff would contract the potentially deadly disease.

In 1907 the Pest House came into high repute as the main building of the hospital. The Naval Hospital was to be reconstructed and orders had come to vacate it. Several other buildings had been added and this forlorn spot had become a lively, though a tiny, village. *An unexpected appropriation came to renovate the old building; patients and doctors were moved to tents behind the building where they remained through a severe winter and storms. The renovation gutted the building, but the old doors, trim and marble mantles were returned. Elevators were added, but they were not big enough for stretchers. Patients on their way to the operating room could, however, now be carried up inside stairways, rather than the outside staircases used before. Inside plumbing was also added to each ward. By the time the interior work was finished almost 1,400 patients had been treated in the outdoor tents.* The whole interior of the building was wrecked *Miss Holladay says*, only the outer walls remaining intact. Those were added to, and the general effect of the Hospital remains pretty much as it was originally. The *Jefferson* dome was, of course, new. *From 1910 through 1940 the main operating room was under this dome. The building was reopened in February 1909.*

In 1908 the Congress adopted a law creating the Navy Nurse Corps and permitting women to serve (previously they had served only as volunteers). The only rank created for the was "nurse." The first twenty women recruited were called "the sacred twenty." Of this group three came to serve at the Portsmouth Naval Hospital in 1909. One of them, Lenah Higbee, became the chief nurse at Portsmouth and later went on to become the second Superintendent of Nursing for the U. S. Navy. It was not until 1964 that men were allowed to join the nursing corps.

By the end of the 1908 the number of female nurses rose to 35. These nurses were housed in the Waverly Apartments, where the new house is now, on the Hampton Row side of Court Street between Waverly Boulevard and North Street. They received vouchers to eat at the restaurant in the building. The Waverly *was the first apartment house built in Portsmouth. It was built in 1909 by L. B. Watley. It later became Parish Memorial Hospital where many Portsmouth babies first saw the world. After that it was converted into a hotel and torn down in the 1960s.*

In 1910 the Naval hospital was again expanded, and a water tower and the power plant with its distinctive chimney added. The old porters' housing was converted into housing for the Marines who guarded the gate.

In 1937 a resident and intern program was added.

A lot of history and construction has taken place in this little idyllic-looking parkland, in view of two major cities, since Miss Holladay's time. I will make a short summary of it at the end of this section.

When the *First* World War came, the Hospital became a small town *with 34 wooden patient pavilions and four new barracks. In one month in 1917 the patient load rose from 200 to 1405. In October 1918 the hospital housed 2,257 patients - half of them suffering from measles and mumps.*

We cannot close our survey without some mention of one of its most interesting features—the old cemetery. The first cemetery was outside of the reservation and the date of the establishment of the present one is not known *(the Navy now places it at 1828)*, but the oldest stone there bears the date of 1838. It marks the grave of an Englishman, George Butler, who fell from the yard of the ship *Constitution*, while coming to anchor in the harbor.

In old days there was a brick wall around the cemetery but this has been replaced by a privet hedge. *Among the 840 burials* there are *113* graves of unknown dead, among them forty-five Confederates. There are also twelve other graves of Confederates whose names are recorded. Captain Holcomb, in his very interesting book, *A Century With The Norfolk Naval Hospital (in the library collection)*, says: "Perhaps no cemetery in this vicinity can claim so romantic a background, for here are inscriptions in English, French, German, Russian and Japanese."

Side by side men lie sleeping who fought on both sides of the conflict in the War Between the North and South, and men who fought on both sides of the Spanish-American War as well as men who belonged to the armed forces on both sides during the Great War *(World War One)*.

Upon the stones of many of these graves are found the names of some of the oldest ships of the United States Navy. Many evidences are afforded of old titles of the Navy now fallen into disuse, such as "Captain of the Forecastle." "Captain of the Afterguard" and "Captain of the Foretop."

Several graves tell part of the story of the visitation of yellow fever. Most notable of these graves is that of a French naval officer, Vincent Louis, serving on the French ship *La Chimere*, then in the harbor. This stone recalls the fact that when the *La Chimere* was in the harbor here there were many cases of yellow fever on board and Dr. Williamson, surgeon in charge of the Hospital, and his past assistant surgeon, James Harrison, were assiduous in their attentions to the stricken. The Emperor of France awarded gold medals to both officers who, by Act of Congress, were permitted to receive the medals in 1856.

In one plot is a cairn of stone, surmounted by a pillar and an urn. This monument was erected to the dead of the *Cumberland* and the *Congress*, three hundred and thirty seven of them as the result of the first day's work of the Ram *Virginia*. "This simple cairn," says Capt. Holcomb, "does more than afford monument to the three hundred and thirty seven officers and men, because it also marks the death of the wooden frigate and the birth of a new epoch in naval warfare characterized by the armored ship and the turreted gun." *It was the custom for a ship to surrender if it lost ten percent of its crew to enemy fire, but the <u>Cumberland's</u> refusal to strike its colors resulted in a loss of 55 percent of its crew before it went to the bottom. The <u>Congress</u> did strike its colors after going aground, but Union soldiers from the shore continued to defend the ship with their fire and so the <u>Virginia</u> fired hot shot into her, signaling an end to the gentler rules of war at sea.*

In another part of the cemetery stones mark the graves of three Germans, one officer and two men. They died at the Navy Yard; Dr Perrenon of the interned ship *Kronprinz Wilhelm* and the others were members of the crew of the *Prinz Eitel Friedrich*.

As we wander on, our attention is caught by four black crosses with inscriptions in Russian. They mark the last resting place of four Russian sailors who died here in 1877 when Grand Duke Michael visited *Portsmouth.*

There are a hundred graves that are marked *Huron.* This ship sank off the Carolina Coast in 1877, in one of the storms. It was in order to aid this ship that Capt. J. J. Guthrie, one of our citizens, formerly an officer in the United States and then of the Confederate States Navy, lost his life. At the time of his death Capt. Guthrie was superintendent of the Sixth Life Saving District. *The Life Saving Service was the predecessor of the Coast Guard and its history will be told in the next chapter.* In 1915 it became a part of the Coast Guard. Capt. Guthrie's wife was Miss Louisa Spratley, of Portsmouth. His son, Dr. Joseph Guthrie was a surgeon in the United States Navy and served through the Spanish American War.

The graves marked with Chinese names simply refer to "messmen" and the romance of shipwrecks and war does not reach them. Two graves are marked. with Japanese characters. There is also an English inscription on each one. At the base of one of these shafts is a small oil cup. It is customary, we are told, in Japan to place these receptacles on the graves and at night they are lighted. There are five Brazilian sailors interred here, having died of beri-beri while attending the Jamestown Exposition *in 1907.*

The cemetery is no longer used for burials, having been closed at the time of the *First* World War, It is beautifully kept and twice a year at least the graves are decorated; on Confederate Memorial Day and on Decoration Day, *or they were in Miss Holladay's time.*

The first Congressional Medal of Honor winner to be buried here was James Avery, so honored for saving crew members of a Union ironclad, but his grave was forgotten until 1990 when it was rediscovered and his name added to the list of Medal of Honor recipients in the cemetery - there are now three.

As World War I began, 40 temporary wooden buildings were added. In the first year of the war the hospital averaged

1,405 patients in residence. It soon rose to 2,250 with only 60 physicians, 80 nurses, 250 corpsmen and 30 yeomen.

When the war ended the great influenza epidemic began - 5,300 Navy men died of it by October 1918. A rumor went around that whiskey was a cure, but there was none as a result of Prohibition. The Governor of Virginia ordered police to sell it for $1.29 a quart and the Portsmouth police station was mobbed. It could be argued that this is the origin of the idea of the ABC (Alcoholic Beverage Commission) stores of today. It was certainly the impetus for the popularity of auto-racing in Virginia. Cars were rebuilt to make the run up from North Carolina to Portsmouth on the Dismal Swamp road faster than any police car.

The Parkview Gate was opened in 1918. The next year a railroad line was extended to the hospital across Scott's Creek.

Veterans were treated for the first time in 1921 under the Veterans Benefit Bill.

The first electrocardiograph was added in 1926. Many new quarters were added, but all were demolished in 1991 to make room for the new hospital. A boathouse was in use to ferry patients until the opening of the Downtown Tunnel. A "Radio Room" was added to entertain the patients - the most popular show being "As the World Turns."

The Second World War brought a $1.5 million expansion. This brought the capacity of the hospital to 3,441 beds and a dental clinic and library were added. The staff rose to 3,055 In August 1944 the patient load fell to 2,997 a day.

At the end of the war the hospital was selected to supervise Medical Discharge Boards for the Veterans Administration, and in 1944 certified a young pilot named George H. W. Bush, later President of the United States, after a physical examination at the hospital.

President Jimmy Carter was also at the Naval Hospital, but as an enlisted man - he would not be President for another thirty years.

A new $15 million building was planned in 1955, to be called simply Building 215. Many old buildings, including Quarters A, were moved to accommodate the expansion, and the high-rise building so visible from the town was finished and opened on 22 April 1960. At seventeen stories it became Hampton Roads first skyscraper and the tallest welded steel frame building between New York City and Miami. It had five hundred beds, a cobbler shop, a navy exchange, a full galley and an auditorium. Many thousands of Navy babies were delivered in this new wing and delivering babies to armed services wives and enlisted women is still one of its major services.

At the close of the Viet Nam War in 1973, 12 former prisoners of war were treated in the new building and a plaque and pictures of them added. The 1960 building is now used primarily for out-patient services and the old building for administration.

In the 1990s work was begun on the $330 million dollar new building and parking facility, the lower red brick structures visible from the city with green roofs. It was completed in 2000 and named the Charette Health Care Center. It was named for Master Chief Corpsman William R. Charette who served with the First Marine Division in the Korean War. He refused to abandon the patients he was working on under hot hostile fire and won the Congressional Medal of Honor. The new building has seventeen operating rooms, three-hundred examining rooms, three-hundred and twenty beds, one hundred and forty special treatment rooms and twenty-six elevators. A long cry from the days when patients were carried up outside stairways by stretcher-bearers in the early days of the hospital.

The hospital, one of three in the nation, now has a staff of 4,000 doctors, nurses, corpsmen, medical officers and civilians and serves 430,000 active duty military, retired military and Navy dependents.

Personnel for hospital ships in the war in Kuwait and in the war in Iraq have been drawn from the Naval Medical Center Portsmouth (the new name given the Portsmouth Naval Hospital after its renovation and expansion).

It is certain Portsmouth will have a poignant connection to all future wars in which the United States Navy will participate.

Just outside the Naval Hospital gate on the corner of Effingham Street and Crawford Parkway a small park was *dedicated on October 12 2006 and called Fort Nelson Park. This is planned to be a stop on the "Path of History" in celebration of the 400th anniversary of the landing of the English at Jamestown. This little park, with an excellent view of the hospital, has a 49,000 pound cannon, Naval anti-aircraft emplacement, buoys and fourteen illustrated markers outlining the history of the hospital.*

For many years citizens of the Olde Towne were used to waking up to revile broadcast from the hospital and taps to lull them to sleep at sunset, but this custom seems to have been abandoned since the 2000 expansion.

COMMANDERS OF THE NAVAL HOSPITAL

1830 Thomas Williamson, Surgeon
1830 William P. C. Barton, Surgeon
1839 George Blacknell, Surgeon
1842 Thomas Williamson, Surgeon
1850 N. C. Barrabino, Surgeon
1852 Thomas Williamson, Surgeon
1855-1858 Lewis W. Minor, Surgeon
1858-1859 Ninian Pickney, Surgeon
1859 Samuel Barrinton, Surgeon
1861 George Blacknell, Surgeon (CSA)
(April 20, 1861 Possession of Confederacy, Retaken by United States, May 10 1862)
1862 Solomon Sharpe, Surgeon
1864 Andrew Henderson, Surgeon
1867 Joseph Wilson, Jr., Surgeon
1869-1872 Marius Duval, Surgeon
1872-1875 Samuel Jackson, Medical Director
1875-1880 Charles Martin, Medical Director
1880-1880 Albert L. Gihon, Medical Director
1880 James Suddards, Surgeon
1883-1886 John Y. Taylor, Surgeon
1886-1887 Delaven Bloodgood, Medical Director
1887-1888 Michael Bradley, Medical Inspector
1888-1891 Christopher J. Cleborne, Medical Director
1891-1894 Thomas N. Penrose, Surgeon
1894-1899 Christopher J. Cleborne, Medical Director

1899-1902 Nelson M. Ferebee, Assistant Surgeon
1902-1906 Remus C. Persons, Medical Director
1906-1909 Phillips A. Lovering, Medical Inspector
1909-1911 William R. DuBose, Medical Director
1911-1913 Charles T. Hibbett, Medical Director
1913-1917 George Pickrell, Medical Director
1917-1921 Leckinski W. Spratling, Captain
1921-1924 George Pickrell, Medical Director
1924-1926 Charles M. DeValin, Captain
1926-1930 Richard C. Holcomb, Captain
1930-1934 James C. Woodward, Captain
1934-1937 Isaac S. K. Reeves, Captain
1937-1940 Richard A. Warner, Captain
1940-1942 Edgar L. Woods, Captain
1940 Dallas G. Sutton, Captain
1943-1943 Daniel Hunt , Captain
1943-1946 Griffith E. Thomas, Captain
1946-1947 William W. Hargrave, Captain
1947-1948 William H. H. Turville, Captain
1948-1950 Albin L. Lindall, Captain
1950-1953 Caldwell J. Stuart, Captain
1953 Gordon B. Taylor, Captain
1953-1955 Sterling S. Cook, Rear Admiral
1955 George N. Raines, Captain
1955-1957 Ocie B. Morrison, Jr., Rear Admiral
1957-1959 Walter H. Schartz, Captain
1959-1963 Hubert J. Van Peenan, Rear Admiral
1963-1964 Martin T. Macklin, Rear Admiral
1964-1972 Joseph L. Yon, Rear Admiral
1972-1974 Willard P. Arentzen, Rear Admiral
1974-1975 Harry P. Mahin, Rear Admiral
1975-1978 William J. Jacoby, Jr., Rear Admiral
1978-1979 Carl R. Bemiller, Captain
1979-1981 George E. Gorsuch, Rear Admiral
1981-1983 Norman V. Cooley, Rear Admiral
1983-1986 John N. Rizzi, Captain
1986-1988 Leon Carey Hodges, Jr., Captain
1988-1990 Charles M. Reinert, Captain
1990-1992 Daniel B. Lestage, Rear Admiral
1992-1995 William J. McDaniel, Rear Admiral
1995-1998 William R. Rowley, Rear Admiral

1998-2000 Marion J. Balsam, Rear Admiral
2000-2002 Clinton E. Adams, Rear Admiral
2002-2005 Thomas K. Burkhard, Rear Admiral

CHAPTER 29: THE COAST GUARD BASE

For this short history I am much indebted to William H. Thiesen, Atlantic Area Historian for the Coast Guard.

Portsmouth was headquarters of the Sixth Life Saving District when that service, which was one of the predecessor to the Coast Guard, was created in 1874. Mr. John J. Guthrie was its first superintendent.

The district was responsible for protecting everything maritime, from the entrance to the Chesapeake Bay to Cape Hatteras on the Outer Banks of North Carolina. It was made up of ten stations: Dam Neck Mills with its commander Bailey Barco whose gold lifesaving medal can be seen at the Virginia Beach museum of the service in its old station, and False Cape in Virginia, Jones Beach, Caffeys Inlet, Kitty Hawk Beach, Nag's Head, Bodie (pronounced as if it were body) Island, Chicomicomico and Little Kinnakeet in North Carolina.

On 18 June 1878 the United States Life Saving Service was made a separate organization under the Department of the Treasury. The President appointed Summer I. Kimball as the first General Superintendent, and the number of stations in all the districts was increased. Some of Sixth District life savings stations can still be seen. The one at 24th Street on the beach at the ocean front is now a museum of the service, as is the one at Chickomicomico on Hatteras Island. The latter not only preserves the station, but its surfboat houses and breaches buoy as well. The Life Saving station at Ocracoke is still in use as a Coast Guard station. In the Sixth District each station had a keeper and as many as six surfmen, the number required to haul out and man one surfboat. These men were required to live in the station from 15 April to 15 December every year. They would patrol the beach on horseback exchanging a chit with the surfman from the next district as proof that they had completed their rounds. They were supplied from Portsmouth.

The Light House Service, which would also become a part of the Coast Guard, was a separate service. It acquired a boat depot in Portsmouth in 1870. The base served as a docking point for lighthouse boats and buoy tenders. This Fifth Lighthouse Service District at Portsmouth served the coast from Maryland to New River, North Carlina. In 1891 an additional buoy yard was added. That old buoy yard remained in service where the nTelos Pavilion now stands into the 1970s. Portsmouth resident Captain Barry Howe, later commander of the tall ship <u>Eagle</u>, recalled there were some large hollow buoys the men did not like placing near the spot where the Chesapeake Bay Bridge Tunnel now runs. When they were hauling in one of these they noticed a fish caught in it. They began to argue light-heartedly about who would take home that fish. Then when the whole buoy was out of the water and dumped on the deck hundreds of fish spilled out and everyone ate heartily when they returned to the yard in Portsmouth. The facilities here were called the Portsmouth Lighthouse Service Depot until 1925.

In 1939 the Lighthouse Service merged with the Coast Guard, and facilities here changed their name to Coast Guard Base Portsmouth. The base at Portsmouth supplied 100 lighthouses and lightships with coal, kerosene, water, food and every other necessity and luxury. The base also maintained all other "Beacons and other minor lights."

The Lighthouse Service is remembered on the Portsmouth waterfront with the big old Second Order Fresnel lense from the Hog Island lighthouse off the Easter Shore mounted in its own enclosure by the seawall. It was the light of the second lighthouse there in 1896. The lighthouse is gone and the island under water now. Earlier in this book the lighthouse which stood on Hospital Point in Portsmouth was mentioned.

The first lightship in the nation was placed off Craney Island on July 14 1820. The early years of that lightship and its first commander were told in the chapter about "Portsmouth Veterans of the War of 1812." The service of that gallant ship is the reason why Portsmouth was selected as a site for the

Lightship Museum in 1967; lightship 101 "Portsmouth" built by Dusey and Jones and added to the <u>National Register of Historic Places</u> in 1989 stands proudly at the foot of London Street and is now a part of the Portsmouth Museums and remains on the list of active lights.

In 1915 the Life Saving Service was merged with the U. S. Revenue Cutter Service and reconstituted as the United States Coast Guard. The Cutter Service had been first requested by Alexander Hamilton in 1780. One of the officers from this services Portsmouth, Captain Travis, was mentioned in the chapter on the War of 1812. This merger made the old services more military in their management and a commissioned officer became its superintendent.

On 6 April 1917, during the First World War, a coded message was sent from Washington to every shore station and in the district advising them of the absorption of the services into the Navy for the duration of the conflict.

In 1939 the Coast Guard Reserve was created, but quickly renamed the Auxiliary, offering training to civilians, and a true Reserve, modeled on that of the Navy was created.

This is the same year the Lighthouse Service became a part of the Coast Guard.

In Hampton Roads the Fifth Coast Guard District was called the Norfolk District, but in 1941, as the United States entered World War Two, the Coast Guard was again made a part of the Navy and the old name was dropped, and the new name was Fifth Coast Guard District in Norfolk. For the duration of the war the harbor pilots were also brought in as Temporary Reserves to the Coast Guard. Technically Portsmouth was considered a part of the Ports of Norfolk. The Coast Guard station, however, despite its name, was still in Portsmouth.

The District served bravely in many fires and torpedoing on the coast during the war. At the end of the war the Coast Guard was returned to the Treasury Department and the name became just The Fifth Coast Guard District. John E. Whitbeck was the first commander of the district after the war. A full list of the commanders appears at the end of this chapter.

When the Department of Transportation was created in 1967 the Coast Guard reported to that department, ending its long association with the Treasury Department.

In 1971 the Marine Safety Office was created to control recreational boating in the Chesapeake Bay, and it is with that part of the Guard the regular Portsmouth citizen has most direct contact. The Marine Safety Officer is also the Captain of the Port. Starting in 1973 this office had responsibility for shipping from the Delaware-Maryland border to Ocracoke Inlet on the Atlantic Coast.

In that same year ground was broken by Admiral Edward C. Allen and U. S. Senator William B. Spong (a Portsmouth native) for the new Coast Guard Base at Craney Island. This is still the home of the Fifth Coast Guard District fleet.

In 1984 the U. S. Coast Guard Area Commander took on maritime defense for the coast with escort, interdiction, port security and surveillance.

The most decorated ship in the fleet, the cutter _Ingham_, was decommissioned at Portsmouth. She had been in service since 1936 and had 18 ribbons on her flying bridge. She is now at the Maritime Museum at Patriots Point, South Carolina.

In 1990 the Coast Guard celebrated its 200th birthday (the founding of the cutter service) by commissioning two ships, the _Forward_ and the _Legare_, at Portside (North Harbor) in Portsmouth.

In 1993 our district conducted 10,500 search and rescue missions and protected three hundred million dollars in property.

The Atlantic Area and Maritime Defense Command, which oversees all Coast Guard operations in the eastern United States, was relocated from Governor's Island off New York City, in 1996 and merged with the 5th District command in Portsmouth. The Governor's Island base was then closed.

As a reslult the three-star admiral in Portsmouth became both commander of the 5th District, in Portsmouth and of the entire Atlantic Area command. His office is in the Federal Building on Crawford Street at High.

The Atlantic command is responsible for an area

encompassing 39 states from the Canadian border to the Gulf of Mexico and west into Wyoming with more than 5 million square miles of ocean, inland waterways and tributaries. It has 2,300 active duty personnel, 1,200 reservists and 6,800 in its auxiliary. It has 38 cutters, helicopters and airplanes and manages them through ten teams and 7,000 aids to navigation. Some of its daring rescues at sea, and dangerous interdiction of the drug trade, can be seen on video.

In 2004 the Coast Guard, including the base at Portsmouth, became a part of the Department of Homeland Security.

The two commands, Atlantic Area and Fifth Coast Guard District, have again been separated, but both still have their headquarters in Portsmouth.

COMMANDERS OF THE FIFTH COAST GUARD DISTRICT IN PORTSMOUTH

1920	Lt. Commander Delef Frederick Argentino deOtte
1924	Captain Andrew James Henderson
1926	Captain Francis Saltus VanBoskerck
1928	Captain Phillip Henshaw Scott
1932	Captain Benjamin Maurice Chiswell
Sept. 1932	Captain William Joseph Wheeler
1934	Captain Roger Chew Weightman
1937	Captain Thaddeus Greaves Crapster (his family settled on North Street at the corner of Dinwiddie)
1940	Captain William J. Keester
1947	Commodore John E. Whitbeck
1950	Captain Lee Baker
1952	Rear Admiral Russell E. Wood
1956	Rear Admiral Harold C. Moore
1959	Rear Admiral Peter V. Colmar
1961	Rear Admiral Henry J. Wuensch
1964	Rear Admiral Oscar C. Rohnke
1967	Rear Admiral Edward C. Allen, Jr.
1971	Rear Admiral Ross P. Bullard (buried in Trinity churchyard)
1975	Rear Admiral Julian E. Johansen (later mayor of the city)
1978	Captain Gilbert L. Kraine
1979	Rear Admiral Thomas T. Wetmore, III

1981	Rear Admiral John D. Costello
1984	Rear Admiral James C. Irwin
1986	Rear Admiral Bobby F. Hollingsworth
1987	Rear Admiral Alan D. Breed
1989	Rear Admiral Paul A. Welling
1991	Rear Admiral W. Ted Leland
1994	Rear Admiral William J. Ecker
1996	Vice Admiral Kent H. Williams (5th District LANTAREA)
1997	Vice Admiral Roger T. Rufe (5th District LANTAREA)
1999	Vice Admiral John E. Shkor (5th District LANTAREA)
2001	Vice Admiral Thad W. Allen (5th District LANTAREA)
2002	Vice Admiral James Hull (5th District LANTAREA)
2003	Rear Admiral Sally Brice-O'Hara
2005	Rear Admiral Larry L. Hereth

CHAPTER 30: A CITY OF NEIGHBORHOODS

This is an appropriate moment to list the history of Portsmouth annexations in old Norfolk County. The city is really a collection of neighborhoods, each with its own character and history. Miss Holladay will describe some of them as we continue in this chapter.

The first annexation to Colonel Craford's town was in 1762 when the lands of Thomas Veale were added and the original town extended to what is now Chestnut Street. On October 18 1784 Gosport was taken in. Parkview, as we will see, joined the list on February 23 1894. In 1909 Scottsville (West Parkview and Shea Terrace) and Prentice Place were added. On March 21 1919 Port Norfolk, Prentice Park, Pinners Point, Piedmont Heights,, Lincoln Park, Truxton, and Brighton were added.

In 1948 Westhaven, West Port Norfolk, River Park, Waterview, Glendale, and Glensheallah extended the city all the way to the Western Branch of the Elizabeth River. On January 1 1960 Cradock, Alexander Park, Simonsdale (named for Rear Admiral Simon), Elizabeth Manor and all of the other developments east of the Western Branch of the Elizabeth River were added. A contentious lawsuit between the new city of Chesapeake (incorporated from the remaining parts of Norfolk County) and Portsmouth ending on January 1 1968 added West Norfolk, Craney Island and large sections of what had been Deep Creek and Western Branch boroughs of the Norfolk County to Portsmouth. In naming this newly annexed section of the county the old popular name of Churchland was used. That name arose from the numerous churches there. When this amalgamation was finished Portsmouth was completely locked in by the other cities of Chesapeake and Suffolk (Suffolk now incorporating *what had been Nansemond County). The boundary between Chesapeake and Portsmouth followed no reasonable traffic flow, but was gerrymandered to arrange the border to keep one county politician's home in Chesapeake. The conflict with Chesapeake was so contentious that the border south of Victory Boulevard was not finally settled until 1991, when industrial land owned by Alcoa Aluminum and McDaniel roofing was still in dispute.*

At one time High Street and those parallel with it ended at Chestnut. Street. Cooke Street, whose name has recently been changed to Elm Avenue, was cut through the plantation of the Cooke family. It was the country home of Col. Mordecai Cooke, *mentioned earlier,* called Misery Thicket, owing to the dense woods which surrounded it. During the Civil War it was seized and used by the Federals as a hospital. Misery Thicket was inherited by Mr. Patrick Henry Cooke, who married Miss Olivia Bilisoly, and their daughter, Miss Virginia Cooke, still lives on part of the old place *(in the 1930s).* All the land west of Pearl Street from Clifford to Oak Grove Cemetery was purchased by Mr. James Gustavus Holladay in the *eighteen* seventies and laid off into streets and lots, conforming in size to those in Portsmouth.

The three streets running north and south were named Godwin, Blount and Gray. The last two are now called Richmond and First Avenue respectively.

Part of this tract of land was known as Oak Grove and it was here that the race-course was situated *described later in this narrative.* Oak Grove Tavern was famous for its good dinners, especially during the *horse*-racing season. After this section was built up this tavern, recently torn down, was used as a hotel for circus people and the rougher element. It stood on South Street just beyond Effingham, and its foundation can still be seen *(these foundations are no longer visible).*

Scottsville was so called from the Scott family who owned the land in that section from the early part of the eighteenth century and had a shipyard there. There is an old house on this farm with the name or rather, the initials of the builder and the date—T. S. 1734. The original name of this place was Church Point and the creek was Church Creek. *This is now called Scott's*

Creek. The old house referred to stands on the portion of the land still used as a farm, and owned by Mr. Shea - *of the family for whom the Shea Terrace neighborhood is named..*

At one time the old name survived in the name of Scottsville Baptist Church, founded in 1889 on Cottage Place and Glasgow Street, but its landmark brick church on the corner of the London-Glasgow Expressway and Constitution, built in 1914, is now called Calvary Baptist.

Shea Terrace, previously just called Scotts Creek for the waterway which runs by it, is a quiet neighborhood from the early twentieth century with its own school, Shea Terrace Elementary, which was added to the National Register of Historic Places in 2002. The architect of the school was Charles M. Robinson in the style called "Late 19th, Early 20th Century Revival." The bridge leading into the neighborhood, Leckie Street Bridge, was a source of annoyance as it was a shortcut to the Midtown Tunnel, until the bridge was taken out in the 1990s making the neighborhood a sort of cul-de-sac to the delight of its residents. For many decades it has had a little hidden treasure, the Flagship Restaurant, originally opened in the 1920s as Saunder's Ship Seafood and then changed to its present name in the 1950s. It is now operated as a part of a small shipyard at the foot of Constitution Avenue.

Portsmouth, being almost an island with the largest amount of waterfront property for its size in Hampton Roads, is dependent upon bridges. At one time there were twenty-five in the city, including the charming little single pedestrian bridge in Glenshellah by the Women's Club of Portsmouth. Not all the essential bridges were publicly owned. Lumberman Carl M. Jordan built the Jordan drawbridge in 1928, which is still a toll-bridge, as is the Gilmerton Bridge built in 1941. Commuters to South Norfolk have often been delayed in recent years when the old mechanically-lifted spans broke down and parts were hard to find. The Churchland Bridge, across the Western Branch of the Elizabeth River was not built until 1952, and much of the span had to be rebuilt in the 1990s because of its fragile design. The Western Freeway Bridge, previously called the West Norfolk Bridge, was completed in 1976 to replace a two-lane wooden bridge with a swiveling draw.

Park View was until the *eighteen* eighties the farm of the Hatton family called Alabama. It was laid off by the owners, Mr. Alexander Hatton, Mr. William Hatton and Dr. James L. Hatton. Mr. John G. Hatton when he became possessed of this property claimed that Fort Lane, then the only way to the Naval Hospital at that time belonged to him. The matter was settled by the Government buying this strip of land.

An advertisement is copied in <u>Portsmouth and Norfolk County Documents</u> *advertising the development of Park View between 1888 and 1892 and illustrating the sort of exuberant Queen Anne and Colonial Revival housing planned for the area. The developers were called the Park View Land Company. Its president was Francis Richards and its members were: John L. Watson, A. J. Phillips, Judge Edward Spalding, S. Meredith, the jeweler C. S. Sherwood and George H. Barrett who was then the president of Virginia Chemical Company in West Norfolk. It had 220 lots to sell. The first "cottage" was completed in 1888 and one hundred and eleven followed in the succeeding decade. It was advertised as being designed for the "Absolute exclusion of every feature of life objectionable to ladies, including the sale of liquor"... with... "its atmosphere of quiet and safety," and " its social advantages." The neighborhood took its name from the 75-acre parkland around the Naval Hospital which it overlooks. The City of Portsmouth annexed the area in 1894 when the trolley line to the Naval Hospital was completed through this neighborhood.*

The neighborhood continued the plan of Olde Towne and Miss Elizabeth West says North Street was the first laid out in it. Her grandfather bought his house there in 1898. North Street was later named Enterprise Way. John Paul Hanbury, whom I quote frequently throughout, tells us some of Portsmouth's notable citizens lived there: Jake Codd; Archie Hutchenson; Dr. Vernon Brooks; Vincent Parker; Roper Lawrence; William Norman; L. McK. Jack; Charles Syer; Gus Morgan; Harry Hunt, for whom a school was named; Charles Hawks; Jimmy Smith; Dr. Thomas Oast, the city's first pediatrician; Judge William Oast; J. Alden Oast one of the city's Commonwealth Attorneys and Dr. George W. Oast.

Frederick Beazley also lived there. He built the housing for low-income families mentioned in the chapter on the Navy Yard. He also began to built Frederick College in 1958, named for his father. In 1968 he donated the campus to the state, causing much controversy. It become the Portsmouth Campus of Tidewater Community College in its Suffolk location, but with a Portsmouth designation. He also founded Frederick Military Academy, which is now the Pines Treatment Center for abused and troubled children created on that site by Dr. Ronald Dozoretz. Beazley also provided the funds to create the Beazley Boys Club on Middle Street. It had a bowling alley and swimming pool. Since it was to promote responsibility and serve the disadvantaged, membership was just twenty five cents a year. The Beazley Foundation, for many years managed by Virginia Supreme Court Chief Justice Red Ianson, still contributes to funding worthy civic projects in Portsmouth. Beazley made his fortune in ice and coal and retired to Portsmouth to spend it on good works.

Two other boys' clubs helped the disadvantaged in the city's past. Vernon Ripley started one in 1930 in tents where the Commodore Theater now stands. It later moved to George Washington Highway and became "Boy's Village" with a miniature town, and crafts were taught until it closed in 1971 and the miniature buildings were sold. The Downtown Kiwanis also operated its "Fresh Air Farm" to offer the camping experience to children who would otherwise never get out of town.

In its heyday Parkview boasted several groceries, the best known being Archie Hudgins; two pharmacies, three churches and Wood's Bakery on the corner of Fort Lane and Glasgow Street.

One of its smaller, but charming, churches is Shelton Memorial Congregational Christian Church on Leckie Street. Organized in 1905 in a firehouse on Holladay Street, the church was completed the following year. This was the first Congregational church in the city. Billie Marie Wood was the first baby christened there. Andrew Carnegie, the nationally known philanthropist, paid a part of the cost of installing the organ. Carnegie offered the city of Portsmouth a library at about the same time, but the City Council, arguing that there must be some strings attached, turned down the offer; one of the few cities in the nation to do this.

The impressive landmark Parkview Methodist was built in 1893. Its organizing committee was made up of E. V. White, T. L. Cleaton, A. A. Martin, J. H. Brownley, M. T. Dill, J. C. Smith, C. W. Hudgins and Joseph E. Bowen. The first minister it called was W. B. Beauchamp, who went on to become a Methodist Bishop.

Some of the other churches in the neighborhood will be described in the section "Getting Religion."

After many years of decline the houses in this neighborhood are being restored to their original splendor. They are some of the best examples of Victorian architecture in South Hampton Roads. The entire neighborhood was designated as a historic site in 1966. This district now includes 310 houses.

West Park View was Matthews' Farm. There was an interesting old house on it which legend tells us was built in one week, Mr. Matthews being particularly anxious to have it ready for some entertainment which could not be postponed. This house was destroyed by fire about ten or twelve years ago *(1910)*. Mr. Alfred Wilson, a grandson of Mr. Matthews, owned this place, and at the death of his widow it became the property of the Guthrie family, who developed it. *Most of the houses are good examples of the architectural styles starting around the time of the First World War.*

Pinner's Point was the home of Mr. John Kearnes, one of the most prominent citizens of the town a hundred and forty years ago *(1790s). He died in 1799 and is buried in Trinity Churchyard.*. Mr. Kearnes' widow married Edwin Gray, of Southampton County, the first representative of his district in Congress, serving there until he moved to Portsmouth. It was Mr. Gray who introduced the bill into Congress to make it unlawful to fight a duel. *One victim of a duel, a thirty-eight year old English sailor named Edward Onley, is buried in Trinity Churchyard. The story of Commodore Barron's duel with Stephen Decatur appears elsewhere in this book.*

Miss Virginia Cooke, a descendant of John Kearnes, has in her possession a picture of Pinner's Point done in needlework by Kearnes' daughter, Margaret, afterwards Mrs. Mordecai Cooke. Pinner's Point was fortified and occupied by troops in the Civil War.

It is now all a part of the Portsmouth International Terminal, in turn a part of the Ports of Hampton Roads and a major export site for Virginia coal, and import and export site for containerized cargo. Virginia coal, being low in sulfur, fetches a premium price on the world market, and in terms of tonnage the ports of Hampton Roads are unrivaled on the Atlantic Coast. The major mover in this development in Portsmouth was John Nix in the early 1960s. The port was opened officially on September 20 1967. It was the world's first completely planned container cargo port and its massive cranes can be seen from the Pinner's Point overpass. The income from the ports, however, goes to the state, not to the city. Portsmouth benefits primarily from peripheral industries such as Daniel Stevens' and Thomas W. McDonough's container hauling and repair business which won them the Small Business Persons of the Year Award in 2006.

In 2001 the vast Danish shipping concern Maersk-Sealand built a terminal on a 200-acre track in Portsmouth, at last benefitting the city tax base for its advantages as a port. The massive cranes of this port dominate the skyline from the "Pinner's Point Connector" highway leading to interstate 164 across the Western Branch of the Elizabeth River to downtown Portsmouth and the Midtown Tunnel.

The Pinner's Point Methodist Church was formed in 1901. Called the "Little Brown Mission," it is now on Caroline Avenue in Port Norfolk.

Another Pinner's Point church was started under a "bush arbor" in that neighborhood in 1887. It was called First Baptist of Pinner's Point, but in 1961 it moved to Cavalier Manor and changed its name to New Bethal Baptist.

Little of the neighborhood remains, except a vestige. A predominantly African American neighborhood called Sugar Hill still survives as a little hidden place beside the massive cranes of Pinner's Point.

One of the longest-running businesses in Portsmouth was David's Seaman's Marine Store. It was founded by a

Lithuanian Jewish immigrant named Henry Dwartz. He started his career as a peddler with a pushcart. He sold work clothes and other goods to the railway workers, stevedores and sailors at Pinner's Point. He opened his shop in 1888 and became so wealthy he was one of the first to finance Gomley Chesed Synagogue in its original location. We will hear about this congregation in the chapter on getting religion. He added a bar to his shop in 1933 when Prohibition ended. His grandson David Schikevitz was the last owner, when in 1990 the business was condemned for development over the objection of its owner and torn down by the city. It is now a parking lot for the International Terminal.

Another maritime business developed in Pinner's Point was Harry E. Lauterbach's custom speedboat business. He built the world's fastest inboard hydroplane racing boats. His original business was approximately where the Midtown Tunnel now crosses the Elizabeth River, but the business moved to Broad Street in Port Norfolk when the tunnel was proposed and remained there for fifty years. The boats were built to his own designs. He won four national titles and is in the speedboat hall of fame called The Power Boat Association Honor Squadron. His son, Larry, set a record in the Grand Prix in one of his father's boats and has gone on to best that record seven times. Lauterbach died in 2006.

Port Norfolk was the glebe of Portsmouth parish, *as we have mentioned earlier,* until after the Revolution, when it was confiscated with the other glebes, by the State of Virginia *and sold in 1802 to benefit education. Glebe is an old term referring to a farm created for the support of the priest of a parish in the Church of England. The "parish" is now Trinity Episcopal Church.* Colonel Craford sold 175 acres here to the church. *At least two of its priests were buried on the glebe, the Reverend Charles Smith and the Reverend John Braidfoot, and their graves later moved to Trinity Churchyard. Their lives will be sketched later in the history of that church.*

It was at this point *(Port Norfolk)* that the British landed when they captured Portsmouth in 1779. The troops upon landing there marched to Scott's Creek, which they crossed and entered Fort Nelson from the rear while *British Admiral* Collier bombarded the fort from the water.

Here, too, was the historic Glebe School where the country children were educated in colonial days; and in fact until the public schools took its place, and did away with the need for this school in the community. The site of the Glebe School is now a playground *which still exists in the Mount Hermon neighborhood on the west side of Mount Vernon Avenue north of London Boulevard.* In the days when it was the glebe, it was surrounded by thick woods *which* added to the feeling of gloom. There was the rumor of it being haunted. In them, too, lived many Indians, who remained in their shelter long after the days of the glebe. Mr. Tee who was born in Portsmouth some eighty years ago *(1850)*, tells us that he remembered seeing the Indians in town. They would follow the market wagons and on market days could be seen in large numbers, under the sycamore trees at the intersection of High and Court streets shooting at pennies put up by interested spectators. The Indians were allowed to keep all the pennies they hit.

The old glebe house *where the priests of Portsmouth Parish lived from as early as the 1730s* stood facing the river on what is now the southeastern corner of Mount Vernon Avenue and the Boulevard, *now overlooking the Pinner's Point Connector to highway I-164.* On its lawn there were immense shade trees; a few of the pomegranate trees still linger in some of the lots on the Boulevard.

Port Norfolk was auctioned off to John Thompson for his brickyard in 1815 for $22. Port Norfolk became the property of a wealthy Norfolk County truck farmer, Alex Skeeter in 1889.

Later The Norfolk Land Company planned an opulent resort with handsome boarding houses on the Western Branch of the Elizabeth River and popular beaches. It was planned to open as a part of the 1893 Naval Rendezvous to commemorate the 400th anniversary of the discovery of America by Christopher Columbus. It was laid out in lots 40 feet wide by 140 feet deep with alleys allowing access to the backs of the properties. A contest was held to name the place and the winner was Port Norfolk to honor both Portsmouth and Norfolk. Among the inducements to settle was a contest in which 12 lots were given away. It is now one of the finest collections of Queen Anne, Colonial Revival, American Bungalow and "Foresquare" houses surviving in Hampton Roads.

There were enough full-time residents in Port Norfolk in 1897 for Portsmouth's Calvary Baptist Church in Portsmouth to open a mission there, which would become Port Norfolk Baptist in the following year.

Port Norfolk was called "Portsmouth's playground." One of the piers built out into the river was hung with gas lamps and had a bathhouse at its end. Another wharf had 'cabaret style entertainment.'" A local group called "Chautauquas" for the famous New York state retreat offered musical evenings and lectures. This group gave its name to Chautauqua Avenue down which the Port Norfolk electric streetcar took Portsmouth residents to the beach. There was even a hotel on the corner of Bayview Boulevard and Chautauqua Avenue.

In the 1890s this was the terminus of the Norfolk and Carolina rail line which we covered in "Where Rail Meets Sail." It dropped off its passengers here to be carried to Norfolk by ferry.

Port Norfolk was later served by the Beltline Railroad and the Atlantic Coastline Railroad.

Among its many industries were a furniture factory, a Heintz pickle factory and Armour's cold storage. Planters Peanuts made crates and bushel baskets for the truck farmers in the area.

The peanut business did not leave Portsmouth until the Skippy Peanut butter company closed its facility on High Street in the 1980s. A landmark of High Street was the immense Skippy Peanut butter jar on the corner of the building which marked Portsmouth as the "home of Skippy." Its building, built in the 1920s, had been a sock factory, but at its zenith it shipped out twenty million pounds of peanut butter to the nation. This was not the only place making Portsmouth "peanut butter city" - Proctor and Gamble opened a plant in Portsmouth in 1931 which, starting in 1957, manufactured Jif Peanut butter. In 1993 that plant was moved to Kentucky, ending Portsmouth's monopoly on this most popular of peanut foods. If you can't get a peanut butter sandwich made in Portsmouth any more, you can get Gwaltney hot dogs. It opened its plant in Portsmouth near Victory Crossing in 1981.

Another famous landmark on High Street was the Tanker Car Gas Station on the corner of High and Elm streets with a full sized oil-tanker railroad car on tracks as its symbol.

Port Norfolk is now a large assemblage of houses, mainly from the first years of the twentieth century, and has emerged as a popular residential neighborhood. A housing development on its west was demolished after drug-gang activity was traced to its residents, and replaced with a new neighborhood of single-family homes in River Edge. Port Norfolk's development was also impacted by the heavy traffic routed through it before the completion of the Pinner's Point Connector, but that problem ended when that flyover was completion in 2005.

The oldest surviving business in Port Norfolk is the Be-Lo grocery opened as an independent grocery in 1921 by Lynwood C. Shelton, Sr. It became a part of the Be-Lo chain in 1955, Sadly the elder Shelton was shot to death in a robbery in the store.

Among its churches are Mount Hermon Baptist, which claims to be the fifth oldest African American church in the city. It was founded April 26 1886 in a house on Cox's farm by eighteen members. It then moved to the old Glebe School House on Broad Street and the "old road," Glasgow Street. In 1893 it moved to a small building on Glasgow and Florida streets called "the little white church." In 1923 it built its current brick building.

Broad Street Methodist Church began with meetings in the old schoolhouse on Broad Street, the old Atlantic Coast Line Railroad Station, and in a pavilion on the beach. In 1897 a retired Methodist minister, I. T. Reed, proposed constructing a permanent building. The new church was called Port Norfolk and Pinner's Point Methodist Episcopal Church South and in the following year a sanctuary was completed. When the Methodist churches were consolidated in 1939 it changed its name to Broad Street Methodist. In 1915 the church moved to the corner of Broad and Second streets.

In the twenty-first century Port Norfolk has a fine restaurant, coffee shop and the bakery, Sweet Temptations, which has put many a pound on a Portsmouthian.

The 3.4 square mile area was annexed by Portsmouth in 1919 from Norfolk County and in 1966 designated as a Virginia Historic Landmark.

The last neighborhood in this group of annexations to be added to the city was Brighton. Lelia Barnes, who lived into her 90s, has written two moving accounts of that neighborhoods called *The Best of Brighton: As I Remember It* and *Oh, Taste and See*, both in the library collection. The Portsmouth African American History Society under Charles Whitehurst named Mrs. Barnes one of the 100 most Influential Americans in 1997.

Zion Bethal United Church on Des Moines Avenue was built in 1898.

Both Prentice Park and Brighton were adversely effected by the construction of interstate 264, which cut the neighborhoods off from the business district of Portsmouth, and by the clear-cutting of Southside which compressed its low-income inhabitants into these two blue-collar communities causing overcrowding.

To compound this the Washington Park housing development was discovered to be built on land so polluted that it became a Super Fund site. It was built on what had been the Abex brass and bronze smelting foundry which manufactured break-shoes and ball-bearings for the railroads. Mrs. Persons, a dedicated advocate for cleaning up the place attended almost every City Council meeting until Washington Park was torn down in 2003 and its citizens relocated.

In 2006 Habitat for Humanity selected Brighton as a location for 10 new homes to jumpstart the revitalization of that old neighborhood which the Civic League under Reggie Allen has long hoped for. A constitutional referendum passed in 2006 will allow tax-breaks for developers working in neighborhoods like Brighton, Prentice Park and Prentice Place.

The next group of annexations begins at the West Norfolk Bridge. The river just west of the current West Norfolk Bridge on the Port Norfolk side was a graveyard for old ships, and as *recently as the 1980s at low tide the gold on old figureheads could be seen there.* An effort has been made here to reintroduce the Chesapeake Bay oyster. The river was crossed by a two-lane wooden bridge with a turnstile type draw before the construction of the modern bridge in the 1970s. Remnants of the old bridge can still be seen.

West Norfolk was laid out on one square mile at the then terminus of the Atlantic and Danville Railroad line in 1890. It had 58 lots planed by the West Norfolk Land Development Company. A railway line still runs through the middle of this neighborhood. The truck gardener Henry Kirn made his great fortune shipping farm goods to Chicago, Cincinnati and St. Louis on this line. He would give his name to the Kirn Building and the New Kirn Building on High Street and his descendants to the Kirn Memorial Library in Norfolk.

In 1891 St. Marks United Methodist Church found its original home on Fifth Avenue in West Norfolk. At first the congregation had permission to meet in the sheds of the West Norfolk Lumber Company. They sat on backless benches and recited hymns from memory as the minister had only one hymnal. They were given wood from the lumber company to build the church, then called West Norfolk Methodist and later Fifth Avenue Methodist. The church eventually moved to Churchland, changed its name to St. Marks and built its building on Twin Pines Road in 1979.

Waterview and Glensheallah are our newest suburbs *Miss Holladay tells us*; but they *were at the time of Miss Holladay's writing* not yet within the city limits.

Waterview was *then called* Dale's Point, the birthplace of that doughty old commodore, Richard Dale*: second in command of John Paul Jones ship the* <u>Bonhomme Richard</u>, *in the Revolution and the hero of the War With the Barbary Pirates. A small marker indicates where the Dale home stood. Much more about Richard Dale appears in the earlier chapter about Revolutionary War Veterans*. It was then his grandfather's farm; and had been the home of the Dale family for several generations.

Glensheallah was part of the Herbert property, and one of Mr. Herbert's heirs sold it to Mr. Beverly Bayton. It afterwards belonged to his grandson, Mr. Beverly Armistead, who made a fine place of it. It was for a long time the show farm of the county. Many attractive homes have been built upon it as well as a country club and the accompanying golf links. *The club house became the Women's Club of Portsmouth and still stands; although the golf links have long ago been replaced by residences. When entering this area from High Street you pass between two brick markers which were the first project of Mary Brown Channel of Portsmouth; the first woman to be licenced as an architect in Virginia. Her father was the rector of St. John's Church and later Bishop of Southern Virginia. When she went into the church every Sunday she would stop by his picture and say, "Good morning, Daddy."*

Cavalier Manor, as mentioned previously, is thought to be the first middle-class suburb in the nation particularly built by and for African Americans. Portsmouth had developed a strong black middle class, primarily as a result of the employment available in the shipyard. It was laid out with many streets named for famous African Americans: entertainers like Dandridge Drive, Belafonte Drive, Horne Avenue for Lena Horne and for athletes such as Liston Lane for Sunny Liston and Alcindor Road for a famous baseball player.

Every city has its share of pleasant suburbs built up in the 1950s to accommodate the newly-formed families after World War II. Among them in Portsmouth are the neighborhoods clustered around Elizabeth Manor Golf Course. The streets in Greenlakes are actually named for famous golfers, some of whom like Sam Sneed, played in Portsmouth.

The oldest golf course in the city is Bide-a-wee built by Fred Findlay in 1956 on a plan drawn by the famous golfer, and longtime Portsmouth resident, Chandler F. Harper and his sister, one of the early well-known women golfers, Lily Harper. Their father, Charles F. Harper, was Portsmouth's City Manager. This course was the site of World Series of Golf Championships six times. A dispute about segregation in the membership of this then private club eventually resulted in the city buying the course as a municipal course in 1997. It was made into a Curtis Strange Signature Course and is to become the jewel in the redevelopment of the old Fairwood Homes site. Fairwood Homes was a World War II housing development which became blighted and was torn down at the opening of the twenty-first century to be developed, with the help of past city manager Robert T. Williams, as a new home for Tidewater Community College, replacing its Suffolk location. The plan is to include, in addition to the golf course and the college campus, upscale housing and a business park. The first section of this development was completed in 2006.

Some areas thought to be new, like Westhaven, are older than you might think. One of the landmarks of this neighborhood is Westhaven Baptist Church. It started with a Sunday School which met by the river in an area then called Battery Park. In 1913 it moved into a tent on the corner of King Street and Caroline Avenue. This tent blew down several times, but that did not deter the congregation. They built the first of several church buildings on County Street in the same year. The 1913 church is now a private home, still standing around the corner from the next sanctuary built in 1923. At that time Westhaven was called Rodman Heights and the church bore that name as well.

Though seven or eight miles from the town, Deep Creek has always been in close touch with Portsmouth, and is by far the *largest Norfolk County* community *(or was in Miss Holladay's time). It is now a part of the City of Chesapeake.*

We get a picture of Churchland from an interview with Miss Emily Duke by William A. Brown III. She tells us that before the Depression this part of what is now Portsmouth was completely rural with its roads, for the most part, unpaved. The farms on the river were in the furthest northern boundry of the Southern growing zone and, therefore, closest to the population concentrations in the North.

The farms were made up of large Victorian houses with long, low, sprawling barns. They were mostly self-sufficient. Hogs were raised and slaughtered in January or February. Every farm had a smokehouse with rafters to hold the parts to be smoked and pits for burning persimmon, or other woods low in tar. Of course fish and oysters were available at hand and every fall the hunting season began - there was plenty of game. A barrel of molasses would be imported from New Orleans once a year and the African American workers would come to the big house with a bucket to get their share. Flour and sugar were also bought annually by the barrel from Portsmouth, and meal by the sack. Apples would be stored wrapped in newspaper and grapes were imported in kegs with cork packing. Wine was generally homemade and a specialty of the area was peach brandy. This was made by putting up peaches and sugar in jars and then burying them to ferment.

When the railroad came in the early part of the nineteenth century it would stop at each of the inland farms to pick up truck goods to be shipped out of Portsmouth to New York, Boston, Baltimore and Philadelphia. Those farms on the water would ship from their wharves on "truck boats," as their ancestors had in Colonial times. These truck boats would also be used as water-borne party boats in summer. They would ship mainly to the North through the Southern Produce Company in Norfolk. Every farm had a pond on which there would be skating in the winter. It was the custom to go visiting, and stay sometimes for a week or even a month.

Housing for slaves and later African American farm workers were separate from the houses. One such community was remembered as the "village of red houses" where the Coast Guard Station now stands.

Social life revolved around the churches and Churchland Academy school.

Boys would walk to school and girls would be taken in buggies. If you were fortunate enough to have a horse of your own the school, then at the corner of Academy Street and Churchland Boulevard, provided a stable. Eventually a streetcar line reached as far into Norfolk County as that school. When the automobile was introduced, drivers' licences did not, Miss Duke tells us, reach as far as Churchland, and more often than not you would see a child behind the wheel. It was not until the fall of 1926 that school buses were provided.

Among the first churches was Churchland Methodist established in 1783 when Francis Asbury, about whom we will hear later, started to meet with thirteen "Faithful souls" at Craney Island. The first church was on the corner of Towne

Point Road and the lane which led to where River Shores now stands. That church burned in 1847. The next church was built just south of the original on land purchased from William Grimes "for the consideration of one dollar of lawful money of Virginia." It was called Wesley Chapel and was one of six churches on a circuit. The chapel was remodeled in 1883 and the name changed to Centenary United Methodist Church. The current church on Cedar Lane was built in 1959. To it was added a new sanctuary, a chapel and more classrooms in 1965. In 1979 the handsome stained glass window was added by the well known local politician Porter Hardy and his wife and a new organ was added in 1982.

Churchland Baptist's long history is mentioned elsewhere in this book, but we can add here some of the events it hosted. It started a Ladies Aid Society. It sponsored an annual excursion to Virginia Beach and a massive Easter Egg hunt planned for many years by Miss Molly Heffington, who hid the eggs. It also helped the African American church called Grove Baptist across the street. This church was first founded by slaves in 1840. Law then required that any black church had to have three white observers at every meeting to insure it would not be a center of slave revolt. Churchland Baptist provided the three, which they called a "commission." This church is described by Miss Maggie Barrett in another interview with Bill Brown in <u>Portsmouth and Norfolk County Documents.</u>

Of course, there were stores. Among those mentioned by Miss Duke were: Trotman's, Lawton's Blacksmith shop and A. W. Johnson's, opened in 1914. Churchland cooks were noted for their Robert E. Lee cake with a filling made from orange juice and nuts, and their Lord and Lady Baltimore cakes. The Carney family, large landowners in Churchland for whom a lane is named were noted for their home-made chocolate ice cream.

Horse collars had to be bought at Parson's store in West Norfolk.

There was even a store exclusively for the African Americans called Terry's.

The advent of the railway refrigerator car meant produce could be shipped from Florida and California which *has longer growing seasons and most of the old farms were sold as suburban housing tracts. Some farms, however, survived into the mid-twentieth century by opening canning operations - like the Eberwine family.*

The agricultural past of this now affluent suburb is now just a memory.

Chapter 31: How We Lived

Having followed up the geographical development of our town for so many years we are naturally interested in the men and women who were responsible for its growth. We are fortunate in having diaries, recollections and other records of bygone days, which not only give us some idea of the traits and characteristics of the people, but paint for us their manner and mode of living. *Unfortunately many of the sources used by Miss Holladay are now lost.*

A writer who lived among them says, "The people of these early days were distinguished for their hospitality and easy good living. There were among these early settlers men of fine talent, sound judgment and, cultivated minds, but noted mostly for incorruptible honesty." Another tells us of the customs that prevailed one hundred and fifty years ago *(the 1790s)*. "In winter," she says, "we were kept warm by wood fires; no coal either bituminous or anthracite was seen on our hearths - but *there was* blazing wood giving comfortable warmth with beautiful flashes of welcome every morning when the household had gotten together, for the hearth was the household altar. Most of the houses had good-sized halls with doors opening into the rooms, and a stairway which however left plenty of space for social gatherings. *This is an architectural style which is best illustrated in the Dale-Reed House built around 1735 on Swimming Point Walk.* In summer one sought the porch or other shady spot, and when teatime rolled around, tea was served in one of these places, never in the diningroom; lamps were not used." Another hand has finished the picture for us and tells us that in the plain simple life of the old regime social visiting was much observed; the old families owning their homes, not only had plenty of room for flowers and fruit, but raised their own vegetables, leaving plenty of space for drying the laundry. The large front porch doors were open from sun-up till bedtime. In porches in the summertime the dropper-in for a chat was entertained. A set table was never prepared, but a servant with a tray of cups filled with tea, was followed by another bringing thin slices of bread and small cakes, to serve the family and guest. Genteel society required the male visitor to practice the art of balancing on one knee, his cup of tea, and on the other his plate of edibles, and join in the conversation. Are their any adepts now? Late hours were not the custom, and bell-ring at nine o'clock closed the scene.

Wood was the only fuel; fires were banked at night for an early morning start. If the fire went out it was no uncommon thing to see the cook hustling around among the neighbors for "a chunk of fire." Matches were later on advertised for twenty-five cents a hundred. They were flat splints of wood about three inches long, ignited between folded sand paper, and it almost required the effort of two people to set them off. One had to hold the paper and the other the match.

The wheaten bread of the family was either beaten biscuits or rising bread made on the premises. Baking powders of any kind were unheard of. The cook's anxiety was the yeast jug, that required constant watching. It would go on the rampage; the stopper would then come out, and yeast like an eruption of lava from Vesuvius, would spread over the floor. There were few bakers of loaf bread here, but the baking of hard bread or hardtack *(sometimes called sea biscuits)* was extensively carried on here. Tradition says that the line-of-battle ship *North Carolina*, commanded by Commodore Morgan, while fitting out at the Navy Yard for a three years' cruise, had to delay sailing for six months by reason of Tildsey Graham's bake-house burning with two thousand barrels of bread which would have been her supply.

This rock-hard bread would last for long voyages, if not forever, without spoiling. The first baker of Portsmouth before the Revolution, John Ewing, is buried in Trinity Churchyard and this was his stock in trade. His business was on the Middle Street side of Courthouse Square. The widow Abigail Moulson also ran a business essential to shipping. She traded in "juniper water:" the brown water brought down Crab Creek from the Dismal

Swamp. *It was high in tannin from decomposing peat and would keep in the barrels on shipboard for the longest of voyages. She is also buried at Trinity.*

Street pumps furnished a meager amount of brackish water, while wells in the yards supplied wash tubs. Those who had no wells caught rainwater in a hogshead. This brand of water was quite popular, it being pleasanter than well water. Our chronicler, Mr. Rowland, refers to the Norfolk water, "for we are told by several travelers who visited Portsmouth that her drinking water was good. First the Frenchman; then an English visitor, Mr. Smith, and the Duc de la Rochefoucauld when he stayed in Portsmouth in 1795 all agreed that the drinking water on this side of the river was much superior to that in Norfolk." Mr. Rowland tells us that no ice was used in the water; but it was cooled in Seville jars. *This is a kind of large ceramic olive jar introduced into the Americas as early as 1554 and common on Virginia sites of the 17th century. It appears first in Virginia records in 1623. It cooled the water by evaporation.*

All through the town pumps were placed at intervals, generally on conspicuous corners. Groups of African Americans stood near at all times and seasons adding a picturesque touch to the scene, with the colored calico dresses and gay bandanas.

The washerwoman was entirely dependent on the corner pump. They generally carried two buckets-full of water at a trip, one on the head and one by hand. A number of little children followed in their wake, to pump the water or help in other ways. At most of these pumps *were like* a watering trough for horses. One of these pumps stood on the corner of Middle and North streets until the days of city water. It was the rendezvous of all the boys and girls in the neighborhood; and many fond recollections cling to the spot, though this pump was not so celebrated in the annals of the town as the old "Boomarlarly" of which we have spoken elsewhere *in this book.*

There too, was a water cart; but the water wagon of that day had no sinister meaning. *Miss Holladay, writing during Prohibition, knew this term. It is the origin of the phrase "on the wagon" meaning you have given up hard liquor and now drink water*. It furnished you with water at the rate of one cent a gallon or three gallons for two cents.

After a while cisterns were built here; but for many a year they were few and far between. *Most of the houses in Olde Towne built before city water still have their cisterns, some full of discarded treasures.* Those who had them, however, gladly supplied their neighbors with a plentiful supply of drinking water. The cistern was not a perfect institution, and few of them were large enough to stand a very dry summer. To get good water in them required care. The first shower must never be turned into them, as it was necessary to wash off the *slate* roof; then rains at certain seasons were *considered* better for the water. At intervals the cistern must be cleaned and this was done by a man who made it his business. The water was all pumped out and then the cleaner went into the cistern by means of a ladder and the manhole.

An English lady who lived in Norfolk for a few years in the 1790's published upon her return to England an account of the life in this section. It is a quaint little volume written in rhyme. She has presented for us many customs of the day. She begins with her life on shipboard and gives us her impressions of the harbor as she approached it. She found the scenery monotonous, as we see by her description of it.

> "When to my wandering view appeared,
> Trees as if on the ocean reared;
> No land I saw but length of way;
> The growing vision seemed to play;
> As on the rough tempestuous tide,
> The tow'ring fir trees seemed to ride.
> But trees on trees in endless rows;
> Without a house to change the scene,
> But green for everlasting green."

She then tells of the cannon that was fired on shipboard as soon as it entered the harbor, which recalls an old custom of the vessels, and one observed until quite recently. The ships of the Old Dominion Line between this port and New York were the last to give it up. Their cannon was duly fired at each end of the line until late in the *eighteen* eighties.

Nothing seemed to have escaped the eye of our poetic lady, who soon became as familiar with our woods as with our towns. She found in them not only singing birds of all kinds, but game ones too in plenty, especially partridges and tom-tits. Red, blue, yellow, and green birds *(this may be a reference to the now extinct North Carolina parakeet)* she found in great numbers.

At market she complained of the beef, finding none there fit to eat, except that brought from New York. It cost fourpence a pound and only the meat was weighed; all else being taken off before it a was put on the scales.

For the poultry she has unstinted praise: the finest turkeys sold for one dollar, while an average one went for much less. Squirrels were extremely good, and so was the other game with the exception of venison, which did not suit her taste. She tells us that,

> "The mutton was tolerably fat,
> The veal as lean as any cat,
> Pork you are always sure is good,
> They live so richly in the wood."

The summer she says brings a feast of peaches; and melons of a fine flavor abounded. They were thought high at ninepence, but in England, she tells us they would have brought seven shillings or more apiece. There were plenty of apples of many kinds; but Father Abrahams were the favorite variety here. The sea food was both good and cheap: soft *shelled* crabs being scarcer than other things, and therefore a little dearer. Hog fish were not caught in the inner harbor; but were brought from some distance by a horseman with

> "a horn proclaims the hog fish near
> Quickly the light horsemen appear
> And on a shabby nag they ride,
> A pannier loaded on each side
> With fish so fresh, the people hunt

Their coming in to hear them grunt
Declaring that if fresh they are found
You may certainly hear that sound."

The Poetess liked Virginia cooking and was charitably disposed when it was not to her taste; thinking,

"Many things you must overlook
When you have a slave as cook."

Anti-slavery campaigns began in England in 1770 and resulted in abolition there in 1833.
She objected to our use of pork, and thought,

". . . They mostly spoil
Whate'er they stew or fry or boil,
In broth, or soup, or hash, or pie
You'll sure a piece of bacon spy.
Whate'er you eat, the same taste,
Bacon for fry and lard for paste;
Hams, greens, puddings oft combine
In the same pot their haste to join."

Candles for common use we made at home; but only those of the finest sperm *whale fat* were used to light the downstairs.

Since bare floors are the vogue again, we might get some helpful hints from her account of cleaning them.

"The floors well laid they seldom scour,
Dryrubbing them at every hour;
scrubbing brush is never seen,
For when they make their flooring clean
A slave with a cocoa shell
Can clean the boards as white an well;
And if of grease they find a spot
An old shoe's directly got;
With which they scrub with all their might,

> Till from the wood it's driven quite;
> Or if too hard for the shoe sole
> A piece of brick concludes the whole."

Much to our pleasure the poet lady attended a wedding in this neighborhood; and she has pictured it for us. Eight o'clock at night was the favorite time for marriage, quite contrary to the English custom, and what was more shocking still was the marriage service, which she says that since the Revolution the ministers perform just as they please.

> "The rooms were dressed with flowers gay,
> The company in best array
> Converse and pass the time away,
> Till Sol withdraws his brilliant ray:
> When entering the diningroom
> The parson shows the hour has come.
> The parents then fetch in the bride
> The bridegroom walking at her side,
> Attended by the bridesmaids fair,
> And bridegroomsmen, in all three pair.
> The preacher saying little more,
> Than you take John and John take thee,
> I give my blessing heartily.
> The laugh, the song, the dance goes forth:
> Till the late evening hours advance,
> When all quit the song and dance,
> Entering the supper room to eat
> Some of the light refreshing treat,
> The table elegantly spread
> With the young couple at its head."

The table she finds a pleasing sight, and kindly furnishes us with the menu, which included many familiar dishes.

> "Chickens, oysters, tarts and fruit,
> With cakes and syllabub *(A popular eighteenth century punch made of white wine, heavy cream, sugar and*

citrus.) to suit:
Confections, trifle *(An English desert of pudding, or custard, cake, jam and fresh fruit with sherry added)*, floating cream.
All there in high perfection seem."

Of funerals, she has given us an equally graphic picture. They usually took place at the house, and to her unfeigned horror, she finds that the burial took place on the third day after death. That the coffin was exposed to view, without any pall, gave her another shock. When preparations for the funeral were made, she tells us,

"Everything with white was hung,
O'er all the glasses *(mirrors)* linen flung;
With all the outward marks of woe
On every box or chest they throw
Sheets, tablecloths; whate'er is white
To hide the furniture from sight."

From the written recollections of a lady who lived to be nearly ninety years old and had spent all her life in Portsmouth, we get glimpses of the town at a later date than that of the poetess. She gives us an amusing account of an incident that happened in the old Portsmouth theater, which stood where the new Professional Building now stands *(on the southeast corner of Washington and High Street)*, in the eighteen thirties.

Her uncle had come to take her to her first play; and as she started off her grandmother said to her, "You are going to see the devil's works tonight." The little girl was too happy to be awed by this wise counsel, and went off in high spirits.

All through the comedy the child was entranced; but tragedy proved her undoing. She stood it silently as long as she could, but when a very realistic shooting scene occurred, she threw up her hands and shrieked at the top of her lungs, "Uncle, Uncle, take me out, take me out. Grandma said it was the devil's work." Her uncle said he could not get her out fast enough to please himself.

The next Sunday, there being no service at the Episcopal church, this little girl was taken to the Methodist church, where a revival of the most exaggerated type was going on, the converted shouting in their joy, the mourners rending the air with their groans and lamentations. This proved too much for the nervous child, and, upon seeing her uncle at some distance, she called in perfectly audible tones, "Take me out, take me out. It is worse than the theater." It was very necessary to get her out without further comment, as there was some feeling at that time between the Episcopal and Methodist churches.

The writer of these recollections has a great deal to say about the strict bounds in which children were kept in her childhood. Playing in the streets was an unheard-of thing for well raised children; and playing in the yard not much more in favor for girls. Once in her life this treat fell to her share: her grandfather was lying, dead in the house and her elders were too much occupied with other matters to know that she had broken bounds. Young girls seldom went in the street alone, and then only to pay a visit. When shopping or walking they must have a grown person with them.

The young men of the day did not escape this surveillance, either. She tells us that her mother was often called on by her neighbor, an intimate friend, for advice. Her son, John Henry, or William Thomas, as the case might be, was calling on some young lady that night, whose parents were not on her visiting list. What should she do? "Send for him at once," was the unwavering answer. Old Mother Patsy was called up and sent to fetch home the errant young master. Young Master would, come, too, very obediently; though it was told by old Mother that he "cussed" her all the way home. William Thomas was not the only one of his associates so protected. It was quite the thing to do when a young gentleman had been daring enough to enlarge the family acquaintance.

One of his friends, when he returned from boarding school, decided to study medicine; and during the summer he was to read in the office of his uncle, a prominent physician in the town. *The most common way to prepare for medicine, or law, at that time was not to go to college for courses, but to apprentice to someone already in practice. This was called "reading" for medicine, or the law.* He was carefully instructed by his mother as to his line of conduct, and, above all, she demanded that he should be home every night before dark. Fortunately for the young gentleman, his uncle held somewhat advanced views; telling his sister that he would allow his pupil to stay out as late as he cared to, adding that he had no intention of instructing babes in the science of medicine.

Of course, a century later the world of young society had completely changed. The first person in town to own an automobile was Dr. George H. Carr in 1902. By the 1950s the automobile craze meant a date was supposed to take place entirely in a car. You could eat without leaving your car go to the movies in the car at a drive-in movie and then complete the date with whatever activity was mutually agreed upon. The drive-in movies are gone, but a memory of the drive-in diner survives in the Circle Restaurant. Started in 1947 by Stewart Mathews and Harry Hopwell, the Circle was designed by Dorothy Morgan with a curved glass wall, perhaps the first in the nation, which gave the restaurant its name. You would pull your car in and a young waitress would take your order while you sat in the car, and bring it to the car on a metal tray with legs designed to hang it from the car window. This kind of drive-in survives at Dumars in Norfolk. Its signature item was hot fudge cake. It was the hangout for the Wilson High School crowd and was open until two in the morning. The Cradock High School crowd drove to the Dixie Drive Inn and the Churchland High School kids went to Rodman's. All three hangouts were within blocks of each other on High Street.

Rodman's had been started by Howard P. Rodman, a blacksmith, June 15, 1929. Although this was the first year of the depression the business has never had a year in the red. In 1937 it moved to the corner of High and Hamilton streets. When all the men were away at World War II Rodmans changed his staff to waitresses rather than waiters. Its signature was its still famous barbecue then served with orange crush. The business was moved by grandson, Judson "Juddy" Rodman to Shoulders Hill Road in Suffolk, but Bones and Buddies across from Maryview

Hospital, which is a collaboration between Stewart Mathews, one of the founders of the Circle and Rodman, keeps the memory of the old high school hangouts alive.

No list of Portsmouth's old fast food places would be complete without mentioning Mosbeth's Chicken on Airline Boulevard. It was started by John A. Mosbeth in 1940 when he rented an old "beer joint" for twenty five dollars a month. It anticipated the "take-out" food trend, and is still in business today. Its larger-than-life chicken on the roof is one of Portsmouth's enduring landmarks.

When the motorcycle craze was revived in the 1990s it was, and still is, served by Portsmouth's Bayside Harley-Davidson dealership opened in 1998. It is the sponsor of the annual "Rumble In the Tunnel where South Hampton Roads highways become impassable for the day with masses of rumbling "hogs."

Chapter 32: Etiquette Lessons From the Past

Portsmouth was not without its pleasures, however, and one of the greatest of them at this period *(the Federal Period)* was "going out to spend the day." This sounds very simple; but what would the housekeeper now say if she had to prepare for one of these incursion? The party would be more agreeable if two or three families came together. Two at least must come; and the invitation included not only the "grown-ups" but all the children, with a servant or two to help look after them.

It was considered complimentary to come early and stay late; the children were sent home in care of the servant at dark, which was their bedtime. The elders lingered until ten o'clock and then the party adjourned to meet the next week at another home. *This was the only form of entertainment, there being neither radio, nor television to fill the time.*

The boys and girls used to enjoy these days immensely, so the recollections tell us, having much more freedom than when at home. Their dinner was served in a separate room and presided over by a female slave of the hostess and the visiting female slaves.

Our mouths water when we hear of the delectable viands served at these all-day feasts. The dinner was formal; but the supper was "handed" according to the old custom; but at this time the simple repast of sliced bread, cakes and tea had been done away with, and much more elaborate food was prepared. There were handy little tables scattered about the rooms and the guest had no longer to balance his plate on his knee as in the days of yore. Some of the old trays from which these suppers were served are still in town, and it would take a careful hand to manipulate them.

The older houses in the town were built with the English basement, that is, with a ground floor, in which the dining room and perhaps a sitting room was situated *and often quarters for the slaves. In Portsmouth separate slave quarters were rare and only two examples survive in the Olde towne..* The drawing-room, for that is what the old people in Portsmouth called the parlor, was on the next floor *reached by a long flight of steps on the outside of the house and then by way of a long side-entrance hall where servants would collect the visitor's wraps.* It was usually a double room. The most noticeable things about *some of* these old houses were halls across the front, thus giving no rooms facing the street. Our grandmothers used to tell us that windows on the street would have been unnecessary, since it would have been ill-bred to have been seen at one.

This architectural style called "English Basement" is the one with the most surviving examples in the Olde Towne today - there are literally dozens of them. They are mainly Federal Period and in the Greek Revival style from 1775 (Captain Pritchett's house in the 500 block of North Street) through 1841 (the Pass, or Murdaugh House on the corner of London and Crawford). Above this second floor, or first floor depending on whether you counted the English basement as a floor rather than a basement, was a set of bedrooms for the adults and above that a set of rooms with ceilings less than six feet high, with sometimes one-quarter-sized-windows, for the children's bedrooms. All the rooms were heated by fireplaces served by two to four chimneys and each; was ornamented with pressed-plaster molding and a pressed-plaster medallions in the middle of the ceiling. The evolution of the pressed-plaster medallions from simple to elaborate in the homes of Olde Towne could make a study in itself, as could the evolving sunburst transom lights above the entrance doors. The plaster used in the houses through the 1860s was made from oyster shell and horsehair. It is about one inch thick and when broken the shell fragments are clearly visible and the horsehair sticks out. An example of the simpler style of English Basement in wood clapboard can be seen in a house from 1795 on Glasgow Street between Middle and Crawford. One of the finest examples of this type is the Trinity rectory from the 1826 on the west side of Court Street between North and Waverly Place.

In glancing back, one finds that a much better class of house was built in Portsmouth before the Civil War; many of that period were fine brick dwellings, both comfortable and city-like. The average house here is not up to what is expected from a city of its size; but the interiors give one a pleasant surprise, for their furniture and fittings have always been unusually good; the people having *made* shopping trips to New York where they had to go in sailing vessels, taking nearly a week to get there. *The closets in many of these houses are very shallow. Clothes were stored in high-standing wardrobes, some of which survive. When traveling the wealthier passengers would sometimes simply move one of their wardrobes onto the steamer. Examples of wardrobes of the time can be seen in the Hill House which is open to the public for tours.*

The shops here handled a high grade of goods, London-made furniture and fine silks and other imported articles. Portsmouth was in a large measure settled by people who came direct*ly* from England. *Many were also Scottish merchants whom Colonel Craford had convinced to move to the clean streets of Portsmouth, to get away from the crowded and dirty streets on the Norfolk side.* This had its influence upon the town, which was in many respects like an English one.

The town was laid out like an English market town. The main street, now Crawford Street, was called Main and ran along the river front; the street leading to the King's highway (a name derived from the Royal highway system built in England) was called High Street,, the streets on either side of the High Street were named King and Queen, The street passing by the courthouse was called Court Street, the street on the south boundary of the original town was called South Street, the one on the north boundary was called North and the street in the middle of everything was Middle Street. The first two streets added to the west were named for English Royal Governors of Virginia: Dinwiddie and Effingham. Dinwiddie was lieutenant governor when the town was laid out. It was he who signed the official document. the other named for Governor General Francis Howard, Baron Howard of Effingham

There was much formality and etiquette here until the Civil War changed everything in the South. Perhaps the most pompous ceremonies were the funerals, which were conducted with as much etiquette as a coronation. There were however, some very trying things connected with them, unknown in these days. They would have been more pleasing to our Poetess than those she witnessed at an earlier period. The dead were not embalmed, but placed in iceboxes made for the purpose. There was but one in town, and its owner rented it to other undertakers. The body remained in it until just before the funeral, when the casket was brought. It was a gruesome custom, the ice had to be constantly renewed, and there was a mournful thud of water dripping in the pail, which had to be carefully watched lest there should be an overflow.

The first preparation for the funeral was the invitation, which was ordered from the printer as soon as the place and hour for the rites had been decided upon. These cards were formal and were printed in most cases on black-bordered paper. They were addressed by members of the family, and sent to all friends and acquaintances,*and delivered* by a servant or some family dependant who could read. This custom was in vogue as late as 1883.

Each night until the deceased was buried, two friends of the family kept vigil over the body. They usually sat in a room adjoining that in which the corpse lay. There was a lavish tray of food placed at a convenient spot for the watchers, so that they could regale themselves from time to time. As a general thing the watchers were men, so liquors and cigars were provided, too.

At the funeral, every relative, no matter how remotely kin, was expected to ride to the cemetery. Every mourner who could muster a black dress and bonnet donned them for the occasion, and all who rode to the grave were "mourners." If the funeral took place at the house it meant much work for those in charge. The undertakers had no chairs, so they had to be borrowed from the various neighbors, and friends were kept busy receiving them and putting them in place. As the funeral hour approached the family standbys were much needed. Box after box of black gloves were there to be fitted to the mourners, for custom required that a pair should be given to each one. Rolls of black ribbon, as well as bolts of crape had to be cut into lengths. About two yards of crape was placed around each man's hat and tied together with narrow black ribbon, thus making long crape streamers to the hat. This material varied in width from six to twelve inches and came in different degrees of thickness; but all this was a matter of expense. Some friend was stationed at the door to receive the hats as the men came to the funeral, so that they could be draped and returned. After the burial the near relatives were expected to take a part of their crape streamers and wear it as an arm band for thirty days.

In the house of mourning the front blinds were kept closed for weeks; sitting on the porch even in the hottest weather would have been direst disrespect. The piano must be silent for months, and if the children took music they must go to a neighbor in order to practice.

The funeral processions were enormously long, the last carriage or two being reserved for old slaves and the family servants. The laws of precedent governing the degrees of kinship were as rigidly observed as those for a coronation. Family feuds have been known to occur because some relative did not get as high a seat at the funeral as the kinship warranted.

Among many of the families not only children and grandchildren, but nieces put on mourning.

As there were no florists in the neighborhood, flowers could not be ordered; but there were always people who sold flowers from their gardens. These flowers were eagerly sought by the friends of the dead, and fashioned into suitable designs.

There was a funeral in town in the eighteen eighties that expressed the ideas of a prominent citizen, who was much opposed to pompous and showy ones. For some years he had cared for an aged cousin in his home. She had outlived all her near relatives, being nearly ninety years old, and there were really none to grieve for her. She was a woman of means, so there was no danger of his being criticized for disrespect to poor relations.

The family connection was immense, for the old lady had married twice, each time a widower with a large family. It is doubtful that the funeral would have been carried out as it was had there been hacks *(horse drawn taxies)* enough in the two cities *(Portsmouth and Norfolk)* to have accommodated the "mourners." Two by two went the family connection and old friends, trailing behind the hearse, from the residence to St. John's Church *(the second of the two Episcopal churches at the time then located on the corner of Curt and London streets, not were it is now)*; and when the services were over there the procession formed again, but this time not with such strict accordance to the rules of kinship. It was actually whispered that some of the young people paired off at the end of the line, and that things were not as doleful there as the occasion required. Two by two they proceeded to Trinity Churchyard; and the saying goes that as the first mourner entered the churchyard the last one left St. John's Church. The churches were nearer together than they are now.

    There was a rigid etiquette that hemmed in the marriages, too. Engagements were held sacred; and to have announced one would have been indelicate in the extreme. The most daring newspaper would never have alluded to a marriage as a coming event.

    Invitations were issued to the wedding exactly one week before the ceremony. They were sent out in proper form, with a great deal of ceremony. A family carriage or hack was requisitioned for the day. The bride's mother, her first bridesmaid, or maid of honor as she would be called now, and another intimate friend were the ones who went in the carriage. A young black man sat with the driver and it was his business to dismount and carry the cards to the doors. He wore spotless white gloves and the invitations were carried on a small silver tray.

    These once out, the bride must go into retirement as far as the public was concerned. Had she appeared on the streets, or even at church, she would have been called unrefined. She came in for her full share of entertainments then, as now, but they took place after the marriage. The day after the wedding was another great day for the bride. It was known as the "second day"; and the dress chosen for that occasion was a matter of almost as much importance as the wedding gown. The bride, assisted by her mother and bridesmaids, received, welcoming all who wished to call.

The wedding receptions of those days were only for relatives and intimate friends of the couple.

It was unusual to take a wedding trip *(honeymoon)* until about the period of the Civil War; and for a long time they were looked upon with disfavor by many people.

One old lady used to tell of the first couple here who took a bridal tour, remarking that it was considered an eccentric performance. These trips evidently created a ripple in editorial circles: and the reporter departed from the strictly formal marriage notice, or rather added to it that the "happy couple had left to consume the honeymoon in New York." Judging by the notices in the papers, most of the weddings occurred at home. Only the barest notice was published: and the public had to be satisfied without knowing what the bride wore or what the groom presented her with. *Through most of the twentieth century wedding notices with photographs were published free of charge as news; but now there is a charge and the detailed descriptions of the wedding, then also considered news, are also a thing of the past. In that era where local people traveled on their vacations and who they visited was also considered newsworthy.*

A rehearsal was an unheard-of event, and would doubtless have shocked the community.

The new babies, perhaps, received no warmer welcome from Portsmouth mothers in the days of yore than is accorded now; but the display of joy was certainly much greater. When the baby was about two weeks old, the mother, arrayed in the daintiest of house gowns, daily received her friends. Cake and wine were served and the baby's health toasted. Every lady on the mother's visiting list was expected to call and pay her respects to the new arrival. Such a visit was as much a social duty as a party call or a call on the bride.

The baptisms passed off more quietly, probably because they took place in church. There was generally a christening robe, which had been passed down for several generations, and in some families there was a christening bowl kept and used in the same way.

Chapter 33: Some Early African American History and the Institution of Slavery

No history of a Southern town could be written without a chapter on the African American population. *Miss Holladay says. I considered omitting this section completely and I have removed some parts of it (I will give you the gist of those sections when we get to them). Some parts of Miss Holladay's presentation would be offensive to the modern reader, although she would be mortified to know that to be the case now, but her attitudes do illustrate the belief among many white Southerners after the Civil War that slaves were somehow happy in their servitude and the institution benign. Of course, we now know from slave narratives and from the fact most left their masters as soon as they could after emancipation, that that was not the case. Miss Holladay believed what she wrote and she does illustrate the lives of some prominent Portsmouth African Americans before the Civil War, and the conflicts which faced them. She also gives some details of the institution of slavery. I cannot cut the section completely because it is the only place where Portsmouth's rich African American heritage gets some of its due. Realize that Miss Holladay is telling these stories from her point of view. I have heavily Bowdlerized the language in this section of her work, as I have in the whole, to try and minimize any offense it might give modern readers . An excellent history of the African American community in Portsmouth's history exists and I recommend it highly to anyone with a special interest in this area of study. I will cite it at greater length in a moment.*

Miss Holladay begins this chapter by the following tribute quoted from a paper published beyond the Mason and Dixon's Line; i. e. in the Northern states, but it is a thoroughly just one and gives a good idea of another of the South's lost treasures. "Typically the African American slave tended her mistress in youth, was her companion in childhood, looked after her in girlhood and shared her confidences in young womanhood. When her charge was married it was not exactly nominated in the bond, but it was understood by the other party to the union that she should be taken over too; and the female slave was taken over in the majority of cases. It was this female slave who managed affairs for the inexperienced bride, bossed the young husband, and as the family grew took charge of it and managed the nursery, entered into the amusements of the small boys and girls and disciplined them only as she could.

 She had always been as well treated as any other member of the family; generally speaking, she shared in its prosperity, and what the family had of comfort, luxury and advantage, she was permitted to claim as her own. When dark days came, or the family was broken up, she clung to her mistress if she might do so, or to the daughter of the house, sharing in the family adversity as she had shared in their prosperity. There was no such thing known as emancipation for this African American slave, for she was always free, *or so the women of Miss Holladay's time fondly believed. Slave narratives contradict this view.*

 As this slave grew older she led an easy life, waited on by the other servants and much looked up to by them. Her "white children" always stood first in her affections, nor did her own children resent it, to them it was a "matter of course." After the emancipation many Portsmouth slaves, like the slaves elsewhere, refused to take their "freedom," as they called it, preferring to remain in the families to which they belonged. Soon after the "Proclamation" was issued an old Portsmouth woman came from church one Sunday and said to her mistress, "Missus, the preacher said today if there was any person in that church not wishing to be free he dared them to stand up." "Did you stand up, Sarah?" said her mistress. "No, I just sat quiet and said to myself Sarah is such a one, but she isn't going to get up." Her mistress, upon going to Sarah's quarters one night, found her small grandchild asleep on the floor. "Why don't you make that child go to bed, Sarah?" "Lord, Missus, do you think I would let her go to bed before I do and wear your sheets out that much more," was the reply. When her young mistress was married, old Sarah had a place not far from the family, while her young grandson edged himself closer and closer to the wedding party, and finally climbed upon the piano, where his form towered above the bride. It was this same Sarah who baked seventeen cakes the day before the wedding; the mere thought of it would send the cook of today home in despair, but the fireplaces of the time had unlimited capacity, and of kitchen help there was no end.

This illustrates the conflict emancipation created for the freedman more clearly than Miss Holladay realized. First we see that no one in the African American community of that church would publicly reject emancipation and most welcomed it; the Black minister certainly did. Sarah, however, had a problem which was probably not unique to her. Her status in the community arose from her job as the female major-domo of that family that held her in slavery. People often identify themselves with the work they do, even today, because it confirms their worth. In a case like Sarah's it must have been wrenching to give that up. It is also clear from this story that Sarah is not young. In the family she served she could count on food and shelter. She surely would have to ask herself, "What else can I do?"

During the *Civil* war *(The Civil War in later times is often called "The War of Northern Aggression," or "The War Between the States" by Southern sympathizers, but Miss Holladay calls it the Civil War more often than anything else throughout her narrative, and in the commemorative dedication to the "Confederate Window" at Trinity church it is also referred to in that way)* the faithful old slave was called and told that her young master was about to run the blockade and join the Confederate Army, and that her help was needed. Grief rent her loving heart and tears filled her eyes, for young Master was nothing but a boy, the baby of the family. Old Sarah wiped her eyes and did her part nobly.

When the Confederates evacuated Portsmouth in 1862, Captain Sidney Lee, who was in command of the Navy Yard, had to leave his post hurriedly; it was to Sarah that his silver was sent to be cared for. It was hidden by her on her mistress' premises, but the secret was not known to her mistress until the war ended and Capt. Lee sent for his silver. Sarah's son was butler at the commandant's house at the *Navy* Yard before the war and for many years afterwards, in fact as long as he was able to serve. Old Sarah never became free, dying just at the close of the war, beloved and respected by all her "white-folks."

Her fame still lingers in the family to which she belonged, and her virtues extolled from one generation to another.

Some Portsmouth leaders did have misgivings about slavery as the following story, quoted from a column by Alan Flanders about John L. Porter, the builder of the ironclad C. S. S. <u>Virginia</u>, *illustrates. Flanders is quoting from a biography of Porter written by his daughter, Martha Buxton Porter Brent.*

"About 1854 my father had saved enough money to buy a piano for my oldest sister (Mary Susan) and she was very happy in the prospect of music lessons from a professor in the fall, but tragedy occurred in the life of the colored members of our family that brought her a great disappointment.

"There were very few slaves in my father's family. His grandfather (William Porter), a very wealthy man, set all his slaves free by his will as soon as they should reach the age of twenty-one. But my mother inherited slaves, among them a man, Willis Hodges, by name, of whom my father and mother thought a great deal, and all the children loved him.

"Willis had married a woman named Matilda, a slave of Col. Binford, a prominent wealthy man of Portsmouth. Matilda and Willis had three children when Col. Binford died. Here arose one of the worst results of slavery.

"The servants had to be sold to settle the estate. So Willis came to my father in great distress and fear of being separated from his family. My father could not stand by and see Willis troubled. So 'Sis' he said, 'you will have to wait for your piano. I cannot have Willis wife separated from him.'"

Brent's memoir continues that her father "arranged for Willis and his family to move into a little plastered house on the edge of town. There Willis preceded to pick up odd jobs to support them. But he had as little idea of making a living for them as his Master had of making money out of them, so it ended in my mother having a rather poor cook in the kitchen, who used the turpentine bottle instead of the essence of lemon, and spoiled the pies first thing."

Flanders continues: "Brent also helped Willis Hodges by teaching him how to read," which was strictly against the law at the time. Brent continues: "Willis Hodges was my first pupil. He developed an ambition to read, so every night in the kitchen he could be seen bending over the book with his Master's little daughter guiding him along in the spelling book.

"The money he earned as a laborer in the Navy Yard came back, much of it, into his own pocket, and many nights I came up from his lessons with my pockets full of peanuts, or with a little peach turnover from those Matilda had made for him to sell to the workmen in the Navy Yard the next day."

Alan Flanders tells us Porter freed all of his remaining slaves in 1861.

Mike Holladay another old standby in the town, a native of Nansemond *County (now Suffolk)*, though he accepted freedom, remained with his master as long as he lived. Mike was a finished butler and served in Portsmouth as a waiter in the hotels and restaurants. He was noted for his fine manners and upright life. He accumulated some means and supported his family in comfort. On Mike's hundredth birthday the newspaper had an article about him and he was the recipient of many attentions from his white friends.

Of Bob Butt, the faithful old grave-digger and sexton we have spoken elsewhere, telling of his unselfish and heroic conduct in the yellow fever epidemic in 1855. In recognition of his faithful services the citizens of the town raised a sufficient sum of money to purchase his freedom. His latter years were spent as sexton of Trinity Church. *Sexton is an official title in the Church of England (in America now called the Protestant Episcopal Church) dating back to the early Middle Ages. It includes janitorial duties, but is not limited to them. In some cases the Sexton is also the Verger who leads the ecclesiastical procession.*

In the *eighteen* fifties Mr. John Neville owned a much-respected slave known as "Old Dick." He worked about his master's store for more than twenty years. His fidelity and politeness won for him the esteem of the community. When Dick died Mr. Neville had him shrouded in a suit of black cloth and placed in a mahogany coffin. On the day of the funeral Mr. Neville closed his store and the whole family went to the burial. There were scores of other white people present besides hundreds of his own race.

Perhaps none of the old time African Americans here was better known or more respected than Ben Godwin, who was not only a man of high principles, but so intelligent that his master, Mr. Robert Godwin, a Suffolk lawyer, felt it his duty to emancipate him. This he did by will in 1814. At that time the law of Virginia required all slaves who had been freed to leave the state at the end of a year. Uncle Ben, who had followed the trade of a barber in Portsmouth from his youth up, was much opposed to giving up his home. So much was he respected that the gentlemen of the town took the matter up and presented to the General Assembly a petition asking that Uncle Ben be allowed to stay in Portsmouth. This document may still be seen in the Archive Room In Richmond, bearing the signatures of the most prominent men of the town. The petition was granted and Ben remained here the rest of his life. He died in 1844, leaving a reputation for integrity equal to any in the town. The papers gave him an obituary that would have done credit to any citizen.

In his life he often received appreciation from former customers, in the form of a small legacy. His shop was on Water Street and we are told by those who remembered it, that it was the resort of gentlemen for a pleasant chat in the afternoon. Ben amassed quite a fortune, which he left to his family at his death. His house stood on the west side of Crawford Street, between Queen and London, where the automobile shop is now located. *That shop is also long gone now and the Wachovia Bank building now stands where his home stood.*

Old Billy Flora was the first of our African Americans to distinguish himself, and this he did by heroic service at the Battle of Great Bridge *in the American Revolution*. At this battle he was the last sentinel to leave the breastworks, not leaving his post until he had fired several times. Then in order to get within the breastworks he had to cross a plank very quickly. He reached this plank which was nothing but a shingle, turned around and fired eight times at the foe, entered the breastworks and coolly pulled in the shingle. *This is slightly different from the tale of William (Billy) Flora told elsewhere. In those accounts it says he held back Governor Dunmore's Ethiopian Brigade at the Bridge, which they attempted to cross three times and were driven back by his fire. This delayed the British just long enough for the militia to draw up before the bridge and to the enemy forces back to Portsmouth.*

Later on when war seemed imminent *in 1812*, Billy offered his services again saying he had the old musket that he had used at Great Bridge; and he'd be buttered if he wouldn't use it. Buttered was the nearest that Billy ever came to using an oath. *He was judged too old for active service in the War of 1812 and was set to blowing up ships in the Elizabeth River to prevent the British from taking them.*

His home was on the corner of Washington and King streets; in his latter days he kept a livery stable. *This livery stable was on Hanover Square where the Olde Towne Commons now stands. Flora was a free black, but his wife was not. He purchased her out of slavery, but the baby she was carrying, having been conceived when his wife was a slave, was, under the law of Virginia, still a slave and so he had to then buy his daughter out of slavery when she was born.* Billy met a tragic death, having been set upon and killed by some toughs of his own race, in a drunken row. *Another version of this states that his death was a result of one of the riots resulting from the hanging of Nat Turner, and Flora was trying to keep the peace.*

Another African American patriot who spent the latter years of his life here was Aberdeen. He served with zeal on shipboard during the Revolution, and rendered such conspicuous service that he won the admiration of Patrick Henry. He, too, was a freed slave. Mr. Foreman in his recollections says he remembered Aberdeen well; he lived on the corner of Court and Columbia streets and was in those days a shipowner and rich man.

I have told of the famous African American spy during the Revolution, James Armistead Lafayette, and of the Civil

War exploits of Mary Luvest. I will tell the story of the opera star Sissieretta Jones and the composer Hiram Simmons in a later chapter. Some other Portsmouth African Americans were: Jeffrey T. Wilson, historian and philosopher, for whom a housing development was named; Ida Belle Barbour, a teacher who in 1911 formed the Miller Day Nursery for the children of working mothers and also had a housing development named for her; Israel Charles (I. C.) Norcum who became principal of the Chestnut Street School in 1884 and
for whom one of the city high schools was named when it was built in 1919; Lavina Miller Weaver, a teacher for whom the Riddick-Weaver School was named. The other person for whom that school was named, William Erhart Riddick, entered the True Reform Building, called High Street School, on the southwest corner of High and Chestnut streets in 1909, then went on to be principal of I. C. Norcum High School for thirty-five years. William E. Waters first came to the city as a football coach, but went on to be principal of Norcum High School and also had a school named for him.

The effort to return local free blacks to Africa which resulted in the founding of Liberia was popular in Norfolk County and some of its early political leaders came from southeastern Virginia counties. Liberia's first president came from Norfolk and a later one from Southampton County. One free black from Virginia Lott Carey went as a missionary to Liberia in 1821 and founded the first church in Monrovia. In 1879 a missionary group was founded named for him, the Lott Carey Foreign Missions Convention, and one of its first missionaries to Africa was Georgia Carter Colley, from Zion Baptist Church in Portsmouth.

For the further and much more complete history of African Americans in Portsmouth, you should start with the three-volume compilation of documents put together by Mrs. Bertha W. Edwards in the local history room at the library. Mrs. Edwards is worthy of particular note herself. She was the first African American professional librarian in Portsmouth and the first paid director of the segregated public library, called the Portsmouth Community Library, then at 801 South Street. For a picture of this old building which still survives, though now moved to a new location, see *The Black America Series: Portsmouth, Virginia* by Casandra Newby-Alexander, Mae Breckinridge-Haywood and the African American History Society of Portsmouth. Mrs. Edwards story illustrates one of the problems of segregation. She had a degree in library science from Hampton Institute and was director of a library. When library licensure was required in Virginia all the library directors with degrees similar to Mrs. Edwards were granted licences. The then State Librarian, Randolph Church, refused to licence Mrs. Edwards, saying she was young enough to go back and get a graduate degree (the newly introduced requirement for a licence). He did not require this of any other library director in the Commonwealth.

On the subject of libraries we should say that two black Portsmouth dentists, James Holley and Hugo Owens, as young men, went into the then segregated public library and demanded service. It was refused. This resulted in a legal case which desegregated the libraries. It was the beginning of their two distinguished political careers. Dr. Owens eventually became the vice-mayor of Chesapeake (old Norfolk County) and Dr. Holley became the longest-serving mayor in the history of Portsmouth.

I have mentioned influential black politicians elsewhere, but must now include one of Portsmouth's most successful, L. Louis Lucas, who started her career in the Shipyard, was elected a member of City Council, went on to the House of Delegates, to the Virginia Senate and ran for the U. S. Senate. W. Nathan Howell from Portsmouth culminated his political career as Ambassador to Kuwait.

African Americans did have a place, if a segregated one, in the *Portsmouth Star*. Its best-known reporter, covering the black community, was Lee J. Rogers. He was his own photographer as well. His photo collection was salvaged by the library after the *Star* went out of business and is the basis of *The Black American Series: Portsmouth, Virginia*. I well remember Mrs. Edwards and your compiler going into the old building to salvage his pictures. There was no electricity and the photographs were ankle-deep on the floor, the filing cabinets that once held them being valued more than the historic images.

Another source for African American history rose from a project also started in the library. The Portsmouth Public Library won the largest grant ever issued a library in Virginia up to that time (1982) by the National Endowment for the Humanities. The project was called Lower Tidewater In Black and White. It hired three historians, Terry Jones, William Paquette, Tommy Bogger and an American Specialist Sarah S. Hughes, to study race relations in Portsmouth and the counties to its south. This resulted in a series of three films, later broadcast on PBS and recently restored to modern format by Tidewater Community College and in use in the school system in Portsmouth: a shorter version produced by the Virginia Endowment for the Humanities and Public Policy and WHRO-TV, a book titled <u>Readings In Black and White: Lower Tidewater Virginia</u> and a compilation of the names and careers of escaped slaves inducted into the U.S. Army at Fortress Monroe (called the Freedom Fort); many of these were among what were later called "the Buffalo Soldiers" in the Indian wars following the close of the Civil War.

Finally, the excellent history of African Americans in Portsmouth mentioned above in the Black America Series has become the best single source for the history of African Americans in the city. Since this source is so complete, I will not try to duplicate it here.

Portsmouth had its brushes with violence in the early days of the desegregation movement. On February 6, 1960, a group of I. C. Norcum students tried to get served at Rose's lunch counter. They were refused and staged a sit-in. The demonstration involved two to three thousand students the <u>Virginian Pilot</u> tells us and was broken up with one of the early examples in Portsmouth of the use of police dogs.

Hugo Owens, the president of the local NAACP when school integration began, admitted that the process had been peaceful in Portsmouth, but that its first year was "tokenism."

When the city planned to convert the traditional black high school (I. C. Norcum) into a trade school there was an angry confrontation between students and the police and a K-9 dog was turned on the leader. This was eventually resolved by making Norcum a magnet school for special training otherwise not offered in the citywide curriculum.

Returning to Miss Holladay: One of the most remarkable of Portsmouth's old slaves was Willis Cromwell, of whom we get a sketch from a little article written many years ago by one of the prominent citizens of our town. The writer begins by describing a great conflagration on the "foreign dock" at Portsmouth; the wharf he tells us was much used by the Italian barks for taking on their cargoes of staves for Palermo. *Portsmouth was in Colonial times a great exporter of wood. It had a contract with Cuba for spars and masts. Even at the end of the nineteenth century the Reed Brothers stave wharves at the foot of High Street did a brisk business with the West Indies. In the Patriot Inn you can see wainscoting almost three feet wide made of solid slabs of heart pine. Random-width heart pine was in use in Olde Towne houses up to the Civil War.* This dock *(the foreign dock)* had been devoted to foreign trade even before the use of steam as a propelling power. The writer goes on to say that, though the fire caused the loss of an immense amount of money, what in his eyes was the most valuable thing burned was the old brick building, a landmark left lonely on the wharf after Dunmore's bombardment of the town in 1776.

An old slave standing by the writer spoke of the great age of the house and its connection with the Revolution. The slave, Uncle John, had lived in this house as assistant to Willis Cromwell.

The passenger ferry as we knew in old times landed at the foot of North Street; but this horse-propelled boat did not carry freight back and forth. This was done by a square-rigged sailboat run by Cromwell. Cromwell then lived in the old brick house on the wharf where the freight from his boat was landed. This man was highly respected in the community and his history is very interesting.

In colonial days, Mr. Yates had left lands and slaves to the church in Nansemond County, as well as funds for a free school. The slaves increased in number as the years went on and some of them were sent to Portsmouth for hire. These slaves were kindly treated by the school authorities. A certain price was fixed on them for a year's term. It varied from $50 to $125, according to the work or capacity of the particular slave.

These "school slaves" were permitted to keep all over that amount that they could earn. Willis Cromwell was rated at $125 and his wife at $50. By frugality and industry they managed year by year to pay their rating and save enough to buy the sloop *Daisy*. As the traffic between the two towns increased Willis needed the help of another man and hired Uncle John. They lived together in the old house. Willis was trusted by the entire community, and held himself among the aristocrats of slavery.

He dreamed of freedom and like a devout Christian prayed for it. After awhile he had saved enough to buy his freedom and that of his wife and their six children and they moved to the North. They were much commended in the town, and their departure from it was universally regretted. Everyone believed that the *Daisy* had purchased their freedom. While watching the fire consume the old landmark Uncle John asked the writer if there would be any harm in telling what had really bought Willis' freedom. He had promised faithfully never to divulge the secret. The narrator told him that all concerned were dead, and there would be no harm in telling the story. Old John, the free black, then started out, "That isn't right: Willis didn't make his free money that way. It's a fact he didn't, for I knows all about it. Willis said one night when the fire was burning in that big old chimney, he was sitting on the bench in the corner and dropped off to sleep. Then he dreamed a dream that told him there was a nail keg of money mighty nigh to him Right there under that hearth. That stirred him early, before day broke. The old woman and the children were fast asleep, so he said to himself, 'I'll just take up a brick or two and scratch under there to see if my dreams is true.' When he grubbed down about a foot he struck something and he said to himself, 'that's it.' He hadn't time then to dig more, so he just put the bricks back where they were and made it look like nothing had troubled it. But he says 'I'll look further tomorrow night.' He studied and he studied and he prayed and he prayed till after midnight and when all was gone to sleep again, he took up the brick hearth and dug with a spade till he uncovered that keg full of gold. That's the way, sir, that Willis got that money that you talk about. Willis said his discovery came from the secret prayers of himself and his old woman. Sir, that money must have been some of old Pirate Kid's belongings, when he used to come up to this place before Nat's War. Yes, sir, Willis always said prayer fetched that money that gave him freedom."

The writer goes on to vouch for the honesty of old John, but he says nothing could ever shake John's belief in Willis' story.

Perhaps the first opinion recorded about the African Americans in our community was expressed by the English Lady so often quoted.. She says:

> "For in the towns where I have been,
> Slaves well-treated I have seen;
> Well clothed and fed they mostly were,
> When sick attended with great care;
> And many bring them up so well
> They go to school to read and spell.

This anti-dates the school for African Americans Miss Holladay will tell us about on Queen Street, and so the "English lady" must be referring to teaching in the home. In 1831, in reaction to the Nat Turner Uprising, the state of Virginia actually made it illegal to teach blacks to read and write, though we know from Miss Holladay that many were literate. For more on this subject and on the African American pioneer educators like Israel C. Norcum, see the chapter "Striving for Education" in <u>Black America Series: Portsmouth, Virginia</u>.

Our English poetess continues:

> For in the church and meeting too,
> They've seats for those who wish to go

In a description of Trinity Church (then Portsmouth Parish) Dr. John Henry Wingfield, he tells us there were pews in the church painted black for the African Americans in the congregation. The Methodist church also had African Americans worshiping with them in Colonial times and the Baptist church had blacks in its congregation from the earliest times ntil emancipation. On December 21, 1863 General Benjamin Franklin Butler ordered that all pews in Trinity church be open to African American soldiers. Even though that ruling ended with the end of Union occupation African Americans continued to worship at Trinity, first sitting in a balcony which has now been removed. As late as December 1926 seating was segregated; we know that because pews 40 and 41 were "rented for blacks." For a time there were no blacks in Trinity's congregation, prompting C. Charles Vaché, then rector, to start one of his sermons, "Have you noticed there are no black people in this congregation?" Fortunately black families have now returned to this old historic church where African Americans have worshiped since Colonial times.

Some of the African Americans in Trinity's congregation, however, decided to form their own Episcopal church in 1890 under the leadership of George Freeman Bragg, as a mission of Grace Church in Norfolk. In 1893 they moved into the Odd Fellows Hall on Court Street, then in that same year into a blacksmith shop on Glasgow Street, in 1897 into a barbershop on London Street near Green and then into their own stand-alone chapel in 1899, called "New Chapel" on High Street near Chestnut. Throughout this time Trinity continued to aid the new congregation financially and there remain strong ties between the two churches. In 1917 the congregation purchased the J. E. Johnson grocery, tobacco, liquor and wine store on the corner of Effingham and Bart streets. The store had been forced out of business by Prohibition. They called the new church St. James. They slowly renovated the building until it appeared as it does today, adding a parish hall in 1982, again with some financial help from Trinity.

Methodism, when it came to Portsmouth in 1772, had blacks in the congregation which later became the congregation of Emanuel African Methodist Episcopal Church, one of the oldest black congregations in the nation. For more about this read _A Brief History of Monumental Methodist Church_ on the INTERNET by Mrs. Margaret Windley and Emanuel's history in the local history room of the library. After the Nat Turner Uprising the Commonwealth made it illegal for any black man to preach to a black congregation. As a result Emanuel A. M. E. was served by white ministers from that time until after the Civil War. The church on North Street is quite beautiful, with murals on the ceiling inspired by ones seen by one of its ministers in Rome and a multistory group of windows made from pieces of blue cathedral glass. It was considered modest when it was finished, but now it seems a masterpiece of modern art.

Our poetess continues:

> In their own church they are allowed
> To meet together in a crowd,
> Where some slaves of the place
> Fired with enthusiastic grace,
> Roars in his motley audience's ears,
> A string of jargon he calls prayers.

(The Methodists were considered unorthodox for their informal style and passionate exhortations, compared to the decorum of the Church of England the author would be familiar with and the decorous words of the <u>Book of Common Prayer</u>)

> For take whatever pains you may,
> They'll only worship their own way,
> And preferred before the rest
> The Anabaptist is the best;
> Dipping on Sunday in the creek
> The converts who that doctrine seek.

When the first Baptist Church in Portsmouth was formed, Court Street Baptist, it included a black congregation with its own preacher. During the Civil War in 1865 a "letter of dismissal" was issued to 318 black members who formed Zion Baptist Church. In 1865 Ebenezer Baptist Church, which claims to be the first black congregation formed after emancipation, was formed. Both have excellent histories in the library collection.

The first pastor of Zion was Reverend E. G. Corprew, who served the church for sixteen years. Land was made available at 527 Green Street by Richard Cox, a member of Court Street Baptist, for the new congregation. The first building burned and in 1876 the new brick building was dedicated. The second pastor, Dr. John M. Armistead, who served the church for forty-three years, organized five "daughter churches."

Ebenezer Baptist Church was started when a small group headed by John W. Godwin secured space in Temperance Hall and organized it as The First Colored Church of Portsmouth. Godwin became its first pastor and it was moved to Sneeds Blacksmith Shop. In 1868 it changed its name to Ebenezer Baptist and in 1871 it acquired the old Wesley Chapel Methodist Church on Effingham and Columbia streets from the white congregation of Central Methodist Church, of which much more later. In 1894 this was replaced with the current brick structure. Two of its pastors, Harvey N. Johnson and Ben A. Beamer, went on to become major players in Portsmouth politics.

Another old African American church is Fourth Baptist. It was destroyed by fire in 1992 but has now been rebuilt and is an excellent example of twentieth century church design.

Miss Holladay now quotes "Mr. Forrest, one of the Norfolk editors, writing between seventy-five and a hundred years ago" (1830 - 1850) an apology for slavery, in which he says local slaves are happy with their lot. I have not included it here, because it is not really Portsmouth history, but an editorial. Some evidence that all was not happy for slaves in Norfolk and Portsmouth, comes from the list of vestry members at Emanuel AME Church listed in the history of that church in the library collection. After each name it says: "ran away", "sold South", or "died happy." Emanuel also prides itself in being one of the stations on the Underground Railway, and in it can be seen the hiding places for slaves and the tunnel bricked up in 1865 through which another source tells us they made their way to the Shipyard, or to railway cars on the line which ran down the middle of High Street, to the wharves where they could stow away on merchant ships.

Miss Holladay goes on to quote a diatribe from the editor of the Norfolk paper against African American forms of worship. To put this in perspective, the memory of the Nat Turner Uprising was still fresh in the minds of local people who feared slave insurrections instigated by black ministers. Virginia had passed laws forbidding blacks to preach to blacks and from what Mr. Fiske says this prohibition was not very successful and the fear still ran close to hysteria.

Miss Holladay continues: When Mr. Fiske published this warning the blacks had just finished their new church on North Street, the African Methodist Episcopal Church *now Emanuel A. M. E. on south side of North Street between Washington and Green. This dates the editorial Miss Holladay quotes to the late 1850s.* This church has been enlarged and improved, but is still the "swell" one, its congregation would tell you. An old man of today *(1935)* tells us that the African Americans had a church for many years on the site now occupied by Briggs School, *(the Briggs School was on Princess Square on the east side of Washington Street at its intersection with King Street. It went out of use as a school and was for a time school board offices; it then burned in the 1960s. It had been the school for downtown children. Miss Holladay has told us the first school for black children was on Queen Street, but the most famous school for them was built in 1878 at 907-917 Chestnut Street and called the Chestnut Street School. Here is where I. C. Norcum started his distinguished career as an educator. There is an engraving of this building in Edward Pollock's* Sketchbook of Portsmouth*)*; but it was closed at the time of the Nat Turner insurrection and never opened again. Today perhaps the African American takes his religion a little more quietly than he did some years ago. We can many of us remember mornings when the maids did not come, or came very late, arriving in a great state of excitement, shouting and singing, "Glory, Glory. Hallelujah my soul is free, I am going to sin no more."

The Invariable comment of the mistress upon hearing the shouts was, "My good servant is gone." All housekeepers would tell you that when a slave got religion that he was worthless for a long time.

The English Lady so often quoted in these pages tells us that the baptisms took place in the nearby creek; but she failed to describe them for us. Now most of the churches have their own pools in them; but the baptisms often take place in the river. One must see the ceremony to appreciate it. A large crowd was usually present; so crowded were the bridges on such occasions that the papers frequently warned the public about the danger of their giving way under the strain. Some forty years ago *(the 1890s)* most of the baptizing was done at the foot of Middle Street, which was more of a beach than it is now. *Crawford Parkway was not extended from the Holiday Inn site to Effingham Street until the 1960s. The beach was gone by Miss Holladay's time, replaced by some sort of business district. The beach on Crawford Harbor now reappears at Crawford Street and Swimming Point Walk, a block away from the site Miss Holladay describes. It gives some idea of what it looked like in the time she is describing. There was, when such baptisms were taking place, a long wooden pedestrian bridge from the foot of Court Street to Swimming Point Walk over Windmill Creek, which is probably the bridge she is referring to. There is a picture of such a scene in* <u>The Black America Series: Portsmouth, VA.</u> It had not been given over to business then. Near the shore was an old brick stable which served the candidates for baptism as a robing room. *There is an old brick fire station at the foot of Middle Street which later was used as an electric substation and has now been handsomely converted into a private home. Miss Louise Tevathan remembered living on the second floor, in an apartment with her mother, before it became a substation. It is certainly in the right place to have been the brick building Miss Holladay describes.* When the calendar announced the coming of spring the time was ripe for the repentant sinner, who did not wait for spring in veritas for his plunge. The Sunday selected generally proved a cold one. By two o'clock, for in the old days the African Americans had church at three o'clock, early dinner being the order of the day so that they could all be present - Middle Street was alive with African Americans of all ages, kinds and conditions, dressed in the finest clothes that they could muster. There was often twenty or thirty candidates to be emersed. Having changed their finery for white raiment they stood in a group on the shore and joined the congregation in singing their wonderful old hymns as only blacks can. Sometimes the favorite song was:

'Sister Mary's got a golden chain,
And every link's in Jesus' name,"

Then again it was "Swing High *(she may mean "low")* sweet chariot" or "These bones shall rise again"

Then the parson would preach his sermon, absolutely leaving no room for doubt as to there being but one form of baptism. His reasoning was entirely convincing. The discourse usually declared that there were three kinds of baptism: emersion, immersion and sprinkling. Only one kind of baptism can be right, Brethren; if emersion and sprinkling is wrong then immersion must be right. Therefore my Brethren, immersion is right." Waxing more eloquent he added further proof "taken right from Scripture," for the "Good Book" does surely tell us that we must be buried in baptism. Now we all know that when we are buried in death we are put under the ground. Then it is sure that when we are buried in baptism we must be put under the water.

Having clearly proven that immersion is necessary, the preacher boldly enters the river, taking his stand where the water is about waist deep. He is then ready to cleanse the penitent and one by one they wade out to him. After a short exhortation he would grasp the sister or brother by the waist and fling him or her as the case might be headlong in the brine. The sisters sometimes went down very reluctantly; hugging the preacher and clinging to him, they would raise their voices in terrific shrieks. They were much subdued, however, when they rose from burial in baptism and waded quietly to shore. In recent years the parson is saved the embraces and harrowing details by an assistant who leads the candidate to him and escorts her back to shore when the rite is over.

There was never a time during the period of slavery when the black was not allowed to hold fairs or use other methods of making money for his church. Of one such venture we have an account written by one who at that time was superintendent of the African Methodist Episcopal Church, the swell church of African American community. "Soon after the War," he says, "we ran an excursion to Soldiers Home, and there were seven or eight hundred people waiting on this side for the boat to come from Norfolk. When it arrived they made rush for it; but the customs officer was on board and he counted every one who came on, even the infants in their mothers' arms he counted as souls under the law. The mothers would not pay for them, and we had a whole boatload of mothers and babies, so the excursion was a failure. No tickets were collected and the proclamation went forth that all tickets would be redeemed, meaning, of course, the tickets of those who did not get on board. We saw many of those who went on the excursion come and exchange their tickets for money. They were members of the church; they are gone now but we don't say where."

After some deletions I will continue with Miss Holladay's description of African American cooking:

Perhaps one of the greatest losses is the art of African American cooking. Here in Portsmouth, once famous for its beaten biscuits, most people have tamely submitted to the yeast powder variety, and one is seldom waked now by the noise of the rolling pin. Loaf bread is following the biscuit into oblivion, as the cooks of today will not come early enough to give it its second rise. Self-raising buckwheat cakes are now served in place of the delicious article made up over night with good old-fashioned yeast.

Old Pats Scott, one of the most noted cooks in the town, used to say a few years back, "You white folks are going to have a bad time one of these days when all us old slaves are dead. There won't be anybody here to tell the other people how to cook." Pats has not been dead very long, but her prophecy is being rapidly fulfilled. Their formulas leave much to the imagination. They do not deal in cupsful and ounces. "Yes, I just take a pinch of butter, and adds a handful of flour. Oh yes, just enough yeast to make it rise."

Pats Scott was quite a character in the town. She was much sought after as a cook until her eyesight failed and then she opened a crab shop, where her crabmeat was much in demand as the freshest and best to be had. She had many quaint sayings, some of them very profane, for Pats' soul had never been set free, and moreover she never seemed to care that it should be.

The old custom of calling the elderly black "uncle" and "aunt" is also a thing of the past. All well-bred children were scrupulously taught to give them these titles. The new generation of African Americans after the war, so disliked the*se terms* that they never applied them to their kin, always calling aunts and uncles "cousin." To them it was one of the marks of slavery. Perhaps the slave was allowed so much freedom in his church because he was so held in elsewhere.

They were subject to very strict laws.

The laws concerning slaves in our town seemed to have been made with care and revised from time to time. No black could be distrained or levied on for debt, if there was sufficient goods or chattels of other kinds within the power of the sheriff to take. *Miss Holladay may have thought this enlightened, but it means that in certain circumstances slaves would be confiscated in payment of a debt.*

Slaves freed by their owners, when they came to Portsmouth, were required to register. There are books at the Clerk's Office which show how carefully the record was kept.

If any of these files survive, and I am not aware of them, they would certainly be very valuable to a genealogist working with records of an African American family and to historians studying free blacks. Records do survive of slaves from Portsmouth and "Crane Island," which is probably Craney Island, who were transported to Nova Scotia at the end of the Revolution; these probably were slaves freed by Governor Dunmore. Among them, though not in the following list because they were not from Portsmouth, are slaves who belonged to Dunmore and were freed by him. Those ex-slaves listed are:

John Pomp, 24, stout fellow, (B. Pioneers). Formerly servant to John Morris, Portsmouth, Virginia; left him in 1779.

Phillis, 20, likely wench, (Black Pioneers). Formerly slave to Willis Wilson, Portsmouth, Virginia; left him in 1778.

Sam, 10, likely boy, (Black Pioneers). Formerly slave to Willis Wilson, Portsmouth, Virginia; left him 1778. Major Willis Wilson, an American artillery officer in the Revolution is buried in Trinity Churchyard.

Betsey, 36, ordinary wench, (Black Pioneers). Formerly slave to William Conner, Crane Island near Norfolk, Virginia; left him in 1778. William Conner is a relative by marriage of Col. Craford's sister Abigail Craford Connor.

Prudence, 11, likely girl, (Black Pioneers). Formerly slave to William Conner, Crane Island near Norfolk, Virginia; left him in 1778.

Mary, 20, likely wench, (Black Pioneers). Formerly slave to William Conner, Crane Island near Norfolk, Virginia; left him in 1778.

John Mosely, 25, likely fellow, (W. M. General Department). Lived with John Cunningham, Portsmouth, Virginia as a freeman; left him in 1776. GMC. We heard about the Cunninghams in the chapter on Portsmouth veterans of the Revolution.

William Dean, 62, ordinary fellow, (W. M. General Department). Formerly slave to William Dean, Crane Island, Virginia; left him in 1779. GMC

Samuel Saunders, 20, likely lad. Formerly slave to John Beans, Crane Island, Virginia; left him in 1778. GBC.

Jane Bush, 17, likely wench, M. Formerly slave to Andrew Stewart, Crane Island, Virginia; left him in 1779. GBC.

Mary Steel, 24, fine wench, (Black Pioneers). Formerly slave to Charles Cannon, Portsmouth, Virginia; left him in 1778. GMC.

In pursuance of two orders from His Excellency Sir Guy Carleton K. B. General and Commander in Chief of His Majesty's Forces from Nova Scotia to West Florida inclusive, both dated Head Quarters, New York, the one 15 April 1783 and the other 2nd May, We whose names are hereunto subscribed do certify that we did carefully inspect the aforegoing Vessels on the 13th June 1783 and that on board the said vessels we found the Negroes mentioned in the foregoing List amounting to Two Hundred and ninety six men, two Hundred and fifty five women and one Hundred and ninety nine Children and to the best of our Judgment believe them to be all the Negroes on board the said vessels and we enquired of the Master of each Vessel whether he had any Records, Deeds, Archives or papers or other property of the Citizens of the United States on board and to each Enquiry We were answered in the negative. And we further certify that

We furnished each master of a Vessel with a Certified List of the Negroes on board the Vessel and informed him that he would not be permitted to Land in Nova Scotia any other Negroes than those contained on the List and that if any other Negroes were found on board the Vessel he would be severely punished and that We informed the Agent for the Transports of this matter and desired him to use means for returning back to this place all Negroes not mentioned in the List.

[Signed]: Gilfillan Armstrong; W. S. Smith, Col., on the part of the United States; Samuel Jones, Secretary. One account says no proper accomodation was made for these slaves in Nova Scotia and many of them died there.

A detailed description of each *freed slave coming to Portsmouth* was recorded, showing any peculiarity or scar. The name and home of the former owner is given, and the manner in which freedom was obtained. Some of the ex-slaves registered had always been free, others gained freedom by the will or during the life of their owners. A few purchased it. Some had Indian mothers, which entitled them to freedom. Speaking of the Indian blood, there are cases on the court record in which persons accused of being African American prove that they have Indian, not African American mothers.

We find that blacks occasionally purchased other blacks. This was done generally to free them, and were relatives of the purchaser; but in other cases it is not clear that any such purpose was the object.

A curious fact is that James Armistead Lafayette, the black patriot spy, about whom we have heard earlier, was himself a slaveholder after the war. We also heard about the free black patriot Billy Flora who bought his wife and daughter out of slavery. In <u>Lower Tidewater In Black and White</u> *there is an interesting story of a shake cutter in the Dismal Swamp named Grandy who had to buy himself out of slavery more than once, due to his master's perfidy.*

All African Americans freed here were obliged to leave the town at the expiration of a year. Failure to comply with this law made them liable to slavery again. They could be sold by process of the law to the highest bidder.

Should a free black fail to register upon his arrival in town, and live here two months without doing so, he was subject to a fine. The employer of an unregistered free black was fined $5 for every day that he employed him.

In most respects the free black and the slave were governed by the same laws. The former if found on the street thirty minutes after "bell-ring" was to be arrested and punished with stripes *(whipping)* or fined.

As far back as 1825, and perhaps before that, there is constant complaint of this class of African Americans. In the *eighteen* fifties they were declared to be a menace. It was agreed by all that this class was thoroughly degraded and had a pernicious influence on both white and colored, especially the latter race, who were much thrown with them in their daily avocations.

If Miss Holladay is correct about the date, this predates the Nat Turner Uprising. This suggest the population felt threatened by free blacks among them from an early time even though, in other parts of her narrative, some of these free blacks were loyal and productive members of society. There is no record of crimes by these free blacks that I can find to justify that fear.

Public meetings irrespective of party were held here, concerning the free black, and petitions were sent to the Legislature, urging that something be done to rid the community of this nuisance.

Another trouble at this time with the African American was the constant interference of the northern abolitionists, who were luring the slaves to the north. The loss from these runaways in 1854 was estimated at one half million dollars in this community. *It is hard to look at this statistic and believe, as Miss Holladay apparently did, that African Americans were happy being held as slaves.*

Male slaves were required to have a license to labor about the town, unless working for their masters, or hired for a term of months. The town clerk received twenty-five cents for issuing such a license.

There were regular printed forms to be filled in when a black was hired. Many of these contracts are extant: one in possession of the writer, shows that the employer agreed to furnish the African American with good clothing, changed to suit the season. The slave was to be returned at the end of his term with a good blanket. The wages agreed upon was ninety dollars for the year (1841).

After the ringing of the town bell at a certain hour, no servant must leave his master's premises, unless it were to go to his usual sleeping place, on any pretense, without a pass. This pass had to designate just where the black was to go, and was good for one night only. If a slave was caught on the street without a pass, he was arrested, put in jail or whipped. *This sentence would have been carried out at the whipping post in Prison Square where the 1846 Courthouse Gallery now stands.* Any African American found smoking in the street was liable to the same punishment. All unlawful gatherings were to be dispersed.

Free blacks that were habitually idle were subject to arrest. The policemen were authorized to hire them to the highest bidder for a term of six or twelve months.

Slaves in Portsmouth were sold in front of the Courthouse, which until 1842 stood on the site of the Monroe Hotel *(now the Tidewater Community College Visual Arts Center).*

In earlier times some slaves were "indentured," that is sold into slavery for a fixed period of time. In 1791 in <u>Portsmouth and Norfolk County Documents</u> *an indenture survives in which a mother sells her "mulatto" (first generation of a white and black parent) son, John Sparrow, "judged to be six years old" to two men who swear to teach him to read the Bible and "the mysteries of a seaman," and at twenty-one free him with "corn and clothes, as the law allows." This form of slavery for a fixed period of time applied to whites and blacks when the nation was first being settled and for many years thereafter. John Sparrow may have learned the mysteries of a seaman. There was a little lane by the shipyard on early maps called Sparrow Lane which might have been named for him if he did..*

Chapter 34: Walking the Streets of the Olde Towne

The old manners and customs naturally recall memories of the men and women of the days long since passed away. In some cases their homes still linger. Strolling down Crawford Street, as we turn into it from North, we soon reach the Barclay house, built in the days when a lot covered one fourth of the square. Its gable faces the street, and like so many of the old homes here the entrance door was in the yard. The Masonic Lodge met in this house before the Barclays bought it. The Barclays, like most of the well-to-do families in Portsmouth had a country home; and theirs was on the site now occupied by Craddock. The house was sold after the death of Mrs. Barclay, the grandmother of Clifford Barclay and of Charles Barclay.

The large house next to the Barclays (now two homes) was owned by Col. Josiah Parker of Isle of Wight. *This house stood on the vacant lot on the northwest corner of Crawford and Glasgow Street. In 2005 Parker's grave was discovered on his farm in Isle of Wight.* It *(Portsmouth)* was his winter home, and he spent the last years of his life here. He was at one time Aide to Gen. Washington. *All of the correspondence between Washington and Lafayette is signed by Josiah Parker, who eventually mustered out of the Continental Army as a Major General.* He was the first representative of this district in Congress. He was one of the *Society of the* Cincinnati *(This society was originally made up of officers in the Continental Army after the Revolution and it is now consists of descendants of officers in that war, one descendent in each name)*; and his certificate of membership in the Society is in the possession of one of his descendants in Portsmouth. After the death of Col. Parker this house was purchased by John A. Chandler, a prominent lawyer here. Mr. Chandler stood high in the estimation of the community, taking an active part in the affairs of the town. The Niemeyer and Hill families are among his descendants. The next to own this old landmark was Mr. John Day. It passed from that family at the death of Miss Laura Day, ten or fifteen years ago *(1920s)*. *The house was torn down before the creation of the Olde Towne Historic District, but the foundations can still be clearly seen in the vacant lot*

On the southwest corner of Glasgow and Crawford streets, set far back from the street is "the last of Irish Row," described in the chapter on the Yellow Fever.

The next two houses are actually modern houses built to conform with their older sisters. Beyond them is the house of the father of Eugene Bunn, who was one of the city's best known Notary Publics (his name is on many legal papers from the twentieth century). The house now belongs to George and Marilyn Brown.

Continuing our walk down Crawford Street, when we reach London there is a large brick house built about seventy-five years ago by Mr. James Murdaugh. Mr. Murdaugh was a prominent lawyer here for many years. He had only one child, the late Judge Claudius Murdaugh of this city. This house is now *(1935)* occupied by Judge Murdaugh's son and daughter. *Currently it is the property of Kathy Revel.* During the Civil War, when the family was away, the basement of this house was used as an office for the provost-marshal. *The house, built in 1841, is now known as the Pass House, as it was here that the Union occupation issued passes to cross the ferry to Norfolk, then belonging to the federal government, and to pass through the Union lines to visit relatives in the Confederate Army when it lay in Suffolk.*

The Pass House was not the first on this site Miss Holladay tells us. On the northwest corner of London and Crawford streets there was once a fine residence belonging to the Seward family. About a hundred years ago *(1835)* its owner, Capt. Joseph Seward was captured by Barbary pirates and never returned home. His fate was never known.

Across London Street from the Murdaugh house was the home of Mrs. Maria Riddick, the sister of Mrs. Murdaugh. *This* is where the Wachovia Bank now stands. The other old houses on this block have been torn down.

The Crawford House, built in 1835, was the leading hotel here for many years. *When it was torn down in the early 1960s it was the only Federal Period hotel still in use as a hotel in the nation. It was five stories tall, unusual for the time, and stood on the corner of Crawford and Queen streets. Several U. S. Presidents stayed there, Martin VanBuren, Zachary Taylor, James Polk, as can be seen on the historical marker on its site; and General Winfield Scott, the hero of the Mexican War was entertained here in 1851. The old hotel was on the <u>Virginia Register of Historic Places</u>, but that did not protect it from demolition by the Portsmouth Redevelopment and Housing Authority. Mrs. Emily Spong, the mother of U. S. Senator William Spong, was aware the state designation could not save it and had made application to have it put the <u>National Register of Historic Places</u> which would have saved it. This came to the attention of the then head of PRHA and he sped up the plan to demolish the building in 1970 so that by the time the papers arrived the building was already in the process of being torn down. Roney Leitner salvaged the front doors with the wrecking ball hanging over him, as he tells it, and they are now the doors to his livingroom on Glasgow Street, complete with marks where a rat had gnawed at them (to get in, or get out is not known). Mrs. Emily Spong was so angered by the loss of the old hotel that she began the process of putting all of the Olde Towne on the <u>National Register</u>. It is through her efforts that Portsmouth can now boast the largest collection of antique houses on the Atlantic Coast between Alexandria and Charleston. No longer "downtown" it was re-christened Olde Towne and added to the <u>National Register</u> in 1970 and expanded in 1983. There is now a parking lot for Towne Bank where the old Crawford House hotel stood and we can only imagine the tourists who would have wanted to sleep in its historic rooms.*

The brick residences opposite were the homes of Mr. Leonard Cocke and Mr. John G. Hatton. *These were removed to build the Federal Building and its parking lot. That building was opened April 29 1961.*

Where the old *Star* Building stands *(torn down to make way for a brick condominium with shops on its first floor in the 1970s)* was the home of Dr. Edward M. Watts, but this was destroyed by fire, many years ago. *Now on this corner is the popular coffee kiosk run by "Miss Betsy" where joggers on the seawall refresh each morning.*

Crossing Queen Street to the north we pass the fine old residence of Dr. R. B. Butt *(now the site of the Federal Building)*, now occupied by his granddaughters, Mrs. Pugh and Miss Nancy Butt. The porch of this house is unusually well designed. The rooms are beautifully proportioned and the hall with its winding stairway is most attractive.

The Crawford Apartment was the site of Drury's Tavern, in bygone days *(we seem to have turned back to the north along the east side of Crawford Street. The building Miss Holladay is now mentioning was also where the Federal Building and its parking lot now stand)*. The apartment was at one time the home of Mr. William Wesson, the grandfather of our late City Manager Gen. Jervey, and the childhood home of his mother. For many years it was the rectory of Trinity Church, next to it. Where the Neely Company formerly had a lumber yard, was the home of Richard Blow, which burned in the great fire of '21.

It was remembered as a hospitable mansion, and the flower garden was long held up as a model of all that a garden should be. The Blows never rebuilt but rented a house in the neighborhood.

Across London Street on the next corner *on the east side* was the home of Mr. Thomas Brooks *(This would be one of the houses in Benthall-Brooks Row which is now used as the emblem of the Olde Towne, and the owner would be the person for whom that landmark of the Olde Towne is named. A mounting block remains with the name "Brooks" on the street side in front of his house)* the father of Mrs. Alexander Grice and Miss Julia Brooks. Miss Brooks was noted for her good work; for wherever sickness and sorrow prevailed, she could be found. Mr. Brooks had a number of sons, but they left Portsmouth in early manhood. *Graves of the Benthals and the Brooks can be found in Cedar Grove Cemetery.*

The vacant lot to the south of this house, now a part of Mr. Norman Cassell's garden was formerly the private burying-ground of the Davis family, who lived opposite this site, where the Murdaugh house *(Pass House)* now stands. *This lot is the enclosed garden of Captain McRae's house on London Street toward the water, across from the post office. We will hear more about this captain and shipbuilder later. The current owners, the Weiss family, have put in a swimming pool, but have not told this author if bones were found in the process.*

Miss Holladay goes on to describe this property; where Mr. Norman Cassell lives, the McRaes lived.. This house was built by Capt. McRae, who went to sea before it was finished, and like his neighbor, never came back. His vessel having been wrecked. *This story is often told about Captain McRae, who was in the business of building ships and sailing them to the Carribean to be sold for rum, but his obituary survives in the Emmerson Papers, telling us he died at his home and was buried at Trinity Church. There is a damaged stone with a partial inscription south of the church annex which is believed to be his. Several members of his family are also buried in the churchyard.*

On the southeast corner of Crawford and Glasgow streets is one of the oldest houses in town, built by Mr. Edmunds Pryor considerably over a century ago *(1735)*, and occupied by his descendants until a few years past. *This house must have stood where the Lafayette Arch and its park now stand.* It originally had a shingled roof, which was so frequently set on fire by sparks from the engines, that the Seaboard Railroad decided that it would be to the road's advantage to cover this venerable mansion with a roof of tin. *In Miss Holladay's time the railroad line ran down the middle of Crawford Street from the Seaboard Airline Railroad terminal at the foot of High Street to the docks which covered the space where the Holiday Inn now stands.*

Across Glasgow Street, on the space now occupied as a shifting yard for the road *(now the Citizens Trust office building - even though Citizens Trust no longer owns it. The line of the old railroad spur can be seen in the eccentric fence line across the street; railroad spikes turn up in these lots, on the off-street parking and in the lots facing Middle Street)*, stood the fine old

Dutch-roof house *(tax dodger house)*, afterwards removed to Middle Street by Mr. D. Ball, and now occupied by Frank Hunter *(1935, but later owned by the elder Mr. Albertson who was City Attorney)*. Col. Nivison built this house about 1784 *(this is what is reported on its state historic marker, but recent research by the Albertson family identifies this date as a bill of sale and the house they believe dates to 1752, making it one of the oldest houses surviving the city)*, and lived in it for ten years and then moved to Norfolk. During the War of '12 it was occupied as barracks. It was at one time the home of a prominent physician, Dr. Harding, whose daughter was the first wife of Dr. Robert Butt. *In 1824 General Lafayette was entertained here on his visit to Portsmouth.*

When Andrew Jackson and his cabinet came to Portsmouth at the opening of the Dry Dock in 1833, they were entertained by Mr. John Murdaugh, who occupied the residence *(now called the Nivison-Ball House)* at that time. *The dry dock in question was Dry Dock Number One at the shipyard, which is the oldest dry dock in the nation and is listed on the <u>National Register of Historic Places</u>.*

The town was astir on this occasion to honor the Chief Executive and to show off the fine dock, the first one ever built by the government. The visitors were met at the County Dock by an escort consisting of two soldier companies, the Grays, commanded by Captain Samuel Watts, and the Portsmouth Rifles under Captain Young. The presidential salute was fired and the President and his party escorted to the Navy Yard. After the ceremonies attendant upon the flooding of the dock were over, there was a reception given the party by Commodore James Barron, then in command of the Yard. In the evening Mr. John Murdaugh also entertained them at a reception, as we have said in this old house. Mrs. Murdaugh was said to have been a charming hostess and the entertainment was long remembered here.

In connection with this visit of Jackson to the yard there is an interesting story told by one of our former citizens, Mr. Ebenezer Thompson, who was at that time about ten years old; *he was* employed to keep the men who were working on the dock supplied with drinking water. He carried with him a bucket and dipper; and as he told us was zealous in his work. On the eventful day while eagerly pursuing his duties he was stopped by a tall gentleman and asked for a drink of water. Seeing at a glance that the request did not come from a workman, he replied, "I haven't the time, Sir; I'm hired by the government to wait on its employees." "Then, my lad, I am entitled to a drink. I am employed by the government as its president, Andrew Jackson, at your service." When Mr. Thompson told us of this incident he was over ninety years old and still an employee at the Navy Yard. He laughed heartily over his adventure and said he remembered it vividly.

After the Seaboard Railroad was built in 1834, the market house was moved from the foot of High Street to Crawford; the house itself being in the middle of the street of the block running from High to King, leaving just room enough on each side for a carriage way. In this building were the butcher stalls. All down the middle of the street, between King and County was a paved way and there the market carts and fowl dealers sold their wares. On Saturday and other busy days the whole street was lined with hucksters' carts. The vegetables came fresh to us from the market gardens nearby and often they reached town before sunrise. The grocers did not sell vegetables and green stuffs, so marketing was a daily task, and usually it fell to the share of the men of the family, as it was not customary for ladies to he seen there. Now one seldom sees a man at market, as they have relegated that job to the ladies. All around the market there were plenty of servants, ready and eager to carry home the market baskets, feeling well repaid with a dime. The market house was again moved to accommodate the road in 1893, and a new building now used as armory was put up at its expense. *This armory stood at the northern extension of WAVY Street, running down County to Crawford across from the present City Hall, and is now a parking lot. It was bounded by Crawford, Bart and WAVY streets. In the mid-twentieth century the upper floors were used by WAVY-TV before it moved to Port Center, and the first floor was still in use as a farmers' market. You could select your Thanksgiving turkey, have it plucked while you were shopping and bring it home, wrapped in butcher paper, under your arm still warm and moist.* In 1924 a new market house and auditorium was erected on Middle Street *presumably behind the armory, or replacing it.*

Starting our walk again, we begin with Middle Street at its northern end, where we find another very old house, known as the Barron House. It was the home of Commodore (James) Barron's widow, who inherited it from her father, Mr. James Wilson. *The house no longer stands.* Mrs. Barron was much beloved in the neighborhood. When a very old lady she was accustomed to take a daily walk, always having plenty of time to talk to the children that she met. At Christmas she always remembered them, giving them each a mug. A local crockery dealer said he had a standing order from her for twelve dozen mugs every Christmas.

The house, number 100 Middle Street *(in the old numbering system - it is on the southwest corner of Middle and North streets)*, in which Mr. Leaven Plummer now lives, *later the home of Mrs. Murdaugh and now of David and Faye Timm*, can be classed with the old residences of Portsmouth though its recent veneer of bricks tends to hide its age. Its interesting history has been told on another page of this book.

The carpenter gothic style house on the northwest corner of Middle and Glasgow streets is another of the Olde Towne's landmarks. Built in 1885 it is still owned by descendants of the same family that built it - J. R. and Frances Gill.

Glasgow Street has always had a special charm. It is the subject of a poem by Virginia's poet Brodie Herndon. It says in part:

> *Wisteria still foams over the old fences of Glasgow Street.*
> *Mosses crevice the old cobble stones,*
> *Damp in early morning.*
> *But never will it be the same in Glasgow Street.*
> *One is not there whose presence,*
> *Casual as the humming of a song,*
> *Was known along the hidden lane.*
> *He no longer pauses where some sagging gate on*
> *overburdened hinges,*

Reveals a garden plot.
The short, familiar cough,
(That we have smiled to recognize in darkened halls, or
crowded auditoriums),
No longer punctuates the morning air.
Nobody goes through Glasgow Street in the morning
now.
Nobody goes the truant way
To the wharves of the side-wheel ferryboats,
And the red railway terminal.

There are two English basement style houses on the north side of Glasgow between Middle and Crawford. The one furthest to the west was built in 1795 and is an excellent example of the style on a less monumental design. It now belongs to Irvin and Dottie Lindley. The other was the home of Marshall Butt Sr., the author of <u>Portsmouth Under Four Flags</u> and Portsmouth's best known historian. It belonged to his son, of the same name, and now to his grandson. The other houses on that side are more modern. On the other side of the street is the Leitner house. The first floor was built in the 1830s to accommodate the second floor, which was the old city market. The numbers of the market stalls can be seen on the inside of its beams.

The old house pulled down to make room for the Rudwall Apartments *on Middle Street* was built by the Forsythes about 1800. In 1830 it became the property of the Watts family. The widow of Dr. Edward M. Watts gave the house to her daughter, Mrs. James G. Holladay, who with her family occupied it until 1909. Mrs. Watts built the two houses next to it on the remainder of the lot for her sons, Dr. Edward M. Watts and Judge Leigh R. Watts. *These houses were removed to make way for a vest-pocket park at the corner of Middle and Glasgow streets when the Olde Towne Historic District was laid out. The Rudwall takes its name from a famous tailor shop in Norfolk, Wallis and Rudolpho. When quality fabric became scarce in the early twentieth century, rather than reduce the quality of their product, the proprietors sold out and built this apartment house.*

What is now the Colonial Apartment was the Odd Fellows' Hall, which was built in 1839. It was a two-story structure, and the third floor was added *in 1901* in a very unusual way. The entire roof with its massive cornice was lifted on supports and the story built under it. The Doric columns of the portico where made higher in the same way and their proportions were somewhat marred by the change. *These three-story pillars are solid brick covered with stucco. After the Odd Fellows left the building it was for a time a seminary for young ladies and is now an apartment house.*

Across the way, next to the Niveson-Ball House, at 413 is a house from 1860 which was built by Henry Hudgins, who was mentioned in the taking of the shipyard as one of the men who went out to sink shipping in the Elizabeth River in a vain effort to keep the Union Navy from burning the Shipyard. He later served as an officer in the Confederate Army, was wounded at Gettysburtg, and buried with military honors from this house. His son, Morgan H. Hudgins, was mayor of Waynesboro, Virginia, and for fifty years head of the Fishbourne Military School there. The house then belonged to the Buchanan family for fifty years - Mrs. Buchanan was known in the neighborhood as "Grandma;" she raised thirteen children in the house and all the children in the neighborhood played there. The house now belongs to the Burgess family. Since it has been owned only by three families it is virtually unchanged inside.

The large brick house on the northwest corner of Middle and London streets built in 1885 was the home of a prominent banker, J. L. Bilisoly, for many years, then became the Balance Dance Studio, where the young ladies of Portsmouth took ballet lessons under the watchful eye of Mrs. Jean Balance. In the 1990 it was the Olde Towne Bed and Breakfast, then again a private residence, and now owned by the Horster family who plan to reopen it as a bed and breakfast in 2007.

Across London Street, where the Olde Towne Commons now stands was the livery stable of William "Billy" Flora who was the hero of the first battle in the American Revolution fought in the South: the Battle of Great Bridge. He was a free black. His story is told elsewhere in this book.

On the southwest corner of Middle and Queen streets was the home of Mr. John Cocke. It was an old-fashioned frame house with an English basement, like so many of the Portsmouth houses of an early day. *This house which would have been across the street from the Virginia Sports Hall of Fame no longer exists.* It was a center of hospitality. One of Mr. Cocke's daughters married Dr. George W. O. Maupin, who built the brick house next door *(also long gone)*. This house is now occupied by the Y. W. C. A. Another daughter married Mr. John R Newton Ashland, and their descendants still live in their old home by the YWCA. *The YWCA is also gone.*

Mr. Cocke had been lame from his childhood, a matter too personal to mention had it not been for the interesting circumstances connected with his lameness. Mr. T. Cocke was born at Shoal Bay, the beautiful Cocke home on the James River; and when he was about ten years old the British Fleet (War of '12) made its appearance in the river and the alarm was given. Fearing that the house would be sacked, the family packed up their valuables and prepared to make a hurried flight from the place. Just as they started to leave the youngster missed his pet hen from his collection of valuables. Declaring that he would not leave her to the mercy of the British, he ran back to find her, chasing her down the long flight of terraces that led down to the shore. He captured his pet, but in doing so fell and hurt his knee seriously.

In the basement of the Cocke house, Miss Mary Anne Bingley kept her historic school. Three generations, it was said, learned their letters at her knee. No pen but Dickens' could have done it justice in describing it. He could have made a glowing picture of it, but the scenes enacted there were often original and comic, but never cruel or false. Miss Bingley was a woman of high spirit and fine intellect. She outlived a large number of brothers and sisters and for many years was entirely alone. She kept house until within a few months of her hundredth birthday; doing her work without even the aid of a servant. At this time she became an inmate of the Home for the Aged, where she died in her hundred and second year. *As we will hear later, much of the education of the 19th century was done by these small private schools.*

In the house still standing on the southwest corner of Middle and County streets *(long ago torn down)* lived Mr. George Veale in the early years of the last century *(the 1800s)*. Once he refused to pay the sum due on a bail bond because the man for whom he had signed had skipped bail. Notice was served; and still he remained obdurate. He had, however to stay at home, for should he appear on the streets he would have been subject to arrest. Day in and day out the old Gentleman sat in his basement doorway chatting with the passers-by. Once in the excitement of an argument, Mr. Veale actually stepped into the street. As he did so the Constable passed and grabbed him. It was said that this officer had a grudge against Mr. Veale and had sought for a long time to catch him out of bounds. The old gentleman was arrested and put in jail, where he remained for some time. *There was a time when a man's home was really his castle.*

Another strange story from County Street is told by Mrs. Barbara Grace who lived in the English basement house which still stands behind the Pythian Castle. She remembered her grandmother telling her that the children of a long ago time would peek into the windows of the home of an old man who lived on County Street near Middle. He could apparently levitate silverware to their amazement and horror.

Beginning at High and going down the east side of Middle Street, we find on the northeast corner of Queen, a quaint old wooden house *(where the Virginia Sports Hall of Fame now stands)* the home of a former citizen of high standing in the community, Capt. Benthall, whose daughter married Mr. William Brooks. Mr. Brooks' grandchildren still live in the house *(1935)* next to the Benthall house *which* is one of the fine old type of house so familiar in Portsmouth in a bygone day; but any history of those who built and occupied it has passed away. On the next corner was the home of Mr. Jack Nash for many years.

The Nivison Ball House and the home of Henry Hudgins have been described earlier.

On the northeast corner of Middle and Glasgow streets is a house built in 1856 which illustrates how cosmopolitan the town was, due to its extensive trade, the Shipyard and the Naval

Hospital. Its original deed of sale was signed in Constantinople. It now belongs to Robert Rea and Maureen Boshier.

Midway between North and Glasgow streets is the home of the Marshall family. Though it is not a very old house it is a well-known one. For Capt. Richard Marshall its former owner was the soul of hospitality; and his home was not only the rendezvous for his friends but for the friends of his family as well. It is now the residence of his son-in-law, Mr. R. Stribling Marshall.

On the east side of Middle Street in this block is a house with verandas in the New Orleans style built in 1860 and still owned by descendants of the Borum family which built it.

On the southeast corner of North Street is the *Washington* Reed home, a handsome brick house, built about a hundred years ago *(1830)* by an old citizen, Capt. Thompson, who owned a brickyard *in Port Norfolk* and had a number of slaves trained to bricklaying. This house, like several others built by Capt. Thompson, was the work of these slaves *who also paved many of the streets in both red and yellow brick..* Mr. Reed purchased it just after the Civil War. *This is the yellow house on the southeast corner of Middle and North, now called the Washington Reed house for its owner at Miss Holladay's time. John Thompson was a Revolutionary soldier and is thought to have built the house soon after his return from the war - this, however, would have made it fifty years older than Miss Holladay says it is. We know its age is, at the latest, in the 1790s. He also built the house behind it on North Street for his adopted son, John Thompson Hill. We know Miss Holiday is wrong about the date of the construction of the Washington Reed house. If it were built, as she suggests, in the 1830s, it would be younger than the house added for his adopted son. Based on the known date of the Hill house it cannot be built later than 1799. It was the home of U. S. Senator William Spong and his mother Mrs. Emily Spong, the mother of Olde Towne, of whom we have spoken earlier. It now belongs to Randy and Lelia Graham Webb.*

Turning to the east on North Street on the south side of it between Middle and Crawford is the home of the Hill family built in the first decade of the nineteenth century in the English Basement style. John T. Hill, the grandfather of Mr. William Hill, was a prominent editor here. *John Thompson Hill was the adopted son of Captain John Thompson. This branch of the Hill family died out in the 1940s, leaving the house with all of its furnishings, even clothes in the closets, to the Portsmouth Historical Society, which keeps it open for tours. Most historical houses are furnished with period pieces. It is quite unusual to have one where all the furnishings are original. This was the town house of the Hill family - they had a plantation on the Lynhaven River in Princess Anne County, now Virginia Beach. The parlors are very elegantly appointed for entertaining. One of the daughters of the family was a horticulture columnist for the old <u>New York Herald Tribune</u>, and endowed the Hill horticulture library on London Blvd.*

On the other side of the street, on the site now covered by several modern houses *(now, of course, more than 100 years old, and some of the best examples of high Victorian architecture in the Olde Towne)* stood the old Wilson house. This residence was placed far back from the street and was surrounded by a large garden, shaded by magnificent trees; among them crepe myrtles fifty feet high. After the house burned down the lot was vacant for many years and was a playground for the children in the neighborhood. It was built by Mr. William H. Wilson, for many years clerk of the court here. Mr. Wilson's family had been prominent in the county for many years, their home being the plantation known as Northwest Landing. Adjoining this place was the home of Mr. Holt Wilson, occupied by his family until recent years. *This would be the house on the northeast corner of Middle and North streets.* One of his daughters Miss Louise Wilson, was organist for Trinity Church for more than fifty years. One of her sisters married Capt. Hugh N. Page, U. S. N., and *the* other was the wife of Dr. Robert Butt.

The large brick house *on the northwest corner of North and Crawford streets*, for so many years the home of the Neelys, was built about eighty years ago *(circa 1860)* by Mr. Frank Grice, a constructor in the Navy. *This is now called the Grice-Neely house, on the northwest corner of Crawford and North. The* ironwork on the front of this house was found in the basement during restoration, and is original; the step to the back yard is a child's gravestone. It has a handsome interior spiral staircase. Frank Grice, with his collaborator Captain Neely, designed and built the steam frigate <u>Powhatan</u> which was Admiral Perry's flagship when he opened Japan as described earlier.

Retracing our steps and crossing Middle Street we find a house recently remodeled by Mr. Frank Crocker. *This is the house now called Dr. Cox's House on the northwest corner of North and Middle streets, owned by Drs. Rob and Susan Hansen.* It was built over a hundred years ago *(actually in the 1790s, based the advertisement for its sale which survives in the Emmerson file)* by Doctor Leigh, who moved later to Norfolk, selling this house to Mr. Swepson Whitehead, a prominent lawyer here, whose daughter was the wife of the Rev. John Wingfield - for so many years the rector of Trinity Church. Among his descendants here are Mrs. John Downing and Mrs. J. W. S. Butt. *The original owner, Dr. William Leigh was a Revolutionary War veteran. He was on the list of Tithables in 1798 and is buried in Trinity churchyard in 1809. The notice for the sale of the house survives. It is described as "A beautiful seat in Portsmouth called 'The Cottage' near the ferry wharf with a view of Norfolk harbour." He also sold a distillery at Gosport in the year he died with four stills, ". . . from which 300 gallons of spirits may be produced . . ." every year. There is an account of a party here with ice sculptures carried from Baltimore on the steamer packed in sawdust.*

Just behind this house on the west side of Middle Street is the home of the owner of the town's largest bank at the outbreak of the Civil War. He refused to divulge to the occupying forces who had money in the bank and was imprisoned at Fortress Monroe. He kept a pencil list of the civilians brought to the fort - a copy is in <u>Portsmouth and Norfolk County Documents</u>. This is the only list of civilians held there. The house was the social center of the Olde Towne when it belonged to James and Ann Douglas Smith. She sold real estate and would have tea parties for all the new residents. It is now owned by one of their sons.

Across the street is the large building divided into apartments described elsewhere in this book as the Macon House Hotel. *It played an important part as a Union Army hospital during the occupation as we have heard earlier.*

On the north side of North Street is the home of Portsmouth's first mayor, John White, when the town became a city in 1856. Continuing west is a row of English basement houses which have been lowered.

Further along this block a small lane enters North Street, which once led to the Portsmouth boat club. It was originally called Gaskins Lane for James Gaskins, the town's first silversmith and a Revolutionary War veteran who lived where the lane intersects the street. Its name was changed to Hunter's Lane until 2004 when it was returned to its original name. Gaskins' silver marks are listed in <u>Silversmiths of Virginia</u> and some of his silver survives in the Virginia Museum in Richmond and in the collection of Saunders and Barbara Early, present owners of his house. Remains of his silver kiln were found in the back yard in the 1960s

On the other side of the lane is the home of Dr. Grice. He built this handsome house set back from the street for his new bride who was the daughter of the Bishop of Southern Virginia. He proposed the city create a Health Department, which seemed an outlandish idea to the town council. Finally Grice opened his own health department for the city, entered from the little side porch which still can be seen on Gaskins Lane. When built the house had a "widow's walk" on its roof from which one could look out and see shipping entering the port, but a fire in the 1960s destroyed the old roof and the walk was not replaced.

The house on the northeast corner of North and Court streets stands where Cornwallis headquarters is reputed to have stood, and is described elsewhere in this work. It is now owned by Amy Manning.

On the northwest corner is the home of Thomas Hume, the first Superintendent of Schools for the city and the minister at Court Street Baptist Church. It is described in Pollard's <u>Sketchbook of Portsmouth</u> in 1888 as the finest house in the city. We will hear more about Hume later in this work.

The same was said in another publication of the Gothic Revival brick house from the 1890s on the southwest corner of North and Court built by the local firm of Hutchins and Moody for Mrs. Laura Armistead. It was for a time the Elks Lodge. During that period the auditorium was added behind it on North Street in the same style. Many young dandies and their dates remember swank cotillions held there. Some invitations survive in <u>Portsmouth and Norfolk County Documents</u>. In the 1960s there was a late night horror show program on television hosted by "Captain Madblood" and featuring the turret of this old house as his "castle." In the 1970s it was remodeled into apartments. The Elks moved to their last Portsmouth home across from I. C. Norcum on London Street. They gave that building up in the 1990s. The old Moose Lodge, often the site of First Citizen's Award Banquets, is in an unremarkable modern building on George Washington Highway.

Hutchins and Moody also built Fourth Street Baptist Church, described elsewhere in this book, on Court Street in Southside (now Port Center).

Some of the old houses are still standing on Court Street, among them number 900 which was known as Webb's Hotel about a hundred years ago. La Fayette was entertained at a banquet there when he visited this section in 1824-5. Mr. Webb's family was prominent in social life, and his daughters were said to have been beautiful women. *This house has not survived, but is described more fully elsewhere.*

The house, number 304 Court Street remodeled by Mr. John Morris, a few years ago was the home of Isaac Luke, the founder of the Methodist Church in Portsmouth. *He saved Robert Williams who was preaching Methodism in 1771 at the foot of Queen Street from a mob, and let him preach from his front porch. Based on that, Monumental Methodist Church is considered the oldest continuously operating Methodist congregation south of the Potomac River and the fourth oldest in the nation. An older congregation existed in Norfolk, founded by the same man before he came to Portsmouth, but that congregation was disbanded when Norfolk was burned in the Revolution and reconstituted after the war. At another point this history goes into greater depth about Monumental Methodist and Miss Holladay tells us the house, which was once an English basement style, was much changed by renovations.* The high English basement, although not apparent in the current facade, survives further back in the house. The Luke family, in its privately published history, tell other stories about Isaac, including the legends that the British made him walk on the shards of broken bottles in his wine cellar in an effort to get him to tell them more about local patriots and that his daughter, who was engaged to a soldier in the Virginia Militia, threw her ring out the back door to keep it from the British - the ring was never found. This Luke house is the second south on Court Street from London on the west side of the street. Isaac Luke and his wife Rebecca are both buried in Trinity Churchyard, just inside the High Street gate on the left.

The house pushed back to make room for the municipal building *(This is the old municipal Building which stood behind the 1846 Courthouse and was torn down in the 1960s)* and now *(1930s)* used for various city offices was the home of Col. James Langhorne, a distinguished lawyer here, and for many years State Senator for this district. The house was a center of hospitality in its day. Col. Langhorne was the grandfather of Mrs. Harry Browne. In later years this residence was the home of Mr. Moss Armistead. *This house no longer exists, but can be seen in old photographs and postcards.*

The two houses now occupied by the Catholic club were built by Mr. William H. Wilson, in 1859, as homes for his daughters, Mrs. Godwin and Mrs. Hodges. *This is the house, now in use by John McGlyn as apartments, on the southwestern corner of Court and Queen streets. The houses were in use starting during the First World War as a predecessor of the USO: an organization which housed and entertained members of the armed forces away from home. It then became the Catholic Club.* After the death of Col. Hodges, his house was purchased by Major (Judge) Crocker. When Judge Godwin moved to Norfolk in the *eighteen* eighties, his home was bought by Mr. O. V. Smith.

On the southwest corner of Court and County streets stood one of the finest of the old houses of Portsmouth; the home of Capt. William Moffat who served in the Virginia Navy in the Revolution. *This was the Navy of the Colony of Virginia in opposition to the British in the Revolution before the Articles of Confederation combined American forces. It has been mentioned elsewhere in this history.* Captain Moffat was much beloved in the town, and often alluded to as a 'Conscript Father.' His son William Moffat had charge of one of the cannon at the Battle of Craney Island *in the War of 1812,* and won a compliment from his state, though only sixteen at the time of the battle. *Captain Moffat married Prudence Dale.* The other son, Robert Moffat was an able editor and a very brilliant man. One of the daughters was the second wife of Dr. George W. Maupin, U. S. A., and the other married David Griffith.

On the northwestern corner of Court and County is the extravagant high Victorian Pythian Castle, designed by Edward Overman, built in 1897 as home for a now-defunct men's club, and added to the National Register of Historic Places *in 1980. It has had several incarnations since them including Thumpers Restaurant, now moved to the north end of the same block, and the offices of the state historical architecture department. The corner is now in use as Patty O'Brien's pub.*

Diagonally across the intersection is a building which was once one of the two old bus stations, later used as an Armed Forces museum, and now vacant. A gas station stood where the parking lot is on the southwest corner of this intersection.

On the next corner *(Court and Columbia)* stands one of the oldest houses in town. *Unfortunately this house no longer stands.* The front has been changed for business purposes and is now *(1930s)* used as a funeral parlor. It was built by Capt. Ralph. Pigott, just after the Revolution, and has been occupied by the descendants until Mr. Wallace Cooke and his brother, Dr. Sanford Cooke, sold it nearly twenty years ago. In his latter years Capt. James Wallace Cooke who won imperishable honor in the Confederate Navy, made this house his home, having married Miss Mary Watts, a descendent of Capt. Pigott. Dr. Cooke built his home on a part of the Pigott property. After the death of Capt. Cooke his wife taught school in the house. She was a woman of broad intellect and fine education; most successful in her work.

The complex of town houses now on this corner was built by William Chick in the 1980s and 1990s.

On the east side of Court between Columbia and South Street was the home of Laban Goffigan *buried in Trinity churchyard,* who served as an officer in the Virginia Navy during the Revolutionary War, and was harbor master for Portsmouth for many years afterwards.

On Court Street the Bannerman couple lived when our town was a village. They kept the community in a stir, leading a cat-and-dog existence, which ended in Margaret Bannerman's taking her troubles to court. It seemed that Benjamin finally turned his wife out of doors minus her wearing apparel and other personal effects. In spite of his wife's persuasions, Benjamin remained obdurate.

The said Margaret must have been either a very stupid woman or a most disagreeable one not to have managed Benjamin to better advantage, since she had already had two husbands to practice her hand on. However, Paul Kingston, one of them did not long survive matrimony, and perhaps John Shreep the second one, did not tarry much longer with the fair Margaret. Both spouses left some property, which fell to the share of Bannerman.

When the domestic grievances came to court, there were numerous witness for both Benjamin and Margaret, and those who testified in behalf of Bannerman abused his wife unmercifully; but Mrs. Bannerman's witnesses were equally vociferous in casting mud at the husband. The Court ordered Bannerman to pay his wife an allowance of sixty pounds a year; she was also to have twenty pounds in lieu of the clothes and personal property which he had forcibly withheld.

The Court found Bannerman hard to manage, too, as it soon received an appeal from the wife, urging that her allowance be paid. This time the Court ordered his property sold by a committee appointed for the purpose, should he further refuse to obey. We hear no more of the quarrel but a few years later in 1774, Benjamin Bannerman is before the Court again, and fined for living in adultery. When the Revolution came the gentleman's sympathy was with England, or at any rate he arrayed himself on that side, and his property was afterwards forfeited. As to Margaret's politics we are left in the dark.

Where the Post Office, *now the main Public Library,* now stands was the O'Neill, or as it was called in later years, the Milligan House. It was built by Barney or Bernard O'Neill, and like so many of the houses of its time it was of the English basement type. Mr. O'Niell who had made quite a fortune, owned the entire frontage of the square on Court Street, and made there a beautiful garden; but enclosed it in such a high fence that the public never even had a glimpse of it. In it were rare shrubs, and plants not usually found in gardens in this section. Midway in the block was an old Dutch-roof house (*Miss Holladay uses this term throughout her history. These houses are now called "tax-dodger houses" as the king taxed you on the number of stories you had on your house. To make their houses seem as though they were one story people would hang a false roof on the front. It looks like a mansard roof, but is actually just a piece of roof hanging down. Two survive in the Olde Towne, one on the east side of Court Street south of the Peters house, with a modern roof added on top of the tax-dodger roof and incorrectly dated to a much later time, and the Nivison-Ball house at 415 Middle Street also incorrectly dated to a bill-of-sale after the Revolution. The houses in this style are all almost certainly from before the Revolution*), in which Mr. O'Niell had lived until he made his money and built on the corner. Mr. O'Neill entered politics and became dispatch bearer under the Tyler regime *(President John Tyler)*, and kept open house. His only child was a daughter, named Jane, who had a very romantic career. She was considered quite a beauty, and at fifteen married a Naval officer who frequented the house. This officer, Dr. Palmer, took as much of her money as his short life permitted and died leaving her with one son, who became a noted sport later on.

Soon after Dr. Palmer's tragic death, a French man-of-war anchored in the harbor and his widow met one of the officers, Capt. Duvayrier, who straightway lost his heart to the Irish beauty. They were introduced by the Priest here and it was said that he interpreted for them, as Mrs. Palmer could speak no French and the Captain no English. They were married in spite of linguistic difficulties before the ship sailed. Captain Duvayrier was not the first of his family to visit Portsmouth; his uncle, General the Count de Moilles, had been here with LaFayette, under whom he held an important command both in this town and at Yorktown, where he was badly wounded. The Captain was also the nephew of another count, to whose title he succeeded the Count Duvayrier.

Life in Paris was not just what the newly made countess fancied. The social code she could not master and her frequent lapses kept her constantly under her husband's reproof. There was one habit that he could not condone—Jane developed a fondness for leaning out of the windows in season and out, to watch the sights of the streets of Paris.

It was finally agreed between the Count and his wife that a divorce would settle their difficulties; and the Countess returned to Portsmouth, bringing with her two children. She was granted a divorce by the Virginia Legislature in 1851. The son, Bernard, died in boyhood, and the daughter Melanie returned to her father by her own choice. She visited Portsmouth occasionally and was most pleasantly remembered by many of the older people of the town. A few years after her divorce the whilom countess again ventured into matrimony. This time she probably married the most congenial of her three husbands, Mr. Milligan. There were two children by this marriage, a son and a daughter. Neither of them married.

The west side of Court Street ended just a few feet beyond the home of Mrs. Ellis Butt, number 30. *All of the street numbers have been changed since Miss Holladay's time and the old City Directories in the library, running back to 1860, must be used to make the old numbers conform with the new. Insurance maps in the library identify the old numbers of the houses.* The east side extended a few feet further. At the foot of Court Street was the "Swimming Point" bridge which started from the middle of the street and ran diagonally to its present terminus. *There is a picture of this bridge a white-painted wooden gently curved span, in the library collection.* Connecting with this bridge was the boathouse of the Portsmouth Boat Club. The lots beyond Mrs. Butt's were all made land; filled in by dumpings from the mud machine. The Dinwiddie Street end was filled in at the same time, in the late *eighteen* seventies. For many years this land was not used and it was known as the "Desert." The bridge route was changed to its present location. In stormy weather the Desert was sometimes under water for days at the time. *In the early 1960s this mud flat was replaced by the extension of Crawford Street to Effingham called Crawford Parkway. During the construction an elderly woman was caught in its quicksand and saved only by the barking of an old white dog name Beau, who was ever after a local hero. The wife of a prominent local grocer, distraught by her husband's death, froze to death in this no-man's land.*

Facing the river on Crawford Street are a set of townhouses built in the 1980s on designs by local architect Kirk Berkeley. The first high-rise apartment tower in the city, now condominiums, was built on this made land in 1964. It is called simply Number One. An effort to build condominiums on Water Street between High and Glasgow languished for many years, then called King's Crossing. Eventually in 1994 it was completed as the elegant Admiral's Landing condominiums.

On the western side of Dinwiddie Street near the corner of London, stood an old house once the headquarters of Cornwallis, but this has long since disappeared. *Modern sources place Cornwallis' headquarters on the northeastern corner of North and Court Streets. Whether Miss Holladay is correct, or Judge Baine, who places it on Court Street, there is no question the Generals headquarters was inside the town and not "near Portsmouth" as another source suggests.*

What is now called Hampton Place was the home of Col. Dempsey Watts, and was called Ben Lomond. This place had been owned by Thomas Veale until purchased by the Watts family, who built the house there in 1799, which stood midway in the square until the place was sold and laid off into lots. It was then taken over and moved to the corner lot by Judge Legh R. Watts, who occupied it until his death. His family still live in *it or did at Miss Holladay's time.*

In continuing our survey of the town we find nothing more changed than the last block on Dinwiddie Street at the northern end. Until very recently it was *under* water, which extended well into the yards of the Court Street lots. *This area still floods and was under water in hurricane Isabel in 2004.*

After the death of Col. Dempsey Watts, Ben Lomond became the home of his son, Capt. Samuel Watts, and in it he entertained many interesting guests, among them Black Hawk the Indian chief, who was imprisoned at Fortress Monroe after his capture. *The Watts house Miss Holladay is speaking of now stands on the northwest corner of Dinwiddie and North streets, having been moved when Windmill Creek was filled in. There is a picture of it in its original location in the library collection. It has a historical marker relating to the visit of Chief Black Hawk.* He dined several times with Captain Watts, and on his first visit bringing with him quite a retinue, Pa-Wa Shee, his adopted son, and interpreter Wa-Ba-Keeship, the Prophet and Na-Pape the great-warrior, as well as others with equally long names. Capt. Watts was one of Black Hawk's escort on his official visit to the Navy Yard, where Mr. Watts said, he showed no interest in any of the sights until he reached the dry dock in which the *Delaware (a battleship under construction in dry dock #1),* was then docked. As his glance fell upon the ship his face lighted up and he exclaimed, "Took big man to build that big canoe."

Black Hawk was chief of the Sac group of the Potawatami tribe. They had used the DesPlains Valley leading from where Chicago now stands to the Illinois River as a migration rout. Settlers moving into the area in the early 1830s, mainly from New England and New York State, blocked this rout. The Sac rose up against them. The war was short and its outcome never in doubt.

Miss Holladay had access to the papers of the Watts family now lost.

Captain Watts had a very fine painting of Black Hawk, which is still in the possession of his family *(its current whereabouts unknown).*

Another visitor to this hospitable old mansion was Henry Clay who was the guest of Capt. Watts during his presidential campaign on *April 24* 1844. When Clay reached Portsmouth he was received with a salute of guns and escorted to the house by the military companies of the town. At night his host gave him a large reception where, like all heroes, he claimed the privilege of kissing all the pretty women. Clay's son was with him, and long before the evening was over the young gentleman had disappeared. At bedtime he was discovered snugly tucked up in bed dressed in all of his clothes even his shoes. The champagne had been too much for him. Clay was much mortified, and profuse in his apologies for his son's shortcomings.

The next morning there was a great meeting at the Whig clubhouse where Clay and his host both made eloquent speeches. A dinner party at Capt. Watts' wound up the festivities. We are told that many brilliant men were present and that, "wit flashed from fluent lips"; but none of the bon-mots have come down to us. A good story however, has reached us from the servants' quarters. Before retiring Capt. Watts was walking through his garden, and saw a bright light in his kitchen. As he drew near he found that the servants were having a party of their own. Clay's body-servant was standing glass in hand, proposing a toast: "Friends, the white folks have been drinking to my Master all night; but there isn't one of them said anything about my Mistress. Here's to her, God bless her."

At the death of Capt. Watts in 1878, Ben Lomond passed to his daughter, Miss Margaret Watts, who sold the place to Dr. Charles T. Parrish in 1908. He developed it as Hampton Place.

The family of Capt. Watts have a permit issued by the Provost-Marshal during the Civil War, allowing him the privilege of hunting in his own grounds, "on the borders of Portsmouth."

We have a fairly accurate idea about when Windmill Creek was filled in, because L. T. Phillips, who was Clerk of the Court of Hustings and Circuit Court and among the first to settle the filled-land is listed as living on the north end of Dinwiddie Street in 1892, but elsewhere in 1886. That puts the development of that end of Dinwiddie Street around 1890. Its development and that of Hampton Place was apparently made by the Dinwiddie Realty Corporation. Its Secretary and Treasurer lived on Hampton Place when it was first laid out. Hampton Place did not exist in 1910, but it did exist in 1911 which absolutely dates its first houses, of which there were seven. By 1917 Hampton Place and Dinwiddie Street were fully-built.

The two lots on the west side of the northernmost block of Court Street, now 328 Court, remained vacant until about this same time. The creek which covered Dinwiddie also made this little section of Court Street unsuitable for building. When this area was drained the Maupin family which had a Federal Period house on the adjacent lot bought the two lots.

In 1895 the widow Mrs. Hester Braxton joined her funds, realized from the sale of her husband's plantation after the Civil War, with those of her son-in-law James F. Maupin and built the house which is now 328 Court Street (in the old numbering 42). Rather large and elaborate for Portsmouth townhouses it is the only house in the city in pure Art Nouveau style, then in fashion. The architect was Charles Cassel who we will meet again when he designs St. John's Church on Washington Street. this house is among the few which are still owned by the family which built it. It has a wide circular staircase which appears to be free standing and twines down from the attic to the entrance hall. This stairway creeks at appropriate moments, announcing the several ghosts about whom you can hear on the annual Ghost Walk on the Friday before Halloween.

From High Street an old landmark has just been removed, the old Emmerson house, built by Parson Emmerson in 1784. *This was in the tax-dodger style and pictures of it survive in the public library collection. It stood where the Commodore Theater now stands. The Commodore Theater takes its name for Commodore James Barron, buried in Trinity Churchyard not far from the east wall of the theater. The theater was built in the 1940s, after the time Miss Holladay was writing. It is one of the best examples of Art Deco architecture in Hampton Roads. It has been lovingly restored by Fred Schonfeld as a working movie theater. He even preserved the murals done by an itinerant Czech artist, with amusing depictions of his view of America, including some presidents on parade. The first Arthur Emmerson was the third rector of Trinity Church, coming to the church just after the American Revolution. A dedicatory window to him, his son and grandson is in the middle of the north wall of Trinity Church on the High Street side and a copy of his ordination papers from England hang in the hallway of the*

Parish Hall. The house is featured in the Bicentennial plaque in the church annex. It can also be seen in a painting of the church, as it originally appeared, in the Parish Hall. In this old house was born Capt. Arthur Emmerson, who distinguished himself in the Battle of Craney Island. The Emmerson family have occupied this house since its erection. Across the street from this house was the home of Mr. Joseph Bilisoly, a prominent citizen in days gone by. The Bilisolys were a French family, who with the Bourkes came over with La Fayette in the Revolution. *In fact, they did not come with Lafayette. Their Bilisoly ancestor, who had settled in the Caribbean, came as a ship's master in the fleet of the Compt Francois Joseph Paul de Grasse, whose fleet blocked entry into the Chesapeake Bay to British ships coming to the relief of General Cornwallis at Yorktown in the last battle of the American Revolution. The naval battle was called the Battle of the Capes.*

A compilation of Miss Gwenn's articles on historic houses at the library can add detail to this walk, as can Mr. Foreman's recollections from the 1820s.

Chapter 35: Amusements

After getting a glimpse of some of the older people of our town, and their homes, we naturally feel an interest in their amusements and recreations. We have been told that they were hospitable and entertained freely and graciously. The two towns were formerly closely allied in their pleasures, and in early days we find the "Norfolk and Portsmouth Jockey Club," and the "Norfolk and Portsmouth Cricket Club."

When there was a good show in Norfolk, its advance agent always made arrangements with the Ferry Manager for night trips. Occasionally the good things came to Portsmouth and similar accommodation was made.

Fox hunting was popular, but horse racing was the chief delight of all, so our English friend tells us. She says a race set the Virginians crazy and no class or condition escaped the contagion.

> "One of their bridges, slight in strength
> Extended half a mile in length,
> Reached from Norfolk to the place
> Where twice a year is held a race.
> The race is a Virginian's pleasure,
> For which he can always find leisure,
> For that they'd leave the farm, the home,
> From every quarter they can come.
> With gentle, simple, rich and poor,
> The race ground soon is covered o'er.
> Slaves the gaming spirit take
> And bet a wager on each stake."

The race course on the Portsmouth side was at Oak Grove, the region beginning at Godwin Street and covering many acres. The old Oak Grove tavern stood on what is now the corner of Chestnut and High streets until it was torn down about ten years ago *(1925)* to make room for a service station. It was, of course, the meeting place of the racing fraternity and the dinners served there during the racing weeks were noted.

The races were generally booked for Easter week and Whitsuntide. For a month or more before they came off, the newspapers were full of them. They were advertised and discussed from every standpoint; and we are thus furnished with many details concerning them. 1808 seems to have been a banner year for this sport. Revised rules were published that year, among them some regulating the costume of the jockeys. No boy *(in order to make the weight as little as possible children were recruited as jockeys)* could ride unless he was clad according to regulations; the marked features being silk jacket, half boots and a jockey cap.

All horses entered for the races were boarded free, and so were the boys. The price of admission certainly put it within the power of everyone to see the races. Those who came on horseback were charged twenty five cents; those in carriages paid fifty cents; while those who were on foot could enter for one fourth of that amount.

The races lasted three days, generally, and the second of them was known as Lady's Day. The runs were mile heats, the best three in five. In the earlier races the purse was usually $100 but occasionally as much as $200; but in 1811 we find $1,000 was the amount offered.

In 1811 we get some idea of the time made by the horses in a very interesting race between Eagle and Sally Hope, when the former made the course in three minutes and fifty seconds.

The horses entered the race at the sounding of a horn; and the two that created most interest in this race (1804) were Mr. Godwin's Catchpenny and Mr. Christian's Bill Beaver; but which won we could not ascertain. Messrs. Murdaugh, Gray and Harrison had horses that won some attention.

The horses usually had interesting names, Whiskey, Daredevil, Æolus, Virago, Firefly, Bumper Ranger, Cockfighter, etc.

Another very popular sport was cockfighting, which was done openly and aboveboard; and one might think at first sight, aided and abetted by the church, when the newspapers of the day announce that: "Elizabeth River Parish challenges any other parish or county, to fight a main of cocks at any time in the ensuing month, for several hundred dollars. Joel Cornick—At the Gardens." The invitation was quickly accepted; the Hampton cocks rising to the occasion.

When the old Red Lion Tavern on London Street between Middle and Crawford was being restored a cockfighting pit was found in its basement.

Hayward's at Lambert's Point and the Strawberry Bank at Hampton were great resorts for cockfighters. Their Mecca on this side of the river was the Edwards farm, especially toward the middle of the last century *(the 1800s)*. In later days these mains were opened to the public at large.

The owner of this farm Mr. John Edwards was a character in the town. He lived alone and lived as he pleased, accepting no rule of life but his own will. He was a man of splendid physique, and well dressed in the style of a former day, wearing ruffled shirts of fine linen, high stockings and trousers fitted close to the calves of his legs, and buttoned from knee to ankle, giving the appearance of knee breeches. His bow was a model of courtesy and his manners most agreeable, but his vocabulary of oaths was inexhaustible. In fact, his conversation was so interlarded with profanity that it required courage to converse with him.

The gentlemen of the community met at Mr. Edwards' for their cockfights, and when the Grand Duke Alexis of Russia was in Norfolk in 1877, Mr. Edwards arranged a main of cocks for his special pleasure. So enthusiastic was the royal visitor over the sport that his host slapped him on the back and called him a "good sport," and afterwards named the two streets that he was cutting through his property, "Cossack" and "Muscovite" in honor of the Grand Duke. The Edwards farm is now a thing of the past, most of it having been laid off into streets and lots and the remainder devoted to the site of the Marine Barracks. The old house is still standing, altered just enough to make it a comfortable residence. Near it stands a veteran tree mounting guard over Mr. Edwards' grave. The old gentleman was buried under it by his own order. *The house, which would have been near the shipyard, is no longer there.*

He died at an advanced age in 1896, leaving a will which is perhaps the most remarkable document ever recorded In Norfolk County. It contains page after page of ribaldry, ridicule and nonsense, interspersed with some kindly remarks and generous bequests. Some of the legacies made the recipients ridiculous, while others were given in a spirit of gratitude.

Mr. Edwards made every arrangement for his own funeral, which was to take place at three o'clock a. m. He forbade religious services of any kind, and desired to be carried to his grave by eight able-bodied African American men, who were to have a dollar each for his services and to be stuffed at a supper after the burial. *He was to be burried standing up.*

There was to be a banquet too, for all who attended the funeral. It happened that the burial took place on the night of one of the Assembly Germans; and as soon as that function was over the gilded youth of the city adjourned to the Edwards obsequies, where an immense number of men had already congregated. At the request of Mr. Edwards' niece one of the clergymen of the town attempted to make a prayer. His effort was in vain, for the mob rushed at him and forcibly turned him from the grave.

The old gentleman was put away just as he desired to be, amidst the shrieks and howls of a drunken mob.

Cockfighting is now a thing of the past. It was taboo long before Mr. Edwards died, and when last engaged in was done on the quiet. *An article in the newspaper morgue, April 1 1962 describes the fights in this way: "The regulated game fights were divided into rounds called 'pits,' which were presided over by a referee. Two lines would be drawn on the ground and the opponents would be placed on them, eagerly facing each other. At a signal from the referee the handlers would release the chickens and they would spring into action. Feathers would fly as each opponent would try to gauge the other with his steel-spurred heels. The pit would last until one of the battlers became entangled and the referee would call 'handle' and the game cocks would be separated. The cocks were then given 20 seconds rest* before being released for another scramble. The fights lasted until one cock killed the other." This usually required about ten minutes, as a result of the spurs. Without spurs the fights could last a full day.

Cricket and quoits were played in the earlier days; these games seemed to be very popular.

Among the rougher element sack-racing and rat-baiting were popular amusements. Card playing and gambling in many forms was carried to such an excess in Portsmouth a little over a century ago *(1830)* that even the parsons were led astray. Old Parson Young *of Trinity* neglected pulpit and parish in pursuit of these pleasures. His sermons were often prefaced with the remark, "Do as I tell you, not as I do."

Soon after the game of baseball was invented it made its way to Portsmouth. The earliest account of a game is told by Alan Flanders. In 1868 the Norfolk Pastime Club met the Virginia Club of Portsmouth on a makeshift baseball diamond in Gosport near the Navy Yard. The Portsmouth team provided breakfast and a light lunch free of charge. By the fifth inning Norfolk was leading five to nothing. In the next inning the score was tied at eight all, but in the ninth inning Portsmouth caught fire and ended the game 27 to 8. These large scoring innings were not all that uncommon since the rules at the time allowed a player to continue running around the bases as long as the opponents failed to tag him out. There was no admission charge to this game, but it did have a printed program and food vendors. These early teams were supported by local taverns and had such fanciful names as the So-Fat Baseball Club of Portsmouth.

The game was not integrated by race and so the famous "Negro League" had some of Portsmouth's best players. Portsmouth's first African American team was the Brighton Blue Socks - named for that neighborhood of the city. It later became the Brighton Firefighter's Team and had its own stadium on Key Street near Truxton. A short history of its players and games is in the clipping file at the library.

The Navy Yard had its own team, which won a league title in 1914.

In 1901 Portsmouth had a professional team in the Virginia Carolina League. When that league went under in 1906 Charles T. Bland reconstituted the team in the Virginia State League as the Portsmouth Truckers. They had their own ballpark between Washington Street and Green, bounded by Lincoln Street and Randolph on what had been the Southern Railway property. It was built for the munificent sum of $3,000. It held 1,200 fans in a covered grandstand and an additional 5,000 seats in uncovered bleachers. The Portsmouth All Stars won the league pennant in 1920. Later the stadium was called Sewanee Stadium for a semi-pro team which played there. It remained virtually unchanged until it was replaced by Frank D. Lawrence Stadium, which stood on part of the land now occupied by I. C. Norcum High School on London Boulevard.

The Lawrence stadium was the first home of the Tidewater Tides baseball team. J. Herbert Simpson, the city's sports cheerleader and a prime mover in getting the Virginia Sports Hall of Fame for the city, remembered the site as a swampy end of Scott's Creek in the 1930s which was used as a dumping yard for old automobiles. When it was built in the early 1940s it was simply called Portsmouth Stadium, but the City Council changed the name to Frank D. Lawrence Stadium in August 1963. Many players went on to the big leagues from this stadium, including: Pie Traymor, Hack Wilson, Ace Parker, Harry Brecheen, Joe Heving, Reggie Otero, Larry Benton, Hal Wagner, Bill Nichols, Jim Turner and Eddie Stanky. The stadium was demolished in the late 1980s.

Another sports figures from Portsmouth was Clarence "Ace" Parker who played for Brooklyn and New York and was named the most valuable player in the National Football League in 1940.

"The great chronicler of the sport in Portsmouth was Abe Goldblatt - himself a player and then a columnist in the _Portsmouth Star_. Fortunately there is a detailed and loving description of Portsmouth's glories and defeats in the book _Baseball In Portsmouth_ by Clay Shampoe and Tom Garrett, starting with 1895 and concluding with its publication date in 2004.

Portsmouth had a Sports Hall of Fame before it was reconstituted as the official Virginia Sports Hall of Fame in 1953 by Frank D. Lawrence and Portsmouth Mayor Irvine Smith. For many years it was housed in the old Clerk of Court's office next to the 1846 Courthouse, now the museum's gift shop, but on April 22 2005, with substantial city financial support added to private donations it was moved to a handsome museum built for the purpose on the northeast corner of Middle and Court streets. The city still subsidizes this museum with an annual donation from the General Fund.

Old inventories in the Clerk's Office here show that most people had wine glasses of various kinds, often far outnumbering the table glasses. Perhaps none of these glasses were more interesting than the julep glass, which was shaped like an ordinary table tumbler, but held about a quart of liquid. They were passed around the family for a swig, somewhat after the manner of the loving cup.

A story was told by one of our citizens of a bishop from a distant diocese, who was visiting one of our country-houses. Opening his bedroom door one morning in response to a tap upon it, he found a young servant with the julep glass filled to the brim with the fragrant toddy. Taking the glass from the boy, he closed the door and disappeared. In vain did the servant wait for his reappearance, and as vainly did the family await their morning portion. At breakfast the bishop announced that he hoped he was not considered unappreciative of the delicious julep; but he really could not drink it all. He was somewhat relieved to know that it was not an individual portion but a family appetizer.

As the gambling spread through the town many people forbade cards in their homes, becoming fanatical on the subject. One old lady used to tell of her father coming into the room and finding them playing whist with their company. Picking up the tongs he seized the cards with them and threw them into the fire; reproving them severely for "handling the dirty things."

Another father of the period was equally horrified when he found his daughter reading Byron; he too had recourse to use the tongs and the volume perished in the flames.

Dancing was the great resource of the gentler sex from early days. The newspapers make frequent mention of assemblies, cotillions and balls, and Drinane's Coffee House, where Maupin's Hall now stands, was the place in which they were given. *Maupin's Hall was situated about where the Children's Museum of Virginia now stands. It was on the southeastern corner of Middle and High. What is now the children's museum was earlier the old Legget's Department Store. On the corner lot was formerly installed a quaint old A&P grocery store with oiled wooden floors with sawdust spread on them and a big red carved wooden pillar at the intersection of the streets. Even earlier this was a Pigley-Wigley. This was the market part of the Kirn Building and Maupin's Hall was the top floor.* There was never a time when there was not a number of dancing masters here, and French ones at that. The "long room" in the taverns served as dancing schools. The poetical English lady thought them a superfluous; dancing, she says, came naturally to the Virginians.

"Dancing is their great 'delight,
They'd jig with pleasure every night,
We often thought in winter weather
Virginia women made of feather;
No trade for dancing master here,
Self-taught are all Virginia's fair."

One of the most elaborate balls ever given here was the Centenary Ball, celebrating the hundredth anniversary of the founding of the town, in February 1852. There is an invitation to it in the possession of the writer. It is engraved on paper with a beautifully embossed border and the following names appear on it, as the committee: Dr. John P. Young, Edward R. Hunter, H. B. Watson, Col. Maurice B. Langhorne, Wm. M. Levy, Dr. Virginius Bilisoly, Col. Winchester Watts, E. T. Blamire, Arthur Emmerson, Dr. Benj. Spratley, Washington Reed *for whom the Washington Reed house on the corner of Middle and North is named* and George Chambers. The ball was given at Oxford Hall. Oxford Hall was remodeled in part by the First National Bank. Grant's

now occupies the remainder of it, and as far as the facade goes on that point is unchanged. The hall always had stores under it."
Grant's Five and Ten in the 1960s went around the corner house thought to be on the site of Benedict Arnold's headquarters on the northwestern corner of Middle and High. That house was once the fondly remembered Fantone's children's clothing store. In Oxford Square there was another children's clothing store also remembers by Portsmouth children called Sears Betty and Bob. This store had a running dispute with Sears Roebuck which claimed trademark infringement. The last five and ten cent store to survive on High Street was Woolworth's, in the building now holding Roger Brown's Sports Bar. Woolworth's closed in 1994.

Although Ocean View and Virginia Beach were nothing but woods and beach until nearly fifty years ago *(the 1920s - see* Recollections of Virginia Beach *by Benjamin Franklin (Bennie) Barco)*, people were not without their pleasure resorts. Perhaps the most popular of them was Vauxhall Gardens in Norfolk. These gardens were situated on Holt and Fenchurch Streets. Set far back from the street was a long pavilion, used for concerts, banquets, speaking and shows of various kinds. Here ice cream, a rarity in those days, was sold and other light refreshments. African Americans, and "women of the town" were not admitted. The place was said to have been crowded every afternoon and all day on Sundays. Fire put an end to Vauxhall in the *eighteen* fifties.

Another place of amusement of similar kind was the Wigwam, at Briggs' Point (end of Holt Street), where there were bowling alleys, cricket and quoit grounds as well as bathing. Liquor could be bought there and the entrance fee charged for a man entitled him to a drink of it. The Wigwam was probably not quite as high-toned a place as Vauxhall.

At an earlier period Lindsay's Gardens and Rousainvine's Bower were frequently mentioned. Their history has not come down to us. They were perhaps earlier names for the other two.

About eighty years ago *(1850)* Ghio's Gardens were popular in Portsmouth. They were situated on Fourth Street, at its extreme north end *by the creek dividing Gosport from Portsmouth*. In addition to the usual amusements there was a ballroom attached. Mr. Ghio was a foreigner; his wife, a native of Portsmouth, was quite a remarkable woman, with unusual mental gifts and a sterling character which won her the esteem of the entire community. She was an orphan at an early age, and *was* befriended by a French lady living here at that time. Upon her return to France she took her protege with her. This young girl had not been long in Paris when her pet bird escaped from its cage. She was much distressed at its loss. Some of the neighbors told her of a family who had a stray bird and would be glad to find its owner. She went at once to the house to which she had been directed, where she found her pet. The house proved to be the home of the celebrated French evangelist Eugene Monad. The Monads were seeking a governess for their grandchildren who could speak English with them. They were delighted to get the little Virginia girl to teach them. Mrs. Ghio always spoke of this opportunity as a wonderful one for her; and always described the Monad home as "Heaven on earth."

Mrs. Ghio's son, Mr. Enoch Ghio, became a prominent man in the town, and was a high official in the Seaboard and Roanoke *(Rail)* Road at the time of his death. He had but one child, a daughter, who lives in New York.

The theater was well patronized on both sides of the river. In Portsmouth it was situated on the southeast corner of High and Washington streets on what was for so many years the jail lot and *is* now occupied by the Professional Building. It was burned down in the late *eighteen* forties and never rebuilt. *Dr. William A. Brown II told his son about watching a public hanging on this site when it was the "jail lot."*

A description of one of these hangings on May 31 1889 survives: Henry A Coleman was sentenced to hang on the jail lot at seven in the morning, a crowd of several thousand gathered to watch, some from as far away as Norfolk and Berkley and even climbing onto house roofs and telephone poles to get a better view. The entire Portsmouth Police Force had to be gathered to control the crowd. Father Brady, the Catholic priest, attended the prisoner and jailer Hutchins brought him his last breakfast consisting of "fish, a piece of beef steak, some oysters, kidney stew, some eggs, fried potatoes, hominy, bread and coffee." The prisoner said of this meal, "I slept well last night and soon I will have the stuffing jerked out of me, so I guess I had better eat." The doctors visited him, he looked out the window on the crowd and then returned to his conversation with the priest. "On entering the jail-yard a deathlike silence prevailed. Coleman walked up the steps (nine in number), with a firm and steady gate. He took his stand upon the trapdoor, showing no sign of weakness. Sheriff Bunting, his deputy John McMahon, Chief of Police G. T. Tynan . . . were on each side of the scaffold. Sheriff Bunting read the death warrant to him and asked if he had anything to say. He hesitated, the question was asked again, and he replied in a clear, calm voice, 'Not a word.'. . . The black cap was placed over his face by Sheriff Bunting, the rope adjusted by Sheriff Lee. After his feet had been tied the signal was given and the trap was sprung by someone concealed in the kitchen. At the expiration of seven minutes an examination was made by the doctors and life was pronounced extinct."

A performer at the theater built on this site whom Miss Holladay does not mention is among the most famous of Portsmouth's daughters, Sissieretta Jones (Matilda Sissieretta Joyner Jones 1869-1933), called the "Black Patti," to indicate her race and the fact that her operatic voice rivaled that of the famous Italian soprano, Angelina Patti. Although she sang in European opera houses, by invitation to royal courts, at a command performance at the White House, and around this country with a touring group she formed called the Black Patti Troubadours, when she sang at Portsmouth the black audience was relegated to the balcony. A picture of her survives in the library and on display in the Renaissance Hotel. During the bicentennial year a national music society honored her with a plaque naming her career as one of the Landmarks of American Music. This plaque hangs in the library. She was also honored with a gold medal by the Republic of Haiti.

Another African American musician who's name is familiar to Methodists is Hiram Simmons (1874-1938). He started his career as a composer and organist with a portable organ on the streets of Portsmouth, where he would play and sing his compositions. Two of his hymns are now in the Methodist

Hymnal and his oratorio "The Lord's Supper" is still performed in churches.

Portsmouth native David Carr Glover worked for Disney Studios as a composer. His best-known work for them is the "Mickey Mouse March." In retirement in his native Portsmouth he opened Music Village on Churchland Boulevard, dedicated to bringing a love of music to the city's children. He gathered a group of piano teachers, including Joan Moore, to teach there, often from Gover's own manuals. Some of his compositions are in the library local history collection.

Some other performers born in Portsmouth are Malcolm Tommy Newsom whose band became famous on "The Tonight Show With Johnny Carson" on late night television: Ruth Weston Brown who grew up on London Street and started her singing career in the choir at Emanuel AME Church and in 1950 was named the top female vocalist in the nation in rhythm and blues; Missy Elliot who won a Grammy Award in 2003 as the best female rap vocalist, William Franklin "Bill" Deal who was "king of beach music" in the late 1950s and Mahlon Clark a clarinetist with several bands before joining Lawrence Welk's famous television band.

In the fashion world Perry Ellis made a splash with his internationally-know mens and women's sportswear line which was initiated in 1978 and outlives his short life.

Among Portsmouth best-known artists was Charles Kenneth Sibley who lived in the city, first in Captian McRae's house on London Street in the Olde Towne and then in a house he built in Simonsdale and the portraitist Ralph Wolfe Cowan who was named by Prince Ranier III as Royal Portrait Painter of Monaco.

Oxford Hall to some extent took *the place of the old Portsmouth Theater*, and on the boards of this old "Hall" trod some of the most celebrated actors of the day; Mrs. Mary Ann Tyrwhitt, Nelly Farren, the great English favorites, and Murdoch and others of the American stage.

The newspapers of the day not only give us a list of the plays presented and the troupes; but make criticisms and comments of both plays and actors. The plays put on the stages of the two towns were generally of a high order, the company stayed two days, but whether they gave matinee performances or not we have been unable to ascertain.

It may be interesting to read a list of some of the plays given in the early years of the last century *(the 1800s)* in this community; and among them we can find a number of familiar friends. Otway's Venice Preserved, Colman's Honeymoon, Don Juan, Raising the Wind, Jane Shore, Douglas, The Fatal Marriage, Love a La Mode, many of Shakespeare's plays, some of Ben Johnson's; and later on Ingomar, The Bride of Lammermoor, Camille and The Lady of Lyons. There were plays of a lighter type; vaudeville, farces and minstrel shows. One farce put on at the Avon Theater in Norfolk, in 1849, is so interesting in the light of present developments, that we can not refrain from giving in full an editorial from the *Portsmouth Daily Whig* concerning it, entitled "Chloroform." "We were amused the other night at the Avon Theatre in Norfolk, in witnessing the play of a hundred years hence. Aminadab Slocum, having been put to sleep by a dentist who practiced magnetism, and hung out a sign, 'Teeth extracted without pain,' is awakened by some of his great-grandchildren and resuscitated. He finds our harbor the greatest port in the world. Women *are* editing newspapers; making stump speeches and running for Congress, while one Sally Dobbs is running in opposition to John Smith the incumbent. Steam is no longer used for propelling power; electricity has usurped its place. Aminadab is treated to a ride in an electric balloon to London and back in two hours at a cost of twenty-five cents. Mexico and Canada are parts of the United States; Great Britain and Australia are territories and the burning political question of the day is the annexation of China. There is no drinking, therefore no need of temperance societies. People only work for amusement or health and nothing is as it was before his sleep. The piece is replete with humor and several of the characters well sustained."

Our grandparents would not be so surprised at all our great inventions as many of us believe, if they could visit us. They had the vision, even though unlike Aminadab, they could not see it become reality.

The replacements for the old venues Miss Holladay tells us about are Willet Hall and the nTelos Pavilion. Built as a part of the old Woodrow Wilson High School, Willet Hall, built in 1988, proved to have unusually good acoustics and is a favorite with local orchestras like the Tidewater Winds which presents an annual concert there. It has also hosted famous entertainers like the comedian George Carlin and touring musicals like <u>Les Miserables</u>. The old Wilson High School became a middle school, called Hunt-Mapp when the new I. C. Norcum High School was completed, and the name Woodrow Wilson High School transferred to what had been Manor High School. In 2005 the middle school was closed and plans begun in 2007 to remove it, but Willet Hall, being too good to lose, there is now a plan to save it as a stand-alone facility. The nTelos pavilion by City Hall was opened in July 2001 as a medium-sized venue for outdoor music concerts. Its simulated tent-like over-structure was very innovative, and had been promised to survive one hundred mile an hour winds. Unfortunately it failed in Hurricane Isabel and had to be rebuilt. It has hosted more world-famous performers than any other venue in Portsmouth's history. On the other hand it was discovered that no one at City Hall was keeping track of the revenues, or what part of those revenues was intended to come to City of Portsmouth. This caused quite a scandal.

We find the circus was no novelty a hundred years ago; and its program differed little from that which is offered now. The sideshows were open all day; and in addition to the animals exhibited there was a collection of paintings on view. The regular performances took place at night, admission being fifty cents. It was plainly stated that no lady, un-escorted by a gentleman, would be admitted. Athletic stunts, wonderful feats of horsemanship, balancing acts, comic songs *and* black extravaganzas were presented to the interested audience, as well as the "Spanish Tranka, performed by real Mexicans." The strongest cards, however, seem to have been dancing and flying *(presumably she means some kind of trapeze act).*

Tradition has passed down a remarkable story in connection with one of these old circuses that visited Portsmouth. First we are told that the elephant could not be accommodated on the ferry boat. He was led to the water and swam across from Norfolk, guided by two rowboats, one on each side of him.

A further incident goes to corroborate the stories told of the wonderful memories attributed to these mighty beasts. As the circus parade passed down Crawford Street, a tailor, scissors in hand, went out to see the show. When the elephant approached him, he stuck his scissors in the hide of the beast, who squirmed a little, it was said, and peacefully went on. *The elephant's* revenge, however, came later; when the circus was over the animals again passed down Crawford Street and the elephant upon reaching the tailor's shop walked over to the gutter and drank all the dirty water found in it. Walking straight way to the shop he deliberately deluged the unsuspecting offender. At the time the tailor was working on a suit which he was making for a naval officer, who had furnished his own cloth, a piece of very fine quality. The dirty shower had somewhat damaged its pristine glory, much to the disgust of the officer, who brought suit against the tailor, for the injury done to his cloth. Unfortunately the legend has not told us in whose favor the suit was decided.

William "Buffalo Bill" Cody with his traveling show made its last performance in the nation at Portsmouth November 11, 1916. This is commemorated by a plaque near the High Street Ferry slip.

Portsmouth must have been a music-loving community from the earliest days, judging by the music clubs and teachers of music and singing. Jules and Hernandez Benedict had a music school here, and later Buck taught in the town, as did other musicians of note and ability.

About a hundred years ago *(1830)* the Apollo Club not only gave good concerts here, but was instrumental in bringing many foreign musicians to play for our people. In 1854 the Italian Opera company, which had visited all the large cities in the country and reaped laurels everywhere, came to Portsmouth and according to custom stayed here three days. This time the ferry boat made night trips for the Norfolk people.

The concerts won unstinted praise, the editorials stating that such music had never been heard in this community before.

Collins, the celebrated Irish comedian, gave delineations of the Irish character, which we are told had never been equaled except by Tyrone Power. It was said by those who heard him that to hear him sing "The Widow Machree" was worth twice the fee for admission.

German soloist Henrietta Sontag, too, thrilled the community with her wonderful voice.

Portsmouth, meanwhile, was training her own musician, the famous Theodore Thomas, who spent his early years in the town. It was on the stage at the old Oxford Hall that he first made his bow to the public, at one of the concerts conducted by his father, who was also quite a fine musician. In the great Centennial in Philadelphia in 1876, it was Theodore Thomas who was chosen to play the opening oratorios. When quite young, Thomas fell in love with one of the Portsmouth girls, a talented musician. His suit was unsuccessful; but he did not forget her.

Some thirty years afterwards when he was giving a series of concerts in Norfolk, he sent complimentary tickets to her and her family. This lady was Miss Ellen Harvey, afterwards Mrs. Hobday. She and her sister Miss Mary Ann Harvey were great favorites in Portsmouth in both social and musical circles. Signor George, a well known musician here later on, dedicated one of his compositions to Miss Mary Harvey.

Musical treats were too numerous in our community some years back, for us to mention them all, but we cannot pass by what was the greatest of them without some note of it—the visit of Ole Bull to Norfolk, in the *eighteen* fifties, accompanied by the "wonderful child musician Adelina Patti. Strackosh conducted this wonderful concert. The price of admission was one dollar.

Sacred music was not slighted. At one time Mr. Potts, the organist of the Court Street Baptist church, made every effort in this direction, opening a school for training in church music. The Porter and Brown families had great musical talent which was always placed at the service of their church.

The organ at Trinity Church, combining the pipes for a Victorian organ and a twentieth-century organ in the 1980s, is now thought to be the largest pipe organ in use in Hampton Roads. It has hosted organ concerts of musicians from all over the world.

A hundred years ago *(1830s)* there was a dramatic club in Portsmouth called "The Thespians." The newspapers of the day occasionally allude to their performances. In 1821 they put on two plays for the benefit of the newly established Masonic Lodge (Naval Lodge). It would be interesting to know who were its members, and something of the plays they chose to act.

About forty or fifty years ago *(1870s)* the Garrick Club was organized, and among its members were many of the prominent people of the town. For a number of years they put on plays.

Later on "The Casino" was established here. There was a large membership in this organization, embracing the social life of the town. There was some entertainment given every Friday night. Sometimes it was a dance, then a concert or a play. Mr. George Curtis was in charge of the dramatic committee, and he proved to be a most able stage manager. Miss Lee Simmons, who afterwards was Mrs. George Curtis rendered him great assistance as leading lady.

The Little Theater of Portsmouth was started in the mid-twentieth century and continues to the present. It earliest performances were presented in a defunct movie theater on High Street across from where Robbie's Hardware store once stood and then moved into the theater of Manor High School, now Wilson High School, when it was built in the 1970s. The inclusion of the Little Theater, the planetarium (now a part of the Childrens Museum of Virginia) and a Public Library branch to the high school was a plan of Michael Alford, then Superintendent of Schools, in an effort to make the school a civic center for the neighborhood.

Portsmouth today has several literary clubs, the Students Club *(still in existence)*, the Forum and the Alumni Association of St. Joseph's School *(the Catholic boys school)*. It was through the untiring effort of the Student's Club that the Public Library was organized here in 1913 *under its first director Miss Esther (Essie) Murdaugh Wilson for whom the local history room is named. The library remained under the ostensible control of that women's club (though fully funded by the city), until 1961 when now Mayor Dr. James Holley and Dr. Hugo Owens, then president of the local chapter of NAACP, requested service and were turned away because of their race. They brought suit against the club officers for discrimination, and to resolve the issue the city took over management of the library, combined it with the segregated black library, then run by Mrs. Bertha Edwards, and opened the new institution to all comers under its third director, Miss Helen Kirkpatrick. Until that time the Portsmouth Public Library was the only private library to serve a community of the size of Portsmouth on the Atlantic Coast.*

The centerpiece of the Churchland neighborhood for many decades was Coleman's Nursery at the corner of High Street and Cedar Road. It was the site of a very large display of automated Christmas figures every year, and a visit to the Coleman's Christmas Shop was a part of the season for every child in Hampton Roads. When the old business closed the automatons were given to the city and now make Christmas happy every year along High Street, in the 1846 Courthouse Gallery and in the Children's Museum of Virginia. The old Coleman's property will become the location of the new Churchland Branch Library in 2007, replacing the old site on Academy Street.

There were debating societies in the town and about ninety years ago *(circa 1840)* the Portsmouth Literary and Library Association was organized here with Capt. Samuel Watts as president and Rev. Thomas Hume, vice-president. These gentlemen were indefatigable in the efforts to make the organization a success; and until the outbreak of the Civil War it was an influence in the town. All through the season there were debates and lectures on political and literary subjects, as well as on other interesting topics of the day. This society was not only instrumental in developing local talent, but gave the people the opportunity of hearing celebrated lecturers from a distance. There was a series of lectures given by Prof. *James* Beard of the Smithsonian Institute on historical subjects. Dr. Armstrong of Norfolk gave each winter a course of talks on science and Prof. Webster, one of our own teachers, gave lectures on

Socrates and Greek philosophy. There were others who spoke on architecture, literature and poetry. G. P. R. James during his stay in Portsmouth was very accommodating in lecturing; and one of his best remembered talks was on "The Anglo-Saxon Race."

Many of the homes had well-filled bookcases, and the advertisements of the bookstores show that this was a reading community. The books had not to be ordered, but were actually on the shelves. From the newspapers we get a good idea of what the people read. Our shops advertised all the noted books of the day on many subjects, nor were French novels eschewed.

The magazines kept in stock show a great variety from which to select. We could find there many of the best foreign publications, such as *Blackwood's Magazine, Westminster Review, London Times, London Lancet, London News, Punch, Dublin Nation*; as well as the best American magazines, *Littell's Living Age, Scientific American, Harper, Frank Leslie, Saturday Evening Post, Spirit of the Times, The Catholic Mirror, Democratic Review, The Illustrated Magazine of Art* and those fashion magazine so dear to our mothers and grandmothers, Godey and Peterson's "Ladies' Books." *Miss Dyson ran a bookstore by the New Kirn Building in the 1960s which also suppled the elder Marshall Butt with hand made bow ties. Unfortunately, the city's last two downtown bookshops selling new books, Pfeiffer's which closed in the 600 block of High Street in the 1990s, and Broad Street Books which moved to Norfolk from Port Norfolk, closed or left the city. Another, however, opened in Churchland in 2006.*

Apart from the historians mentioned in the introduction of this work, Portsmouth has provided many published authors. The following is a short and incomplete list. Among the city's novelists are the best-selling writer of romantic thrillers V. (Virginia) C. Andrews; Tomeka M. Winbourne with <u>Where My Strength Comes From</u>; *Emily Hines known for her short stories and eight books; Zita Winterberg Christian, an author of love stories who was born in Portsmouth and graduated from Portsmouth Catholic High School; James Ives; Nathaniel "Bud" Morrison who is also a poet; the historical novelist Dean Burgess; and Vernon Kitabu Turner, a descendant of* the leader of the Nat Turner Uprising. Portsmouth's best-known non-fiction author, Alf Mapp, has written two novels, one set in Portsmouth's history, but he is better known for his biography of Jefferson, <u>Faith of Our Fathers</u> about the religious beliefs of the Founding Fathers and <u>Frock Coats and Epaulets</u>. Among Portsmouth playwrights who have gone on to fame are Terrence Arer Anderson and the scriptwriter Sheri Bailey and Robert H. Buckner with fifty-seven pictures to his credit. Portsmouth poets include: Raheema Turner Ahabazz, of <u>Trials and Tribulations of the Downtrodden</u>; David Jeddie Smith a nominee for the Pulitzer Prize and Poet Laureate of Portsmouth; Peter LeCompte; Earl Virginia Bundy and City Councilman Charles Whitehurst. Portsmouth resident Foredeh Goldin has written about her childhood as a Jew in Iran; and journalist Nathan McCall whose very controversial memoir <u>Makes Me Want To Hollar</u> about black men dying young and often violently is set partly in the Cavalier Manor neighborhood of Portsmouth. Hubert J. Davis, winner of the Paxton Award from Torch International, published a series of light-hearted stories and children's books drawn from the stories gathered in the mountains of Virginia by the WPA. Among children's book authors from Portsmouth are Theodore Taylor, a Cradock High School graduate with 32 books to his name, and the couple Cheryl Willis and Wade Hudson who published through their own New York press - Afro-Bets. Virginia's expert on covered bridges is also a Porsmouth resident: Leola Pierce. G. Douglas Johnston, from Portsmouth, became the publisher of <u>Vanity Fair</u> and William Schneider a well known columnist for the <u>Los Angeles Times</u>... .

    It may be surprising to know that the people of this community had the opportunity of seeing good painting which was exhibited in Norfolk occasionally. These exhibitions were held in the ballroom of Johnson's Hotel; and the pictures shown in the early years of the last century were part of a collection being made for an English nobleman. The collector was traveling through this country with it before turning it over to his patron. Most of the painting listed were originals, and so marked. These embraced works by Rembrandt, Guercino, Domenchino,

Vernet, and Carlo Dolci. In 1831 we find an account of a similar exhibition in Norfolk.

We know that artists of note came to the two towns from time to time in order to paint the portraits not only for the townspeople themselves, but for those in the vicinity. Sharpless was in Norfolk for many months, where in addition to painting pictures he gave drawing lessons. Raphael Peale and his more celebrated brother both spent some months in Portsmouth painting many portraits which are still owned by the descendants of the sitters. Raphael Peale, too, advertised for pupils, though tradition has given us no list of those who studied under him. *Laurence Sully, the brother of the more famous Thomas, worked for some time in Norfolk and Portsmouth. Before photography became popular it was common for well known artists to settle in a city and create portraits of local leaders.*

In 1819 Mr. Browne introduced the fashion here of cutting silhouettes and it is interesting to note that the price of this article has not advanced in the course of one hundred and ten years; the cost being then, as now *1935)*, twenty-five cents each. Mr. Browne would come to your house and cut you for the same price if you preferred it.

Chapter 36: Getting Educated

People who were as cultivated as those of our town must have been deeply interested in education, and generous in their support of it, promptly adding to their numerous private schools a substantial system of public ones as soon as the need for them became apparent.

The history of our schools is a long and interesting one, going back in some instances to colonial days, when part of the glebe land was set aside for school purposes. This site is on Mount Vernon Avenue *in what is now the Mount Herman neighborhood*, and has been turned over for a playground *(which still exists)*, the property having been so given that it could only be used for educational purposes.

The introduction of public schools in Port Norfolk did away with the usefulness of the old Glebe School.

Interestingly in 2006 the Port Norfolk Elementary School was torn down and the area is proposed to become a park in 2007. This reflects a decline in school population which was first addressed by Superintendent Wilbert Hawkins in a plan for school closings and realignments.

We know nothing of *the glebe's* early history, as far as its teachers and pupils are concerned; it was, of course, under the church (Trinity Church), as were all parish schools; but after the Revolution it was responsible for the education, at least in their early years, of many of our best citizens.

The Sunday schools, after this, instructed the children, who had no other opportunity of learning, in reading, but at best could only teach them enough to puzzle out a few verses in the Bible.

Early in the nineteenth century when the confiscated glebes *(church-owned land used for the support of the priest)* were sold by the order of the State of Virginia, the money arising from the sales was added to certain other sums of money set aside by the State to be used in educating the poor.

The Marine Hospital at Washington Point (Berkley) was sold to the United States Government in 1799 by the State, and the money was divided between the towns of Norfolk and Portsmouth, to be used for an educational fund.

Portsmouth's share was to be used in building a schoolhouse for poor children. This sum of money was placed in the hands of a body of men, known as "School Commissioners." The school was not built immediately, in fact not for many years; but the children of the poor did not lose their opportunity for an education. Such children as could not afford to pay their tuition, attended some of the private schools, and their expenses *were* paid by the Commissioners out of the "Funds."

This privilege was evidently abused as time went on; for in 1843, and perhaps earlier, the Commissioners through their clerk issued a notice saying that this body would refuse to pay for any child entered at schools unless it was done with their authority.

It was just at this time (1843) that a novel system of education was introduced in Portsmouth, by the "Odd Fellows", who established a school under the direction of Mr. T. O. Connoly. *The Odd Fellows' Lodge, as Miss Holladay has already told us, was in the building that is now the Colonial apartment house in the 400 block of Middle Street (with the white pillars). She does not, however, tell us whether the school they founded started there. When next mentioned it is in Court Street Baptist Church. The Odd Fellows was a national fraternal order. It may have gotten its peculiar name from the fact it included members of the working class who otherwise were not eligible for membership in such clubs and, therefore, were "odd." The earliest mention of an Odd Fellows lodge was in 1748, but its founding predates that. Their motto is friendship, love and truth.* The course was entirely preparatory, claiming as its peculiar advantage the ability to teach a hundred children at the same time and by the same person This method of teaching so reduced the cost of education that a pupil was only charged one dollar a quarter for tuition and the Lodge furnished all the books and stationery required.

The Odd Fellows' school was probably the germ of the public schools in Portsmouth; as there is strong evidence to show that our system developed from it. The life of this school was brief as a separate institution, it being merged into the public schools established here a year or two later. This is plainly shown by the recollections of one of our oldest citizens, Mr. John C. Tee, who says, "My first appearance at the public schools commenced when I was very young, not more than seven years of age. My first teacher was Miss Martha Thompson, and the schoolhouse was in the basement of the old Baptist Church, on the site of the present one. *That is Court Street Baptist Church in one of its earlier incarnations.* She taught the primary grades under the auspices of the Odd Fellows." Mr. Tee has furnished some other interesting notes about the schools which will be quoted in due order.

The Public, or as they were then called Free Schools, were established in Norfolk County and Portsmouth by an act of the General Assembly on *February 17* 1845. The law provided that their quota of the "Literary Fund" should be turned over to the commissioners as soon as the schools were in working order. *The Literary Fund was a fund created by Thomas Jefferson from the earnings of the state lottery. It still exists, and still lends money to localities for building schools. When the Virginia lottery was revived in the mid-twentieth century its income was also designated for education.* This sum was to be divided between County and Town on a basis of population. Should there have been any dispute about this question, the census of 1840 was to be accepted until a new one was taken. The money from this fund was to be used entirely for educating poor children. This act furthermore authorized the town trustees to raise an additional tax yearly for operating the schools.

This tax however, was subject to the vote of those who formed the electorate of the town. The first levy was placed at two dollars for every white male over sixteen years old. Within two years this tax was increased to two dollars and fifty cents, the State of Virginia agreeing to add one dollar and thirty-three and a third cent for every two-fifty raised by the town.

The Court of Norfolk County, *just moved to the 1846 Court House at Court and High streets,* was required to turn over all its surplus funds to the Commissioners. This amount was divided between County and Town, on the same basis as their other sums. Portsmouth received from this source three thousand dollars and her share of the taxes was nearly twelve hundred dollars.

In 1846 the old Portsmouth Academy was ordered to be sold, and the proceeds of the sale divided between Portsmouth and the County portion of Portsmouth Parish. *A school called Portsmouth Academy in memory of this institution stood on Academy Avenue and Churchland Boulevard as late as the 1970s, next to the Baptist church, where there is now a parking lot and shopping center.*

In 1848 the entire control of the Free Schools was given to a board elected to manage them. The trustees of the town elected this board, and were themselves eligible to serve on it. It was to be composed of not less than five, nor more than ten citizens. The first school board included the following gentlemen: Capt. Samuel Watts, Dr. William Cocke, Messsrs. Stephen Cowley, George Chambers, Henry Phillips, Joseph Porter and Robert Scott. Rev. Thomas Hume, pastor of the Court Street Baptist Church, was elected superintendent for both county and town, and for his services received the sum of five hundred dollars a year. The superintendent was required to visit each school twice a year, and also to give lectures on subjects specified.

The examining board was composed of Capt. Watts, Dr. Cocke, Mr. Hume and Mr. Cowley.

The schools were open to all white children under certain conditions. It was agreed upon that all children who could afford to pay a small amount for their tuition should do so. These rates were fixed at six and one-quarter, twelve and one-half, and eighteen and three-quarter cents a month, according to the grade. At this time there were three grades and six divisions, each grade being divided into male and female departments.

At this time in the Northern states coeducational free public schools already existed. In the South, however, private education was the rule, as Miss Holliday will soon tell us.

We know very little about the number of pupils who attended these schools in the first two years of their existence;

but in 1847 there were eighty-three girls in the third or highest female division, only fourteen of these being indigent. About five years later in 1852 we get a more extensive view of the schools. In that year there were nine hundred children who remained in school the entire term. The total amount spent at this time by the board was $5,194.91. Of this sum $2,600 was expended in teachers' salaries, the individual salary being only $300 a year. The board in its report apologizes for this meager sum, alluding to it as a "mere pittance."

In 1849 the teachers in the three female grades were Mrs. Eliza Turner, Mrs. Eliza Bain and Miss Towne. Miss Towne was a graduate of the celebrated Williard School of Troy, New York. The boys were taught by Miss Martha Thompson, Zelotus Lockwood and Isaac V. Pratt; the latter, owing to his excessive use of the rod, was called Isaac Vengeance Pratt by the youngsters.

At this period we get some interesting glimpses from Mr. Tee's recollections. We have already heard from him that the primary grades were taught in the basement of the Baptist Church, and when this grade was abolished the third grade moved there.

The Masonic Temple, which stood on the site of the present one, was used for the second grade. *This is the Masonic Lodge on the east side of the 500 block of Court Street behind the Tidewater Community College Visual Arts Center (the old Famous Department Store) and three doors from Queen Street, now the banquet facility for Brutti's Restaurant.* Mr. Tee tells us that when Mr. Lockwood resigned Mr. Addington of Berkley was called to fill his place. He goes on to say: "He was the best teacher that ever held this position. The course of study given by Mr. Addington included English grammar, arithmetic, algebra, astronomy, geography and Latin. In addition to these subjects, there were lectures on the Constitution of the United States, and on the Holy Bible. The best Biblical knowledge that I ever received was from him. He was truly a devout man, deeply interested in all his pupils."

Mr. Andrew Simmons was in charge of the Newtown (South Portsmouth *once Gosport Village*) schools, assisted by

Miss Mary Simmons. The first school built in Newtown was just off Fourth Street at its intersection with Wythe, near the site of the present Friends' Church. It was erected in 1850 and was, so we learn from specifications advertised in a newspaper of the time, built of wood and was seventy feet in length and forty feet wide. *All of this neighborhood was demolished in the 1960s and is now part of Port Center industrial park.*

It was in this year that Free Schools took over the old "Academy," which is still standing on Glasgow Street, near Middle. This building has several times been injured by fire, besides passing through vicissitudes of various kinds. Its exterior has been little changed, though it has been used for residential purposes for some years, for which it was well suited as the building was in two parts—one for boys and the other for girls. It has been in comparatively late years that boys and girls were taught together. *Where it stood is now the off-street parking lot next to the playground on the east side of the corner of Middle and Glasgow and the south side of Glasgow Street. Mr. Robert Albertson has an inkwell from this school he found in his back yard and your editor has found clay marbles, used by the students, in his back yard.*

The Academy was built about a hundred years ago for a private school, serving this purpose for many years. In the awful summer of 1855, *the year the yellow fever killed a tenth of the population,* it housed the refugees from the plague-stricken parts of Gosport who sought purer air and cleaner quarters. Later in that summer when the fever had killed its hundreds, it was the official orphan asylum of the town, sheltering at one time nearly three hundred children. When war was declared in 1861, the Academy was turned into barracks; and many are the stories told of the pranks of the soldiers quartered there. The Louisiana Tigers made an indelible impression on the neighborhood. Some of the old inhabitants still talk of their wild behavior.

When the Confederates evacuated the Federal soldiers took over the Academy. The star regiment among the enemies was one from New York, who candidly said that it made them "sore" to have to fight for the slaves. It was plain that they gave the slaves no quarter, making things as hard for them as they could. *Although Miss Holladay is quoting people who lived in Portsmouth at the time we cannot assume that she, or her informants were objective viewers of the Union Army and its views on slavery. Some Union soldiers were certainly ambiguous about slavery, but many were abolitionist at this early date. The war was being fought at this time to decide whether slave state would remain a part of the Union, not to bring about emancipation per se.*

When Green Street School was finished in 1886 the Academy was vacated and it soon fell upon evil days, being used for an yeast powder factory. The building was outwardly unchanged, and the neighborhood much quieter without the noise of the children. Once or twice a year the factory made war upon its rats and the houses were overrun with the exiles for a while.

The County schools, as we have said, were established in 1845; and from a letter written some years ago we get a picture of one of these schools, near Wallaceton *(now in Chesapeake near Bunch Walnut Road)* in the late forties *(1840s)*. "I had to walk three miles to the schoolhouse," says the writer, "and then had to sit on a bench without any back, with a long desk in front of it. When we were not using our books we could put them on the shelf under the top of this desk. We had to stand up in front of the teacher to recite our lessons. The teacher always looked fierce and kept a bunch of switches stuck in the weatherboarding behind him. The room was not plastered, and there were cracks in the boards through which the wind used to come to make us shiver. We carried our dinners in tin buckets, and when we finished eating, we had to cut wood with a dull axe, to keep fire in the stove. Our parents took turns in furnishing the wood and we boys had to cut it in short lengths for the stove."

Many of these conditions prevailed in the country schools until very modern times.

From the first "free schools" were made a campaign issue in Norfolk County and Portsmouth. The Whigs were strongly in favor of them; and as far back as 1850, one of their slogans was "Better Free Schools, and more money for them." *The Whig Party was particularly strong in New England, where free public schools had existed from a very early date.* The Democratic party opposed spending so much for them and their nominee for the Legislature, Dr. Smith, spoke against it publicly. At this period the public and private schools worked together most harmoniously; teachers in both institutions were members of the same "Teachers Association." The first meeting of this body was in 1853, when all the teachers of Norfolk, Portsmouth, Nansemond *(now the City of Suffolk)*, Norfolk County *(now partly the City of Portsmouth and partly the City of Chesapeake)* and Princess Anne County *(now partly the City of Norfolk and partly the City of Virginia Beach)* were invited to a meeting at Deep Creek, to organize a "Teachers' Association." So successful was this meeting that the next year they held an anniversary meeting in Portsmouth. Essays and other papers were read, one of them on the vexed subject of teaching spelling. Various methods were suggested and discussed. At this session it was agreed that the organization should become a permanent one, and be called "The Virginia Seaboard Teachers' Association." *At this time British spelling was being replaced with American spelling introduced by Noah Webster in his famous spelling book. That is why Americans spell "theatre," as " theater" and many words spelled in Britain with "our" as "or," as in "honour" and "honor."*

Of course the Civil War disorganized everything in the South; but the schools of Portsmouth were kept open as long as possible. In 1870 free schools became compulsory in Virginia but only for the African Americans. There were many changes made in the system at this time and a little later the adjective "free" was objected to in many quarters, and by common consent rather than by law the name was dropped, and the term "public" took its place.

It may be interesting to note that Portsmouth had a well-organized system of free schools several years before Norfolk succeeded in establishing them.

The first schoolhouse used for teaching the African Americans was "Webster's Hall," formerly used by Mr. Webster for his well-known private school. This building is still standing on Queen Street between Effingham and Green. It is now a tenement, and in very bad repair. *I have tried to find Webster's Hall with little success. The added yellow brick facade on the corner of Queen and Dinwiddie streets says "Tidewater Building 1906," but the building is older, with granite sills, and may be a remnant of the Hall. The rest of the block is made up of modern buildings and parking lots now. A historic marker should be put up in this block to mark the site of the first school for teaching African-American in Portsmouth.*

Our private schools have also a long and honorable history. The first one in Portsmouth after the Revolution was taught by a veteran of that War, Capt. Jesse Nicholson, who won distinction both at *the Battles of* Brandywine and Germantown.

We know nothing of his methods, neither do we know what studies his curriculum included; but we do know that many of the boys of the town were his pupils, and they loved him and revered his memory.

At this time school books were not easily procured, and the master himself had much of the work to do. Often the book was compiled by him, and written out in his hand. From it he gave out exercises or copy. We have seen an old arithmetic of this period carefully written out in a blank book.

Private schools like taverns were plentiful here a hundred years ago *(1830s)*. Those for advanced pupils were usually in a house built for the purpose, the primary school was generally taught in the parlor of the school-mistress. An interesting account of one of these "Dame Schools" has come down to us from an old lady of several generations ago. She could not tell us much about her studies; but her teacher, a stern old Scotch lady, made a deep impression upon her. A maid was stationed at the door each morning when the children arrived. She saw that the little feet were carefully wiped, for "Missus" would tolerate no dirt. When this ceremony had been performed, the pupils assembled in the drawing room, and seated themselves in small chairs grouped about the schoolmistress. Each child recited its lesson when called upon to do so, and did it alone, there being no classes. When eleven o'clock arrived the maid again appeared, this time armed with dry-rubbing brush and cloth. Orders were then issued to the pupils to go and study on the stair-steps for a while.

After the floors had been sufficiently polished, the children were permitted to resume their seats in the drawing-room, and lessons continued without further interruptions. Dry-rubbing the floors at eleven o'clock had been a life-long habit in that household, and this methodical Scotch lady could not change her customs for the comfort or convenience of the children.

Occupying the site of what is now Mrs. Charles Nash's residence on Middle Street was a schoolhouse built for Mr. Anson Brooks' school in *Number 817 by the old numbering system. Based on the old house-numbering system used at that time this would be several blocks south of High Street on Middle. The house no longer exists.* Mr. Brooks had a well-equipped school for older boys. His curriculum was a broad one, including Latin and Greek, as well as ancient and modern geography, with the use of globes, mathematics, science, history, reading, writing, composition and rhetoric. Associated with Mr. Brooks in teaching was a competent assistant for smaller boys.

Mr. Brooks was not a native of Portsmouth but he married a daughter of Mr. Swepson Whitehead, a distinguished lawyer of the town. Mr. Swepson Brooks their only child died a very few years ago at his farm in Princess Anne County *(Virginia Beach)* at the ripe age of ninety.

About this same time in Gosport, then a fashionable residential section, Mr. and Mrs. Ben Smith had a school. Mr. Smith taught the boys and Mrs. Smith had charge of the girls. Besides the usual English branches the young ladies were taught sewing, both plain and fancy. French music and painting were included in the course; but an extra charge was made for them. The opportunity for studying these subjects was excellent in Portsmouth. French was always taught by a native of France, for the town was at this time filled with exiles, who had either fled from the terrors of the French Revolution, or who had come at the downfall of Napoleon. The newspapers of the day are filled with advertisement for teaching French music and dancing.

A noticeable advantage in these old-fashioned schools was the male teacher for the boys. Except in the Dame Schools, we find there was always a "competent" master to take charge of the boys.

Mrs. Bowles had a school on High Street near Crawford; but as her course of study was similar to others mentioned there is no need of describing it. She too, had the "competent gentleman" to teach the boys. In 1825, Mrs. Bowles' school was taken over by Mrs. Butler, and for the first time we get some idea of the cost of an education, as well as learn something of the school hours. In the highest grade she taught grammar, arithmetic, history, geography and sewing, for which she charged six dollars a quarter. The intermediate grade had practically the same course, but tuition was only four dollars. This too, was the cost of the primary grade, in which nothing was taught but reading, writing and spelling. French was taught in the school; but there was an extra charge for it. The school hours were long; work commenced at nine o'clock, and at twelve there was a recess of two hours. The second session ended at four o'clock. There seems to have been no vacation given. In some instances the schools closed for two weeks in August; and later on the whole month was given. This was the usual vacation in some of the private and in all the public schools until sometime in the *eighteen* eighties.

Mr. Henry Robinson opened a school here in 1820, for "Young Ladies," and after teaching in Portsmouth for many years he moved to Norfolk. So great was his reputation as a teacher, that his pupils followed him; and his influence in educating Portsmouth girls was in no way diminished. He educated mother and daughter in turn. His curriculum was not crowded and his methods were very thorough. His pupils, many of them had not forgotten their Latin at eighty; and their knowledge and use of English was remarkable. These two subjects were his hobby; and his young ladies parsed *Paradise Lost* and other masterpieces word for word.

Arithmetic he taught, but he frankly admitted that he saw no use in teaching young ladies any mathematics. He was exceedingly careful about the manners and bearing of his young ladies, not only when they appeared in school but generally. From time to time some of the girls would be noisy on the street, or make themselves conspicuous in some other way. If Mr. Robinson heard of it, and we are told that he always did hear of it, the offenders were warned; and if they continued to misbehave their parents were asked to withdraw them from school.

Some years ago the writer had the pleasure of hearing three ladies, each over eighty, who had been schoolmates at Mr. Robinson's, talk over their school days. They spoke affectionate words of their old Master, for whom they professed the greatest admiration.

There was a man who lived on Washington Street in the block between North and Glasgow who had as his specialty preparing young men of the town to pass the entrance exam at the Navy Academy in Annapolis.

The tradition of a teacher running a private school persisted with the Stokes Academy. Isaiah Stokes came to Portsmouth from Ireland, and served in the Confederate Army - in the Grays. His wife, whom he met in America, was also Irish. There son William Henry Stokes was purported to be the smartest man in the city, and in 1868 opened a school on County Street between Court and Dinwiddie. In 1873 it was moved to a spot on Court Street across from the old location of St. John's church and finally in 1887 to the southeast corner of Crawford and London where a part of the Federal Building now stands. The first floor of Mr. Stokes home on Crawford Street consisted of two classrooms with as many as forty students in all the grades. He also had a night school to prepare students for passing the exam to become bookkeepers at the Navy Yard. In the 1880s he edited the <u>Portsmouth Record</u> and then, with John Porter, the short lived <u>Portsmouth Enterpriser</u>. The school survived into the twentieth century and his grandson, Dr. Ralph Stokes, the husband of the artist E. Ann Stokes, still lives in the city.

The last of the private schools in Portsmouth to survive was Frederick Military Academy, established by Frederick Beazley and described in greater detail elsewhere in this work. If was in business from 1956 to 1985.

In 1825 the Portsmouth Academy incorporated by act of the General Assembly. The academy building was erected on Glasgow Street near Middle with money received from the sale of the glebes.

Mr. Freeman in his announcement sounded no uncertain trumpet, declaring that he wished to give the boys and girls entrusted to his care, a practical education, but that he intended to lay special stress upon cultural subjects. We know little of the curriculum; but like most of the schools of the day it had the three departments, primary, intermediate and senior, and different divisions for girls and boys. The charge for the highest grade was seven and a half dollars a quarter; the intermediate cost five dollars and the primary four dollars a quarter. A charge of ten dollars was made for Greek and Latin.

A list of those who passed their examinations at the close of the first year will interest many now living. The first class wore pink ribbons and the successful young ladies were Misses Rebecca Schoolfield, Ritchie Swift, Susan Wilson, Mary Jane Wilson, Ann Webb and Clara Crocker. Messrs John T. Hill and William Benthall were the successful boys. Blue ribbons distinguished the second class, and in it were Misses Carmi Watts, Mary Frances Blow, Emily Wilson, Elizabeth Wilson and Mary Chandler. The boys who passed were Dempsey Hatton, William Freeman and Thomas Hopkins.

In 1840 the Academy became a military school under Mr. Patridge and its opening day was a gala one in the town. There was a great parade, in which the military companies of both towns took part, as well as the navy and army corps, town trustees and the ministers. After marching through the town the procession adjourned to the theater, where speeches were made by prominent men.

It was during this year 1840 that the teachers complained officially of the long hours spent in teaching, urging that they might be shortened. The newspapers published letters from various sources in regard to their plea; and many suggestions were made for remedying this evil, but nothing was found to show us whether or not the teachers were successful.

About 1850 the Academy was taken over by the public schools and used by them until 1886.

Webster's Collegiate Institute followed next in our list of schools. Its principal Professor Webster was an able and gifted man, who labored faithfully in his own particular field, and was zealous in keeping up the cultural standards of the town. Mr. Webster was at the head of the boys' department and under him were three assistants. Mrs. Webster had charge of the girls' division, assisted by several other ladies. In 1853 there were one hundred and fifty pupils in this school.

At this time the school game was cricket, and much interest was manifested in it. There were frequent games with the teams from the Norfolk schools. Among the names listed in the cricket club, we find many that are yet familiar ones in Portsmouth, Blister Gayle, Levin Gayle, William Fiske, James Parrish, Louis Boutwell, C. T. Phillips, and Arthur Collins. After the Civil War Mr. Webster took charge of a school in Norfolk and Mr. C. T. Phillips succeeded him in Portsmouth. It would be impossible to mention all the schools that have helped to promote education in Portsmouth.

A Norfolk school that was a great favorite here, was Mrs. Hackeley's. This lady was a niece of Thomas Jefferson and was brought up under his care. Her school was a good type of the fashionable boarding school of the day; and some account of it may be interesting. Young ladies were there trained for social life; but useful things were much stressed. Sewing, both plain and ornamental were requirements of the curriculum. These with the usual English branches and science cost ten dollars a quarter. Spanish and French were taught, at the price of eight dollars each, a term. Painting, too, was an extra, and that cost twenty dollars a term. Music was fifty cents a lesson, and a charge of three dollars was charged for the use of the piano in practicing. Board was set at one hundred dollars a year but bedclothes were furnished by the pupils.

John Paul Hanbury fondly remembers the two schools built in Parkview. The Ann Street School which covered the first to the fourth grade stood where Parkview Elementary now stands, and Cooke Street School took on the fifth to the seventh graders. That school's principal, Florence Hall, is said to have climbed a twenty-foot ladder every morning to ring the school bell and was so punctual in this task that the neighbors set their clocks by her. Alf Mapp tells us the bell survives in the backyard of Raymond Wimbrough in Park Manor.

An excellent review of the modern history of the Portsmouth Public School system appears in Alf and Remona Mapp's *Picture History of Portsmouth* and another in the library collection by Miss Deans, and so there is little point in going into detail here. The Superintendents in modern times were as follows. James Francis Crocker who served from 1871 through 1882. He opened the Newtown Academy, the first coeducational school in the city, and the Chestnut Street School, mentioned earlier, which was the first school for African Americans, opened in 1879 at the corner of Chestnut and South streets. Gifford R. Edwards served from 1882 to 1886. He opened a combined elementary and high school at the corner of Green and Columbia streets in 1886 and the first public high school in the old Academy building on Glasgow Street in 1885. He was followed by James C. Ashton who built the Cooke School, already mentioned and Portsmouth High School on the east side of Washington Street between High and King streets in 1908. Next came Harry A. Hunt, for whom Hunt-Mapp Middle School was later named. He was the longest serving Superintendent - serving from 1909 through 1950. The first Woodrow Wilson High School opened on May 18, 1917. Alf J. Mapp served from 1950 to 1965. During his tenure the Portsmouth School system was selected by the Office of Education as one of three model systems for its emphasis on reading skills and education for the handicapped. The first I. C. Norcum was built during his tenure as was the new Woodrow Wilson in 1953. He added five elementary schools and nine more through annexation. Dr. M. E. Alford, who has been mentioned elsewhere in this book, served from 1965 to 1984. In his tenure Manor High School, later to become the current Woodrow Wilson High School, was built.

  Catholic schools played an important part in Portsmouth's educational system. The building of St. Joseph's Academy for boys still stands on the south side of King Street between Dinwiddie and Washington, although no longer in use as a school. The Catholic elementary school is still in operation on King's Highway in Oregon Acres off Airline Boulevard. The original Catholic High School was built in 1891 on the southeast corner of London and Washington streets. In the 1950's the *old building was encased in a newer structure, and it became a neighborhood high school for the children of Olde Towne of all faiths. In the 1990s Bishop Sullivan of the Diocese of Richmond decided to close the school. It stood vacant until the land was purchased by Monumental Methodist Church in order to demolish the building to make space for a parking lot for the church. A public effort was made to save the historic core of the building. Then City Attorney G. Timothy Oksman describes the events as follows: "The controversy over possible demolition of this historic structure was intense. It pitted the legitimate interests of one of Portsmouth's oldest and most respected churches, Monumental United Methodist Church, against the equally legitimate interests of historic preservationists. The controversy raged for the better part of a year, turning neighbor against neighbor. When the City Council, after several fractious meetings, ultimately denied a demolition permit, it was by a slender 4-3 margin. Denial of the demolition permit led to a lawsuit brought by the church. The lawsuit was a classic clash of towering legal issues, free exercise of religion, and rights under the federal Religious Land Use and Institutionalized Persons Act on one side against the rights of a community to protect its important historic resources on the other side. The case received national attention and was the subject of several seminar discussions. Ultimately, it was resolved with no losers: the church received much-needed additional parking and the old Catholic school was deeded to the city for restoration; legal expenses for both sides were moderate and the healing process for the community began. This commendable outcome was possible only because of the judges involved in the case: Jerome B. Friedman, U.S. District Court, Tommy E. Miller, magistrate judge: and E. Everett Bagnell, settlement judge. Special credit is also due to the late Joe Lyle, attorney for the church, for his statesmanlike and enlightened advocacy." The old school, now in use as an office building, is one of the special ornaments of the Olde Towne.*

The library has almost a full run of the annuals of Woodrow Wilson High School and I. C. Norcum High School, the predominantly African American school until integration and of the other newer high schools as well.

CHAPTER 37: THE TOWN'S BUSINESS BEGINS

Portsmouth, as Col. Crawford foresaw, was fortunate in her situation, her hinterland covered by vast forests of oak and pine, ready to build the ships which should bring a great trade to the magnificent harbor at her shores. In an address some years ago one our citizens said in speaking of Portsmouth, "Nature has done much for us, and it only requires energy and enterprise to utilize these advantages; and turn them to good account. With a climate of unsurpassed salubrity and healthfulness, a soil of unrivaled fertility and productiveness, a location unsurpassed by any on the Atlantic Coast—why should we not attain a position of great commercial importance and prosperity?"

This question is still asked; and as we study the history of the development of the town, we shall see that the answer is not hard to find.

Few perhaps ever realized the great advantages of this port more than the numerous Scotch and English settlers who flocked to Col. Crawford's little town as soon as it was established. It is astonishing how rapidly Portsmouth developed up to the Revolution, and for many years after it. As far back as 1770 the merchants of town in conjunction with those of Norfolk, established a board of trade for the "better conduct of business". The meeting for organizing it took place at the house of Mr. Anthony Hay in Norfolk; but a Portsmouth citizen, Mr. Andrew Sprowle, *the founder of the Gosport Yard, now the Norfolk Naval Shipyard in Portsmouth and, at this time, agent for the British Navy and the wealthiest merchant in Virginia,* was appointed chairman of the board. The other merchants from Portsmouth present at the meeting were, James Marsden, German Baker, Humphrey Roberts, David Ross, Robert Sheddon and Thomas Hepburn. *Some of these were identified as Tories earlier in this work, but Miss Holladay says -*

When Great Britain levied the oppressive taxes, our merchants were indignant and the majority of them signed the "Association", which was an agreement of some kind refusing to purchase from the English merchants. *In various of the colonies this was a document called the Association of the Sons of Liberty Written in 1773 in opposition to the taxation on tea; other material, like paper had be included in the original tax, but all but tea removed from this extra taxation in 1770. In the Association the merchants agreed not to buy the materials taxed in the act from England.*

When war was actually a fact these merchants were forced to take a stand. Some of them played fast and loose with both sides; finally going with the one with which they could make the best bargain. *As we illustrated in the chapter called "The Royal Capital."* A few threw in their lot with the Colony, or as she then was the State of Virginia. The remaining number returned to their homes across the sea, fully intending to return when hostilities ceased and resume their former vocations. After the war was over many of them made application to return to Portsmouth and later some of them evidently did do so. These men were not interested in politics; but each one wished to build up a successful business regardless of the flag under which he lived.

It was at this time that Portsmouth made her first and perhaps greatest mistake. If the Revolution caused a setback to our commercial growth, it certainly offered us an advantage in the burning of our sister town, *Norfolk*, which was leveled to the ground in January 1776. Mr. Forrest in his *History of Norfolk*, says that Portsmouth should have grown more rapidly under these conditions, but for the injudicious behavior of some of the best citizens in the town.

When the Scotch families came to this section to settle after the war, they were ordered to leave Portsmouth at once. They came in such numbers that houses could not be found for them all, so many families encamped on the open square in front of the ferry, at the foot of North Street. These settlers were much annoyed by the rougher element, who visited the *Scottish* people, asking after King George, making enquiries about Cornwallis, while some of them even stooped to personal violence, throwing rocks and stones at individuals.

The citizens of the town at large sought to rid the town of these Tories in a more dignified way; and it has been our proudest boast that Portsmouth drove out the Tory settlers.

We learn from a document recently found in the State Archives at Richmond, just what measures were taken by the town for this purpose. A meeting of the citizens was called in order to fix upon some plan to prevent the "Tory Invasion" of the town.

The record just alluded to was addressed to Mr. John Kerr, a former resident of Portsmouth: "We the subscribers, the inhabitants of the town of Portsmouth, having yet very recent in our memory, the treasonable and most traitorous act perpetrated by these execrable miscreants called Tories, and to our great astonishment now see a number of them and have reason to believe that many more will have the audacity to attempt to settle in our town; and it is a measure as insolent and as audacious as their late past actions have been treasonable and diabolical; we find it indispensably necessary for measures to be immediately adopted to stop the same; for it is morally impossible for Whigs and Tories to live and coincide together. One or the other must be expelled from this town. Therefore we the subscribers, pledge to each other our faith and honor that we will first by gentle measures do all that we can to prevent these perjured villains from effecting a settlement among us; and if that will not do; we will make every effort that we hitherto have done against the British Army and its adherents. We herewith beg you to leave this town immediately or measures very disagreeable to us as well as to yourself will be taken."

At this period 1783-4 only twelve houses had been rebuilt in Norfolk; and she realized that her opportunity had come. The people of the town banded together and offered the exiled settlers from Portsmouth lots on very advantageous terms, and extended to them every facility to aid them in their business careers. "In consequence," says Mr. Forrest, in his *History of Norfolk*, "Norfolk soon rose from her ruins and acquired an ascendancy over Portsmouth, both in commerce and population. " These Scotch merchants became the leading factor in the success of Norfolk and some of the most prominent citizens of the city today are their descendants.

An old citizen of a bygone day used to tell of another of Portsmouth's mistakes: when in the period between 1816 and 1821, the country was making every effort to recover from the War of 1812, her people who had done such a noble part in her defense wasted their time and energy in disputes over the "Embargo Act," "Right of Search," the injustice of Congress to the navy. "Party spirit in Portsmouth has often sacrificed the interests of the community." *The Embargo Act of 1807 was a response to the rise of Napoleon in which Britain and France restricted neutral merchant shipping. Thomas Jefferson hoped, by forbidding all foreign trade to enter U. S. ports to convince the combatants to lift their restrictions on American merchants. The impact of stopping international trade on a seaport like Portsmouth is obvious. In 1809 the prohibition was limited to England and France by the Nonintercourse Act; even that was thwarted by American Merchants and finally defeated in 1810 when the restrictions to trade were rescinded by the second Macon Act. The "Right of Search" allowed a warring nation to stop the ships of a neutral nation and search them for contraband which might aid their opponent.*

A few years after the close of the Revolutionary War, we are told that it was dangerous to cross the ferry, owing to the great number of vessels in the harbor. Ships from foreign parts *were* bringing in luxuries and commodities of other kinds, *and* carrying away from this port in return lumber, cattle, pork and shipstores. Our coasting trade besides employed hundreds of vessels, and the question asked at the numerous shipyards that surrounded Portsmouth was not how much will it cost to build a ship, but how soon you can do it. Vessels were too much in demand to haggle about the price of one. *Mr. Foreman tells us in his walk around Portsmouth in the 1820s that the Elizabeth River front was a row of shipyards. Each yard was led by a captain, among them Captain Benthal and Captain McRae, who would build one ship, send it to the Caribbean where they would sell it for rum, import the rum and sell it to pay themselves, their crews, their sailors, and their shipwrights and still have enough left to build another ship. Among the shipyards here in 1829 were Joseph Porter's, John Overton's, Miles Chambers& Hathaway, Ryan & Gales and Guy C. Wheeler.*

Private shipbuilding continued in small yards at Portsmouth through the end of the nineteenth century, when Lewis A. Hoagland ran a shipyard at the foot of South Street where he built tugboats, dredges and even schooners. Alf Mapp tells us that a well-known Philadelphia figurehead carver Henry Wells from Philadelphia moved his business to the Portsmouth bank of the Elizabeth River.

As far back as our newspaper records have been preserved, 1804, the front page of the paper was given up to shipping news, and the things pertaining to it. *Although these newspapers were available to Miss Holladay, most are now lost.* Sailing dates were published, boats advertised for charter, lists of cargoes *were* carried out and brought in and so on. At this date 1804 there were ships in port at one time from Isle de Re, Lisbon, Cadiz, Surinam, Bordeaux, Liverpool, London, Glasgow, Madeira, Bermuda, Bahama, Rotterdam, Antwerp and other places. *In a description of Dickson's Wharf at Gosport in the 1820s John Foreman says, "I have seen more rum, sugar and molasses landed in one day than you can see in the port now (the 1890s) in six months. The whole river was lined with vessels trading from foreign ports." In 1803 Portsmouth had a rum distillery of its own with a capacity of 600 gallons a year. Among the Portsmouth ships listed in the Caribbean trade in 1807 were the <u>Flora</u>, <u>Anacreon</u>, <u>Elizabeth</u>, <u>William and Mary</u>, <u>Malvina</u>, <u>Modoc</u>, <u>Margaret Wright</u>, and <u>Constitution</u>.*

The waterfront at Gosport, we are told, was lined with warehouses belonging to those dealing with the West Indies. The Dickson family owned several there and kept a fleet of ships going and coming. *Captain John Dickson, his wife Sarah and their sons; Captain William Dickson, who owned a block full of warehouses in Gosport, and Captain Henry Dickson and his wife Hannah are all buried in Trinity churchyard.* Capt. John Coxe of Revolutionary fame, too, had warehouses on the waterfront.

In 1784 the Government ordered tobacco warehouses built in Portsmouth and the lots selected for their site were those numbered on the plat of the town *in* 1834. They were at the extreme southern end of Court Street just below Bart, fronting on Crab Creek, which was navigable at that time far to the west. All tobacco had to be inspected at and shipped from a warehouse owned by the State Government, which also appointed its own inspectors. John Cowper was made inspector in Portsmouth.

In 1783 the citizens of Portsmouth applied to the General Assembly, feeling that they needed some "internal policy for government," asking that an act might be passed authorizing the town trustees to levy an annual tax which was not to exceed three shillings on every tithable, *Several early lists of Tithables survive in Portsmouth and Norfolk County Documents in the library history room. They are lists of those heads of families (including some single women) who were required to contribute to the support of Portsmouth Parish (now Trinity Church).* They also requested that the forfeited lands be laid off and sold for the improvement of the town, under the authority of the trustees, who should be empowered too, to regulate the markets, remove nuisances, as well as be allowed to punish those who misapplied money which came into their hands.

The next year (1784) Laban Goffigon, who had served as a lieutenant in the Navy during the Revolution, was appointed harbor master for Portsmouth. Goffigon was much interested in this harbor and, seemed to have studied its advantages very carefully. At this time it was urged that Portsmouth be made a "capital port," by building a canal. Goffigon urged that it should be done, and among other advantages declared that between Devil's Reach and the Navy Yard there was ample room for five large shipyards. We have not been able to locate the "Reach," beyond what Goffigon tells us. It was he says five miles above the town on the Southern Branch. *His wife Mary Goffigan is buried in Trinity Churchyard. She is believed to have been a member of the Veale family who inherited some of Col. Crawford's remaining lots after his death. He married again after Mary's death to Elizabeth Hansford.*

In the opening years of the nineteenth century the old provost prison had been taken over by a company who established a sugar refinery in it and was then known as the Sugar House. *We have heard about a daring escape from this property when it was a prison in the chapter on Revolutionary War veterans and on the fire which destroyed it in the chapter on fires..* Business was carried on a large scale; and only the best quality of sugar sold. The shops supplied this commodity in small quantities; the Sugar House would only supply the wholesale trade. *This Sugar House was opened in 1802 at the corner of Crawford and First streets.*

At this period other advantages accrued to the town; the court was moved here and Portsmouth became the county seat in 1800. At this date the United States Government purchased the old

Marine Yard from the State, with the intention of equipping it for a large Navy Yard.

It was thought that it would be a great asset for the town; but unfortunately it has been largely the source of Portsmouth's undoing. *It is interesting that Miss Holladay says this more than 75 years ago. Today most of the Yard's employees live outside the city and it still takes a large chunk of prime Portsmouth development land off the tax rolls.*

There were distilleries in Gosport, making hundreds of gallons of rum a day. *This trade continued into the next century. John Mahoney came from Ireland to Portsmouth in 1850 and began J. & E. Mahoney's Liquor House at 11-13 High Street where he distilled rye whiskey and gin. He expanded to a larger facility in Alexandria, but continued to live, brew and sell spirits in Portsmouth. Several of his descendants are buried in Cedar Grove Cemetery.*

An old citizen Walter T. Brennan remembered that when prohibition became law on November 1 1916, Mahoney was required to take all of the bottles in his distillery and in the warehouse on the southwest corner of Water and High streets out into the street, break them and pour out the alcohol on the pavement. When the building was being cleaned many bags of coffee were found hidden above the ceilings in the rafters. At the time it was thought they had been hidden there during the Civil War for transport to the Confederate Army and forgotten after the war ended. Because of the blockade of Southern ports coffee was unavailable and Confederate soldiers had to invent alternative herb brews.

The brewery building, which had a bridge across Water Street to the Seaboard Railway station, became the offices of the <u>Portsmouth Star</u>. The first issue of the <u>Star</u> came out on September 4, 1894. The paper was run by Paul L. Trugien and William S. Wilder out of offices at 409-11 Crawford Street at that time, and was later moved to High Street and then into the old Mahoney distillery in 1926. The then owner and editor, Norman R. Hamilton, started selling subscriptions to the paper when he was a young boy, getting ten cents for every subscription he sold. He was owner and publisher for 31 years. The paper was sold to the <u>Virginian Pilot</u> and <u>Ledger Star</u> in March 1955 leaving Portsmouth for the first time without a newspaper of its own; and the old building was torn down in 1973 and is now the site of the High Street Landing information center - Betsy's coffee kiosk and the Crawford Street Parking Ramp, built in 1987.

The earliest-known newspaper editor from Portsmouth was Alexander Scott from Gosport, buried in Trinity churchyard and, in fact, the oldest burial there - 1763; but nothing is known about his paper except it was published in Norfolk.

The first paper actually published in Portsmouth was *The Virginia Palladium and Portsmouth Commercial Advertiser.* Its history was of the shortest; its first number appearing on May 1, 1827, and the last one in May, 1828. Its publisher was Robert Geddes and it was published at its office on High Street just below the Courthouse, so it stated; but the Courthouse then stood on the site of the Hotel Monroe *(now the TCC Visual Arts Center).* It was issued every Tuesday, Thursday and Saturday. Of its editor we know nothing; but we are fortunate in having a volume of this paper in the Public Library, where those who are interested can see it. The tri-weekly paper was a custom of the day, not only at that time but for many years later.

The Portsmouth and Norfolk papers were not delivered until 12 o'clock. This was because they waited for the latest news from the North and from foreign parts, which arrived here early in the morning *on the Old Bay Steamship Line.*

After *the Palladium* quite a crop of Portsmouth newspapers appeared, until midway in the nineteenth century when the town supported three of them at once. Politics were a great issue at this time and the papers were strongly partisan.

There were no personal notices. A formal notice was all that the newspaper printed about any wedding. In some of these notices, however, thanks from the editor appeared for some of the wedding cake which came to him with the notice.

In the thirties (1835) The *Portsmouth Times* first published in Portsmouth, edited by Mr. Bland, and was issued on Wednesdays and Saturdays. Two years later Bland was succeeded by Mr. John Thompson Hill, who became editor of the *Times* in 1837.

Mr. Hill, though born in the North, came to Portsmouth in his childhood. He was a graduate of Yale College and practiced law in his adopted city. He was a brilliant intellect and *The Times* was ably edited during his regime which unfortunately was a very short one, ending with Mr. Hill's death in 1839.

He married Miss Mary Eliza Chandler, daughter of Mr. John A. Chandler, a noted lawyer of Portsmouth. Mrs. Hill was a woman of fine intellect and of attractive qualities. They lived in the fine old brick house now number 221 North Street, the town house of their grandchildren, the Misses Hill and the late William C. Hill. *This is the Hill house, now open for tours. One of the daughters was for many years garden editor of the <u>New York Herald Tribune</u>.*

About 1838 or 1839 another paper was started in Portsmouth, *The Clay Banner and Naval Intelligencer*. Its editor was Mr. John Murdaugh, a prominent lawyer in the town. Mr. Murdaugh's paper, as its name would indicate, was strongly partisan - *Clay meaning Henry Clay*. Mr. Murdaugh had been prominent in politics and had several times served in the State Legislature. His home was a social center and his wife was remembered as a charming hostess, who was admired and loved in her circle of friends. Mr. Murdaugh was the father of Mrs. Washington Reed, Mrs. Fanny Downing and of Capt. W. H. Murdaugh. He died in 1842 and his cousin, another John Murdaugh, succeeded him as editor of the *Clay Banner*. We have not ascertained just when this paper ended its career. The second John Murdaugh lived but a short time after he became its editor.

In 1840 we learn from an advertisement in one of the Norfolk newspapers that Mr. Theophilus Fiske had resigned as editor of the *Portsmouth Chronicle* and Mr. D. D. Fiske would succeed him in the editor's chair. It became known as the *Transcript*, a paper which appeared in 1840, published at number 59 Crawford Street, in the block between High and Queen Streets, *opposite the building mentioned earlier as the original home of the <u>Portsmouth Star</u>.*

When the Civil War came both of Mr. Fiske's sons entered the Confederate Army and Melzar Fiske lost his life. The other son Mr. William Fiske spent his life in Portsmouth and died when he was over ninety years of age. He never married..

The Transcript probably ended its days in the early years of the Civil War. We have seen a copy of it dated as late as April 1861.

In the 1850s Portsmouth supported three newspapers: the *Transcript*, the *Democrat* and the *Old Dominion*. Of the *Democrat* we know nothing except that it was edited by Mr. Orr. Of the *Old*

Dominion we know even less; but that it was still issued in 1864 is certain as there is in existence an "Extra" published by it announcing the assassination of Lincoln: "HON. ABRAHAM LINCOLN ASSASSINATED: Secretary Seward and His Son Stabbed.
"Lt. Col. O. L. Mann. our Provost Marshall, has furnished us with a dispatch which has just been received announcing the awfully solemn intelligence of the assassination of President Lincoln, with the attempted murder of members of his Cabinet. While at the Theatre in Washington. The following is the dispatch: Fort Monroe, April 15, 1865. Brig. Gen Geo. H. Gordon, Commanding, &c., Norfolk Va.
Not knowing whether the sad intelligence we have received here has yet reached you, I thought proper to send you this by special boat.
"President Lincoln was shot last night at Ford's Theatre and died at 7:30 this a.m.
Secretary Seward may recover. His son was also stabbed, and will probably not recover.
We have no further particulars here.
I have the honor to be
Your ob't Serv't,
W. S. JAMES,
Brevet Major & A. Q. M."

After the Civil War it was some little time before business in any form was reorganized and newspapers were not published at once. Through the *eighteen* seventies and eighties there were two daily papers published in Portsmouth, The *Portsmouth Times* and *The Enterprise* and in addition there was published in the *eighteen* eighties a weekly, newspaper, *The Portsmouth Observer*.

The Times was owned by the Bain Brothers and one of its unique features was a woman as its editor. This editor was Mrs. Fanny Murdaugh Downing of Portsmouth, whose literary gifts and attainments had already made her prominent. On the staff of this paper at one time was the late Julius H. Wilcox, a man of marked intellect, though rather eccentric.

Returning to the <u>Portsmouth Star</u> saga Miss Holladay shares Mr. Trugien's difficulties in starting the paper: "One of the founders was a consistent member of the Methodist Church and the other a copper fastened Presbyterian who would not work on Sundays." *This was resolved by making it an evening paper.* The gas engine to run the press, rather than hand power, the first engine of its kind in Portsmouth, became temperamental and says Mr. Trugien, "The damn thing, as it was known around the *Star* building, came up to no single expectation, or fond anticipation that was indulged in when it was purchased. For days on end it would run with the smoothness and regularity of a watch - then for days on end it would refuse to budge. Everybody, editors, reporters, passing well-wishers would turn and turn again on the flywheel -then when the point of exhaustion was reached, when profanity grew blue and unabashed - off she'd go - just in time to make the paper late."

There were ropewalks on South and on Bart streets. *A ropewalk was a very long narrow roofed enclosure. The rope makers would walk backward in it spinning hemp yarn from a coil of combed fiber wrapped around their waste; then in another pass they would braid the rope in various weights called sheets, cables and hawsers for use in rigging sailing ships. the walks had to be long enough to make the rope meet the standard for the time of 120 fathoms, or 720 feet.* Brick kilns were scattered through the town, one of the best known being on the northwest corner of Middle and High streets. There were several windmills here and in the 1820s Commodore Barron built one of the most approved type for his son-in-law, Mr. Hope, the father of James Barron Hope, the poet and noted editor. *Commodore James Barron's interesting story is told elsewhere. He is buried in Trinity churchyard with his grandchildren. The Commodore Theater is named for him. Among his grandchildren buried with him is George J. S. B. Hope. That George Hope died in infancy. His daughter, Ann Ballard Maupin, is also buried in Trinity churchyard as she was the first wife of Dr. George Washington Maupin and died in childbirth with her first child.* This *wind*mill, which Barron built, was at what is now the intersection of South and Chestnut streets; *of course, long gone,* but it was not a success financially and was consequently soon abandoned.

A soap and tallow factory carried on an extensive business on High Street in the very early years of the *nineteenth* century. *In the early part of the twentieth century Portsmouth was home to another soap business: a large Proctor and Gamble factory was in business here for several decades. Many citizens of the village of Truxton worked there.*

Our first real estate firm was established, though it did not trade under that name. The partners were Capt. Davis, a retired sea captain and Mr. James Young, an officer in the Revolution. They were both wealthy and influential men. In addition to their dealings in real estate, they insured ships.

As early as 1827 we had commenced to build steamboats here. At that time one was launched from Mr. Joseph Porter's shipyard at the foot of High Street. The vessel was named *Fredericksburg* and was intended for travel on the Rappahannock River. *For more information on steam navigation in this area see John Clloyd Emmerson's books on the coming of the steamboat to the Chesapeake Bay.*

Portsmouth was the pioneer in this section in handling Maine ice. In 1830, Capt. Samuel Watts and his brother established the ice business here. The ice was cut from ponds in Maine and brought to Portsmouth in schooners. In 1832 this firm built an icehouse on Queen Street, on the site of the one still standing there between Middle and Crawford streets, *now parking for two banks and the Virginia Sports Hall of Fame.* The capacity of this house was only about twenty or thirty tons; but three years later it was enlarged and held about three hundred tons. Maine ice having proved successful in Portsmouth, Norfolk decided to supply her people in the same way; and we learn from an apology made by Mr. Watts for the shortage of ice in Portsmouth that Norfolk had not furnished a sufficient quantity of ice and had called on the Portsmouth firm to help her out The newspapers of 1835 published a statement from the Watts to this effect, adding that their supply had been adequate for their own city.

In 1855 the ice house was burned but immediately rebuilt. It again fell a prey to the flames in —— (the omission of a date is in the original) but was restored and improved. It is now used as an office for the George W. Maupin Ice and Coal Company. Mr. Maupin purchased the ice business from the Watts family.

In these progressive days *(1930s)* we make our own ice and the Maupin's have a large and well equipped plant here for manufacturing it. The Portsmouth Ice and Coal Company and Isaac Fass, *a wholesake fish merchant with offices on Crawford Street,* too, have large plants here. *Another ice manufacturer, Orlando B. Baker of the Hygenic Ice Co. on High and Armstrong streets had an innovative York and St. Clair compression ice machine run on coal with water drawn from six artesian wells on his property which could turn out ten tons a day in 1892. All of this, of course, became obsolete after the introduction of electric freezers and home refrigerators. There were horse-drawn wagons delivering the ice blocks around Portsmouth until World War II, and children ran behind them to glean ice slivers from the sawdust to cool themselves on hot summer days.*

In the *early* days of Maine ice there were of course, no deliveries in the town; and everyone went for or sent for their own ice. The number of pounds desired was cut off the block by *an African American called* Uncle Jacob, and weighed. It was then dipped in a barrel of water, which was part of the equipment of the ice house, to cleanse it from the sawdust *in which it was stored.*

When this was properly done, a groove was cut all around the ice, to hold the string with which it was tied. A slip knot was made in the end of the string and a small stick of wood was placed in the knot; this was done to keep from cutting the hand with the string.

The various ceremonies incident to the purchase of five or ten pounds of ice being thoroughly carried out, the ice was turned over to the purchaser, who went home dangling a lump of ice from its long string. Ice at this time was kept in an immense loft and covered with sawdust for protection. This loft was a great place for storing watermelons in order to get them cold. In summertime not only the ice but the melon had to be sent for at dinnertime.

Another industry carried on to a great extent here in early days was oyster pickling. The pickled oysters were shipped in large quantities to the West Indies, New York and New Orleans. One of the largest shippers in Portsmouth was Mr. John Benson whose plant was on the Western Branch *of the Elizabeth River*. He advertised to furnish this commodity in any quantity up to three thousand gallons. The shops in the two towns furnished his pickled oysters in smaller quantities. *Oysters were a staple of families even in the Midwest. Your editor has a letter from Illinois in this period which tells of oysters being regularly served on the dinner table. Our local oysters were the best available. An elderly lady in Princess Anne County whose father was in the trade said the New York hotels would send an order by telegraph. Some unscrupulous suppliers learned the Morse Code and sat around the telegraph office listening for a big order. They would then deliver first, stealing the trade. Her father outfoxed them, however, by using homing pigeons sent out to and from his hotel customers in New York City. The pirate oyster suppliers were mystified as to how he managed to get his orders around them.*

The Virginia *General* Assembly enacted very strict laws forbidding the sale of oysters between May and October. If the luscious bivalves were found on any ship during that season the masters of the vessels were subject to a heavy fine. This clause of the act caused some excitement among the "Picklers"; who demanded that the clause be altered, and amended; declaring that pickled oysters did not come within the law *because they did not require refrigeration.*

The oyster business survived in Portsmouth into the twentieth century. W. C. Dutton and then White and Fleming Oyster Packers shipped 150,000 bushels a year from the foot of Middle Street, which may explain why you cannot put a shovel down in Olde Towne without brining up some oyster shell.

It will probably come as a surprise to many of us to know that Portsmouth was one of the pioneers in building "ready to put up houses." During the gold rush in California in 1849 and 1850, when people were clamoring for houses there; several cities undertook to send them this type of building. A company to build such houses was formed here under the leadership of Mr. Henry V. Niemeyer. The necessary parts for constructing a house were cut and fitted ready to be set up. These parts were then bundled and shipped to California by sailing vessels *around the Horn, as the Panama Canal did not exist at that time.* One of these "ready to build houses" is standing in Portsmouth today. It was formerly the home of Mr. William A. Niemeyer, now known as number one Swimming Point. *Although this example of Mr. Niemeyer's handiwork no longer survives here, at least two others do. One is on the southeast corner of Court Street and Glasgow Street and another is on South Street at the corner of Dinwiddie. It is reported that these "pre-fabs" did badly in the California earthquakes.* The *remaining ones* were left on the hands of the company, California having then been sufficiently supplied with homes. *Many of the Niemeyer family can be found buried in Cedar Grove Cemetery.*

We know that the ladies of Portsmouth did not do all of their own sewing, in *those* days when all of it was done by hand; but we hear little of the mantua-makers; dressmaker was an unknown word; at that period. If there were any *fashionable French dressmakers* here their fame did not pass down to us. In the *eighteen* thirties, we learn from their advertisements in the newspapers, that there were two fashionable mantua-makers in Norfolk, who evidently had a clientele on this side of the river, as they refer to their Portsmouth patrons. One of them Mrs. James announced that she had just returned from New York with models of the latest fashions, which she would be pleased to show to her customers in Norfolk and Portsmouth. Mrs. Dentzil in the same issue of the paper makes a similar announcement. She makes no reference to "model" but she goes Mrs. James one better in having the latest London fashions as well as those of New York.

The gentlemen did not neglect their dress. They had their fashions too, the papers advertised a most useful book, called *The Art Of Tying The Cravat*. It was published in London and gave sixteen illustrated lessons in tying it. The cravat of 1830 was a complicated affair judging by the portraits of that day, and doubtless required some skill in the handling.

The most famous men's store in Portsmouth in the twentieth century was the Quality Shop, later a chain with stores in the other Hampton Roads cities; started by Morris Rapoport in 1917 as a men's hat shop it, soon became the place to buy a business suit. Once when faced with an overstock of straw hats Rapoport froze one in a block of ice and put it in his window, soon his whole stock of straw hats was sold out. Paintings of the founder and his wife may be seen in the Children's Room of the Public Library where their children and grandchildren have sponsored the summer reading club for many decades in their name. The Portsmouth shop closed in 1997.

In the *eighteen* forties and fifties hoop-skirts were the rage. *Some Olde Towne houses still have chairs called "ladies' chairs" designed with small splayed arms and a low seat particularly made to accommodate hoop-skirted sitters.* If hoop-skirts added style to the ladies they certainly furnished fun for the men who made them the subject of jokes of all kinds. The fun caused by the hoopskirt was nothing to be compared with the dismay inspired by the much-heralded garment to be worn in the "coming winter" -1870. The first rainy day brought forth the garment to the eye of all. This shocking piece of raiment, called a "Balmoral", proved to be nothing worse than a red flannel petticoat, with a border striped in gay colors. Hitherto ladies wore only white undergarments; colored ones were called "vulgar." *The columnist on local history George Tucker always enjoyed quoting the doggerel common among his peers: "Norfolk girls wear ruffled drawers, Portsmouth girls wear plain. Berkley girls wear none at all, but they get there just the same."*

The next fashion to set the male element talking was the Dolly Varden craze. These gaily-flowered materials were rather expensive; and husbands and fathers rebelled at their cost. It is related that one gentleman who was shopping with his wife complained of having to pay a dollar a yard for a cotton print. Whereupon the dealer replied, "Not dear when you get a whole conservatory of flowers at that price."

The confectionery shops sold, in addition to candy and sweetmeats, toys and ornamental chinaware. In the *eighteen* fifties some of them added an "ice-cream parlor" where delicious Baltimore cream was served much as it is in the drug stores today *(1930s)*, the greatest difference being the price of the cream was then twenty-five cents a saucer. Ice cream up to this time had been a rarity; once in a while some enterprising person would make a small freezer full. It was carried forth on the head of an African American woman, who measured it out in a wineglass and sold it for three or four cents a measure. The freezer was soon emptied, but the proceeds hardly justified the venture.

By 1886 in Portsmouth the baker F. Rieger had a fashionable "ice cream saloon" on High Street.

The grocery stores here outnumbered all others; and while they kept serviceable chinaware and crockery, they handled no fresh vegetables. With the majority of them the drawing card was liquor. In old times no one ever had to go to Norfolk for that commodity, for Portsmouth had it in great variety and great quantity. One of the grocers of the day announced through the newspapers that he had just received twenty barrels of flour, and forty of whiskey. In the *eighteen* fifties we read another advertisement that fairly makes our mouths water—London Dock Brandy, Cognac, Monongahela *(a special variety of high quality rye whiskey)* and Old Rye whiskey, Old Port, Madeira, Amontillado Sherry and Malaga wines, as well as claret and champagne. Many of the grocery stores' accounts showed that it was a common occurrence for their customers to owe more for liquor than for the needful commodities. When the Milligan or O'Niell house was torn down to make room for the new post office *(now the main Public Library)*, an old ledger was found in the attic which showed this to be true in many instances.

The ledger was about one hundred years old *(1830s)*; but the name of its owner did not appear at all. Mr. O'Niell was probably the proprietor of the shop in his early days. The account is interesting, in as much as it gives us an insight into the prices of many necessary articles. Sugar proved to be an inexpensive item at 12½ cents a pound, the loaf variety being double that price. Shoulder and bacon cost 9 cents and pork 10 cents a pound; butter was worth 25 cents and coffee 35 cents a pound.. Flour sold for $5.75 a barrel, while meal was 18 cents a peck. A pound of tea was worth $1.50 and herrings a penny apiece; mackerels sold for 5 cents each. White flannel, corduroy and homespun sold respectively for 35, 45 and 16 cents a yard. Rum was the favorite drink of the customers of this shop. Four good glassfuls could be had for 12½ cents, while whiskey brought seventy cents a gallon. Brandy was a trifle cheaper, while beer cost 6 cents a quart and cider half of that amount. *A recent study of American drinking habits finds our ancestors could drink us under the table, most often in rum, of which they would take several tots as the day progressed. On the other hand, you must remember that most water was not potable.*

The account of one John Bird is a typical one. His grocery bill for two weeks was seven dollars; and his daily supply of rum totaled four dollars in that length of time.

There were many *wind powered* mills for grinding corn in and around the town and meal was shipped from Portsmouth in large quantities. *This was important in Hampton Roads, where the estuary rivers provide no running water for water-milling, as in other parts of the country.*

The shoe shops advertised extensively and had snappy, and taking notices, Jenny Lind pumps and blue gaiters being the leaders one season. There were a number of clothing stores here before the Civil War, and two jewelry shops. There was a millinery establishment on Crawford Street, occupying the same quarters for over sixty years, and passing from mother to daughter. There was another shop of this kind on High Street, where the same milliner presided for over fifty years. There were a number of milliners who worked at home, making hats and bonnets especially for older people who*se tastes* did not change with the fashions.

There were foundries and machine shops here in plenty and a factory for making tools. *John Forman in his description of Portsmouth in the 1820s tells us there were several foundries on the Elizabeth River front providing fittings for the sailing ships.*

At Page and Allen's shipyard on *April 14* 1853 the largest clipper ship ever built south of New York was launched. *It was Called Neptune's Car and was the only such ship ever built in the South. It sailed to New York and from thence to San Francisco under Captain Forbes in 117 days, a record speed at the time; and then five years later reduced the time to 99 days. Of course, at this time it would have made the trips around the horn of South America. It sailed from Calcutta to New York in only 109 days in command of Captain Joshua Patten and then from Penang to New York under Captain Caleb Sprague in 92 days. In 1860 it was sold to Barclay & Co. in Liverpool for £8,000 and broken up.*

As mentioned elsewhere in this book the engines and boilers for the United States ship *Powhatan* were made at Mahaffy's Iron Works in Gosport. *This was Admiral Perry's flagship when he opened the ports of Japan, as mentioned earlier.*

Before the Civil War coal played but little part in the trade of Portsmouth; it was occasionally advertised at 25 cents a bushel.

All the firewood was brought to the town in lighters or vessels and had to be landed at the wood wharf (this wharf was on the waterfront just south of King Street and is now a part of the Seaboard Railroad property) and weighed by the wharfmaster, who received 6¼ cents for each cord weighed. The wood brought in by the cars was weighed on them.

The Seaboard Airline Railroad Building and station was later the Municipal Building and now houses a restaurant, art gallery and condominiums. It is the round-fronted building facing the High Street ferry landing. It was added to the <u>National Register of Historic Places</u> in 1985. South of it along Water Street on the east, across from the current court houses and jail, were its passenger-train platforms. This is the area Miss Holladay is referring to. Elegant travel was available from this station; in 1915 when steel dining cars with electric lights began served on the Seaboard from Portsmouth to Birmingham, Alabama.

The first woodyard established in the town was in 1854, when the Council gave Mr. Harrison permission to start one here.

Our merchants thoroughly believed in the advantage of advertising a hundred years ago *(1830)*. Some of these inserted in the papers of that period were often snappy and humorous. The dry goods shops kept many things that they would not dare handle today, handmade laces, canton crape shawls, embroidered velvet cloaks and other handsome articles. The best Irish linen could be had at three prices, 25 cents, 37½ cents and 50 cents; the finest kid gloves sold for 75 cents a pair and could often be bought for half that amount at "clearing sales." These "clearing sales" correspond to our bargain sales and were quite as much advertised.

We know nothing of the salaries which the clerks in these various stores received, but are in no doubt about their hours of service.

On the eleventh day of May, 1858, the grocery clerks and the dry-goods clerks met to discuss a plan for having their hours of service shortened.

A committee composed of George W. Oast, Ed B. Blamire, Edgar Ashton, Richard Hume and Columbus Lassiter, drafted resolutions to present to the merchants. They petitioned their employers to close their establishments at eight o'clock p. m. during the summer months, Saturdays and mechanic's days excepted. It was agreed furthermore that should the petition be granted, each clerk was to pay ten cents a month to defray the cost of ringing the town bell every night at eight o'clock. *This bell was probably in the tower of what is now the Bangle law building on Market Square.*

Our merchants, being a very accommodating set of men, immediately complied with the request of their clerks; and shorter hours were declared in order.

It is needless to say that these enterprising clerks were in after years some of our leading merchants.

We do not know whether the custom prevailed in the *eighteen* fifties that was in vogue for many years after the Civil War. Every morning when the shops were opened the dry goods boxes were placed in a neat pile on the sidewalk in front of the stores, very close to the curbstone, so as not to block the way of the pedestrian. The clerks when not otherwise engaged could be found lounging upon them during the day. From these seats came much of the news and gossip of the time. Politics and religion too received their share of attention from these rostrums. The clerk of the *eighteen* seventies doubtless had long hours and small pay, but he was not worked to death; moreover, he had plenty of fresh air. Just before closing time the packing cases or boxes were carried back into the shop, and the loose goods put in them for the night. In good time the city passed an ordinance forbidding the main street of the town to be thus littered with the conveniences of the merchants, who henceforth had to procure other quarters for their boxes.

Among the High Street merchants was Wilson and Fiske Printing in the 100 block, founded in 1840. G. Breslauer and Emanuel Anthony founded their clothing store on the east side of Crawford on High in 1860, making theirs the oldest of its kind in the city. During the Second World War the Red White and Blue restaurant stood in this block with its country-style checkered table-cloths, next to the Greyhound Bus Terminal with its narrow winding entry so hated by bus drivers.

C. S. Crawford was in the two-hundred block. He sold furniture and claimed his to be the largest store of its kind south of Washington, D. C.. It was probably very close to where Crockin's Furniture now does business. Crockin's was started by Meyer Crockin in 1889. He started his business selling window shades and carpets from a pushcart. Around 1900 he opened his shop. It was rebuilt after it was destroyed by fire in 1965, and now may be the oldest business on High Street and among the oldest continuously operated furniture store in Hampton Roads.

Levy and Jacobs clothiers was in the same block. William C. Nash, in the old Kirn Building, sold "dry goods, notions and gentlemen's furnishings, dress goods and lady's wraps." W. L.

Crump sold musical instruments, typewriters and books in that same block. He was also Director of the YMCA founded in 1886.

The original YMCA was on the second floor of the old Kirn Building, but in 1914 the handsome YMCA building was built in the 500 block of High for $100,000. It had marble steps, a grand entrance hall with a fireplace, billiard rooms, a racetrack and bleachers to seat up to 900 people. The Y moved to Churchland in the 1980s, in the administration of Benn Boyd Griffin, leaving only the Effigham Street "Y" to serve downtown. The Effingham Y, once the social center for African Americans, is now a fixture for everyone in the downtown and in collaboration with the Girls Club Inc. even offers swimming once provided by the city in its recreation centers at Elm Avenue and Manor. In 2006 the new Churchland Y began a major expansion. The YMCA on High Street has been converted into condominiums, but the old tiled swimming pool where most Portsmouth children learned to swim is still in its basement.

Hoffheimer's shoe store opened in Norfolk in 1885 and three years later opened its shop in the 200 block of High Street in Portsmouth. It was a family-owned company until it was sold to a British conglomerate in 1988. The Portsmouth store closed in 1990.

T. S. Lawrence and B. F. Welton had matching women's and men's clothing stores in the 300 block of High. The Welton name would be added, in the twentieth century, to the local department store chain, Smith & Welton, which had it main store in Norfolk and a branch in the Midcity Shopping Center in Portsmouth.

Portsmouth had a number of other department stores. The Famous and Leggetts have been described elsewhere in this book, as has Sears Betty and Bob, but further up High Street in the 800 block was the Philzer Department Store founded in 1919 by Harry Philzer and his wife Sophye and later run by his son Harry and his wife Bernice. Beyond that in the 900 block was Laderberg's Department Store, founded in 1925. After that closed the space was used by the Victory Tavern, the Brass Rail and the Blue Rose Café. Across the street on the south side was Sutton's Furniture Store which once held a movie theater and something like a shopping arcade.

Among the city's first plumbers were W. R. Whitehurst and P. J. Riley who added the elegance of indoor plumbing to the new city market and the jail.

Probably the city's shortest-lived business was the Princess Ribbon Company which relocated to Portsmouth from New York City in 1984, giving a hope of industrial revival at a low point in business growth. It burned to the ground in 1989 and did not rebuild.

Chapter 38: More Businesses, Cemeteries and the Courts

The *American Beacon*, a newspaper whose subtitle was "*The Norfolk and Portsmouth Advertiser*," states that Portsmouth was growing very rapidly and, from this time on until the yellow fever epidemic of 1855, the growth of the town was steady and great. It was during this period that most of the civic improvements started. The first railroad in this section had been opened up here in 1834 (the Seaboard Airline). *Although "railroads" date back to the 1720's, the first real steam-engine-drawn line in America was built in 1829. Several other communities claim early railroads, but Miss Holladay is correct in calling it the earliest in "this section."*

The Dale house on Swimming Point had been purchased for a "poorhouse." *This is the brick house, now the Robert Reed home described earlier. It is usually called the Dale house, for Col. Crawford's overseer David Dale..* A "pest house," *or hospital for people with contagious diseases, was built. A new* cemetery *was laid out to replace the burying ground at Trinity (It is the walled enclosure called Cedar Grove at the foot of North Street, added to the <u>National Register of Historic Places</u> in 1992),* and a *powder* magazine was added to the municipal holdings. *There had been a powder magazine during the British occupation where the entrance to the tunnel now opens, but where it was in the 1830s Miss Holladay does not tell us.* New streets had been opened and many lots added to the town. A "Potter's Field" too, *for people too poor to be given a regular burial,*, had been bought for an African American burial-ground. This was in the southern extremity of the city, and with some additional land still serves the *African American population one hundred years later. I don't know where this was; it may be part of a larger cemetery now. The "south side of town" would probably mean south of Crab Creek.* A part of the original Potter's Field was reserved for white paupers. This section was kept entirely apart from that used by the African

Americans. Until 1832, there was no public burial place for the dead excepting the various churchyards *at Monumental Methodist Church on Glasgow Street, now a vest pocket park, with a memorial marker and three gravestones, Trinity churchyard and around Court Street Baptist*. Many people had a private plot in their own gardens, where members of the family were buried, but for sanitary reasons, this was forbidden, as we have said, in 1832, when the Legislature of the States authorized the town trustees to forbid the burial of the dead within the city *limits. Miss Holladay has already pointed out two of these private cemeteries, but there were others in the city and in what is now Churchland. An exception is now made for cremated remains, and which allowed Trinity Church to reopen its churchyard for these burials in the 1990s.*

Cedar Grove Cemetery was purchased in 1833, laid out and sold in lots. Space was kept in the cemetery where one grave could be purchased. This was for the convenience of nonresidents who had no need of a whole lot. The regular price for opening a grave was eight dollars; but a nonresident was charged ten dollars for burial. *Cedar Grove is known for its handsome sculpture, and for the graves of many men and women of national prominence. It is on the Virginia and National Registers of Historic Places and occasionally open for guided tours. Oak Grove off London Street will be described in a moment. It is now one of several burial places. One is primarily for Roman Catholic burials, another primarily for Jewish burials, off George Washington Highway near Cradock and Olive Branch Cemetery in front of City Park. Some lists of burials, but not all, in these grounds, are on record in the Library and at city offices.*

When the cemetery was first established, the keeper was the town sergeant, who held the position in virtue of his office, and for "the faithful performance of his duty," received the lucrative salary of fifty dollars a year. There came a time however, when the town sergeant begged to be excused from his position as keeper of the cemetery, and in the *eighteen* fifties a woman signed in his stead. We learn from the records of the town council at that time one Mrs. McEwen held the job, and like all women in business she was imposed upon, receiving ten dollars less a year than the town sergeant's salary when he was keeper.

Cedar Grove Cemetery was several times enlarged, even after a site for a new cemetery had been purchased. The new cemetery was a tract of land bought from the Portlock family in 1851, and its purchase made a stir in the Town Council; several of its members heartily opposed the scheme. Mr. George Grice, president of the body, refused to sign the legal papers in connection with the transfer. It was soon shown, however, that the town had made a snug bargain. Portlock's, or Oak Grove Cemetery, has been enlarged several times; and part of the Bunting tract was laid off for a cemetery and given the name of Olive Branch from the district in which it was situated. In accord with the modern custom then there are to be no mounds; the earth has been turfed and is to be kept level. *It was thought in Victorian times that cemeteries would become parks where ladies and gentlemen would walk of an evening enjoying the sculpture and quietly communing with their dear departed. Death was always with them.*

A market house was one of our early possessions, and it was first built on the lot given for that purpose, where the New Kirn Building now stands - *on the southeast corner of High and Court Street. This block is called "Market Square."* In 1821 the market had for some years been at the foot of High Street. The market house was burned there at this time. The next location was in the middle of Crawford Street between High and King. *This seems to contradicts the current belief that the second floor of the Leitner house on the south side of Glasgow Street between Middle and Crawford is the original city market from 1752. Both contentions are probably true, the second being constructed from the remains of the first. If Miss Holladay is correct, it is that second city market from the middle of Crawford Street. The market which is the second floor of the Leitner house has the numbers of the stalls scratched on the inside of its beams. As mentioned earlier it was purchased when the Seaboard Airline Railroad came in 1834 and the first floor of that house built to accommodate it.*

Again the market changed its site. This was done at the request of the Seaboard Airline Road, which built a new market house with an armory above it on the corner of Crawford and South Streets. *Although the armory was gone by the 1960s, the WAVY building on that same corner did have a farmers; market on its first floor. A picture of this old Armory survives in the Library. The current Armory is behind Cradock near the Regional Jail.*

A few years ago a new market house was built on *the southeast corner of* Middle Street *and High*, over it is a large auditorium. *A photograph of it survives. It is called The Kirn Building, not to be confused with the New Kirn Building a block away, and the date of construction can be seen carved on its facade as 1887.*

A new courthouse was built in 1842 on the site of the former jail, which has been rebuilt on the lot now occupied by the Professional Building. *Construction of the courthouse may have been started as early as 1842, the date Miss Holladay gives, but it was completed in 1846 on "Prison Square", the northwest corner of Court and High Streets, site of the former jail and place of public execution. The new courthouse was designed by William B. Singleton, from the same firm which drew the plans for the Norfolk Courthouse on City Hall Avenue, now the MacArthur Memorial. It was built by Willoughby G. Butler. Singleton was a Portsmouth native. the design is supposed to be based on the temple of Jupiter Stater, but anther way to look at the building is to see it as a modification of the English basement house with the family rooms (clerks offices) in the basement entered by a ground floor door and the public rooms on the second floor entered by a long exterior staircase. To add to this supposition, it is believed the exterior staircase was once on the southeast corner of the front of the structure, off to the side, as it would have been in a house of the Federal period. The first day court was held in the new building was July 20 1846. The 1846 courthouse is now the 1846 Courthouse Gallery. It was replaced as a working courthouse in 1970 by the municipal complex on the east side of Crawford Street between South and Court streets which included the courthouses, jail, police headquarters and city hall. The new complex was designed by local architect Glen Yates.*

The 1846 courthouse was the court of Norfolk County, Portsmouth being the county seat, until Portsmouth became a city in 1858, when the court's interior was divided down the middle, one side being the Portsmouth City courts and the other remaining the court of Norfolk County. When Norfolk County became the City of Chesapeake the county court was moved to Great Bridge. Charles Cross, then the Clerk of the County Court, took all the records, including the Portsmouth deed and will books to Great Bridge. Recently the Olde Towne Civic League acquired copies on microfilm for the Portsmouth library. A full history of the courts was published by Charles Cross, and a list of all of its judges appears on a plaque in the entryway of the 1846 Courthouse Gallery. Many of these judges had distinguished careers and one Portsmouth judge, "Red" Ianson went on to become Chief Justice of the Virginia Supreme Court.

Alf Mapp tells us the first bank opened in Portsmouth was the Portsmouth Savings Society in 1827. In 1835 Portsmouth petitioned for the authority to establish here one of the Virginia Banks, but the legislature refused permission. There was a great deal said in the newspapers of the period about the unfairness of the decision. It was not, however, until 1845 that the town established a Virginia Bank. A fine old building, where the new Kirn Corner stands, *New Kirn was built in 1911, on the southeast corner of High and Court Streets,* was built for the bank. For many years after the bank had gone out of existence the building was used for the post office.

A few years after the bank was established it was robbed of fifty thousand dollars. The thief was captured after some time had elapsed, but the money was never recovered.

Around the corner on Court Street is the New York Delicatessen which first started business at High and Green streets in 1938, moved to its current location in 1964, and still provides fast business lunches.

In 1837 Portsmouth's brick sidewalks were laid with cobbled gutters and flagstone curbs and street crossings. In the earliest days most streets in America were still dirt with stepping stones across the intersections; sometimes young children would sweep these stepping stones and expect a tip for their labors.. The streets of Portsmouth have always been her especial pride, and justly so, in some respects. Wide they certainly are, and straight, and before so many leafy trees were felled in grading the sidewalks, they might have been called beautiful; but there was an obverse side to the picture. Unfavorable criticisms have been passed upon them from time to time, we regret to say most fairly. The newspapers often called attention to their neglected condition; and the *Portsmouth Daily Transcript* in 1850 made an urgent appeal to the "City Fathers," to take a turn through some of the city streets, especially Middle, south of High, and Queen between Middle and Court streets. They were warned not to attempt the journey on foot, as it would be impossible for any pedestrian to make the trip. Mules were recommended for the journey. *When many of the sidewalks were re-bricked between the 1960s and 2005 happily the trees were returned to them, and to the medians.*

It is a comfort to know that though our streets were not kept in an immaculate condition, our morals were above reproach; and we find in an issue of the same paper a few days later how Portsmouth welcomed improper characters. The article says, "Two nymphs of the pavement visited our town last night, and the appearance of such characters in our streets is altogether a novelty. No sooner was the fact of their arrival known than they were duly honored with an escort. Wherever they moved they were followed by the jests, groans and laughs of a crowd of men and boys. At the ferry when these 'ladies of easy virtue' essayed to depart they were duly sprinkled with salt water, and it is evident that the crowd would have ducked them, but for the interference of the police. *This may have been true of the town in the 19th century, but in the 20th it had its share of brothels, one on North Street surviving into the 1960s and a retired madam from Gosport, still well known in the community, traveled in a chauffeured car. At the end of the twentieth century there was a problem with prostitution on High Streeet itself. During World War II even the old Parish Memorial Hospital on Court Street, then in use as a hotel, had an unsavory reputation, I am told. It was, after all, a sailor's town. It may be that Miss Holladay was sheltered from such things.*

Even at this time our Town Council was not utterly indifferent to the care of our streets. Mr. William May's petition to that body asking that his hogs might roam at large in our thoroughfares was promptly refused, some law to keep hogs and cattle from sharing our streets equally with the humans having recently gone into effect. We hear, however, of an ordinances concerning the crops of grass that grew so abundantly in our highways. Perhaps it did not grow so luxuriantly in the *eighteen* fifties as it did in the next three decades. *Major* Gen. *John A.* Lejeune, *later Commandant of the Marine Corps.* tells us that when he came to live in Portsmouth in the *eighteen* nineties, that he did not see the bustling streets that one sees now. "High Street," he says, "was paved with Belgian block as far as Court, and there were cobblestones on Crawford Street, if you could cut down enough weeds to find them." *When the cobblestones were removed some were saved and they decorate some curb cuts in the Olde Towne and some intersections, as they do where Glasgow Street enters Crawford. Some streets were paved in hard yellow brick, of which a sample can be seen at the northern end of Middle Street.*

The property owners of Portsmouth are fortunate in not having to share with the city the expense of keeping up the streets. The money received by the town from the ferries cares for the street improvement. Alas, the ferries, now belonging to Hampton Roads Transit (HRT), no longer contribute to

The town was, of course, lighted at first with oil lamps, which often furnished another topic for eloquence. The usual complaint, dirty lamps making the lights useless, was followed by another of unlighted lamps, many of them being overlooked by the lamplighter who was the ubiquitous town sergeant. The papers nobly defended this much overworked officer, demanding that Portsmouth should have an official "lamplighter," as did all other towns of her size. The Council did about this time appoint an official "chimney sweep." He probably did his work in a fairly satisfactory manner as we have seen no criticism of him in the newspapers. We have not been able to ascertain whether chimney sweeping was done by the town sergeant prior to this appointment. *The handsome lamps now seen in the Olde Towne were purchased from London in the 1960s, when Olde Towne was placed on the National Register. The lamps placed in front of houses then thought to be of historic interest. They are not reconstructions, but authentic 18th century street lamps. The cross bar on them served to lean the ladder against when climbing up to trim the wick.*

In 1854 the first exhibit of gas was made in Portsmouth when one of our enterprising firms illuminated their store. This firm was then engaged in putting fixtures in some of the homes and shops of the town. *Some Olde Towne houses still have their gas lamp fixtures, and probably the piping to them.*

The Council agreed to light all streets where the property owners would pay two-fifths of the costs of installing the fixtures, as well as the same proportion of the lighting costs.

Many of our citizens responded to this proposition; and a number of the streets were quickly in line for gas. The lamplighter still went the rounds with his short ladder and little bag of matches. When electricity came he was succeeded by a man with a pony. Most of us can remember his successor, a very large man, who drove the tiniest of white ponies as he drove through the town each morning, taking out the old carbons and replacing them with new ones. The pony was so well-trained that, as soon as its master took a carbon out of the bag and started up the pole, he would meekly amble down to the next pole and there await his master.

The Portsmouth Gas Company opened in 1854 near Green and Washington streets on a short street called Gas House Lane. In 1961 the property, near the Swimming Point neighborhood, was sold to the Portsmouth Redevelopment and Housing Authority for their proposed redevelopment of Lincolnsville. That neighborhood is now only a memory and the location became a federal Super Fund site because of the pollution remaining in the soil from the gasworks. An apartment complex on the land was demolished and the land stripped in 2005. In 2006 it was opened as park to be used in the celebration of the four-hundredth anniversary of the Jamestown landing in 2007. It is called Fort Nelson Park.

Lincolnsville was a predominantly African American neighborhood outside the Naval Hospital gate. Its shopping street was Effingham. A French map of Portsmouth from before the American Revolution marks the same spot as a village for blacks. Although the neighborhood is long gone in 2007, an effort was begun to build a "town center" again on Effingham Street at its intersection with County. The plan was championed by Circuit Court Judge Johnny Morrison, Kenneth Wright, lawyer Eric Moody and Rev. Melvin O. Marriner.

Had it not have been for the epidemic of yellow fever here in the summer of 1855, we should have had waterworks in our town forty years sooner than we did get them.

The Town Council in 1854 appointed a committee headed by Col. Winchester Watts to enquire into the costs of furnishing the town with water. In considering this scheme, the engineers gave approximate costs of three different plans of procuring water for the city. They found that to bring the water from the basin between Deep Creek and Gilmerton would cost seventy thousand dollars. From the basin just beyond Scott's Creek it would cost fifty thousand dollars; and if the third plan, artesian wells, was adopted, the cost would amount to forty eight thousands. The water committee had not reached any conclusion in the matter when the yellow fever scourge appeared, and turned the hands of Portsmouth's clock backward for a long time.

In the second decade of the twentieth century Portsmouth wisely bought a private water company's rights to the spring-fed lakes in Suffolk. This was the Portsmouth, Berkley and Suffolk Water Company pumping its water from Lake Kilby in Nansemond County (three miles long and eight to ten feet deep) with Lakes Cahoon, Phillips and Burnt Mills in reserve. As a result Portsmouth has some of the finest water in the area, as it did in Colonial times, and was not subject to the shortages Norfolk and Virginia Beach experienced before the pipeline to Lake Gaston was completed in the 1990s. In fact Portsmouth sold water to the City of Chesapeake, which had an ongoing problem with salt in its water drawn from the Northwest River and even sold water to Suffolk, where its lakes are located. The downside to this was the fact that the equipment to pump the water was also manufactured before 1920 and by the 1990s replacement parts were not available. When a storm came through that threatened the pumping station, an alert worker shut it down before it was destroyed, but this still left the whole city without water for a week. Some people dipped water out of the Elizabeth River to flush their toilets, as their ancestors had done.

When High Street was excavated to repair water lines in the 1970s it was found that some old lines had completely disappeared. The then director of the water system, James Spacek, recalled that they had even found some wooden pipes in old water system excavations. They were simply logs with the middles reamed out. This valiant water man, when he was young on the job, decided to be hands-on and went down into a manhole himself to look at a problem and he came very close to being washed away. There are still storm drains under the Olde Towne from the nineteenth century.

My son used to climb down into them and secretly go from one place to another underground, to the amazement of adults. He said you could still see the old brick arches in the system.

It may be a surprise to most of us to know that Portsmouth in 1860 was sufficiently able to stand alone to the extent of having her own city directory; and in a volume for that year we find a classified list of business houses. *This Directory survives in the Public Library collection.*

In 1860 there were nine commission merchants, *who resold other people's goods for a commission*; fourteen confectioners, *candy stores, often with a soda fountain, or ice-cream parlor*; thirteen dry goods stores; three bake-shops *(Rather than cook at home some people in Victorian times would buy the goods for their dinner and take them to a bake shop to be cooked. Of course, some people did not have the luxury of a kitchen in their house furnished with a stove for cooking. This example can be seen in Dicken's "Christmas Carol" when the goose is taken to a bake shop to be cooked)*; two foundries; four barber shops; three book stores; the same number of banks; several insurance agencies; one public accountant; two auctioneers; five merchant tailors, *(A merchant-tailor is a person who keeps and sells the fabric for clothes as well as tailoring it. You could buy material separately and carry it to a regular tailor - as Miss Holladay described under "Entertainment" in the case of the tailor who teased the circus elephant.)*; three tailors, three undertaking establishments, three milliners, *(women's hat makers - men's hats were sold by a haberdasher, or made by a hatter)*; four tin and stove shops; seventy five grocers, *(Unlike modern groceries they would normally not sell fresh meat, or produce. Some who did sell fresh stuff would have been called greengrocers. You would get vegetables and meat at the farmer's market on Crawford Street, fresh from the field. As late as the 1960s some farmers would go around the Olde Towne in horse-drawn wagons piled high with produce hawking their wares by calling out "strawr-awr-awr-berries," or "watermelon man!" These little corner groceries might devide a pack of cigarettes and sell two for a penny. They would also weigh your baby in their hanging scales if you asked and give you credit with no interest if you were a little short that day)*; two lumber merchants, and several sawmills *(the last of this class to survive is Portsmouth Lumber on*

High Street, still in business today). There were sixteen restaurants licensed to sell drinks, as well as ten barrooms, in the town - *it was a sailor's town as I remarked earlier.*

By the end of the nineteenth century the town could also boast three wood-planing mills (one belonging to L. C. Godwin), three shingle mills (one belonging to J. T. Halstead on Race Street outside the city limits and another to E. B. Taylor at Race and Chestnut streets), a basket factory, iron works, a fertilizer plant and two chemical plants. From the earliest time the Great Dismal Swamp, just south of the city, was a major place for cutting "shakes," as they were called in earlier times (shingles). Slave owners set their charges to cutting shingles in the swamp from its cypress trees, these thought to last longer than normal shakes. It was relatively easy for these slaves to escape and by the middle of the nineteenth century there was a community of "maroons" (run away slaves in the wilderness) living in the swamp, as documented by Professor Tommy Bogger in the project "Lower Tidewater In Black and White." The basket and fertilizer plants depended on the important truck garden business in what is now Churchland. It shipped all over the East Coast. That is the reason the Churchland High School teams are called "the Truckers." That business was lost to suburban sprawl in the late twentieth century - the last to hold out being the Eberwine canning company.

One chemical company, originally Virginia Chemical, now Hoechst Ceylonese, still does business in West Norfolk. The Eustice family of Boston had copper mines in Southwest Virginia and needed a place to smelt the ore and ship it out. The patriarch of the family, Abraham Eustice, was a Union officer posted at Fortress Monroe in the Civil War, when he became aware of the deep water and railroad lines in Portsmouth. The original smelter was built on the site of the Atlantic and Danville Railroad roundhouse in West Norfolk in 1890. It was soon discovered that the byproduct of the smelting was sulfur dioxide which was central to the production of many other chemicals. That transformed the copper business into a chemical business. The last of the family to run the business was Peter Eustice who was influential in Portsmouth for many years, although he and his wife Anne still returned every summer to the family's roots at Buzzard Bay on Cape Cad. In 1981 the business was sold to the Ceylonese

Corporation, which in turn merged with the German chemical giant Hoechst in 1987.

The professions were also well represented, there being fifteen practicing physicians, ten lawyers and two dentists here.

Portsmouth meanwhile had not been without its booms, the first one dating back to 1790, when refugees who had fled from the "Reign of Terror" in France, upon coming into our town had planned wonderful agricultural schemes. They were aided in their plans by an inrush of emigrants from Italy and the West Indies. Sugar cane and tropical fruits they decided to plant, even persuading some of our own farmers to enter into their schemes. Oranges and olives grew apace for a while; and the pomegranate too flourished; but, just as the wise heads had said such crops could not grow to any extent in this climate *then colder than it is today*. All the toil and money was thrown away.

Again there was an exodus from Europe; and many more Frenchmen and Italians came to Portsmouth during the Napoleonic Wars. *Of course, there had been Frenchmen in Portsmouth since the end of the Revolutionary War. Bernard Magnien, Lafayette's aide, mentioned earlier, buried in Trinity Churchyard, had founded a French Masonic lodge on Middle Street south of High soon after the end of the war (see his obituary in the Emmerson Papers and his mention elsewhere in this book).*

This time fortunes were to be made from the almond trees, which they insisted upon planting, in spite of all our farmers could say. Time and money were again thrown away. This experiment was remembered many years, said one of the old inhabitants, "because the almond trees long survived their planters, though the nut was but little better flavored than a peach kernel." Even with these failures fresh in mind, another set of foreigners imported merino sheep from the mountains of Spain, only to realize their mistake too late. *Marino wool was so popular in America in the 1860s that a sort of shawl made from it with a blue and white pattern was simply called "a marino." It is frequently mentioned in letters, North and South, from around the time of the Civil War.*

The next venture of this kind could not be attributed to the folly of foreigners; for the scheme set the whole population wild. It was the mulberry boom of 1838. The newspapers devoted columns to accounts of the mulberry, discussing it from every angle. There was a large cocoonery (for raising silk worms and gathering their silk) built just outside of the town and another in Norfolk.

One of our citizens, George M. Bain, sold fifty thousands of these trees in one day. They were one foot high and brought thirty cents each. Within the week the purchaser sold the entire lot for fifty cents apiece. At the same time another citizen sold trees to the amount of eighteen thousand dollars in one lot; and so the mania spread. This boom accounts for the number of gnarled and worthless mulberry trees found in the gardens of the older Portsmouth homes, for even flowers and vegetables were uprooted to make room for the trees. As almost everybody in the community was interested in the scheme in a greater or less degree - the mulberry was a sore subject with all for a long time. *Miss Holladay mentioned mulberries as among the trees in Colonel William Craford's garden at the foot of High Street before the town was laid out, as well, but I believe it was a later introduction as she here suggests. Mulberries are still a common weed tree in Olde Towne to this day, but loved by the birds who get drunk on its fermented berries late in the summer.*

We get an interesting account of this boom from a lady living in Portsmouth when it was at its height. She tells us that, "Mr. Jones, a chaplain in the navy, owned a farm just where the southeast end of the town joins the Deep Creek Road. He was a pioneer in planting the mulberry, or as he called it "the *morus multicaulis*. Beginning on his little farm the spirit of speculation grew rife, spreading through town and county. The excitement was not long in reaching fever heat; every vacant lot in town was in demand; and much of the farming land in the country was turned into mulberry plantations. The fever ran into an epidemic; those who had laughed at it as a wild fancy now caught the contagion; men, women, and children laid down cuttings, counted the number of joints on each stick, made estimates of trees to be produced, and the dollars to be realized. Ladies thought that silk dresses would be as common in this country as cotton prints. The servants believed that the time had come when they would wear silk bandanas on their heads. Then the bubble burst and what subject was as disgusting as the silk worm?"

In the twentieth century Portsmouth's central location in the area caused it to develop as an emporium. Photographs of High

Street from the first half of the twentieth century show a bustling street jammed with cars, buses and streetcars. In the previous chapter and elsewhere some of these businesses were described, but here is a place to spotlight some other famous old Portsmouth shopkeepers.

Chapman's Jewelry on Courthouse Square was opened in 1937 and survived until 2006. One of the early High's Ice Cream parlors was opened in 1960 on Portsmouth Boulevard and is still in business. Among Portsmouth's many movie theaters was the Colony which was the first to show moving pictures in color in the city. This old movie theater became David's nightclub and finally closed in 1993. Now only the Commodore Theater remains; built by John J. Zink it is now owned and managed by Fred Schonfeld and Jean Haskell, showing first-run movies in a dinner theater format.

Further up High Street Janet's Office Supply dealt in typewriters from 1951 to 2004. Their primary stock in trade had, by that time, become obsolete.

Harrels Sporting Goods first opened its doors in 1899 under I. M. Harrell as a bicycle shop. There was a boom in the interest in bicycles in the 1890s. In 1950 it changed its specialty to team uniforms. Many a Portsmouth ball player or boy scout bought his uniform from this old company.

Hagwood's dry cleaning was started in 1922 by Akey Mahlon and Hazel Hagwood on Elm Avenue. In its early years it specialized in cleaning uniforms for sailors.

The father of Speros Caravas immigrated from Greece and opened a small restaurant on Crawford Street called The Elite in 1917. His two sons immigrated in 1946 and expanded the business. In 1949 the business was taken by Portsmouth Redevelopment and Housing, which offered them a meager price. The Caravases refused and sued PRHA. The case was found for them and the property on the southeastern corner of Middle and High streets was given them in compensation. They opened the Merrimac Cafeteria, well known to the lunch crowd and shoppers at Leggetts Department Store across the street. The business was closed in 1987 and its space eventually became the home of the China Garden Restaurant.

T. O. Williams used to deliver meat from his market on South Street in a horse-drawn wagon. In 1927 the business was taken over by Paul "pigs" Stokley, who was convinced to convert the business *into a wholesale meat processing company. After its old location was taken during the construction of the Downtown Tunnel it moved to its location at Wythe and Court streets. In 1977 the business was sold to a Korean businessman H. J. Chai who still operates it.*

The old Oxford Square Restaurant was on Oxford Square, the northwest corner of Dinwiddie and High, when it was purchased by Robert and Linda Huguelet and renamed the Baron's Pub, for Mr. Huguelet's nickname. It started business there in 1987 and is still a regular downtown watering hole. Another old favorite, now gone, on Dinwiddie Street was the Tip Toe Tearoom.

Ogg Stone Works was founded in 1896 on Glasgow Street and then moved by the founder's son and successor, Malcolm Ogg to its current location on London Boulevard.

Radio first came to Portsmouth in 1943 with the first broadcast of WSAP . This was to become WAVY in 1953 and in September 1957 WAVY-TV broadcast for the first time. This television station was first located on WAVY street in the old market, but with the completion of PortCenter it moved to its current location in its own building in PortCenter. WAVY-TV would become one of the three major network providers for the whole of Hampton Roads.

Another major television broadcaster started its life in Portsmouth. In 1960 the evangelist Pat Robertson started his Christian Broadcasting System with its hallmark 700 Club in a radio station in an abandoned garage in Chesapeake as WYAH. The name was drawn from the Hebrew name for God: Yahweh. On July 31 1967 the fledgling broadcaster broke ground in the Parkview neighborhood in Portsmouth for its television station WYAH-TV the first television location for what would become an international broadcaster. Its studio still stands.

Starting in the late 1960s many of the city's merchants were put out of business, or bought out, by national franchises with shops in covered malls, or by national chain big box stores like Wal-mart. Portsmouth's answer was the strip shopping center called Mid-City and the covered mall called Tower Mall.

In 1975-76 Portsmouth won the "All American City Award" due to the hard work of then Mayor Richard Davis and his staff. This was particularly based on its creative redevelopment of the Mount Hermon neighborhood. In the following year a committee was formed to expand on the city's triumph. Many of the projects developed, however, turned out to be as much wishful thinking as the silk industry plans described by Miss Holladay. This was not surprising in the context of the decline of central cities taking place in the 1970s. In this decade Portsmouth Redevelopment and Housing Authority purchased the property in Southside, the old Gosport Village, and demolished everything, making way for PortCenter Industrial Park. By 1984 the industrial park was open, and was given its present name in 1987.

In 1987 Portsmouth became the first city to go on national television to attract new industrial development with an add called "The right place - The right time."

Although the Free Trade Zone in PortCenter did develop, the effort to attract an oil refinery to vacant land in West Norfolk to dramatically increase the city's tax base was too strongly opposed by the citizens, and the city eventually used the land for the more environmentally friendly steam generation plant called Cogentrix. Planned commercial development of the downtown river front also proved anemic at best, due in part to the location on prime waterfront land of the jail and courts. Efforts to get the Federal government to turn over the Craney Island Landfill to the city also failed.

These efforts did, however, result in the creation of the Portsmouth Partnership in 1984 with the express purpose of raising money for Portsmouth urban development and attracting industry.

In that same year the state created "Enterprise Zones" in Danville, Lynchburg, Newport News, Norfolk and Portsmouth to benefit "economically distressed areas" and combat the national trend toward decay in old core cities. The zone stretched from Water Street to MidCity along the High Street corridor, bounded on the north by London Street and on the south by the interstate highway. It consisted of 238 acres and included the 70 acres in the PortCenter industrial park.

Efforts to revitalize this area had mixed success in the next decade, but Portsmouth built back its downtown with fine restaurants, specialty shops and antiques. This effort started with the plans for the development of the 600 block of High Street in 1997, spearheaded by Arden and Pat Pfeiffer who opened their book and fine wine store there and Peter Barr who moved his antique store from Norfolk. Among the best-known of the early galleries to open was the Olde Towne Gallery operated by Nate and Heather Moewhinney in the New Kirn Building at the corner of Court and High Street where the To Life specialty grocery now stands. Among the early restaurants was Brutti's, opened by Charles Greenhood, and the finest restaurant in Hampton Roads: the Café Europa with its charming French owner Veronique.

This initiative has been replaced by the federal HUBZone project now extended to 2010 to revitalize shopping of the High Street corridor.

Some businesses located in PortsCenter industrial park as well in this decade, among them Kerma Medical Products Inc. which supplies the military, KMC: a Korean manufacturer of ball valves, and Wright Engineering/MES Marine.

The incentives to start new businesses included a ten-year state income tax credit, a refundable real property improvement tax credit, an investment tax credit and a jobs creation grant.

The city also made a bold speculative venture in PortCenter, reminiscent of Colonel Craford's building of a court house in the hope it would attract the real thing. City Council actually built an eight and a half million dollar office building with no particular client in mind in 1998. Fortunately, with the help of past City Manager Robert Williams, it sold two years later.

Recently this effort paid off with the relocation from Connecticut of the headquarters of the Lindab USA manager and manufacturer of sheet metal

In 1992 the K-Mart which was the anchor of the MidCity shopping center closed, sounding the death knell of that thirty-year-old experiment in combining shops into a mall. Two years later in 1994 the city attempted to involve citizens in setting development plans for the city with the City Vision 2005 Project, based on town meetings. In an effort to answer the decline in local business the city Economic Development Department has encouraged PRHA to purchased the defunct Mid-City Shopping Center in 2004. The old empty stores were torn down, the street pattern redesigned and it was offered for sale. Wal-mart purchased 23 acres of the site and will open a 204,000 square foot superstore there in 2007. PRHA also purchase the old Tower Mall enclosed mall site in 2001, removed the *mall and redesigned the space. It is now a vibrant shopping center called Victory Crossing built around Lowes which opened at Victory Crossing in 2002 and a FarmFresh supermarket relocated to the site.*

CHAPTER 39: TAVERNS AND HOTELS :

Old residents of Portsmouth have pointed out so many sites once occupied by taverns that we wonder who filled them, or why so many were needed in such a small town. For even in early days there were several to chose from.

The tax list of 1784 gives Portsmouth 584 white males: this, of course, refers only to property owners, but nevertheless we get from it some idea of the number of the inhabitants. That year there were five ordinary licences issued. Some of these probably were boardinghouses where the constant influx of the men coming here for work in the shipyards and the other industries could find a home. Portsmouth at this time carried on a large foreign trade, and we learn from letters of this period that the harbor was so crowded with ships that it was dangerous to cross by the ferry. From the same source we learn, too, that for miles around the country was taxed to feed the people.

Some of our taverns sheltered the homeless mariners who came to our shores, while others were frequented by the throng of travelers passing through our town on their way north or south.

The Craford Apartment on Crawford Street stands on the site of Drury's Tavern, one of the best known here in its day more than a hundred years ago. It was a large brick building; but who it housed and fed we are not told. Drury's was burned down in the great fire of 1821, and never rebuilt as a tavern.

The Globe Tavern, later called the High Street Hotel, was kept by Captain Reynolds on the north side of High Street.

On Crawford Street near North stood another old tavern. Though its name is forgotten, memories and tales of the wild doings there still linger. It was the meeting place of pirates and other outlaws of the sea. It finally became so disreputable that it was ordered to be closed.

The two houses formerly belonging to the Peed and Moloney Families, numbered 211 and 213 London Streets, *now known as the Red Lion Tavern, on Red Lion Square on the north side of London Street between Crawford and Middle streets,* were remodeled on a rambling Dutch roof house once a tavern. Under different management it probably changed its name; however, in 1804 it bore a double sign - General Washington commanding his army on one half, and General Washington planting his field on the other. We suppose it was known familiarly as the General Washington. *Washington is said to have stayed in the town while working on The Washington Ditch in the Great Dismal Swamp before the Revolution and this may have been his favorite stop.* We are not told whether this elaborate production was the work of the town painter or not. We are at liberty to believe that some stranded artist painted it in lieu of his board. It was not an uncommon thing for painters of note to be found in the old inns. They often selected a good center and there remained many months painting portraits in the neighborhood.

In 1804 the keeper of this tavern was one Edward Hanson; and, beyond the fact that he married a Portsmouth girl Ann Kyd by name, his story is a blank. *Ann Kyd, may be the daughter of John and Mary Kid buried in Trinity churchyard. In 1762 John Kid (or Ked) owned land on Argyle Square near Crab Creek.* Mrs. Hansford afterwards kept a fashionable tavern in Norfolk, on East Main Street, then an exclusive section of the town. It was at this tavern that LaFayette stayed when he visited Norfolk in 1824. *The description of Lafayette's visit to Portsmouth at this was described earlier.*

On the southwestern corner of Middle and High street where Street's Hall now stands was Drinane's, a great place for assemblies and cotillions. There the gentlemen of the town met every evening for a social chat. Drinane's was in fact a coffee house, and provided no accommodations for lodgers. *Street's Hall is long since gone. In the later half of the 20th century all the buildings on this side of the block were torn down and replaced by "Middle Street Mall:" a pedestrian street with a row of storefronts for rent (site of a barber shop and the offices of the then Portsmouth Chapter of the Chamber of Commerce, now the offices of the annual Todi Arts Festival. Previously on the site of the China Garden Restaurant (southwest corner of Middle and High Streets) in this row was the Merrimac Cafeteria, a popular cafeteria style restaurant described earlier. Another famous old restaurant, Hodges', was here until it moved to the end of the Holiday Inn pier and changed its name to The Deck. On the northwest corner of Middle and King Streets was a popular curiosity and used book shop and across King Street where the Children's Museum of Virginia Parking Ramp (once called the Edinburgh Square Parking Ramp for one of the two squares on which it stands) was a curious building with a sign painted on it, identifying it as a livery stable long after horse-drawn vehicles were a thing of the past. It was the one time place of business of D. Sullivan, an Irishman who started making carriages there in 1866.*

Another house in this block, 516 Middle Street, in the old numbering system, belonged to H. E. Culpepper, who, at the end of the nineteenth century could be said to have built all the wharves on the Norfolk side of the river and many of the bridges.

On the opposite side of the street, where the stores numbers 314, 316 and 318 *in the old numbering system* now stand was the site of Runald's Tavern, a very popular resort in the early days of the last century, *the 1800s,* frequented by the sportier element of the community. In Runald's 'long room' one could always have dancing lessons taught by a French master. Mons. Duccoing and others whose names are long since forgotten held classes in this room.

I think Miss Holladay means the west side of Bloomsbury Square, the east side of Middle Street Mall between High and King Streets. On September 3, 1937 the shops she refers to would be replaced by Leggett's Department Store, known and loved as one of the magnets of the Downtown. Children loved it because it had the only escalator in the city. In the 1990s the Leggett Company made an executive decision to move all of its stores into enclosed malls and shut down the Portsmouth store, even though at the time it had the highest sales per square foot of any store in the system, and they owned the building outright. It opened a store in Chesapeake Square Mall, but soon went out of business. The old Leggett's Department Store stood empty for many years, occasionally used by the city to host events like the Christmas crafts shop, and the annual gathering of college rowing teams for the sculling competition on the Elizabeth River, until it became the home of the Children's Museum of Virginia on December 10 1994, during the museum directorship of Betty Forbes. The children's museum was the brainchild of the Portsmouth Service League. They presented the idea to Portsmouth Museums, but it was rejected, the then director saying, "Our business is art, not children's education." The city then turned the idea down. Your gentle editor was Director of Libraries at that time and, recognizing that the idea had great potential, welcomed it into the basement of the main public library on Court Street, next to the library Children's Room. Its first director, Patricia Pfeiffer, with the energetic volunteers from the Service League, made the hands-on museum such a success that the museum department changed its mind and welcomed it into the basement of the 1846 Courthouse Gallery. Soon it was clear that space was too small for the audiences it attracted and the city moved it into the old Leggett's building, incorporating a planetarium previously housed at Manor High School (currently Wilson High School). Later the model railroad collection which had been housed in Trainland and was one of the largest on the east coast was willed by its owner, Junie Lancaster, to the museum where it is now on display. In 2004 the museums added the famous collection of automated exhibits so dear to generations of Portsmouth children in the holiday season at Coleman's Nursery in Churchland where the Churchland Library branch now stands. This display of what some call "Christmas robots" is displayed seasonally at the 1846 Courthouse Gallery, the Children's Museum, local churches and in the store windows along High Street. Another expansion of the museum was initiated in 2006.

The house still standing, but sadly changed, *(Miss Holladay is still describing the east side of the Middle Street Mall - the house, of course, is also long gone)* was Webb's Hotel. The military patronized it; and the Fourth of July banquets were given there. These banquets were very elaborate affairs, so we judge from an account of one of them that has been passed down. In 1824 a newspaper of the day tells us a sumptuous repast was served, presided over by Col. Dempsey Watts and Lieut. Col. Kay. The food was not described in detail and nothing was said about the liquor; but we counted twenty-four toasts, and feel assured of its plentifulness. The toasts were nearly all patriotic, and one to Greek Liberty caused much applause. *The Federal Period is also called Greek Revival. The new American nation thought itself the midwife of a new world of democracy on the ancient Greek model, and details from Greek architecture illustrated this grand surmise. On March 25, 1831, after 400 years of Ottoman rule, the modern state of Greece came into existence. The origin of the rebellion, however, is dated to 1814 with the activities of the "Philikií Etaireíia" (Friendly Brotherhood). It was a patriotic conspiracy founded in Odessa (now in Ukraine). The revolt began in March 25 of 1821.* The last toast was to the 'Fair Sex.'

When LaFayette visited Portsmouth in 1824 he was entertained at a banquet at Webb's. Mr. Webb was prominent in the town and had several beautiful daughters, long remembered here. *He was also entertained at the Nivison-Ball House on Crawford Street, later moved to Red Lion Square on Middle Street between London and Glasgow where you will see his visit commemorated on a state historical marker. It was described earlier.*

Between 1826 and 1840 there was an occasional mention made in the newspapers of Wyatt's Hotel; but it seems to have passed entirely out of memory; not even its location is known. We get one interesting glimpse of it, however, recalling an almost forgotten custom, when the tablecloth was changed for the wine course. In old times when the dessert was finished the white cloth was removed from the table and a red one put in its place before the wine was brought out in quantity.

The oldest of all the Portsmouth hostelries was the Mansion House; once called the Bell Tavern. It stood on the corner lot designated and given by Col. Crawford for a market-house and hotel. It occupied part of the space on which the New Kirn Building was erected, and was torn down to make way for that building.

The bank, afterwards the Post office, occupied the remainder of the lot, but in early days that site was part of the inn yard. *Miss Holladay is now talking about the southeastern corner of the intersection of High and Court streets, across from Trinity Church. An illustration of the bank which stood here, later the post office, can be seen in <u>Images of America: Portsmouth, Virginia</u> by Robert Albertson, from an engraving in Pollock's <u>Sketchbook of Portsmouth</u> from 1886. Dr. Albertson's book also has an illustration of the New Kirn Building as it appeared soon after construction in 1911. In that picture you can see the fire hall previously mentioned, next to it,* *with the fire apparatus on display.* The Mansion House survived all the other taverns as far as the buildings were concerned, remaining with its moss-covered roof right in the heart of the busiest section of the town. In later years it was altered to suit business purposes. Lawyers took possession of its rooms and turned them into offices; and until the end it was popular with them. The well-known firm of Edwards and Happer were the last to leave it. The lower floor was turned into stores and thus the front was slightly altered. One of the tavern's greatest assets was the "pump right at its door." This was the celebrated Boomarlarly *(or Boomerlarly)* Pump once so prominent in the annals of Portsmouth. This old pump stood guard on the corner until the water plant made it useless.

Speaking of this old pump recalls an old story current a hundred years ago *(1830s)*. "Few of the present generation," said the narrator, "have heard of the incidents connected with the central point of our town and its historical corners. In the old time our friend Boomarlarly was an adjunct of the tavern that stood on the southeast corner of High and Court streets, opposite was the courthouse; and where the courthouse now stands was the jail. The fourth corner then as now was crowned by Trinity Church. About 1830 there was a school for midshipmen at the Navy Yard, and the elder midshipmen were in the habit of warning the younger ones of their fate should they go to the tavern. They would get drunk; and then would have to be carried to the courthouse and tried for drunkenness; jail would follow, where they would stay until church time. They would then be taken there to be converted. They must not yet think that they were out of durance—by no means—they had to "box the compass" *(i. e. visit all four of the cardinal directions)* and this could not be done until the church wardens had conducted them to the Boomarlarly Pump, where *they would be sprinkled with its water to cleans them of their sins. Worse yet they would have to drink from the old public pump, most often used for horses and* their dismissal would *then* be public. *It was thought a drink from the old pump cured drunkenness forever.*

Court Street before the Civil War was notorious for flooding. One citizen who had waded from the old pump to Trinity Church suggested that subscriptions should be solicited to make drawbridges across Court Street. Advised that the newspapers, who favored the city administration, would not publish the notice; to encourage them it was suggested they be offered a dipper of water from the old pump as a bribe, since it cured all that might ail you.

The sycamore trees have gone from this location, yet there are some who still remember it as the parade ground, where before the *First* World War the nurses and children would gather to hear the band play—hence the Boomarlerly *(for the sounds of the brass and drums). This was a nightly event and the bands were drawn from the militia companies. . .*

In 1804 Mrs. Lucy Taylor kept the Mansion under the name of Taylor's Tavern, and such good dinners did she serve and such liquor that the fame of them has been handed down. The stagecoaches left from the Mansion House and their booking office was there.

Evil times fell upon this old inn; modern hostelries were built and the lease was not taken up. It then became a private residence, rented first to one family and then another. In the late *eighteen* thirties it was the home of a Jewish family, and Rachel the beloved daughter of the house was dying of consumption. To this poor girl the thought of being shut up in the grave was the chief horror of death. She seemed to get some little comfort when h*er father* promised her that when she died he would bury her in her own garden in a spot that he pointed out to her as one upon which the sun always shone. He assured her that her grave should always be kept green. Rachel passed away and was laid to rest as her father had promised her. As long as he lived Rachel's grave was tenderly cared for, and the old people say that when the father had gone the grave still remained fresh and green, no matter how cold the winter nor how warm the summer sun. When the bank was built it did not encroach on the grave, which was in the alley back of it, and the sun shone on all day just as before. The New Kirn Building has left but a narrow lane and Rachel lies under it, but no grass grows there and only a few rays of afternoon sun reach it. *Your compiler was speaking to a workman working on the Atrium Building, designed by local architect Kirk Berkeley, in the middle of Market Square on the south side of High Street between Court and Middle, now "The Studio" where artists can be seen creating and selling their wares; this workman told me he had come upon a grave in the alley behind the building. He knew nothing of Miss Holladay's account of Rachel's story. Timid fellow* *that I am, I have never trespassed down that narrow alley to see if I could find any remnant of her grave.*

In this same block is a quaint storefront with a sort of little round courtyard entry and a pattern in its stone floor. This was the business of the jeweler C. S. Sherwood. Sherwood was also president of the Portsmouth and Deep Creek Turnpike Commission, Portsmouth and Norfolk County Building and Loan and auditor for the city and, as we have seen earlier, keeper of the town clock.

The Harp and The Eagle was another Portsmouth tavern in the early days of the nineteenth century. In Gosport there were several boarding houses for the convenience of naval officers' families, before quarters were built in the yard.

In 1835 the Crawford House, the first five story house in town, was opened, and was long the fashionable hotel here *described elsewhere in this book.*

In 1851, Mr. Wm. H. Wilson built the Macon House, which opened with Mr. Tyler as proprietor. This hotel was beautifully furnished and equipped with every convenience. The opposite side of North Street had not then been built up to any extent; and *this gave* an attractive outlook for the Macon House, as the shore, then was a beach, and not encumbered with the shanties which cover it today. *Apparently these long-gone rundown houses Miss Holladay mentions were on the river front where Crawford Parkway now runs and where there are now townhouses designed by the architect Kirk Berkeley in the 1990s. She does not mean the elegant houses on Elizabeth Row.* There was a bathing house near the beach for the pleasure of the hotel guests *and the hotel had bathing machines: little horse-drawn houses on wheels with an open floor so ladies could be drawn out into the river and bath without being seen..* Many banquets and balls did our townspeople enjoy in this hotel; and the stranger who lodged there had all that could be desired in comfort of all kinds. G. P. R. James, who was at the time British Consul at Norfolk, moved over to Portsmouth and took up his quarters at the Macon House, writing one of his books at this hotel. Mr. James and his family were popular in social circles and left pleasant memories here. *The Macon House* still stands on Elizabeth Square on the south side of North Street between Court and Middle Streets. *It is now in use as apartments.*

When the Civil War came the Macon House, like the Ocean House, was filled with Confederate officer and their families, and others connected with the Army. Gaiety reigned for awhile; but after the Confederate evacuation it became a *Union hospital*. People who lived within a wide radius of the building had harrowing tales to tell of the agonized shrieks that issued from its walls. Investigations were made and the groans came from the African American patients, who were operated on without an anaesthetic. Chloroform and similar drugs were not plentiful, and were not to be used on the African Americans - *or so Miss Holladay tells us*.

The old house on Middle Street number 100 *in the old numbering system and most recently called Mrs. Murdaugh's house and now the property of David and Faye Timm on the southwest corner of North and Middle Streets*, recently encased in brick and now the residence of Mr Levin Plummer, was the private residence of the hotel proprietor. During the War it was occupied by the officers in charge of the hospital. The floors still show marks of the occupation; regimental numbers and other marks have been burnt in them.

The exterior of the Macon House is little changed *(its balconies were removed in the 1970s)*. Soon after the Civil War it was turned into four residences; now with additions it makes four apartment houses, the Macon, Chelsea and Angayle. *The current Director of Libraries, Susan Burton, once lived in one of the apartments in the Macon House and told me that regimental numbers also could be seen on the woodwork in the main part of the hotel.*

The Ocean House, *later the Famous Department Store, now the site of the Tidewater Community College Visual Arts Center on the northeast corner of Court and High streets* was finished in 1856 at a cost of $70,000. The building covers the site of the old courthouse, as well as some leased ground. Gen. Hamilton, a former resident of Portsmouth, has recently recalled an old story about the contractor for the erection of this hotel. Joshua White, he tells us, was declared the successful bidder, his price being five thousand dollars less than any other bid.

Everyone marveled that there should be such a great difference in the cost. The matter was explained when Mr. White looked into his own figures and found that he had actually forgotten to calculate for the bricks to go into the structure.

The chief promoters of this enterprise were Mr. Arthur Emmerson and Col. Winchester Watts. These gentlemen never married, and their greatest ambition was the advancement of their native city; and for this end they spared neither time nor money. The hotel was opened with great eclat with Mr. White as proprietor. Monsieur Monserrat a French chef presided over the culinary department. The hotel maintained a fine band under the leadership of Signor George, a talented musician.

The entrance in "old times" was on High Street; it opened into a large lobby or office in which the main staircase started. The steps ran right up to the top of the house, with a landing on each floor. On these platforms the wall was covered by immense mirrors, which gave rise to many jokes about the length of time required to go up and down stairs. Flanking the outer doors of the entrance were two great iron New Foundland dogs, the same ones that for a while mounted guard at the Catholic Club *(the double house still standing across from the hotel on court Street and described elsewhere in this book)*, but recently removed to a residence at the northern end of Dinwiddie Street. *These dogs survive in a little park on the Western Branch of the Elizabeth River between the water and Riverview Street in Glensheilah.* An iron-railed balcony extended around the entire front and side of the hotel; the part directly over the entrance was covered with a trellis like canopy of wrought iron.

The Ocean House balcony was a most desirable place for watching parades and shows of various kinds. Many fine speeches have been delivered from it, among them one by President *Franklin* Pierce who was a guest of the house.

His speech aroused great enthusiasm and he was forthwith made an honorary officer of the Old Dominion Guards, a crack *Portsmouth* company of that day.

President *John* Tyler with his family, too, were guests of the hotel and he also made a stirring speech from the balcony.

The ballroom on the third floor was the scene of nightly dancing. Once a month a hop was given there and many of the invitations to them are extant. An old bill of fare or menu has been preserved and we reproduce it here *(unfortunately it was not included with the article, but it survives in a copy in <u>Portsmouth and Norfolk County Documents</u>)* to tell its own story and make our mouths water.

The ladies' entrance was on Court Street and by its side was the hospitable arch that led to the Ocean House bar. No history of the hotel, nor even of the town, could be written without a mention of that popular institution.

Gen. Le Jeune found that out some thirty years ago *(1900)*, when he came to Portsmouth to live and took up his quarters at the Ocean House. He says, "I think the chief sport in those days was taking a drink at the Ocean House bar. I believe I got acquainted with the whole population, certainly with half of it, by sitting still and watching the procession file back to the bar. I must admit that I sometimes joined it myself; but all that is changed now."

Old newspapers tell us of many balls and entertainments celebrated at this popular hostelry, but perhaps none of them surpassed the banquet given in honor of Thomas Webster, Esq., of Philadelphia in 1857. Mr. Webster had been untiring in his efforts to aid the towns of Norfolk and Portsmouth in the epidemic of yellow fever in 1855. From the *Philadelphia Ledger* we get an account of this banquet. The writer starts out by saying that the supper was beyond his powers of description. After giving a list of the viands served, and praising them highly, goes on to say: "We have sat down to many suppers, but to none that equaled this one. Bouquets were placed at each plate and larger ones in ornamental vases graced the center of the table. The waiters were dressed in white, gloved, and their jackets tied with sashes of blue silk ribbon.

"Mr. James Gustavus Holladay presided, assisted by Col. Winchester Watts. At his right was our townsman, Thomas Webster, Jr., flanked by Commodore Dornin and other naval officers. Surgeon Minor in command of the Naval Hospital was present as were some of the most distinguished men of Virginia. The health of Mr. Webster and the prosperity of Philadelphia was given as a toast, and drunk with applause. Mr. Webster refused the honor for himself but accepted for his city, saying that he was glad that she could help us out in 1855. Speeches, songs and well-told stories kept the company together until 3 o'clock."

At the outbreak of the Civil War the Ocean House was the headquarters for the Confederate officers, and General *Marcus Joseph* Wright and General Huget made it their home, while in the town. In spite of the hovering war clouds the young people were having a gay time. Camps extended for miles in this vicinity and the town was full of strangers.

The dark days came soon enough and everything was changed. Portsmouth fell into the hands of the Federals, and their officers took charge of the hotel. In course *the* of time the hotel became a hospital and the rooms that so recently had echoed with merriment were filled with the wounded and dying. The building was used as a hospital until after the war ended. The Federal order restoring the Ocean House to its owners is now in the possession of a descendant of one of them. Among other things the document states that the share of "one Arthur Emmerson is not to be turned over to him as he has not taken the oath of allegiance to the Government and refuses to do so." *These oaths of loyalty to the United States were issued in the Pass House, on London and Crawford Streets.*

For some years after the *Civil* War the hotel had a precarious existence; it was closed for a number of years, but the great dining room on the first floor was in frequent use for balls, fairs and other functions. The barroom lived on and prospered until the detestable prohibition laws went into effect. The hotel was sold to a company and reopened. Soon afterwards some changes were made in the building. The eastern portion was used for offices and a club called the "Business Men's Association." At the same time a lot was purchased on Court Street, and an annex built there and another story added. Two of the stores under it were changed to make an entrance to a theater, which was built at the back of the hotel, *called the Orpheum*. This theater burned some years ago but was repaired and is now a moving picture house. *Before this an area of the hotel approximately where Brutti's restaurant now stands was in use as a movie theater. It can be seen on the insurance plat of that year, as can the Orpheum.* At the time of these changes the hotel was re-christened "Hotel Monroe," a great mistake we think as the old name had so many associations for the town. There is in existence a piece of music called the "Ocean House Schottische," composed by Signor George George and dedicated to Messrs. Watts and Emmerson. It is interesting because it contains a print of the hotel as it originally appeared, and in addition to this shows our old friend the Boomarlarly Pump. *This illustration survives.*

The Gates Theater which appears in several pictures in <u>Images of America: Portsmouth, VA</u> *by Robert Albertson, was a part of the old hotel, but is now gone. The Monroe Hotel, also pictured by Albertson, burned on August 9 1957 and was replaced by the Famous Department Store, also pictured by Albertson. Started by Isaac and Belle Goodman in 1916 at 316 High Street it moved to the corner of High and Court in 1940, where it was long kowned by Bernard and Zelma Rivin. Isaac Goodman told of one morning when he was arranging a window display and a woman tapped on the glass, then came in and asked him the price of the silver fox scarf he had just put out. He quoted her a price and then when he looked at his records found it had cost him much more than that,. When the woman returned, however, he did not raise the price. He had given his word. Women of a certain age will remember this wonderful old institution with nostalgia. The staff was very professional; they would meet you at the door and they always knew each woman's taste. Mrs. Ferabee, in the clothing section on the second floor, knew my wife's taste so well she would call her if something came in which she might like and was always correct. The first floor, flooded with light from the plate-glass windows, sold perfume, jewelry and shoes. You then went up in the elevator, with a real elevator operator, to the girls' and women's fashions. Its famous wedding gowns, once presided over by Mrs. Hannah Phelps, were on the third floor. Many a Portsmouth girl started her wedding plans there. In December they had a fashion show "for men only," by invitation. - sometimes demurely including lingerie. There was a day of mourning when the store closed in 1991.*

The hotel on the southwest corner of Dinwiddie and High streets was first opened as the Hotel Portsmouth in 1946. It is believed that President Harry Truman roomed there during his visit to the shipyard, but the old hotel books are now lost and so that cannot be proved. The name was changed a decade later to the Hotel Governor Dinwiddie to honor that Colonial Governor of Virginia, mentioned earlier. Four decedents of the governor were present at the renaming ceremony. It became a residence for the elderly and low-income, and was purchased by the Winbrough family who had just redeveloped the interior of the old YMCA building in the same block. In 2005 it was opened as a hotel again, now called Hawthorne Suites.

The Holiday Inn was built in the late 1960s and is slated for removal. A request for proposals was issued by the city in 2006. The property offered by the city includes the Holiday Inn, the parking ramp beside it, the city's only visitors center and the green space where the popular recreation area called Portside once stood. Development of the latter two parcels has been opposed by many citizens who point out that the tourist trade served by the visitor's center is important to the city's economic development and that the green space in question is the last of the bucolic gathering-places left on the city's waterfront and is frequently the cite of programs which bring money and attention to this old port city.

Portsmouth's newest hotel is the Renaissance Portsmouth Hotel and Waterfront Conference Center on the Elizabeth River at North Harbor, opened January 10, 2001.

This site was originally intended to house a tower matching the Harbor Tower apartments on the north side of the inlet. When Harbor Tower was built in 1983 it was the tallest apartment building in Hampton Roads and is still a centerpiece of the skyline, particularly when Portsmouth and Norfolk buildings are illuminated for the Christmas season.

Chapter 40: Getting Religion

Portsmouth has so many churches to describe all of them would require another book of this length and so I will limit this chapter to the old churches described by Miss Holladay. Most of them can be entered on the Steeple To Steeple walk on the first Saturday of October each year.

Trinity Church

A detailed history of the church was written by the Right Rev. C. Charles Vaché, rector of the church for 19 years before he became Bishop of Southern Virginia. The following is a brief history by Miss Holladay.

Trinity Church was originally the parish church of Portsmouth Parish. This parish had been carved out of Elizabeth River Parish on *March 5* 1761, and in that year the Rev. Charles Smith gave up his charge of St. Paul's, Norfolk *which he had held for almost twenty years* in order to become rector of the Portsmouth church, which he served until his death in 1773. According to the custom of the day, Parson Smith lived at the Glebe *(Port Norfolk)*, or farm owned by the church and used as a home for the minister. In the garden at the Glebe he found his last resting place, in a spot chosen in his will for this purpose. The will furthermore states that he wished to be buried in a "plain pine coffin." Parson Smith's son-in-law James Taylor was executor of this will, and his daughter Alice Taylor and her two children Margaret and Abigail were legatees. All memory of Mr. Smith has passed away, though he has many descendants in Norfolk, his granddaughter Abigail Taylor having married Mr. Benjamin Pollard of that city, in 1784. Some years ago Mr. Smith's remains were moved from Port Norfolk and reentered in Trinity churchyard. *His stone at Trinity reads, "Here lies interrd the Revd. CHARLES SMITH rector of Portsmouth Parish who died the 11th of January 1773 in the 61st year of his age. He officiated as minister upward of 30 Years and his conduct through Life was Unexceptionable. He was a sincere friend a most tender Husband an affectionate Father and a humane good Man. He was Esteemd and beloved when alive and died universally Lamented. In testimony of their tender regard his son in law JAMES TAYLOR and Daughter ALICE TAYLOR have erected this Monument."* James Taylor is called a Dr..

The first vestry for the new parish was elected in 1761, and those chosen for this duty were Col. William Craford *founder of the town*, John Tatem, John Ferebee, Jeremiah Creetch, Thomas Creetch, James Ives, Giles Randolph, John Herbert, George Veale, Thomas Veale, Thomas Grimes and Richard Carney. *In Anglican churches the vestry manages all the affairs of the church other than worship. On 12 June 1938 a Celtic Cross was erected in the churchyard by the Neeley family on which these vestrymen are listed.*

After *Royal Governor* Dunmore's arrival in this section, the church like everything else, was more or less affected, and we find in Richmond in the archives a petition from "sundry inhabitants of Portsmouth Parish."

This document says that during the alarm of November, 1775, many of the inhabitants of Portsmouth moved farther into the country for safety, among them several members of the vestry. Owing to this there had been no vestry-meetings, and the levy had been neglected. As there had been no tax collected for them, the poor were in a bad way. The object of the petition was to have the General Assembly dissolve the old vestry, and order the election of a new one. *At this time the Church of England was still the state church. It collected the tithe, or tax, primarily used for the education and support of the poor; all oaths were to be sworn there and any citizen who did not attend the church could be brought into court and fined for not attending holy worship. The only other church tolerated was the Methodist, it being considered a prayer meeting of the Church of England. Thomas Jefferson would soon draft an act guaranteeing freedom of religion in the state, but Virginia was still a colony of England at this time.*

There are many signatures attached to this document, and we print the names as they will be interesting since we have no directory for those days. The signers were Paul Owins, Robert

Ives, Abner Ballance, Samuel Ballance, Thos. Bruce, John Bruce, Thos. Moore, Fred Moore, Joseph Stafford, Wm. Stafford, Wm. Buntin, Wm. Hoffler, Thos. Hoffler, Tenant Scott, Thos. Best, James Hodges, Benjamin Dingley Gray, Sol. Deans, Sr., John Bayne, Wm. Ballentine, Elisha Eastwood, Sol. Hodges, John Joliffe, Nath. Wright Burgess, Demsy Veale, Alexander Montgomery, Richard Blake, Herbert, Maximilian Grimes, John Wiat, Jos Bailey and Sam Ballentine.

The second rector of the parish was John Braidfoot, a Scotchman *from Wigtown (now a sister church to Trinity)*, who threw in his lot with the Patriots and served them faithfully as a chaplain throughout the war. He died in 1784 and like his predecessor was buried at the Glebe; but reentered in Trinity churchyard, where the D. A. R. have placed a marker over his grave. The Rev. Mr. Braidfoot has a number of descendants in Portsmouth, among them Mrs. Wm. Hartt, Mrs. E. A. Hatton and Mrs. Beverley Armistead. *Braidfoot joined the Virginia Militia, breaking his oath of loyalty to the Bishop of London, and was chaplain in the Continental Army throughout the war. He returned to Portsmouth when the British left. The bell at Trinity was cracked ringing the victory at Yorktown. Ironically no one could be found to repair it and so it was sent back to England for repairs. A bronze plaque was added to honor Braidfoot in the nave during the 1990s. As I have mentioned earlier, during the British occupation of the city a British Army chaplain William Andrews was the officiant at Trinity, and the church is mentioned in the diaries of two Hessian soldiers who attended services in the church. Braidfoot's granddaughter told a ghost story she had been told about the parson which appears in <u>Virginia's Ghosts</u>. It has been the lead story told in Portsmouth's annual Ghost Walk since the walk began. It is told by your humble compiler, who was one of the committee to initiate the Ghost Walk in 1980. The second year 6,000 people attended the Ghost Walk and then attendance was limited to 2,000 by tickets. It has sold out most years since. It was first planned to have only the one narrator, but it quickly became apparent it was too popular for that, and several actors were hired to tell the ghost stories all over the Olde Towne. The Olde Towne Civic League has sponsored the walk ever since and used the proceeds to beautify the Historic District.*

Mr. Braidfoot, as we have said, died in 1784 and was succeeded by Rev. A*rthur* Emmerson, father of the gallant defender of Craney Island. Mr. Emmerson went to England to be ordained and his ordination papers are in possession of his family here, *and a copy is on display in the church Parish Hall.* He was ordained to the deaconate upon his arrival, and to the priesthood on the day following, at Fulham Palace Chapel. Mr. Emmerson came to Portsmouth from the churches in Nansemond County. He purchased the lot on High Street next to Trinity Church and built the house there which was still standing, and occupied by his descendants until recently torn down. *A photograph of it survives in the library collection. It stood where the Commodore Theater now stands. It was a tax dodger style house. It is the model for the house pictured on the marble plaque in the church installed during the bicentennial year. That plaque was designed by John Temple Witt, the artist who did the Bo Jangles monument in Richmond, and it was the last stone cut by the sculptors at the National Cathedral. The plaque includes many symbols of the city's history. It is surrounded by stars for the states and dogwood blossoms for Virginia; in the center a young girl representing the Church of England presenting the* <u>Book of Common Prayer</u> *to the baby in its mother's arms, representing the Protestant Episcopal Church in America. The male figure is uniformed for the Revolutionary War. On the left is a ship of the sort which came into the harbor at this time, and the tobacco on the wharf represents the export of Col. William Crawford's plantation which was listed in his bill of lading in the first year of the town. When this plaque arrived from Washington, D. C., planking had to be laid to roll it in, so its great weight would not damage the tile floor. A hole was then knocked in the annex wall to insert supports to hold it and, to everyone's surprise, a verger's wand was found concealed in that wall. The verger is the church officer who opens the church (getting any sleeping dogs and cats out) and then leads the procession with his wand of authority held diagonally across his chest. With the end of the wand he may then tap anyone in the congregation who might fall asleep during the sermon. The church now uses the wand on important occasions, designating a member as the verger.*

The central window on the north side of the church, sometimes rudely called the "Father, Son and Holy Ghost" window commemorates Rev. Emmerson, his son and grandson. In 2006 the latest in the line of Arthur Emmersons came back to visit the church.

The Rev. Arthur Emmerson died in 1800. The next pastor was the Rev. George Young, known as the "Sporting Parson." He spent much of his time in gambling and drinking. He was wont to close his sermons with the following admonition, "Brethren, do as I tell you, not as I do." Owing to the unpopularity of all English institutions after the Revolution, the congregation of the church had declined rapidly, and little interest was manifested in it, so when Parson Young died in 1811, *on a hunting trip to the Peaks of Otter*, no rector was called to succeed him.

At this time the Presbyterians who had no church of their own borrowed Trinity for their services, once or twice a month. *You may remember that earlier Miss Holladay quoted a Frenchman as saying that most of the citizens were really Scottish Presbyterians, but had to attend the Church of England as they had no alternative. Trinity has experienced the conflict between "high" and "low" church throughout its history, as you will soon see when we speak of St. John's, and this ongoing quarrel probably has its roots as far back as those Colonial Scottish Presbyterians forced to worship at Trinity.*

The Rev. Benj. Grigsby had come here from Scotland and lived in Gosport. He was afterwards called to Norfolk, to take charge of the first *Presbyterian church* in that city. At this period the church building was used as a schoolhouse in the week. The Presbyterians decided to take over Trinity formally, now that they had a minister. *Grigsby and his successor, Hugh McPherson, are both buried in Trinity churchyard under un-Anglican obelisks.* The chance of losing their church awakened the slumbering loyalty of the Episcopalians, who rallied their forces and called a rector, the Rev. John H*enry* Wingfield, then a young deacon, in 1821.

It might be interesting now to hear something about the old church before it was almost entirely rebuilt by Mr. Wingfield. The original structure occupied the site of the present church, or a portion of it. Built In 1761, the chapel faced the west, opposite to the entrance door. There was no doorway to the street and the church could only be entered by the yard. *This is the prefered orientation for parish churches in England since ancient times, with the churchyard and entrance on the south, but a description of the church by Wingfield survives in the church records and it isn't exactly what Miss Holladay says here. In that plan the entrance door is where the central High Street window now is (the only nineteenth century window in the church which cannot be opened - the others, although stained glass, are double hung). To your right as you entered from this door was the chancel and the sanctuary, protected by a rood screen. A high pulpit stood next to the entrance on the right, and pews painted black for the African Americans in the congregation on the left of the entrance. Directly across from the High Street entrance was the door to the churchyard, which Miss Holladay tells us was the only entrance. The barrel vault above the nave is original. The original pews were destroyed during the Union occupation when it became a hospital for African American soldiers.* In 1829 the church was practically rebuilt on the old foundations and enlarged. The vestry was fortunate in getting much of the building material from the ruins of old Fort Nelson, which had recently been torn down to make room for the Naval Hospital. *The extent of the stone wall on the High Street side of the church was illustrated when the bronze plaques at the east end of that wall were moved to the choir end to make room for the plaque honoring Rev. Braidfoot. At both ends the workman was able to easily insert the outer screws, but burned up his drill bit on the inner ones as it hit the solid granite from Fort Nelson.* The building was stuccoed in order to hide the unsightly material used for it. About thirty five years ago *(1893)* when the building was remodeled the workmen expressed great astonishment at finding the church built of what they termed rubble. The old people then recalled the fact long forgotten, that the only tangible memory of old Fort Nelson was built in the walls of Trinity Church.

In January, 1830, the church was ready for occupancy; all the pews but eleven having been sold or rented; and these were advertised in the daily papers. *Some of the rent notices survive. William Dickson in 1822 paid $30 for the rental of his pew. He was a wealthy man, owner of a wharf in Gosport.* On the tenth of the month the church was re-consecrated under the name of Trinity Church. Christ Church, Norfolk, was closed for the day and its rector Rev. Henry Ducachet conducted the morning service at Trinity, with Rev.

W. H. Jones of Isle of Wight. *Wingfield would give Rev. Ducachet's last name as a second middle name to his eldest son.* The bishop of the diocese the Right Rev. Richard Channing Moore presided. The instrument of endowment was read by Rev. Jacob Keeling, of Suffolk, and Holy Communion celebrated by the rector Rev. John H. Wingfield, assisted by Rev. Henry Ducashet and Rev. Mark Cheevers of Hampton. During the service Rev. Zachariah Goldsmith of Accomac *on the Eastern Shore of Virginia* was ordained to the priesthood by the imposition of hands of all the clergy present.

The church was again greatly changed during the rectorship of Rev. James B. Funsten in 1893. The quaint old belfry was done away with, and the annex and tower added to the church. The galleries which ran all around three sides of the building, placed there in 1840 to accommodate the increase in the congregation, were removed, and a new gallery built at the east end of the building. *In this same year the handsome marble baptismal font in the shape of an angel (called Elizabeth by the congregation) was added and the original font from 1762, in the form of a simple marble bowl with carving on its lip was moved to the All Saints Chapel, where it can still be seen. Miss Holladay will tell us more about this font in a moment. The balcony was apparently where the African Americans in the congregation sat until the establishment of the predominantly African American Episcopal church, St. James, described earlier. One of the Trinity rectors said this balcony obscured all of the painted and stenciled windows from the 1850s on the east side of the church, but that when he was in the pulpit (then to the left of the steps to the chancel, but moved in 2003) he could just see the Holy Spirit descending and the eye of God at the top of one of the windows - when he gave a particularly good sermon, he said, God's eye would wink at him. This balcony was removed in the mid-twentieth century renovation when C. Charles Vaché became rector and the church was returned to its colonial appearance.*

The fine Luke slab was taken from the yard and placed on the wall *of the annex* inside the church. It had been originally fixed to the outside wall with copper bolts; during the Civil War the Yankees tore down the slab to get the copper. In doing so they broke it into eight pieces. After the war it was carefully mended - only one piece was lacking. In remodeling the church the vestry-room steps were moved, and under them was found the long-lost fragment. The architect in charge of the interior decorations of the church said this slab was one of the finest pieces of memorial carving that he had ever seen in this country.

His son has a sad story to tell of a brokenhearted mother, Nancy Luke, wife of Isaac Luke, Jr., who died September 1st in her 25th year, of grief for the death of her little two year old son and her two little daughters all within the space of a few days Capt. Luke, who was master of a ship brought the slab with him from London on one of his voyages and had it put over his wife's grave. He left town immediately after this was done on another cruise, from which he never returned. It was not known whether he was shipwrecked or captured by pirates. *Very faintly on the table at the foot of this memorial you can read, "Since my son is dead, my only hope is in God."*

The handsome Italian marble font, *Elizabeth, mentioned above,* an angel holding a shell, was given as a memorial by Mrs. Oscar Smith to her husband, a devoted member of Trinity Church.

Near the chancel is the tablet to the Rev. George Young, and on the north wall another tablet given by the Sunday school in memory of Mr. Edward N. Wilcox, its faithful superintendent for many years. The chancel window was placed there as a memorial to the Rev. John Henry Wingfield, rector of the church for more than fifty years. *The story told about this window over the alter, although it may be apocryphal, is that Wingfield was high church, which he was, and the congregation was low church, which we have seen it was (in fact heavily Presbyterian). The congregation demanded that he not place a cross on the altar, as it would be Papist; and so Wingfield stipulated the design of the window, with its large red cross, so they would have a cross over the altar whether they liked it or not. this conflict about the placement of crosses was hotly contested over the centuries in England. Anyone might think that the six superb windows by Louis Comfort Tiffany, or the "White Friars'" windows at the back of the annex, said to be the only windows by that famous English glass house in America, would be the most valuable; but an insurance examiner told the vestry that, in fact, the hand-painted and stenciled windows on the High Street and Court Street side of the nave, being unique, are more valuable."* There are *several* windows to *the memory of* families and individuals connected with the church; among the most interesting of them is the window commemorating those in Trinity Church who gave their lives for the Confederacy. Of this window we will let one speak who was present at its unveiling. "On Easter Sunday 1867, a large congregation gathered at Trinity; a great surprise awaited most of them; a new memorial window had been placed there since the last Sunday. On this beautiful window was a majestic matron of noble feature and sorrowful expression, standing in her own land, clad in rich robes and costly jewels. This mother of great men bows over the tomb of her sons. The Mother of States has become a Rachel weeping for her children, refusing to be comforted. After service many bereaved ones approached the window and exclaimed, 'It is Virginia. It is our State!'"

Virginia was at this time simply a military district of the United States; and Portsmouth was of course under Federal authority. The *Union army and navy quartered in town* took umbrage at the inscription on this window, issuing an order that the inscription must be changed or else the window would have to be removed from the church. This order caused quite a stir in the town at the time. *The U. S. Congress threatened to close the shipyard and Naval hospital if the inscription saying "For those who died in defense of their native state of Virginia against the invasion of the U. S. forces" was not removed. After removal it was, but saved by a parishioner and it was restored to the sill of the window in the 1980s.*

The communion table was formerly the tombstone of Mrs. McFarland, one of the old-time members of the church. The additions to the building in 1893 covered the space in which the grave was situated and the stone had to be removed; it was thought best to preserve it in this way. *The effort of the national church to move altars out so the priest could face the congregation during the communion raged in the last decade of the twentieth century. Trinity's congregation opposed moving the table. Then a much loved interim priest Rev. Mr. Christopher Wilson quietly had it done while other work was in progress on repairs. In the late 1990s the chancel was expanded and the pulpit and large brass epistle stand moved. During this process a dedication stone from an earlier renovation was found and can now be seen outside the vesting area door in the churchyard.*

During the Civil War Trinity Church was taken over by the Federals when in occupation of the city, and used as a hospital. The pews were ripped up and made into beds for the patients; and the building carelessly handled. The church was reimbursed for these damages by the Government, which awarded twelve hundred dollars about twenty-five or thirty years ago *(the 1890s)*.

Surprisingly, Miss Holladay does not tell the most interesting story about the church during the Union occupation. It is told in great detail by its subject, Dr. John Henry Ducachet Wingfield, the oldest son of Rev. John H. Wingfield, in C. Charles Vaché <u>A History of Trinity Church</u> which I will summarize here.

When the war broke out the elder Wingfield went to North Carolina to be near his sons and son-in-law in the Confederate Army. He left his oldest son, also an Episcopal clergyman, to keep the church in Portsmouth. As I have noted earlier, he blessed the officers of the CSS <u>Virginia</u> in the church and later the ship itself in dry dock number one. This story, however, starts with the Union occupation. Wingfield says his congregation was now made up mostly of Union soldiers and their wives. He had been praying for the President of the Confederacy, rather than for Lincoln, but now stopped mentioning anyone in the place where the President is prayed for, or if another read the prayer raised his head in protest.

Wingfield tells us that he was sitting in his "robing room" when he noticed a lady and two Union officers walking around the grounds and inquiring about the times of the services. At Morning Prayer they "took the most prominent pew" and at the prayer for the President one of them stood up and threw his <u>Prayer Book</u> on the floor. After the service one of these officers, whom he later found out was a Baptist chaplain, came to his office and said, "Why did you not pray for the President of the United States?" and Wingfield replied, "I am now a member of the Confederate States, and have been ordered by my Bishop to pray for our President," and that he might as well "pray for Queen Victoria, or some other foreign potentate." The chaplain reported him to every commanding officer after that. Finally one of them, General Barnes, listened and called Wingfield in, but after talking to him took no action. But Wingfield tells us "At last 'the Beast' was sent to take charge," by which he meant General Benjamin Franklin Butler. Lincoln in December

1863 issued a letter saying that it was not the business of the Army to take over churches, but Butler issued his General Order #3 in which he ordered, "All places of public worship in Norfolk and Portsmouth are hereby placed under the control of the Provost Marshals of Norfolk and Portsmouth respectively." That placed Trinity under General Wild. Only five of the male citizens of Portsmouth refused to take the oath of allegiance required by Butler. They were: "the Cashier of the 'Portsmouth Saving Bank Society;' the Cashier of the 'Merchants and Mechanics Savings Bank;" Arthur Emmerson, Esq., Clerk of the County and City Court; Dr. Arthur R. Smith, a distinguished Physician and the Reverend Associate Rector of Trinity Church," Mr. Wingfield. Anyone who refused the oath was to forfeit all property and the right to make a living.

On Christmas Eve two soldiers turned up at the rectory and took the key to the church from the younger Wingfield. He held services in homes until he worried lest this put his parishioners in danger. The church was taken over by the Rev. Mr. Jones, a Union chaplain of the New Hampshire Volunteer, with the permission of his supervisor, the Bishop of Massachusetts, maintaining that the war was "for God and country." Wingfield argued this was in opposition to the Cannons of the Church to no avail.

But the Union was not through with Rev. Wingfield. It issued Special Order #44 which reads in part, "It having been reported to the General Commanding that J. H. D. Wingfield of Portsmouth is an avowed secessionist, and that he takes every opportunity to disseminate his traitorous dogma . . . at a place of worship, while a prayer for the President of the United States was being read, his conduct was such as to annoy and disgust the loyal portion of the congregation . . . It is therefore ordered that the Provost Marshal arrest Dr. J. H. D. Wingfield and that he be turned over to Colonel (Daniel W.) Sawtelle to work for three months cleaning the streets of Norfolk and Portsmouth." This is signed by General E. A. Wild. Despite a petition signed by "Dr. Robertson, M. M. Shouthgate, A. A. Cowdery, James Cornick, Richard Dickson, W. Hoalbut, W. Whiting, John Cocke, (acting Warden of Trinity), Samuel Cutherell, James Williamson MD, James L. Hatton MD and Samuel Watts, the sentence was executed. and he gives a description of it. He was marched through the street and taken on the ferry to Norfolk and *put in what was called "Hall's Jail," now converted by Butler from a prison for African Americans into a penitentiary. The uniform required was "a brown skull cap with a broad red band around it, and one half of the body covered with rough gray cloth and the other with black." When taken out he swept the streets while the other inmates carried cobblestones. Newspaper accounts, and the subsequent account told before the Virginia legislature, say he was forced to wear a ball and chain.*

After the war he went west and became the first Bishop of California. His portrait hangs in the Bishop's office by Grace Cathedral in San Francisco.

The records of the church were completely destroyed, with the exception of a few fragments. *All the vestry books but the first survive.*

There is extant a deed selling one of the pews of the church to Col. Winchester Watts In 1840. The document is a printed form with blanks to be filled in. It names the rector and the vestrymen, who signed the deed. The Rev. John Wingfield was rector. The wardens were Holt Wilson and S. W. Latimer. The other vestrymen were Dr. Robert Butt, Dr. Edward Watts, Charles Grice, William Bogart, James Murdaugh, Stephen Cowley, and John Cocke. The pew was number 44 and the purchaser was required to pay down fifty dollars and agreed to pay twenty dollars a year for its use.

Trinity Church has been called a training school for bishops, as several of her rectors have been called to fill that office. Two of them, Rev. James B. Funsten and Rev. Arthur C. Thomson *who lived on Hampton Place*, were chosen while in actual charge of Trinity and were consecrated in that church. *Since Miss* Holladay's *time several more have been added to the list. She may not have known that the younger Wingfield, who had been left in charge of the church and whom we have quoted several times, went on to become the first Bishop of California. The most recent to be elevated was C. Charles Vaché, who was elected Bishop of Southern Virginia while serving as rector of Trinity.*

The 1893 renovation was credited to the firm of Cassell & Cassell when the church building was added to the <u>National Register of Historic Places</u> in 1973.

We have said so much about the church building and its adjoining yard, that the services and customs of the church have been passed over apparently. Fortunately, however, one who was a member of the congregation a hundred years ago *(1830s)* has left in writing some account of the services and things connected with them "The wardens," she says, "did not pass the plate at every service, but only once a month, when each adult present was expected to give a silver half dollar or quarter. The children put in such an amount as their parents saw fit." In these days of free pews one might fail to understand that the offerings were not the support of the church; that came from the pew rent. The pews that were privately owned required a certain amount from their owners annually. The Churches she tells us were not heated in her childhood, "In winter once," she goes on to say "I saw two old ladies, thin and pale, enter the church followed by their little maids carrying their warm foot stoves which were deposited in their nistress's pew. The child looking on remembered the pale-faced ladies and was moved that day to bring up the subject of foot stoves and requested that one might be placed in each pew, but the little one was silenced with the old proverb of being seen and not heard."

In regard to the music she says, "As far back as we can go Miss Christian Davis was organist; and she with a few ladies, Mrs. Wingfield, Mrs. Galt, Mrs. Langhorne and Miss Livingstone managed the choir. After Mrs. Davis Mrs. Langhorne became organist, and in turn was succeeded by her young cousin, Miss Louisiana Wilson, who served in this position for sixty years, This lady was gifted with a great talent for music and soon gathered around her the best singers in the church. These were Mrs, Page, Mrs. Rutter, and Mrs. Cowley, who with the organist made a fine quartet. Bishop John *Johns* called this choir the best in the Diocese. " *Trinity in the last half of the twentieth century and into the twenty first is still noted for its fine music program under Frank Liebolt and then James Derr. The choir has recorded two CDs. The church still has organ recitals periodically, and hosts international music groups and internationally known organists. The organ, which combines the pipes from the Victorian organ with a modern organ, is thought to be the largest pipe organ in* a church in Hampton Roads. A history of this fine instrument written by James Derr is available at the church.

Miss Holladay goes on to list the burials in the old churchyard, which was the city's graveyard until the opening of Cedar Grove in 1835, but, this information being more fully covered in <u>Surviving Gravestones at Trinity Church</u> in print and on Donna Bluemink's INTERNET site, is not repeated here. She does, however, report one stone which was lost and is not in <u>Surviving Gravestones</u>, The stone long since gone told of Major LeRoy Opey's tragedy. He was an officer in the United States Army who had married a Portsmouth lady. He left her and her infant daughter to go to Carolina by stage coach, carrying a large sum of government money. He had not gone far when the coach was held up by a highwayman and robbed. Major Opie was killed. *She also tells the story of a duelist's grave in more detail than that given in <u>Surviving Gravestones</u>.* We learn that in October 1806 "His Britannic Majesty's" ship *Chichester* was anchored off the Navy Yard, and while there young Ottleys *(Edward Onley in the Vestry records)* the first lieutenant and the second lieutenant, Cornell by name, had a falling out; but the cause of the ill feeling is not now known. The duel was fought in the dense woods that were then west of the Navy Yard. Ottleys was killed and his antagonist and both seconds disappeared immediately after the duel.

Many strangers too found a resting pace in Trinity Churchyard, for there was much coming and going here as in other ports. We find record of those from over the sea and of others from the North, and one stone tells us another sad story. Capt. Le Conte was stationed at Fort Nelson. With his wife and little daughter he started to visit relatives in Georgia. They had scarcely reached the Carolina border when Mrs. Le Comte became alarmingly ill and died in a few hours. Her remains were brought to Portsmouth and interred in Trinity Churchyard.

Attention has been called to the shortness of the lives recorded in the churchyard; few of those buried there reached the ago of fifty. This was probably not peculiar to this cemetery, but was due to the time when tuberculosis roamed broadcast.

Trinity is the mother church to Emanuel, the Episcopal mission church in Cradock, mentioned earlier, and St. Christophers in Churchland, started in 1948 on land donated by Mrs. Bernard Ferguson on Cedar Lane and completed in an austere modern style, unusual for an Episcopal church, in May 1962. It also opened a mission in Port Norfolk in the 1890s called All Saints. This ended its life as an Episcopal church, however, in the darkest days of the Depression. The building remains and has been loved by several other denominations since. Its memory survives in the name of the chapel at Trinity..

Bishop C. Charles Vaché has published a full history of Trinity church.

St. John's Church.

The great Oxford Movement which started in 1833 and caused such a stir in the Anglican church was not without its effect in this country, and many of our churches were in sympathy with its doctrines.

In the early *eighteen thirties* many members of the old Parish Church of Portsmouth, known as Trinity Church since the Revolution, had become dissatisfied with this church and finally decided to form a congregation themselves. They withdrew from the church in 1848 and elected a vestry; and planed to build a new church.

In order to have the congregation recognized as a branch of the Episcopal Church, it was necessary to have an action at the Council of the Dioceses. This Council sat in Norfolk in May 1848, and at the meeting of St. John's Vestry in the home of Mr. James Murdaugh on the 18th of May it was ordered that the entire Vestry be present at the Council and present the petition that a new church might be established in Portsmouth, to be known as St. John's. This vestry was comprised of the following gentlemen: Mesers. James Murdaugh, John G. Hatton, Charles Grice, Dr. Edward M. Watts, Stephen Cowley, William G. James Riddick and Dr. George W. Maupin.

On the twentieth of May, after due consideration, the Council decided in favor of the new congregation and steps were taken to build a new church. The lot purchased for this purpose was on the northeast corner of Court and London streets, running about seventy feet on Court. This lot cost two thousand five hundred dollars. The building was to be erected on the northern half of the lot and the southern portion to be reserved for a rectory. The Rev. David Caldwell, rector of St. Paul's Church, Norfolk, was asked to take charge of the congregation until they were in a position to call a rector. This flock remained under his pastoral care until 1850, when the church was finished and a rector called. *A picture of this church survives in the library collection.*

The cornerstone of the church was laid October 28, 1848. The Reverend David Caldwell laid the cornerstone and made the address.

In a short time the new church had been paid for and was ready for consecration. This ceremony was performed by the Right Reverend John Johns on May 20, 1850.

Later in the year the first rector came to St. John's, the Reverend James Chisholm *whose story of heroism during the yellow fever epidemic was told at length in chapter seventeen.* He was born in Salem, MA in 1815, entered Harvard College and graduated in 1836. While in the Latin School he received a prize which was presented to him by Judge Story, who remarked at the time he had promise of unusual intellect. . . . He had a remarkable memory and facility for languages . . . Mr. Conrad in his *Life of Chisholm* says he kept a diary, or common pleasebook, in which entries were made sometimes daily in Hebrew, Greek, Latin, French, Spanish, German and Italian.

Mr. Chisholm came to Virginia as a tutor, or assistant teacher, in Charleston, Virginia (now West Virginia). In the 1830s he entered Virginia Theological Seminary and in 1845, having finished his course at the seminary, he was ordained deacon by Bishop Meade, *the great reforming bishop in the cause of the "low church" and one of Virginia's finest early genealogists. His seminal book <u>Old Churches and Families of Virginia</u> is in the library's history collection..*

Chisholm was called to St. John's Church from Martinsburg, now in West Virginia. He had married Miss Jane Page in 1847. Mrs. Chisholm, like her husband, was much beloved in Portsmouth. She died in April, 1855, and it was said that during the funeral services there was not a dry eye in the church. Before the last hymn was over the choir broke down and it was finished to the accompaniment of the organ alone.

Mr. Chisholm's work in Portsmouth was successful, and he built up a congregation that was numerically small when he took charge of it, but one working under great difficulties.

In the summer of 1855 he was called to Cumberland to see his little son who was desperately ill. He started on the journey, but turned back to Portsmouth, hearing that the yellow fever had been pronounced epidemic.

A life of Mr. Chisholm has been written and it tells in detail of his services to the town of Portsmouth and of his own sufferings. During the latter part of the epidemic he was the only minister left in town. All of the churches closed early in the summer. The Catholic Church and St. John's alone held services. Worn out in body Mr. Chisholm contracted the fever when the disease was on the wane; he was admitted to the Naval Hospital and died there on September 17th.

The Rev. Mr. Hume, pastor of the Baptist Church, came in from the country and performed the burial service at the grave side, where about twenty people were present.

St. John's quietly went on its way, doing the work of the Master until it was halted almost by the sword; for in October 1863 came an order from the Provost-Marshal demanding that St. John's be turned over to them in order that their soldiers might have a place in which to worship. The order promised that nothing should be removed from the church and that, moreover, what had already been taken would be restored. The Rev. Mr. Willing, it was stated, would hold divine service in the church. Enclosed with the order was another from the Provost-Marshal to an officer in command on this side of the river, commanding him to send sufficient guard to the church to see that his orders were obeyed.

The congregation of St. John's, though deprived of their own house of worship, continued their services, holding them in the Presbyterian Church, which had been lent to them, the Presbyterians being at this time without a minister.

At the close of the Civil War St. John's was returned to its owners by the federal authorities. The building, which had been used for religious purposes only, had not been injured.

A rector was called almost immediately, the Rev. Randolph McKim, who had himself served through the war in the Confederate Army.

When Rev. McKim resigned in 1868, the Rev. John Dalrymple Powell came to St. John's and for twenty-seven years served the church.

In 1895 when Mr. Powell resigned as pastor of St. John's, the church building was in very great need of repair and it was decided very soon after the new rector Rev. Z. S. Farland had been installed in 1895 that a new church should be erected. It was not without regret that many of the congregation saw the old building razed. While the church was not perhaps a fine piece of architecture, it had a certain dignity and the lines were good.

The exterior was in the Greek style, the porch was recessed and extended to the roof, supported by two Doric columns. The exterior of the building was exceedingly plain; the large windows had panes of plain glass, and there was a gallery across the back of the building in which the organ was placed and where the choir assembled. There was no chancel, properly speaking, but a raised platform that served as such. The only ornamentation of any kind seems to have been the fresco painting at the back of the chancel. It was the work of an Italian painter named Oliviero and was said to have been a fine piece of work. Unfortunately, not many years after it had been painted, the church was injured by a storm and the fresco ruined. It was replaced by one that was not in any way attractive. The pulpit was an immense affair, and when the sermon was preached from it only the parson's head could be seen.

The font was the gift of Commodore Warrington, of the U. S. Navy, who was a member of the congregation *and one of the officers who had selected the site for the Naval Hospital in Portsmouth*. It was made of wood that had been taken from the noted old vessel the *Constitution*, and both bowl and pedestal were of live oak. *This old font still survives at St. John's.*

When the church was finished the congregation could not afford a large bell, and purchased a small one that hung in a temporary tower in the yard of the building. This structure proved to be an unsafe place for the bell.

On one occasion there was a fire in the neighborhood;

and, in order to give the alarm, St. John's bell, being within easy reach, was rung so frantically by the excited people that it was badly cracked as a result.

The bell was thus rendered useless. But St. John's did not have to bear the loss. Another and much larger bell was purchased and given to the church, the same bell that is now in use. This newly-bought bell was sold by the congregation of the old Presbyterian Church in Norfolk, who had just built a new church and made no use of it. In order to hang the new bell a new belfry was built on the roof of the church near the front of the building.

When plans were made for the new church it was deemed best to build in another section of town, and consequently a lot was bought on the northwest corner of Washington and London streets, and in 1897 the building was commenced. The architect was Charles Cassell, a member of the vestry. The vestry was at the time composed of the following: Judge Legh R. Watts, Dr. Joseph Grice, M. D. Eastwood, Legh R. Powell, Alexander Warner, Jefferson Hudgins, Dr. Gray G. Holladay, Charles Cassell and Zach Green.

The church was opened for services in September 1898 and the sermon was preached by Rev. Beverly D. Tucker, later Bishop of the diocese. The first St. John's church was consecrated on May 29 1850, and on the seventy-first anniversary of this occasion the new St. John's was consecrated. Bishop Beverly Tucker performed the office of consecration and the service was conducted by the rector, Dr. William A. Brown, *who would also become Bishop of the diocese of Southern Virginia (one of Miss Holladay's relatives).* The Bible used was the same that had been used for the first consecration.

Bishop Brown is remembered fondly in Portsmouth for his sometimes outrageous sense of humor. When at the Lambeth conference in England he roomed with a British clergyman who, hearing Brown was from the diocese of Southern Virginia, asked him if that was in Africa. Brown said it was not and that the Englishman might remember one of its small towns, called Yorktown. He also said he did not like funerals, because the corpse tended to be the center of attention. We have mentioned Parson Brown's Punch earlier: an incendiary concoction of apple brandy still served in Olde Towne, with which he initiated unsuspecting young priests when they came to the diocese.

Among the many treasures of this church is what is thought to be the largest window by Tiffany and Company in the nation. It was placed over the sanctuary and illuminated from the back, since the parish hall, when it was built, blocked the sun from shining through it.

There is a complete history of the church in the library collection.

The London House, originally designed as a residence for the elderly, was a joint project of Trinity and St. John's. When the number of residents declined it became a children's hospice.

Monumental Methodist

The first record that we have of a Methodist minister preaching in Portsmouth was in 1764, when Mrs. Helen Calvert Maxwell of Norfolk, tells us that *George* Whitefield preached here. Mrs. Maxwell gives the following account of the man and his sermon. "There was a sermon which I had the happiness to hear from the great Mr. Whitefield when I was about thirteen years old. He preached in Portsmouth, and stood out I remember on the steps of a house not far from the ferry wharf (North Street), for such a crowd of people had come to hear him that no house could have held them all. And there he held his white handkerchief in his hand and talked in a loud sweet voice, which I shall never cease to be hearing. His text was from the third chapter of John - 'Ye must be born again.' 'Poor Nicodemus, a ruler of the Jews, did not know ye must be born again.' At another time he broke out 'Alas, I might as well think to stop this vessel under full sail' waving his handkerchief at her while be spoke, 'as one of you think to get to Heaven without being born again.' All the people were much moved, and as for me I never heard anything like it before."

George Whitefield was a companion of Wesley until 1741 when the two parted ways on the subject of predestination; Whitefield being the more Calvinist. Whitefield died in Newburyport in 1770. .John Wesley preached at his funeral on the text "Let me die the death of the righteous."

The apostle of Methodism in Portsmouth, however, was Robert Williams, who preached his first sermon here from the porch of Isaac Luke in 1772. Mr. Luke lived in the old house remodeled by Mr. John Morris, number 304 Court Street. *This is, of course in the old numbering system. The house still stands, much changed as Miss Holladay will tell us, on the west side of Court Street between London and Queen streets. It is now divided into apartments. The descendants of the Luke family have written a small book on the house including not only this event, but its history during the American Revolution.* The Luke family occupied this house until about fifteen years ago *(1920)*. Mr. Morris made many changes in the house, adding rooms at the back and taking away the basement by lowering the first floor. *A remnant of the original "English basement," however, survives in the back of the house.*

Mr. Williams afterward held his meetings where South and Effingham Streets intersect, under the shade of a sycamore tree that grew in the space there.

A class was formed which met at Mr. Luke's for some time, and great interest was aroused in Methodism. In 1792 the class had become a congregation and a church was needed. The lot on Glasgow street between Court and Dinwiddie, still owned by the church *(now a vest-pocket park with a marker identifying the location of the church)* was purchased and on it was erected a wooden building forty feet long and thirty feet wide. The space around the church was used as a burying ground *(only three of the stones remain)*. Here many soldiers of the Revolution found their last resting place: Captain Jesse Nicholson, Captain Porter, among others. Here too was buried the victim of the War of '12, Lieutenant Ball *whose story was told earlier*. This churchyard, like Trinity's, fell into disrepute and the graves were overgrown and the stones for the most part broken. A few have been removed to the yard of the Monumental Methodist *and from thence to Cedar Grove Cemetery.*

In this old building the first Sunday School was established in 1818. This was said to have been the first school of its kind in Portsmouth. It was organized by the first pastor of the church, James McAden. Mr. Henry Singleton was chosen its superintendent and Miss Betty Cooke Paul was directress.

Some of the books and slates used in this school are still in existence, for as it has been shown secular learning went hand in hand with religious instruction. Among the slates preserved is that of Mr. Andrew Simmons, and recalls the story of the first organ used by the Methodists.

The older members of the congregation adhered to the good old rules of simplicity and accordingly disliked the tuning fork which had come into use. An organ was an undreamed-of innovation to them, but the younger members looked forward to the day when they would be able to buy one. Mr. Simmons, a lover of music, was the prime mover in getting the organ. He laid his plans and smuggled the organ that he had succeeded in purchasing, right into the church when nobody was near.

Before leaving the old church we must say something of the noted men who preached there. Perhaps the most famous of them was Francis Asbury, who served the church in 1775-1776. The history of this remarkable man is too well known to be told here. Eight years after he came to Portsmouth he was ordained bishop. *There is a plaque to his memory in Monumental Methodist, the new church, on Dinwiddie Street.*

Capt. Jesse Nicholson, the Revolutionary soldier, served this congregation in 1791. At various times he preached when the church was without a pastor, and was always ready to lend his aid. Capt. Jesse Nicholson was a very capable man and useful citizen. Besides his duties as postmaster and surveyor he was a schoolmaster. The surveyor's chain and compass of Capt. Nicholson are in the possession of the writer, as well as a beautiful map of one of his surveys.

The next pastor of note was William McKendree, who served in 1790 and again in 1792. Like Asbury he became a bishop, the first native-born American bishop in the Methodist Church. Three more of Monumental's pastors have filled the office of bishop. These were John Early, Richard Westcoat and V. B. Beauchamp.

In 1853 the church had established a mission in Gosport. As work developed and plans were on foot to build another church it was deemed wiser to change the site, so the lot on which the present Wright Memorial stands was bought and a small church erected. Wright Memorial is its outgrowth. *The life and death of this congregation is outlined later in this chapter.*

The next offshoot of this church was Central Church. This church was organized by Mr. Nathaniel Owens and his class of twelve, who agreed to support it for one year. Central Church was on County Street between Washington and Dinwiddie, and some years ago it was sold to the Jewish people who altered it and use it for a synagogue. *The history of this congregation will be told under synagogues.* The new Central Church was built on the northwest corner of Washington and South streets. *Its sad history will come up later in this chapter.*

Returning to the Glasgow Street Church, in 1831 the original or Glasgow Street Church was moved to Dinwiddie Street on the site of the present church. *The old church became the home of Emanuel A. M. E. Church, one of the oldest African American congregations in the nation, whose story is told elsewhere in this book.* The minister *of the Methodist congregation* at this time was Rev. John Kerr and the stewards were George K. Bain, Nathaniel Owens, John Talbot, William Outten, Joseph Culpepper, Jesse Culpepper, Robert H. Tatom and Overton Bernard

During the Civil War this church was taken over by the "Northern Methodists" and some very objectionable doctrines *to the members at the time* emanated from the pulpit. While thus occupied it burned by accident and *was* not rebuilt until 1866. *A portion of the wall of the old building survives in a small closet near the sanctuary.* The greater part of this structure was removed to the lot which it now occupies on Queen Street in 1872, to make room for a new church which was to be called "Monumental," and built as a monument to the hundred years of Methodism in Portsmouth. The old church was fitted up for a chapel and Sunday School and is now one of the best equipped in town. *So much new construction has followed that identifying the spaces Miss Holladay describes can only be done by the church historian, Margaret Windley.*

This church was dedicated on September 3 1876, when the trustees were: John L. Porter *(the builder of the C. S. S. Virginia, called the Merrimac)*, George W. Reynolds, James Brown, William Dyson, Willis H. Neville *(his family supplied ministers to the church and, as mentioned earlier, provided heroes of the Boxer Rebellion, the invasion of Nicaragua and the First World War) and* W. V. H. Williams..

In 1918, to celebrate the hundredth anniversary of the founding of the Sunday School, the church and Sunday School were opened and such artifacts shown as Isaac Luke's Bible and mementos of the Neville family including those of Samuel Peed, who served on General Pershing's staff in World War I.

The most modern of the Methodist churches in the city is Centenary on Cedar Lane in Churchland. Its sanctuary is quite remarkable. Its history was covered earlier when describing Churchland.

Again, as a full history of Monumental Methodist church survives, there is no need to repeat it here.

First Presbyterian

Earlier the French visitor was quoted in saying that there were many Presbyterians in both Norfolk and Portsmouth, but that they had no church of their own and were forced to worship in the Church of England, then the state church, now Trinity.

About 1811 or 1812 the rector of the parish church died, and the Episcopal church had fallen into disfavor with many people who looked upon it as a part of the old regime, and recalling the rule of Great Britain. As a result of these conditions, the few who remained faithful to their church were unable to call a minister and it was only occasionally that the church was used by the Episcopalians.

The Presbyterians by this time were very numerous in the town, owing to a great influx of Scotch settlers who moved here after the Revolution. The Presbyterians asked that they might hold service in the church occasionally and their request was granted. For some years the building was used by both denominations. The lukewarm Episcopalians let the church fall into a sad state for lack of repairs. At this juncture the Presbyterians called a minister, the Rev. Benjamin Grigsby from Scotland, and decided to take over the church entirely, repair, and use it for their own denomination alone.

This thought of losing their church awakened the loyalty of the Episcopalians, who immediately took steps to renovate it. Rev. Mr. Grigsby who lived in Gosport served his congregation there, but no church was built at this time.

Norfolk soon after this built a church and Grigsby was called to take charge. He remained in that town during the remainder of his life, and his family made it their home after his death, *but he is buried with another of the early Presbyterian pastors in Trinity churchyard. Their graves are quite distinctive, being tall pillars.* Hugh Blair Grigsby, Esq., the noted editor and distinguished citizen of Norfolk, was his son.

Hugh Blair Grigsby built a beautiful old house in Norfolk, for many years the residence of the Whitehead family, who were related to him. Some years ago Mrs. Washington Taylor (Miss Emily Whitehead) presented the Presbyterian Church in Norfolk with some silver which had been used first in Gosport and, being private property, had been carried to Norfolk by the Grigsby family, from whom it passed to the Whiteheads.

The Presbyterians of Portsmouth, when they found that a rector had been called to the Parish church, made plans to build one for themselves. They purchased the lot on the northwest corner of Middle and London streets from Mrs. Barbary Douguld of Aberdeen, Scotland, paying her the sum of five hundred dollars for it.

While the church was building the congregation worshiped in Mr. Anson Brooks' schoolhouse, which stood on the site now occupied by Mrs. Charles Nash's residence, 313 Middle street *(in the old numbering and unfortunately now gone)*. The leading spirits in building this church were Mr. and Mrs. Frank Grice and Mr. Anson Brooks.

Mr. Grice was a naval constructor at the yard here *about whom we heard earlier*, and uncle of Major George Grice. Mr. Grice was considered a very able man and was much respected in Portsmouth. His home here was at number 206 North Street, for many years the residence of the Neely family. *That is on the northwest corner of North and Crawford streets, now called the Grice-Neely House.*

Mr. Brooks was the head of a large school for boys here and married a daughter of Mr. Swepson Whitehead, the prominent lawyer.

Mr. Singleton was the architect who designed this church. It was finished in 1822 and used for worship immediately. Its first minister was the Rev. Mr. Price, and the service of dedication was presided over by the Rev. Benjamin Rice of Petersburg.

At the opening of the church there were but five

communicants: Mr Grice and his mother, Mrs. Mary Grice, Mrs. Abigail Maulson *(this may be Paulson)*, Mrs. Jane Dickson and Mrs. Dorothy King. The first person baptized in the church was Mr. Grice's little daughter Virginia.

From 1826 to 1830 the Reverend Richard Cleveland was pastor of the church. His home was on High Street, approximately on the site of the Citizens Trust Company. There are old photographs extant which show the house.

Mr. *Richard F.* Cleveland had a school for young ladies, which he taught in his own home. He had a sister Mrs. Emily Knox, who lived with him and assisted him in teaching. When his son Grover Cleveland became prominent in public life, citizens here recalled that Portsmouth was his birthplace. When Cleveland was elected President of the United States a prominent citizen of the town wrote and asked if he was born here. He set the matter straight by saying that he was born in New Jersey while his mother was visiting her grandfather there, *but his family was living in Portsmouth at the time.*

For fifty years the congregation worshiped in this little church, but in 1872 a larger building took its place. Among the mementos placed in the cornerstone of new church was a silver plate engraved with the names of the ruling elders: Messrs. Henry V. Niemeyer, Owen D. Ball, Jesse Carr, Wm. H. Stokes and Dr. M. J. Daughtery.

In 1874 a 2,500 pound bell made at the McShane Bell Factory in Baltimore was added in a separate bell tower.

The congregation did not enjoy long their new quarters, for in 1877 it was burned down. The fire was discovered one Sunday morning just as the pastor, Mr. Rose, had commenced his sermon. Mr. Paul Trugein noticed smoke issuing from a corner of the building, and with great presence of mind quietly dismissed the congregation.

The church bell rang and rang lustily, giving the alarm, which was taken up by the fire bells. The excitement was great, but the excitement at St. John's was greater than among the Presbyterians, for that church was on Court Street almost directly behind the Presbyterian church and several families in St. John's lived on the same block on which the burning church was situated;

and the rushing of the crowds and the noise of engines made it plain that the fire was close at hand. Everyone lost interest in the service. One by one the men left the church and soon the women commenced to follow suit. Only two or three remained and were about to received the Communion. Just then the doors of St. John's opened and an excited woman screamed, "The Presbyterian church is on fire." The faithful few needed no other call but sprang to their feet with alacrity.

The church itself could not be saved but the furniture was carefully removed with the other fittings. *Among these were the 200-year-old pews which had been purchased from a church in England, the unusual stenciled windows, also imported from England, and the bell.*

When the congregation planned a new church it was decided to change the site, and accordingly a lot on the northeast corner of Court and King streets was bought and the new church erected there. In recent years the congregation of the First Presbyterian church has bought another lot on its Court Street side and built a chapel and a most convenient Sunday school. *The interior of the church has a very distinctive look. It appears to be a square. Everything is symmetrical, but that is an illusion, because two of the doors are there only to complete the design, and lead to nowhere.*

This church has been served by number of pastors, but perhaps none of them were more beloved than Dr. McMurran. Dr. McMurran served the congregation a number of years, dying while its pastor. His family, too, took prominent part in the life of the town and shared his popularity. Mr. Robert McMurran, the new Commonwealth's Attorney is his. grandson. *Robert McMurran and his son Dennis would both go on to be judges in the court at Portsmouth.*

The new church was at first called Court Street Presbyterian, but in 1897 it changed to its current name: First Presbyterian. In 1974 the educational building was added, wrapping around the church, and another major renovation was completed in 2003.

There was another Presbyterian church started on the southwest corner of High and Dinwiddie streets in 1852 during what was called the "Old School-New School controversy" which developed in the Presbyterian denomination in 1839. The two churches, however, reunited during the upheaval of the Civil War.

A full history of the church can be found in the library collection.

Court Street Baptist

The Baptist Church was established in Portsmouth September 5 1789 by a committee, composed of four elders and four laymen. The elders were David Barrow, Thomas Armistead, Elijah Baker and William Morrice. The laymen were James McClenny, Lavan Blake, John Moore and Etheldred Lancaster. Two days later the Church Covenant was read and Thomas Craft, Harrison Benthal, John Foster and George Billups agreed to join the organization. It is to be noted that this congregation was established without any women in its fold.

Before the year was out Elder Thomas Armistead became pastor of the church, with a congregation of sixty-eight members. Mr. Armistead Semple, the historian of the Baptist Church, tells us he was a man of means and a member of an influential family. He had been an officer in the Revolutionary Army and always retained his love of things military. His military zeal was sometimes a stumbling block in his way.

It was decided to divide the Kehukee Association, which included in its membership the Baptist Churches throughout Virginia. This body was in session in Portsmouth when the decision was made and the new organization was named "The Portsmouth Association" and included the counties of Princess Anne, Norfolk, Nansemond, Isle of Wight, Surry, Sussex, Northampton, Dinwiddie and Prince George.

About 1792 Mr. Armistead resigned, partly owing to bad health and partly to other reasons. He left Portsmouth and lived in King and Queen County, where he became a merchant, though he preached when the occasion arose. When Mr. Armistead left the church here there were one hundred thirteen members, thirteen of them having been baptized the year before.

The missionary spirit had been present in the church and it had early established a mission in Norfolk. This little body, however, had many setbacks in its early days, being unfortunate in its choice of ministers.

There were several pastors in charge of the Portsmouth church before the Rev. Davis Biggs became its pastor, but none of these were inspired with the zeal to build a house of worship. Mr. Biggs, who was in charge of the Baptist Churches in both towns, soon set his congregation to work and in October 1799 the lot on the northeast corner of Court and Queen streets was purchased for this purpose, and a small wooden church was built facing Queen Street. There were galleries and a pulpit with a stairway. The congregation grew rapidly and an addition was built to the church, giving it the shape of a "T." For forty years this little structure served as a house of worship.

In 1833 Elder Thomas Hume was called to the church and remained its pastor for twenty-one years. Mr. Hume was educated at the Baptist Seminary, now the Richmond College. He was not only a man of great piety but of unusual executive ability. Mr. Hume's services extended beyond the bounds of his own congregation, and he did much for his adopted town, especially in the field of education. He was much interested in the establishment of public schools, and was the first superintendent of those in Portsmouth *as we have seen earlier. There was a friendly rivalry between Hume and the then minister at Monumental Methodist named Waller. There was a little verse repeated by the Baptists: "While Waller studied his Greek, Hume was baptizing down by the creek." Thomas Hume's house is the brick house on the northwest corner of North and Court streets. The unusual comradery among Portsmouth's downtown churches sometimes startles those who have not experienced it. When a representative of Court Street Baptist recently mentioned in a church conference that Court Street regularly had joint services with Monumental Methodist some in attendance could not imagine such a thing.*

The congregation of the Court Street Church had increased so greatly under Mr. Hume's administration that a new church became a necessity and the large brick church, which was torn down to make way for the present structure, was built. This brick church was finished and used for divine service in 1842, but the basement had been finished and was in use in 1839. There was one service performed in the new church before it was finished. The occasion was the marriage of Miss Rebecca Schoolfield and Col.

D. G. Potts. In the Summer of 1855 when the town was scourged by the yellow fever epidemic, Mr. Hume went with his family to the country, there being less danger of taking the disease there; but he came into town each morning and faithfully discharged his duty to his flock and rendered aid to the sick and dying of other congregations. Mr. Hume spent the remainder of his life in Portsmouth, where he died in 1874. He has many descendants here and in Norfolk. His son Mr. Thomas Hume also became a. Baptist minister and at one time was a professor at the University of North Carolina at Chapel Hill.

It may be interesting here to note that a church was built for African Americans at this period. This was Zion Baptist Church, which was built on the corner of Green and King streets, on a lot bought by Mr. Richard Cox and given to the African Americans for this purpose. *This church now claims to be the oldest African American church founded after the Civil War in Portsmouth and one of the oldest from its period in the state. More about this in a moment.*

In 1855 the Church sent out her first colony, releasing sixty-three members from her rolls for the purpose of establishing a church in Newtown (South Portsmouth, *old Gosport Village*). A lot had already been purchased by Mr. Hume for this purpose on Fourth Street, and a wooden building was erected on it. Rev. Mr. Hume then resigned the charge of the larger church in favor of his mission. About 1890 this little church was razed to make room for the brick one standing on the site at the present time. *Unfortunately Fourth Street Baptist, in its handsome brick building, was disbanded and the church removed to make way for PortCenter. This author has a piece of its stained glass in his home.*

At the outbreak of the Civil War the pastor of the Court Street Church was Rev. M. R. Watkinson of New Jersey, who boldly declared himself in favor of "secession." So vociferously did he preach this doctrine that many of his congregation, who bitterly opposed this movement, were much upset.

About this time Mr. Watkinson's family had gone North. After Virginia seceded, the people in the town who wished to remain loyal to the Union could be transported to parts north.

One or two steamers were to convey these people to the Union Territory, and on April 23 1861 the last of these boats was to leave, thus ending all friendly communication between the North and the South. When the steamer was making ready to leave the dock that day Mr. Watkinson quietly went aboard, saying good bye to his church. Though many condemned his action the majority of his congregation held him in affectionate memory. After the Confederate evacuation of the town it was occupied by the Federals and when they took over the Baptist Church they called Mr. Watkinson to its pastorate. But, as said one of its members, "He wisely declined to come." Many years later he was asked to become pastor of Fourth Street Church and this call he declined, too.

M. R. Watkinson went on to a church in Pennsylvania but, remembering the struggles of his old congregation in Portsmouth, had an idea. "The Rev. M. R. Watkinson of Ridleyville, Pennsylvania, was the first of many pastors to write a letter to Salmon P. Chase, the Secretary of the Treasury. suggesting that the words, 'God, Liberty, Law; be used in government documents."

"Two years later, in 1863, Chase asked James Pollock, the Director of the Mint, to put together a suitable motto for Union coins to be used during the Civil War. Pollock suggested several, including 'Our Trust Is In God,' and 'God Our Trust.' Chase decided that 'In God We Trust' would be used on some Union coins, as a way of reminding people that the Union was on God's side with regard to the issue of slavery."

During the Civil War, as was to be expected, the Baptist Church, like the other churches in the town, fell upon hard times. Elder Dobbs, who was in charge of the Court Street Church, was arrested and put in the military prison at Old Point *Comfort (probably Fortress Monroe)*. The African Americans of the congregation were in a rebellious state, constantly making trouble between the church authorities and the officers, demanding that they should have their due. In the midst of all this turmoil the church building was taken over by the Provost Marshal and put into use as a military hospital. The minister here at this time, though under the Federal Authority, proved acceptable to the Baptist people of the town. He made every endeavor to regain their building for the congregation and finally succeeded in having it returned to use for Divine Service and had it repaired and made fit for such services. The services of this gentleman, Elder Gregory, ended in 1865, after the Surrender. At this time (1865) the African American brethren at their own request were allowed to withdraw from the Court Street congregation in order to establish one of their own.

The newly-formed congregation was known as Zion Baptist Church, *described earlier in this book,* and their building was erected on the lot already alluded to on the northeast corner of Green and King streets, which had been purchased by Richard Cox and presented to the African Americans for this purpose. Mr. Cox was a man of weight and influence in the county where be resided. He was the father of Mrs. T. J. Barlow and John Cox.

Before this time the African Americans used the basement of the church for early services on Sunday mornings and held services there every Sunday afternoon at 4 o'clock. Two of the prominent elders were appointed each week to preach to them. There was a gallery reserved for them in the main church.

The building of a baptistry had long been the aim of this congregation and in 1870 this goal was reached and the baptistry was built that year at a cost of $1,225. The first persons baptized in it were converts, one from the Methodist Church and the other from the Presbyterian Church.

The Rev. A. E. Owen assumed charge of Court Street Church in 1871 and served the church longer than any other pastor *up to that time* with the exception of Mr. Hume. *The current pastor Dr. Wilbur Kersey has served longer than any of his predecessors.*

The music of the church has had an interesting history, beginning in 1835 when Brother William Forbes was appointed to line out the hymns and lead the singing. The next venture was a "choir;" and this body urged that the two front benches be allotted to them for seats. A great innovation followed, and racks for hymn books were asked to be put in the choir benches, for now singing by note was to be the order. In 1841 another bench was turned over to the choir, that body having increased in number. The leader used a flute and it was accompanied by forty-eight voices. The next proposition from the choir caused a stir. There were some of them venturesome enough to ask for a melodeon. Much discussion ensued; and after considerable deliberation, John Clark was allowed to install his melodeon in the church for the use of the choir.

The Baptist Church in Portsmouth was the mother church in this section and her missions lay spread over a large area. This historic old brick church built while Mr. Hume was in charge of the congregation was replaced by present stone building while A. E. Owen was pastor of church. In addition to this church there is a fine and well-equipped Sunday School building facing on Queen Street. *The current church is one of only two Baptist churches in this exuberant Romanesque Revival style in the nation. The other is in Tennessee. The stained glass is also exceptional, being all of a piece in its design, with yellow and shocking pink predominating, The ensemble of glass is so designed that curved stained glass windows go up the stairwells to the towers. When hit by full sunlight this creates a golden glow in the church that is quite unique. Dr. Kersey and his wife started Court Street Academy - a private school next to the church.*

By the first old brick church there were graves and tombstones in the churchyard; and we learn that it was the custom in its early days for the church to sell single graves and allow burials in its yard.

The pastor of the church at this present time *(1930s)* is the Rev. Archer Bass. The parsonage of this church is at 527 Hampton Place.

Again, a full, and more accurate history of the church is in the library and so I will not expand further on Miss Holladay's notes.

South Street Baptist Church on the corner of Effingham and South streets was first organized in 1889. In 1969 the congregation sold the church for $55,000 to Fourth Street Baptist Church and the original congregation moved to Chesapeake where it is now known as Western Branch Baptist Church.

St. Paul's Church

Portsmouth hadn't been established many years before a church was built by the *Roman* Catholics.

In the latter part of the eighteenth century many French families and a smaller number of Italians sought refuge here from their war-ravaged homes in Europe. Again a few years later an influx of French people, fleeing from the outrages in San Domingo and other places of the West Indies, greatly added to our French population. *Miss Holladay is probably referring to Santo Domingo the capital of the Dominican Republic, but people coming from there would be Spanish, not French. The 'Dominican Republic, however, shares the Island of Hispaniola with Haiti which was a French Colony. She probably means French refugees came to Portsmouth fleeing the successful slave uprising in Haiti led by Touissaint l'Ouverture. Wordsworth said of l'Ouverture:"Thou hast great allies. Thy friends are exaltations, agonies and love and man's unconquerable mind." This could be true of the slaves in revolt and of those French they drove from their lands, some to Portsmouth.*

These families at first worshiped in the church in Norfolk, but in the early years of the nineteenth century Mr. Patrick Robertson gave the land on which the present church is built *on the* northeast corner of High and Washington streets, so that a Catholic church could be erected there. He also gave the land on the north side of High Street, extending from Middle Street to the present bounds of the Hotel Monroe *(now the cite of the Tidewater Community College Visual Arts Center).*

It is not known just when a church was built, but it was a small brick structure which faced the east and was set back from each street, so we are told by Mrs. Olivia Cooke, a daughter of Mr. Joseph Bilisoly, a prominent citizen in bygone days.

Mrs. Cooke adds that the church was built on the ground level, with a thick floor. The whole interior of the church was very plain. The sacristy was in the northeast corner of the building and separated from the body of the church by tongue-and-grooved boards. There was no organ and no pulpit. Near the doorway was the grave of Mr. Robertson, who had given the land.

The church was dedicated to St. Paul and was served by a priest from Norfolk, Father de Lacy, a refugee from San Domingo. The congregations in both cities were mainly French and Irish. *We know that Irish settled in Portsmouth at this early date from renunciations of allegiance to the English throne issued by them, preserved in <u>Portsmouth and Norfolk County Documents</u>.*

In 1824 the congregation had increased to such an extent that the need of a priest was apparent and the Rev. Joseph Van Horsigh, a native of Antwerp, was called to this charge. Father Van Horsigh served here for ten years and at the end of that period was sent to Washington. He was succeeded in this parish by a young German, Father Burgess, who spoke broken English. He remained at the church but a few months.

Before Father Horsigh left a new church had been built. It was a very attractive building facing High Street, its floor level being about four or five feet above the ground. This, too, was built of brick but was stuccoed all over. A row of cedar trees was planted on all but the High Street side of the building, and gave it a picturesque appearance. There was a willow tree on each side of the entrance steps. There was a gallery over the door for the organ; for this church, unlike its predecessor, not only had an organ and a pulpit, but a bell, too. The Sanctuary was opposite the door and over its altar in large gilt letters was written," Reverence My Sanctuary."

There were several priests who served the church for a few months each, and then for about two years it looked almost as if the parish had been forgotten. The church was without a priest. In 1839 Father Moriarty was sent to care for the congregation and under him much was done to beautify the interior of the building. The church was frescoed. The design over the altar was the crucifixion, while on one side of it was *painted* the immaculate conception and on the other side the annunciation. The twelve apostles were pictured on the side walls, six on each side.

In August Father Moriarty was sent to another charge, and after another interim without a priest Father Devlin came to this church. Father Devlin remained here the rest of his life, dying in 1855, a victim of the yellow fever scourge.

One of his parishioners writes this tribute to his memory:

"In 1855, when the two cities of Norfolk and Portsmouth were visited by the awful scourge yellow fever, the good Father was indefatigable in his efforts to relieve the sick of all grades, classes and religions, without any distinction, until overcome by the terrible strain upon his system, he too fell a victim to the fever. After rallying twice, the third attack conquered and he was called to fill a martyr's grave." There is a slender Gothic monument in the churchyard that marks his grave *(it is on the High Street side of the church today)*.

Father Devlin, while in charge here, built a new church, too. The congregation had grown so rapidly that the old one had to be torn down and a very much larger one was built. This church fronted on High Street and was not on the street line.

In 1853 the first Mass was celebrated there. The sermon was preached by a very dear friend of Father Devlin's, Father Joseph Plunkett, who later succeeded him in charge. Though the flock had been greatly diminished by the yellow fever when Father Plunkett took charge, the congregation grew rapidly and galleries had to be built on the east and west sides of the building.

Father Devlin's church did not survive him many years; for in 1859 it fell a prey to flames and was burned to the ground. It was the work of an incendiary, and for a while it was attributed to those who were opposed to the Catholic faith. It proved later to be the work of men who were plotting to get some of their companions out of jail. The city and county jail at this time was on the opposite corner to the church, occupying the site of the Office Building *(the Professional Building)* and Briggs School *(itself burned much later)*. The plan of the incendiaries was to start a fire in the church and cause an excitement which would divert attention from their plans to reach and free the prisoners. The prisoners escaped.

The new church which was started in 1860 was not completed for many years, owing to the Civil War. It was, however, very quickly arranged for holding services. The Washington Street end of the lot which had hitherto been a marsh, *at the end of Windmill Creek which reappears at high water to this day,* was at this time filled in and the new church faced on Washington Street. There were entrance doors on both streets. Father Plunkett did not live to see his church finished. He died here in 1870.

Many people here who were not Catholics remembered Father Plunkett with gratitude. When Portsmouth was under military rule this kindly priest, who had some influence with those in power, was untiring in his efforts to aid those who fell under the displeasure of those in authority. Father Plunkett is buried at the foot of the altar in the church which he had loved so much.

On Sunday, March 28 1898 this building too fell a prey to the flames. Again the fire was of incendiary origin, but the enemies of the church had no hand in the fire; it was one of about forty buildings burned. A gang of firebugs started fires simultaneously in different sections of the town, and changing winds caused fires in the most unexpected quarters.

The pastor of the church at this time was Father Brady, who had served the parish for many years, and was much beloved by his flock and greatly respected in the town. He was much cast down by this calamity. No time was lost, however, in starting a new church and the result is the handsome edifice that the Catholics now worship in. The plans were drawn by the well-known firm of Architects *John R.* Carpenter and *John K.* Peebles *(this is Miss Holladay's spelling - when it was added to the <u>National Register of Historic Places</u> in 2002 the name was spelled Peeples)*, of Norfolk. Built of granite and beautifully proportioned, it is one of the finest Catholic churches in the South. Father Brady celebrated his Jubilee here after fifty years of faithful service. At this time the congregation presented him with a chalice of gold set with gemstones, as a memento of their appreciation.

The interior of the building was not finished for some time, that is to say, it was not decorated until a few years ago *(1930s)*. The many memorial windows were given by the different families of the church; the organ, a very fine instrument, was the gift of the late .John Mahoney *the Portsmouth distiller of whom we heard earlier*. The beautiful mural paintings, the work of a well-known fresco painter, were the gift of the Misses Maupin and of Mr. George W. Maupin and the Parker family.

In addition to their handsome church, the Catholics own two commodious school buildings, where some five or six hundred children are studying, a home for the Sisters of Charity who teach in them and a home for the priest. *One of the schools, from 1891, was recently restored on the corner of Washington and Queen streets. The Sisters of Charity cite is now the Parish Hall.*

In recent years a school has been established for African American children and a church opened for people of that race. Mrs. Cooke tells us that the first class ever confirmed in Portsmouth was in 1830, and that Archbishop Whitefield of Baltimore was the celebrant. Mrs. Cooke was one of that class. The first marriage ceremony performed was in the second of the churches and was that of Miss Virginia Bilisoly, daughter of Mr. Antonio Bilisoly, and Dr. Laurensco Jose Moniz of Lisbon,. Portugal, in 1833. Mrs. Cooke's own marriage was the second one. She was married to Patrick Henry Cooke in 1844. Father Magri is at present *(1930s)* in charge of this parish, and is admired and respected all throughout the community.

A major renovation of the church was completed in 2006. The original manufacturer of the stained glass was discovered in Germany and their records consulted in the on-going restoration of these spectacular works of art. The statue of St. Paul over the Washington Street entrance is considered one of the finest pieces of religious sculpture in the area. A parishioner of this church, Debbie Schwind, began the popular annual tour of Portsmouth's downtown churches called "Steeple To Steeple."

Again, I have not updated Miss Holladay's account, as there is an excellent new history of the church available.

First Lutheran

Lutheranism was late to come to Portsmouth. Rev. V. W. Shuey came to the city in 1908 and organized the First Evangelical Lutheran Church in the great room on the second floor of the Pythian Castle on the southwest corner of Court and County streets. One little irony of that location is the fact that on the Saturday before Lutheran services were held, that space was used as a municipal dance hall. Shuey convinced J. E. Cooper from central Virginia to buy lots on the southwest corner of High and Dinwiddie streets. In 1908 the congregation changed its name to The Luther Memorial Church and two years later renovated a building at 510 Dinwiddie Street. The current church site at Washington and King streets was purchased in 1925 and eventually named First Evangelical Lutheran Church. It is still a small congregation.

This is far from a comprehensive list, as Portsmouth has had more than 150 churches, of which 60 have pictures or histories on file in the library history room. Some others not mentioned by Miss Holladay were described earlier when covering their neighborhoods in old Norfolk County. A few more, however, cannot go unmentioned:

Shoulders Hill Baptist, now Churchland Baptist Church, is worth special mention because it was founded in 1785 and it has its day-book starting in the 1700s on file at the library (the originals were donated to the Library of Virginia). It is not only a fascinating diary of the church, but it gives an insight into the peccadilloes which could get a member banished from its stern faith, among them gossiping, which would certainly have left Miss Holladay and your compiler out in the cold. It had more black members than white in its early years. In 1824 it had 32 white members and 108 blacks. In 1829 it moved from Shoulders Hill in Suffolk to its present location on land donated by Colonel William Wright called Sycamore Hill. It retained its old name, Shoulders Hill Baptist, until 1890 when it changed its name to Churchland Baptist. The 1829 church was destroyed by fire in 1863. It is thought this was set deliberately in part because many in the church members were opposed to slavery. A new church was built in 1868. This was replaced in 1884 by another wooden structure and that burned in 1910. In the next year a brick church was put in its place. this was razed in 1978 after sharing the land with its newer sisterbuilt in 1963 for fifteen years.

Two old Methodist churches had sad endings. One started in a carpentry shop on Wyth Street in the 1840s. A new church was built in 1883 and called Wright Memorial. Many people remember when it was torn down in 1987 to make was for the industrial park called Port Center. It supposedly had a cornerstone with mementoes in it but, even with the aid of the fire department's long ladder, the stone was never found. For a time during the decline of Southside this was the home of the Wesley Community Service Center, which offered services to those displaced by the

Port Center redevelopment. The need for services like day care, meals and pre-school classes continued after Wright Memorial was torn down, and so the center moved to its current location in Martin Luther King Memorial Church on Elm Avenue.

The other Methodist congregation, called Central Methodist, has had a very strange history. It located its church on Effingham and Crabb (now called Columbia) streets. This church was to be started in 1854 and to be called "Wesley Chapel." Construction was again delayed by the advent of the Civil War. This little chapel soon was considered too small and a new church was built on County Street, and opened April 22, 1870. The old church was turned over to an African American congregation described earlier in this book. Work was soon begun on yet another sanctuary and the County Street church was sold to a Jewish congregation, to become the first synagogue in Portsmouth, about which we will hear more in a moment. The handsome stone structure which still stands on the northwest corner of Washington Street and South was opened on November 2, 1902. Although the church was struck by lightning three times it survived. The congregation, however, eventually succumbed to suburban flight and relocated to Suburban Drive in Westwood, then in Norfolk County but now in the City of Chesapeake. The old church was sold to Bishop Willis, an evangelical African American cleric from Norfolk, and operated as "Garden of Prayer." That church also closed and the building, a very visible Portsmouth landmark from interstate 264, stood vacant for many years. It then became a cause celebre when Reverend Joseph Chase, who had been ordained in the old church, and his wife applied to open the church again in 2002. The request went before City Council. The City Attorney, Timothy Oksman, advised the Council that if they turned down the application they would be open to a civil rights suit based on recently passed federal legislation. Four members of Council ignored this sage advice and voted not to allow its use as a church. A Federal lawsuit did follow. The city attempted to quash the suit, but that effort failed. One of their arguments was that the building was not now a church. Judge Dumar said, "Are you kidding? All you need to do is drive by to see it is a church." Eventually, in 2006, it became apparent the Council must reverse *itself and allow its use for what would be called Friendship Temple. The resulting action exercise required the city not only to allow the use of the building, but to pay damages of $850,000 to the new congregation for violating their civil rights.*

Another curious church story is that of West End Methodist. During World War II there was a shortage of lumber and so on September 1, 1944 this congregation purchased Bethany Methodist-Episcopal Church in Cape Charles on the Virginia Eastern Shore and had the whole church disassembled and shipped by the Cape Charles ferry across the mouth of the Chesapeake Bay and rebuilt in Portsmouth.

St. Mark Church of Deliverance on the corner of Washington and County streets was originally the site of The Christian Church organized in 1901. The building is from 1909.

Portsmouth Synagogues

Portsmouth developed a large and affluent Jewish population. So strong was it that there was even Beck's Kosher butcher store, serving its special needs on High Street near where I. C. Norcum High School now stands. One of Mr. Beck's descendants remembers that he would go home in a horse ad buggy each day until long after automobiles had become popular. One day, however, he fell asleep in the shop and the horse, very well trained over the years, took the buggy home without him.

Many Jewish owned businesses identified on High Street in an earlier chapter and many small groceries, like Lerman's near Lincoln Street, served Portsmouth. Many professionals in the city today are Jewish and they are prominent on any list of cultural events, charitable organizations, civic clubs and are among the recipients of the First Citizen Awards.

Although Jewish immigration to Portsmouth started in the eighteenth century, a synagogue was not opened here until 1896 when Gomley Chesed, meaning "doer of good deeds" opened above a store in the 600 block of High Street. In 1901 the congregation purchased the Central Methodist Church building, about which we have already heard, on County Street. This old synagogue, which some remember had a pair of lions with illuminated eyes, survives and is now in use as the Knights of

Columbus Hall.

Gomley Chesed was a Conservative congregation, and in 1917 a group who wanted something more Orthodox began to build the small brick building on the east side of Effingham Street between High and Queen. They called the new congregation Chevra Thellem. Although the active life of this congregation ended in the 1980s, it is now being restored as a museum by a committee headed by Zelma Rivin. The synagogue is a treasure. Its interior is not only handsome, with the traditional raised center sanctuary called a bimah and galleries in which the women were segregated from the men at worship, but it is built to copy the design of the synagogues of Eastern Europe. The originals on which this unique little building are based were almost all destroyed during the Holocaust. Rebecca Foreman remembers that "once in a while you would drop something from the balcony and the boys would have to bring it back to you and that's how I got my little dates." A long-time member remembers the occasion when the women decided to quietly, on one Day of Atonement, leave the gallery and sit by their husbands. "There was no argument, no dissension and from then on, without a word, we sat together." In another break with tradition, an organ was added, over the objections of many members, reminiscent of the same controversies over the organ at Monumental Methodist and the melodion at Court Street Baptist.

Charles Greenhood, the owner of Brutti's Restaurant remembered that they would have a little schnapps at the end of the service, even the children would take a taste, make a face and get their cheeks pinched by the old members."

Gomley Chesed built a large modern building on Sterling Point Drive in Churchland in 1955. However the number of families in the congregation dropped from 500 to 100, and then in 2003, to save the congregation's investment, they reached an agreement with the Torah Day School of Virginia to use its now mainly empty classrooms and to acquire ownership of the building over a thirteen-year time period. The original sanctuary, built to seat 750 will become a gymnasium and the congregation will meet in what was a side chapel. The memorial plaques from the original were moved into the chapel. In the hallway can still be seen artifacts from the County Street location including the famous "lions of Judah" mentioned earlier with their illuminated eyes.

In 1954 a new synagogue was started. It is the Reform liberal progressive temple called Temple Sinai on two acres in Hatton Point. The original committee was made up of Zelma and Bernard Rivin, Rachael Blachman, Lewis and Isabel Brenner, Esther and Irving Duffen, Catherine and Sol Fass, Belle Goodman Rosetta, Karl Mark, Julia and Morris Rapoport and Roberta and Ted Steiner. The design of the temple is unusual, made to resemble a tent, reminiscent of those used in ancient times.

Its longest-serving rabbi is Arthur Steinberg, who has served the congregation since 1980 and lives with his wife, Kitty Wolf, on Hampton Place in the Olde Towne. This witty and urbane man has more than one string to his bow - he has also served as a classical music disc-jockey for the local public radio station.

CHAPTER 41: A LIST OF MAYORS, MANAGERS AND FIRST CITIZENS

Since many City Managers and Mayors have already been mentioned in the text they will simply be listed here, but one not previously mentioned deserves our attention. Soon after G. Robert House became City Manager he, his assistant Chet McGinnis and the Head of Public Works Ralph Hester decided they would fly to Annapolis in 1982 to see the highly-praised waterfront development there, hoping to duplicate it in Portsmouth. They were flown by a Portsmouth Police pilot. Apparently the pilot took a wrong turn on approaching the landing and they were all killed in the crash. When news reached City Hall all work stopped in stunned silence. A memorial to those lost in the flight can be seen on the north side of North Harbor.

The City Manager form of government was adopted in Portsmouth on February 19, 1916.

I have mentioned City Manager Bob Williams earlier, as he is still active in plans for Portsmouth development.

Phin Horton is worth particular mention because in his short term he created much of the infrastructure of City Hall. Managers before his time tended to make all decisions themselves, running the city out of the Manager's desk.

V. Wayne Orton was the first African American to serve in this post in the city.

George Hanbury has also been mentioned earlier for his willingness to take the risks needed to revive a declining city, but Ron Massey should also be remembered for taking chances which later paid off with the Renaissance Hotel and the nTelos pavilion.

V. Wayne Orton and Luke McCoy were the earliest modern Managers to come up through the ranks, Wayne from Social Services and Luke from Public Works. Many other managers,

House, Hanbury, Massey and Oliver among them, came to the city after managing other Hampton Roads cities.

City Managers

Tyrell B. Shertzer	*1917*	
W. B. Bates	*1917-1920*	
J. P. Jervey	*1920-1926*	*whose home on Crawford Street is mentioned in "Walking the Streets."*
Frank C. Hanrahan	*1926-1932*	*His father was in the Portsmouth militia company at the execution of John Brown.*
Harold B. Anderson	*1932-1935*	
Edward B. Hawks	*1935-1936*	
Charles F. Harper	*1936-1941*	*whose son, Chandler F. Harper was the professional golfer who started Bid-a-Wee golf course in Portsmouth.*

M. E. Haug   *1941-42*
R. C. Barclay (acting)   *1942*
Arthur S. Owens   *1942-1947*
R. C. Barclay (acting again) 1947-1948
W. Guy Ancell   *1948-1949*
I. G. Vass   *1949-1958*
Aubrey P. Johnson   *1958-1974*
H. M. Myers, Jr. (acting) 1974
Phineas Horton   *1974-1976*
Robert T. Williams   *1976-1981*
Steven Lieberman (acting) 1981
G. Robert House   *1982*
George Lafayette Hanbury 1982-1990
V. Wayne Orton   *1990-1995*

Ronald W. Massey	1995-2000
David M. Stuck	2000-2002
C. W. "Luke" McCoy	2002-2005
James B. Oliver, Jr.	2005-

Before Portsmouth became a city on March 1 1858 it was the county seat for Norfolk County, and the town was governed by a Town Council which selected a member to conduct meetings from its ranks. Portsmouth had been incorporated as a town in 1852, one hundred years after its founding. When it became a city its connection to Norfolk County ended, because of an obscure Virginia law making cities separate from counties. Portsmouth elected its first directly-elected Mayor, or President of the Common Council as it was called then, before incorporation as a city was completed on February 17 1852. That mayor, John L. Porter, would later become famous as the builder of the ironclad C. S. S. <u>Virginia</u>, called the <u>Merrimac</u>. The account of his election, from his daughter's biography, quoted earlier, however, contradicts the list of mayors listed in the City Manager's Office and so I will use the city list omitting Porter.

Mayors

John S. White	1852-1854	
Hezekiah Stoakes	1854-1855	
D. D. Fiske	1855-1856	editor of a Portsmouth newspaper, who warned about the danger of free blacks. He was also on the Yellow Fever Relief committee. His sons served in the Confederate Army and one was killed.
Dr. James J. Hodges	1856-1857	
Major George Washington Grice	1856-1861	
John O. Lawrence	1861-1862	

John Nash	*1862-1863*	*One of the young ladies who welcomed Lafayette in an earlier chapter of this book would become Nash's wife.*
Daniel Collins	*1863-1866*	
James C. White	*1866-1868*	
James E. Stoakes	*1868-1869*	
E. W. Whipple	*1869-1870*	
P. J. Thomas	*1870-1872*	
A. S. Watts	*1872-1876*	
John O'Connor, Jr.	*1876-1878*	
J. Thompson Baird	*1878-1894*	*Starting in 1883 the annual messages of the mayors survive in the library collection.*
L. H. Davis	*1894-1896*	
J. Thompson Baird (again)	*1896-1904*	
Jefferson Davis Reed	*1904-1911*	
Dr. Frank Stanley Hope	*1912-1916*	
James Thomas Hanvey	*1916-1920*	
Robert A. Hutchins, Jr.	*1920-1924*	
Luther Gehrman White	*1924-1926*	
Dr. Vernon Asbury Brooks	*1926-1936*	*Some of his achievements have already been cited.*
John Powell Leigh, Sr.	*1936-1944*	
Leslie Talbot Fox	*1944-1950*	
Fred A. Duke	*1950-1956*	
Albert C. Bartlett	*1956-1958*	
Barnabas William "Billy" Baker	*1958-1960*	*One of the best known historian of Portsmouth who did much to collect and arrange the materials in the library history room.*

R. Irving Smith	1960-1968	He promoted the program which gave Portsmouth the "world's first completely planned container cargo port" Alf Mapp tells us.
Jack P. Barnes	1968-1974	Mayor Barns secured federal funding to build the seawall, completed the Civic Center in 1970 and was President of the Virginia Municipal League.
Richard J. Davis	1974-1980	During his time as Mayor Portsmouth won the All American City Award. After he retired as director of world trade for the state he served as chairman of the state Democratic Party, was elected Lieutenant Governor of the Commonwealth and narrowly lost the election to become U. S. Senator.
Julian E. "Joe" Johansen	1980-1984	A past commander of the Coast Guard Base; in his tenure ferry service to Norfolk was reinstituted.
Dr. James W. Holley III	1884-1987	Portsmouth's first African American Mayor.

Gloria O. Webb	*1987-1997*	*Portsmouth's first female Mayor came into the position after serving as Chirperson of the School Board; she championed education and the arts.*
Dr. James W. Holley III (again)	*1997-*	*Portsmouth's longest serving Mayor.*

The First citizen's award has been given since 1933. For a long time it was given by, and the banquet held at the Moose Lodge. More recently it has been given by the Downtown Kiwanis Club and the Rotary Club.

First Citizens

1932 Norman R. Hamilton — mentioned elsewhere in the text owned the <u>Portsmouth Star</u> newspaper and was South Hampton Roads representative to the U. S. Congress.

1939 John A. Morris

1940 Edward W. Maupin, Jr. worked for the Portsmouth Lumber Company, served on City Council, was the first President of Rotary and the first chairman of the Community Chest in 1915 - now United Way.

1941 Right Reverend Monsignor F. Harold Nott was the founder of Maryview Hospital in 1944. He donated his family's land in Richmond for one of Virginia's first tuberculosis treatment centers.

1942 Frank D. Lawrence was one of the founders of the Sports Hall of Fame and the person for whom Lawrence Stadium was named

1943 Rear Admiral Felix X. Gygax, USN was commander of

the Navy Yard throughout most of World War II. He was so committed to saving much needed fuel and so he did his rounds in the shipyard on bicycle.

1944 George T. McLean, the best known contractor in the city. Along with Manley H. Simons he founded the Portsmouth Housing Authority and was instrumental in building Swanson Homes, Dale Homes, Highland Biltmore and Cavalier Manor. He was given the job of salvage of landing craft at the Shipyard after World War II where he salvaged barracks and made them over to homes in Truxton. He built 5,000 homes in Hampton Roads, Town & Country and MidCity shopping centers and many apartment houses. He was first president of the Portsmouth Sports Club, started Tidewater Teleradio Corporation and attracted WAVY to Portsmouth.

1945 T. A. Willett was an educator for whom Willett Hall was named

1946 Chief Justice Lawrence W. I'Anson, chief justice of the Virginia Supreme Court, was on the committee which wrote the handbook for jurors still in use throughout the commonwealth and was President and Director of the Beazley Foundation described earlier.

1947 Leslie T. Fox

1948 Sol Fass manager of Fass Borthers Coal and Ice, he was a wholesale

	fish merchant and benefactor of Travelers Aid. He was one of the founders of The Portsmouth Industrial Foundation and the vice-president of B'nai B'rith for whom the local chapter was named.
1949 Maywood O. Lawrence	
1950 Abner B. Hill	*was active, as most on this list were, with the Chamber of Commerce. He was also active with USO and the national United Services Organization.*
1951 Porter Hardy, Jr.	*was a farmer and businessman elected to the U.S. Congress from the 2nd District in 1946. He spent twenty-two years in office.*
1952 Lewis C. Warren	*was police chief of the city from 1950 through 1960.*
1953 Reverend Ernest K. Emurian	*was the minister at Elm Avenue Methodist Church (later Martin Luther King Church). He doubled the congregation in his time, but was best known as a hymn writer, having written ninety-eight hymns, including "Bless Thou the Astronauts" sung at the Coco Beach United Methodist Church in Florida before each launch and played at the memorial in Houston for those lost in the crash of the shuttle <u>Challenger</u>.*
1954 J. Roy Rodman	*of the famous family of restauranteurs mentioned elsewhere in the test for whom Rodman Shopping Center and Rodman Street are named.*
1955 O. B. Wooldridge	*vice-president of the Bank of Virginia who was chairman of*

History of Portsmouth, Virginia

	the combined Community Chest-Red Cross drive and active in the Executives Club founded in the 1950s. The Executive Club building is on the corner of London Boulevard and Peninsula Avenue.
1956 Harry A. Hunt	*for whom Hunt-Mapp Middle School was named.*
1957 Right Reverend William A. Brown	*Who was the Bishop of Southern Virginia mentioned elsewhere in this book.*

1958 A. J. Lancaster

1959 Fred Beazley   who built Frederick Military Academy and Frederick College. His charitable foundation still donates to Portsmouth's growth.

1960 Arthur L. Cherry   of Cherry Carpet Company.

1961 Richard F. Wood   with the Bank of Virginia who was influential in the starting of the Portsmouth Partnership.

1962 Russell Mills Cox, M. D.
after serving in World War I he became president of Parish Memorial Hospital and then of the King's Daughter's Hospital which would become Portsmouth General Hospital.

1963 George T. Ewell   with the Planters Peanut Company became Chairman of the Board of the bank of Virginia and help raise money for a two-million dollar expansion of Portsmouth General Hospital.

1964 Lester Lloyd Knight   with the Seaboard Airline Railroad was a city councilman and later an advisor to the nation of Ecuador on the development of its railway system.

1965 George Tidings Nix

1966 Willfred Fleming McGann a member of the Portsmouth Port Authority he went on to champion the Colonel Crawford Common project. Its goal was to remake twenty-six blocks of High Street into a late twentieth century shopping center. The shops on the west side of Middle Street between High and King illustrate what this group had in mind. Many historically important buildings were lost in this effort. Fortunately they never got beyond Middle Street because this sort of development was doomed by the development of covered shopping malls. Its failure left the handsome old main street which is now such a draw for tourists, small specialty shops and fine restaurants.

1967 Robert Monroe Campbell, M. D. a much loved local doctor who has devoted his retirement to combating drug addiction in the city.

1968 Judge John Ashton MacKenzie a civic activists and long time Judge of the Federal court in Norfolk.

1969 E. Saunders Early mentioned earlier served on city council and for many years owned Robbie's Hardware.

1970 Robert Murdaugh Reed retired from the Seaboard Airline Railroad when it moved to Richmond, he became the financial officer for most of Portsmouth's best known charities.

1971 Mearle A. Kise was Vice-President for Research for the Virginia Chemical Company, treasurer of the Tidewater Science

	Council and active with the Old Dominion Research Foundation and the Humane Society.
1972 Paul Curtis Stokley	*mentioned earlier in this work made his money in meat packing in Portsmouth and used it in support of many charitable ventures.*
1973 Richard J. Davis	*mentioned many times in this book.*
1974 Herbert K. Bangel	*a prominent local lawyer for whom the Bangel Law Building is named.*
1975 P. Stockton Fleming	*who won a bronze star in the Korean War became the president of the Welton, Duke and Hawks Insurance Agency, a councilor on the Portsmouth Redevelopment and Housing Authority, the Chamber of Commerce and Chairman of the Board of the Red Cross.*
1976 Emily Nichols Spong	*the first woman to receive this honor has been frequently mentioned in this book for her work in historic preservation.*
1977 Frank Langley Kirby	*seriously wounded in the Second World War returned to his native Portsmouth to be manager of the local Red Cross chapter a member of City Council and Director of the Portsmouth Community Trust to which citizens can contribute, the funds being invested and used to improve the community.*
1978 George Delman Eastes	*a major general in the Virginia Army National Guard, member of City Council and Vice-Mayor he served as General Manager of Community Action committed to improving the quality of life in the city and active with the Portsmouth*

	Industrial Development Authority and the Norfolk-Portsmouth and Virginia Development Corporation..
1979 Daniel W. Duncan	*Director of the Virginia Chemical Company was active in many civic organization and on the grand-jury examining problems in the city jail. He later became chairman of the Jail Advisory Board.*
1980 Robert William Wentz	*a banker and civic leader, but best known for assembling tens of thousands of negatives of photographs from Portsmouth's history and publishing a picture history of the city. His negative collection is in the library.*
1981 Rear Admiral Jamie Adair	*a past commander of the Navy Yard who settled in Portsmouth and became an advocate for and advisor to many of its charities.*
1982 Emile S. Sayegh	*born in Egypt he was a much loved local doctor involved in many charities, but particularly in Portsmouth General Hospital.*
1983 Peter Eustis	*the owner of Virginia Chemicals whose contribution to the city has been mentioned earlier.*
1984 Bradford L. Cherry	*of Cherry Rug Company, who was chairman of the School Board and a prime mover in the moving of Churchland High School to its new location in 1990.*
1985 John Paul Conwell Hanbury	*a nationally known architect with a particular interest in historical restoration, he has been frequently mentioned and quoted in this book.*

1986 J. Herbert Simpson will be remembered for planning many decades of Memorial Day parades and as the father of the Virginia Sports Hall of Fame.

1987 Anne Hyde Long devoted herself to developing low-income housing in the city Mrs. Long was chair of the Wesley Community Service Center board which, with its first director Ruth Mayhall and its current director John Hatcher has helped many low-income families get on their feet.

1988 W. Ashton Lewis planned to be a farmer in Norfolk County, but during the Second World War when automobiles were not available he entered business with his uncle on Effingham Street in Davenport-Lewis Chevrolette. The business became Bill Lewis Chevrolette, named for his father. Mr. Lewis was an active force in the development of the Medical College of Eastern Virginia.

1989 P. Ward Robinette, Jr. a banker with Central Fidelity Bank, is a member of City Council and chairman of Portsmouth Redevelopment and Housing Authority. he was the first chairman of the Portsmouth Partnership, a $2.5 million public-private project to improve Portsmouth. He also was the Portsmouth representative when the old Portsmouth Chamber of Commerce was merged into the Hampton Roads Chamber of Commerce.

1990 Arthur J. Lancaster, Jr. was mentioned earlier as an officer *of Coleman's Nursery whose model train collection was donated to the Children's Museum of Virginia and whose Christmas display called "Winter Wonderland" started at the nursery in 1966 was transferred to the city and can still be seen on High Street, at the Children's Museum and at the 1846 Courthouse Gallery every November and December. He also was influential in starting Holiday House for severely mentally handicapped children.*

1991 Herber A. Haneman, Jr., President of Western Branch Diesel, worked with a dozen charities, but is best known for his work in relocating the YMCA from downtown to a modern facility in Churchland.

1992 Morton V. Whitlow an active member of City Council who was the moving force in starting the annual Cock Island Race and sailing regatta in the Elizabeth River, convincing Tidewater Community College to locate its Visual Arts Center in downtown, chairing the Seawall Festival and the Portsmouth Events Board.

1992 Maury Wise Cooke retired while still young from the presidency of the Community Trust Bank and started the Portsmouth Community Development Group to build new homes in Prentis Place and improve the quality of life for all Portsmouth's citizens.

1994 Zelma Goodman Rivin carried on the tradition of the

Famous Department Store mentioned earlier and is in the process of restoring the downtown orthodox synagogue as a museum. She was the first woman to become President of Temple Sinai, and among the first in the nation to hold such a post. She also was among those who started the Portsmouth Little Theater and president of the Portsmouth Chapter of the American Association of University Women.

1995 Junius H. Williams, *an employee of Virginia Power was the first African American recipient of this award. He was appointed to City Council and is credited with raising tow million dollars for urban renewal.*

1996 J. Hunter Brantley, Jr. *after retiring from the Norfolk Naval Shipyard went into city government as liaison between the shipyard and the city in the decade at the end of the Cold War when funding for the yard was in decline. He served on fifteen city boards and commissions. He was one of the moving forces in developing the "Path of History," mentioned earlier.*

1997 Ernest F. Hardee *a realtor started the Shorty Stallings Scholarship Fund and worked with Meals On Wheels for the elderly, Big Brothers/Big Sisters and the American Heart Association.*

1998 Horace S. Savage, Jr. *frequently mentioned earlier in this book, was a respected educator*

	as coach at Harry Hunt Junior High School and Vice-Principal at Woodrow Wilson High School, President of the Portsmouth Schools Foundation, and then the moving force and primary presenter for the Vann Lefcoe city management development program.
1999 G. Robert Aston, Jr.	of Citizens' Trust Bank, was one of the founders of Commerce Bank, now BB&T and spearheaded the organization of Towne Bank.
2000 David R. Tynch	a lawyer who, through the Portsmouth Development Corporation helped renew the old Woolworth store into Roger Brown's Sports Bar (named for its owner who was Portsmouth's most famous contribution to professional football), helped attract Hawthorn Suits (part of the Doubletree chain) to renovate the old Hotel Governor Dinwiddie and in the redevelopment of what had been Tower Mall into Victory Crossing.
2001 Michael J. Blachman	a well known local lawyer who took on the management of the Vann Lefcoe workshop, was president of the United Jewish Fellowship of Tidewater and served on Portsmouth Partnership, PRHA and the board of Child and Family Services..
2002 Diane Pomeroy Griffin	was one of the first women to enroll in the University of Virginia and Portsmouth's first practicing woman lawyer. She served as

	registered agent for Girls Inc., Help and Emergency Response (the HER shelter for battered women) and the Portsmouth Service League.
2003 P. Scott Morgan	*the President of Towne Bank served as chairman of PRHA, President of the Tidewater Winds, the Virginia Arts Festival (an annual Hampton Roads wide event) and on the board of Saint Christopher's School in Churchland.*
2004 Nancy Glisson Wren	*served with the Portsmouth General Hospital Foundation, the Portsmouth Community Foundation, Sports Hall of Fame and the Todi Music Festival (an annual music festival held in Portsmouth).*
2005 Dr. Arthur A. Kirk	*was Portsmouth's first orthopedic surgeon and with Grace Cone in 1954 started the Kirk-Cone school for disabled children unable to attend the public schools. This is now a foundation. He was also influential in the early years of the Eastern Virginia Medical School.*

INDEX

numerals

1st Coast Guard District 281
1st Marine Division 274
3rd Virginia Regiment 264
4th Marine Regiment 267
4th U. S. Colored Troops 132
4th Virginia Regiment 38, 108, 220
5th Army Air Force 132
5th Coast Guard District 99
5th Lighthouse Service District at Portsmouth 280
6th Life Saving District 272, 279
6th Virginia Regiment 214
7th Virginia Regiment 112, 114
9th Virginia Regiment 214
29th division, U. S. Army 221
42nd Prince Charles Own Hessian Regiment 42
42nd Royal Highlanders 42, 46
56th North Carolina Regiment 214
102 Regiment on infantry 97, 108
600 Block of High Street 452
700 Club 451
1846 Courthouse Gallery 13, 38, 120, 202, 347, 366, 394, 401, 440, 458

A

A & P Grocery 384
A. M. & C. Railroad 179
Aberdeen 329, 493
Abex brass and bronze smelting 296
abolition 203, 308, 346, 405 *see also* emancipation
absentee landlords 251
Academy Bar 244
Academy Park 250
Academy, the 159, 413
accidents on the railroad 142
Adair, Jamie (Rear Admiral) 256, 524
Adams, (Chaplain) 236
Adams, Clinton E. (Rear Admiral) 277
Adams, John (President of the United States) 230
Adams, John Quincy (President of the United States) 234
Adder (sumarine) 241
Addington, K(Mr.) 403

Admirals' Landing Condominiums 60, 102, 231, 371
adultery 368
Adventurers for Draining the Great Dismal Swamp 148
African American fire company 122, 125
African American History Society of Portsmouth 331
African Americans 122, 125, 127, 132, 155, 187, 201, 203, 205, 209, 226, 245, 291, 295, 298, 300, 301, 305, chapter 33, 380, 381, 385, 387,406, 413, 414, 427, 430, 435, 437, 444, 463, 474, 475, 480 *see also* slavesAfro-bets 396, 491, 498, 506, 508, 513
Afton Theater 244
Agnew, John (the Reverend Mr.) 32, 33, 34, 35, 36, 50, 124
Agnew, John (fire engine) *see* John Agnew (fire engine)
Agnew, Stair (Lieutenant) 34, 50, 58
Ahabazz, Raheema Turner 396
aircraft carrier, first 247 *see also* flight deck, first
airplanes 283
Ajaaccio, Corsica 78
Ajax (railroad engine) 141
Alabama (plantation) 38, 42, 288
Alabama (ship) 249
Albermarle (ship) 177
Albermarle and Chesapeake Canal 149
Albermarle Canal 148
Albertson, Robert VIII, 125, 223, 354, 404, 459, 467
Alcoa Aluminum 286
Alcoholic Beverage Commission 273
Alert (ship) 233
Alexander Hamilton (shp) 133
Alexander Park 285
Alexandria 421
Alford, Michael E. (Dr., Superintendent of Schools) 393, 413
Algerian pirates *see* War With the Barbary Pirates
All American City 451, 452 , 517
All Saint's Chapel (Trinity Church) 115, 475
Allen, Edward C., Jr. (Rear Admiral) 133, 282, 283

Allen, Gardner W. 25, 40
Allen, Henry 177
Allen, Reggie 296
Allen, Thad W. (Vice Admiral) 284
Allert (ship) 70
Alliance (ship) 71, 72, 75
almond trees 448
American Association of University Women. 527
American Beacon: Norfolk & Portsmouth Advertiser 119, 236, 437
American Bungalow style 294
American Heart Association 527
American House 130
American National Bank 131
American Revolution *see* Revolution, American
amphibious assault 238
Amphitrite (ship) 241
Ancell, W. Guy (City Manager) 514
Ancient and Honorable Artillery Company of Boston 106
Anderfuren, Marian X
Anderson, Harold B. (City Manager) 514
Anderson, Terrence Aver 396
Andrew Caldwell (ship) 226
Andrews, Philip (Rear Admiral) 255
Andrews, Virginia C. (V. C.) 395
Andrews, William (the Reverend Mr. Chaplain at Trinity Church) 50, 471
Anabaptist 337
Anacreon (ship) 419
Ann Street School 412
annexation 166, chapter 30
Annapolis 105, 218, 234, 266, 410, 513
Anspach Regiment 57 *see also* 42nd Prince Charles Own Hessian and Anspach Regiment
Antarctic expedition of Admiral Byrd 249
Anthony, Emanuel 434
Antigone (ship) 243
Antigua 78
antique stores 452
apartment houses, first in Portsmouth 270
Apollo Club 391
apothecary 165
apples 307
Arbuthnot, Marriot (Admiral) 55,56
arch *see* Lafayette Arch
architect, first woman 298
architects *see* them by name (i. e. Hanbury, John Paul; Yates, Glen;

Berkeley, Kirk)
archives, state *see* Library of Virginia
Ardurias (Lieutenant) 221
Arentzen, Willard P. (Rear Admiral) 276
Ariel (ship) 75
Arizona (ship) 247
Armed Force Museum 367
Armistead, Beverly 298, 471
Armistead, Francis 172
Armistead, James *see* Lafayette, James Armistead
Armistead, John M. (Dr.) 337
Armistead, Laura 365
Armistead, Lewis A. (Brigadier General) 213
Armistead, Moss 366
Armistead, Theodorick 254
Armistead, Thomas (Reverend) 77, 78, 496
Armistead, William 59
armory 67, 355, 439, 440
Armour's Cold Storage 294
Armstrong, Gilfillin (Colonel) 345
Army *see* Confederate States Army and units by name (i.e. Portsmouth Rifles, Light Infantry Grays of Portsmouth)
Army and Navy Union 267
Arnold, Benedict (Major General, Commander of His Majesty's Forces in Virginia) chapter 7, 64, 130, 384
Arnold, Peggy 56
Art Deco style 374
Art Nouveau style 374
artesian wells 445
Articles of Confederation 367
artillery companies *see* Grimes Battery
artists 388, 397, 410, 456
"As the World Turns" 273
Asbury, Francis (Bishop) 66, 300, 490
Ashbrook, (Lieutenant) 247
Ashland, John R. Newton 359
Ashton, Edgar 433
Ashton, James C. (Superintendent of Schools) 413
Ashton, John N. , Sr. 110
aspirin 268
Assembly Germans 380
Association of the Sons of Liberty 416
Aston, G. Robert, Jr. 528
Atkins, Edna Falls 246
Atkinson, Archibald 100
Atkinson, James 110

Atkinson, Richard 106
Atlantic and Danville Railroad 146
Atlantic Area and Maritime Defense Command 282
Atlantic and Beltline Railroad 294
Atlantic and Danville Railroad 297, 447
Atlantic coast 146
Atlantic Coast Line Railroad 295
Atlantic Hotel fire 124
Atlantic Intercoastal Waterway 149
Atrium Building 461
auctioneers 446
"aunt" 343
authors 395
auto racing 273
automobile dealers
automobiles 300, 312
Avery, James 78, 272
Avery, Mary 18, 78
Avery, William Halley 78
Avon Theater in Norfolk 389
Azores 226

B

babies 321
baby carriages 92
Bacon, Nathaniel 5
Bacon's Rebellion 3, 4
badges *see* rosettes of ribbons and Patriot badges
Bagley (ship) 248
Bagnell, E. Everett 414
Bailey, Joseph 471
Bailey, Sheri 396
Bain Brothers 424
Bain, Eliza 403
Bain, George K. 491
Bain, George M. 167, 449
Bain, James (Corporal) 172
Bainbridge, William (Commodore) 262
Baine, (Judge) 371
Baine's Bank 130
Baird, J. Thompson (Mayor) 220, 516
bake houses 257, 304, 446
Baker, Barnabas William "Billy" (Mayor) IX, 121,516
Baker, Elijah 496
Baker, German 415
Baker, Lee (Captain) 283
Baker, Orlando B. 426, 427
Baker, W. H. 167

Baker Salvage Company 185
bakers *see* bake houses
Baldwin, Loammi (Colonel) 234
Ball, Owen D. 143, 144, 354, 494
Ball, William, Jr. (Lieutenant) 108, 109
Ballance, Abner 471
Ballance Dance Studio 358
Ballance, Jean 358
Ballance, Richard 172
Ballance, Samuel 471
Ballentine, Samuel 471
Ballentine, William 471
ballet school 358
ballroom 464, 466
Balmoral 430
Balsam, Marion J. (Rear Admiral) 277
Baltic Fleet 71
Baltimore 155, 161, 300, 363
Baltimore and Ohio Railroad 171
Baltimore Riots 205
banana pier 149
bands 461
bandstands 244, 252
Bangel, Herbert K. 523
Bangel Law Building 120, 176, 433
Bank of Virginia 520, 521
bank robbery 441
banks 461 *see also* banks by name
Bannerman, Benjamin 368
Bannerman family 368
Bannerman, Margaret 368
baptismal fonts 475
Baptists 5, *see also* Court Street Baptist Church and other churches by name
baptizing 340, 341
Barbary Pirates *see* War With the Barbary Pirates
barbers 165, 328, 336
Bargour, James 262
Barbour, Fort 98
Barbour, Ida Belle 330
Barclay, Charles 349
Barclay, Clifford 349
Barclay family 244
Barclay house 349
Barclay, R. C. (Acting City Manager) 514
Barco, Bailey (Captain) 279
Barco, Benjamin F. 385
Barker, Albert S. (Rear Admiral) 255
Barlow, (Mr.) 167
Barlow, T. J. 500
Barnard, William 172

Barnes, James (General) 478
Barnes, George H. (Colonel) 214
Barnes, Jack P. (Mayor) 517
Barnes, Lelia 296
Barnett 209
Baron's Pub 451
Barr, Peter 452
Barrabino, N. C. (Surgeon) 275
Barrett, George H. 288
Barrett, Maggie 301
Barrington, Samuel *see* Barrinton, Samuel (Surgeon) 183, 264, 275
Barrinton, Samuel (Surgeon) 183, 264, 275
Barron, James (Captain) 44
Barron house 356
Barron, James (Commodore) 43, 67, 75, 78, 82, 115, 226, 228, 229, 236, 254, 290, 354, 356, 374, 425
Barron, Samuel (Captain) 225, 228, 238, 254
barrooms 202, 447 *see also* Taverns
Barrow, David D. (Seaman) 132, 496
Bartle, Rees 223
Bartlett, Albert C. (Mayor) 516
Barton, William P. C. (Surgeon) 263, 275
baseball 381, 382
baseball parks 96 (Harbor Park), 381, 382 *see also* Frank D. Lawrence Stadium
basket factory 294, 447
Basilan, Philippines 267
Bass, Archer 501
Bates, W. B. (City Manager) 514
bath houses 462
bathing machines 462
Battery Park 299
battles are arranged by their names omitting "Battle"
battleship, first 241
battleships *see also* battleships by name
Baugh, Richard 110
Bay Line Steamship Company 154, 171, 422
Bay Shore, Battle of 172
Bayea, (Engineer) 89
Bayne, John 471 *see also* Bain and Baine
bayonets 212
Bayside Harley-Davidson 313
Bayton, Beverly 297
BB&T Bank 528
beach music 388
beaches 293, 340, 462

beak 192
Beamer, Ben A. (Reverend) 338
Beans, John 344
Beard, James 394
Beast butler *see* Butler, Benjamin Franklin (General)
Beatty, Frank E. (Rear Admiral) 255
Beatty, Henry (Colonel) 99
Beauchamp, W. B. (Bishop) 290, 490
Beau (dog) 371
Beaufort (ship) 177, 193
Beavan (Clerk) 113
Beazley Boy's Club 289
Beazley Foundation 289, 519
Beazley, Frederick 250, 289, 410, 521
Beckwith, Sidney (Sir) 97, 105
bed and breakfasts 358 *see also* Patriot Inn, Glen Coe, Olde Towne Bed and Breakfast
Bedinger, Daniel 254
bees 31
Belgium, King and Queen of 247
Bell, Charles H. (Captain) 254
Bell Tavern 137, 459
bells 61, 125, 196, 347, 433, 471, 494, 503
Be-Lo Grocery 295
Beltline Railroad 294
Bemiller, Carl R. (Captain) 276
Ben Franklin (ship) 151
Ben Lomond 166, 371
Benedict, Hernandez 391
Benedict, Jules 391
Bennett, (Quartermaster) 219
Bennett, W. L. 126
Benson, Francis 172
Benson, John 427
Benthal-Brooks Row 118, 352
Benthal, (Captain) 360, 418
Benthal family 352
Benthal, Harrison 496
Benthal, William 411
Benton, Larry 382
Benton, Odell (Fire Chief) 122
beri-beri 272
Berkeley 13, 85, 87, 90, 224, 233, 386 *see also* Washington Point
Berkeley, Kirk 371, 461, 462
Berkeley, William (Sir, Royal Governor of Virginia) 6
Berkey, Richard D (Captain) 256
Berkley, (Mr.) 403

Berkley *see also* Berkeley
Berkley Bridge 87
Bermuda 62, 97, 225, 228
Bernard, Overton 491
Berrien, John M. (Captain) 255
Berry, Robert H. (Rear Admiral) 255
Best, Thomas 471
Bethany Methodist Episcopal Church in Cape Charles 509
bicentennial of the nation 472
bicycle route 267
bicycle shops 450
Bide-a-wee Golf Course 250
Bielenstein, Gabrielle Maupin IX
Big Bethel, Battle of 205
Big Brothers/Big Sisters 527
Biggs, David (Reverend) 497
Bilisoly, (Dr.) 158
Bilisoly, Antonio 506
Bilisoly, Antonio Sylvestre 78
Bilisoly, Belle 184, 208
Bilisoly Blues 214
Bilisoly, Charles 78
Bilisoly family 375
Bilisoly, J. L. 358
Bilisoly, Joseph 375, 502
Bilisoly, Olivia 78, 286
Bilisoly, Virginia 506
Bilisoly, Virginius (Dr.) 384
Bill Lewis Chevrolet 525
Billups, George 496
Binford, (Colonel) 326
Bing 137
Bingham, James 172
Bingley, Anne 359
Bird, John 431
bird watching 99
Birmingham, Alabama 433
Birmingham (ship) 242
Bishop Brown's Punch 487
Blachman, Michael J. 528
Blachman, Rachael 511
Black Hawk (Chief) 372
"Black Patti" *see* Jones, Matilda Sissieretta Joyner
Black Patti Troubadours 387
Black Pioneers 344
Blacknell, George (Surgeon) 183, 200, 275
blacks *see* African Americans
blacksmiths 164, 312, 336
Blake, Levan 496

Blake, Richard 471
Blamire, E. T. 384
Blamire, Ed B. 433
Bland, Charles T. 382, 422
Bland, Esquire (Lieutenant) 5, 6
blind horses *see* horse boats
blockade, Union 191, 200, 239, 325
Blonde (ship) 51

Bloodgood, Delaven (Medical Director) 275
Blow, Frances 411
Blow, (Miss) 200
Blow, Richard (Colonel) 117, 142, 352
Blue Ridge Mountains 171
Blue (ship) 248
Blue Rail Café 435
Bluemink, Donna 151, 482
B'nai B'rith 520
boarding houses 462
Bodie Island 279
Bogart, William 480
Bogger, Tommy 332, 447
Bohemia 1
boilers bursting 136
Bold (ship) 251
bombardment 180, 257, 333
bombing target 253
Bon Homme Richard *see* Bonhomme Richard
Bon Secours 260
Bonaparte *see* Napoleon, Bonaparte (Emperor of France)
Bones and Buddies 312
Bonhomme Richard (ship) 70, 71, 72, 73, 226
Bontakoff, (Admiral) 241
bookkeeping 410
bookstores 395, 457
Boomarlarly Pump 305, 460, 467
Borum family 361
Borum, John 110
Boshier, Maureen 361
Boston 44, 149, 229, 300
Boston (ship) 47
Bougeous, Arnie (Lietenant) 62
Bourke family 375
Boutwell, Edward 172
Boutwell, Louis 412
Bowen, Joseph E. 290
Bowers, James 110
Bowers, Thomas 82

box stores 451
Boxer Rebellion 132, 267, 268, 491
boxing the compass 460
Boy Scouts 109
Boy's Village 289
Brackenridge, (Lieutenant) 100
Braddock, Edward (General) 24
Bradley, Michael (Medical Inspector) 275
Bradshaw, John 61
Brady, (Reverend Father) 505
Bragg, George Freeman 336
Braidfoot, John (the Reverend Mr.) 50, 55, 61, 82, 292, 471
Brandywine, Battle of 407
Brandywine (ship) 235, 263
Brannon, John 37, 78
Brantley, J. Hunter, Jr. 527
Brass Rail 435
Braxton, Hester 374
Brazilians 272
breaches buoys 279
bread 201
Brecheen, Harry 382
Breckinridge, John C. 205
Breckenridge-Haywood, Mae VIII, 331
Breed, Alan D. (Rear Admiral) 284
Breese, Samuel L. (Captain) 254
Brennan, Walter T. 421
Brenner, Isabel 511
Brenner, Lewis 511
Brent, Martha Buxton Porter 326
Breslauer, G. 434
Brice-O'Hara Sally (Rear Admiral) 184
brick making 37, 111, 293, 361, 425
"Bride of Lammermoor" 389
bridges 165, 166, 223, 224, 233, 244, 266, 287, 340, 377, 457 *see also* by name (i.e. Union Bridge, Gosport Causeways, Lafayette Bridge, Churchland Bridge, Jordan River Bridge, West Norfolk Bridge)
Briggs Point 114, 385
Briggs School 339, 504
Brighton 285, 296
Brighton Blue Socks 381
Brighton Firefighter's Team 381
Bristol Square Office Complex 18
Britton, (Mr.) 156
Broad Street Books 395
Broad Street Methodist Church 295
bronze star 133
Brooke, Francis 190

Brooke, John Mercer (Lieutenant) 190
Brooklyn 382
Brooks, Anson 408, 493
Brooks family 352
Brooks, Julia 352
Brooks, George (Captain) 217, 219
Brooks, Thomas 352
Brooks, Swepson 408
Brooks, Vernon Asbury (Dr., Mayor) 86, 149, 288, 516
Brooks, William 360
brothels 442 *see also* prostitution
Broughton, William 172
Boutwell, Edward 172
Brown, George 350
Brown, George (Commodore & Rear Admiral) 255
Brown, James 183, 491
Brown, James (Captain) 185
Brown, James A. (Rear Admiral) 256
Brown, John chapter 19, 212
Brown, Marilyn 350
Brown, Roger 528 *see also* Roger
Brown's Sports Bar
Brown, Ruth Weston 388
Brown, William A. Jr., (Dr.) 386
Brown William A. (Right Reverend, Bishop of Southern Virginia) 487, 521
Brown, William A. III IX 54, 102, 299, 386
Browne, Harry (Mrs.) 366
Browne, Joe Sam 177
Brownley, J. H. 290
Bruce, Alexander 87
Bruce, John 471
Bruce, Thomas 471
Brumby, Frank H. (Rear Admiral) 255
Bruno (Sister) 162
Brutti's Restaurant 403, 453, 466, 510
Bryant, Harvey 245
Buchanan family 358
Buchanan, Franklin (Commodore) 190, 193
bucket brigade 118
Buckner, Robert H. 396
Buffalo Bill *see* Cody, Buffalo Bill
Buffalo Soldiers 205, 209, 332
Building #215 273
Bulgaria (ship) 243
Bull, Ole 392
Bullard, Ross P. (Rear Admiral) 283
Bullock, Elias 110

Bulwark (ship) 251
Bundy, Earl V. 396
Bunker Hill Day 234
Bunn, Eugene 350
Buntin, William 471
Bunting, (Sheriff) 387
Bunting tract 439
buoy tenders 280
buoy yard 63, 280
buoys 275, 280
Burch, J., Jr. 132
Burgess, Dean IV X, 395
Burgess family 358
Burgess, (Father) 503
Burgess, Marguerite Barco IX
Burgess, Nathaniel 94
Burgess, Nathaniel Wright 471
Burkhard, Thomas K. (Rear Admiral) 277
Burnt Mills, Lake 445
Burrage, Guy H. (Rear Admiral) 255
Burton, Susan H IX, 128, 463
burying grounds 353 *see also* grounds by name (i.e. Trinity Churchyard, Cedar Grove Cemetery, Oak Grove Cemetery, Lincoln Memorial Cemetery)
bus station *see* Greyhound Bus Station, Trailways Bus Station
buses, horse drawn 166
Bush, George W. H. (President of the United States) 230, 273
Bush, Jane 112, 344
Business Men's Association 466
Bustin, Thomas 20, 223
butchers 355
butler 327
Butler, Benjamin Franklin (General) 204, 205, 206, 207, 208, 238, 336, 478
Butler, George 270
Butler, Jane 37, 38
Butler, (Mrs.) 409
Butler, Willoughby G. 440
Butt, Bob 156, 327
Butt (Dr.) 130
Butt, Ellis (Mrs.) 370
Butt, J. W. S. (Mrs.) 363
Butt, James B. (Sargent) 106
Butt, Marshall, Sr. VIII, 6, 10, 13, 14, 253, 357, 395
Butt, Nancy 352
Butt, R. B. (Dr.) 352
Butt, Robert (Dr.) 354, 362, 480
Byers, (Captain) 202

Byrd, Richard E. (Admiral) 249
Byron, (Lord) 383

C

Café Europa 453
Caffey's Inlet 279
Cahoon, Lake 445
Cain, M. T. 126
Caldwell, David (the Reverend Mr.) 484
California 301, 480
California gold rush 428
Call, Daniel 94
Callao (ship) 218
Calvary Baptist Church 287, 294
Cameron, Daniel (Corporal) 106
Camilla (ship) 47
"Camille" 389
Camp Carson *see* Carson, Camp
Campbell, Joseph (Captain) 256
Campbell, Robert Monroe (Dr.) 522
Campbell, William (Colonel) 58
Canada 34, 49, 58, 283
Canadian Chasseurs 97
canals chapter 16, 147, 148, 149, 216, 420 *see also* canals by name (i.e. Albermarle and Chesapeake Canal, Dismal Swamp Canal)
cane 110
Cannon, Charles 344
cannons 36, 45, 60, 101, 102, 129, 135, 139, 180, 183, 184, 190, 218, 228, 235, 247, 248, 253, 258, 275, 306, 367
Cape Breton 10
Cape Charles 149
Cape Fear 149
Cape Hatteras 279
Cape Horn 233
Cape Lookout 149
Capes, Battle of the 78, 375
Capital Port 420
Captain of the Port 282
Caravas, Speros 450
card playing 381, 383
careening ships 20
careening ground 223
Carey, (Lieutenant) 230
Carey, Lott 330
Carleton, Guy (Sir, General) 344
Carlin, George 390
Carmichael, Edith IX
Carnegie, Andrew 289

Carney family 302
Carney, Richard 470
Carney, Samuel 111
Carpenter, John R. 505
Carr, George H. (Dr.) 312
Carr, Jesse 494
Carr, Thomas 185
Carr, William N. 132
carriages 457
Carribean 234, 353, 418
Carson, Camp 61
Carson, Johnny *see* Johnny Carson Show
Carson, Robert 111
Carter 151
Carter, Edward (Captain) 110
Carter, Jimmy (President of the United States) 273
Carthage 29
Cartier, Betsy 352
Carver, Richard 4
Carver, William (Captain) 3, 4, 5, 6, 7
Carvette Pucelle (ship) 78
Casino 393
Cassell and Cassell 480
Cassell, Charles 110, 197, 374, 487
Cassell, Norman 353
Cassin, John (Captain) 254
Casteen, John 245
Catholic Club 366, 464
Catholic High School 413
Catholic schools 413
Cavalier Manor 245, 291, 298, 396, 519
Cavilla (submarine) 133
Cedar Grove Cemetery 78, 80, 82, 106, 107, 117, 161, 177, 231, 240, 352, 421, 429, 437, 438, 482
Celtic cross 470
cemeteries chapter 38 *see also* cemeteries by name (i.e. Cedar Grove, Trinity, Portsmouth Naval Hospital Cemetery)
Cemetery Ridge, Battle 211
Centenary Ball 384
Centenary United Methodist Church 301
Centennial in Philadelphia 392
Centipede (ship) 102, 103, 105
Central Fidelity Bank 525
Central Methodist Church 338, 490, 508
Cevera, Pasqual (Admiral) 217, 266
Ceylonese Corporation 447, 448
Chai, H. J. 451
chain to protect the harbor 98
Challenger (Space Shuttle) 520

Chamber of Commerce 456, 523, 525 *see also* Portsmouth Chamber of Commerce and Hampton Roads Chamber of Commerce
chamber pots 207
Chambers *see* Miles, Chambers and Hathaway
Chambers, (Fire Chief) 121
Chambers, George (Captain) 95, 120, 121, 158, 384, 402
Chambers Fire Company 121, 125
Chandler, John A. 349, 423
Chandler, Mary 411
Chandler, Mary Eliza 423
Channel, Mary Brown 298
Chapel Hill (plantation) 26
chaplain, British Army *see* Andrews, William
chaplain, Confederate *see* Peterson, P. A. (Reverend)
chaplain, Virginia Militia *see* Braidfoot, John (the Reverend Mr.)
Chapman's Grocery 244
Chapman's Jewelry 450
Charette Health Care Center 274
Charette, William R. (Master Chief Corpsman) 274
Chariot, Pierre Raphael (Captain) 61
Charles I (King of England) 257
Charleston, South Carolina 49, 50, 135, 192
Charleston, West Virginia 58, 171
Charlotte, North Carolina 201
Chase, Joseph (Reverend) 508
Chase, Salmon P. 499
Chasseurs Britanique 97
Chateau Thierry, Battle of 24, 63
Chautauquas 294
Cheevers, Mark (the Reverend Mr.) 475
chemical plants 447, 448
Cheriton 44
Cherub (ship) 233
Cherry, Arthur L. 521
Cherry, Bradford L. 524
Cherry Carpet Company 521, 524
Cherry, Dempsey 172
Cherry, Roy 128
Chesapeake 285, 331, 405, 440
Chesapeake Bay 279
Chesapeake Bay Bridge Tunnel 280
Chesapeake (ship) 9, 122, 227, 228, 229, 230

Chesapeake Square Mall 457
Chesapeake Tribe 2
Cheshire Grill 18
Chester's Station, Battle of 214
Chestnut Street School 330, 339, 413
Chestnut Street Station 140
Chevra Thellem 510
Chicago 297, 372
Chichester (ship) 482
chicken 313, 359
Chicomicomico Life Saving Station 279
Child and Family Services 528
Children's Museum of Virginia 143, 384, 393, 457, 458, 526
Childs (Engineer) 89
Chimere, La (ship) 161, 271
chimney sweeps 443
Chimo/Piscataqua (ship) 252
China Garden 450, 456
Chinese 272
Chisholm, James (the Reverend Mr.) 152, 153, 484, 485
Chiswell, Benjamin Maurice (Captain) 283
chloroform 389, 463
choirs 481, 484, 500, 501
Christ Church Norfolk 474
Christ Church Philadelphia churchyard 76
Christian Broadcasting Network 451
Christian Church 509
Christian, Zita Winterberg 395
Christian's Bill Beaver (horse) 378
Christmas Craft Shop 457
Christmas decorations *see* Winter Wonderland
Christmas illumination 468
Christmas mugs 356
Chuckatuck Church *see* Saint John's Chuckatuck
Church (Lietenant) 68
Church Creek 7, 286
Church of England 337, 470
Church Point 286
Church, Randolph (State Librarian) 331
Churchland 111, 123, 297, 299, 300, 301, 394, 435, 438, 458, 483
Churchland Academy 300
Churchland Baptist Church 301, 507
Churchland Branch Library 394, 458
Churchland Bridge 287
Churchland High School 312, 447, 524

Churchland Methodist Church 300
churches chapter 40 *see also* churches by name
Cicero 29
Cienfuegos, Cuba 132
Cimarron (ship) 253
Cincinnati 297
Circle Restaurant 312
Circuit Court 127, 373
circumnavigation 241
circus 286, 390, 391
cisterns 265, 306
Citizens' Trust Bank 353, 494, 528
City Council 197, 290, 414, 508
city directories 446
City Hall 355
city managers chapter 41
City Park 4, 133, 438
City Point 55
City Vision 2005 Project 453
Civic Center Complex 163, 517
Civil Court 127
Civil Rights 508
Civil War 26, 92, 125, 132, 146, 170, 176, 205, 219, 232, 252, 270, 286, 291, 337, 350, 363, 373, 421, 434, 447, 463, 478, 485, 491, 499, 504, 508
Civil War veterans chapter 25
Clark, David H. (Rear Admiral) 256
Clark, John 501
Clark, Mahlon 388
Clay Banner and Naval Intelligencer 423
Clay, Henry 372, 373, 423
clay marbles 404
Cleaton, T. L. 290
Cleborne, Christopher J. (Medical Director) 275
Clerk of Court's Office 383
Cleveland, Grover (President of the United States) 494
Cleveland, Richard (Reverend) 494
Clinton, Henry (Sir, Commander of His Majesty's Forces) 42, 46, 47, 49, 53, 56, 57
clipper ships 432
clock, town 120
closets 317
Cluverius, Wat T. (Rear Admiral) 255
coal 289, 291, 303, 432, 519
Coast Guard 107, 133, 272, chapter 29
Coast Guard Base Portsmouth 280, 282, 517

Coast Guard Buoy Yard 280
Coast Guard Reserve 281
Coast Guard Station *see* 5th Coast Guard District and 6th Coast Guard District
Coast Guard Station at Craney Island 282, 300
Cobbler Shop at the Naval Shipyard 274
Cock Island Race and sailing regatta 20, 526
Cockburn, George (Sir, Rear-Admiral) 97, 105, 112
cockfighting 379, 380, 381
cockfighting pits 379, 380
Cocke, (Dr.) 158
Cocke, John 359, 479, 480
Cocke, Leonard 351
Cocke, William 402
Coco Beach United Methodist Church in Florida 520
Codd House 245
Codd, J. A. 245
Codd, Jake 288
Cody, Buffalo Bill 391
Cofer, Thomas W. 186
coffee 39, 421
coffee houses 384, 456
coffins 157, 209, 238
Cogentrics 452
Cold War 527
Cole, Cortlandt (Dr.) 161
Cole, William C. (Rear Admiral) 255
Coleman, Henry A. 386, 387
Coleman, John C. (Dr.) 161, 264
Coleman's Nursery 394, 458, 526
Colley, Georgia Carter 330
Collier, George (Sir, Commodore of His Majesty's Fleet) chapter 5, 223, 258, 261, 293
Collins, Arthur 412
Collins, Charles W. 214
Collins, Daniel (Mayor) 516
Collins, George 172
Collins, John 119
Collins, Nancy 130
Collins, William 143
Colman's Honeymoon 389
Colmar, Peter V. (Rear Admiral) 283
Colonial Apartments 358
Colonel Crawford Common project 522
Colonial Revival style 288, 293
Colony Theater 450
Colorado (ship) 239

Colored Troops 132 *see also* 4th U. S. Colored Troops
Colquitt, Alfred (Colonel) 183
Colter family 76
Columbia, PA 161
Columbia (ship) 240
Columbian (ship) 235
Columbus, Christopher 293
Columbus Life Guards of Georgia 183, 184
Comfort Inn 127
Commandant's House *see* Medical Director's House and Quarters A
Commander of the Marine Corps *see* Marine Corps, Commander of the
Commerce Bank 528
Commercial Place in Norfolk 86, 87, 141
commission merchants 446
Commissioners of the Navy 224
Committee of Claims (House of Burgesses) 10
Committee of Safety *see* Virginia Committee of Safety
Commodore Richard Dale Chapter of the DAR 77
Commodore Theater 146, 229, 289, 374, 450, 472
Community Action Committed 523
Community Chest 518
Community Trust Bank 526
Concas, Victor M. (Captain) 221, 266
Cone, Grace 529
confectioner's shop 430, 446
Confederacy (ship) 47
Confederate Army 176 *see also* Confederate States Army
Confederate Memorial Day 197, 272
Confederate monument, Norfolk 87, 141
Confederate monument, Portsmouth 197
Confederate Navy *see* Confederate States Navy
Confederate States Army 177, 265, 270, 325, 351, 358, 410, 421, 486, 515
Confederate States Navy 177, 180, 182, 187, 191, 197, 198, 201, 272, 367
Confederate States (ship) 184
Confederate Veterans *see* Stonewall Camp Confederate Veterans
confederate Window at Trinity Church 213, 325, 477
Congregational church 289
Congress *see* United States Congress

Congress (ship) 192, 193, 252, 271
Congressional Medal of Honor 132, 176, 227, 267, 272, 274
Congreve rockets 97, 102
Conner, Abigail (Craford) 8, 344
Conner, Betsey 344
Conner, Keader 9
Conner, Mary 344
Conner, Prudence 344
Conner, William 344
Connoly, T. O. 400
Conrad's Life of Rev. James Chisholm 160
Consort (ship) 235
Constable see Town Constable
Constantimopal 361
Constellation (ship) 98, 100, 107, 227, 233, 252
Constitution (ship) 228, 235, 237, 270, 419, 486
consumption 461
containerized cargo 291, 517
Continental Army 35, 91, 349, 471
Cook, James 177
Cook, Sterling S. (Rear Admiral) 276
Cooke family 286
Cooke, Giles Buckner (Reverend) 185
Cooke, James Wallace (Captain) 367
Cooke, John K. 185
Cooke, Maury Wise 526
Cooke, Mordecai 93, 119, 286, 291
Cooke, Olivia 502
Cooke, Patric Henry 286, 506
Cooke, Sanford (Dr.) 367
Cooke Street School 412, 413
Cooke, Virginia 286, 290
Cooke, Wallace 367
cooking 308, 309, 310, 342, 343
Cooley, Norman V. (Rear Admiral) 276
Cooper, J. E. 506
Cooper, Willie 128
Cooper, Willis 128
Copeland, Allen (Corporal) 172
copper mines 447
copyright X
cordwayner 38
corn 215
Cornick (Captain) 89
Cornick, James 479
Cornick, Joel 379
Cornwallis, Charles Earl (General) 37, 49, chapter 8, 78, 80, 364, 371, 375, 416

Cornwallis (prison ship) 67
Cornwallis (ship) 40, 41, 50
Corprew, E. G. (Reverend) 338
Corprew, G. M. 126
Corps of Engineers 149
Corregidor, forts 218
Corsica 78
Costello, John D. (Rear Admiral) 284
cotillions 365, 384, 456
cotton 146, 183, 196
Cotton, Charles S. (Rear Admiral) 255
cotton oil 146, 194, 201
Countess of Scarborough (ship) 71
Coupes 77
Court Marshal 229
Court of Hustings 167
Court Street Academy 501
Court Street Baptist Church 78, 158, 336, 337, 364, 400, 438, chapter 40
Court Street Presbyterian 495
Courthouse 13, 118, 163, 176, 202, 347, 422, chapter 38, 452, 460 see also 1846
Courthouse Gallery
Courthouse Annex 120
Courthouse, Norfolk 440
Courthouse Square 13
Courtland Library 170
courtroom 127
Covington, Richard W. 132
Cowan, Ralph Wolfe 388
Cowdery, A. A. 479
Cowley, Stephen 402
Cowpens, Battle of 37
Cowper Brothers 65
Cowper, John 63, 64, 65, 419
Cox family 23
Cox farm 295
Cox, John (Captain) 62, 63, 78, 225, 500
Cox, (Mrs.) 201
Cox, Richard 338, 498
Cox, Russell Mills (Dr.) 521
Coxe family 23, 24
Coxe, Godfrey 94
Coxe, John see Cox, John (Captain)
Cox's Island 20, 23
Crab Creek 7, 20, 23, 166, 223, 304, 419, 437
Crab Creek Bridge 23
Crab Shop 342
Crab Square 7
crabs 307, 342
Cradock 244, 245, 247, 285, 349

Cradock Branch Library 244
Cradock, Christopher (Sir, Admiral) 244
Cradock High School 244, 312, 396
Cradock Methodist Church 244
Cradock Presbyterian Church 244
Crafford family 8 *see also* Craford and Crawford
Crafford house 8
Craford, Abigail *see* Conner, Abigail (Crawford)
Craford, Abigail (Mason) 9
Craford family 8 *see also* Crafford and Crawford
Craford, George 9
Craford, William (Colonel) Chapter 2, 85, 87, 453, 470 *see also* Crawford, William
Craft, Thomas 496
Cramton Gap, Battle of 211, 215
Craney Island 96, 99, 107, 111, 196, 280, 282, 285, 300, 344, 452
Craney Island, Battle of chapter 11-12, 146, 176, 261, 367, 375, 472
Craney Island Artillery 213
craps 128
Crapster, Thaddeus Greaves (Captain) 283
Crater, Battle of the 179, 215
cravats 429
Crawford, Abigail *see* Conner, Abigail (Crawford)
Crawford Bay 37, 54, 149, 231, 340
Crawford, C. S. 434
Crawford House Hotel 351, 455
Crawford Parkway 340, 371
Crawford Street Parking Ramp 422
Crawford, William chapter 2, (Colonel) 472 *see also* Craford, William (Colonel)
Creech, Jeremiah 470

Creech, Thomas 470
creeks *see* creeks by name (i.e. Crab Creek, Windmill Creek
Creighton, J. Blakeley (Commodore) 255
creosote plant 231
Creyke, (Captain) 45
cricket 377, 381, 412
Crocker, Clara 411
Crocker, Frank 363
Crocker, James Francis (Superintendent of Schools(413
Crocker, Major (Judge) 366
Crockin, M. M. Furniture 434

Crockin, Meyer 434
Cromwell, Willis 333, 334, 335
Cross, Charles 9, 440
Crown Prince Wilhelm (ship) *see* Kronprinz Wilhelm (ship)
Crump. W. L. 435
Cuba 266, 333 *see also* Havana
Cubicle Two 268
Culpepper, H. E. 457
Culpepper, Henry 37
Culpepper, Jesse 491
Culpepper, Joseph 491
Cumberland (ship) 179, 180, 191, 192, 193, 271
Cummings, Southall 127
Cunningham (Captain) 67, 68
Cunningham, Alexander 110
Cunningham, John 344
Curle, Joshua 7, 257
Curtis, George 393
Curtis, George (Mrs.) 393
Curtis-Dunn Marine Shipyard 3
Cutherell, Samuel 479
cutters 283
Czech artist 374

D

Dahlgren guns 185, 186, 189
Dakota (ship) 239
Daily Grind Coffee Shop 53
Dale (ship) 77
Dale, Ann 68
Dale, David 10, 11, 36, 106
Dale Homes 250, 519
Dale, Prudence 367
Dale, Richard (Captain) 68, 69, 70, 71, 72, 73, 74, 75, 76, 77, 226, 254, 297
Dale-Reed House 11, 303, 437
Dale, Winfield 68
Dale's Point 297
Dam Neck Mills Life Saving Station 279
Dame Schools 407
dancing 384, 457, 464, 506
Daniels, Josephus 238
Danville 146, 452
Daughters of the American Revolution 77, 115, 265, 471 *see also* Fort Nelson Chapter of the DAR and Commander Richard Dale Chapter of the DAR
Daughters of the Confederacy *see* United Daughters of the Confederacy

Daughtery, M. J. (Dr.) 494
Davenport-Lewis Chevrolet 525
David's Night Club 450
David's Seaman's Marine Store 291
Davis, (Captain.) 426
Davis, Charles H. (Rear Admiral) 255
Davis, Edward 4
Davis family 353
Davis Farm, Battle of 214
Davis, Hubert J. 396
Davis, Jefferson (President of the Confederate States of America) 195, 205, 206
Davis, L. H. (Mayor) 516
Davis, (Mrs.) 481
Davis, Rachel 4
Davis, Richard J. (Mayor, Lt. Governor) 451, 452, 517, 523
Day, David 78
Day, John 350
Day, Laura 350
Deal, Peter 172
Deal, William Franklin "Bill" 388
Dean, William 344
Deane (ship) 47
Deans, Benjamin 110, 172
Deans, (Miss) 413
Deans, Solomon 471
debating societies 394
debts 343
Decatur, Stephen 75, 180, 229, 235, 236, 290
Deck, the 457
Decoration Day 272
Deep Creek 23, 89, 175, 285, 299, 406
Deerfield, New Hampshire 205
de Grasse, François Joseph Paul, compte (Admiral) 59, 78, 375
DeLacy, (Father) 503
de la Roche, George F. (Master) 103, 108
Delaware (ship) 233, 234, 235, 240, 372
Delight (ship) 51
Democrat 423
Democratic Convention in Charleston, SC 205
Democratic Party 125, 406, 517
Denby, Edward 172
dental clinic at the Naval Hospital 273
dentists 448
Dentzil, (Mrs.) 429
deOtte, Delef Frederick Argentino (Lt. Commander) 283

Department of Homeland Security 283
Department of the Treasury 279, 281, 282
Department of Transportation 282
Department of Virginia and North Carolina 207
Depression 299, 312
Derr, James 481
desegregation 331 *see also* segregation
Desert, the 371
deserters 104, 209
designers 388
DesPlains Valley 372
deSteiguer, Louis R. (Commodore) 255
de Tilley (Admiral) 55
DeValin, Charles M. (Captain) 276
Devil's Reach 420
Devlin, Francis (Reverend Father) 152, 153, 158, 503
Dewey, (Admiral) 218
Diadem (ship) 102
Diamond, Jarred M. 155
Dickey, (Lieutenant) 43, 44
Dickenson, Thomas Bowers 78, 82
Dickson family 23, 24, 419
Dickson, Hannah 419
Dickson, Henry (Captain) 419
Dickson, Jane 494
Dickson, John (Captain) 419
Dickson, Richard 479
Dickson, Sarah 419
Dickson, Selina 88
Dickson, William (Captain) 419, 474
Dickson's wharf 419
Dictionary of Virginia Biography 9
Diligence (ship) 49
Diligent (ship) 40
Dill, M. T. 290
dining cars 433
Dinwiddie Courthouse, Battle of 212, 214
Dinwiddie Hotel *see* Governor Dinwiddie Hotel
Dinwiddie Realty Corporation 167, 373
Dinwiddie, Robert (Royal Governor of Virginia) 14
Discovery (ship) 3
Dismal Swamp 12, 41, 147, 304, 447, 456
Dismal Swamp Canal Company 148
Dismal Swamp Rangers 211, 264
Dismal Swamp Road 273 *see also* Washington Oak
Disney Studios 388

distilleries *see* Liquor, rye, gin and rum
District of Columbia 105
divorce 370
Dixie Drive Inn 312
Dixon, David 237
Dobbs, (Elder) 499
Doctor Cox's House 363
Doehla, Johann Conrad 50
dogs 30
dogs, iron Newfoundland 464
Dolly Vardens 430
Dolphin (ship) 180, 185, 240
Dominican Republic 502
Don Juan 389
Donohue, David P. (Commodore) 256
Doolittle, James H. 250
Doolittle, James H. (Mrs.) 250
Dornin, Thomas (Commodore) 254, 465
Doubletree hotel chain 528
Doughty, William 184
Douglas, Catherine (Sprowle) *see* Sprowle, Catherine
Douglas, Francis 30
Douglas, Jane Shore 389
Douguld, Barbary 493
Doulton, Caroline 263
Downing, Fanny Murdaugh 423, 424
Downing, John (Mrs.) 363
Downs (ship) 248
Downtown Tunnel *see* tunnel, downtown
Dowson, Johnny 128
Doyle, Robert M. (Rear Admiral) 255
Dozoretz, Ronald (Dr.) 289
dramatic clubs 393
drawbridge from Berkeley to the Shipyard 233
dressmakers 429
Drinane's Coffee House 384, 456
drive-in movies and restaurants 312
Driver, I. 127, 137, 148
drug addiction 522
drug trade 283, 295
drunkenness 122, 180, 329, 460, 473
Drury, William (Sargent) 106
Drury's Bluff, Battle of 214
Drury's Tavern 352, 455
Dry Dock #1 181, 182, 225, 234, 243, 354, 478
Dry Dock #2 241
Dry Dock #3 241
Dry Dock #4 243
Dry Dock #5 243

Dry Dock #6 243, 247
Dry Dock #7 243, 247
Dry Dock #8 249, 251
dry docks 20, 249
dry goods 433, 446
dry rubbing floors 408
DuBose, William R. (Medical Director) 276
Ducachet, Henry (the Reverend Mr.) 474, 475
Duccoing, (Mons.) 457
duels 229, 236, 290, 482
Duffen, Esther 511
Duffen, Irving 511
Duke, Emily 299
Duke, Fred A. (Mayor) 516
Duke of Kent 249
Dulany, Blanden (Midshipman) 103
Dumar, (Judge) 509
Dumar's Restaurant 312
Duncan, Daniel W. 524
Dunmore, John Murray, Viscount Fincastle, Barron of Blair, of Moulin and Tillymount, Earl of (Royal Governor of Virginia) chapter 4, 112, 224, 257, 329, 333, 343, 470
Dunmore (ship) 46
Dunmore's Proclamation 34 *see also* emancipation
Dunn, Edward (Ensign) 172
Dusey and Jones 281
Dutch 3
Dutch Roofed Houses 166 *see also* Tax Dodger Houses
Dutton, W. C. 428
Duval, Marius (Surgeon) 275
Duvayrier, Bernard 370
Duvayrier, (Captain) 369, 370
Duvayrier, Melaine 370
Dwartz, Henry 292
Dyson, George 88, 172
Dyson, (Miss) 395
Dyson, William 95, 491

E

Eagle (ship) 135, 280
Eagle House 181, 240
Eagle Tavern 95
Earl Industries 251
Early, Barbara 364
Early, John (Bishop) 490

History of Portsmouth, Virginia

Early, E. Saunders 164, 364, 522
East India trade 23
Easter Egg Hunt 301
Eastern Branch of the Elizab4eth River 223
Eastern Shore 27, 32, 62, 475, 509
Eastern Virginia Medical School 529
Eastes, George Delman (Vice Mayor, General) 523
Eastwood, Elisha 471
Eastwood, M. D. 487
Ebenezer Baptist Church 337
Eberwine Canning Company 302, 447
Eccles, James (Sargent) 172
Ecker William J. (Rear Admiral) 284
Economic Development Department 453, 468
Ecuador 521
Edinburgh Square Parking Ramp 457
Edo Bay 236
Edwards, Amos (Corporal) 110, 172
Edwards and Happer 460
Edwards, Belle 208
Edwards, Bertha W.3 IX, 330, 331, 394
Edwards farm 379
Edwards, Gifford R. (Superintendent of Schools) 413
Edwards, Griffin F. 184
Edwards, John 379
Edwards, Thomas 78
Effingham, Fancis Howard, Barron Howard (Royal Governor General of Virginia) 15, 317
Effingham YMCA 435
Egypt 75
electrical substation on Middle Street 340
electricity 265, 444
electrocardiograph 273
elephant 390, 391
elevators 269, 274, 467
Elite, the 450
Elizabeth City 137, 148, 154
Elizabeth City County 80
Elizabeth City State University 246
Elizabeth Manor 285
Elizabeth Manor Golf Course 298
Elizabeth River 1, 8, 85, 87, 148, 149
Elizabeth River Ferry *see* ferries
Elizabeth River freezes *see* Great Freeze
Elizabeth River Parish 95, 379, 469
Elizabeth River Project 231
Elizabeth (ship) 186, 202, 419

Elk's Lodge 365
Elliot, Missy 388
Elliot, Robert (Captain) 78
Ellis, Perry 388
Ellygood, Jacob 26
Elm Avenue Methodist Church 520
Elm Avenue Recreation Center 435
Ely, Eugene B. 242
Ely, (Miss) 142
emancipation 27, 323, 405 *see also* abolition
emancipation, voluntary 4, 326, 328
Emanuel A. M. E. Church 109, 158, 336, 337, 338, 339, 341, 342, 388, 491 *see also* Glasgow Street Methodist Church
Emanuel Episcopal Church 244, 482
Embargo Act 418
Emmerson, Arthur (Captain) 99, 101, 102, 103, 106, 119, 129, 145, 146, 200, 375, 384, 464, 473, 479
Emmerson, Arthur (the Reverend Mr.) 146, 374, 472, 473
Emmerson files VIII
Emmerson House 374
Emmerson, John Clloyd VIII, 135, 426
Emmerson, Louisa 10, 129
Emory, William H. (Rear Admiral) 241
Empress of China *see* Tsu Si
Emurian, Ernest K. (Reverend) 520
engagement 320
engines, railroad *see* locomotives
English Basement style 8, 19, 315, 369, 440, 489
English Channel 227
Enterprise 424
Enterprise (ship) 75, 252
Enterprise Zones 452
Episcopaleans 311, 483 *see also* trinity Church, Stain Johns Church, Emanuel Episcopal Church, Saint James and Saint Christophers
Epps, (Lieutenant) 219
Ericson, Leif
Ericsson, John 189
Ericsson's Folly 189
escalator 457
Escambria (ship) 186, 202
Eskridge, (Reverend) 158
Essex (ship) 233
Etherage, Alexander 172
Etheridge, Amos 20, 35, 36, 79
Etheridge, Hannah 36

Etheridge, Moses 172
Etheridge, Powers 36, 79
Ethiopian Brigade 26, 27, 329
Eustalea 79
Eustis, Abraham 447
Eustis, Anne 447
Eustis family 447
Eustis, Fort 8
Eustis, Peter 447, 524
Evans, George 94
Evans, Robley D. (Rear Admiral) 241
Evans, Samuel (Captain) 254
Ewell, George T. 521
Ewing, John 304
Executives Club 521

F

F. W. Woolworth *see* Woolworths Five and Ten
Fairfax, (Captain) 185
Fairwood Homes 250, 299
Fajardo, (Lieutenant) 221
False Cape 279
famine 156
Famous Department Store 13, 403, 435, 463, 467, 527
Fanning, Edmond (Lt. Governor of the Island of St. John) 50
Fantone's children's clothing store 385
Farland, Z. S. (the Reverend Mr.) 486
FarmFresh Grocery 454
Farquhar, Norman H. (Rear Admiral) 255
Farragut, David (Admiral) 233, 238, 239
Farrin, James M. (Rear Admiral) 256
Farrin, Nelly 388
fashion show 467
fashions 429, 430
Fass, Catherine 511
Fass, Isaac 426
Fass, Sol 511, 519, 520
Fass Borthers Coal and Ice 519
"Fatal Marriage" 389
Faulkner, James (Major) 99, 101, 102, 103
Fechtele, Augustus F. (Rear Admiral) 255
Federal Building 351, 352, 410
Federal Period 262, 316, 352
Ferabee, (Mrs.) 467
Ferebee, John 470
Ferebee, Nelson M. (Assistant Surgeon) 276

Ferguson, Patrick (Major) 50
Ferries 10, 22, chapter 10, 130, 140, 147, 183, 204, 216, 273,333, 350, 357, 363, 377, 391, 418, 443, 455, 479
Ferry Point 13, 18, 90, 141
Ferry Street 18
fertilizer plants 447
Fifth Avenue Methodist Church 297
Fifth Coast Guard District *see* 5th Coast Guard District
figureheads 234, 240
Fin Castle (ship) 46
Findlay, Fred 298
fire departments, private 110 chapter 13 *see also* Independent Fire Company, Phoenix Fire Company, Chambers Fire Company, Rescue Fire company and Resolute Fire Company
fire engines 118, 119, 122 *see also* hose engine and water set
fire stations 340, 460
"Fireman's Bride" 122
fireplaces 316
fires 30, 45, chapter 13, 143, 147, 290, 333, 352, 385, 404, 426, 434, 436, 455, 466, 467, 486, 487, 491, 494, 504, 507
First Baptist Church 246
First Baptist Church of Pinners Point 291, 362
First Citizens Award 365, chapter 41
First Colored Church of Portsmouth 338
First Evangelical Lutheran Church 506, 507
First National Bank 384
First Presbyterian Church 237, 485, chapter 40, 487
fish market 95, 520
Fishborne Military School 358
Fishel, Frederick H., Jr. 82
Fisher, Fort, Battle of 207
Fiske, D. D. (Editor, Mayor) 158, 166, 339, 423, 515 *see also* Wilson and Fiske Printing
Fiske, Melzer 423
Fiske, Theophilus 423
Fiske, William 211, 212, 412, 423
Five Forks, Battle of 205, 212, 214
flagpole at High Street Landing 132
flags 73, 101, 132, 175, 176, 184, 192, 195, 202, 203, 212, 213, 214, 225, 228 *see also* Grand Union Flag, Palmetto Flag, Don't Tread On Me flag,

Confederate Flag
Flagship Restaurant 287
flagstaff at Town Square 175, 176
Flamborough Head 71, 73
Flanders, Alan VII, 11, 125, 188, 226, 230, 326, 327, 381
Fleet Emergency Corps 243
Fleming *see* White and Fleming Oyster Packers
Fleming, P. Stockton 523
Flemish bond 111
flight deck, first fitted on a ship 242
flint lock muskets 212
flooding 37, 460
floors, maintaining 408
Flora (ship) 419
Flora, William "Billy" 27, 328, 329, 245, 358
Florida 146, 149
Florida (ship) 252
florists 319
flu *see* influenza
Flying Squadron, Schley's 217
foot stoves 481
football 382
Forbes, Betty 458
Forbes, William 500
Ford's Theatre 424
foreign docks 333
Foreman, (General) 112
Foreman, John 113, 115, 165, 419, 432
Foreman, Rebecca 510
Foresquare style 294
Forest, (Mr.) 338, 416
Forestal (ship) 252
Forrest, French (Captain, VA State Navy & CSN) 254
Forsythe family 357
Forsythe, (Mrs.) 38
Fort *see* forts by name (i.e. Eustise, Fort)
Fort Nelson *see* Nelson, Fort
Fort Nelson Chapter of the DAR 260
Fort Nelson Park 265, 274, 275, 444
Fort Norfolk *see* Norfolk, Fort
Fort Point 258
fortifications 54
Fortunatus (ship) 43
Forward (ship) 282
Foster, John 496
foundries 432
Fourth Baptist Church 338
Fourth Street Baptist Church 365, 498

Fowler, James (Captain) 115
Fowler, Samuel (Captain) 115
fox hunting 377
Fox, Josiah 228
Fox, Leslie Talbot (Mayor) 516, 519
France 34, 70, 226, 448, 502, 503
franchises 451
Frank D. Lawrence Stadium 382, 518
Franklin, Benjamin 76
Franklin (fire engine) 124
Franklin (ship) 252
Frederick Military Academy 289, 410, 521
Frederick College 289, 521
Fredericksburg 58
Fredericksburg, Battle of 214
Fredericksburg (ship) 426
Frederickton, New Brunswick 34
Fredly, Michael 37, 38
free blacks 346
free exercise of religion 414
free schools 401, 405
Free Trade Zone 452
Freedly, Michael 37, 38
Freedom Fort *see* Monroe, Fortress
Freeman, Charles S. (Rear Admiral) 256
Freeman, William 411
French and Indian War 24
French government 21, 161
French language 408
French mercenaries 105
French Revolution *see* Revolution, French
French sailors 270
French West Indies 62, 502 *see also* Haiti
Frenchtown and Newcastle, Deleware 146
Fresh Air Farm 289
Fresnel lense 280
Friedman, Jerome B. 414
Friend's Church 404
Friendship Chapel 509
Fulham Castle Chapel 472
funeral parlors 367
funerals 310, 318, 319, 320
Funsten, James B. (the Reverend Mr.) 475, 480
furniture factory 294

G

Galena (ship) 132, 195

Galt, (Mrs.) 481
Gambier, James (Commodore of His Majesty's Fleet) 40
gambling 128, 257, 381, 383, 473 *see also* cock fighting, horse racing
Gamewell Police Telegraph 128
Ganges (ship) 75, 227
garbage-fueled power-plant 252
Garden of Prayer 508
Garrett, Tom 382
Garrick Club 393
Gartert, Order of the *see* Order of the Garter
Gas House Lane 444
gas lamps 127, 443, 444
gas stations 367 *see also* Tanker Car Gas Station
Gashouse Creek 265
Gaskins, James 79, 364
Gaskins' Lane 37, 364
gaslights 265, 294
Gaston, Lake 445
Gates Theater 467
Gathorne-Hardy, G. H. 1
Gayle *see* Ryan and Gayle
Gayle, Blister 412
Gayle, Levin 80, 412
Gayle, Nat (Captain) 172
Geddes, Robert 422
George III (King of England) 104, 235, 416
George Post & Sons 244
George, George (Signor) 392, 464, 467
George W. Maupin Ice and Coal Company 426, 427
George Washington (ship) 247
Georgia Navy 49
Georgia Troops 185
Germain, George (Lord) 40, 48
German sailors 242, 270, 271
German spies 124
German Village 242, 243
Germans *see* the various Heeian regiments
Germans interned at the Shipyard 242, 243
Germantown, Battle of 407
Germantown (ship) 180, 185
Germany 506
gerrymandered 286
Gettysburg, Battle of 211, 213, 214, 358
Ghio, Enoch 386

Ghio, (Mr.) 386
Ghio's Garden 385, 386
Ghost Walk 374, 471
ghosts 38, 262
Gibbs family 108
Gibralter 75
Gihon, Albert L. (Medical Director) 275
Gill, Frances 356
Gill, Franklin 96
Gill, J. R. 356
Gilbert, Thomas 5
Gill and Thomas 89
Gill House 37
Gilmerton 445
gin 421
Girls Club 435
Girls Inc. 528
Glasgow, Scotland 30
Glasgow Street Methodist Church 109, 335, 491 *see also* Monumental Methodist Church and Emanuel A. M. E. Church
Glasgow Street Pier 123
Gleason, (Lieutenant) 211, 238
Gleason, James 94
glebe, the 7, 42, 83, 292, 399, 469
Glebe Church 33
Glebe House 293
Glebe School 293, 295, 399
Glencoe Bed and Breakfast 36
Glendale 285
Glensheallah 285, 287, 297, 464
Globe Tavern 455
Glover, David Carr 388
Gluse, Michael R. (Captain) 256
Godspeed (ship) 3
Godwin, Ben 328
Godwin, John W. 338
Godwin, (Judge) 366
Godwin, L. C. 447
Godwin, (Mrs.) 366
Godwin, Richard 142
Godwin, Robert 328
Godwin, Thomas (Major, Lietenant) 34, 101, 106
Godwin's Catchpenny (horse) 378
Goffigan, Laban 80, 358, 420
Goffigan, Mary 420
Gokey, Noah W. (Captain) 256
gold 334
Gold Rush 428
Goldblatt, Abe 382
Goldin, Foredeh 396

goldsmith 165
Goldsmith, Zachariah (the Reverend Mr.) 475
golf courses 250 *see also* by name (i.e. Bide-a-wee Golf Course, Elizabeth Manor Golf Course)
Gollihue, Alan 260
Gomez, (Dr.) 221
Gomley Chesed Synagogue 292 , 491, 508
Good, Edward 5
Goodman, Belle 467
Goodman, Isaac 467
Goodrich family 31, 46, 47
Goodrich, John 25, 31, 35, 36. 47
Gordon, George H. (General) 424
Gorsuch, George E. (Rear Admiral) 276
Gosport 8,20, 22, 26, 45, 88, 151, 181, 223, 363, 381, 385, 408, 419, 422, 462, 474, 490, 493, 498
Gosport Creek 54
Gosport Iron Works 124, 237
Gosport Navy Yard 7, 22, 43, 45, 46, 49, 61, 78, 79, 113, 223, 233, 415 *see also* Norfolk Navy Yard, Portsmouth Navy Yard, Norfolk Navy Yard in Portsmouth
Gosport (ship) 95
Gosport Village 7, 21, 163, 165, 285, 403, 452
gossiping 527
Gothic Revival style 365
Governor Dinwiddie Hotel, 467, 468, 528
Governor's Island (Gwynn's Island) 29
Governor's Island off New York City 282
Grace, Barbara X, 360
Grace Cathedral in San Francisco 480
Grace Church in Norfolk 336
Graham, R. W. 161
Graham, Tildsey 304
Grammy Award 388
Granberry, Louis (Sargent) 172
Grand Union Flag 132
Grant, George 172
Grant, Jordan W. 125
Grant Multiversal Nozzle 125, 126
Grant, Ulysses S. (General and President of the United States) 207, 239
Grant's, W. T., Five and Ten 384, 385
gravedigger 156
graving dock 234
Gray, Benjamin Dingley 471
Gray, Edwin 290

Gray, J. P. 132
Gray's horses 378
Grays see Light Infantry Grays of Portsmouth
Grayton (Commodore) 51
Great Bridge, Battle of 26, 27, 37, 66, 78, 81, 328, 329
Great Dismal Swamp *see* Dismal Swamp
Great Fire of 1821 chapter 13 *see also* fires
Great Freeze 96
Great White Fleet 241
Greece 450
Greek Liberty 458
Greek Revival style 316, 458
Green, Nathaniel (General) 50
Green Point, Long Island 189
Green, Zach 487
Greenback Party 205, 207
Greenhood, Charles 453, 510
Greenlakes 298
Gregory, (Elder) 500
Gregory, John 34
Grenville, Richard (Sir) 1
Greyhound Bus Stations 367, 434
Grice, Alexander 352
Grice, Alexander P. 111
Grice, Charles 110, 119, 480, 483
Grice, (Dr.) 364
Grice, Francis 237
Grice, Frank 362
Grice, George 439, 493
Grice, George Washington (Major, Mayor) 515
Grice, Joseph (Dr.) 487
Grice, Mary 494
Grice-Neely House 36, 237, 362, 363
Grice, Virginia 494
Griffin, Ben Boyd 435
Griffin, Diane Pomeroy 528
Griffith, David 200, 367
Grigsby, Benjamin (Reverend) 473, 492
Grigsby, Hugh Blair 493
Grimes Battery 106, 183, 211, 219, 264
Grimes, Cary F. (Captain) 211, 213
Grimes, Maximilian 471
Grimes, Thomas 470
Grimes, William 301
grocers 165, 431, 446
Grove Baptist Church 301
Guantanimo 217
Guards Regiment 42

Guerriere (ship) 233, 235, 236
Gulf of Mexico 283
Guthrie family 290
Guthrie, John J. (Captain) 272, 279
Guthrie, Joseph (Dr.) 272
Guy, Henry 94
Guy, William R. 110
Gwaltney hot dogs 295
Gwynne, Walter 37
Gwynn's Island 29, 36
Gygax, Felix X. (Rear Admiral, Mayor) 256, 518, 519

H

Habitat for Humanity 296
hack (hackney cab) 208, 320
Hackeley, (Mrs.) 412
Haerlem (ship) 40
Hagwood, Hazel 450
Hagwood's Dry Cleaning 450
Haiti 502 *see also* San Domingo and French West Indies
Hakluyt, Richard 1
Halifax, North Carolina 110
Halifax, Nova Scotia 29, 229
Hall, Elizabeth 37
Hall, Florence 412
Hall of Fame *see* Virginia Sports Hall of Fame
Hallahan, John M. 98
Hall's Jail 480
Halstead, J. T. 447
Ham, William, Sr. (Lieutenant) 80
Hamilton, (Mr.) 201, 203
Hamilton, Alexander 281
Hamilton, (General) 463
Hamilton, Norman R. X, 86, 421, 518
Hamilton, Richard 232
Hammerhead Crane 249
Hammond (ship) 46
Hammond, Andrew (Captain) 29, 30
Hampton 12, 39, 47, 49, 50, 105, 129
Hampton (ship) 177, 186
Hampton Place 373
Hampton Roads VII, 2, 99, 198
Hampton Roads Chamber of Commerce 525
Hampton Roads Transit Authority 87, 96
Hanbury, George Lafayette (City Manager) 11, 85, 87, 513, 514
Hanbury, John Paul Conwell VIII, 163, 288, 412, 524
Hanchett, John (Captain) 102, 103, 104
Hancock, Sophia 37
Handy, (Miss) 213
Handy, (Reverend) 158
Haneman, Herbert A., Jr. 526
hanging 386, 387
Hanging Tree Road 170
Hanrahan, Frank C. (City Manager) 171, 514
Hanrahan, J. W. 172
Hanrahan, Lucille 171
Hanrahan, William 177
Hansen, Susan (Dr.) 363
Hansen, Rob (Dr.) 363
Hansford, Elizabeth 420
Hanson, Edward 456
Hanvey, James Thomas (Mayor) 516
Happer *see* Edwards and Happer
harbor 21
Harbor Master 368, 420
harbor tours 468
Harbor Tower Apartments 85, 141
Hardee, Ernest F. 527
Harding, (Mr.) 354
hardtack 235, 258, 304
Hardy, Porter, Jr. (Congressman) 301, 520
Hargrave, William W. (Captain) 276
Harlem (ship) 40, 46
Harmony (ship) 185
Harp and Eagle Tavern 462
Harper, Charles F. (City Manager) 298, 514
Harper, Chandler F. 298
Harper, John 172
Harper, Lily 298
Harper's Ferry 171, 172
Harper's Ferry, Battle of 212, 214, 215
Harpers Weekly 175, 181
Harrell, I. M. 450
Harrell's Sporting Goods 450
Harrington, Purnell F. (Rear Admiral) 255
Harriet Lane (ship) 184, 213
Harrison, James F. (Dr.) 161, 264, 271
Harrison, (Mr.) 433
Harrison, Randolph (Dr.) 161, 264
Harrison's horses 378
Harry Hunt Junior High School 528
Hartt, Beverly 237
Hartt House 54, 237

Hartt, Samuel 158, 237
Hartt, William (Admiral) 237, 471
Harvey, Ellen 392
Harvey, Mary Ann 392
Haskell, Jean 450
Hatcher, John 525
Hathaway *see* Miles, Chambers and Hathaway
Hatteras Island 206, 238
Hatton, (Dr.) 158
Hatton family 42, 288
Hatton, Alexander 288
Hatton, Dempsey 411
Hatton, E. A. 471
Hatton, Francis 37, 38
Hatton, James L. 288, 479
Hatton, John 160, 161
Hatton, John D. 288
Hatton, John G. 351, 483
Hatton, William 288
Haug, M. E. (City Manager) 514
Havana, Cuba 21, 227
Haviland, John 262
Hawkins, Wilbert (Superintendent of Schools) 399
Hawks, Charles 288
Hawks, Edward B. 514
Hawthorn Suits 468, 528
Hay, Anthony 415
Hay, Joseph 80
Haynes, Alice IX, 86, 253
Haywards at Lamberts Point 379
health department 364
heart pine 333
Heath and Smith 146
Heffington, Molly 301
Heintz pickle factory 294
helicopters 283
Helm (ship) 248
Help and Emergency Response 528
hemp yarn 425
Hen Island 227
Henderson, Andrew (Surgeon) 275
Henderson, Andrew James (Captain) 283
Henley, Robert (Lieutenant) 254
Hennings Documents 99
Henry, Patrick (Governor of Virgnia) 62, 82, 329
Hepburn, Thomas 415
HER *see* Help and Emergency Response
Herbert, John 470
Herbert property 297

Herbert, William 211
Hercules 240
Hereth, Larry L. (Rear Admiral) 284
Hernden, Brodie 356
Hessian Regiment Von Bos 50 *see also* 42nd Prince Own Hessian and Anspach
Hessians 51, 471
Hester, Ralph 513
Heving, Joe 382
Hibbett, Charles T. (Medical Director) 276
hieroglyphics 169
Higbee, Lenah (Superintendent) 269
high school, first 413
High Street 11
High Street Hotel 455
High Street Landing 86
High Street School 330
Highland Biltmore 519
High's Ice Cream 450
highwaymen 482
highways *see* interstate highways and King's Highway
Hill, Abner B. 520
Hill and Ferguson 244
Hill, C. W. 128
Hill family 350, 362
Hill Horticultural Library 362
Hill House VIII, 317, 362, 423
Hill, John Thompson 361, 362, 411, 422
Hill, William 362
Hill, William C. 423
Hilton, James 250
Himalaya Mountains 250
Hindenburg (Zeplin) 136
Hines, Emily 395
Hispaniola 502
Historical Association *see* Portsmouth Historical Association
Historical Commission of the City of Portsmouth III
History Central 207
Hitchcock, Robert B. (Commodore) 255
Hoagland, Lewis A. 418
Hoalbut, W. 479
Hobday, John (Captain) 214
Hodges, Christopher 172
Hodges, (Colonel) 366
Hodges, Leon Carey, Jr. (Captain) 276
Hodges, James 471
Hodges, James J. (Dr. Mayor) 515
Hodges, Joel 94

Hodges, Matilda 326, 327
Hodges, (Mrs.) 366
Hodges Restaurant 457
Hodges, Solomon 471
Hodges, Thomas 211
Hodges, William 172
Hodges, Willis 326, 327
Hoechst-Ceylonese 447, 448
Hoffheimer's Shoes 435
Hoffler, (Major) 100
Hoffler, Thomas 471
Hoffler, William 471
Hoffler's Creek 100, 101, 245
hog fish 307
Hog Island lighthouse 280
hogs 61, 299
Hokwood, John 172
Holborn, F. K. 126
Holcomb, Richard C. (Captain) 261, 276
Holderness, George A., Jr. (Rear Admiral) 256
Holiday House 526
Holiday Inn 18, 54, 118, 340, 353, 457, 468
Holladay, Anthony (Colonel) 34
Holladay, Gray G. (Dr.) 237, 265, 487
Holladay, Gustavus 158
Holladay, James Gustavus 92, 158, 175, 286, 357, 465
Holladay, Mike 327
Holladay, Mildred M. X
Holladay Point 137
Holland, Bob 194
Holland, Charles 172
Holland (submarine) 241
Holley, James W., III (Dr., Mayor) 245, 331, 394, 517, 518
Hollingsworth, Bobby F. (Rear Admiral) 284
Holmead, Charles H. (the Reverend Mr.) 82, 115
Holy Angels Church *see* Roman Catholic Church of the Holy Angels
Home for the Aged 359
homespun 39
honeymoons 321
Hood's Battery 54
hoop skirts 429
hop 464
Hope, Frank Stanley (Dr., Mayor) 126, 516
Hope, George J. S. B. 425

Hope, James Barron 236, 425
Hopkins, Thomas 411
Hopwell, Harry 312
horse boat 88, 95, 333
horse collars 301
horsehair 316
horse racing 286, 377, 378
horses 88, 122, 140, 166, 180, 300, 305, 378, 460
Horster family 358
Horton, Phineas (City Manager) 513, 514
hose cart 122
Hospital Corps 268
Hospital Point 29, 35, 38, 227, 239 *see also* Windmill Point, Mosquito Point
hospital ships 266
hospitals 152, 183, 286, 463, 466, 474, 478 *see also* hospitals by name (i.e. King's Daughters, Portsmouth General Hospital, Marryview Hospital)
hotels 294, 327, 351, 364, chapter 39 *see also* hotels by name (i.e. Oak Grove Tavern, Mansion House, Ocean House, Robert's Ordinaty, Monroe Hotel, Macon House)
House, G. Robert (City Manager) 513, 514
House of Burgesses 10, 80
House of Delegates *see* Virginia House of Delegates
Houston Space Center 520
How, Archibald B. (Barry) (Captain) 280
Howard Association 159, 161
Howard, William E., Jr. (Rear Admiral) 256
Howe, Robert (Colonel) 29
Howell, Jesse 172
Howell, W. Nathan (Ambassador) 331
Howie, Parke G.(Lieutenant, Captain) 101, 106
Howie, Thomas P. (Dr.) 161
HUBzone Project 453
Hudgins, Archie 289
Hudgins, C. W. 290
Hudgins, Henry C. 177, 358
Hudgins, Jefferson 487
Hudgins, Morgan H. 358
Hudson, Wade 396
Hugel,1Mark A. (Captain) 256
Huger, Benjamin (General) 196, 201, 466
Hughes, Aaron K. (Commodore) 255
Hughes, Sarah 332

Huguelet, Linda 451
Huguelet, Robert 451
Huguenot's Bridge 54
Hull, England 9
Hull, James (Vice Admiral) 284
Humane Society 522
Hume, Richard 433
Hume, Thomas (Reverend) 158, 364, 394, 402, 485, 497, 498
hummingbirds 31
Humphries, Joshua 184
Hunley, Evan 220
Hunley (submarine) 192
Hunt, Daniel (Captain) 276
Hunt, Harry A. 288, 521
Hunt-Mapp Middle School 390, 521
Hunter, Edward R. 384
Hunter, Frank 354
Hunter, John 28, 30
Hunter (Mr.) 80
Hunter, William 80
Hunter, William F. 136
Hunter's Lane 37
hunting 307, 373
Hunt, Harry A. (Superintendent of Schools) 413
Hunt-Mapp Middle School 413
Huron (ship) 252, 272
hurricanes 37
Hurst, Logan 201
Husen, William 161
Hutchins and Moody 365
Hutchins Robert A., Jr. (Sargent, Mayor) 211, 212, 516
Hutchinson, Archie 288
Hutchison, Benjamin (Captain) 255
Hutchinson, (Lieutenant) 219
hydroplane racing boats 292
Hygenic Ice Company 426, 427
hymn writer 330, 387, 520
hymns 340, 341
Hyslop, J. C. 111

I

I. C. Norcum High School 246, 330, 332, 333, 382, 390, 413, 414
I'Anson, Lawrence W. (Red) (Chief Justice) 289, 441, 519
ice 157, 289, 305, 426, 427, 519
ice age *see* little ice age
ice boxes 318

ice cream 301, 385, 430, 446, 450
Iceland 133
Idaho (ship) 247
Illinois River 372
impeachment 207
"In God We Trust" 499
incendiaries 117, 119
indentured servitude 347
Independence (ship) 227
Independent Steam Fire Company 122, 123, 125, 147
India, governors general 60
Indian Wars 209, 332
Indians *see* Native Americans and tribes by name (i.e. Chesapeake tribe, Nansemond tribe)
Infanta Maria Theresa (ship) 217, 221, 266
influenza 273
Ingersoll, Charles J. 104
Ingham (ship) 282
Ingomar 389
Ingstad, Helge 1
insurance salesmen 446
integration 414
Intercoastal Waterway *see* Atlantic Intercoastal Waterway
International Terminal *see* Portsmouth International Terminal
INTERNET VIII
interstate highways 147
Iraq, War in 274
Ireland 36, 152, 410, 421, 457, 503
Iris (ship) 75
Irish Republican Army 249
Irish Row 32, 151, 152, 153, 160, 350
iron works 447
ironclads, Battle of the 186, 188, chapter 23
Irwin, James C. (Rear Admiral) 284
Isaac Bell (ship) 147
Isabella (Sister) 162
Isadore (Sister) 159
Island Creek 7, 259
Isle of Wight County 81, 349
Italian Opera Company 391
Italy 333, 448
Ives, James 395, 470
Ives, Robert 470, 471

J

J. & E. Mahone Liquor House 421
J. B. White (ship) 202
Jack, Eugene Alexander 177
Jack, L. McK. 288
Jackson, Andrew (President of the United States) 235, 354, 355
Jackson, C. 132
Jackson Light Infantry 215
Jackson, Samuel (Medical Director) 275
Jacob, "Uncle" 427
Jacobs *see* Levy and Jacobs
Jacoby, William J., Jr. (Rear Admiral) 276
jail 119, 124, 127, 163, 386, 435, 440, 452, 461, 480, 504 *see also* prison and regional jail
Jail Advisory Boar 524
James I (King of England) 1, 2
James, G. P. R. 395, 462
James, (Mrs.) 429
James River 196, 359
James, W. S. (Major) 424
Jameson 31
Jamestown 44
Jamestown Colony 2
Jamestown Exposition of 1907 272
Jamestown Exposition of 2007 275, 444
Jane Smith (ship) 177
Janet's Office Supply 450
Jangles, Bo 472
Japan 133, 235, 236, 250, 363, 432
Japanese held islands in the Pacific 250
Japanese sailors 270, 272
Jaques, John (Captain) 227
Jarvis, James (Captain) 89, 110, 118, 172
Jarvis, John 172
Jarvis Papers 98, 108
Jasper, Hummingbird 31
Java (ship) 235
Jean Sands (ship) 132
Jeffers, William N. (Captain) 255
Jefferson Dome 269
Jefferson, Thomas (Governor of Virginia and President of the United States) 29, 51, 66, 75, 227, 401, 412, 418, 470
Jenkins, Jone 4
Jenkins, Richard 172
Jenkins, William 172
Jenny Lind shoes 431
Jervey, J. P. (General, City Manager) 352, 514
jewelry shops 432
Jewish cemetery 437

Jif Peanut Butter 294
Joannaou, Johnny (Delegate, Senator) 125
Jockey Club 377
jockeys 378
Joe Sam (railroad engine) 141
Johansen, Julian E. (Rear Admiral, Mayor) 283, 517
John Adams (ship) 235
John Agnew (fire engine) 124
John Barnett (railroad engine) 140
John, Uncle 333, 334, 335
Johnny Carson Show 245, 388
Johns, John (Right Reverend, bishop of Southern Virginia) 481, 484
Johnson, A. P. (General) 201
Johnson, A. W. 301
Johnson, Andrew (President of the United States) 206, 207
Johnson, Aubrey P. (City Manager) 121, 514
Johnson, Ben 389
Johnson, Harvey N. (Reverend) 338
Johnson, J. E. 336
Johnson, (Lieutenant) 100
Johnson, Lucy 161
Johnson, Thomas 110
Johnson's Hotel in Norfolk 396
Johnston, G. Douglas 396
Joliffe, John 471
Jones, C. ap R. (Lieutenant) 191, 196
Jones, Carl H. (Rear Admiral) 256
Jones, John Paul (Admiral) 70, 71, 72, 73, 74, 76, 226
Jones, Lewis 110
Jones, Matilda Sissieretta Joyner 330, 387
Jones, Robert 165
Jones, Samuel 345
Jones, Sissieretta *see* Jones, Matilda Sissieretta Joyner
Jones, Terry 332
Jones, (the Reverend Mr.) 479
Jordan Bridge 287
Jordan brothers 87, 96
Jordan, Carl M. 287
Jordan, David 87, 96
Jordan, Francis 122
Jordan, Ida Kay VII
Jordan, Thomas H. 132
Judaism chapter 40
julep 383

History of Portsmouth, Virginia

Junior Military Company 89
Junior Volunteers of Norfolk 169
juniper water 304

K

K9 units *see* police dogs
K-Mart 453
Kay, (Colonel) 458
Kay, Jesse (Corporal) 172
Kay, John (Captain) 80, 82, 172
Kearnes, John 290
Kearnes, Margaret 291
Kearney, Lawrence (Captain) 254
Kearns, (Captain) 213
Kearsarge (ship) 252
Keeling, Jacob (the Reverend Mr.) 475
Keeling, Thouroughgood 32, 33
Keester, William J. (Captain) 283
Kehukee Association 496
Kelly, Will 106
Kelsey, H. P. 246
Kelsick, John 172
Kelsick, Richard (Captain) 172
Kempff, Clarence S. (Captain) 255
Kemp's Landing 26, 45
Kent, England 8
Kentucky (ship) 249
Kerma Medical Products 453
Kerr, John 417, 491
Kerry, John (Senator) 124
Kersey, Wilbur (Reverend, Dr.) 500
Key, Francis Scott 102
key to the city 220
Key West 149
kid gloves 131
Kid, John 456
Kid, Mary 456
Kidd, John M. (Corporal) 106
Kilby, Lake 445
Kilty, Augustus H. (Commodore) 255
Kimball, Summer I. (Superintendent) 279
King Cotton 146
King, Michael 110
King, Randolph W. (Rear Admiral) 256
King's American Regiment 49, 50
king's banner, the 26
King's Council 63
King's Crossing 371
King's Daughters' Hospital 259, 260, 521
King's Highway 11
King's Mountain, Battle of 50, 58

Kingston, Paul 368
Kinkead, Thomas C. (Captain, Admiral) 61
Kirby, Frank Langley 523
Kirby, William 80
Kirk, Arthur A. (Dr.) 529
Kirk-Cone School for Disabled Children 529
Kirkpatrick, Helen 394
Kirn Building *see* New Kirn Building, or Old Kirn Building
Kirn, Henry 297
Kirn Memorial Library in Norfolk 297
Kise, Mearle A. 522
Kiser, Abednigo 98
Kitty Hawk Beach Life Saving Station 279
Kiwanis, Downtown 289, 518
Klemm, Willam R. (Captain) 256
KMC 453
Knight, Lester Lloyd 521
Knights of Columbus 510
Knott, (Captain, Fire Chief) 122, 125
Knox, Emily 494
Korean companies 453
Korean War 132, 251, 274, 523
Kosslier, Herman Joseph (Rear Admiral) 133
Kraine, Gilbert L. (Captain) 283
Kronprinz Wilhelm (ship) 242, 271
Kuwait 331
Kuwait, War in 274
Kurzenhauser, Alfred (Captain) 256
Kyd, Ann 456

L

Laderberg's Department Store 435
Ladies Aid Society 301
Ladies Day at the races 378
"Lady of Lyons" 389
La Fayette (ship) 63, 64, 65
Lafayette Arch 129, 130, 353
Lafayette Bridge 130, 165, 166
Lafayette, James Armistead 53, 59, 329, 345
Lafayette, Marie Joseph Paul Yves Roch Gilbert du Motier, Marquis de 55, 57, 58, 59, 63, 81, 113, chapter 14, 349, 354, 365, 370, 375, 456, 516
Lake Champlain (ship) 249
Lake Erie, Battle of 239

lakes *see* lakes by name (i.e. Kilby, Cahoon, Phillips, Burnt Mills)
Lamb, William (Colonel) 77
Lambert's Point 4, 98
Lambeth Conference 487
lambs 44
lamplighter 443
Lane, Ralph (Governor) 1
Lancaster, A. J., Sr. 521
Lancaster, Arthur J. "Junie", Jr 458, 525, 526
Lancaster, Etheldred 496
Lancaster School of Portsmouth 130
landing craft 250, 519
Landmarks of American Music 387
Langhorne family 209
Langhorne, (Captain) 129
Langhorne, James (Colonel) 141, 366
Langhorne, Maurice B. (Colonel) 384
Langhorne, (Mrs.) 481
Langhorne, William S. 209
Langley (ship) 247
Langley Air Force Base 230
Langton, G. H. 132
L'Anse au Meadow 1
Larramore, Thomas (Captain) 5, 6
Lassiter, A. E. 132
Lassiter, Columbus 433
Latimer, S. W. 480
Laurel Hill Cemetery, Philadelphia 76
Laurence (ship) 235
Lauterback, Harry E. 292
Lauterback, Larry 292
Lawrence, Frank D. 382, 383, 518
Lawrence, James (Captain) 229
Lawrence, John O. (Mayor) 515
Lawrence, Maywood O. 520
Lawrence, Roper 288
Lawrence, T. S. 435
Lawrence Welk Show 388
Lawton, John 106
Lawton's Blacksmith 301
le Soucy (ship) 61
Leahy, William H. (Captain & Rear Admiral) 256
Leckie Street bridge 287
LeCompte, (Captain) 482
LeCompte, (Mrs.) 482
LeCompte, Peter 396
Ledger-Star XI, 421
Lee, Charles (General) 26, 29, 30, 31, 33
Lee Hall 186

Lee, Richard Henry 27, 46
Lee, Robert E. (General) 181, 185, 204, 216
Lee, Sidney Smith (Captain) 181, 254, 325, 326
Lefcoe, Vann *see* Vann Lefcoe Progam
leg found at Craney Island 108
Legare (ship) 282
Leggett's Department Store 126, 384, 435, 450, 457
Legislature of Virginia *see* Virginia General Assembly
Leigh, John Powell, Sr. (Mayor) 516
Leigh, William (Dr.) 63, 363
Leigh's Row 160
Leitner house 351, 439
Leitner, Ronney 351
Lejeune, John A. (General, Commandant of the Marine Corps) 442, 443, 465
Leland, W. Ted (Rear Admiral) 284
Lello, John 37, 38
Lello, Susan 38
Leonard Wood (ship) 133
Leopard (ship) 228
Lerman, Arhur 242
Leslie, George (Sargent) 172
Lesley, Alexander (Major General) chapter 6, 57
Lesley, George 37, 38, 172
Lestage, Daniel B. (Rear Admiral) 276
Lester, (Colonel) 108
Letcher, John (Governor of Virginia) 176, 203
Leviathan (ship) 247
levitation 360
Levy, William M. 384
Lewis, Bill 525
Lewis, Samuel 110
Lewis, W. Ashton 525
Levy and Jacobs 434
Lexington (ship) 69, 70
Liberia 330
Liberty (ship) 43
liberty ships 249
library *see* Portsmouth Public Library, Portsmouth Community Library
library at the Naval Hospital 273
Library of Congress IX, 105
Library of Virginia 28, 328, 417, 470, 507
Lieberman, Steven (Acting City Manager) 514
Liebolt, Frank 481

Life Saving Service 272, 279, 280
Lifesaving Medal 279
Light Infantry Grays of Portsmouth 129, 141, 169, 171, 183, 212, 264, 354
lighthouse at Hospital Point, 218, 267, 280
Lighthouse Service 280, 281
lightning 508
Lightship Museum 281
Lightship Portsmouth 107 *see also* Lightship Museum
lightships 107, 280 *see also* Lightship Portsmouth
Lincoln, Abraham (President of the United States) 175, 205, 424, 478
Lincoln Memorial Cemetery 206
Lincoln Park 285
Lincolnsville 444
Lindab USA 453
Lindall, Albin L. (Captain) 276
Lindley, Dorothy 357
Lindley, Irvin 357
Lindsay's Gardens 385
Linscott, Edward 233
L'Insurgente (ship) 227
lions 131, 511
liquor 136, 180, 202, 238, 288, 305 336, 421, 430, 458 *see also* rum, rye, gin, whiskey
Lisbon 506
Lishman, Richard 38
literary clubs 393
Literary Fund 401
Lithuanian 292
Little Ice Age 96
Little Kinnakeet Life Saving Station 279
Little Theater of Portsmouth 393
Lively, Charles R. 126
Liverpool marines 26, 28
livery stables 329
Livingston, John W. (Commodore) 255
Livingston, (Mrs.) 481
Livingston, Samuel (Sargent) 101, 106
Lockwood, Zelotus 403
locomotive 140, 141
London, Bishop of 471
London, England 56, 317, 429, 443
London House 488
Long, Anne Hyde 525
Long Island, NY 189, 226
Lord and Lady Baltimore cake 301
Lord North (ship) 46

Lossing's Field book of the Revolution 53
lottery 22, 401
Louis XVI (King of France) 76
Louis, Vincent 271
Louisiana Territory 227
Louisiana Tigers 404
Lousedo, Francis 106
L'Ouverture, Touissaint 502
Louveste, Mary 187, 188, 330
"Love a la Mode" 389
Love, Alexander 35
Lovering, Phillips A. (Medical Inspector) 276
Lovitt, (Dr.) 158
Lower Tidewater In Black and White 205, 332
Lowes Hardware 454
lowering houses 364, 366
Loyal, (Miss) 238
loyalists 26, 33 *see also* Tories and rosettes of ribbons
Loyall, Paul 224
Lucas, L. Louise (Senator) 331
Luke family 76, 366
Luke, G. G. (Colonel) 214
Luke, Isaac 35, 36, 365, 366, 488, 492
Luke, Isaac, Jr. 476
Luke, John 110, 172
Luke, Nancy 476
Luke, Rachel 36, 366
Luke slab at Trinity 475
Luke, William 172, 234
lumber 148, 352, 446 *see also* wood
Lumber, W. H. (Captain) 211
Lundey's Lane, Battle of 105
Lunville, France 114
Lutheran Memorial Church 506
Lutherans chapter 40
L'Vengeance (ship) 227
lyle, Joe 414
Lynch, William Francis (Commodore) 215
Lynchburg 452
Lynn 220
Lynn Haven River 26, 55, 362
Lynnhaven *see* Lynn Haven

M

M. M. Crockin Furniture 126
MacArthur, Douglas (General) 265

MacArthur, Malcolm 265
MacArthur Memorial 202, 440
MacCauley, Charles S. (Commodore) 254
Macedonia (ship) 180, 235
Macelefield (Plantation) 81
machine shops 23, 432
MacKenzie, John Ashton (Judge) 522
Macklin, Martin T. (Rear Admiral) 276
Maclin, John 110
Macon Act 418
Macon House Hotel 88, 201, 203, 364, 462, 463
"Madblood (Captain)" 365
Madison, Dolley 105
Madison, James (President of the United States) 105
Maersk-Sealand 291
Magnien, Bernar 82, 113, 448
Magnion, Bernard *see* Magnien, Bernar
Magri, (Father) 506
Mahaffy's Iron Works 237, 432
Mahin, Harry P. (Rear Admiral) 276
Mahlon, Akey 450,
Mahone, William (General) 179, 215
Mahone's Brigade 215
Mahone, John 421, 505
Mahone'e Liquor House 421
Mahopac (ship) 252
mail 135 *see also* stamps
Maine ice 426
Majestic (ship) 247
Majette, (Private) 219
malaria 11
Malata Fort 218
Malay 72
Mallory, Stephen Russell (Secretary of the Confederate Navy) 187
malls, covered shopping 451, 453
Maltese 72
Malvern Hill, Battle of 196, 211, 212, 214
Malvina (ship) 419
Manassas, Second Battle of 212, 214
Manassas (ship)177
Manhasset (ship) 92
Manhattan (ship) 101
Manilla Bay, Battle of 218, 241
Mann, O. L. (Colonel) 424
Manning, Amy 37, 364
Manor Branch Library 393
Manor High School 393, 413, 458
Mansion House 137, 459, 460

mantua makers 429
Mapp, Alfred J. ,Sr (Superintendent of Schools) 413.
Mapp, Alfred J. ,Jr. VIII, 126, 132, 133, 170, 216, 396, 412, 413, 419, 441
Mapp, Ramona 133, 413
Marblehead, Massachusetts 116
Marchant, Jordan 93
Margaret Wright (ship) 419
Margaretville 142
Maria Theresa (ship) *see* Infanta Maria Theresa
marinas 149, 248, 270 *see also* marinas by name (i.e. Tidewater Yacht Marina, Ocean Marine)
Marine Barracks 252, 267, 379
Marine Committee 46, 47
Marine Corps, Commanders of the 267, 442, 443
Marine Hospital at Washington Point 400
Marine Parade Ground (Trophy Park) 242
Marine Safety Office 282, 283
Mariners' Museum 194
Marines 248, 266
marino sheep 448
Marion Rifles 264
Maritime Museum at Patriot Point, South Carolina 133, 184, 282
Mark, Karl 511
market house 35, 117, 165, 293, 307, 355, 435, 439
Markham, Claud 220
maroons 447
Marquis de LaFayette (ship) 225
marriage 309, 320, 323, 325
Marriner, Melvin O. (Reverend) 444
Mars (ship) 227
Marsden, James 36, 415
Marshall, (Dr.) 161
Marshall family 361
Marshall, R. Stibling 361
Marshall, Richard 220, 361
Marshall, William A. (Rear Admiral) 248, 255
martial law 203
Martin, A. A. 290
Martin, Charles (Medical Director) 275
Martin Luther King Church 208
Maryview Hospital 164, 260, 312, 518
Masling, William 110
Mason, Abigail *see* Craford, Abigail (Mason)

Mason, James R. (Lieutenant) 115
Masonic Lodge 123, 161, 349, 393, 403
see also Scottish Rite
Masonic Lodge, French 114, 448
Massachusetts (ship) 241
Massey, Ronald W. (City Manager) 513, 515
"Master and Commander" 235
Master at Arms 122
masts 21, 333
matches 304
Mathew, Edward (Major General) 40, 41, 42, 43, 46, 258, 261
Mathews County 29
Mathews, Joel 172
Mathews, Stewart 312, 313
Mathews, Thomas (Lieutenant) 80
Matthews family 42, 290
Maulson, Abigail 494
Maupin, Alliene 206
Maupin, Ann Ballard 63, 117, 425
Maupin, Dawson 206
Maupin, Edward W., Jr. 518
Maupin family 374
Maupin, George W. 505
Maupin, George W. (Dr.) 63, 117, 367, 426, 483
Maupin, George W. O. (Dr.) 152, 359
Maupin, George Washington (Dr.) 158, 425
Maupin, George Washington Virginius 206
Maupin Hall 384
Maupin house 167, 374
Maupin, James F. 374
Maupin, William G. 128
Maxwell, George 186
Maxwell, Helen Calvert 488
May, William 442
Mayhall, Ruth 525
Maynard, Horace (Congressman) 266
Mayo, William K. (Commodore) 255
mayors chapter 41
Mayrant (Midshipman) 73
McAden, James 489
McAdow, Aaron 106
McAlpin, Charles (Captain) 214
McAlpine, Kenneth (Captain) 77, 217, 218
McCabe, Ned IX
McCall, Nathan 396
McCauley, Charles S. (Commodore) 179, 254
McClellan, George Brinton (Major General) 190
McClenny, George 111
McClenny, James 496
McClenny, (Miss.) 142
McClenny's Station 142
McCoy, Basset 172
McCoy, C. W. Luke (City Manager) 513, 515
McDaniel Roofing 286
McDaniel, William J. (Rear Admiral) 276
McDonough, Thomas W. 291
McEwen, (Mrs.) 438
McFarland, (Mrs.) 477
McGann, Willfred Fleming 522
McGinley, Edward S. (Captain) 256
McGinnis, Chet 513
McGlynn, Anne 36
McGlynn, John 366
McGun, John 172
McKee, Logan (Rear Admiral) 256
McKeever, Issac (Captain) 254
McKendree, William (Bishop) 490
McKim, Randolph (the Reverend Mr.) 486
McKinley, William (President of the United States) 268
McLean, George T. 519
McLean, Walter (Rear Admiral) 255
McMahon, John 387
McMurran, Dennis (Judge) 495
McMurran, (the Reverend Doctor) 495
McMurran, Robert (Judge) 495
McNiell, Duncan 35, 36
McPherson, Hugh (Reverend) 473
McRae, John W. (Captain) 115, 353, 418
McShane Bell Factory 494
Meade, William (Right Reverend Bishop of Southern Virginia) 76, 484
Meals On Wheels 527
measles 270
meat packing 450, 451
mechanics 211
Mechanic's Union 111
Mechanicsville, Battle of 212
medallions, ceiling 316
Medical College of Eastern Virginia 525
Medical Director's House 258
Medical Discharge Board 273
medicine 201
Meljde, M. 1

melodeon *see* organs
Memorial Day Parades 124, 525
Mercer, Singleton 161
Mercereau, (Mrs.) 210
Merchants and Farmer's Bank 14, 126
Merchants and Mechanics Savings Bank 479
Merchants family 238
Meredith (Captain) 64
Meredith, S. 288
Merrimac Cafeteria 450, 457
Merrimac (ship) 180, 185, 187, 189 *see also* Virginia, C. S. S. (ship)
Merritt (ship) 218
Methodist hymnal 387
Methodists 5, 36, 65, 311, 365, 370, 487, 488, 489 *see also* Monumental Methodist Church, Glasgow Street Methodist Church and other churches by name
Mexico 176
Mexican Navy 233
Mexican War 77, chapter 19, 170, 172, 185, 262, 351
Mexicans 390
Miami 274
"Mickey Mouse March" 388
Mid City Shopping Center 435, 453, 519
Middle Street Mall 456
midshipmen's school 460
Midtown Tunnel *see* tunnel, midtown
Miles, Chambers and Hathaway shipyard 418
militia *see* Norfolk County Militia, Virginia Militia
Mill Prison 70
Miller Day Nursery 330
Miller, E. Perry 161
Miller, Francis 20, 32, 87
Miller, Nelson 172
Miller, William (Captain) 110
Milligan House 369, 431
Milligan, (Mr.) 370
milliners 210, 432, 446
mills 10, 230
minesweepers 251
Minnesota (ship) 193, 194
Minor, Lewis W. (Surgeon) 161, 264, 275, 465
minute men 80
Misery Thicket 286
Mississippi River 239
Mississippi (ship) 247

Mitchell, Joseph 132, 267
Mitchell, Rosell Edward 246
Mobile Bay, Battle of 132, 234
Moccasin (submarine) 241
model train collection 143, 458
Moewhinney, Heather 453
Moewhinney, Nate 453
Moffat, Robert 367
Moffat, William (Captain, Corporal) 78, 79, 101, 106, 367
Moffat, William 367
Moilles, the Compt de (General) 370
molasses 31, 299
Moloney family 456
Monad, Eugene 386
Monaco 388
Monitor (ship) 184, chapter 23
Monitor-Merrimac Bridge Tunnel 147
Moniz, Laurensco Jose (Dr.) 506
Monk (ship) 75
Monroe, Dorothy 77
Monroe, Fortress 205, 206, 209, 261, 332, 372, 447, 499
Monroe, Hotel 13, 347, 466, 467, 502 *see also* Ocean House
Monroe, James (Governor of Virginia and President of the United States) 230
Monrovia 330
Monserrate, M. D. 212, 464
Monterey Apartments 38
Montgomery, Alexander 471
Monticello Hotel fire 124
Monumental Methodist Church 66, 109, 158, 183, 203, 336, 365, 414, 424, 438, chapter 40 *see also* Glasgow Street Methodist Church
Moody, Eric 444
Moody, George 246
Moon Engineering 251
Moore, Fred 471
Moore, Harold C. (Rear Admiral) 283
Moore, J. Brewer IX, 137, 267
Moore, Joan 388
Moore, John 496
Moore, M. S. 110
Moore, Richard Channing (Right Reverend, Bishop of Southern Virginia) 475
Moore, Thomas 169, 471
Moose Lodge 365, 518
Moran, William, 211
Morgan, Charles W. (Commodore) 304

Morgan, Dorothy 312
Morgan, Fleet Murdaugh Carney IX
Morgan, Gus 288
Morgan, P. Scott 529
Moriarty, (Father) 503
Morrice, William 496
Morris, Charles (Commodore) 262
Morris, George U. (Lieutenant) 181
Morris, Hank (General) VIII
Morris, John 35, 343, 365, 489
Morris, John A. 518
Morris (ship) 249
Morrison, Johnny (Judge) 444
Morrison, Nathaniel "Bud" 395
Morrison, Ocie B., Jr. (Rear Admiral) 276
Morse Code 428
Mosbeth, John A. 313
Mosbeth's Chicken 313
Moseley, Edward (Colonel) 55
Moseley, Samuel 94
Mosely, John 344
Mosquito Fleet 238
Mosquito Point 35, 257 *see also* Hospital Point
mosquitos 57, 162
motorcycles 128, 313
motto 139
Moulson, Abigail 304
Mount Carmel Baptist Church 246
Mount Hermon 293, 399, 451
Mount Hermon Baptist Church 295
Mount Washington (ship) 132
Mountbatten, Louis (Lord) 249
mounting block 352
movie theaters 450, 466, 467
Mowat, Farley 1
mud machine 88, 371
Muhlenberg, Peter (General) 55
mulberry boom 448, 449
Mulberry Point 8
mumps 270
Municipal Building 121, 366, 432, 433 *see also* City Hall and Seaboard Building
Murdaugh, Claudius (Judge) 110, 350
Murdaugh house 204, 316
Murdaugh, James 80, 130, 180, 350, 480, 483
Murdaugh, James (Captain) 80
Murdaugh, John 354, 423, 423
Murdaugh, John L. (Captain) 177
Murdaugh, Mrs. house 463
Murdaugh, William Henry (Captain) 95, 177, 423
Murdaugh's horses 378
murders 5, 109, 295
Mushfeldt, Fred 161
Music Clubs 391
Music Village 388
Musket Point 258
Myers, George 66
Myers, H. M., Jr. (Acting City Manager) 514

N

Na Pape 372
NAACP 394
Nags Head 252, 279
Nansemond County 10, 33, 80, 231, 286, 327, 445, 472
Nansemond River 5, 64, 100, 158
Nansemond (ship) 177, 186, 243
Nansemond Tribe 3
Napier, Charles (Lieutenant Colonel) 97
Napoleon Bonaparte (Emperor of France) 112, 135, 408, 418, 448
Napoleon III (Emperor of France) 112, 271
Nash (Captain) 66
Nash, Abner 106
Nash, Charles 493
Nash, Charles (Mrs.) 408
Nash, Jack 360
Nash, John (Mayor) 128, 516
Nash, John (Mrs.) 130
Nash, William C. 434
Nashville (ship) 132
Natches (ship) 233
National Cathedral 472
National Endowment for the Humanities 332
National Football League 382
National Grays *see* Light Infantry Grays of Portsmouth
National Historical Landmarks 107 *see also* Virginia Historical Landmark Commission and the National Register of Historic Places, and the National Rigister of Historic Districts
National Industrial Recovery Act 248
National Register of Historical Places 177, 181, 232, 243, 246, 262, 281, 287, 351, 367, 433, 437, 480, 505
National Ship Repair and Construction

Corp. 251
Native Americans 2, 155, 257, 293, 345, 372
Naugatuck (ship) 195
Naval and Maritime Museum at Patriot Point *see* Maritime Museum at Patriot Point South Carolina
Naval Hospital 7, 8, *see* Naval Medical Center Portsmouth and Portsmouth Naval Hospital
Naval Hospital Cemetery 270, 271, 272
Naval Medical Center Portsmouth 263 *see also* Portsmouth Naval Hospital 2
Naval Medical Service 261
Naval Post Band 219
Naval Rendezvous 293
Naval Shipyard *see* Norfolk Naval Shipyard in Portsmouth and Gosport Shipyard
Naval Shipyard Museum *see* Portsmouth NavalShipyard Museum
Naval Training Station at Saint Helena 239
Navy *see also* Confederate States Navy and ships by name (i.e. Chesapeake (ship) C.S.S. Virginia (ship)
Navy Citation 133
Navy Nurse Corps 269
Neal, Charles 128
Neale, (Lieutenant) 100, 103, 106
Neckar (ship) 243
needlepoint 290
Neely, (Captain) 363
Neely Company 352
Neely family 470, 493
Negro League 381
neighborhoods Chapter 30
Nelson, Fort 35, 39, 41, 42, 43, 44, 46, 54, 62, 98, 113, 257, 259, 260, 261, 292, 474, 482
Nelson, Horatio (Lord, Admiral) 75
Nelson, Thomas (General) 55
Neptune (ship) 78, 79,
Neptune's Car (ship) 432
Nestor, Richard 259
Netherlanders 122, 236 *see also* Dutch
Nevada (ship) 247
Neville, John 327, 328
Neville, Wendell Cushing (General) 24, 63, 132, 267, 491
New Bethal Baptist Church 291
New Brunswick 34

New England 49, 149
New Hampshire Volunteers 479
New Kent County 59
New Kirn Building 175, 297, 395, 439, 453, 459, 461
New Orleans 121, 206, 299, 427
New River 280
New York (ship) 233, 240, 247
New York City 45, 47,49, 56, 64, 78, 135, 147, 234, 248, 274, 300, 306, 317, 321, 344, 382, 386, 427, 429, 436
New York Delicatessen 441
New York Herald 209, 362, 423
Newark (ship) 132
Newberne, Battle of 214
Newby-Alexander, Casandra VIII, 331
Newell, John 106
Newport, England 143
Newport, RI 55
Newport News 8, 65, 158, 184, 191, 266, 452
Newport News Shipbuilding and Dry Dock Corporation 251
Newsome, Malcolm Thommy 245, 388
Newton, George (Captain) 169
Newton, (Mr.) 230
Newton, Thomas 257
Newtown 165, 403, 498
Newtown Academy 413
Niagara Falls 105
Nicaragua 267
Nichols, Bill 382
Nicholson 177
Nicholson, (Captain) 47
Nicholson, (Dr.) 158
Nicholson, Jesse (Captain) 65, 66, 81, 172, 258, 407, 489, 490
Nicholson, Patience 37
Nicholson (ship) 80
Niemeyer family 350, 429
Niemeyer, Henry V. 170, 428, 494
Niemeyer, John Christian 213
Niemeyer, William A. 428
Nimmo, Gersham 17
Nine O'clock Gun 247, 248, 253
Nivison-Ball House 144, 354, 360
Nix, George Tidings 521
Nix, John 291
Nobal (Lieutenant) 221
Nonintercourse Act 418
Norcum High School *see* I. C. Norcum High School

Norcum, Israel Charles (I. C.) 330, 339
Norfolk 10, 26, 27, 29, 35, 85, 90, 93, 123, 129, 141, 142, 208, 220, 234, 238, 257, 264, 416, 417, 452, 456
Norfolk and Carolina Railroad 146, 294
Norfolk and Portsmouth Cricket Club 377
Norfolk and Western Railroad 179
Norfolk County 3, 15, 147, 175, 247, 285, 296, 330, 401, 440, 515
Norfolk County and Portsmouth Ferries 91
Norfolk County Ferries 90
Norfolk County landholders 6
Norfolk County Militia 10, 82
Norfolk Courthouse 440
Norfolk Fire Department 118
Norfolk, Fort 98, 110
Norfolk Harold 104
Norfolk Land Company 293
Norfolk Landmark 236
Norfolk Naval Shipyard in Portsmouth 7, 25, 28, 67, 78, 92, 98, 118, 130, 132, 153, 155, 160 175, chapter 21, 183, 194, 197, 212, 218, chapter 27, 244, 325, 327, 338, 354, 372, 381, 386, 410, 418, 420, 421, 460, 477, 519, 524, 527 *see also* Portsmouth NavalShipyard, Marine Barracks, Trophy Park and Gosport Shipyard
Norfolk Nary Base 230
Norfolk Navy Yard 223 *see also* Norfolk Naval Shipyard in Portsmouth
Norfolk Pastime Club 381
Norfolk-Portsmouth & VA Development Corporation 523
Norfolk (ship) 95
Norfolk War 98
Norman, William 288
Normandy invasion 250
Norse settlement 1
North Africa 133 *see also* War With the Barbary Pirates
North Carolina 50
North Carolina (ship) 235, 304
North Carolina Sounds 209, 215 *see also* Outer Banks of North Carolina
North Harbor 13, 85, 141
North Landing, Norfolk County 82
North Pole 251
North River, Battle of 47
North Street A. M. E. Church *see* Emanuel A. M. E. Church
Northrup-Grumand 251
Northwest Landing 362
notaries public 350
Nott, F. Harold (Right Reverend Monsignor) 518
Nova Scotia 112, 229, 343
nozzle 125, 126
nTelos Pavilion 24, 63, 143, 149, 180, 390
Number One 371
nurses 269

O

Oak Grove 377
Oak Grove Cemetery 152, 286, 439
Oak Grove Tavern 286, 378, 438
Oast, George W. 288, 433
Oast, J. Alden 288
Oast, Thomas (Dr.) 288
Oast, William (Judge) 288
Oath of Loyalty 91, 208, 466, 471
oaths 470
Obici, Amadeo 137
Oblinski, Prince 241
O'Brien, Patrick 235
occupation *see* Union occupation
Ocean House Hotel 13, 127, 203, 463, 464, 465, 466, 467 *see also* Monroe, Hotel
Ocean House Schottische 467
Ocean Marine Yacht Center 149
Ocean View 385
Oceana Air Base 230
O'Connor, James F. 132
O'Connor, John, Jr. (Mayor) 516
Ocracoke Island 279, 282
Odd Fellow's Lodge 123, 336, 358, 400
Odean, David 172
Odessa 459
Ogg, Archibald 77
Ogg, Malcolm 451
Ogg Stone Works 451
O'Hara, Sally Brice (Rear Admiral) 284
Ohmson, August (Master At Arms) 132
oil cotton *see* cotton oil
oil lamps 443
oil refinery 452
oilers 253
Oksman, G. Timothy (City Attorney) 414, 508

Old Bay Line *see* Bay Line Steamship Company
Old Dick 327, 328
Old Dominion 423, 424
Old Dominion Guards 177, 213, 214, 217, 219, 464
Old Dominion Research Foundation 522
Old Dominion Steamship Company 147, 306
Old Kirn Building 175, 384, 434
Old Point Comfort 64, 191, 195, 196, 202, 499
Old School-New School Controversy 495
Olde Towne VIII, 210, chapter 34, 471
Olde Towne Bed & Breakfast 358
Olde Towne Civic League 441, 471
Olde Towne Common 329, 358
Olde towne Gallery 453
Olde Towne Ghost Walk 38
Olive Branch Cemetery 438, 439
Oliver, James B., Jr. (City Manager) 514, 515
Oliver, M. 132
olives 448
Oliviero, Pietro? 486
omnibuses 166
On Line Institute for Advanced Loyalist Studies 26
"on the wagon" 305
O'Neill, Bernard 369
O'Neill House 369, 431
O'Neill, Jane 369
Onley, Edward 82, 290, 482
opera 387
Opey, LeRoy (Major) 482
oranges 448
Order of the Garter 60, 112
ordinaries 21, 32, 37.455
Oregon Acres 413
organs 289, 362, 392, 393, 481, 486, 490, 500, 501, 502, 510
orphan asylum 159, 263, 404
Orr, (Mr.) 423
Orton, V. Wayne (City Manager) 513, 514
Ostfriesland (ship) 253
Otero, Reggie 382
Otter (ship) 29, 40, 41, 45, 46
Ottoman Empire 459
Otway's Venice Preserved 389
Ouley, Edward *see* Onley, Edward
Outer Banks of North Carolina 193, 279
see also Hatteras Island
Outten, William 491
Overman, Edward 367
Overton, Delores 246
Overton, John 418
Owen, A. E. (Reverend) 500, 501
Owens, Arthur S. (City Manager) 514
Owens, Edwin W. (Captain) 219
Owens, Hugo (Dr.) 331, 332, 394
Owens, John (Captain) 219
Owens, Lame 106
Owens, Nathaniel 490, 491
Owens, Richard P. 172
Owens, Williams 172
Owins, John C. (Captain) 213
Owins, Paul 470
oxen 180
Oxford Hall 384, 388, 392
Oxford Movement 483
Oxford (ship) 44
Oxford Square Restaurant 18, 451
Oxford University X
oyster shell 316
oysters 297, 299, 427, 428

P

Pa Wa Shee 372
Pacific Ocean 233
Page and Allen's Shipyard 151, 432
Page, Hugh Nelson (Captain) 239, 362
Page, Jane 484
Page, John 29
Page, (Mrs.) 481
painting exhibitions 396
Palermo 333
Palladium 164
Pallas (ship) 71
Palmer, (Dr.) 369
Palmer, George O'Neill 121
Palmette flag 176
Panama Canal 428
Panco Villa, capture of *see* Villa, Pancho
Paquette, William 205, 332
parade carriage 125
parade grounds 54, 175, 239, 461
parades *see* Memorial Day Parade
Paradise Creek 7, 230, 244
Paris 370, 386
Parish, Charles T. 373
Parish, James 412
Parish Memorial Hospital 270, 442, 521

Park Manor 412
Park View 8, 38, 42, 260, 285, 288, 412, 451
Park View Elementary 412
Park View Gate to the Naval Hospital 273
Park View Land Company 288
Park View Methodist Church 290
Parker, Clarence "Ace" 382
Parker family 505
Parker, George W. 111
Parker Hosiery Company 146
Parker, Josiah (Major General) 81, 349
Parker, Vincent 288
Parkview *see* Park View
Parrett, Edwin (Dr.) 161
Parson Brown's Punch *see* Bishop Brown's Punch
Parsons, Merritt 110
Parson's Store 301
partial genetic immunity 155
Partridge, (Mr.) 411
Pasha of Tripoli 75
Pasquotank River 9
Pass House 91, 204, 316, 356, 466
passports 91
Path of History 253, 264, 275, 527
patriot badge 35
Patriot Inn 32, 333
Patriot Point *see* Naval and Maritime Museum at Patriot Point
Patten, Joshua (Captain) 432
Patti, Adelina 392
Patti, Angelina 387
Patti, the Black *see* Jones, Matilda Sissieretta Joyner
Patty O'Brien's Pub 367
Paul, Betty Cooke 489
Pauling, (Captain) 180
Paulsin, John 115
Paulson, Abigail 494
Pawnee (ship) 177, 179
"Pawnee War" 177, chapter 21
Paxton Award 396
PBS 331
peach brandy 300
Peaks of Otter 473
peanut butter 294
Pearl (ship) 69
Pearl Harbor 249
Pearson, Richard (Commander) 73, 74
Peddlers 292

Peebles, John K. 505
Peed family 456
Peed, George (Dr.) 126, 220
Peed, Samuel 492
Peeples, John K. 505
Peggy (ship) 49
Pegram, Robert B. (Captain, Virginia State Navy) 184, 254
Pell, George 106
Pell, John 172
Pendelton, Celestia 237
Pendleton, Edmond 30
Pennock, William 226, 230, 232, 254
Pennsylvania 58 *see also* Philadelphia
Pennsylvania Historical Museum 76
Pennsylvania (ship) 180, 181, 239, 240, 252
Penrose, Thomas N. (Surgeon) 275
Perrenon, (Dr.) 271
Perrott guns 185, 252
Perry, Matthew Calbraith (Admiral) 236, 237, 363, 432
Perry (ship) 235
Pershing, John L. (General) 221, 492
Persons, (Mrs.) 296
Persons, Remus C. (Medical Director) 276
Pest House 268, 437
Peters and Reed Stave Wharf 123
Peters house 207, 369
Peters, William H. 180, 201
Peters, William N. (Mrs.) 37
Petersburg 54, 57, 137, 179, 214, 264
Petersburg and Weldon Railroad 142
Petersburg, Siege of 179
Petersburg (ship) 129
Peterson, P. A. (Reverend) 183, 184
petticoats 200
pews 474, 481, 495
Pfeiffer, Arden 452
Pfeiffer, Patricia 452, 458
Pfeiffers Book Store 395, 452
Phelps, Hannah Burgess 467
Philadelphia, PA 56, 75, 76, 82, 135, 143, 156, 161, 240, 300, 465
Philadelphia Ledger 465
Philadelphia Shipyard 184, 226
Philip, John (Captain) 217
Philippine Islands 218
Phillips, A. J. 288
Phillips, C. T. 167, 412
Phillips, Henry 402

Phillips, L. T. 373
Phillips, Lake 445
Phillips, William (General, Commander of His Majesty's Forces in Virginia) 54, 55, 56, 57
Phillis 343
Philzer, Bernice 435
Philzer, Harry 435
Philzer, Sophye 435
Philzer's Department Store 435
Phoebe (ship) 233
Phoenix Fire Company 122
photograph collection at the Portsmouth library VIII, 331, 524
physicians 448
pianos 206, 319, 325, 326, 388
Pickett's Brigade 211
Pickney, Ninian (Surgeon) 275
Pickrell, George (Medical Director) 276
Piedmont Heights 285
Pierce, Franklin (President of the United States) 464
Pierce, Leola 396
piers, amusement 294
Pig Point 184, 213
pigeons, homing 428
Pigly Wiggly 384
Pigott, Ralph (Captain) 367
pikes 199, 212
Pilot (ship) 235
pilots, harbor 281
pine tar 45
Pines Treatment Center 289
Pinners Point 146, 184, 213, 285, 290, 291, 295
Pinners Point Connector 96, 291, 293
Pinners Point Methodist Church 291
Pioneer (ship) 235
pirates 25, 31, 36, 46, 227, 233, 234, 334, 335, 455, 476 *see also* privateers and War With the Barbary Pirates
pivot gun 192
planetarium 393, 458
plantations 12
Planters Peanut Company 294, 521
pleasure boating 148
Plumer, Leaven 356, 463
Plunket, (Father) 505
Plymouth, England 9
Plymouth (ship) 180, 185, 240
Pocahontas (ship) 129
poets 236, 395, 396, 425

Point Comfort *see* Old Point Comfort
police cars 128
Police Court 127
Police Department chapter 13, 386 *and see* Portsmouth Police Department
police dogs 332, 333
police motorcycles 128
police radios 128
police station 163
police uniforms 128
Polk, James (President of the United States) 351
Pollard, Benjamin 469
Pollard, John H. 100, 110
Pollard, Thomas 81
Pollock, James 499
Pomp, John 343
poorhouse 437
pork 45
Port Center 7, 24, 181, 251, 355, 365, 404, 451, 498, 507
Port le None, Ireland 113
Port Norfolk 7, 42, 145, 147, 285, 292, 293, 361, 395, 399, 469
Port Norfolk and Pinners Point Methodist-Episcopal Church South 295
Port Norfolk Baptist Church 294
Port Norfolk Electric Railway Company 145
Port Norfolk Elementary School 399
Port Side *see* Portside
PortCenter *see* Port Center
Porter, David (Commodore) 233
Porter, George 183
Porter, John (Captain) 81, 410, 489
Porter, John L. (Captain) 81, 182, 187, 190, 203, 326, 491, 515
Porter, John W. H. VIII. 176
Porter, Joseph 402, 418, 426
Porter, Mary Susan 326
Porter, Sally Macon 207
Porter, William 81, 326
Portlock's Cemetery 152, 439
Portnorfolk *see* Port Norfolk
Ports of Hampton Roads 99, 291
Ports of Norfolk 281
Portside 13, 468
Portsmouth 3, 14, 17
Portsmouth Academy 402, 404, 405, 410
Portsmouth African American History Society 296
Portsmouth All Stars 382

Portsmouth and Deep Creek Turnpike Commission 462
Portsmouth and Norfolk County Building and Loan 462
Portsmouth and Norfolk County Documents IX
Portsmouth and Roanoke Railroad company 139
Portsmouth and Weldon Railroad 263
Portsmouth Artillery 106
Portsmouth Association 496
Portsmouth Bank 206
Portsmouth, Berkeley and Suffolk Water Company 445
Portsmouth Boat Club 364, 370
Portsmouth Catholic High School 395
Portsmouth Chamber of Commerce *see also* Chamber of Commerce and Hampton Roads Chamber of Commerce
Portsmouth Chronicle 423
Portsmouth Community Development Group 526
Portsmouth Community Foundation 529
Portsmouth Community Library 330, 331
Portsmouth Community Trust 523
Portsmouth Cotton Oil Refinery Corporation 146
Portsmouth Daily Transcript 441
Portsmouth Daily Whig 389
Portsmouth Development Corporation 528
Portsmouth Enterpriser 410
Portsmouth, England 8, 22, 261
Portsmouth Events Board 526
Portsmouth Forum 393
Portsmouth Gas Company 444
Portsmouth General Hospital 260, 521, 524
Portsmouth General Hospital Foundation 260, 529
Portsmouth Grays *see* Light Infantry Grays of Portsmouth
Portsmouth Hardware 164
Portsmouth High School 413
Portsmouth Historical Association IX, 86, 362
Portsmouth History Commission, dedication
Portsmouth, Hotel 467
Portsmouth Housing Authority 519
Portsmouth Ice and Coal Company 426
Portsmouth Industrial Development Authority 523
Portsmouth Industrial Foundation 520
Portsmouth International Terminal 147, 291
Portsmouth Light Infantry Grays *see* Light Infantry Grays of Portsmouth
Portsmouth Lighthouse Service Depot 280
Portsmouth Literary and Library Association 394
Portsmouth Little Theater 527
Portsmouth Lumber Company 446, 518
Portsmouth Marine Terminal 265
Portsmouth Museums 253, 281, 458 *see also* 1846 Courthouse Gallery, Children's Museum of Virginia, Lightship Museum and the Portsmouth Naval Shipyard Museum
Portsmouth Naval Hospital 2, 26, 142, 153, 159, 183, 200, 221, 233, chapter 28, 288, 400, 465, 474, 477 *see also* Naval Medical Center Portsmouth, Naval Hospital
Portsmouth Naval Hospital Cemetery 200
Portsmouth Naval Shipyard Museum IX, 24, 60, 86, 102, 186, 253
Portsmouth Navy Yard 223 *see also* Norfolk Naval Shipyard in Portsmouth and Gosport Shipyard
Portsmouth Observer 424
Portsmouth Parish 95, 292, 420, 469
Portsmouth Partnership 452, 521, 525
Portsmouth Police Department 273, 442, 520 *see also* Police Departments, private
Portsmouth Port Authority 522
Portsmouth Public Library IX, 289, 369, 393, 394, 431, 458
Portsmouth Record 410
Portsmouth Redevelopment and Housing Authority 132, 351, 444, 450, 452, 453, 528
Portsmouth Relief Association 160
Portsmouth Rifles 118, 129, 172, 183, 203, 212, 213, 217, 219, 354
Portsmouth Savings Society 441
Portsmouth Schools Foundation 528
Portsmouth Service League 458
Portsmouth (ship) 95
Portsmouth Service League 528
Portsmouth Sports Club 519
Portsmouth Stadium 382
Portsmouth Star IX, 86, 421, 424, 518 *see*

also Star Building
Portsmouth Street Railway 145
Portsmouth Theater 310, 388
Portsmouth Times 422, 424
Portsmouth Transcript 166
Portsmouth Truckers 382
Portsmouth's Own *see* Washington Company F, First Regiment, Virginia Foot, Portsmouth's Own
Portuguese 72
Post Office 369, 431, 459
postmaster 65, 81, 185, 490
Potawatami Tribe 372
Potomac (ship) 235
Potter, Edward E. (Captain) 255
potter's field 437
Potts, D. G. 497
Potts, (Mr.) 392
powder magazine 54, 259, 437
Powell, John Dalrymple (the Reverend Mr.) 486
Powell, Legh R. 487
Power, M. 132
Powerboat Association Honor Squadron 292
Powhatan (ship) 136, 236, 237, 363, 432
Powhatan Confederation 2
Pratt, Isaac V. 403
predestination 488
prefabricated buildings 245, 246
prefabricated houses 428
Prentice Park 285, 296
Prentis Place 285
Presbyterians 22, 424, 473, 492 *see also* First Presbyterian Church
Presidents of the United States who have visited Portsmouth: George Washington, John Tyler, Zachary Taylor, Andrew Jackson, Franklin Pierce, Martin VanBuren, James Polk, Grover Cleveland, Theodore Roosevelt, Franklin D. Roosevelt, Harry S. Truman, Jimmy Carter, George W. H. Bush
presidents, prayers for 478
pressed plaster molding 316
Price, (Reverend Mr.) 494
Prince Charles' Own Hessian Regiment *see* 42nd Prince Charles Own Hessian Regiment
Prince Eitel Frederick (ship) *see* Prinz Eitel Frederick

Princess Anne Courthouse 202
Princess Anne County 9, 26, 27, 49, 406
Princess Anne Rangers 26 *see also* Queen's Own
Princess Ribbon Factory 436
printers 434
Prinz Eitel Frederich 242, 271
Prison Square 13
Prison Square Antiques
prisoners of war 103, 104, 110, 242, 265, 266, 274
prisons *see also* jail
Pritchard, William 93
Pritchett house 316
Pritchett, Joseph 167
private schools *see* schools, private
privateers 61, 75, 227
Proctor and Gamble 294, 425
Professional Building 119, 124, 386, 440, 504
Prohibition 163, 273, 292, 305, 336, 420, 466
propellers 253
prostitution 20, 207, 442
Protestant Episcopal Church in America 472
Provincial Light Infantry 50
Provost Marshall's Office 91, 204, 208, 350, 373, 479, 485, 499
Provost Prison 67, 420
Pryor, Edmunds 353
pub 230
Public Ledger
Pugh, (Mrs.) 352
Pully, John 106
pumping station 445
pumps 304, 305
punch 487
Purcell, David (Dr.) 20, 22
push carts 292, 434
Pythian Castle 360, 367, 506

Q

Quakers 4, 108
Quality Shop 429
Quarters A 232, 253, 273
Quarters B 232, 268
Quarters C 232, 257, 268
Quasi War With France 98, 226, 228, 233
Queen Anne style 288, 294
Queen's Own loyal Virginia Regiment

26, 28, 34, 50, 58
Queen's Rangers (Canadian Army) 26, 34
Queensbury, Duke of 30
quoits 381
Quonset hut 109

R

racecourse 286, 378
Rachel's story 461
racing boats 292
racing silks 378
radio 128, 250, 451
Radio Room at the Naval Hospital 273
Rae, James 20
railroad accidents 142
railroad cars on the Underground Railway 338
railroad museum 143
railroad terminal 357 *see also* Seaboard Airline Railway Terminal
railroad track 186
railroads chapter 16, 148, 273, 296, 300, 437 *see also* railroad lines by name (i.e. Petersburg and Weldon Railroad, or Portsmouth and Roanoke Railroad
railway station 143
railway workers 292
Rainbow (ship) 40
Raines, George N. (Captain) 276
'Raising the Wind" 389
Raisonable (ship) 40, 41, 47
Rakowski, Edward IX
Raleigh (ship) 193, 218, 241
rams 192
Ramsay, Henry Ashton (Captain, Chief Engineer) 188, 190, 191, 194, 196
Randolph, Giles 470
Ranier III (Prince of Monaco) 388
rap music 388
Rapoport family 511
Rapoport, Julia 511
Rapoport, Morris 429, 511
Rappahannock River 426
Raritan (ship) 180, 240
rat baiting 381
rats 405
rattle 127
Rawls, Marion 197
Rea, Robert 361
"reading" for medicine and the law 311, 312
reading, forbidden to slaves 327
receiving ships 218
Reconstruction 127
Red Cross 521, 523
Red Lion Tavern 117, 379, 456
red shirts 29
Red White and Blue Restaurant 434
Red's Drug Store 244
Reed Brothers Stave Wharves 333
Reed, I. T. 295
Reed, J. David 76
Reed, George 119
Reed, Robert Murdaugh 76, 522
Reed, Jefferson Davis (Mayor) 516
Reed, Robert 437
Reed, Shippie 76
Reed, Walter (Dr.) 154, 162
Reed, Washington 361, 384, 423
Reeves, Isaac S. K. (Captain) 276
refrigerator cars on the railroad 301
regional jail 128, 440
Registry of Historic Places 243
Registry of Virginia Landmarks 243
Reign of Terror 448
Reina Mercedes (ship) 218, 241
Reine (ship) 243
Reinert, Charles M. (Captain) 276
Relief (ship) 235
Religious Land Use and Institutionalized Persons Act 414
Remus (railroad engine) 143
Renaissance Portsmouth Hotel and Waterfront Conference Center 131, 387, 468
Renown (ship) 62, 78, 79
Renshaw, James (Captain) 254
Republican Party 207
Rescue Fire Company 125
Resident and Intern Program 270
Resolute Fire Company 120, 122
restaurants 452
Reuben James (ship) 249
Revanche de Ceri (ship) 227
Revel, Kathy 350
Revenue Cutter Service 281
revile 275
Revolution, American 25, chapters 4, 5, 6, 7, 8, and 9 113, 131, 226, 257, 329, 333, 361, 363, 364, 368, 369, 370, 375, 399, 426, 472, 489, 492
Revolution, French 227, 408, 448

revolver 186
Reynolds, (Captain) 455
Reynolds, George W. 491
rhythm and blues 388
Rice, Benjamin (Reverend) 494
Richards, Francis 288
Richardson, William Harvey (Captain) 99
Richardson's "Wild cats" 212
Richmond 54, 57, 94, 104, 129, 135, 136, 145, 159, 161, 186, 191, 201, 203, 209, 470, 472
Richmond (ship) 132, 239, 252
Richmond Mutual 123
Riddick, Joseph 350
Riddick, Louisa 200
Riddick-Weaver School 330
Riddick, William Erhart 330
Riddick, William G. James 483
Ridleyville, PA 499
rifled guns 190
Right of Search 418
Riley, P. J. 435
rioting 175, 205, 207
Ripley, Vernon 289
River Edge 295
river freezes 96
River Shores 301
Riverpark 285
Rivin, Bernard 13, 467, 511
Rivin, Zelma Goodman 13, 467, 510, 511, 526, 527
Rizzi, John N. (Captain) 276
Roanoke 146
Roanoke Island, Battle of 196
Roanoke Island Colony 1
Roanoke (ship) 193, 239
Robbie's Home Center Hardware 164, 522
Robert E. Lee cake 301
Roberts, Ann 32
Roberts, Burrell (Captain) 99
Roberts, Humphrey 20, 31, 37, 415
Roberts (Miss) 142
Roberts Ordinary 21, 32, 37
Roberts, William 37
Robertson, (Dr.) 479
Robertson, W. F. 164
Robertson's Hardware 164
Robinette, P. Ward, Jr. 525
Robinson, Charles M. 287
Robinson, Henry 409, 410
Robertson, Pat 451

Rrochambeau, Jean Baptiste Donatien de Vemeur, comte de (General) 55
Rochefoucauld, Duc de la 305
rockets 139 *see also* Congreve Rockets
Rocky Mount 146
Rodgers, (Captain) 135
Rodman Heights 299
Rodman, Howard P. 312
Rodman Judson "Juddy" Roy 520
Rodman Shopping Center 520
Rodman's Restaurant 312
Rodney (Admiral, His Majesty's Navy) 51
Roebuck (ship) 25, 29
Roger Brown's Sports Bar 385, 528
Rogers, Lee J. 331
Rohnke, Oscar C. (Rear Admiral) 283
Roman Catholic Cemetery 437
Roman Catholic Church of the Holy Angles 244
Roman Catholics 502
Romanesque Revival style 501
Romanov, Alexis, Grand Duke of Russia 241, 379
Romanov, Constantine, Grand Duke of Russia 241
Romanov, Michael, Grand Duke 272
Romulus (railroad engine) 143
Romulus (ship) 51, 55
rood screen 474
Roosevelt, Franklin D. (President of the United States) 250
Roosevelt, Theodore (President of the United States) 149, 221, 241, 267, 268
rope walk 21, 425
Roper, John 106
Rose Hall (plantation) 26
Rose, (Reverend) 494
Rosell Edward Mitchell 246
Rose's Lunch Counter sit-in 332
Rosetta, Belle Goodman 511
rosettes of ribbons (Revolution) 34
Ross, David 415
roster, Spanish American War 221
Rotary Club 251, 518
Rourke, (Captain) 101
Rousainvine's Bower 385
Rowan (ship) 248
Rowan, Stephen C. (Rear Admiral) 247, 255
rowing race 457
Rowland, (Mr.) 305

Rowland, Thomas 88, 121
Rowley, William R. (Rear Admiral) 276
Royal Marine Brigade 97
royalist *see* loyalist and tories
Rudwall Apartments 38, 357
Rufe, Roger T. (Vice Admiral) 284
rum 45, 115, 363, 419, 431
Rumble In the Tunnel 313
Runald's Tavern 119, 457
Rush, John 240
Russell County 98
Russia, Grand Dukes of 241, 272
Russian grippe 265
Russian sailors 270, 272
Russo-Japanese War 268
Rutter, (Mrs.) 481
Ryan and Gayle shipyard 418
rye 421

S

saboteurs 243
Sabine (ship) 252
Sac War 372
sack racing 381
"sacred twelve" 269
Saint Brides Parish 95
Saint Christopher's Church 482
Saint Christopher's School 529
Saint Croix 62
Saint Helena, Naval Training Station at 239
Saint James Church 336, 475
Saint John's Church 152, 158, 203, 236, 237, 298, 320, 374, 473, chapter 40, 495
Saint John's Church, Chuckatuck 33, 34, 201
Saint Joseph's Academy 413
Saint Joseph's School Alumni Association 393
Saint Julian's Creek 231
Saint Lawrence (ship) 193
Saint Louis 297
Saint Mark's Church of Deliverance 509
Saint Marks United Methodist Church 297
Saint Martin 79
Saint Mery, Moreau de *see* St. Mery, Moreau de
Saint Paul's Catholic Church 119, 123, 124, 152, 153, 244, chapter 40
Saint Paul's Church in Norfolk 22, 469
Saint Vincent's Hospital 124, 265
Sally Norton (ship) 62, 225
salt 44
San Domingo 19, 104, 502
Sandfoot, Samuel, 37
Sandy Grove, Battle of 214
Sanfoot, Samuel 37
Sanfoot, William 37
San Francisco 432
Sanger, William P. (Captain) 172
Sanitary Committee 152, 153
Santiago de Cuba, Battle of 217
Santo Domingo 502
Sarah 324, 325, 326
sargent *see* Town Sargent
Saunders, Samuel 344
Saunder's Ship Seafood 287
Savage, Horace S., Jr. 245, 527, 528
Savannah (ship) 186
Sawtelle, Daniel W. (Colonel) 479
Sayegh, Emile S. (Dr.) 260, 524
Saylor's Creek, Battle of 214
Scarborough, England 73
Schartz, Walter H. (Captain) 276
Scheib, Timothy E. (Captain) 256
Schikevitz, David 292
Schley, W. S. (Commodore, Admiral) 217
Schmitz, Pierre 131
Scheineder, William 396
Schonfeld, Fred 374, 450
school 300, 333, chapter 36, 493, 497
School Board 518
School buses 300
School Commissioners 400
school, first African American 339
school slaves 333, 334
Schoolfield, Joseph (Dr.) 153, 158
Schoolfield, Rebecca 411, 497
schools 95, chapter 36, 473 *see also* schools by name (i.e. Glebe School, Woodrow Wilson High School, Churchland High School)
schools, private 367, chapter 36
Schottische 467
Schultz (Mr.) 143
Schwind, Debbie 506
Scientific American 188
Scorpion (ship) 80
Scorpion (submarine) 251
Scott, Alexander 422
Scott family 286
Scott, George 172

Scott, Nicholas 106
Scott, Pats 341, 342
Scott, Tenant 172, 471
Scott, Phillip Henshaw (Captain) 283
Scott, Robert 402
Scott, Winfield (General) 351
Scottish merchants 13, 22, 35
Scottish Rite 123
Scottish transports 44
Scott's Creek 7, 86, 149, 265, 273, 286, 292, 382, 445
Scottsville 285, 286
Scottsville Baptist Church 287
sculling race 457
Sea Bird (ship) 215
Seaboard and Roanoke railroad 143, 216, 386
Seaboard Airline Railroad 118, 120, 123, 126, 132, 145, 166, 208, 216, 219, 263, 353, 355, 421, 432, 433, 439, 521, 522
Seaboard and Roanoke Railroad 386
Seaboard Building 126 see also Municipal Building
Seaboard Shops 143
Seaboard Warehouses 18
Sears Betty and Bob 385, 435
Sears Roebuck 385
Seatack 97
Seawall 149
Seawall Festival 526
Secession 173 chapter 20, 498
Secretary of the Navy 230, 238, 262
segregation 245, 250, 298, 330, 336, 394 see also integration
Semple, Armistead 496
September eleventh see Twin Towers
Serapis (ship) 71, 72, 73, 74, 226
Seven Pines, Battle of 196, 214
Seville jars 305
Sewall's Point 177, 184, 202
Sewanee Stadium 382
Seward family 350
Seward, Joseph (Captain) 117, 350
Shady Grove, Battle of 214
shakes 447
Shakespear, William 389
Shampoe, Clay 382
Shangri-La (ship) 249, 250
Shannon (ship) 229
Sharp (Colonel) 112
Sharpe, Solomon (Surgeon) 275
Sharpe, William 61

Sharpless 397
Sharpsburg, Battle of 211, 214, 215
Shea family 287
Shea, Richard T., Jr. (Lieutenant) 132
Shea Terrace 285, 287
Shea Terrace Elementary School 287
Shedden, Robert 31, 35, 415
Sheeler, A. L. 244
Shelton, Lynwood C. 295
Shelton Memorial Congregational Christian Church 289
Shepard, John 172
Sheridan, Philip H. (General) 214
sheriff 128
Sherman, L. K. 245
Shertzer, Tyrell B. (City Manager) 514
Sherwood, C. S. 120, 288, 462
shingle mills 447
ship graveyard 296
shipbuilding 3, 21, 23, 37, 95, 115, 286, 353, 415, 418, 426, 455
shipping 62
shipwrecks 34, 231, 476
shipyards see shipbuilding
Shkor John E. (Vice Admiral) 284
Shoal Bay 359
shoe shops 431, 435
shopping 311
Shorty Stallings Scholarship Fund 527
Shoulders Hill Baptist Church 507
show farm of Norfolk County 298
Shreep, John 368
Shrieve, Charles 161
shrouds 155
Shubrick, William B. (Captain) 254
Shuey, V. W. (Reverend) 506
Sibley, Charles Kenneth 388
"sic semper tyrannis" flag 176, 181
Sicily 133
sick babies 92
sidewalks 441
signature golf course 298
silhouettes 397
silk worms 448, 449
silver, hidden 325
silversmith 79, 364
Simcoe, John Graves (general) 58
Simmonds, J. H. 106
Simmons, Andrew 403, 490
Simmon's Directory of Norfolk 258
Simmons, Hiram 330, 387
Simmons, Mary 404

Simmons, Lee 393
Simmonsdale 285, 388
Simons, Manley H. (Rear Admiral) 249, 256, 285, 519
Simpson, J. Herbert 382, 525
Singapore 219
Singleton, Henry 119, 489
Singleton, (Mr.) 493
Singleton, William B. 440
Sissisky, Norman (Congressman) 230
Sisters of Charity 159, 265, 506
sit-ins 332
Skate (submarine) 251
skating, ice 300
Skeeter, Alex 293
Skinner, Charles W. (Captain) 254
skins 128
Skippy Peanut Butter 294
skyscrapers 274
slate roofs 306
slave states 170
slaves 3, 4, 10, 12, 25, 27, 28, 51, 53, 59, 88, 112, 148, 156, 159, 169, 171, 201, 205, 216, 300, 308, 315, 319, 320, chapter 33, 361, 377, 404, 447, 499
Sleepy Hole 95
Sleepy Hole Golf Course 137
Sloat, John D. (Captain) 254
slums 3, 251
Small Business Person of the Year 291
Small, Lisle F. (Commodore) 256
smallpox 155, 268
smelters 447
Smith, A. St. Clair (Rear Admiral) 256
Smith and Welton 435
Smith, Ann Douglas 363
Smith, Arthur R. (Dr.) 479
Smith, Benjamin (Mrs.) 408
Smith, Charles (the Reverend Mr.) 292, 469, 470
Smith, David Jeddy 396
Smith, (Dr.) 406
Smith, J. C. 290
Smith, J. Clarkson (Dr.) 161
Smith, Jimmy 288, 363
Smith, John (Captain) 2, 257
Smith, O. V. 366
Smith, Oscar (Mrs.) 476
Smith, R. Irving (Mayor) 383, 517
Smith, Samuel 172
Smith, W. S. (Colonel) 345
Smithfield 12, 154

Smithsonian Institution 394
smoking 347
Sneed, Sam 298
Sneed's blacksmith shop 338
So Fat Baseball Club of Portsmouth 381
soap 425
Society of Cincinnati 349
Solace (ship) 266
Soldiers Home in Norfolk 342
Sontag, Henrietta 392
Soul's Point 20, 26, 29, 223
South Carolina 50
South Carolina Naval District 133
South Norfolk 287
South Street Baptist Church 501
Southampton County 12, 142, 169, 170, 330
Southard, Samuel (Secretary of the Navy) 262
Southern Produce Company 300
Southern Railway 382
Southgate, M. M. 479
Southside 165, 250, 365, 452, 498
Spacek, James 445
Spalding, Edward (Judge) 288
Spanish American War 24, 77, 132, chapter 26, 239, 241, 265
Spanish sailors 221, 265, 266
Spanish ships 219
Spanish Tranka 390
Sparrow, John 347
spars 333
speedboats 292
spelling 406
Sperry, Charles S. (Rear Admiral) 241
spies 31, 50, 58, 59, 124, 185, 187, 188, 200, 209, 329, 345
spinning wheel 39
Spong, Emily Nichols 351, 361, 523
Spong, William B. (Senator) 282, 351, 361
Spoons Butler *See* Butler, Benjamin Franklin (General)
Spraque, Caleb (Captain) 432
Spratley, Benjamin (Dr.) 384
Spratley, Louisa 272
Spratling, Leckinski W. (Captain) 276
Spratly, Benjamin 110, 119
Spriggman, Henry 181
Sprowle, Andrew 13, 20, 22, 25, 28, 31, 35, 67, 223, 224, 415
Sprowle, Catherine 28, 30

Sprowle's Marine Yard 35
SPSA 253
squares (named blocks) map follows the introduction, 18
squirrels 307
St. *see* Saint
Stack (ship) 248
Stafford, Joseph 471
Stafford, William 471
stagecoachs chapter 15, 154, 461, 482
stained glass 474, 501
stamps, Confederate 185
Stallings, Shorty *see* Shorty Stallings Scholarship
Stanky, Eddie 382
Star building 352
"Star Spangled Banner" 102, 218
Starboard's Coffee Kiosk 352, 422
"stars and bars" *see also* flag
staves *see* Peters and Reed Stave Wharf
StClair, O. 132
steamships VIII, chapter 15, 236, 426
Steel, Mary 344
Steele, Thomas H. (Dr.) 161, 264
Steeple To Steeple 469, 506
Steinberg, Arthur (Rabbi) 511
Steiner, Roberta 511
Steiner, Ted 511
Steuben, Friedrich von (General) 55, 58
Stevens, Daniel 291
Stevens, Thomas H. (Commodore) 255
Stewart, Andrew 344
Stewart, Charles 20, 81
Stewart, (Colonel) 202
Stewart (ship) 132
Stewart, William H. VIII
Stimers, Allan 189
St. Mery, Moreau de 19, 88
Stoakes, Hezekiah (Mayor) 515
Stoakes, James E. (Mayor) 128, 516
Stoat, John D. (Commodore) 238
Stobo, Jacob (Captain) 82
Stoddard, David 78, 224
Stokes Academy 410
Stokes, E. Ann 410
Stokes, Ralph 410
Stokes, William Henry 410, 494
Stokley, Paul Curtis 450, 523
Stonewall Camp Confederate Veterans 176, 197, 215
stoning houses 208
Stony Point, Battle of 47

stop lights 128
storm water 445, 446
Stormy Petrel (ship) 209
stove shops 446
Strackosh 392
Strange, Curtis 298
straw hats 429
Strawberry Banks at Hampton 379
streetcars 87, 145, 244, 294, 300 *see also* companies by name (i.e. Portsmouth Street Railway, Port Norfolk Electric Railway)
streetcars, horse drawn 145
street lamps 443
Street's Hall 456
streets, paving 361, 441, 442
Stringham, Silas H. (Captain) 232, 238, 254
Strutton, Randi 245
Stuart, Caldwell J. (Captain) 276
Stuart, Elizabeth (Queen of Bohemia) 1
Stubbs, John F. 200
Stuck, David M. (City Manager) 515
Students Club 393
SuBig Bay, Battle of 218
submarine, first 241
submarines 251, 253 *see also* the ships by name (i. e. Cavilla (submarine0 and u-boats)
suburbs 223, 245, chapter 30
Suddards, James (Surgeon) 275
Suffolk 3, 10, 12, 31, 45, 63, 91, 137, 140, 141, 154, 196, 202, 225, 250, 286, 406, 445
Suffolk Road 137, 154
sugar cane 448
Sugar Hill 291
Sugar House 67, 118, 420
sulfur dioxide 447
Sullivan, (Bishop of the Diocese of Richmond) 414
Sullivan, D. 457
Sully, Laurence 397
summer reading club 429
Sumter (ship) 252
Sunday school, first 489
Superfund site 296, 444
Superintendent of Nursing for the U. S. Navy 269
superintendents of schools 364
surfboats 279
surfmen 279

Surry 12
Surveyor (ship) 104
Susan Constant (ship) 3
Susquehanna (ship) 235, 243
Sutton, Dallas G. (Captain) 276
Sutton's Furniture Store 435
Svetlana (ship) 241
Swanson Homes 250, 519
Swanton, John R. 2
Sweden 189
Sweeny, George 106
Sweet Temptations 296
Swift (Mrs.) 62
Swift, Richie 411
swimming 259, 293, 435
Swimming Point 8, 428, 444
Swimming Point Walk 259, 266, 303, 370
swine flu 155
Sword presented to John Paul Jones 76
Sycamore Hill 507
Syer, Charles 288
syllabub 309
synagogues chapter 40
syncrolift 149

T

Tabb, Maurice 111
tablecloths 459
tailors 165, 391, 446
Talbot, John 491
Talbot, Thomas 225
Talbot, William 227
Taliaferro, William Booth (General) 180
Tallapoosa (ship) 132
tallow 425
tank landing ships 250
Tanker Car Gas Station 295
taps 275
Tarawa (ship) 249
Tarbell, Joseph (Captain) 100
Tarlton, Banastre (General) 58
Tarrant, William T. (Captain) 255
Tatem, John 470
Tatom, Robert H. 491
Tatnall, Josiah (Commandant) 195
Taussig, Edward D. (Admiral) 242, 255
Tavern sign 456
taverns chapter 39 *see also* taverns by name (i.e. Eagle, and barrooms)
tax-dodger houses 369, 472 *see also* Dutch roofed houses

taxes 127, 231, 401, 416, 420, 452, 453, 455, 470
Taylor, Abigail 469
Taylor, Alice 469, 470
Taylor, E. B. 447
Taylor, Gordon B. (Captain) 276
Taylor, James (Dr.) 469, 470
Taylor, James L. (Rear Admiral) 256
Taylor, John Y. (Surgeon) 275
Taylor, Lucy 461
Taylor, Margaret 469
Taylor, Robert 142
Taylor, Robert Barraud (General) 100, 114
Taylor, Theodore 396
Taylor, Washington 493
Taylor's Tavern 461
Tayler, Zachary (President of the United States) 351
tea 39, 304, 416
Teachers Association 406
Tecumseh (Chief) 234
Tee, John C. 108, 143, 177, 293, 401
Tee, William (Captain) 107
telegraph 428 *see also* Gamewell Police Telegraph
television 451
Temperance Hall 338
Temple Sinai 511, 527
Tennessee (ship) 252
Terry's Store 301
Texas (ship) 77, 217, 218, 241, 247
theaters 310, 311, 389, 390, 466
Thespians 393
Thiesen, William H. (Atlantic Area Historian) 179
Thomas, Charles M. (Rear Admiral) 241
Thomas, Cornelius 96
Thomas, Griffith E. (Captain) 276
Thomas, John S. 128
Thomas, P. J. (Mayor) 516
Thomas, Theodore 392
Thompson, Arthur C. (The Reverend Mr.) 480
Thompson, (Captain) 161
Thompson, Ebenezer 354, 355
Thompson, John (Captain) 81, 293, 361, 362
Thompson, Martha 401, 403
Thoroughgood, Adam 85
Thumpers 367
Tides baseball team 382

Tidewater Building 407
Tidewater Community College 213, 250, 289, 299, 332, 526 *see also* Pig Point
Tidewater Community College Visual Arts Center 13, 197, 203, 347, 403, 422, 463, 502
Tidewater Knitting Mills 146
Tidewater Rapid Transit 87
Tidewater Science Council 522
Tidewater Teleradio Corporation 519
Tidewater Tides 382
Tidewater Winds 390, 529
Tidewater Yacht Marina 149
Tientsin, Battle of 267
Tiesen, William H. (Atlantic Area Historian for the Coast Guard) 179
Tiffany and Company 488
Tiffany, Louis Comfort 476
Timm, David 356, 463
Timm, Faye 356, 463
timber docks 236
Tip Toe Tearoom 451
Tishman, Richard 37
Tithables 363, 420
To Life Specialty Grocery 453
tobacco 12, 45, 61, 87, 419, 472
toddy 383
Todi Music Festival 456, 529
Tokyo 236, 250
"Tonight Show" *see* Johnny Carson Show
Toomer, Thomas 37
Torah Day School of Virginia 510
Torch International 396
Tories 25, 28, 30, 31, 33, 35, 56, 224, 416, 417 *see also* loyalists
Tortola 62
tourists 93
Tower Mall 451, 453, 454, 528
Town and Country 519
Town Clerk 346
town constable 127
Town Council of Portsmouth 142, 151, 439, 515
town sergeant 126, 151, 438, 443
town trustees 20, 29, 32, 36, 230
Towne Bank. 8, 14, 351, 528, 529
Towne, (Miss) 403
track laid on Crawford Street 144
Trainland 458
traitor 202
Transcript 423
transoms, sunburst 316

trapeze acts 390
Travelers Aid 520
travelift 149
Travis, Joseph 170
Travis, William (Captain) 104, 281
Traymor, Pie 382
Treadwell, Lawrence P. (Captain) 256
Tredigar Mills 186, 190
Trenton (ship) 252
Trevethan, Louise 340
Trevett, Samuel (Captain) 115, 116
trifle 310
Trinity Church 7, 22, 36, 50, 54, 55 177, 203, 234, 260, 292, 320, 327, 335, 336, 353, 362, 381, 392, 393, 399, 461, chapter 40, *see also* Portsmouth Parish
Trinity Churchyard 32, 36, 38, 79, 80, 81, 82, 115,223, 229, 233, 236, 290, 304, 343, 363, 366, 358, 419, 420, 422, 456, 473, 482
Trinity Rectory 316, 352
Tripoli 75, 77
Tripoli (ship) 75
trolley tours 252, 254
trolleys *see* streetcars
Trophy Park 252, 253, 254 *see also* Marine Parade Ground
Trotman's 301
truck farming 294, 296, 300, 447
True Reform Building 330
Trugien, John (Dr.) 152
Trugien, Paul L. 421, 424, 494
Truman, Harry S. (President of the United States) 467
Trumbull (ship) 75
trumpet, silver 121
trustees *see* town trustees
Truxton 226, 245, 246, 247, 285, 381, 425, 519
Truxton, Thomas (Captain) 226
Truxton, William T. (Commodore) 255
Tsu Si, (Dowager Empress of China) 268
Tucker, Beverly D. (Right reverend) 487
Tucker, George VII, 31, 225, 430
Tucker, (Judge) 62
Tucker, Robert 257
Tucker (ship) 248
Tucker, StGeorge 225
Tucker, Thomas 245
Tucker, William 257
Tucker's Mill 26, 257
tugboats 418

tuning fork 490
tunnel, Downtown 86, 93, 96, 118, 147, 273, 451 *see also* tunnel, Midtown and tunnels
tunnel, Midtown 96, 147, 287 *see also* tunnel Downtown and tunnels
tunnels chapter 10, 147, 437 *see also* tunnel, Downtown, tunnel Midtown
Turkey 233
turkeys 307
Turner, Eliza 403
Turner, Jim 382
Turner, Nat chapter 19, 329, 335, 339, 346, 396
Turner, Samuel 169
Turner, Vernon Kitabu 395
turning basin 247
turret 193, 271
Turville, William H. H. (Captain) 276
Twin Towers disaster in New York City 248, 252, 266
Tyler, John (President of the United States) 464
Tyler, (Mr.) 462
Tynch, David R. 528
Tynan, G. T. (Police Chief) 387
typhoid fever 268
Tyrwhitt, Mary Ann 388

U

u-boats 133, 249
U. S. Naval Institute at Annapolis *see* Annapolis
U. S. Naval Museum 197
U. S. Shipping Board 243
Ulrich-Ricardi, J. 259
"uncle" 343
underground railroad 201, 338
undertakers 155, 318, 446
uniforms for the police 128
uniforms, sports 450
Union Army, African Americans in the 205, 209
Union Bridge 165, 166
Union candidates 175
Union Car Words 212
Union occupation chapter 24
Union (ship) 95
United Daughters of the Confederacy 197
United Jewish Fellowship of Tidewater 528

United Services Organization *see* USO
United States *see also* U. S.
United States Coast Guard *see* Coast Guard
United States Coast Guard Buoy Yard *see* buoy yard
United States Congress 81, 87, 207, 251, 253, 290, 349, 418, 518, 520
United States Housing Corporation 243, 245
United States Navy *see* Navy and Naval
United States (ship) 180, 184, 240
University of North Carolina, Chapel Hill 498
University of Virginia, 264, 528
unknown dead 270
Urbana (Sister) 162
urinals 111
Usher, Nathaniel R. (Rear Admiral) 255
USO 366, 520

V

Vaché, C. Claude (Right Reverend, Bishop of Southern Virginia) 188, 251, 336, 469, 475, 478, 480
Valentine, Jacob 81
Valentine Museum in Richmond 59
Valparaiso 233
VanBoskerck, Francis Saltus (Captain) 283
VanBuren, Martin (President of the United States) 351
VanHorsigh, Joseph (Father) 503
Van Peenan, Hubert J. (Rear Admiral) 276
Vann Lefcoe Program IX, 528
Vass, I. G. (City Manager) 514
Vaudeville 389
Vaughan, Mattie 170
Vauxhall Garden 121, 385
Veal, Charles (Sargent) 132
Veale 177
Veale, Annie 108
Veale, Demsy 471
Veale family 420
Veale, George 360, 470
Veale, Mary 9, 10
Veale, Samuel 35, 36, 37
Veale, Thomas 20, 36, 285, 371, 470
Vengeance (ship) 71
Vera Cruz 267

verger 472
Vermillion, John 213
Vestry of Trinity Church 470 *see also* Trinity Church
veterans chapter 9 (American Revolution) chapter 12 (War of 1812) *see also* veterans by name
Veterans Administration 273
Veterans' Benefit Bill 273
Viceroy of India and Pakistan 249
Victoria (Queen of England) 249, 478
Victorian style 290, 362
Victory Crossing 528
Victory Tavern 435
Viele, Egbert L. (General) 204
Viele, (Mrs.) 204
Viet Nam War 252, 274
Vigilant Fire Engine 122
Vignier, Louis (Lietenant) 62
Villa, Pancho 221
Virginia Army National Guard 523
Virginia Artillery 212
Virginia Arts Festival 529
Virginia Bank 441
Virginia Beach 9, 26, 49, 301, 362, 385
Virginia, C. S. S. (ship) 177, 187, 188 chapter 23, 207, 240, 252, 271, 326, 478 *see also* Merrimac
Virginia Carolina League 382
Virginia Chemical Company 288, 447, 448, 522, 524
Virginia Club 63
Virginia Club of Portsmouth 381
Virginia Committee of Safety 29, 31
Virginia Defenders 214
Virginia Department of Archaeology 86
Virginia Endowment for the Humanities and Public Policy 332
Virginia (fire engine) 147
Virginia Fireman's Association 125
Virginia flag *see* "sic semper tyrannis" flag
Virginia General Assembly 95, 139, 141, 230, 328, 346, 366, 370, 401, 419, 428, 438, 470, 480
Virginia House of Delegates 59
Virginia Landmark Commission 243, 296
Virginia Legislature *see* Virginia General Assembly
Virginia Militia 29, 55, 57, 366, 471
Virginia Municipal League 517
Virginia Museum in Richmond 364

Virginia Navy 44, 62, 78, 79, 224, 225, 367, 368
Virginia Palladium and Portsmouth Commercial Advertiser 422
Virginia Pension List 30
Virginia Power 527
Virginia Rangers 215
Virginia Register of Historic Places 351
Virginia Seaboard Teachers Association 406
Virginia Sports Hall of Fame 145, 176, 359, 360, 382, 383, 426, 518, 525, 529
Virginia State League 382
Virginia State University 246
Virginia Supreme Court 519
Virginian Pilot IX, 421
Vollet, Pierre (Lieutenant) 62
Volunteers of Ireland 42, 46
von Steuben, Friedrich (General) *see* Steuben, Frederick von
Vulture (ship) 47

W

WPA 396
W. T. Grants *see* Grant's, W. T. Five and Ten
Wa Ba Keeship (Profit) 372
Wachovia Bank 328, 351
Waggoner, Andrew (Major) 99
Wagner, Hal 382
Wagner, Joseph 172
Wagner, Lon 151
Wainwright (ship) 249
waitresses 312
Wakefield, (Mr.) 165
Walke, Frank Anthony (Dr.) 161, 264
Walker, Chichester 110
Walker, Nathaniel 106
Wallacton 80, 405
Waller, (Reverend) 497
Wallin, Homer N. (Rear Admiral) 256
Wallis and Ruddalfi 357
walls of the town 54
Wal-Mart 451
War of 1812 75, 76, chapters 11and 12, 117, 132, 229, 233, 261, 329, 354, 359, 418, 489
War On Terror 283
war reparations 253
War With the Barbary Pirates 76, 77, 180, 226, 228, 234, 350

Warden, John (Captain) 195
wardrobes 317
warehouses 144 *see also* wharves
Warner, Alexander 487
Warner, Richard A. (Captain) 276
Warren, John Borlase (Sir, Admiral) 97, 104, 112
Warren, Lewis C. (Chief of Police) 520
Warrenton Springs, Battle of 214
Warrington, Lewis (Captain) 232, 236, 254, 262, 486
Washington Company F, First Regiment Virginia Foot, Portsmouth's Own 170
Washington, D. C. 153, 184, 195, 205, 207, 267, 472
Washington Ditch, 148, 456
Washington, George (General, President of the United States) 31, 53, 55, 59, 105, 130, 132, 147, 148, 184, 226, 349, 456
Washington Oak 148
Washington Park 296
Washington Point (Berkeley) 13, 41, 90, 400
Washington Reed house 361
watchmen 127
water set 123
Water Street 23
water supply 265, 305, 306, 444, 445 *see also* juniper water
water wagon 305
watermelons 427
Waters, William E. 330
Waterside 87
Waterview 68, 285, 297
Watkinson, M. R. (Reverend 498, 499
Watley, L. B. 270
Watson, H. B. 384
Watson, John 50
Watson, John L. 288
Watt Engine 140
Watts, A. S. (Mayor) 516
Watts, Carmi 411
Watts, Dempsey ((Major) 112, 371, 372, 458
Watts, E. M. (Mrs.) 37
Watts, Edward 480
Watts, Edward M. (Dr.) 352, 357, 483
Watts family 371
Watts House 167
Watts, James S. 128
Watts, John 110, 172
Watts, (Judge) 127

Watts, Legh R. (Mrs.) 37, 357, 371, 487
Watts, Margaret 373
Watts, Mary 367
Watts, Samuel 78, 142, 166, 169, 180, 394, 402, 479
Watts, Samuel (Captain) 119, 141, 354, 372, 373
Watts, Winchester 130, 158, 159, 384, 444, 464, 465, 480
Waughop, James 172
Waverly Apartments 269, 270
WAVY-TV 7, 253, 355, 439, 440, 451, 519
Waynesboro 358
Weaver, Aaron W. (Commodore) 255
Weaver, Joseph 181, 182
Weaver, Joseph E. 215
Weaver, Lavina Miller 330
Webb, Ann 411
Webb family 365
Webb, Gloria O. (Mayor) 518
Webb, Lelia Graham 361
Webb, Randy 361
Webb, Tapley 93
Webb's Hotel 131, 365, 458
Webster, Noah 406
Webster, (Professor) 411, 412
Webster, (Mrs.) 412
Webster, Thomas 465
Webster's Collegiate Institute 411, 412
Webster's Hall 406
weddings 309, 320, 321, 325, 422, 467
Weed, T. Phillis 183
weed trees 11, 448, 449
Weedon, George (General) 55
Weightman, Roger Chew (Captain) 283
Weiss, Denton 115
Weiss, Michelle 115
Weiss, Ronald 33
Weiss, Verle 33
Weldon 142
Welling, Paul A. (Rear Admiral) 284
wells 305, 445
Wells, Gideon (Secretary of War) 187, 189
Wells, Henry 419
Welton, B. F. 435
Welton, Duke and Hawks Insurance Agency 523
Wentz, Robert William VIII, 524
Wesley Chapel 301, 508
Wesley Chapel Methodist Church 338

Wesley Community Service Center 507, 508, 525
Wesley, John (Reverend) 488
Wesson, William 352
West End Methodist Church 509
West, Elizabeth 288
West Indies 228, 419, 427, 448, 502 *see also* French West Indies, Antigua, Haiti, Cuba, San Domingo, Saint. Croix, Saint Martin, Bahamas, Tortola, Bermuda and Haiti
West Norfolk 147, 285, 288, 297, 301, 447, 452
West Norfolk Bridge 287, 296
West Norfolk Land Development Company 297
West Norfolk Lumber Company 297
West Norfolk Methodist Church 297
West Park View 42, 290
West Port Norfolk 285
Westcoat, Richard (Bishop) 490
Western Branch 22, 285
Western Branch Baptist Church 501
Western Branch Diesel 526
Western Freeway Bridge 287
Westfall, Elmer T. (Rear Admiral) 256
Westham Foundry 54
Westhaven 285, 299
Westhaven Baptist Church 299
Westover Plantation 54
Wetmore Thomas T., III (Rear Admiral) 283
whale fat 308
wharves 10, 12, 18, 21, 22, 23, 65, 144, 146, 154, 224, 236, 294, 333, 357, 419, 432, 457, 474 *see also* timber dock, banana pier, stave wharf
Wheeler, Guy C. 418
Wheeler, William Joseph (Captain) 283
"Where Rail Meets Sail" 139
Whidbee, William 110
Whig Clubhouse 373
Whigs 373, 405, 417
whipping 346, 347
Whipple, E. W. (Mayor) 516
Whipple, William 46
whiskey 273, 421, 430
whist 383
Whitbeck, John E. (Commodore) 281, 283
White and Fleming Oyster Packers 428
White, E. V. 290

White Fleet *see* Great White Fleet
White Friars stained glass 476
White House 105, 387
White, James C. (Mayor) 516
White, John S. (Mayor) 364, 515
White, Joshua 463
White, Luther Gehrman (Mayor) 516
White Oak Swamp, Battle of 196
White, Richard 81
White, William H. 175
Whitefield, (Archbishop) 506
Whitefield, George (Reverend) 488
Whitehead, Emily 493
Whitehead, Swepson 94, 363, 408, 493
Whitehurst, Charles 296, 396
Whitehurst, J. S. 132
Whitehurst's Hall 123
Whitehurst, Nathaniel 172
Whitehurst, W. R. 435
Whiterock, Joseph 106
Whiting, W. 479
Whitlow, Morton V. "Mo" 526
Whittier, Clive (Mrs.) 161
WHRO-TV 332
Wiat, John 471
Wickham, Hampshire, England 230
Wickham, John 94
"Widow Machine" 392
Widow's Point 18
widow's walk 364
Wigtown, Scotland 471
wigwam 385
Wilcox, Edward N. 476
Wilcox Farm, Battle of 214
Wild, Edward A. (Brigadier General) 479
Wilder, Douglas (Governor of Virginia) 86
Wilder, William S. 421
Wilkerson, Jesse (Commodore) 231, 254
Wilkins, John 111
Wilkins, James 172
Wilkins, Raymond H. (Major) 132
Wilkinson, Jesse (Captain) 254
Willett Hall 390, 519
Willett, T. A. 519
William and Mary (ship) 419
William G. Anderson (ship) 252
Williams, David A. 181, 182
Williams, Edward 119
Williams, James 479
Williams, James A. 81, 110, 172
Williams, Joe, Jr. (Rear Admiral) 256

Williams, Junius H. 527
Williams, Kent H. (Vice Admiral) 284
Williams, Lemuel (Corporal) 213
Williams, Robert 365
Williams, Robert T. (City Manager) 299, 453, 513, 514
Williams, Sally Macon Porter 207
Williams, (Sargent) 219
Williams, T. O. 450, 451
Williams, Thomas (Captain) 254
Williams, Thomas McDowell 207
Williams, W. V. H. 491
Williamsburg 13, 29, 58, 62, 225, 257
Williamson, James 479
Williamson, Mattie 200
Williamson, Thomas (Surgeon) 142, 200, 233, 262, 275
Williard School of Troy, New York 403
Willing, (the Reverend Mr.) 485
Willis, (Bishop) 508
Willis Cooper and Brothers 63
Willis, Cheryl 396
Willoughby Point 65
Willoughby Spit 202, 242
Willoughby, William 257
Wilson, Alfred 290
Wilson, Christopher (the Reverend Mr.) 477
Wilson and Fiske Printing 434
Wilson, Elizabeth 411
Wilson, Emily 411
Wilson, Esther "Essie" Murdaugh 393
Wilson, Hack 382
Wilson High School see Woodrow Wilson High School
Wilson, Holt 93, 158, 362, 480
Wilson house 362
Wilson, James 356
Wilson, Jeffrey T. 330
Wilson, John 81, 127
Wilson, John (Colonel) 66
Wilson, Joseph, Jr. (Surgeon) 275
Wilson, Louise 362
Wilson, Louisiana 481
Wilson, Mary Ann 236
Wilson, Mary Jane 411
Wilson, Phillis 343
Wilson, Sam 343
Wilson, Susan 411
Wilson, W. H. 88
Wilson, William 95
Wilson, William H. (Clerk of Courts) 362, 366, 462
Wilson, Willis 82, 343
Wilson, Woodrow (President of the United States) 243
Winbrough family 468
Wimbrough, Raymond 412
Winbourne, Tomeka N. 395
Winchester, Frederick County 109
Windley, Margaret VII, 203, 336, 491
Windmill Creek 37, 54, 166, 340, 372, 373, 504
Windmill Point 257 see also Hospital Point and Mosquito Point
windmills 36, 37, 54, 257, 425, 431
windows 495 see also stained glass
Windsor, Charles (Prince of Wales) 249
wine 300, 383, 431
wine cellars 366
Wingfield, John Henry (the Reverend Dr.) 5, 238, 363, 473, 475, 476
Wingfield, John Henry Ducachet (Bishop) 188, 205, 474, 478, 479, 480
Wingfield, (Mrs.) 481
Wingina (Chief) 1
Winter Wonderland 394, 526
Wise, George (Captain) 102
Wise, Nicholas 93, 94
Wise's Creek 101, 102
witchcraft 4
Witt, John Temple 472
Wolf, Katherine "Kitty" 511
woman, first woman mayor 518
woman's order 206
women 19
women at the shipyard 243
woman, first licenced as an architect 298
women golfers 298
women in law 528
Women's Club of Portsmouth 287, 298
wood 432, 433, 447 see also lumber
Wood, Billie Marie 289
Wood, Don and Demming architects 262
Wood, James 172
Wood, John 3
Wood, Russell E. (Rear Admiral) 286
Wood, Richard F. 521
Wood, William 110
Woodford, William (Colonel) 29, 81
Woodis Rifles 171
Woodley, (Mrs.) 167
Woodrow Wilson High School 220, 312, 390, 413, 414, 458, 528

Wood's Bakery 289
Woods, Edgar L. (Captain) 276
Woods, Samuel 132
Woodward, James C. (Captain) 276
Wooldridge, O. B. 520, 521
Woolford, William (General) 66
Woolworths Five and Ten 385, 528
World Series of Golf 298
World War I 24, 92, 93, 132, 218, 221, 226, 239, 242, 243, 246, 253, 270, 271, 281, 290, 366, 492
World War II 132, 133, 249, 250, 251, 265, 273, 281, 298, 299, 312, 427, 434, 509, 519, 523
Wotten, Thomas 172
Wren, Nancy Glisson 529
Wren, Thomas 110
Wright Engineering/MES Marine 453
Wright, Kenneth 444
Wright, Marcus Joseph (General) 466
Wright Memorial Church 207, 508
Wright, William (Colonel) 507
WSAP 451
Wuensch, Henry J. (Rear Admiral) 286
WYAH 451
Wyatt, John (Sargent) 82, 172
Wyatt, Sarah 82
Wyatt, Spivey 65, 82
Wyatt's Hotel 459
Wyoming 283
Wyoming (ship) 252
Wysham, (Dr.) 200

X

x-ray machine 266

Y

yacht repair facilities 253
Yadkin (ship) 202
Yates, Glen 163, 440
Yates, (Mr.) 333
yeast jug 304
yeast powder factory 405
yellow fever 121, 127, 172, 238 chapter 17, 263, 271, 350, 404, 444, 484, 485, 497, 504
yellow fever flies 162
Yellow Fever Relief Committee 515
YMCA 435, 468, 526
Yon, Joseph L. (Rear Admiral) 276

York and St. Clair compression ice machine 427
York County 80
Yorktown 57, 58, 61, 78, 80, 113, 129, 370, 375, 471, 487
Yorktown (ship) 235
Yost, Jon 212
Young Creole (ship) 228
Young, Edward E. G. 146
Young family 23
Young, (Captain) 129
Young, George (the Reverend Mr.) 381, 473, 476
Young, James (Captain) 23, 24, 63, 82, 426
Young, John (Captain) 185
Young, John P. (Captain) 172, 384
Young, Moses 183
Young, William D. (Captain) 172
Young, William P. (Sargent) 101, 106, 119
YWCA 359

Z

Ziegemeier, Henry J. (Rear Admiral) 255
Zion Baptist Church 330, 337, 498
Zion Bethol United Church 296
Zink, John J. 450